Handbook of Research on Demand–Driven Web Services:

Theory, Technologies, and Applications

Zhaohao Sun
University of Ballarat, Australia & Hebei Normal University, China

John Yearwood
Federation University, Australia

A volume in the Advances in Web
Technologies and Engineering (AWTE)
Book Series

Managing Director:	Lindsay Johnston
Production Editor:	Jennifer Yoder
Development Editor:	Vince D'Imperio
Acquisitions Editor:	Kayla Wolfe
Typesetter:	Christina Henning
Cover Design:	Jason Mull

Published in the United States of America by
Information Science Reference (an imprint of IGI Global)
701 E. Chocolate Avenue
Hershey PA 17033
Tel: 717-533-8845
Fax: 717-533-8661
E-mail: cust@igi-global.com
Web site: http://www.igi-global.com

Library of Congress Cataloging-in-Publication Data

CIP Data - Pending
ISBN 978-1-4666-5884-4 (hardcover)
ISBN 978-1-4666-5885-1 (ebook)
ISBN 978-1-4666-5887-5 (print & perpetual access)

This book is published in the IGI Global book series Advances in Web Technologies and Engineering (AWTE) (ISSN: Pending; eISSN: pending)

British Cataloguing in Publication Data
A Cataloguing in Publication record for this book is available from the British Library.

All work contributed to this book is new, previously-unpublished material. The views expressed in this book are those of the authors, but not necessarily of the publisher.

For electronic access to this publication, please contact: eresources@igi-global.com.

Advances in Web Technologies and Engineering (AWTE) Book Series

Ghazi I. Alkhatib
Princess Sumaya University for Technology, Jordan
David C. Rine
George Mason University, USA

ISSN: Pending
EISSN: pending

MISSION

The **Advances in Web Technologies and Engineering (AWTE) Book Series** aims to provide a platform for research in the area of Information Technology (IT) concepts, tools, methodologies, and ethnography, in the contexts of global communication systems and Web engineered applications. Organizations are continuously overwhelmed by a variety of new information technologies, many are Web based. These new technologies are capitalizing on the widespread use of network and communication technologies for seamless integration of various issues in information and knowledge sharing within and among organizations. This emphasis on integrated approaches is unique to this book series and dictates cross platform and multidisciplinary strategy to research and practice.

The **Advances in Web Technologies and Engineering (AWTE) Book Series** seeks to create a stage where comprehensive publications are distributed for the objective of bettering and expanding the field of web systems, knowledge capture, and communication technologies. The series will provide researchers and practitioners with solutions for improving how technology is utilized for the purpose of a growing awareness of the importance of web applications and engineering.

COVERAGE

- Case Studies Validating Web-Based IT Solutions
- Data Analytics for Business and Government Organizations
- Human Factors and Cultural Impact of IT-Based Systems
- Knowledge Structure, Classification and Search Algorithms or Engines
- Mobile, Location-Aware, and Ubiquitous Computing
- Ontology and Semantic Web Studies
- Security, Integrity, Privacy and Policy Issues
- Software Agent-Based Applications
- Strategies for Linking Business Needs and IT
- Web Systems Engineering Design

IGI Global is currently accepting manuscripts for publication within this series. To submit a proposal for a volume in this series, please contact our Acquisition Editors at Acquisitions@igi-global.com or visit: http://www.igi-global.com/publish/.

Titles in this Series

For a list of additional titles in this series, please visit: www.igi-global.com

Demand-Driven Web Services Theory, Technologies, and Applications
Zhaohao Sun (University of Ballarat, Australia & Hebei Normal University, China) and John Yearwood (University of Ballarat, Australia)
Information Science Reference • copyright 2014 • 374pp • H/C (ISBN: 9781466658844) • US $195.00 (our price)

Evaluating Websites and Web Services Interdisciplinary Perspectives on User Satisfaction
Denis Yannacopoulos (Technological Educational Institute of Piraeus, Greece) Panagiotis Manolitzas (Technical University of Crete, Greece) Nikolaos Matsatsinis (Technical University of Crete, Greece) and Evangelos Grigoroudis (Technical University of Crete, Greece)
Information Science Reference • copyright 2014 • 354pp • H/C (ISBN: 9781466651296) • US $215.00 (our price)

Solutions for Sustaining Scalability in Internet Growth
Mohamed Boucadair (France Telecom-Orange Labs, France) and David Binet (France Telecom, France)
Information Science Reference • copyright 2014 • 288pp • H/C (ISBN: 9781466643055) • US $190.00 (our price)

Adaptive Web Services for Modular and Reusable Software Development Tactics and Solutions
Guadalupe Ortiz (University of Cádiz, Spain) and Javier Cubo (University of Málaga, Spain)
Information Science Reference • copyright 2013 • 415pp • H/C (ISBN: 9781466620896) • US $195.00 (our price)

Public Service, Governance and Web 2.0 Technologies Future Trends in Social Media
Ed Downey (State University of New York, College at Brockport, USA) and Matthew A. Jones (Portland State University, USA)
Information Science Reference • copyright 2012 • 369pp • H/C (ISBN: 9781466600713) • US $190.00 (our price)

Performance and Dependability in Service Computing Concepts, Techniques and Research Directions
Valeria Cardellini (Universita di Roma, Italy) Emiliano Casalicchio (Universita di Roma, Italy) Kalinka Regina Lucas Jaquie Castelo Branco (Universidade de São Paulo, Brazil) Júlio Cezar Estrella (Universidade de São Paulo, Brazil) and Francisco José Monaco (Universidade de São Paulo, Brazil)
Information Science Reference • copyright 2012 • 477pp • H/C (ISBN: 9781609607944) • US $195.00 (our price)

E-Activity and Intelligent Web Construction Effects of Social Design
Tokuro Matsuo (Yamagata University, Japan) and Takayuki Fujimoto (Toyo University, Japan)
Information Science Reference • copyright 2011 • 284pp • H/C (ISBN: 9781615208715) • US $180.00 (our price)

IGI GLOBAL
DISSEMINATOR OF KNOWLEDGE
www.igi-global.com

701 E. Chocolate Ave., Hershey, PA 17033
Order online at www.igi-global.com or call 717-533-8845 x100
To place a standing order for titles released in this series, contact: cust@igi-global.com
Mon-Fri 8:00 am - 5:00 pm (est) or fax 24 hours a day 717-533-8661

List of Contributors

Table of Contents

Section 1
Theory of Demand-Driven Web Services

Section 3
Applications of Demand-Driven Web Services

Detailed Table of Contents

Section 1
Theory of Demand-Driven Web Services

Chapter 1

Zhaohao Sun, University of Ballarat, Australia & Hebei Normal University, China
John Yearwood, Federation University, Australia

Web services are playing a pivotal role in business, management, governance, and society with the dramatic development of the Internet and the Web. However, many fundamental issues are still ignored to some extent. For example, what is the unified perspective to the state-of-the-art of Web services? What is the foundation of Demand-Driven Web Services (DDWS)? This chapter addresses these fundamental issues by examining the state-of-the-art of Web services and proposing a theoretical and technological foundation for demand-driven Web services with applications. This chapter also presents an extended Service-Oriented Architecture (SOA), eSMACS SOA, and examines main players in this architecture. This chapter then classifies DDWS as government DDWS, organizational DDWS, enterprise DDWS, customer DDWS, and citizen DDWS, and looks at the corresponding Web services. Finally, this chapter examines the theoretical, technical foundations for DDWS with applications. The proposed approaches will facilitate research and development of Web services, mobile services, cloud services, and social services.

Chapter 2

Kenneth David Strang, APPC Research, Australia & State University of New York, USA

This chapter provides literature-grounded definitions of contemporary Web services and marketing theories, which can model business demand through procurement decision-making behavior. First, the literature was reviewed to identify contemporary Web 2.0 and Web service ontology alongside marketing theories, which can describe individual decision making in an organizational or personal context. The Web services included cloud computing, social networking, data storage, security, and hosted applications. Then selected models for assessing procurement decision-making behavior were discussed in more detail. The constructed grounded theory method was applied by interviewing Chief Information Officers (CIO) at large organizations across four industries in the USA: healthcare, higher education, energy creation, and banking. The purpose was to determine which marketing theories could effectively model their Web service procurement behavior. An empirical procurement decision-making model was developed and fitted with data collected from the participants. The results indicated that Web service procurement decision-making behavior in businesses could easily be modeled, and this was ratified by the CIOs. The chapter proposes a state-of-the-art ontology and model for continued empirical research about organizational procurement decision-making behavior for Web services or other products.

Chapter 3

Innovations in services often emanate from service encounters (i.e. the touch points between the service producers and the customers). Two different types of service encounters are dealt with: face-to-face and ICT-based service encounters. The aim of the chapter is to examine the specific conditions for innovations from ICT-based service encounters. The service encounter research tradition is mostly concerned with customer satisfaction. The perspective of the present chapter is on innovations in the service encounter. The specific contribution of the chapter is to establish a conceptual foundation for innovations in ICT-based service encounters.

This chapter has the goal of showing how multi-agent systems can be a suitable means for supporting the development and the composition of services in dynamic and complex environments. In particular, the chapter copes with the problem of developing services in the field of social networks. After an introduction on the relationships between multi-agent systems, services, and social networks, the chapter describes how multi-agent systems can support the interaction and the collaboration among the members of a social network through a set of active services.

Section 2
Technologies of Demand-Driven Web Services

Chapter 5

Highly developed economies are based on the knowledge society. A variety of software tools are used in almost every aspect of human life. Service-oriented architectures are limited to corporate-related business solutions. This chapter proposes a novel approach aimed to overcome the differences between real life services and software services. Using the design approaches for the current service-oriented architecture, a solution that can be implemented in open source systems has been proposed. As a result, a new approach to creating an agent for service composition is introduced. The agent itself is created by service composition too. The proposed approach might facilitate the research and development of Web services, service-oriented architectures, and intelligent agents.

Chapter 6

Zakaria Maamar, Zayed University, UAE
Noura Faci, Claude Bernard Lyon 1 University, France
Ejub Kajan, State University of Novi Pazar, Serbia
Emir Ugljanin, State University of Novi Pazar, Serbia

As part of our ongoing work on social-intensive Web services, also referred to as social Web services, different types of networks that connect them together are developed. These networks include collaboration, substitution, and competition, and permit the addressing of specific issues related to Web service use such as composition, discovery, and high-availability. "Social" is embraced because of the similarities of situations that Web services run into at run time with situations that people experience daily. Indeed, Web services compete, collaborate, and substitute. This is typical to what people do. This chapter sheds light on some criteria that support Web service selection of a certain network to sign up over another. These criteria are driven by the security means that each network deploys to ensure the safety and privacy of its members from potential attacks. When a Web service signs up in a network, it becomes exposed to both the authority of the network and the existing members in the network as well. These two can check and alter the Web service's credentials, which may jeopardize its reputation and correctness levels.

Chapter 7

Evan Morrison, University of Wollongong, Australia
Aditya Ghose, University of Wollongong, Australia
Hoa Dam, University of Wollongong, Australia
Alex Menzies, Expert and Decision Support Systems Institute, Australia
Katayoun Khodaei, University of Wollongong, Australia

Adaptive case management addresses the shift away from the prescriptive process-centric view of operations towards a declarative framework for operational descriptions that promotes dynamic task selection in knowledge-intensive operations. A key difference between prescriptive services and declarative services is the way by which control flow is defined. Repeatable and straight-thru processes have been successfully used to model and optimise simple activity-based value chains. Increasingly, traditional process modeling techniques are being applied to knowledge intensive activities with often poor outcomes. By taking an adaptive case management approach to knowledge-intensive services, it is possible to model and execute workflows such as medical protocols that have previously been too difficult to describe with typical BPM frameworks. In this chapter, the authors describe an approach to design-level adaptive case management leveraging off existing repositories' semantically annotated business process models.

Chapter 8

Provisioning of applications and value-added services for mobile (remote) monitoring and access to measurements data is supported by advanced communication models such as Internet of Things (IoT). IoT provides ubiquitous connectivity anytime and with anything. IoT applications are able to communicate with the environment, to receive information about its status, to exchange and use the information. Identification of generic functions for monitoring management, data acquisition, and access to information provides capabilities to define abstraction of transport technology and control protocols. This chapter presents an approach to design Web Services Application Programming Interfaces (API) for mobile monitoring and database access. Aspects of the Web Services implementation are discussed. A traffic model of Web Services application server is described formally. The Web Services application server handles traffic of different priorities generated by third party applications and by processes at the database server's side. The traffic model takes into account the distributed structure of the Web Services application server and applies mechanisms for adaptive admission control and load balancing to prevent overload. The utilization of Web Services application server is evaluated through simulation.

This chapter focuses on a new business model in social networking, uses platform strategy to discuss possible business models, evaluates the optimal model for partnering with social networking service providers. This research develops a new revenue business model in social networking with a case study and discusses its potential monetization business model. The chapter reviews five business models including: 1) social media startups; 2) challenges social networks face: must monetize or die; 3) a case study of the new effective social business model – Facebook; 4) monetization: Facebook revenue and business model; and 5) a discussion of monetizing social networks: the four dominant business models and how you should implement them in the future. Through a comprehensive review, the chapter proposes a social media monetization model as the reference for firms to implement new business models of social networking.

Securing a cloud network is an important challenge for delivering cloud services to enterprise clouds. There are a number of secure network protocols, such as VPN protocols, currently available, to provide different secure network solutions for enterprise clouds. For example, PPTP, IPSec, and SSL/TLS are the most widely used VPN protocols in today's securing network solutions. However, there are some significant challenges in the implementation stage. For example, which VPN solution is easy to deploy in delivering cloud services? Which VPN solution is most user-friendly in enterprise clouds? This chapter explores these issues by implementing different VPNs in a virtual cloud network environment using open source software and tools. This chapter also reviews cloud computing and cloud services and looks at their relationships. The results not only provide experimental evidence but also facilitate the network implementers in deployment of secure network solutions for enterprise cloud services.

Chapter 11

Chellammal Surianarayanan, Bharathidasan University, India

Gopinath Ganapathy, Bharathidasan University, India

Manikandan Sethunarayanan Ramasamy, Bharathidasan University Constituent College, India

Semantic Web service discovery provides high retrieval accuracy. However, it imposes an implicit constraint to service clients that the clients must express their queries with the same domain ontologies as used by the service providers. Fulfilling this criterion is very tedious. Hence, a WordNet (general ontology)-based similarity model is proposed for service discovery, and its accuracy is enhanced to a level comparable to the accuracy of computing similarity using service specific ontologies. This is done by optimizing similarity threshold, which refers to a minimum similarity that is required to decide whether a given pair of services is similar or not. The proposed model is implemented and results are presented. The approach warrants clients to express their queries without specifying any ontology and alleviates the problem of maintaining complex domain ontologies. Moreover, the computation time of WordNet-based model is very low when compared to specific ontology-based model.

Section 3
Applications of Demand-Driven Web Services

Chapter 12

Dong Dong, Hebei Normal University, China

Lizhe Sun, Boston Consulting Group, Australia

Zhaohao Sun, University of Ballarat, Australia & Hebei Normal University, China

This chapter examines Web services in China. More specifically, it examines the state-of-the-art of China's Web services in terms of cloud services, mobile services, and social networking services through exploring several leading Web service providers in the ICT industry, including Alibaba, Tencent, China Mobile, and Huawei. This research reveals that the Chinese culture has played an important role in the success of China's Web services. The trade-off ideology and communication conventions from Chinese traditional culture, as well as Mao Zedong thought, greatly influenced the development of China's Web services. The findings of this chapter might facilitate the research and development of Web services and better understanding of the growth in China's ICT industry, as well as future trends.

Mohd Hisham Mohd Sharif, University of Adelaide, Australia

Indrit Troshani, University of Adelaide, Australia

Robyn Davidson, University of Adelaide, Australia

The increasing diffusion of social media is attracting government organizations worldwide, including local government. Social media can help local government improve the manner in which it is engaged with community and its responsiveness whilst offering cost savings and flexibility. Yet, there is paucity of research in relation to the adoption of social media Web services in local government organizations. The aim of this chapter is to investigate the factors that drive the adoption of social media Web services within Australian local government. Using qualitative evidence, the authors find technological, organizational, and environmental factors that drive the decisions of local government organizations to adopt social media Web services. In addition to extending the existing body of knowledge, this chapter offers insight concerning important managerial implications for helping local governments to better understand social media adoption in their organizations.

Juan Boubeta-Puig, University of Cádiz, Spain

Guadalupe Ortiz, University of Cádiz, Spain

Inmaculada Medina-Bulo, University of Cádiz, Spain

The Internet of Things (IoT) provides a large amount of data, which can be shared or consumed by thousands of individuals and organizations around the world. These organizations can be connected using Service-Oriented Architectures (SOAs), which have emerged as an efficient solution for modular system implementation allowing easy communications among third-party applications; however, SOAs do not provide an efficient solution to consume IoT data for those systems requiring on-demand detection of significant or exceptional situations. In this regard, Complex Event Processing (CEP) technology continuously processes and correlates huge amounts of events to detect and respond to changing business processes. In this chapter, the authors propose the use of CEP to facilitate the demand-driven detection of relevant situations. This is achieved by aggregating simple events generated by an IoT platform in an event-driven SOA, which makes use of an enterprise service bus for the integration of IoT, CEP, and SOA. The authors illustrate this approach through the implementation of a case study. Results confirm that CEP provides a suitable solution for the case study problem statement.

Shah Jahan Miah, Victoria University, Australia

Technology development for process enhancement has been a topic to many health organizations and researchers over the past decades. In particular, on decision support aids of healthcare professional, studies suggest paramount interests for developing technological intervention to provide better decision-support options. This chapter introduces a combined requirement of developing intelligent decision-support approach through the application of business intelligence and cloud-based functionalities. Both technological approaches demonstrate their usage to meet growing end users' demands through their innovative features in healthcare. As such, the main emphasis in the chapter goes after outlining a conceptual approach of demand-driven cloud-based business intelligence for meeting the decision-support needs in a hypothetical problem domain in the healthcare industry, focusing on the decision-support system development within a non-clinical context for individual end-users or patients who need decision support for their well-being and independent everyday living.

Patrizia Lombardi, Politecnico di Torino, Italy & Università di Torino, Italy
Andrea Acquaviva, Politecnico di Torino, Italy
Enrico Macii, Politecnico di Torino, Italy
Anna Osello, Politecnico di Torino, Italy
Edoardo Patti, Politecnico di Torino, Italy
Giulia Sonetti, Politecnico di Torino, Italy & Università di Torino, Italy

ICT is recognized as being a key player against climate change: pervasive sensors and actuators can efficiently control the whole energy chain. On the other side, advances on 3D modelling, visualization, and interaction technologies enable user profiling and real-time feedback to promote energy-efficient behaviours. The study presented in this chapter illustrates the development of a Web service-oriented, open platform with capabilities of real-time district level data processing and visualization. The platform will allow open access with personal devices and A/R visualization of energy-related information to client applications for energy and cost-analysis, tariff planning and evaluation, failure identification and maintenance, energy information sharing. The expected results are a consistent reduction in both energy consume and CO2 emissions by enabling more efficient energy distribution policies, according to the actual characteristics of district buildings and inhabitants as well as a more efficient utilization and maintenance of the energy distribution network, based on social behaviour, users lifestyles, and singular demands.

Edwin Iroroeavwo Achugbue, Delta State University, Nigeria

This chapter is anchored on previous research to examine e-business in education, with emphasis on the Delta State University Abraka, Delta State, Nigeria. The study focused on the concept of e-business, e-business in education, and explored the various educational routines, such as e-learning, tele-learning, research, and administration. The study examined classification of e-business, e-business tools, such as e-mail, Websites, message boards, online catalogs, and telephone and e-business activities in education. It also focused on e-payment of fees, students' registration, checking of results, and online application as part of e-business routines in administration. Finally, the study looked at the barriers to e-business adoption in education using diffusion theory of innovation. A conclusion and recommendations are then made.

Cloud applications have been gaining popularity in recent years for their flexibility in resource provisioning according to Web application demands. The Elastic Application Container (EAC) system is a technology that delivers a lightweight virtual resource unit for better resource efficiency and more scalable Web applications in the Cloud. It allows multiple application providers to concurrently run their Web applications on this technology without worrying the demand change of their Web applications. This is because the EAC system constantly monitors the resource usage of all hosting Web applications and automatically reacts to the resource usage change of Web applications (i.e. it automatically handles resource provisioning of the Web applications, such as scaling of the Web applications according to the demand). In the chapter, the authors firstly describe the architecture, its components of the EAC system, in order to give a brief overview of technologies involved in the system. They then present and explain resource-provisioning algorithms and techniques used in the EAC system for demand-driven Web applications. The resource-provisioning algorithms are presented, discussed, and evaluated so as to give readers a clear picture of resource-provisioning algorithms in the EAC system. Finally, the authors compare this EAC system technology with other Cloud technologies in terms of flexibility and resource efficiency.

Industrial and environmental research will always involve the study of the cause-effect relationship between emissions and the surrounding environment. The techniques of artificial intelligence such as artificial neural network can be applied in the industrial and environmental research. Chemical facilities have high risks to originate air emission events (e.g. intensive flaring and toxic gas release). They are caused by various uncertainties like equipment failure, false operation, nature disaster, or terrorist attack. Through an air-quality monitoring network, data integration is applied to identify the possible emission source and dynamic emission profiles. In this chapter, the above-mentioned application has been illustrated. It has the capability to identify the potential emission profile and characterize spatial-temporal pollutant dispersion. It provides valuable information for accidental investigations and root cause analysis for an emission event; meanwhile, it helps evaluate the regional air quality impact caused by such an emission event.

Preface

Service is the lifeblood for individuals, industry, community, and society; demand-driven services are paramount. An industy is inevitably defined by customer demands. Similarly, citizen and community demand inevitably define the government in a country. Therefore, meeting the demand from government, community, and customers at a social level is a grand challenge for computing, service, and management in the Internet age. Meeting the demand from individuals, businesses, transactions, and projects at an activity level is also a grand challenge for services, analytics services, mobile services, e-services, cloud services, and social networking services in the Internet age. With these challenges in mind, *Demand-Driven Web Services* will address the following significant issues arising in the smarter customers-driven age. What are the demands of governments for Web services? What are the demands of communities for Web services? What are the demands of organizations in general, and specific enterprises for Web services? What are the demands of customers' Web services? Taking these demands into account, what are the Web services that can meet each of these mentioned demands?

Web services are playing a pivotal role in service computing, mobile computing, analytics computing, cloud computing, and social computing (for short SMACS computing); for all these computing, e or electronic is at the center over the past decade. This is also the case in the traditional FREG (Foods, Resources, Energy, and Goods) services, because almost all traditional services are fully or partially replaced or improved by Web services. Demand-driven Web services as a computing paradigm, a service paradigm, and a management paradigm is becoming important for service computing, mobile computing, Web computing, cloud computing, and social computing. However, many fundamental issues in developing demand-driven Web services remain open. For example, what are the theory and technlogies of demand-driven Web services? How should real world demands be classified? How should Web services be classified? How can an ontology of Web services be developed? How can we combine the theory and technologies of demand-driven Web services with real-world applications including e-supply chain, e-marketing, e-commerce and e-government, cloud services, big data management, and social networking services.

In tandem with resolving these issues, this book on demand-driven Web services can meet the demand of various professionals' understanding of Web services in the Internet age more comprehensively. More specifically, this book will address these above-mentioned issues by exploring the theory of demand and various demands from governments, communities, organizations, and individuals, and then look at the various demand-driven Web services. This book further provides applications of the proposed theory, technologies, and methodologies to successful demand-driven Web services in the real world. The approach proposed in this book will expand the field of mobile services, e-business services, Web services, cloud services, and social networking services through the proposed theory, technologies, and methodologies of demand-driven Web services with applications. The proposed approaches will facilitate research and development of electronic computing, mobile computing, analytics computing, cloud computing, and social computing (for short, eSMACS computing). The proposed approach in this book will also benefit readers by providing an understanding of demand-driven Web services and their impacts on e-commerce, e-services and e-government, and cloud computing.

In the past two decades, commerce has evolved from traditional commerce through e-commerce to smarter commerce thanks to the dramatic development of the Internet and the Web. In the meantime, services have also evolved from traditional services through electronic services to Web services. Currently, Web services emphasize e-services, smarter services, mobile services, analytics services, cloud services, and (online) social networking services (for short, eSMACS services). However, demand is the driver of the economy, marketing, and any business/services activities. Demand-driven Web services are the effective computing, management, and service paradigm, and provide significant solutions to business, marketing, and services through effective theory, technologies, methodologies, and applications. This book is the first book to reveal the cutting-edge theory, technologies, methodologies, and applications of demand-driven Web services in the Internet age in an integrated way. This is also the first book demonstrating that demand-driven Web services are an important computing, management, and service paradigm for developing smarter commerce, business, and services in the digital age.

There are a large number of books on Web services and e-services. They focus either on describing a few global successful companies in Web services in the world or on exploring technological Web services. Unlike the existing books, this book will explore the cutting-edge theory, technologies, methodologies, and applications of demand-driven Web services using the novel classification of demands and Web services and their interrelationships based on the effective contributions of international scholars from a perspective of computing, service, business, and management. The emerging mobile services, analytics services, cloud services, and social networking services are centered in the current Web services. More real world Web services will be examined in this book because of the characteristics of this book and the contribution of international peers.

This book's primary aim is to convey the ideas, thoughts, and methods as well as results of demand-driven Web services to scientists, engineers, educators and university students, business, service and management professionals, policy makers and decision makers, and others who have interest in traditional services, e-services, mobile services, analytics services, cloud services, social networking services, and Web services. Primary audiences for this book are undergraduate, postgraduate students, and variety of professionals in the fields of computing, commerce, business, services, management, and governance. The secondary audience(s) for this book is the variety of readers in the fields of government, business, and trade as well as the readers from all the social strata.

This book presents a collection or original, rigorous, and significant contributions on demand-driven Web services. Nineteen chapters are selected and included in this book after double anonymously blinded reviewing by the international peers due to the limitation of the allotted pages published. The chapters are organized into three sections: Section 1: "Theory of Demand-Driven Web Services," Section 2: "Technology of Demand-Driven Web Services," Section 3: "Applications of Demand-Driven Web Services." In what follows, we briefly summarize each chapter included in each section.

Section 1: Theory of Demand-Driven Web Services

Section 1: "Theory of Demand-Driven Web Services" consists of four chapters.

Chapter 1, by Zhaohao Sun and John Yearwood, provides a theoretical foundation of demand-driven Web services. More specifically, this chapter addresses two fundamental issues: what is the unified perspective to the state-of-the-art of Web services? What is the foundation of Demand-Driven Web Services (DDWS)? Chapter 1 answers these questions by examining the state-of-the-art of Web services and proposing a theoretical and technological foundation for demand-driven Web services with applications. This chapter also presents an extended Service-Oriented Architecture (SOA), eSMACS SOA, and examined main players in this architecture. This chapter then classifies demand-driven Web services as government demand-driven Web services, organizational demand-driven Web services, enterprise demand-driven Web services, customer demand-driven Web services, and citizen demand-driven Web services, and looks at the corresponding Web services. Finally, this chapter examines the theoretical, technical foundations for demand-driven Web services with applications.

Chapter 2, by Kenneth David Strang, explores marketing theories to model business Web service procurement behavior. This chapter provides literature-grounded definitions of contemporary Web services and marketing theories, which can model business demand through procurement decision-making behavior. The constructed grounded theory method was applied by interviewing Chief Information Officers (CIO) at large organizations across four industries in the USA: healthcare, higher education, energy creation, and banking. The purpose was to determine which marketing theories could effectively model their Web service procurement behavior. An empirical procurement decision-making model was developed and fitted with data collected from the participants. The results indicated that Web service procurement decision-making behavior in businesses could easily be modeled, and this was ratified by the CIOs. The chapter proposes a state-of-the-art ontology and model for continued empirical research about organizational procurement decision-making behavior for Web services or other products.

Chapter 3, by Jannick Kirk Sørensen and Anders Henten, examines co-creation of innovations in ICT-based service encounters. Innovations in services often emanate from the service encounters (i.e. the touch points between the service producers and the customers). This chapter deals with two different types of service encounters: face-to-face and ICT-based service encounters, and examines the specific conditions for innovations from ICT-based service encounters. This chapter establishes a conceptual foundation for innovations in ICT-based service encounters.

Chapter 4, by Enrico Franchi, Agostino Poggi, and Michele Tomaiuolo, looks at multi-agent active services for online social networks. This chapter demonstrates how multi-agent systems can be a suitable means for supporting the development and the composition of services in dynamic and complex environments. In particular, this chapter addresses the problem of developing services in the field of social networks. After an introduction to the relationships between multi-agent systems, services, and social networks, this chapter describes how multi-agent systems can support the interaction and the collaboration among the members of a social network through a set of active services.

Section 2: Technologies of Demand-Driven Web Services

Section 2: "Technologies of Demand-Driven Web Services" consists of seven chapters.

Chapter 5, by Mihai Horia Zaharia, examines generalized demand-driven Web services through proposing a novel approach for overcoming the differences between real life services and software services. Using the design approaches for the current service-oriented architecture, a solution that can be implemented in open source systems has been proposed. As a result, a new approach to creating an agent for service composition is introduced. The agent itself is created by service composition too.

Chapter 6, by Zakaria Maamar, Noura Faci, Ejub Kajan, and Emir Ugljanin, examines Social Web services management. This chapter sheds light on some criteria that help Web services select a certain network to sign up over another. These criteria are driven by the security means that each network deploys to ensure the safety and privacy of its members from potential attacks. When a Web service signs up in a network, it becomes exposed to both the authority of the network and the existing members in the network as well. These two can check and alter the Web service's credentials, which may jeopardize its reputation and correctness levels.

Chapter 7, by Evan Morrison, Aditya Ghose, Hoa Dam, et al, looks at declarative service modeling through adaptive case management. Adaptive Case Management addresses the shift away from the prescriptive process-centric view of operations towards a declarative framework for operational descriptions that promotes dynamic task selection in knowledge-intensive operations. By taking an adaptive case management approach to knowledge intensive services, it is possible to model and execute workflows such as medical protocols that have previously been too difficult to describe with typical BPM frameworks. This chapter proposes an approach to design level adaptive case management leveraging off existing repositories' semantically annotated business process models.

Chapter 8, by Evelina Pencheva, discusses design of Web services for mobile monitoring and access to measurements. Provisioning of applications and value added services for mobile (remote) monitoring and access to measurements data is supported by advanced communication models such as Internet of Things (IoT). IoT provides ubiquitous connectivity at any time and with anything. IoT applications are able to communicate with the environment, to receive information about its status, to exchange and use the information. This chapter presents an approach to design Web services Application Programming Interfaces (API) for mobile monitoring and database access, discusses the aspects of the Web services implementation, and describes a traffic model of Web services application server. The Web services application server handles traffic of different priorities generated by third party applications and by processes at the database server's side. The traffic model takes into account the distributed structure of the Web services application server and applies mechanisms for adaptive admission control and load balancing to prevent overload. This chapter also evaluates the utilization of Web services application server through simulation.

Chapter 9, by Te Fu Chen, develops a new revenue business model in social network through a case study of Facebook and discusses its potential monetization business model. The study reviews five business models including: 1) social media startups, 2) social networks face challenging: must monetize or die, 3) a case study of the new effective social business model – Facebook, 4) monetization: Facebook revenue and business model, and 5) a discussion of monetizing social networks: the four dominant business models and how one should implement them in the future. Through the above comprehensive review, this chapter proposes a social media monetization model as the reference for firms to implement new business models of social networking.

Chapter 10, by Chengcheng Huang, Phil Smith, and Zhaohao Sun, examines secure network solutions for enterprise cloud services. Securing a cloud network is an important challenge for delivering cloud services to enterprises cloud. There are a number of secure network protocols, such as VPN protocols, currently available to provide different secure network solutions for enterprise clouds. For example, PPTP, IPSec, and SSL/TLS are the most widely used VPN protocols in today's securing network solutions. However, there are some significant challenges in the implementation stage. For example, which VPN solution is easy to deploy in delivering cloud services? Which VPN solution is most user-friendly in enterprise clouds? This chapter explores these issues by implementing different VPNs in a virtual cloud network environment using open source software and tools. This chapter also reviews cloud computing and cloud services and looks at their relationships.

Chapter 11, by Chellammal Surianarayanan, Gopinath Ganapathy, and Manikandan Sethunarayanan Ramasamy, proposes a practical approach to enhancement of accuracy of similarity model using WordNet towards semantic service discovery. Semantic Web service discovery provides high retrieval accuracy. However, it imposes an implicit constraint to service clients that the clients must express their queries with the same domain ontologies as used by the service providers. Fulfilling this criterion is very tedious. Hence, a WordNet (general ontology)-based similarity model is proposed for service discovery, and its accuracy is enhanced to a level comparable to the accuracy of computing similarity using service-specific ontologies. This is done by optimizing similarity threshold, which refers to a minimum similarity that is required to decide whether a given pair of services is similar or not. The proposed model is implemented and results are presented in this chapter. The approach warrants clients to express their queries without specifying any ontology and alleviates the problem of maintaining complex domain ontologies.

Section 3: Applications of Demand-Driven Web Services

Section 3: "Applications of Demand-Driven Web Services" consists of eight chapters.

Chapter 12, by Dong Dong, Lizhe Sun, and Zhaohao Sun, examines Web services in China. More specifically, this chapter examines the state-of-the-art of China's Web services in terms of cloud services, mobile services, and social networking services through exploring several leading Web service providers in the ICT industry, including Alibaba, Tencent, China Mobile, and Huawei. This research reveals that the Chinese culture has played an important role in the success of China's Web services. The trade-off idea and communication conventions from Chinese traditional culture, as well as Mao Zedong thought, have greatly influenced the development of the China's Web services. The findings of this chapter might facilitate the research and development of Web services and better understanding of the growth in China's ICT industry as well as future trends.

Chapter 13, by Mohd Hisham Mohd Sharif, Indrit Troshani, and Robyn Davidson, discusses adoption of social media services using the case of local government organizations in Australia. The increasing diffusion of social media is attracting government organizations worldwide, including local government. Social media can help local government improve the manner in which it is engaged with community and its responsiveness whilst offering cost savings and flexibility. Yet, there is paucity of research in relation to the adoption of social media Web services in local government organizations. This chapter aims to investigate the factors that drive the adoption of social media Web services within Australian local government. Using qualitative evidence, this chapter finds technological, organizational, and environmental factors that drive the decision of local government organization to adopt social media Web services. In addition to extending the existing body of knowledge, this chapter also offers insight concerning important managerial implications for helping local government to better understand social media adoption in their organizations.

Chapter 14, by Juan Boubeta-Puig, Guadalupe Ortiz, and Inmaculada Medina-Bulo, examines approaching the Internet of Things (IoT) through integrating Service-Oriented Architectures (SOA) and Complex Event Processing (CEP). IoT provides a large amount of data, which can be shared or consumed by thousands of individuals and organizations around the world. These organizations can be connected using SOA; however, SOA do not provide an efficient solution to consume IoT data for those systems requiring on-demand detection of significant or exceptional situations. In this regard, CEP technology continuously processes and correlates huge amounts of events to detect and respond to changing business processes. This chapter proposes the use of CEP to facilitate the demand-driven detection of relevant situations. This is achieved by aggregating simple events generated by an IoT platform in an event-driven SOA, which makes use of an enterprise service bus for the integration of IoT, CEP, and SOA. This chapter illustrates the proposed approach through the implementation of a case study. The research results confirm that CEP provides a suitable solution for the case study problem statement.

Chapter 15, by Shah Jahan Miah, discusses demand-driven cloud-based business intelligence for healthcare decision-making. More specifically, this chapter introduces a combined requirement of developing intelligent decision support approach through the application of business intelligence and cloud-based functionalities. Both technological approaches demonstrate their usage to meet growing end users' demand through their innovative features in healthcare. As such, the main emphasis in this chapter goes after outlining a conceptual approach of demand-driven cloud-based business intelligence for meeting the decision support needs in a hypothetical problem domain in healthcare industry, specially focusing on decision support system development within a non-clinical context for individual end-users or patients who need decision support for their well-being and independent everyday living.

Chapter 16, by Patrizia Lombardi, Andrea Acquaviva, Enrico Macii, et al., examines Web and cloud management for building energy reduction toward a smart district information modeling. This chapter illustrates the development of a Web service-oriented, open platform with capabilities of real-time district-level data processing and visualization. The platform will allow open access with personal devices and A/R visualization of energy-related information to client applications for energy and cost-analysis, tariff planning and evaluation, failure identification and maintenance, and energy information sharing. The expected results are a consistent reduction in both energy consumption and CO_2 emissions by enabling more efficient energy distribution policies, according to the actual characteristics of district buildings and inhabitants as well as a more efficient utilization and maintenance of the energy distribution network, based on social behaviour, user lifestyles, and singular demands.

Chapter 17, by Edwin I. Achugbue, examines e-business in education, with emphasis on the case of the Delta State University Abraka, Delta State, Nigeria. This chapter focuses on the concept of e-business, e-business in education, and explores the various educational routines, such as e-learning, tele-learning, research, and administration. The study also examines classification of e-business and e-business tools, such as e-mail, Websites, message boards, online catalogs, and telephone and e-business activities in education. This chapter focuses on e-payment of fees, students' registration, checking of results, and online application as part of e-business routines in administration. Finally, this chapter looks at the barriers to e-business adoption in education using diffusion theory of innovation.

Chapter 18, by Sijin He, Li Guo, and Yike Guo, examines an Elastic Application Container (EAC) system. EAC system is a technology that delivers a lightweight virtual resource unit for better resource efficiency and more scalable Web applications in the cloud. It allows multiple application providers to concurrently run their Web applications on this technology without worrying the demand change of their Web applications. This is because the EAC system constantly monitors the resource usage of all hosting Web applications and automatically reacts to the resource usage change of Web applications (i.e. it automatically handles resource provisioning of the Web applications, such as scaling of the Web applications according to the demand). This chapter describes the architecture, its components of the EAC system, in order to give a brief overview of technologies involved in the system. It then presents, explains, and evaluates resource-provisioning algorithms and techniques used in the EAC system for demand-driven Web applications. Finally, this chapter compares this EAC system technology with other cloud technologies in terms of flexibility and resource efficiency.

Chapter 19, by Tianxing Cai, discusses the artificial neural network for industrial and environmental research via air quality monitoring network. Industrial and environmental research will always involve the study of the cause-effect relationship between the emission and the surrounding environment. The techniques of artificial intelligence such as artificial neural network can be applied in the industrial and environmental research. Chemical facilities have high risks to originate air emission events (e.g. intensive flaring and toxic gas release). They are caused by various uncertainties like equipment failure, false operation, nature disaster, or terrorist attack. Through air-quality monitoring network, this chapter applies the data integration to identify the possible emission source and dynamic emission profiles. This chapter also provides valuable information for accidental investigations and root cause analysis for an emission event; meanwhile, it helps evaluate the regional air quality impact caused by such an emission event as well.

It clearly is impossible to cover the full range of issues related to demand-driven Web services theory, technologies, and applications in a single book, and hence, no attempt has been made to do so. We hope that the readers will find some interesting and valuable ideas, methods, techniques, models, and insights for stimulating new research and development of demand-driven Web services.

Demand-driven Web services is still an emerging area for research and development in terms of eS-MACS computing. There are still many issues that need to be addressed in the near future, for example, fundamental concepts, models, architectures, frameworks, schemes, or theories for planning, designing, building, operating, or evaluating, managing demand-driven Web services. As technologies for demand-driven Web services, AI-based technologies, including rule-based systems, ontology-development systems, machine learning techniques, multi-agent systems techniques, neural networks systems, fuzzy logic systems, cased-based reasoning systems, genetic algorithms techniques, data mining algorithms, intelligent agents, user intelligent interfaces, Web technologies, service technologies, social networking technologies, decision-making technologies, DSS technologies, need to be incorporated into demand-driven Web services. As applications of demand-driven Web services, case studies and applications in using the above-mentioned technologies and fundamental theory in the representative service domains such as: e-business services, mobile services, social networking services, cloud services, financial services, legal services, healthcare services, logistics services, educational services, e-FREG services, and military services taking into account demands from government, organization, enterprise, community, individual, customer, and citizen, need to be undertaken. Finally, trends and challenges on demand-driven Web services include emergent AI-based technologies, big data technologies, social networking services, integrations of these technologies, and the implications, challenges for demand-driven Web services, emerging demands, emerging technologies, including human computation and big data management, methodologies for demand-driven Web services, require more attention in research and development.

Zhaohao Sun
University of Ballarat, Australia & Hebei Normal University, China

John Yearwood
Federation University, Australia
December 2013

Acknowledgment

The publication of this book reflects the wisdom and hard work of many researchers worldwide. We first thank all the members of editorial board for their erudite comments and guidance. We heartily thank all the high quality contributors for their time and submission of manuscripts; they have made this book possible and transformed our concepts to reality. We would also like to thank all those who have contributed their proposals, drafts, ideas, and insights to this book. Our gratitude extends to the international team of referees who reviewed the book chapters selflessly. Our sincerest thanks go to our good friends at IGI Global, Mr. Vince D'Imperio, Ms. Christina Henning, Ms. Allyson Gard and Ms. Kayla Wolfe, who have given us outstanding support through the book development process. Their support, patience, and encouragement during its production have been very important for us.

Finally, Zhaohao would like to express his deep appreciation for the support and encouragement of his wife, Dr. Yanxia Huo. Without her lasting support and patience, writing and editing this book would not have been possible. John would like to express his thanks and appreciations to Zhaohao for his energy and commitment, but particularly his wonderful sense of collaboration that saw this come together so smoothly.

Zhaohao Sun
University of Ballarat, Australia & Hebei Normal University, China

John Yearwood
Federation University, Australia

December 2013

Section 1
Theory of Demand-Driven Web Services

Chapter 1
A Theoretical Foundation of Demand Driven Web Services

Zhaohao Sun
University of Ballarat, Australia & Hebei Normal University, China

John Yearwood
Federation University, Australia

ABSTRACT

Web services are playing a pivotal role in business, management, governance, and society with the dramatic development of the Internet and the Web. However, many fundamental issues are still ignored to some extent. For example, what is the unified perspective to the state-of-the-art of Web services? What is the foundation of Demand-Driven Web Services (DDWS)? This chapter addresses these fundamental issues by examining the state-of-the-art of Web services and proposing a theoretical and technological foundation for demand-driven Web services with applications. This chapter also presents an extended Service-Oriented Architecture (SOA), eSMACS SOA, and examines main players in this architecture. This chapter then classifies DDWS as government DDWS, organizational DDWS, enterprise DDWS, customer DDWS, and citizen DDWS, and looks at the corresponding Web services. Finally, this chapter examines the theoretical, technical foundations for DDWS with applications. The proposed approaches will facilitate research and development of Web services, mobile services, cloud services, and social services.

1 INTRODUCTION

Web services are playing a pivotal role in business-es, governments, communities and organisations, and societies with the dramatic development of the Internet and the Web. Technically, Web services are Internet-based application components

published using standard interface description languages and universally available via uniform communication protocols (ICWS, 2009). Generally, Web services refer to all the services provided on the Web. With the dramatic development of the Internet and the Web in the past decade, Web services have been flourishing in e-commerce, e-

DOI: 10.4018/978-1-4666-5884-4.ch001

business, artificial intelligence (AI), and service computing. They have also offered a number of strategic advantages such as mobility, flexibility, social-ability, interactivity and interchangeability in comparison with traditional services (Hoffman, 2003). Web services are playing a pivotal role both in e-business, service computing and social networking services and cloud computing. This is also the case in the traditional FREG (foods, resources, energy and goods) services, IT services (Kauffman, Srivastava, & Vayghan, 2012), because almost all traditional services are fully or partially replaced by Web services.

The fundamental philosophy of Web services is to meet the needs of users precisely and thereby increase market share and revenue (Rust & Kannan, 2003). Web services have helped users reduce the cost of information technology (IT) operations and allow them to closely focus on their own core competencies (Hoffman, 2003). At the same time, for business marketers, Web services are very useful for improving interorganizational relationships and generating new revenue streams (Sun & Lau, 2007). Furthermore, Web services can be considered a further development of e-business (Gottschalk, 2001), because they are service-focused business paradigms that use two-way dialogues to build customized service offerings, based on knowledge and experience about users to build strong customer relationships (Rust & Kannan, 2003). However, one of the intriguing aspects of Web services is that any Web service cannot avoid similar challenges encountered in traditional services such as how to meet customer's demands in order to attract more customers.

Demand-driven Web services (DDWS) as a computing paradigm (Currie & Parikh, 2006) and a service paradigm are becoming important for Web services, service computing, cloud computing and social networking computing. However, many fundamental issues in developing DDWS remain open. For example, the following research problems arise in Web services:

- What is a unified perspective to the state of art of Web services?
- What are the main players in various Web services?
- What are the theoretical, technological foundations for Web services?

These problems remain open in Web services in general, and DDWS in particular. This chapter addresses these issues. This chapter was motivated by our early work (Sun, Dong, & Yearwood, 2011), in which we proposed a demand-driven architecture for Web services and a demand-driven Web service lifecycle for the main players in Web services respectively, we also looked at mathematical analysis of demands in Web services. As the further development of our early work, the remainder of this chapter is organized as follows. Firstly we examine state of art of Web services. Then we propose an extended service-oriented architecture (SOA): eSMACS (e + social (networking) + mobile + analytics + cloud + service) SOA and discuss the main players in this architecture. We also classify demand-driven Web services (DDWS) as government DDWS, organizational DDWS, enterprise DDWS, customer DDWS and citizen DDWS and look at the corresponding Web services in detail. Finally, we examine the theoretical and technical foundations for DDWS with applications. We end this chapter with providing some concluding remarks and discussing some future research directions.

2 THE STATE OF THE ART OF WEB SERVICES

2.1 E-Services and Web Services

E-services are "electronic offerings for rent" made available via the Internet that complete tasks, solve problems, or conduct transactions (Hoffman, 2003). Song (2003) demonstrates that e-services have the following features: integration, interaction, customization, self-services, flexibility and automatic response. Interaction is an important feature of e-services. Each e-service interacts with others to fulfill customer requests. Self-services are another feature of e-services (Song, 2003). Websites offering e-services allow customers to review accounts, monitor shipments, edit profiles, schedule pick-ups, adjust invoices, return merchandises and so on, as computer-mediated rather than interpersonal transactions. E-business services are important e-services that include e-buy services, e-intermediary services, e-sell services, e-supply chain services, e-marketing services, e-procurement services, e-banking services.

Some e-services, e.g. Amazon.com, are integrated with e-commerce applications such as shipping information, package tracking and rate inquiries (Song, 2003). E-services are seamlessly integrated with e-commerce applications to make the shipping experience simple and convenient. Therefore, from a business viewpoint, e-services are a further development of traditional e-commerce (Sun & Lau, 2007). In other words, traditional e-commerce is giving way to e-service. The majority of e-business or e-commerce activities can be considered e-services, which can be also considered as e-commerce services. E-commerce services have matured with the dramatic development of the Internet and e-commerce.

Web services are defined from an e-commerce or a business logic viewpoint at one extreme, in which case, Web services are the same as e-services (Sun & Lau, 2007). At another extreme, Web services are defined from a computer science or IT viewpoint as "A standardized way of integrating Web-based applications using the XML, SOAP, WSDL, and UDDI open standards over an Internet protocol backbone. XML is used to tag the data. SOAP is used to transfer data. WSDL is used for describing the e-services available. UDDI is used for listing what services are available." (Alonso, Casati, Kuno, & and Machiraju, 2004, p. 125). Between these two extremes, many different definitions of Web services have been

proposed at an intermediary level based on the understanding of different authors. For example, Web services are a way of publishing an explicit, machine-readable, common standard description of how to use a service and access it via another program using some standard message transports (Petrie & Genesereth, 2003). A Web service is "a self-describing, self-contained software module available via a network, such as the Internet, which completes tasks, solves problems or conducts transactions on behalf of a user or application" (Papazoglou, 2008, p. 5)

Hereafter, Web services refer to all the services on the Web. The reason for it is that e-commerce, e-marketing, e-selling are preferred in (Chaffey, 2009), whereas commerce on the Web, marketing on the Web and selling on the Web are preferred in (Schneider, 2013). However, e-commerce is commerce on the Web, e-marketing is marketing on the Web and e-selling is selling on the Web, respectively. In other words, the terms Web services, e-services and electronic services are used interchangeably in this chapter. We prefer to the usage of Web services, e-services rather than that of electronic services. E-commerce or e-business services include e-banking, e-procurement, e-supply chaining management, e-marketing, e-government, and so on (Kauffman, Srivastava, & Vayghan, 2012; Chaffey, 2009). Different from e-commerce services, a few new emerging kinds of Web services have been at the center for government, business, computing, and society in recent years. These new emerging Web services as the state of art include service as a Web service (services services), social networking services (SNSs), mobile services, analytics services, and cloud services. These Web services and their relationships can be illustrated using a model of e-SMACS services, as shown in Figure 1.

In the next section we argue the Web services as eSMACS services, which can be considered as a state of art of Web services, addressing the first research problem mentioned in the first section.

Figure 1. A model of e-SMACS services

2.2 Web Services = eSMACS Services

In this model, the Web is a new form of electronic (e) things, underpinned by the Internet, different from the traditional electronic age including telephone and TV, because the latter can be also considered as electronic products. Therefore, e is at the center. E-services are at the center of all the Web services, this means that e-services can be considered the first kind of Web services accompanying the inception of e-commerce in the middle 1990s. E-services have been popular since, and are all the services on the Web. All the new emerging Web services constitute the state of art Web services, that is, social networking services, mobile services, analytics services, cloud services, and service as a Web service. For brevity, we can represent these new emerging Web services as Web services = eSMACS services, where eSMACS = e + social (networking) + analytics + cloud + service. In what follows, we will examine each of these in some detail.

2.2.1 SNS

A social networking service is an online service that focuses on facilitating the building of social networks or social relations among people who, for example, share interests, activities, backgrounds, or real-life connections (Turban & Volonino, 2011). Social networking services (SNS) can be called social networking as a WS (SNaaWS), which further includes friending services, blog services, game services, photo sharing services. A SNS is also a website where individuals, who are defined by a profile, can interact with others (Turban & Volonino, 2011, p. 223). Technically, a SNS is a group of Internet-based applications (apps) that allow for the creation and exchange of user-generated content (Dong, Cheng, & Wu, 2013). The Internet-based apps include social software that mediates communication and interaction among the users on the online social networking websites. The current popular websites for SNS are Facebook, Twitter, Google+ and QQZone. More generally, a SNS is a Web service that facilitates the building of social networks or social interactions among people through sharing ideas, activities or virtual or real-life interactions (Dong, Cheng, & Wu, 2013). The most common SNSs at the moment consist of mediator of activities and events, developer of interests within their individual networks on the SNS websites and beyond. Twittering, blogging, photo and text sharing are also common SNSs. That is, the Web users in SNS can express themselves by posting blogs or experiences or photos, interact with each other, share information and multimedia, and establish their social networks (Lu, Zhao, & Wang, 2010) creation, sharing and exchange of information (e.g. photos, texts, and messages), thoughts, opinions and experiences (e.g. comments, opinions, ratings and playing games) among individual users (Smyth, Briggs, & Coyle, 2009; Kaplan & Haenlein, 2010). SNS websites such as Facebook and Twitter have reshaped communication and interaction among people and have had a profound impact in the way people interact with each other (Sun, Yearwood, & Firmin, 2013).

2.2.2 Mobile Services

Mobile services can be considered as the first kinds of Web services following e-services. Mobile services have evolved rapidly over the past two decades (Turban & Volonino, 2011, p. 192). Mobile devices, mobile operating systems and software, and wireless networks have facilitated the dramatic development of mobile services, thanks to the tremendous growth of use of smart phones and tablets which are connected to the Web (Schneider, 2013, p. 175). Mobile Internet access devices include smartphones, iPads and other tablet computers (Laudon & Traver, 2013, p. 164). A smartphone becomes not only a general-purpose computer, but also a shopping tool for a consumer, as well as an entirely new marketing and advertising platform for vendors. The most popular mobile services include mobile financial

or banking services, mobile commerce services, mobile information services and mobile SNS (Turban & Volonino, 2011, pp. 197-211).

Mobile financial or banking services means that customers can use smartphones to receive a wide range of financial or banking services (Turban & Volonino, 2011; Baltzan, Phillips, Lynch, & Blakey, 2013), which includes account balances management and updates, bill paying, fund transfers and transaction verification, to name a few. Mobile financial services can be considered as a mobile application of e-financial services. Different from e-financial services, mobile financial services are free from laptop, and desktop computers. A smartphone is enough for receiving financial services at any time and at any place. In such way, a smartphone has replaced laptop, and desktop as a mobile computing device.

Mobile commerce services include mobile shopping, advertising, and entertainment (Schneider, 2013, p. 175). Mobile advertising or marketing services include advertising campaigns, discounts, promotions and marketing messaging services (Baltzan, Phillips, Lynch, & Blakey, 2013). Mobile entertainment services include downloads of music, videos, games and ring tones, as well as messaging services (Baltzan, Phillips, Lynch, & Blakey, 2013). Mobile games mean that an individual can play any online games using a smartphone or other mobile devices (Turban & Volonino, 2011). Therefore, replacing desktop, PlayStation and X-box, smartphone has been used to play online games at any time at any place. In such a way, mobile games can be considered as an integration of online games and mobile games.

Mobile information services include information services for news, city events, weather, and sports reports, online language translation, tourist attractions and emergency services, to name a few. For example, users spent 95% of their time accessing travel information from their mobile apps in the travel area (Laudon & Traver, 2013, p. 165).

Mobile SNS is a SNS in which two or more individual converse and connect with one another using smartphones and other mobile devices (Turban & Volonino, 2011, pp. 192-203). In such a way, mobile SNS can be considered as integration between mobile services and SNS.

2.2.3 Analytics Services

Generally speaking, analytics is a method or technique that uses data, information, knowledge to learn and predict something (Turban & Volonino, 2011, p. 341). More specifically, data analytics encompasses a wide range of mathematical, statistical, and modeling techniques to extract knowledge from data (Coronel, Morris, & Rob, 2013, p. 569). Analytics can be then considered as data-driven discoveries (Demirkan & Delen, 2013). Analytics always involves historical or current data and visualization. This requires analytics to using data mining (DM) to discover knowledge from a large database or data warehouse (DW) or a big database in order to assist decision making (Turban & Volonino, 2011, p. 344). DM employs advanced statistical tools to analyze the wealth of data now available through DWs and other sources to identify possible relationships, patterns and anomalies and discover information or knowledge for rational decision making (Coronel, Morris, & Rob, 2013, p. 539). DM includes Web mining and text mining (Turban & Volonino, 2011). DW extracts or obtains its data from operational databases as well as from external sources, providing a more comprehensive data pool including historical or current data (Coronel, Morris, & Rob, 2013). Analytics is also required to use statistical modeling (SM) to learn something that can aid decision making (Schneider, 2013, p. 183). Only these are not enough for decision making in general, business decision making in specific, because a business decision maker such as CEO and CFO have not time to read discovered knowledge or patterns in long text. They hope to get succinct and vivid knowledge or patterns in

a form of figure or table presented by either ppt or spreadsheet or dashboards or scorecards or barometer. They require analytics to use visualization technique to make any knowledge patterns and information for decision making in a form of figure or table. In summary, analytics can facilitate business decision making and realization of business objectives through analyzing current problems and future trends, creating predictive models to foresee future threats and opportunities and analyzing/optimizing business processes based on involved historical or current data to enhance organizational performance (Delena & Demirkanb, 2013). Therefore, analytics can be succinctly represented below.

$$Anylytics = DM + DW + SM + Visualization \tag{1}$$

There are many analytics that have drawn increasing attention in academia and business field. The most popular analytics comprise data analytics, information analytics, knowledge analytics, business analytics and Web analytics. Data analytics might be the oldest among all these analytics (Kauffman, Srivastava, & Vayghan, 2012; Delena & Demirkanb, 2013). Business analytics consists of descriptive, prescriptive and predictive analytics (Delena & Demirkanb, 2013). Descriptive analytics, also called business reporting, addresses what happened, and what is happening? Prescriptive analytics answers, what should we do, and why should we do it? Predictive analytics focuses on forecasting trends by providing a business solution to what will happen, and why will it happen (Delena & Demirkanb, 2013; Turban & Volonino, 2011)? Web analytics, a general form of website analytics, focuses on the collection, analysis and reporting of Internet data traffic or online customers behaviors of a website by providing a business solution to "what happens after they click" (Baltzan, Phillips, Lynch, & Blakey, 2013).

Analytics as a service (AaaS) is a relatively new concept, has emerged as a rapidly growing business sector of Web analytics industry, which provides efficient Web log analytic services for firm-level customers (Park, Kim, & Koh, 2010). AaaS or analytics service means that an individual or organization uses a wide range of analytic tools wherever they may be located (Delena & Demirkanb, 2013). AaaS has the ability to turn a general analytic platform into a shared utility for an enterprise with visualized analytic services (Demirkan & Delen, 2013). An analytics service can be available on the Web or used by smartphone. Therefore, analytics services include e-analytics services or Web analytics services (WAS) (Park, Kim, & Koh, 2010) and mobile analytics services.

AaaS is gaining popularity rapidly in business and management in recent years. For example, AaaS model has been adopted by many famous Web companies such Amazon, Microsoft, and eBay (Demirkan & Delen, 2013). The main reason is that the traditional hub-and-spoke architectures cannot satisfy the demands driven by increasingly complex business analytics (Demirkan & Delen, 2013). AaaS promises to provide decision makers with much needed information and knowledge with visualization (Delena & Demirkanb, 2013). Cloud analytics is an emerging alternative solution for large scale data analytics (Demirkan & Delen, 2013).

It should be noted that AaaS often referred to as agile analytics which is a service model of integrating computing utility with visualization (Delena & Demirkanb, 2013). Organizations are turning to social media as the new source for social data, information and knowledge to gain competitive advantage, then big data analytics has drawn increasing attention. Vertica, AsterData and Netezza are examples of big data analytics vendors (Coronel, Morris, & Rob, 2013).

2.2.4 Cloud Services

"Cloud" is a metaphor for an Internet accessible platform of shared resources hidden from users for scalable service provision. Cloud services are one of the critical components of cloud computing which has drawn increasing attention over the past few years (Turban & Volonino, 2011, pp. 47-50). Briefly, a cloud service is any service provided anywhere anytime in the cloud. More specifically, a cloud service, or called a cloud computing service, is any computing resource or service provided by the cloud computing providers over the Internet (Rouse, cloud services, 2011). Cloud services are designed to provide flexible, scalable to applications, resources and services, and fully managed by a cloud services provider based on "pay-as-you-go" models (Coronel, Morris, & Rob, 2013). Therefore, a cloud service can dynamically scale to meet the needs of its customers so that the customers do not need to deploy their own resources such as hardware and software for the service nor allocate IT staff to manage the service. Cloud services broadly comprise three different types of services: Infrastructure as a Service (IaaS), Platform as a Service (PaaS) and Software as a Service (SaaS) (Buyya, Broberg, & Goscinski, 2010).

2.2.4.1 Infrastructure as a Service (IaaS)

IaaS allows users to gain access to different kinds of infrastructure. Typically, the service providers provide different services by dividing a very large physical infrastructure resource into smaller virtual resources for access by the users (Halpert, 2011). For instance, the service provided can be a virtual machine with an operating system, application platforms, middleware, database servers, enterprise service busses, third-party components and frameworks, and management and monitoring software (Kommalapati, 2010).

2.2.4.2 Platform as a Service (PaaS)

PaaS allows users who want to develop and run custom applications as services by offering scalable hosted application servers that have large resource pools. In this form of cloud services, developer do not necessarily need to pay special attention on how many processors or how many memories that applications will be using when they are in deployment and deployment stage (Kommalapati, 2010). PaaS also provides necessary supporting services such as storage, security, integration infrastructure and development tools for a complete platform. The largest platform is the Web or the Internet. Therefore, the Web as a service (WaaS) is the most important PaaS. The other common platforms include the social networking platforms provided by SNS website such as Facebook, Twitter and QQZone.

2.2.4.3 Software as a Service (SaaS)

SaaS is a cloud model in which software is available to users as needed (Turban & Volonino, 2011, p. 49). SaaS is also on-demand and hosted service. The key idea behind it is that instead of buying expensive software, users can access software on the Web based on the "pay-as-you-go" business model, just as you pay the electricity bill based on your consuming electricity.

2.2.4.4 Other Cloud Services

Cloud services are expanding rapidly (Turban & Volonino, 2011, p. 49). Aside from the aforementioned cloud services, IaaS, PaaS, and SaaS, Network as a service (NaaS) and Storage as a Service (StaaS) are examples of the latest cloud services. NaaS aims to outsource to the cloud networking service providers in order to limit the cost of data communications for cloud consumers, as well as to improve network flexibility (Costa, Migliavacca, Pietzuch, & Wolf, 2012). NaaS offers the cloud consumers to use network connectivity services and/or inter-cloud network connectivity services. It includes flexible and extended VPN, and bandwidth on demand(Focus Group, 2012). StaaS is a cloud service that an individual or an organization rents the storage space(Rouse, 2009). StaaS is also being recognized as an alternative way to mitigate risks in disaster recovery, as well

as offering long-term preservation for records for businesses, which improves both business continuity and availability.

2.2.5 Services as a Service

It is strange to read Services as service because this is against English grammar, based on the search for "services as a service" using Google Scholar, because there is no scholarly research on this topic (searched on 27 September13). However, we say services as a service (SeaaS) on the Web or services of services or services as a Web service, cloud services as a service, then few are against such a usage any more. In fact, Kapustka (2013) argues that SeaaS is a direction where cloud is going. Then SeaaS can be considered as the most general term for all the x services as a service. Where x can be data, cloud, software, information, consulting, knowledge, to name a few. Therefore, SeaaS can cover all what we already discussed in the previous subsections: SNS as a service, mobile services as a service, analytics services as a service, cloud as a service.

More generally, we can look at SeaaS in terms service as a Web service and meta-services. Service as a Web service can be considered in such a way that a traditional service have been moved to the Web or replaced by a Web service. This traditional service has been dead or replaced by a form of new service, for example, eSMACS service. Delivering electricity bill to the customer used to be an important post service. However, this service delivery has been replaced by Web services, in which the customer accesses the attached file on the bill in the email from the electricity company and paid the bill online or using mobile phone. FREG services are traditional services including food services, resource services, energy services, and goods services. e-FREG services are the FREG services online, which include e-food services, e-resource services, e-energy services, and e-goods services. e-FREG services can be considered as a part of e-services or e-business services.

Meta-services are the methods, techniques and process of how to use the services. These services are in particular, provided to the service providers on the Web or on the cloud. In order to explain this in more detail we will discuss the extended SOA in the following section.

2.3 A Hierarchy of Web Services

Web services (WS) can be considered in a hierarchical way from an evolutionary viewpoint, as shown in Figure 2. WS is at the top level and represented an integrated form of all the services on the Web, as the state of art. The next higher level consists of e-SMACS services, that is, e-services, SeaaS, mobile services, analytics services, cloud services and SNS, e-services includes e-business services, and e-FREG services as well as decision services. This implies that Web services reflects the new and refined representation of services in e-services, services in service computing, mobile computing, analytics computing, cloud computing and social computing. The bottom level is traditional services which are still basis or resource for the majority of Web services. Data WS, information WS and knowledge WS are the fundamentals for any e-SMACS services. Data WS, information WS, and knowledge WS correspond to data as a WS, information as a WS, and information as a WS respectively. Data, information and knowledge

(Chaffey, 2011) are the fundamentals of any e-SMACS services and then data WS, information WS and knowledge WS are at the lower level or penultimate level.

3 AN EXTENDED SOA AND MAIN PLAYERS IN WEB SERVICES

This section will review the service-oriented architecture (SOA) and present an extended SOA. Different from the extended SOA of (Papazoglou & Georgakopoulos, 2003), we extended the SOA by adding the players to the SOA taking into account eSMACS services.

3.1 Overview of SOA

The service-oriented architecture (SOA) is a basic concept for Web services (Papazoglou, 2008). The most general SOA is shown in Figure 3.

This SOA is simple because it only includes three players, and three fundamental operations for Web services. The three players in the SOA are Web service providers, Web service requestors and Web service brokers (Sun, Dong, & Yearwood, 2011). The Web service provider is the owner of the Web service. The Web service requestor is the consumer of the Web service. The Web service broker is an intermediary that facilitates the discovery, selection, composition, recommendation, transfer or delivery of Web

Figure 2. A hierarchy of Web services

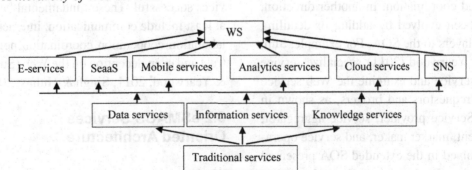

Figure 3. A general SOA

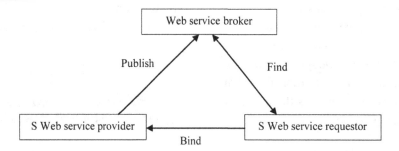

services from the service provider to the service requestors (Tabein, Moghadasi, & Khoshkbarforoushha, 2008). The three fundamental operations are; publish, find and bind.

- **Publish Operation:** The Web service provider publishes the Web service to the Web service broker (so that the Web service can be found by the Web service requestor).
- **Find Operation:** The Web service requestor discovers Web services from the Web service broker.
- **Bind Operation:** The Web service requestor invokes the found Web services from the Web service provider.

Since its inception in 1999-2000 (Kreger, 2001), SOA have been evolved significantly along three directions. In one direction, SOA has been evolved by adding more operations to the SOA. For example, Papazoglou (2003) proposed an extended SOA by adding many new operations including discovery, selection, assurance, support, and coordination. In another direction, SOA has been evolved by adding or detailing the main players to the SOA. For example, Sun, Dong, and Yearwood (2011) specialize service into Web service and examine the Web service providers, requestors and brokers, as shown in Figure 3. Service provider, service aggregator, service client, market maker, and service operator are involved in the extended SOA presented by Papazoglou (Papazoglou & Georgakopoulos, 2003). From the viewpoint of multiagent systems

(Wooldridge, 2002), there are still other players involved in Web services, such as Web service advisors, Web service managers, Web service composers, Web service recommenders, Web service consultants (Sun, Dong, & Yearwood, 2011), Web service quality analyser (Tabein, Moghadasi, & Khoshkbarforoushha, 2008) and so on. We mainly focus on Web service providers, brokers and requestors hereafter in this chapter.

The third direction is to provide more sophisticated computing techniques and intelligent techniques to realize these three fundamental operations and to automate the roles of the three players in the SOA (Papazoglou, 2008). For example, an activity or operation of Web services usually is implemented by a few intelligent agents within a multiagent Web service system (Sun & Finnie, 2004). Therefore, more and more intelligent players or agents will be involved in Web services with the development of automating activities of Web services (Sun, Dong, & Yearwood, 2011). Some behaviour operations of Web service agents are also fundamentally important to make Web services successful. These fundamental behaviours at least include communication, interaction, collaboration, cooperation, coordination, negotiation, trust and even deception on the Web (Sun, Dong, & Yearwood, 2011; Singh & Huhns, 2005).

3.2 eSMACS Services Oriented Architecture

We have examined Web services = eSMACS services as the state of art of Web services in the previous section. Now we use eSMACS services to extend SOA to an eSMACS service-oriented architecture (an eSMACS SOA), as shown in Figure 4. The key idea behind this extended SOA is that we detail the main players in the SOA taking into account the eSMACS services. That is, different from other proposed SOAs (Papazoglou, 2008), in our proposed eSMACS SOA, the service providers are eSMACS service providers; the service brokers are eSMACS service brokers; and the service requestors are eSMACS service requestors. In such a way, one can further elaborate this extended SOA taking into account of each kind of eSMACS services with concrete applications. In what follows, we will examine each of the main players in the proposed eSMACS service-oriented architecture. Firstly, we look at e-service requestors, brokers, and providers from a most general viewpoint.

3.3 Main Players in eSMACS Services Oriented Architecture

This section will look at the requestors, brokers, and providers of eSMACS services in some detail and then each of the following subsection can be considered as a new extension of the SOA in the corresponding eSMACS service sector.

3.3.1 e-Service Requestors, Brokers, and Providers

Web service providers, requestors, brokers, and UDDI are the most integral players in Web services transactions (Deitel, Deitel, DuWadt, & Trees, 2004, p. 52). Web service requestors also denote Web service users, buyers, customers, consumers, receivers, clients, and their intelligent agents. Web service requestors retrieve the information from the registry and use the service description obtained to bind to and invoke the Web service. Web service brokers maintain a registry of published Web services and might introduce Web service providers to Web service requestors. They use universal description discovery integration (UDDI) to find the requested Web services, because UDDI specifies a registry or "yellow pages" of services (Singh & Huhns, 2005, p. 20).

According to the Macmillan Dictionary (2007, p. 181), a broker is "someone whose job is to organize business deals for other people". Web service brokers denote Web service intermediaries, middle agents, registry (Kreger, 2001), discovery agency (Sun, Dong, & Yearwood, 2011), Web service platform and their intelligent agents (Burstien & et al, 2005). The service broker or registry contains additional information about the service provider, such as address and contact of the providing company, and technical details about the service. Web service providers may integrate

Figure 4. An eSMACS service-oriented architecture

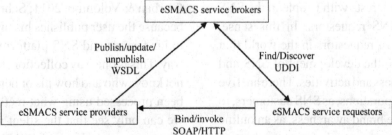

or compose existing services using intelligent techniques (Sun, Dong, & Yearwood, 2011). They may also register descriptions of services they offer, monitor and manage service execution (Dustdar & Schreiner, 2005).

Web service providers denote Web service owners, sellers, senders, firms and their intelligent agents (Sun, Dong, & Yearwood, 2011; Currie & Parikh, 2006). Web service providers create Web services, and advertise them to potential Web service requestors by registering the Web services with Web service brokers, or simply offers Web services (Dustdar & Schreiner, 2005). The Web service provider needs to describe the Web service in a standard format, and publish it in a central service registry. One of the well-known Web services providers is Amazon Web Services (AWS).

It seems that there is a trend that Web service provider and broker are integrated as a unified presence. For example, AWS is not only a Web service provider but also a Web service broker.

3.3.2 Social Networking Service Requestors, Brokers, and Providers

If we apply the general SOA to social networking services (SNS), then we should look at requestors, brokers and providers of SNS, for short, SNS requestors, brokers and providers. In what follows, we will examine each of them in some detail.

Generally speaking, SNS requestors are all the consumers of SNS. More specially, anyone that has built a profile in any SNS and interacted with others to share ideas, pictures, posts, activities, events, and interests with people in the SNS belongs to the SNS requestors. In this sense, there are billions of requestors in the world that are contributors to the development of SNS and SNS-driven business and activities. There are five major uses for corporations, as SNS customers, to use SNS: to create brand awareness, as an online reputation management tool, for recruiting, to learn about new technologies and competitors,

and as a lead generation tool to intercept potential prospects (Nimetz, 2007).

Based on the statistical information summarized by Wikipedia (Wikipeidia-SN-List, 2013), 5.5 billion people in the world have been a registered member of at least one SN website of the listed 200 SNS websites. The most populous SN website is Facebook with more than 1 billion registered users, following by China's QZone with about 800 million users. Removing the repetitive calculation, about 50% of the world's population have become the netizens of the SNS world. The repetitive calculation is based on the fact that one might registered a few SNS websites because of his or her social interests and behaviors. For example, an overseas Chinese scholar might register Facebook, LinkedIn and QZone. From this list, we can also see that every social interest or behavior might lead to the birth of a new SNS website. Therefore, there is currently no stagnating phenomenon evident in SNS.

Without the selfless contribution of individual customers to the SNS, there would not have dramatic development of SNS and big data. Strictly speaking, every SNS provider including Facebook and QZone only provides a SNS platform that can be used to build social networks or social relations among people who share social interests, social activities, backgrounds, or real-life connections through video interactions (Wikipedia-SNS, 2013). Although this platform has technological components, it is similar to a warehouse that are collecting all the online data and information including private information from its users using Opt-in or Opt-out approach (Turban & Volonino, 2011; Schneider G., 2011), because the user publishes his or her information to his friends and SNS platforms in a voluntary way. This is one way collection, because one does not know who and how his or her information has been processed using what method. In this way, we can only see that the silent majority of SNS requestors are living in the SNS world blindly.

SNS brokers are all the brokers of organizing SNS deals for other people. More generally, a SNS broker is an intermediary that helps companies and individuals to promote their SNSs in the SNS marketing to the customers and at the same time, s/he encourages customers to accept the SNS of a company. For example, is it Mark Zuckerberg who made Facebook successful? The answer is not completely right. To some extent, the broker of Facebook has also been allocated very profitable shares as an award for their successful brokerage within a short term. Have a look at IPO of Facebook in 2012, one can find who is the awarded SNS broker of Facebook. In fact, in the Internet era, a function of a traditional broker has been so decomposed that a great number of different brokers are around a company to support its development and success. In this sense, the SNS brokers consist of media reporters, consulting companies, bankers, investors, scholars, even governments.

SNS providers are all the providers of SNS. The largest SNS providers in English world are American-based providers such as Facebook, Twitter, LinkedIn, Google+, pinterest, and Instagram (Laudon & Traver, 2013). Facebook is not only the number one of SNS providers but also the number one social marketing tool for brands at 83%, followed by Twitter at 53% (Creotivo, 2013). Pinterest is an image-based social media network, and had become the third largest social network in the United States (Creotivo, 2013; Wikipedia-SNS, 2013). However, different countries and regions have their own SNS providers, which are experiencing the fast development and will become the future trend. For example, Hi5 in The Netherlands, iWiW in Hungary, Glocals in Switzerland; Mxit in Africa; and Cyworld, Mixi, Orkut, renren, weibo and Wretch in Asia and the Pacific Islands. As a counterpart of Facebook, QQ provides the ability to create groups that share common interests or affiliations such as university classmates, upload or stream live videos, and hold discussions in forums as well as hold real time

party using the QQ group's video function and real time chatting function. The real-time SNS of QQ meet the social requirement of Chinese for simultaneous communication and interaction rather than planned ones (through appointment making) popular in the Western countries (Dong, Sun, & Sun, 2014). In reality, China has all the SNS providers that correspond to every most famous America-based SNS provider. For example, the counterpart of Twitter is Sina.weibo. The counterpart of youTube is Tudou.com.

3.3.3 Mobile Service Requestors, Brokers, and Providers

Everyone using mobile devices including mobile phone is a requestor of mobile services. In this sense, there are billions requestors of mobile services in the world. One of the basic mobile services is short messaging service (SMS). SMS allows mobile phone users to send short text message to each other (Schneider, 2013). Mobile service brokers include mobile services developers, companies, bankers, investors, scholars, social media, etc. Mobile service brokers facilitate the healthy development of mobile services. The providers of mobile services includes mobile services vendors, social networking service providers such as Facebook, Qoogle+, and youTube, and QZone, because they have successfully provided social mobile services to the smartphone users. In terms of mobile services, smartphones have replaced PCs and laptops and become more convenient than the latter regardless of time and place to receive mobile services. A mobile services developer might be a company that develops application software (apps) that can run on a mobile phone. The mobile service developer uses software as a service (SaaS) strategy to generate revenue by giving the license of apps to mobile phone companies. Mobile phone companies generate revenue by charging subscribers a monthly usage fee for each app (Schneider, 2013, p. 257).

As mentioned earlier, the most popular mobile services include mobile financial services, mobile entertainment services, mobile commerce services, mobile information services and mobile SNS (Turban & Volonino, 2011). Therefore, the mobile service requestors, brokers, and providers can be considered as requestors, brokers, and providers of mobile financial services, mobile entertainment services, mobile commerce services, mobile information services and mobile SNS. For example, requestors of mobile financial services are all the customers that use mobile devices to accept the financial services such as paying bills, manage bank account information. Brokers of mobile financial services include mobile services developers, banking companies, investors, scholars, social media, etc. Providers of mobile financial services include financial services companies, e-commerce companies and mobile phone companies. E-commerce companies such as e-Bay, QQ (http://www.qq.com/) provides mobile financial services through their special platform.

3.3.4 Analytics Service Requestors, Brokers, and Providers

Based on the analysis in the previous section, analytics service requestors include organizations, governments and all level business decision makers such as CEO and CFO as well as managers. Analytics service requestors require data analytics services, information analytics services, knowledge analytics services, business analytics services to use visualization technique to make any knowledge patterns and information for decision making in a form of figure or table or report (Kauffman, Srivastava, & Vayghan, 2012). More generally, analytics service requestors include anyone who likes to make any decision or acquire information based on analytical reports provided by analytics service provider. Therefore, a person with smartphone receiving analytics services is also an analytics service requestor (Delena & Demirkanb, 2013).

Analytics service brokers are all the entities that facilitate the development of analytics services, which include popular press, traditional media and social media, consulting companies, scholars and university students and so on. All these use a variety of methods to improve the better understanding of analytics in general and data analytics, business analytics, and Web analytics in particular, all these have been offered to university students as a course material or content in business and computing areas to some extent in recent years. McKinsey Consulting (http://www.mckinsey.com/) and Boston Consulting Group (BCG) as analytics service brokers will play an important role in adopting AaaS in business, just as they promote "big data". Gartner and Forrester are also famous analytics service brokers in the world (Demirkan & Delen, 2013).

Analytics service providers includes analytics developers, analytics vendors, and other intermediaries that can provide analytics services. Recently, Web analytics service (WAS) providers are important analytics service providers. A WAS provider, for example, Adobe Marketing Cloud (http://www.adobe.com/au/solutions/digital-marketing.html), aggregates and analyzes weblog data about the online behaviors of users who visited the client's website, and evaluate a variety of analytical reports the client's customer online activities characteristics that the client wishes to understand, this can then facilitate the business decision making of the client (Park, Kim, & Koh, 2010). Application service providers (ASPs) can also provide Web analytics in a hosted ASP model with quicker implementation and lower administrative costs (Park, Kim, & Koh, 2010). Analytics developers provide analytic tools with extensive data extraction, analytics and reporting functionality such as Piwik, CrawlTrack (Laudon & Traver, 2013, p. 212; Loukis, Pazalos, & Salagara, 2012). Google not only is a search engine provider, but also a WAS vendor, because Google provides Google Analytics (http://www.google.com/analytics/) with good tracking tools for any advertisement on Google. In fact, most hosting websites also provide these similar services as well. A mobile phone company is an intermediary that can provide analytics services to the customers with smartphone (Delena & Demirkanb, 2013). For example, Mobile App Analytics (http://www. google.com/analytics/mobile/) is a part of Google Analytics. It is also a mobile analytics services provider that helps the smartphone customers to discover new and relevant users through traffic sources reports and Google play integration, to get engaged through event tracking and flow visualization, and set and track the goal conversions one wants most: purchases, clicks, or simply time spent on the app. More generally, every information system or intelligent systems has contained a system component used to generate table, diagram or report. All these kinds of information systems can be considered as analytics service providers. For example, predictive analytics is a component of Web mining systems that sifts through data to identify patterns of e-customer behaviors that predict which offers customers might respond to in the future or which customers the company may be in danger of losing in the near future (Turban & Volonino, 2011, p. 345). Microsoft Excel is a powerful analytics service tool that can be used to conduct data analytics and business analytics for companies and businesses.

3.3.5 Cloud Service Requestors, Brokers, and Providers

As mentioned early, cloud services mainly include Infrastructure as a Service (IaaS), Platform as a Service (PaaS), and Software as a Service (SaaS), here we look at the service providers, brokers and requestors of each of these respectively below.

IaaS service providers include government agencies, individual ICT infrastructure vendors, and other organizations. The example of government agencies is China's Telecom, which has national infrastructure for telephony and the Internet. The most popular ICT infrastructure vendors includes Huawei, CISCO, BEA systems

(Currie & Parikh, 2006), AWS (Amazon Web Services), Google Compute Engine, HP Cloud, Joyent, Linode, NaviSite, Rackspace, Windows Azure, ReadySpace Cloud Services, and Terremark. Typically, the IaaS service providers provide different services by dividing a very large physical infrastructure resource into smaller virtual resources for access by the users (Halpert, 2011).

A cloud service broker provides the brokering services between cloud providers and cloud requestors that assist companies in choosing the services and offerings that best suits their needs in terms of IaaS, PaaS and SaaS. Cloud service brokers may also assist in the deployment and integration of apps across multiple clouds or provide a choice and possible cost saving function which includes multiple competing services from a catalog. The most famous cloud service broker is Gartner (http://www.gartner.com/technology/home.jsp).

The IaaS service requestors include individuals, enterprises, communities and governments. Different kinds of IaaS service requestors have different demands to the IaaS service providers. The solutions to the demands of IaaS service requestors are normally provided by the IaaS service brokers.

PaaS service providers allow a PaaS service requestor who wants to develop and run custom applications as services by offering scalable hosted application servers that have large resource pools. PaaS service providers also provide necessary supporting services such as storage, security, integration infrastructure and development tools for a complete platform. The PaaS service requestor in general and developer in specific do not necessarily need to pay special attention on how many processors or how many memories that applications will be using when they are in deployment and deployment stage (Kommalapati, 2010).

SaaS service providers provide, typically, a rich Web-based interface to their consumers for using their software (Halpert, 2011). SaaS providers includes salesforce.com(Currie & Parikh,

2006), IBM, Microsoft, Adobe and others. The consumers are SaaS service requestors that can obtain the same software services and functionally on-line rather than locally installed computer program(Buyya, Broberg, & Goscinski, 2010). There are no upfront commitments or any long-term contracts for the SaaS service requestors. There are also many free SaaS. For example, we use Internet email communication software freely. We also use Google as a search engine freely.

Recently, there is a fierce completion in terms of cloud services providers. Every cloud services provider pursues to provide a comprehensive cloud services to the cloud requestors. The most famous cloud services providers are AWS and Google cloud services (GCS).

AWS offers a complete set of infrastructure and application services that enable the user to run virtually everything in the cloud: from enterprise applications and big data projects to social games and mobile apps (Amazon, 2013). In this way, AWS can be considered to provide a combination of IaaS, PaaS, and SaaS, because AWS provide the following free cloud services: Elastic Compute Cloud (EC2); Simple Storage Service (S3), DynamoDB, Relational Database Service (RDS), ElastiCache; Simple Workflow (SWF); Simple Queue Service (SQS) and Simple Notification Service (SNS), Amazon Elastic Transcoder, Data Transfer; CloudWatch, Data Pipeline in the tier of Compute & Networking, Storage, Database, Application Services, Development & Management respectively (Amazon, 2013). AWS has then been considered as a successful exemplar of cloud computing and mobile computing as well as mobile cloud computing.

GCS provides integrated cloud services including IaaS, PaaS and SaaS. GCS provides IaaS through Google Compute Engine, PaaS through Google App Engine, and SaaS through Google Apps. Google Compute Engine is an infrastructure as a service that allows the customer run his or her large-scale computing workloads on Linux virtual machines hosted on Google's infrastruc-

ture. Google App Engine allows the customers to run Web applications on Google's infrastructure. Google Apps is a service from Google providing independently customizable versions of several Google products under a custom domain name.

3.3.6 SeaaS Requestors, Brokers, and Providers

As we mentioned in Section 2, SeaaS can be considered as the most general term for all the x services as a service. Therefore, the SeaaS requestors include all the service requestors mentioned in the previous subsections. Furthermore, SeaaS requestors also include the traditional service requestors in the physical world and also requestors for transforming traditional services to Web services such as cloud services, analytics services, and mobile services as well as SNS.

SeaaS brokers include all the service brokers mentioned in the previous subsections. SeaaS broker systems provide coordinating service systems to reduce the costs of service creation, production, provision and delivery (Demirkan & Delen, 2013). Furthermore, SeaaS brokers also include those that help transformation of traditional services to Web services. For example, adventure investors are SeaaS brokers. Without early adventure invest, Facebook could have not developed itself as a successful public company with 1 billion registered users.

SeaaS providers include all the service providers mentioned in the previous subsections. Furthermore, SeaaS providers include Xerox, which provides business services to its customers, besides printer services.

In this section, we have extended the SOA in terms of eSMACS services. Then we examined the requestors, brokers, providers for e-services, SNS, mobile services, analytics services, cloud services, and SeaaS respectively. All these requestors, brokers and providers for the mentioned services are still in an early stage from marketing, demand, integrated perspective. Nonetheless, we can conclude that all the requestors, brokers, providers for eSMACS services are the strategic asset for developing any Web service.

It should be noted the role of a player in Web services is not unique, for example, a SNS broker might be also a SNS requestor. A SNS provider might be a requestor of a mobile service. An e-service provider might be a SNS requestor. For example, a majority of e-business companies are branding themselves using the marketing function of Facebook, and then they are the SNS requestor. In this sense, we do not go into requestors, brokers, providers for eSMACS services any more.

4 DEMAND DRIVEN WEB SERVICES: A 2D REPRESENTATION

According to the Macmillan Dictionary (2007, p. 1356), service is

1. A system provided by a government or official organization for the needs of the public, e.g. police service, emergency service and health service.
2. Help that you give someone in need, especially by using your skills, ability, or knowledge.

Demand is

1. A very firm statement that you want something.
2. (pl) the things that need to be done in a particular situation.
3. The amount of a product or service that people want.

Based on these two definitions, any service is related to need or demand and can be considered as a solution or response to a demand. For example, a business service is a business solution or response to a need or demand from its customers. More generally, a service is a combination of response, r, (or solution) with a demand, d, donated by

$$S = (r, d)$$

Demands in DDWS can be at least classified into government demands, organization demands, enterprise demands, community demands and customer/individual demands. The individual demands include citizen's demand. Correspondingly, services in DDWS at least includes government demand-driven Web services, organization demand-driven Web services, enterprise demand-driven Web services, community demand-driven Web services, customer demand-driven Web services and citizen demand-driven Web services. Services in DDWS can also include business demand-driven Web services, transaction demand-driven Web services and project demand-driven Web services, if we consider business demand, transaction demand and project demand at an activity or process level. Here activity is the basis of transaction and business process (Schneider, 2013). Demand-driven Web services can be a solution to any government demand, organization demand, enterprise demand, community demand, customer demand and citizen demand. Therefore, demand-driven Web services are fundamental Web services for these mentioned demands. Government DDWS, organization DDWS, enterprise DDWS, community DDWS, customer/individual DDWS, and citizen DDWS provide eSMACS services as the solutions to the government demand, organization demand, enterprise demand, community demand, customer demand and citizen demand, as illustrated in Table 1.

Every intersection cell in Table 1 is a specific X demand-driven Web services, where X = {government, Organization, Enterprise, Community, Customer, Citizen}. For example, when x = government, the intersection cell of government and cloud services is government demand-driven cloud services (GDDCS). More detailed, government demand-driven IaaS, PaaS, DaaS and SaaS, so does government demand-driven SNS, e-business services and eFREG services. Therefore, the interrelationship among the mentioned various demands and Web services form a complex system

Table 1. A 2D representation of demand-driven Web services

	Web Services (WS)					
	E-Services	**SeaaS**	**Mobile Services**	**Analytics Services**	**Cloud Services**	**SNS**
X demand -driven (DD)	e-services	SeaaS	mobile services	Analytics services	Cloud services	SNS
Government (GDD)	GDD e-services	GDD SeaaS	GDD mobile services	GDD Analytics services	GDD Cloud services	GDD SNS
Organization (ODD)	ODD e-services	ODD SeaaS	ODD mobile services	ODD Analytics services	ODD Cloud services	ODD SNS
Enterprise (EDD)	EDD e-services	EDD SeaaS	EDD mobile services	EDD Analytics services	EDD Cloud services	EDD SNS
Customer (CDD)	CDD e-services	CDD SeaaS	CDD mobile services	CDD Analytics services	CDD Cloud services	CDD SNS
Community DD	CoDD e-services	CoDD SeaaS	CoDD mobile services	CoDD Analytics services	CoDD Cloud services	CoDD SNS
Citizen (CiDD)	CiDD e-services	CiDD SeaaS	CiDD mobile services	CiDD Analytics services	CiDD Cloud services	CiDD SNS

of demand-driven Web services, and a challenging topic for information systems, information technology and business, services and management.

It should be noted that in what follows, for brevity, we merge organization DDWS, community DDWS, enterprise DDWS as enterprise DDWS. This is because organizations, communities, and enterprises targets customers and enterprises have closer relationships with customers. Further, we cannot enumerate all the services in every category that we will discuss. The services that we mention are only used to illustrate viability of our classifications. It should be also noted that government DDWS and citizen DDWS have a demand-supply relationship, that is, the requestors of government DDWS are citizens (although including enterprises to some extent), the providers of citizen DDWS are governments and their agencies. Similarly, enterprise DDWS and customer DDWS have a demand-supply relationship, that is, the requestors of enterprise DDWS are customers (although including governments and their agencies to some extent), the providers of customers DDWS are enterprises.

4.1 Government DDWS

Government DDWS consists of government demand-driven (GDD) e-services, SeaaS, mobile services, analytics services, cloud services and SNS. The ultimate goal of GDDWS is to improve government-citizen interaction in terms of business, governance, information sharing and communication effectiveness (Huang, Chang, & Kuo, 2013).

Government demand-driven e-services include all the public services on the Web from governments to their citizens. Australian Government demand-driven e-services (australia.gov.au) includes information provision, information exchange, payment processing (Government, 2012)

Government demand-driven SeaaS include the upgraded social services, public services and international aid services through the Web, mobile devices, the cloud and SNS.

Government demand-driven mobile services include more effective and efficient services through more sophisticated mobile devices. Based on this, mobile services, mobile life and mobile learning become most important government demand-driven mobile services. One of such mobile services are free Wi-Fi services provided in popular tourist spots including airports and hotels (Huang, Chang, & Kuo, 2013). The difference between government demand-driven e-services and government demand-driven mobile services is that the latter allow relatively more mobile communication elements (Huang, Chang, & Kuo, 2013).

Government demand-driven analytics services include services of predictive analytics and big data analytics software (Coronel, Morris, & Rob, 2013), and services of dashboard and governance activity monitoring, portals, data analysis and reporting tools. Predictive analytics uses advanced statistical and modelling techniques to predict future governance and business outcomes with great accuracy (Coronel, Morris, & Rob, 2013).

Government demand-driven cloud services include all the main three cloud services IaaS, PaaS and SaaS. For example, some governments demand better to communicate continuously with their citizens, customers and agencies through upgrading networking infrastructure such as Australian NBN despite the fact that mobile communication anytime and anywhere is crucial in improving performance of Web services (E-Government, 2010).

Government demand-driven SNS include blogging, twitting, social media services and social interaction services provided by SNS companies to interact with its citizens, organizations, and communities. Social media services can help the government to be more responsive to its citizens, engage with its communities through promoting both accountability and transparency. Governments can also offer cost savings and efficiency through improving services delivery and obtaining community feedback effectively and efficiently using social media services (Sharif, Troshani, & Davidson, 2014).

It should be noted that decision as a WS (DaaWS) is a new service paradigm that will play more and more important role in e-government and e-democracy.

4.2 Citizen DDWS

Citizen DDWS consists of citizen demand-driven e-services, SeaaS, mobile services, analytics services, cloud services and SNS. More specifically, citizens demand their governments to provide high quality WS that they are seeking to them timely. For example, citizen demand-driven e-services include e-welfare services to assist low-income citizens, strengthen families and children's well-being, and help elderly and disabled citizens (Medjahed, Rezgui, & Bouguettaya, 2003). These services can be efficiently accessed through smartphones as mobile services and cloud services while preserving citizens' privacy, because the government provided e-social services are normally resided in public cloud. Another example, a few years ago, an Australian permanent resident must visit the related government office in metropolitan cities such as Sydney and Melbourne to renew his/her permanent residency in Australia. Now he or she can complete this renewal online. This is a kind of citizen demand-driven e-services. Australian citizen demand-driven e-services (australia.gov.au) include information seeking, information exchange, payment receiving (Government, 2012). For example, two in five of those who have completed some form of post secondary study used the Internet in their most recent contact with government (Government, 2012).

Citizen demand-driven mobile services include that citizens use smartphones to access governments' information and social services from governments. The governments' information includes policy, regulations and parliament debates. These have been available to smartphone, although they can be accessed through desktops and laptops. Social services include the welfare services from the government through mobile devices.

Citizen demand-driven analytics services include the diagram or table based on decision making process or statistics results relating to budget, interest change, real estate trend, and social welfare benefits analysis. Citizen demand-driven cloud services include the services through the national ICT infrastructure, government provided free software and e-platform to its citizens so that its citizens can access the social and public e-sources through these public clouds (Huang, Smith, & Sun, 2014).

Citizen demand-driven SNS include that the interaction between government and citizen through social networking websites such as Facebook and Twitter through dialogue, online discussion and debate. For example, recently, in the national election, every candidate of the prime minister in Australia does his or her best to interact with citizens in Facebook and Twitter to pursue the support from the citizens. Remote area citizens, homebound, low computer-literacy, or chronic illness citizens have a significant demand of utilizing e- services or mobile services provided by governments or their agencies (Huang, Chang, & Kuo, 2013).

4.3 Enterprise DDWS

Generally, enterprise DDWS consists of enterprise demand-driven e-services, SeaaS, mobile services, analytics services, cloud services and SNS.

Enterprise demand-driven e-services include various types of Web information systems to help run their daily operations (Baltzan, Phillips, Lynch, & Blakey, 2013, p. 331). These Web information systems include knowledge management software, customer relationship management software and supply chain management software (Schneider, 2013), data mining, database, data warehouse software and enterprise resource planning (ERP) software (Baltzan, Phillips, Lynch, & Blakey, 2013).

Enterprise demand-driven SeaaS include transition, update, upgrade and integration of existing enterprise services. As a process of weeding out and fixing or discarding inconsistent, incorrect or incomplete information, information cleansing is

also an enterprise demand-driven SeaaS (Baltzan, Phillips, Lynch, & Blakey, 2013).

Enterprise demand-driven mobile services include all the services that provide to the enterprise through mobile devices including smartphones and tablets. Message exchange, SMS, blog and discussion through mobile devices can be also considered as enterprise demand-driven mobile services. Enterprise demand-driven mobile services, cloud services and SNS are being integrated based on mobile cloud computing, because smartphones and tablets are replacing desktops and laptops as an integrated platform.

Enterprise demand-driven analytics services include Web analytics software and benchmarking services. Web analytics software has built-in analytical services such as data collection, extraction, analytics and reporting for firms. Web analytics software includes big data analytics software, which is emerging as an important analytics service (Hakes, 2012). Benchmarking services allow users to learn from other competitive website (Park, Kim, & Koh, 2010).

4.4 Customer DDWS

Customer DDWS consists of customer demand-driven e-services, SeaaS, mobile services, analytics services, cloud services and SNS.

Customer demand-driven e-services include e-commerce services, online shopping services (Schneider, 2013), e-travel services (e-services for flight booking, hotel reservation, car rental (Tabein, Moghadasi, & Khoshkbarforoushha, 2008). Customer demand-driven SeaaS includes e-brokering or e-intermediary services in all the services sectors such as real estate, financial services, and legal services, to name a few (Sun & Finnie, 2004; 2010).

Customer demand-driven mobile services include weather reports, SMS services, mobile SNS services (to individual customers), mobile analytics services, mobile cloud services, and

GPS navigation as well as Customer demand-driven SNS.

Customer demand-driven analytics services include business analytics services, information analytics services, data analytics services (Delena & Demirkanb, 2013) and Web analytics services as well as personal analytics (Coronel, Morris, & Rob, 2013). Personal analytics as a service is deployed to mobile users who are closer to customers to let customers understand the business better. MiscroStrategy, QlikView and Achuate are the examples of personal analytics vendors.

Customer demand-driven SNS include blogging, twittering, chatting and multimedia information sharing with laptops, notebooks, and hand-held devices including smartphones (Turban & Volonino, 2011).

It should be noted that all these mentioned demand-driven Web services should be improved through theoretical development, technological development, and methodologies in order to meet the different demands from different parties or individuals.

5 FOUNDATION OF DEMAND-DRIVEN WEB SERVICES

This section briefly looks at theoretical and technological foundations of demand-driven Web services with their applications.

5.1 A Theoretical Foundation of Demand-Driven Web Services

Theory of demand-driven Web services is mainly underpinned by mathematics, computational theory, theory of artificial intelligence, social networking theory, business theory and management theory. All the mentioned theories have been developed independently in different disciplines for over decades. For developing theory of demand-driven Web services, we need the fundamental concepts, models/architectures, frameworks/schemes or theories for planning, designing, building, operating or evaluating, managing demand-driven Web services. For example, the presented eSMACS SOA is one attempt to provide an integrated perspective to look at eSMACS services as Web services. In what follows, as a theoretical foundation we propose a mathematical foundation of demand-driven Web services.

Demand is an important concept in microeconomics. Jackson and McIver (2004, p. 74) defines demand as "a schedule that shows the amounts of a product that consumers are willing and able to purchase at each specific price in a set of possible prices during some specified period of time". The basic law of demand is "All else being constant, as price falls, the corresponding quantity demanded rises". Alternatively, the higher the price is, the less corresponding quantity demanded.

Demand analysis has drawn attention in e-business. Chaffey (2007) defines demand analysis as "assessment of the demand for e-commerce services among existing and potential customer segments" (p. 218). He then analyzes the factors that affect demand for e-commerce services (Chaffey, 2007, pp. 150-60.) and uses demand analysis to examine current projected customer use of each digital channel with different markets (Chaffey, 2007, p. 344).

Demand, in particular "on-demand" (Dan, et al., 2004), has drawn increasing attention in Web services. For example, Burstein, et al. (2005) examine functional and architectural demands or requirements for service discovery, engagement and enactment in terms of the semantic Web service architecture. However, in the above-mentioned discussion, it seems that the subject of the demand and its objective are ignored to some extent. For example, who demands what from where is usually unclear. It may not be critical for traditional economics and e-commerce. However, it is useful for Web services to know who, what and where exactly for Web services. Further, there has not been a mathematical theory or analysis of demand in Web services. In what follows, we examine the mathematical foundation of demand in order to fill this gap and then use it to develop demand-driven Web services.

We can analyze "demand" mathematically as follows. A person M demands something S provided by N. In other words, from a mathematical viewpoint, demand is a 3-ary relation that can be denoted as *Demand* (m, n, s). In the context of Web services, we can explain *Demand* (m, n, s) as: a player m demands Web service s provided by player n. For example, "service requestor r demands Web service consultation c provided by service broker b" can be denoted as *Demand* (r, b, c). More generally, demand as a 3-ary relation can be denoted as: Let M, N, and S be a non-empty set respectively, $M = m_1, m_2, \cdots, m_p$, $N = n_1, n_2, \cdots, n_j$, $S = s_1, s_2, \cdots, s_K$, then any subset D^3 of $M \times N \times S$, $D^3 \subseteq M \times N \times S$, is a demand relation. In Web services, N and M can denotes all the service requestors and all the service providers or brokers respectively. S represents all the Web services provided on the Web.

In business practice, this 3-ary demand relation is usually simplified as a binary relation D^2 or a unary relation D^1: For example, in B2C Web services, we only focus on: who demands what, that is, $D^2 \subseteq M \times S$ represents "customers m demands a Web service s," where M denotes all the service requestors or all the service providers. Further, in B2C Web services, we usually do not care about "who demands what" but only care about "what are demanded," that is, $D^1 \subseteq S$ represents the good or service that is demanded. Therefore, from a demand's perspective, there are three different types of Web services: D^1 Web services, D^2 Web services and D^3 Web services.

- D^1 Web services only focuses on the goods or services that are transacted. Such a Web service is usually used for statistical analysis and data analytics.
- D^2 Web services only focuses on the customer and the goods or services that are purchased by the customer or the buyer. Therefore, D^2 Web services correspond to a B2C e-commerce and B2B e-commerce.
- D^3 Web services focuses on all the service providers, requestors, and goods and services that are transacted. Therefore, D^3 Web services is an organization that runs or oversees the activities in Web services or e-commerce. D^3 Web services correspond to e-commerce or e-service company.

In fact, taking into account the amount and payment associated with demand relation, we introduce demand functions respectively for D^1 Web services, D^2 Web services and D^3 Web services. For example, let A and P be non-empty sets, then any function $d^1: S \to A \times P$, $d(s) = a \cdot p$, is a demand function taking into account the amount A of demand and the corresponding price P per a unit demand. For example, in D^1 Web services, a customer demands 100 textbooks on e-commerce, and the price is AUD\$100.00 per textbook. Then, the corresponding demand function value is

$$d^1(book) = 100 \cdot 100 = 10,000$$

where the customer and provider are technically ignored. This demand function represents the total price for the demanded 100 textbooks.

Similarly, in D^2 Web services, $d^2(David, book) = 100 \cdot 100 = 10,000$ represents that David demands 100 textbooks on Web services with the price of AUD\$10000.00, where the providers are technically ignored.

In D^3 Web services, $d^3(David, Amazon, book) = 100 \cdot 100 = 10,000$ represents that David demands 100 books on Web services provided by Amazon.com with the price of AUD\$10000.00. This is a complete form for demand in a transactional Web service.

From the above discussion, we can see that there is an inclusion relationship among D^1 Web services, D^2 Web services, and D^3 Web services.

5.2 A Technological Foundation for Demand-Driven Web Services

Technologies for demand-driven Web services include intelligent technologies, computational technology, Web technology and Internet technology, social networking technology, cloud technology, Web technologies, data analytics, big data technologies, service technologies, social networking technologies, decision making technologies, DSS technologies, management technologies and business technologies, to name a few. We have mentioned some technologies in the early section to some extent, for example, Web technology and Internet technology, social networking technology, cloud technology. In what follows, we look at intelligent technologies in some detail.

Intelligent technologies are AI-based technologies or intelligent techniques such as rule-based systems, ontology-development systems, machine learning techniques, intelligent agents and multi-agent systems, neural networks systems, fuzzy logic systems, cased-based reasoning systems, genetic algorithms, data mining algorithms,. Many intelligent techniques have been developed in both AI and IS. Some of the most useful intelligent techniques are listed in Table 2. Each of the intelligent techniques listed has its own strengths and weaknesses for solving real world DDWS problems (Moutinho, Rita, & Li, 2006). A few of the intelligent techniques mentioned are usually integrated or hybridized in order to solve a class of DDWS problems in the real world (Moutinho, Rita, & Li, 2006). For example, Casillas and Martínez-López (2009), and Martínez-López and Casillas (2009) developed a marketing intelligent system for marketing services. Their system was also used for consumer behavior analysis, based on integrating knowledge base systems, genetic fuzzy systems, multiobjective optimization, data mining and knowledge discovery from databases (KDD). These intelligent techniques have also aided managers by extracting useful patterns of

Table 2. Intelligent techniques

Intelligent Techniques	Citations
Knowledge representation	(Schalkoff, 2011)
Expert systems and knowledge-based systems	(Moutinho, Rita, & Li, 2006)
Case-based reasoning (CBR)	(Sun & Finnie, 2004)
Genetic algorithms	(Martínez-López & Casillas, 2009; Casillas & Martínez-López, 2009)
Machine learning	(Schalkoff, 2011)
Neural networks	(Moutinho, Rita, & Li, 2006; Negnevitsky, 2005)
Fuzzy logic and fuzzy expert systems	(Casillas & Martínez-López, 2009; Martínez-López & Casillas, 2009; Orriols-Puig, Martínez-López, & Casillas, 2012; Negnevitsky, 2005)
Intelligent agents and multiagent systems	(Russell & Norvig, 2010)
Data analytics and business analytics	(Delen & Demirkan, 2012)
Data mining and KDD	(Martínez-López & Casillas, 2009; Casillas & Martínez-López, 2009)
Multiobjective optimization	(Martínez-López & Casillas, 2009; Hu, Almansoori, Kannan, Azarm, & Wang, 2012)
DSS	(Hu, Almansoori, Kannan, Azarm, & Wang, 2012; Delen & Demirkan, 2012)
Knowledge management and knowledge base systems	(Moutinho, Rita, & Li, 2006; Russell & Norvig, 2010),

information(Martínez-López & Casillas, 2009; Casillas & Martínez-López, 2009), capturing knowledge, discovering knowledge, and generating solutions to problems encountered in planning, organizing, leading, controlling, and corresponding decision making (DM). These intelligent techniques have also enhanced information systems by providing organizations with intelligent techniques and systems to automate business activities of organizations, and improve human-machine activities (Sun & Firmin, 2012).

As mentioned early, data analytics or business analytics are based on statistical modelling, therefore, various statistical methods or techniques such as calculation of averages, correlations and Cronbach alpha values and regression, to name a few, are useful for analysing Web services evaluation data and calculating new types of business analytics on Web services' requestors' online and mobile activities (Loukis, Pazalos, & Salagara, 2012).

5.3 Applications for Demand-Driven Web Services

Applications of demand-driven Web services cover all the applications and case studies of demand-driven Web services in e-commerce, social networking, big data, cloud computing and other real world problem solving. For example, cases and applications for using the mentioned fundamental theory and technologies for planning, designing, building, managing and operating or evaluating of demand-driven Web services in the main service domains such as social networking services, cloud services, financial services, legal services, healthcare services, logistics services, educational services, and military services taking into account demand from government, organization, enterprise, community, individual, customer and citizen.

It should be noted that all mentioned theories, technologies and applications might bring new emerging demands, emerging technologies, methodologies for demand-driven Web services. Every chapter in this book can be considered as example of emerging demands, emerging technologies, methodologies for demand-driven Web services. Although some of these research areas have been covered in the chapters of this book, as a whole, they represent an excellent starting point, and perhaps, a seminal reference for future research and development in DDWS. In this regard, all these mentioned theoretical foundations, technological foundations and applications of

demand-driven Web services should be improved through theoretical and technological development and development of methodologies in order to develop DDWS with applications.

6 CONCLUSION

This chapter, firstly examined the state of art of Web services and argued Web services = eSMACS services. Then it proposed an extended service-oriented architecture (SOA), eSMACS SOA and examined main players in this architecture: eSMACS service providers, eSMACS service brokers, and eSMACS service requestors, taking into account eSMACS services. This chapter also classifies DDWS as government DDWS, organizational DDWS, enterprise DDWS, customer DDWS and citizen DDWS and looked at the corresponding Web services. Finally, this chapter examined the theoretical, technical foundations for DDWS with applications. The proposed approach might facilitate the understanding, research and development of Web services, e-business, e-government, service computing, mobile computing, analytics computing, cloud computing and social computing. The proposed approach in this chapter might also facilitate the engineering and management of Web services, and the research and development of Web services, e-services, service intelligence, and service science.

We have witnessed the continuing global transition from manufacturing economies to service economies (Kauffman, Srivastava, & Vayghan, 2012). Therefore, services in most general, and demand-driven Web services in specific will be playing more important role in developing a healthy society and harmonious world. Understanding the demand of stakeholders of Web services is a critical factor for further development of Web services. This chapter looked at eSMACS service providers, eSMACS service brokers, and eSMACS service requestors. In fact, these demands from these service providers, brokers, and requestors should be further elaborated combining with concrete real-word problems. These demands also require to be met from more stakeholders of Web services, in particular, the Web service developers. These developers provide business and technological solution for the main activities of Web service lifecycle such as Web service description and discovery (Garcia & Toledo, 2006), composition (Papazoglou, et al, 2006), billing, contracting. For example, the engineering of Web service composition and recommendation are a research direction (Papazoglou, et al, 2006). In future work, we will explore implementation issues for engineering of Web service composition and recommendation.

Applying intelligent techniques to Web services and automating the process stages in the demand-driven Web service lifecycle is another research direction (Sun, Dong, & Yearwood, 2011). In future work, we will integrate Web service discovery, composition and recommendation using soft case based reasoning taking into account eSMACS services.

Demand as a service and management of demand (Demirkan & Delen, 2013) are at least an important topic for any service provider and service broker to provide and broke services to service requestors. In the future work, we will elaborate the proposed e-SMACS SOA with the real world case study. We will also develop demand-driven framework for Web services by extending Table 2 to taking into account the stages or activities of Web services life cycle.

REFERENCES

Alonso, G., Casati, F., Kuno, H., & Machiraju, V. (2004). *Web Services: Concepts, Architectures and Applications*. Berlin: Springer-Verlag.

Amazon. (2013). *Amazon Web Services*. Retrieved 9 8, 2013, from http://aws.amazon.com/

Baltzan, P, Phillips, A., Lynch, K., & Blakey, P. (2013). Business Driven Information Systems. Sydney: McGraw Hill Australia.

Barr, J., Varia, J., & Wood, M. (2006). *Amazon EC2 Beta*. Retrieved Nov 27, 2012, from Amazon Web Services Blog: http://aws.typepad.com/aws/2006/08/amazon_ec2_beta.html

Burstien, M. et al. (2005). A semantic Web services architecture. *IEEE Internet Computing, 9*(5), 72–81. doi:10.1109/MIC.2005.96

Buyya, R., Broberg, J., & Goscinski, A. M. (2010). *Cloud Computing Principles and Paradigms*. Hoboken: John Wiley & Sons, Inc.

Carr, P., May, T., & Stewart, S. (2012). *Australia's Trusted Infrastructure-as-a-Service Cloud Provider Market 2012*. Retrieved Nov 28, 2012, from longhaus: http://www.longhausshop.com/reports/single-user-online-version-1.html

Casillas, J., & Martínez-López, F. J. (2009). Mining uncertain data with multiobjective genetic fuzzy systems to be applied in consumer behaviour modelling. *Journal of Expert Systems with Applications, 36*(2), 1645–1659. doi:10.1016/j.eswa.2007.11.035

Chaffey, D. (2009). *E-Business and E-Commerce Management: Strategy, Implementation and Practice* (4th ed.). Harlow, England: Prentice Hall.

Chaffey, D. (2011). *Business Information Management* (2nd ed.). Harlow, England: Prentice Hall.

Computenext. (2013). *What is Cloud Service Brokerage?* Retrieved 9 8, 2013, from https://www.computenext.com/cloud-service-brokerage/

Coronel, C., Morris, S., & Rob, P. (2013). *Database Systems: Design, Implementation, and Management* (10th ed.). Boston: Course Technology, Cengage Learning.

Costa, P., Migliavacca, M., Pietzuch, P., & Wolf, A. L. (2012). NaaS: Network-as-a-Service in the Cloud. *In Proceedings of the 2nd USENIX conference on Hot Topics in Management of Internet, Cloud, and Enterprise Networks and Services, Hot-ICE* (pp. 1-1). Berkeley: USENIX Association.

Creotivo. (2013). *100 Social Networking Statistics & Facts for 2012*. Retrieved 9 24, 2013, from http://visual.ly/100-social-networking-statistics-facts-2012

Currie, W. L., & Parikh, M. A. (2006). Value creation in web services: An integrative model. *The Journal of Strategic Information Systems*, *15*(2), 153–174. doi:10.1016/j.jsis.2005.10.001

Deitel, H. M., Deitel, P. J., DuWadt, B., & Trees, L. (2004). *Web Services: A technical Introduction*. Upper Saddle River, NJ: Prentice Hall.

Delen, D., & Demirkan, H. (2012). Data, information and Anlytics as services, available online. *Decision Support Systems*. doi: doi:10.1016/j.dss.2012.05.044 PMID:23552280

Delena, D., & Demirkanb, H. (2013). Data, information and analytics as services. *Decision Support Systems*, *55*(1), 359–363. doi:10.1016/j.dss.2012.05.044

Demirkan, H., & Delen, D. (2013). Leveraging the capabilities of service-oriented decision support systems: Putting analytics and big data in cloud. *Decision Support Systems*, *55*(1), 412–421. doi:10.1016/j.dss.2012.05.048

Dong, D., Sun, L., & Sun, Z. (2014). Web Services in China. In Z. Sun, & J. Yearwood, Demand-Driven Web Services: Theory, Technologies and Applications. IGI-Global.

Dong, T.-P., Cheng, N.-C., & Wu, Y.-C. J. (2013). A study of the social networking website service in digital content: industries: The Facebook case in Taiwan. *Computers in Human Behavior*. doi:http://dx.doi.org/10.1016/j.chb.2013.07.037

Dustdar, S., & Schreiner, W. (2005). A survey on web services composition. *International Journal Web and Grid Services*, *1*(1), 1–30. doi:10.1504/IJWGS.2005.007545

Focus Group. (2012). *Focus Group on Cloud Computing Technical Report Part 1*. Geneva: International Telecommunication Union.

Fremantle, P., Weerawarana, S., & Khalaf, R. (2002). Enterprise services. *Communications of the ACM*, *45*(10), 77–82. doi:10.1145/570907.570935

Gottschalk, K. e. (2001). *Web Services architecture overview. retrieved*. Retrieved July 15, 2009, from http://www.ibm.com/developerworks/webservices/library/w-ovr/

Government, A. (2012). *Interacting with Government: Australians' use and satisfaction with e-government services—2011*. Retrieved 11 11, 2013, from http://www.finance.gov.au/publications/interacting-with-government-2011/index.html

Hakes, W. (2012). *Big Data Analytics: The Revolution Has Just Begun*. Retrieved 10 20, 2013, from Analytics 2012 Conference: http://www.youtube.com/watch?v=ceeiUAmbfZk

Halpert, B. (2011). *Auditing Cloud Computing A Security and Privacy Guide*. Canada: John Wiley & Sons, Inc. doi:10.1002/9781118269091

Hoffman, K. D. (2003). Marketing + MIS = E-Services. *Communications of the ACM*, *46*(6), 53–55. doi:10.1145/777313.777340

Hu, W., Almansoori, A., Kannan, P. K., Azarm, S., & Wang, Z. (2012). Corporate dashboards for integrated business and engineering decisions in oil refineries: An agent-based approach. *Decision Support Systems*, *52*(3), 729–741. doi:10.1016/j.dss.2011.11.019

Huang, C., Smith, P., & Sun, Z. (2014). Securing network for cloud services. In Z. Sun, & J. Yearwood, Demand Driven Wen Services. IGI-Global.

Huang, S.-Y., Chang, C.-M., & Kuo, S.-R. (2013). User acceptance of mobile e-government services: An empirical study Government Information Quarterly,. *Vol.30(1), pp.33-44, pp.77-82.*

ICWS. (2009). *ICWS2009*. Retrieved from http://conferences.computer.org/icws/2009/

Kaplan, A. M., & Haenlein, M. (2010). Users of the world, unite! The challenges and opportunities of Social Media. *Business Horizons*, *53*, 59–68. doi:10.1016/j.bushor.2009.09.003

Kapustka, P. (2013). *Where cloud is going: Service as a service.* Retrieved 9 27, 2013, from IT World: http://www.itworld.com/cloud-computing/348931/where-cloud-going-service-service

Kauffman, R. J., Srivastava, J., & Vayghan, J. (2012). Business and data analytics: New innovations for the management of e-commerce. *Electronic Commerce Research and Applications*, *11*, 85–88. doi:10.1016/j.elerap.2012.01.001

Kommalapati, H. (2010). *Windows Azure for Enterprises.* Retrieved Nov 28, 2012, from MSDN Magazine: http://msdn.microsoft.com/en-us/magazine/ee309870.aspx

Kreger, H. (2001). *Web Services Conceptual Architecture (WSCA 1.0).* Retrieved 8 27, 2013, from http://www.cs.uoi.gr/~zarras/mdw-ws/WebServicesConceptualArchitectu2.pdf

Laudon, K., & Traver, C. (2013). *E-Commerce 2013: Business, Technology, Society* (9th ed.). Harlow, England: Pearson.

Liu, D. (2008). Models on Web-based information gap between e-goverment and citizens. *2008 ISECS International Colloquium on Computing, Communication, Control, and Management* (pp. 156-160). It is a very low quality CP paper. Read 02 10 13: IEEE Computer Society. doi:DOI 10.1109/CCCM.2008.61

Loukis, E., Pazalos, K., & Salagara, A. (2012). Transforming e-services evaluation data into business analytics using value models. *Electronic Commerce Research and Applications*, *11*(2), 129–141. doi:10.1016/j.elerap.2011.12.004

Lu, Y., Zhao, L., & Wang, B. (2010). From virtual communities members to C2C e-commerce buyers: Trust in virtual communities and its effect on consumers' purchase attention. *Electornic Commerce Research and Applications*, 346-360.

Macmillan. (2007). *Macmillan English Dictionary for Advanced Learners.* London: Macmillan.

Martínez-López, F. J., & Casillas, J. (2009). Marketing intelligent systems for consumer behaviour modelling by a descriptive induction approach based on genetic fuzzy systems. *Industrial Marketing Management*, *38*(7), 714–731. doi:10.1016/j.indmarman.2008.02.003

Medjahed, B., Rezgui, A., & Bouguettaya, A. (2003). Infrastructure for E-Government Web Services. *IEEE Internet Computing*, *7*(1), 58–65. doi:10.1109/MIC.2003.1167340

Moutinho, L., Rita, P., & Li, S. (2006). Strategic diagnostics and management decision making: A hybrid knowledge-based approach. *Intell. Sys. Acc. Fin. Mgmt*, *14*, 129–155. doi:10.1002/isaf.281

Negnevitsky, M. (2005). *Artificial Intelligence: A Guide to Intelligent Systems* (2nd ed.). Harlow: Addison-Wesley.

Nimetz, J. (2007). *Emerging Trends in B2B Social Networking*. Retrieved 9 24, 2013, from Marketing-jive: http://www.marketing-jive.com/2007/11/jody-nimetz-on-emerging-trends-in-b2b.html

Orriols-Puig, A., Martínez-López, F. J., & Casillas, J. (2012). (in press). A Soft-Computing-based Method for the Automatic Discovery of Fuzzy Rules in Databases: Uses for Academic Research and Management Support in Marketing. *Journal of Business Research*.

Papazoglou, M. P. (2003). Service -Oriented Computing: Concepts, Characteristics and Directions. In Proceedings of 4th Intl Conf on Web Information Systems Engineering (WISE2003). pp. 3-12.

Papazoglou, M. P. (2008). *Web services: Principles and Technology*. Harlow, England: Pearson Prentice Hall.

Papazoglou, M. P. (2008). *Web Services: Principlies and Technology*. Prentice Hall.

Papazoglou, M. P., & Georgakopoulos, D. (2003). Service-orented computing. *Communications of the ACM, 46*(10), 25–28.

Park, J., Kim, J., & Koh, J. (2010). Determinants of continuous usage intention in web analytics services. *Electronic Commerce Research and Applications, 9*(1), 61–72. doi:10.1016/j.elerap.2009.08.007

Petrie, C., & Genesereth, M. e. (2003). Adding AI to Web services. In D. V. van Elst L, AMKM 2003, LNAI 2926 (pp. 322-338).

Rainbird, M. (2004). Demand and supply chains: The value catalyst. *International Journal of Physical Distribution & Logistics Management, 34*(3/4), 230–250. doi:10.1108/09600030410533565

Rouse, M. (2009, Feb). *Storage as a Service (SaaS)*. Retrieved July 11, 2013, from SearchStorage: http://searchstorage.techtarget.com/definition/Storage-as-a-Service-SaaS

Rouse, M. (2011, 09). *cloud services*. Retrieved 07 03, 2013, from SearchCloudProvider: http://searchcloudprovider.techtarget.com/definition/cloud-services

Russell, S., & Norvig, P. (2010). *Artificial Intelligence: A Modern Approach* (3rd ed.). Upper Saddle River: Prentice Hall.

Rust, R. T., & Kannan, P. K. (2003). E-service: A new paradigm for business in the electronic environment. *Communications of the ACM, 46*(6), 37–42. doi:10.1145/777313.777336

Schalkoff, R. J. (2011). *Intelligent Systems: Principles, Paradigms, and Pragmatics*. Boston: Jones and Bartlett Publishers.

Schneider, G. (2011). *Electronic Commerce* (9th ed.). Australia: Course Technology.

Schneider, G. P. (2013). *Electornic Commerce* (10th ed.). Australia: Coourse Technology CENGAGE Learning.

Shan, T. (2009, 02 19). *Cloud Taxonomy and Ontology*. Retrieved 08 1, 2013, from Ulitzer: http://tonyshan.ulitzer.com/node/1469454

Sharif, M., Troshani, I., & Davidson, R. (2014). Adoption of Social Media Services: The Case of Local Government Organizations in Australia. In Z. Sun, & J. Yearwood (Eds.), *Demand-Driven Web Services: Theory, Technologies, and Applications*. IGI-Global.

Singh, M. P., & Huhns, M. N. (2005). *Service-oriented Computing: Semantics, Processes, and Agents*. Chichester: John Wiley & Sons, Ltd.

Singh, M. P., & Huhns, M. N. (2005). *Service-oriented Computing: Semantics, Processes, and Agents*. Chichester: John Wiley & Sons, Ltd.

Sitaram, D., & Manjunath, G. (2011). *Moving To The Cloud Developing Apps in the New World of Cloud Computing*. Burlington: Elsevier Science.

Smyth, B., Briggs, P., & Coyle, M. (2009). A Case-Based Perspective on Social Web Search, LNCS. In *Case-Based Reasoning* []. Berlin: Springer.]. *Research for Development*, *5650*, 494–508.

Song, H. (2003). E-services at FedEx. *Communications of the ACM*, *46*(6), 45–46. doi:10.1145/777313.777338

Sun, Z., Dong, D., & Yearwood, J. (2011). Demand Driven Web Services. In H. Leung, D. K. Chiu, & P. C. Hung (Eds.), *Service Intelligence and Service Science: Evolutionary Technologies and Challenges* (pp. 35–55). Hershey, PA: IGI Global.

Sun, Z., & Finnie, G. (2004). *Intelligent Techniques in E-Commerce: A Case-based Reasoning Perspective*. Heidelberg, Berlin: Springer-Verlag. doi:10.1007/978-3-540-40003-5

Sun, Z., & Finnie, G. (2004; 2010). Intelligent Techniques in E-Commerce: A Case-based Reasoning Perspective. Heidelberg Berlin: Springer-Verlag. Reprinted

Sun, Z., & Firmin, S. (2012). A strategic perspective on management intelligent systems. In J. Casillas et al, Management Intelligent Systems, AISC 171 (pp. 3-14). Springer.

Sun, Z., & Lau, S. K. (2007). Customer experience management in e-services. In J. Lu, D. Ruan, & G. Zhang (Eds.), *E-Service Intelligence: Methodologies, Technologies and Applications* (pp. 365–388). Berlin, Heidelberg: Springer Verlag. doi:10.1007/978-3-540-37017-8_17

Sun, Z., Yearwood, J., & Firmin, S. (2013). A technique for ranking friendship closeness in social networking services. In ACIS2013 Conference proceedings Melbourne.

Tabein, R., Moghadasi, M., & Khoshkbarforoushha, A. (2008). Broker-based Web service selection using learning automata. *2008 International Conference on Service Systems and Service Management, June July 2008, pp.1-6*.

Thirumaran, M., Naga Venkata Kiran, G., & Dhavachelvan, P. A. (2012). Collaborative Framework for Managing Run-Time Changes in Enterprise Web Services. *International Journal of Web & Semantic Technology*, *3*(3), 85. doi:10.5121/ijwest.2012.3306

Thomas, P. Y. (2012). Harnessing the Potential of Cloud Computing to Transform Higher Education. In L. Chao (Ed.), *Cloud Computing for Teaching and Learning Strategies for Design and Implementation* (pp. 147–158). USA: IGI Global. doi:10.4018/978-1-4666-0957-0.ch010

Turban, E., & Volonino, L. (2011). *Information Technology for Management: Improving Performance in the Digital Economy* (8th ed.). Hoboken, NJ: John Wiley & Sons.

Turban, E., & Volonino, L. (2011). *Information Technology for Management: Improving Strategic and Operational Performance*. Hoboken, NJ: John Wiley & Sons, Inc.

Turban, E., & Volonino, L. (2011). *Information Technology for Management: Improving Strategic and Operational Performance* (8th ed.). Wiley.

Waters, D. (2006). Demand chain effectiveness-supply chain efficiencies: A role for enterprise information management. *Journal of Enterprise Information Management*, *19*(3), 246–261. doi:10.1108/17410390610658441

wikipedia-CP. (2013). *Cloud Computing*. Retrieved 8 28, 2013, from wikipedia: http://en.wikipedia.org/wiki/Cloud_computing

Wikipedia-SNS. (2013, 9 20). *Social Networking Service*. Retrieved 9 24, 2013, from Wikipedia: http://en.wikipedia.org/wiki/Social_networking_service

Wikipeidia-SN-List. (2013, 7 26). *List of social networking websites*. Retrieved 9 24, 2013, from Wikipeidia: http://en.wikipedia.org/wiki/List_of_social_networking_websites

Wilkinson, N. (2005). *Managerial Economics: A Problem-Solving Approach*. Cambridge: Cambridge University Press. doi:10.1017/CBO9780511810534

Wooldridge, M. (2002). *An Introduction to Multiagent Systems*. Chichester, England: John Wiley & Sons Ltd.

ADDITIONAL READING

W3C (2013). Web Services Activity. Retrieved November 18, 2013, from http://www.w3.org/2002/ws/

Bell, M. (2008). *Service-Oriented Modeling (SOA), Service Analysis, Design, and Architecture*. Chichester, England: John Wiley and Sons Ltd.

Benatallah, B., Reza, H., & Nezhad, M. et al. (2006). A model-driven framework for Web services life-cycle management. *IEEE Internet Computing*, (July/August): 55–63. doi:10.1109/MIC.2006.87

Cheng, R., & Su, S. Yang, F., & Li, Y. (2006). Using case-based reasoning to support Web service composition. In V.N. Alexandrov, & et al. (Eds.), ICCS 2006, Part IV, LNCS 3994, pp. 87 – 94, Berlin Heidelberg: Springer-Verlag.

Erl, T. (2006). *Service-Oriented Architecture (SOA), Concepts, Technology, and Design*. Upper Saddle River, NJ: Prentice Hall.

Guruge, A. (2004). *Web Services: Theory and Practice*. Amsterdam: Elsevier Inc.

Han, W., Xingdong Shi, X., & Chen, R. (2008). Process-context aware matchmaking for Web service composition. *Journal of Network and Computer Applications*, *31*(4), 559–576. doi:10.1016/j.jnca.2007.11.008

Henderson-Sellers, B., & Giorgini, P. (Eds.). (2005). *Agent-Oriented Methodologies*. Hershey, PA: Idea Group Publishing. doi:10.4018/978-1-59140-581-8

Jackson, J., & McIver, R. (2004). *Microeconomics* (7th ed.). Australia: McGraw-Hill.

Jeong, B., Cho, H., & Lee, C. (2009). On the functional quality of service (FQoS) to discover and compose interoperable Web services. *Expert Systems with Applications*, *36*(3), 5411–5418. doi:10.1016/j.eswa.2008.06.087

Kajan E., Lazic, L. Maamar, Z. Software Testing as a Service: The BISA Approach, Proceedings of Telsiks 2011, October 2011, Nis, Serbia, pp. 204-207.

Ladner, R. et al. (2008). Soft computing techniques for Web service brokering. *Soft Computing*, *12*, 1089–1098. doi:10.1007/s00500-008-0277-0

Lau, R. Y. K. (2007). Towards a Web services and intelligent agents-based negotiation system for B2B eCommerce. *Electronic Commerce Research and Applications*, *6*(3), 260–273. doi:10.1016/j.elerap.2006.06.007

Lawler, J. P. (2007). *Service-Oriented Architecture: SOA Strategy, Methodology, and Technology*. Hoboken: Taylor & Francis Ltd. doi:10.1201/9781420045017

Lu, J., Ruan, D., & Zhang, G. (Eds.). (2006). *E-Service Intelligence*. Berlin, Heidelberg: Springer Verlag.

Madhusudan, T., & Uttamsingh, N. (2006). A declarative approach to composing Web services in dynamic environments. *Journal of Decision Support Systems*, *41*(2), 325–357. doi:10.1016/j.dss.2004.07.003

Mamar, Z., Hacid, H., & Huhns, M. (2011). Why Web Services need Social Networks. *IEEE Internet Computing*, (March/April): 90–94. doi:10.1109/MIC.2011.49

Mudunuri, S. (2012). Imbibing Java Web Services: A Step by Step Approach for Learning Web Services. CreateSpace Independent Publishing Platform.

Papazoglou, M. (2012). *Web Services and SOA: Principles and Technology* (2nd ed.). Pearson Education Canada.

Park, C.-S., & Park, S. (2008). Efficient execution of composite Web services exchanging intensional data. *Journal of Information Science*, *178*(2), 317–339. doi:10.1016/j.ins.2007.08.021

Pfleeger, S. L., & Atlee, J. M. (2006). *Software Engineering: Theory and Practice* (3rd ed.). Beijing: Pearson Education, Inc.

Platzer, C., Rosenberg, F., & Dustdar, S. (2009). Web Service Clustering using Multidimensional Angels as Proximity Measures. *ACM Transactions on Internet Technology*, *9*(3), 11. doi:10.1145/1552291.1552294

Sun, Z., & Finnie, G. (2005). A unified logical model for CBR-based e-commerce systems. *International Journal of Intelligent Systems*, *20*(1), 29–46. doi:10.1002/int.20052

Tagarelli A., & Greco S. Semantic Clustering of XML Documents. ACM Transactions on Information Systems, Vol. 28, No. 1, Art. 3. (January 2010).

Talukder, A. K., & Yavagal, R. R. (2007). *Mobile Computing: Technology, Applications and Service Creation*. New York, NY: McGraw-Hill Inc.

Ting, I.-H., & Wu, H. J. (Eds.). (2009). *Web Mining Applications in E-commerce and E-services*. Berlin, Heidelberg: Springer Verlag. doi:10.1007/978-3-540-88081-3

KEY TERMS AND DEFINITIONS

This section provides eight terms related to the topic of this chapter. Frankly speaking, there are many definitions for each of the terms to be mentioned in this section. Therefore, we can only provide one or two for each of them owing to the space limitation. Further, this is not the place for reviewing the existing definitions for each of the term. For detailed information on each of the terms please read the related books or papers.

Demand Theory: A part of microeconomics. It examines demand curves, demand equations, demand analysis, demand chain, impact factors on demand, demand estimation and so on. Demand analysis assesses current and projected demand for e-commerce services amongst existing and potential customer segments.

E-Commerce: Buying and selling on the Web and associated activities.

eSMACS: It is abbreviated for electronic, service, mobile, analytics, cloud and social networking. This chapter uses eSMACS services as the state of art of Web services. More generally, eSMACS computing can be considered as the state of art of computing in the age of the Internet.

Intelligent System: A system that can imitate, automate some intelligent behaviours of human being. Expert systems and knowledge based systems are examples of intelligent systems. Currently intelligent systems is a discipline that studies the intelligent behaviours and their implementations as well as impacts on human society.

Multiagent Systems: An intelligent system consisting of many intelligent agents. An intelligent agent can be considered as a counterpart of a human agent in intelligent systems.

Service Computing: A research field about service science, science intelligence, service technology, service engineering, service man-

agement, and service applications. It is the most general representation form of studying service in computing discipline. Service computing and service-oriented computing are used interchangeably.

Service Oriented Architecture (SOA): It is a high level description for services, service-oriented systems, which is free of concrete implementation of a Web service system.

Web Services: Generally speaking, Web services are all the services available on the Web or the Internet. From a technological perspective, Web services are Internet-based application components published using standard interface description languages and universally available via uniform communication protocols.

Chapter 2
Exploring Marketing Theories to Model Business Web Service Procurement Behavior

Kenneth David Strang
APPC Research, Australia & State University of New York, USA

ABSTRACT

This chapter provides literature-grounded definitions of contemporary Web services and marketing theories, which can model business demand through procurement decision-making behavior. First, the literature was reviewed to identify contemporary Web 2.0 and Web service ontology alongside marketing theories, which can describe individual decision making in an organizational or personal context. The Web services included cloud computing, social networking, data storage, security, and hosted applications. Then selected models for assessing procurement decision-making behavior were discussed in more detail. The constructed grounded theory method was applied by interviewing Chief Information Officers (CIO) at large organizations across four industries in the USA: healthcare, higher education, energy creation, and banking. The purpose was to determine which marketing theories could effectively model their Web service procurement behavior. An empirical procurement decision-making model was developed and fitted with data collected from the participants. The results indicated that Web service procurement decision-making behavior in businesses could easily be modeled, and this was ratified by the CIOs. The chapter proposes a state-of-the-art ontology and model for continued empirical research about organizational procurement decision-making behavior for Web services or other products.

DOI: 10.4018/978-1-4666-5884-4.ch002

INTRODUCTION

Business Web services are a relatively new phenomenon, despite the first Internet - ARPAnet - was developed in 1966 by the US Department of Defense (Usdod, 2013). Ironically Internet TCP/IP protocol and Domain Name Service (DNS) were developed in 1983, while Nexus the first World Wide Web (WWW) browser came online available in 1991, followed by Netscape in 1993 (Estrin, 2009). Despite this, we know very little about how businesses make procurement decisions for WWW services.

The pervasiveness of personal computer technology such as Apple's iPhone which debuted in 2007 (Yan, 2008) make it easy to forget that business and government are large purchasers of Web services. In 2011, IBM announced Smart Planet Cloud Computing, designed to promote the sharing of application and data through the Internet. Google recently released a new 3D beta version of their maps and earth Web 2.0 applications, which allow users to contribute to the database (Google, 2013). Some researchers have argued that there business demand for these modern Web services are just as high as personal consumption, but for different reasons (Ante, 2012; Buera & Kaboski, 2012; Yeo, 2008).

As a case in point, one of the most successful business-oriented applications used by businesses in all sectors was the *Enterprise Resource Planning System* (ERP) that was developed in 1972 by German-based System Analyse und Programment-wicklung which we commonly know today as SAP R/3 (Buyya, Broberg, & Goscinski, 2011). When SAP became a Web-enabled hosted service by 2000, this enabled more affordable access to small businesses and non-profit organizations (Buyya et al., 2011). The affordable access to Web-serviced applications led to the modern e-business term, which means that business processes strategically leverage Internet-enabled ERP software to effectively and efficiently transform resources to produce and supply products or services to their clients and partners around the world (Strang, 2008). ERP's and e-business are synonymously associated with Web services for businesses.

ERP's are expensive, often costing millions of dollars, but in the early 2000's they became available online as hosted solutions from application service providers which made them more affordable to non-profits, small businesses and government (Golicic & Smith, 2013). Therefore, the question remains, do we know how to gauge this business consumer demand for Web services or how decisions are made?

The majority of 21st century Web-services seem to have been designed for the individual consumer. This raises the question about how key executives, such as CIO's, make Web service procurement decisions. Decision making for Web services is a complex task, especially given the social versus economic level conflicts in organizations (Sun, Zhang, Dong, Kajan, Dorloff & Bedini, 2012). This is why the researcher has attempted to explain executive CIO decision making for Web services through a consumer behavior model, which has been shown to explain individual behavior in businesses. In fact a number of researchers have applied marketing theories to understand individual consumer behavior for Web service purchases (Strang, 2011a). Thus, it was hypothesized that some marketing theories could be used to model business procurement behavior of Web services.

Research Purpose and Method

First, though, what are Web services? What models and techniques should Web service designers use to understand procurement decision making behavior by government, profit and not-profit organizations? Certainly no service provider would want to build a million dollar hosted business application without knowing there would be a market for that and understanding how consumers make purchase decisions.

This was the challenge facing the researchers of this handbook. There was a collaborative effort to document theories, techniques, and models for understanding the Web service procurement behavior of business, government and non-profit consumers. We already know a lot about consumer behavior but there are few empirical studies concerning procurement behavior of business consumers.

The purpose of this chapter was to qualitatively and quantitatively explore organizational decision making for Web services using demand theories from consumer behavior (and somewhat from micro economics). The exploration was empirically-driven, based on a literature review followed by a small sample of Chief Information Officers (CIO) at large USA-based corporations across four different industries. The four industries were healthcare, higher education, banking, and energy creation.

Exploratory best described this type of research because there was very little known about business consumer procurement decision making behavior in the modern Web 2.0 service context. The researcher believed that a more 'ground roots' approach was needed (based on 30 years of technology and research experience). An exploratory approach is appropriate when taxonomies and survey instruments do not yet exist (at least if they are not proven in the study context - which was the case here). Interviews with subject matter experts is an effective approach to uncover or validate best-practices and perceptions underlying decision making behavior, especially when some *a priori* models in related disciplines exist (Creswell, 2009; Glaser & Holton, 2005). Therefore, an interpretative constructed grounded theory research design was used, since there was a wealth of empirical literature for individual consumer behavior but very little about the procurement behavior for Web services in the business context.

BACKGROUND

The literature review first defined the core ontology for Web services. Next, the marketing theories were discussed; with elaborations of the models which, retrospectively, were found to be more relevant for understanding Web service procurement decision making behavior in organizations. The following section then applied a constructed grounded theory method to interview four theoretically-sampled CIO's from different industries, to develop an interpretation of how they make procurement decisions for Web services.

Constructed Grounded Theory is a well-documented formal research methodology (Creswell, 2009), and it is well-suited for this type of research where theories already exist but remain untested in a new cross-disciplinary practitioner context. Charmaz (2006) is a subject matter expert often cited in the literature for constructed (constructivist) grounded theory. Based on the interviews, an empirical model was designed (informed by theory grounded in the literature) and tested by the researcher using data collected from the participants, in a collaborative discussion.

Web 2.0 and Business Web Services

The term 'Web 2.0' emerged in the 21st century from the World Wide Web Consortium to refer to collaborative applications, or software linked together over the WWW where end-users may contribute both data and processes (Buera & Kaboski, 2012; Buyya et al., 2011; Yeo, 2008). Web 2.0 applications depend on an implicit, lightweight, flexible, and shared semantic model between Web-linked application elements or programs (Buera & Kaboski, 2012). Web services are the commercial applications offered to individuals and organizations, such as social networking, cloud computing, data storage, hosted ERP's, security, and so on. The most significant aspects of Web 2.0 and Web services are discussed below.

Web 2.0 has quickly matured during the last three years leading into 2013, and it has reinforced itself because of promotions from software developers. Web-based applications include mashups, blogs, wikis, feeds, tagging systems, user-created publication systems, and social networking applications. Several Web 2.0 interaction methods are available to the individual and business consumer market. The most popular include, Software as a Service (SaaS), Gleaning Resource Descriptions from Dialects of Languages (GRDDL), Really Simple Syndication (RSS), Asynchronous JavaScript and XML (AJAX), micro formats, and Representational State Transfer (Buyya et al., 2011). Interaction methods are used for managing process and data flow.

Web innovations are not necessarily based on new technology as much as new Web services with revisions to failed technology concepts. For example, Apple innovated the iPad and collaborated with service providers, which was a new brand rather than a new product. Apple improved Microsoft's failed tablet concept by innovating how the service was provided to individual and business consumers.

However, even Apple's ideology may not unequivocally apply to every market. Steve Jobs made an interesting comment during an interview before he died, "people don't know what they want until you give it to them" (Wolf, 2004). The refers to the psychological, motivational underpinning of decision making, where choices are made without a high degree of cognitive evaluation.

The key benefit of Web 2.0 applications is their openness. These applications are intended to unlock data, letting Web users work with and get significant value from untapped knowledge sources (Ante, 2012; Yeo, 2008). Hundreds of companies have announced support for Web 2.0 principles, which has motivated venture capitalists to begin funding associated start-ups, and bookstore shelves are crowded with Web 2.0 programming guide design books (Ante, 2012; Yeo, 2008).

Web 2.0 applications require and provide open shared meaning to link their various components and data sources. The techniques with which these applications represent and share meaning are extremely broad, ranging from the syntactic relationships users perceive among natural-language tags to precise algorithmic transforms that can accurately fuse with graphic information system location information.

The attraction of Web 2.0 for business consumers is that users are able to promote their data using tag systems. Businesses generally use tags and cross links in blogs, wikis, and social networking sites to increase exposure of their products or services (Buyya et al., 2011). Businesses generally like to use tags and links for knowledge management, collaboration and market promotions (Yeo, 2008).

The underlying philosophy of many Web 2.0 applications is to build participatory ecosystems of content that are supplied and developed in large part by their users. Web 2.0 provides and is dependent on URL's and content. A good example of this is that eBay uses massive numbers of individual user rated-tags of buyers and sellers to create the foundation of trust necessary to conduct commerce (Yeo, 2008). Wikipedia amasses expert knowledge from millions of contributors to form an information resource that is unmatched in breadth and coverage. Flickr integrates user contributions and links to bundle more photos than any other site. Social networking sites such as Facebook and non-profit wikis depend on user content and traffic in exchange for their services.

Social networking sites are a form of publicly-shared knowledge sharing through the Internet generally using micro-blogging in communities of interest or practice, whereby user share information, ideas, personal messages, and other content such as videos. As seen by Facebook, Twitter, Youtube and MySpace, social networking sites have become popular as a Web service to both individuals and businesses. Businesses use social network sites to advertise their services or products yet sometimes they solicit resources (e.g., employment or partnering opportunities). There are over a billion active users of social media channels (Ante, 2012; Barbot, 2013). The instant and global popularity of social networking impacts the way people communicate, as well as the market for products and services.

Social networking has led to the development of cloud computing. A cloud is formed by an unlimited base of Internet developers providing powerful datacenters (Yan, 2008). The cloud uses API's to allow providers to offer services (generally free) and to provide advertising for subscribers (Yeo, 2008). Data storage, data conversion and other office automation utilities are generally offered in the cloud.

All significant Web 2.0 technological revolutions have been associated with building large companies, changing millions of people's behavior along with many organizations too (Ante, 2012; Buera & Kaboski, 2012; Yeo, 2008). Web 2.0 Web service providers clearly thrive in this context of talented hackers whom have left their day jobs to stay up late in Silicon Valley garages building mashups (Ante, 2012).

Traditional companies that build Web services usually have a business model that equates users with individual purchasers. In this ideology, vendors, traditional media organizations, and other organizations create compelling Web sites, they try to attract large numbers of users to view their sites, and they create most of their revenue through user transactions on the site. This has given rise to Web service advertising industries exploited by Google which are devoted to banner placement, click-stream tracking, and republishing content onto the Web from more traditional media (Yeo, 2008).

Most types of Internet-driven organizations earn revenue from content providers and Web services based on how long an end-user remains on the site (after clicking on the URL to get there, and the conversion rate proportion of site visitors who actually make a transaction. Google's 'Ad-

Sense' and 'AdWords' are good examples of this marketing-related Web services behavior. This motivates traditional Web services companies to transform their business models into subscription-based access as well as to provide advertising for other Web service sites. Some Web services providers develop (or purchase) open API's to facilitate other businesses and consumers contributing content.

Marketing Theories and Web Service Business Behavior

Web service consumers are individuals but these people are also making procurement decisions as part of their work in organizations. This chapter is focused on the business, government and non-profit sectors. It was clear from the literature review that both individual and business-level consumer demand drives Web services. Individual consumer behavior studies were prolific in the marketing literature, although there were few studies published about business consumer procurement behavior for Web services.

Therefore, from a product/service design perspective, it would be useful to identify theories and models to understand business consumer procurement behavior for Web services. A key assumption made here is that business consumer behavior is similar for Web services as compared to traditional services. This research was informed by several studies about e-businesses who were consumers of Web services (Strang, 2009; 2010a; 2011a; 2011b; 2012a; 2012b; 2012c; 2012e; 2008; Strang & Chan, 2010). The most important business consumer demand models are discussed based on these studies and from an independent literature review.

Marketing theory procurement behavior is interdisciplinary because it integrates psychology, anthropology (culture), sociology, economics and statistics with marketing theories (Diewert, 2012; Foxall, Yan, Oliveira-Castro, & Wells, 2011), as illustrated in Figure 1. Procurement behavior analy-

Figure 1. Family of interdisciplinary marketing theories related to purchase behavior (author)

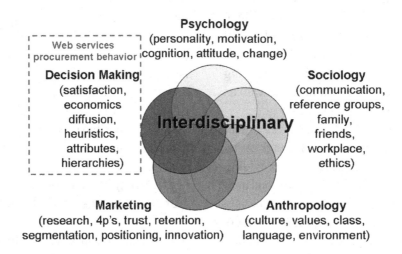

sis occurs before the design phase in new product development, and the results feed into design as well as marketing of the product/service (Strang & Chan, 2010). Procurement behavior theory does not include innovation or creativity, as the focus is on understanding perception, motivation and decision making (Kotabe & Helsen, 2010).

The business procurement behavior demand theories focused on in this chapter are in the 'decision making' category (from Figure 1). The three major strategic tools of procurement behavior marketing are market segmentation, targeting, and positioning. The marketing mix consists of a company's service and/or product offerings to consumers and the pricing, promotion, and distribution methods needed to accomplish the exchange.

The core marketing theories related to procurement decision making behavior are listed in Table 1, by category. These are a detailed breakdown of the decision making theories from Figure 1. The 'explored' column in table 1 contains a 'yes' if the topic is discussed at length in this chapter, due to its perceived relevance for understanding business Web service procurement behavior. The purpose of listing the procurement decision making theories which are not examined in this chapter is to inform future research.

The theories and models in procurement behavior are mixed in the sense that they are both qualitative as well as quantitative. This means that qualitative approaches as well as quantitative techniques are relevant for assessing Web service business consumer demand behavior. Qualitative consumer research often uses focus groups and interviews; one of the popular specialized qualitative methodologies is the Zaltman Metaphor Elicitation Techniques (Kotabe & Helsen, 2010). Quantitative consumer research includes observation, experimentation and surveys followed by statistical analysis of the responses based on *a priori* theories (Kotabe & Helsen, 2010), such as the Net Promoter Score and Fishbein Attitude Models.

Market segmentation is defined as the process of dividing a potential market into distinct subsets of consumers with a common need or characteristic and selecting one or more segments to target with a specially designed marketing mix (Kotabe & Helsen, 2010). The benefit of segmenting for Web services consumers is to redesign or reposition existing products/services or to create promotional appeals through selected advertising media. However, segmentation begins with measuring business consumer preferences and attitudes.

Table 1. Marketing theories for explaining procurement decision making behavior (author)

Generally-Accepted Procurement Decision Making Theories	Explored
Customer retention, loyalty and trust	
Projective techniques [interpretative data collection]	No
Assessing customer loyalty [Net Promoter Score quantitative analysis]	Yes
Perceptual maps [quantitative data collection & analysis: bubble maps]	No
Memory, cognition and learning	
Information overload [memory]	No
Just noticeable difference [memory]	Yes
Behavioral learning - classical and operant conditioning [learning]	No
Memorable taglines [memory]	No
Memory models and promotional strategies [learning]	No
Customer experience management - touch point analysis [	No
Personality, motivation and psychogenic factors	
Personality [traits, innate, content and process theories]	No
Maslow needs hierarchy, customer motivation	No
Appealing to Freud id, superego, ego & + psychogenic needs	No
Self-concept	No
Socio-cultural factors and lifestyles	
Forms of reference group influence [power styles]	No
Types of reference groups	No
Consumer behavior diversity	No
Diffusion of innovation	No
Socio and geo-demographic factors [PRIZM]	No
VALS segmentation categories	No
Group/family decision making	No
Attitude and perception	
Balance theory and spokesperson strategies	No
Social judgment theory and attitude change	No
Cognitive dissonance	
Attribution theory	
Adopter life cycle categories & consumer attitude	No
Decision making rules	
Hierarchies of effects	No
Fishbein model of attitude measurement	Yes
Extended fishbein model	Yes
Elaboration likelihood model	No
Decision heuristics [espoused vs. Theories-in-use]	No
Decision rules	No
Multi-attribute models attitude change strategies	No
Research and segmentation	No
Research methods [qualitative, mixed, quantitative]	
Positioning strategies [segmentation]	No
Laddering interviews & means-end analysis	No
Information display boards	No

Consumer-rooted behaviors, cognitions, consumption-specific facts and attitudes can be used to segment consumers. The most common categories used for individual consumer segmentation are demographics and psychographics (or lifestyles). However, in most cases, hybrid segmentations are used. The primary examples of hybrid frameworks are VALS™ and the PRIZM™ geo-demographic clusters (Kotabe & Helsen, 2010). Other consumer-rooted variables used to segment markets are personality traits, socio-cultural values and beliefs. In contrast, the most important factors for segmenting business consumers are likely to be usage behavior (including usage rate and situation), benefit segmentation, brand loyalty and relationship building. These are unlikely to be key factors to analyze for Web services business consumers.

Contemporary procurement behavior models analyze consumer perceptions using mapping, Internet/subculture influences, memory/conditioning, multicultural consumer motivation, purchase attitudes, segmentation/branding/advertising impacts, and multi-attribute decision making (Kotabe & Helsen, 2010). After a brief introduction to the economics of procurement behavior, the most important theories and models from Table 1 which are related to Web services procurement are discussed.

The economics dimension of procurement behavior is concerned with explaining the purchasing decisions of rational consumers under combinations of limited resources allocated to different commodities (Diewert, 2012). Together with the theory of the firm (which is really a theory of supply), it forms the basis of microeconomics (Kotabe & Helsen, 2010). Money is not necessarily an explicit component of economics in consumer behavior decision making because decision making is a procedure that makes choice from several alternatives, which could be for motivational rationale or instinctive response (Diewert, 2012).

The cardinal utility approach was superseded by indifference-curve analysis (ordinal utility), which dispensed with the need for an absolute measure of utility (Diewert, 2012). Revealed preference is a third approach which is largely a re-expression of indifference-curve analysis, in which no explicit notion of utility is used at all (Kotler & Keller, 2009). All these approaches give rise to the same qualitative analysis of procurement behavior and support the laws of demand and supply, which is simply that as price rises it leads to drops in demand.

Most procurement behavior models are built on demand functions. A demand function is a mathematical expression of the relationship between the quantity of a good or service that is demanded, and changes in a number of factors, such as price, substitute prices and complementary goods, income, credit terms, etc (Ruscitti, 2012). The quantity demanded or purchase intention is the dependent variable while the other factors are independent variables (Strang, 2012e). The effect of each independent variable on the dependent variable may be estimated statistically by time-series regression analysis or cross-sectional factor analysis (Strang, 2012e). Demand is relatively simple to model and is not discussed here.

Although cognition, perception, and motivation are the driving forces within individual consumers that impel them to action, it is worth discussing a few of the key psychological procurement behavior theories since humans are still the decision makers in Web services. These driving forces are produced by a state of uncomfortable tension, which exists as the result of an unsatisfied need. All individuals have needs, wants, and desires. The individual's subconscious drive to reduce need-induced tensions results in behavior that he or she anticipates will satisfy needs and thus bring about a more comfortable internal state (Kotler & Keller, 2009). Motivation can be either positive or negative.

Innate needs—those an individual is born with—are physiological (biogenic) in nature; they include all the factors required to sustain physical life (e.g., food, water, clothing, shelter, sex, and physical safety). Acquired needs—those an individual develops after birth—are primarily psychological (psychogenic); they include love, acceptance, esteem, and self-fulfillment (Kotler & Keller, 2009).

All behavior is goal oriented (Kotabe & Helsen, 2010). Goals are the sought-after results of motivated behavior. The form or direction that behavior takes—the goal that is selected—is a result of thinking processes (cognition) and previous learning (e.g., experience). There are two types of goals: generic goals and product specific goals. A generic goal is a general category of goal that may fulfill a certain need; a product-specific goal is a specifically branded or labeled product that the individual sees as a way to fulfill a need.

Product-specific needs are sometimes referred to as wants. For any innate or acquired need, there are many different and appropriate goals. The specific goal selected depends on the individual's experiences, physical capacity, prevailing cultural norms and values, and the goal's accessibility in the physical and social environment. Needs and goals are interdependent and change in response to the individual's physical condition, environment, interaction with other people, and experiences. As needs become satisfied, new, higher-order needs emerge that must be fulfilled. A similar process takes place within businesses, whereby decision makers are goal-driven, except the goals are based on personal experiences and accountabilities toward the institution, policies and peer pressures from organizational stakeholders.

Failure to achieve a goal often results in feelings of frustration. Individuals react to frustration in two ways: fight or 'flight' (Kotler & Keller, 2009). They may cope by finding a way around the obstacle that prohibits goal attainment or by adopting a substitute goal (fight); or they may adopt a defense mechanism that enables them to protect their self-esteem (flight). Defense mechanisms include aggression, regression, rationalization, withdrawal, projection, daydreaming, identification, and repression.

Motives cannot easily be inferred from procurement behavior. People with different needs may seek fulfillment through selection of the same goals; people with the same needs may seek fulfillment through different goals. Although some psychologists have suggested that individuals have different need priorities, others believe that most human beings experience the same basic needs, to which they assign a similar priority ranking. Maslow's hierarchy-of-needs theory proposes five levels of human needs: physiological needs, safety needs, social needs, egoistic needs, and self-actualization needs. Other needs widely integrated into consumer advertising include the needs for power, affiliation, and achievement (Kotabe & Helsen, 2010).

There are self-reported and qualitative methods for identifying and "measuring" human motives and researchers use these techniques in tandem to assess the presence or strength of consumer motives. Motivational research and its current extended form seeks to delve below the consumer's level of conscious awareness, and to identify underlying needs and motives. Moreover, quantitative research has proved to be of value to marketers in developing new ideas and advertising copy appeals. It is possible this may be relevant for assessing Web services business consumer demand.

Personality of the consumer is sometimes analyzed as a motivational-psychological characteristic that both determine and reflect how a person responds to his or her environment. Although personality tends to be consistent and enduring, it may change abruptly in response to major life events, as well as gradually over time (Kotabe & Helsen, 2010).

Three theories of personality are prominent in the study of procurement behavior: psychoanalytic theory, neo-Freudian theory, and trait theory (Kotabe & Helsen, 2010). Freud's psychoanalytic theory provides the foundation for the study of motivational research, which operates on the premise that human drives are largely unconscious in nature and serve to motivate many consumer actions. Neo-Freudian theory tends to emphasize the fundamental role of social relationships in the formation and development of personality. Alfred Adler viewed human beings as seeking to overcome feelings of inferiority. Harry Stack Sullivan believed that people attempt to establish significant and rewarding relationships with others. Karen Horney saw individuals as trying to overcome feelings of anxiety and categorized them as compliant, aggressive, or detached.

Trait theory is a major departure from the qualitative or (subjective) approach to personality measurement. It postulates that individuals possess innate psychological traits (e.g., innovativeness, novelty seeking, need for cognition, materialism) to a greater or lesser degree, and that these traits can be measured by specially designed scales or inventories. Because they are simple to use and to score and can be self-administered, personality inventories are the preferred method for many researchers in the assessment of consumer personality. Product and brand personalities represent real opportunities for marketers to take advantage of consumers' connections to various brands they offer. Brands often have personalities—some include "human-like" traits and even gender. These brand personalities help shape consumer responses, preferences, and loyalties (Kotabe & Helsen, 2010).

Each individual has a perceived self-image (or multiple self-images) as a certain kind of person with certain traits, habits, possessions, relationships, and ways of behaving (Kotler & Keller, 2009). Consumers frequently attempt to preserve, enhance, alter, or extend their self-images by purchasing products or services and shopping at stores believed to be consistent with the relevant self-image(s) and by avoiding products and stores they perceive are not. With the growth of the Internet, there appear to be emerging virtual selves or virtual personalities. Consumer experiences with chat rooms sometimes provide an opportunity to explore new or alternative identities.

Perception is the process by which individuals select, organize, and interpret stimuli into a meaningful and coherent picture of the world (Kotler & Keller, 2009). Perception has strategy implications for marketers because consumers make decisions based on what they perceive rather than on the basis of objective reality.

The lowest level at which an individual can perceive a specific stimulus is that person's absolute threshold. The minimal difference that can be perceived between two stimuli is called the differential threshold or just noticeable difference (Kotabe & Helsen, 2010). Generally speaking, a price discount should be at least 15% for an individual consumer to 'notice' the difference. Consumers perceive most sensory stimuli above the level of their conscious awareness; however, weak stimuli can be perceived below the level of conscious awareness (i.e., subliminally). Research refutes the notion that subliminal stimuli influence consumer-buying decisions (Kotler & Keller, 2009).

Consumers' selections of stimuli from the environment are based on the interaction of their expectations and motives with the stimulus itself (Kotler & Keller, 2009). People usually perceive things they need or want, and block the perception of unnecessary, unfavorable, or painful stimuli. The principles of selective perception include the following concepts: selective exposure, selective attention, perceptual defense, and perceptual blocking.

Consumers organize their perceptions into unified wholes according to the principles of Gestalt psychology: figure and ground, grouping, and closure (Kotler & Keller, 2009). The interpretation of stimuli is highly subjective and is based on what the consumer expects to see in light of previous experience, on the number of plausible explanations he or she can envision, on motives and interests at the time of perception, and on the clarity of the stimulus itself. Stereotypes that distort objective interpretation stem from physical appearances, descriptive terms, first impressions, and the halo effect (Kotler & Keller, 2009).

Just as individuals have perceived images of themselves, they also have perceived images of products and brands. The perceived image of a product or service (how it is positioned) is probably more important to its ultimate success than are its actual physical characteristics (Kotler & Keller, 2009). Products and services that are perceived distinctly and favorably have a much better chance of being purchased than products or services with unclear or unfavorable images.

Compared with manufacturing firms, Web service marketers face several unique problems in positioning and promoting their offerings because services are intangible, inherently variable, perishable, and are simultaneously produced and consumed. Regardless of how well positioned a product or service appears to be, the marketer may be forced to reposition it in response to market events, such as new competitor strategies or changing consumer preferences from global Web service providers.

Consumers often judge the quality of a product or service on the basis of a variety of informational cues; some are intrinsic to the product (such as color, size, flavor, and aroma), whereas others are extrinsic (e.g., price, store image, brand image, and service environment). In the absence of direct experience or other information, consumers often rely on price as an indicator of quality. How a consumer perceives a price—as high, low, or fair—has a strong influence on purchase intentions and satisfaction. However, the senses beyond visual are unlikely to influence Web service business consumers. In fact, business consumers often rely on both internal and external reference prices when assessing the fairness of a price.

Consumers often perceive risk in making product selections because of uncertainty as to the consequences of their product decisions. The most frequent types of risk that consumers perceive are functional risk, physical risk, financial risk, social risk, psychological risk, and time risk

(Strang, 2012d). Consumer strategies for reducing perceived risk include increased information search, brand loyalty, buying a well-known brand, buying from a reputable retailer, buying the most expensive brand, and seeking reassurance in the form of money-back guarantees, warranties, and pre-purchase trial. The concept of perceived risk has important implications for marketers, who can facilitate the acceptance of new products by incorporating risk-reduction strategies in their new-product promotional campaigns. Risk may be a factor for Web service business consumers - this could be assessed from their attitudes.

Consumer demand is sometimes assessed from a customer satisfaction perception standpoint. The rationale for this is because it is typically five to ten times more costly to obtain a new customer than to retain an existing one (Kotabe & Helsen, 2010). This would seem especially relevant for assessing Web services demand from business consumers where trust and loyalty are key factors.

Net Promoter Score (NPS) (Reichheld, 2013) is one of the best-known models for measuring customer perception of satisfaction and to predict loyalty, particularly for services rather than products. NPS integrates micro economics with consumer behavior. NPS is calculated using an *a priori* survey instrument, which asks customers to rate their perceptions of satisfaction for 10 attributes, using a Likert scale where 0 is lowest and 10 is highest. "Detractors" are respondents who answered 0-6 on a survey item while "promoters" are clients who answered 9-10 (Reichheld, 2013, p. 1). Responses for items 7-8 are dropped since they are considered neutral.

NPS is interpreted according to industry benchmarks, for example, 16 is a borderline NPS for retail. A study from a New York camping outlet is illustrated in Table 2 where the NPS was 0.159 (N=704) which is rounded and reported as 16 percent, indicating an acceptable result for the retail industry (author, 2013). The 'responses' column were counts of those survey responses customers, detractors were 0-6 while promoters

were 7-10. NPS was calculated by summing the detractors, promoters and both; then dividing the former by the total, the latter by the total, and then subtracting these subtotals (ignoring the sign). For example, based on Table 2, NPS = (205 / 704) - (317 / 704) = 0.159 rounded to 16%.

Consumer learning is the process by which individuals acquire the purchase and consumption knowledge and experience they apply to future related behavior (Kotabe & Helsen, 2010). Although from the author's experience some learning is intentional, much learning is incidental. Basic elements that contribute to an understanding of learning are motivation (drives), cues, response, and reinforcement (Kotabe & Helsen, 2010).

There are two schools of thought as to how individuals learn—behavioral theories and cognitive theories (Strang, 2010b). Both contribute to an understanding of procurement behavior. Behavioral theorists view learning as observable responses to stimuli, whereas cognitive theorists believe that learning is a function of mental processing.

Table 2. NPS for New York camping outlet store (N=704, author)

Scale Value	Responses	Detractors	Detractors
0 (not at all likely)	38	38	**0.291**
1	10	10	
2	13	13	
3	9	9	
4	16	16	
5 (neutral or unsure)	72	72	
6	47	47	
7	82	**205**	
8	100	*Promoters*	*Promoters*
9	198	198	**0.450**
10 (extremely likely)	119	119	*NPS:*
Totals	**704**	**317**	**0.159**

Three types of behavioral learning theories are classical conditioning, instrumental conditioning, and observational (vicarious) learning. The principles of classical conditioning that provide theoretical underpinnings for many marketing applications include repetition, stimulus generalization, and stimulus discrimination. Neo-Pavlovian theories view traditional classical conditioning as cognitive associative learning rather than as reflexive action (Strang, 2010b).

Instrumental learning theorists believe that learning occurs through a trial-and-error process in which positive outcomes (i.e., rewards) result in repeat behavior (Strang, 2010b). Both positive and negative reinforcement can be used to encourage the desired behavior. Reinforcement schedules can be total (consistent) or partial (fixed ratio or random). The timing of repetitions influences how long the learned material is retained. Massed repetitions produce more initial learning than distributed repetitions; however, learning usually persists longer with distributed (i.e., spread out) reinforcement schedules.

Cognitive learning theory holds that the kind of learning most characteristic of humans is problem solving (Strang, 2010b). Cognitive theorists are concerned with how information is processed by the human mind: how is it stored, retained, and retrieved. A simple model of the structure and operation of memory suggests the existence of three separate storage units: the sensory store, short-term store (or working memory), and long-term store. The processes of memory include rehearsal, encoding, storage, and retrieval.

Involvement theory proposes that people engage in limited information processing in situations of low importance or relevance to them, and in extensive information processing in situations of high relevance. Hemispheral lateralization (i.e., split-brain) theory gave rise to the theory that television is a low-involvement medium that results in passive learning and that print and interactive media encourage more cognitive information processing (Kotler & Keller, 2009).

Measures of consumer learning include recall and recognition tests and attitudinal and behavioral measures of brand loyalty. Brand loyalty consists of both attitudes and actual behaviors toward a brand, as both must be measured. For marketers, the major reasons for understanding how consumers learn are to teach them that their brand is best and to develop brand loyalty... Brand equity refers to the inherent value a brand name has in the marketplace (Kotler & Keller, 2009).

An attitude is a learned predisposition to behave in a consistently favorable or unfavorable way with respect to a given object (e.g., a product category, a brand, a service, an advertisement, a Web services site, or a physical establishment). Each property of this definition is critical to understanding why and how attitudes are relevant in procurement behavior and marketing.

The structure of attitude is important in understanding the role of attitudes in individual as well as business procurement behavior. Attitude is considered a key factor for assessing Web services business procurement behavior. Four broad categories of attitude models have received attention: the tri-component personal attitude model, multi-attribute attitude models, trying-to-consume attitude model, and attitude-toward-the-ad model (Kotabe & Helsen, 2010).

The tri-component model of attitudes consists of three parts: a cognitive component, an affective component, and a conative component. The cognitive component captures a consumer's knowledge and perceptions (i.e., beliefs) about products and services. The affective component focuses on a consumer's emotions or feelings with respect to a particular product or service. Evaluative in nature, the affective component determines an individual's overall assessment of the attitude object in terms of some kind of favorableness rating. The conative component is concerned with the likelihood that a consumer will act in a specific fashion with respect to the attitude object. In marketing and procurement behavior, the conative component is frequently treated as an expression of the consumer's intention to buy.

Multi-attribute attitude models (i.e., attitude-toward-object, attitude-toward-behavior, and the theory-of-reasoned-action models) have received much attention from market researchers. As a group, these models examine consumer beliefs about specific-product attributes (e.g., product or brand features or benefits). Recently, there has been an effort to better accommodate consumers' goals as expressed by their 'trying to consume' (i.e., a goal the consumer is trying or planning to accomplish). The theory of trying is designed to account for the many cases in which the action or outcome is not certain. The attitude-toward-the-advertisement models examine the influence of textual as well as visual messages on the consumer's attitudes toward the brand (Kotabe & Helsen, 2010).

Attitudes are learned and different learning theories provide unique insights as to how attitudes initially may be formed. Attitude formation is facilitated by direct personal experience and influenced by the ideas and experiences of friends and family members and exposure to mass media. In addition, it is likely that an individual's personality plays a major role in attitude formation, which would be exponentially impacted by the size of the group for Web services decision making in businesses.

These same factors also have an impact on attitude change; that is, attitude changes are learned, and they are influenced by personal experiences and the information gained from various personal and impersonal sources. The consumer's own personality affects both the acceptance and the speed with which attitudes are likely to be altered. Likewise, individual personalities impact group decisions in businesses.

Attitudes can be classified into six distinct categories: (1) changing the basic motivational function; (2) associating the attitude object with a specific group or event; (3) relating the attitude object to conflicting attitudes; (4) altering components of the multi-attribute model; (5) changing beliefs about competitors' brands; and (6)

the elaboration likelihood model. Each of these strategies provides the marketer with alternative ways of understanding and potentially changing consumer attitudes (Kotabe & Helsen, 2010).

One of the best-known models to measure individual consumer intention to purchase behavior is the *Theory of Reasoned Action* (TRA) (Ajzen, 1978), as adapted for this study and conceptually depicted in Figure 2. TRA was developed by Martin Fishbein first as *Attitude Theory* (Ajzen & Fishbein, 1969), based on the principles of *Expectancy Theory*, *Subjective Expected Utility Theory*, and the *Theory of Propositional Control* (Ajzen, 2012).

In Figure 2 the personal norms are the beliefs and attitudes of the key decision maker(s) toward the requirements based on personal experience, knowledge, moral ethics and institutional job accountabilities. In other words, decision makers will likely do what is required in their job above all else, but only to the extent that these actions are balanced with their personal moral standards and belief that the action will be successful for the organization and for themselves. The personal norms are considered experiential deductions, personal attitudes, or personal requirements. These are impacted by (weighted) by the importance (priority) or likelihood the individual feels each is needed for achieving a successful outcome in the organization.

The subjective (objective) norms in Figure 2 in the two lower blocks on the left are distinctive to this adapted TRA model. A business decision maker has beliefs about what others think they should do and also have differing levels of how likely they will follow those beliefs, also known as their motivation to comply with the referents. In an organizational setting, the beliefs of others would be collected as stakeholder requirements. The priorities of others would be recorded as priorities (weights), which is traditionally done through group brain storming sessions or another comparative form of joint collaboration. The subjective norm is now combined with the consumer's

Figure 2. Theory of Web services procurement behavior (adapted from Strang, 2013a, p. 7)

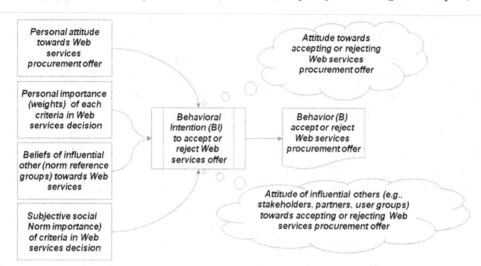

personal attitude toward a behavior to form an intention to perform a behavior. In this context, it would represent the Web services procurement decision making behavior in business. The intention may or may not lead to the actual behavior. Note this is not the actual behavior because only a retrospective study of past behavior would truly explain actual behavior. Therefore, the correct interpretation of the TRA model is that businesses would likely behave in the manner indicated according to the probability calculated by the model, on a comparative basis between alternatives.

This model proposes that the immediate determinant of behavior or action is a person's intention to perform the behavior, or attitude. Intention, was a function of two determinants, personal attitude toward performing that behavior, and perceived social approval, which is referred to as a subjective norm (Ajzen, 1978; Ajzen & Fishbein, 1969).

Most empirical studies applying TRA have shown a strong link between attitudes and intention, as well as between behavioral intention and actual behavior (Ajzen, 2010; Ajzen & Fishbein, 2004). Since individual personality characteristics and socio-demographic factors are often linked to behavior, these may be reflected in attitude and subjective norms within business teams making Web services purchase decisions.

The *Theory of Reasoned Behavior* (TRB) was an extension to TRA developed by Ajzen and his mentor Fishbein (Ajzen & Fishbein, 1969; Ajzen & Fishbein, 1973). TRB added behavioral control to the factors, which affected behavior (Ajzen, 1974; Ajzen, 1976, 1977). The weakness of TRB is that it is based on the assumption that behavior is under complete volitional control. Recent studies have shown that the addition of a measure of perceived behavioral control into the theory of reasoned action does improve the prediction of intention (Ajzen, 1978; Ajzen & Fishbein, 2004). TRB is not likely to be a relevant model for Web services decision making in a group context since cooperation would be more important than control, otherwise a decision would not be made.

The TRA model was argued (here in this chapter) to parallel procurement decision making behavior for strategic Web services in businesses where executive actions are impacted by their own considerable personal experiences and institutional accountabilities, along with professional ethics norms and social pressure from their boards, staff subject matter experts, as well as from other organizational stakeholders. The TRA model was a perfect conceptual fit for this business problem, so additional research was performed to understand how to apply it for procurement decision making.

TRA can be implemented to assess the business consumer attitudes toward Web service procurement using equation 1 which is called the Fishbein Extended Attribute Model. The general formula below was adapted from Ajzen and Fishbein (2008) as well as Strang (2013a, p. 9).

Behavioral intention = $\sum$(attitude toward behavior * object importance * importance weight W_b) + $\sum$(norm belief * norm importance * subjective norm weight W_s).

In this equation, behavioral intention (BI) [is a predictor of behavior]=attitude toward behavior [subjective importance weight of attitude on +1 to +7 scale * likelihood of outcome on -3 to +3 nonzero scale] + subjective norm [weight of object normative belief on a +1 to +7 scale * motivation to comply on -3 to +3 nonzero scale]. In this equation, the personal importance weight is W_b and subjective norm weight is W_s. In this model, weights W_b and W_s are statistical compliments, which sum to 100%. In order to apply the equation to business procurement decision making, the sum of all criteria or requirements, would need to be calculated and aggregated (added) to form an overall BI toward procurement.

Theories and extensions to TRA and TRB exist in the literature, such as the Technology Acceptance Model (Davis). The TAM was adapted from TRB to measure acceptance of information technology changes. In this chapter, TRA was applied to illustrate how this popular marketing consumer behavior model could be implemented. By doing this, the foundation would be established for other researchers to directly utilize TRA, extend it, or adapt one of the similar models cited here.

Finally, it should be noted that cognitive dissonance theory and attribution theory provide alternative explanations of attitude formation and change that suggest that behavior might precede attitudes. Cognitive dissonance theory suggests that the conflicting thoughts, or dissonant information, that following a purchase decision might propel consumers to change their attitudes to make them consonant with their actions (Kotabe & Helsen, 2010). Attribution theory focuses on how people assign causality to events and how they form or alter attitudes as an outcome of assessing their own behavior, or the behavior of other people or things (Kotabe & Helsen, 2010).

WEB SERVICES PROCUREMENT BEHAVIOR

Issues, Controversies, Problems

There are no empirically-grounded models in the literature to explain business Web service procurement decision making. The marketing literature reviewed above was focused on explaining individual consumer decision making or attitude driven behaviors within group contexts. The Web service procurement decision making processes are not necessarily different from individual consumer behavior, because humans are the decision makers, and everyone is influenced by personal as well as social factors. Therefore, several models in the marketing literature were examined in the previous section to understand Web service business procurement decision making.

Constructed Grounded Theory (Charmaz, 2006) was applied as a research methodology to answer the questions concerning Web service procurement decision making that would best apply to explain individual behavior by key executives within the organizational level of analysis.

Grounded theory starts with a proposition for a theory as the unit of analysis, or in some cases *a priori* concepts serve as the theoretical lens in modifying our understanding of a model (Strang, 2013b). As with all empirical research, the literature must be reviewed to determine if this is a unique goal (gap in current theories), and to identify the extent that other researchers have explored the levels of analysis (Strang, 2013b). Qualitative data is collected from participants and then the researcher attempts to organize the data into a categorical taxonomy of themes or factors (Glaser & Holton, 2005). The researcher then reviews the literature to determine if the taxonomy is equivalent to existing theories or constructs, and if so, cites these (Charmaz, 2006). If this is a new finding then it is proposed as a theory grounded to the data with a recommendation that positivists and constructivists further study this (Glaser & Holton, 2005). This variation that theory may already exist to guide the modification of a new model has become known as Constructed Grounded Theory or it is sometimes called Constructivist Grounded Theory (Glaser & Holton, 2005).

Constructivist grounded theory, as stated by Charmaz (2006), "sees both data and analysis as created from shared experiences and relationships with participants and other sources of data" (p.130). A research takes a constructivist perspective to better understand how and why perceptual constructs develop and the resulting theory is dependent on the researcher's view as part of the construction from the data (Charmaz, 2006). Charmaz (2006) stated, "the constructivist approach theorizes the interpretive work that research participants do, and acknowledges that the resulting theory is an interpretation" (p.130). In this chapter, the constructivist grounded theory approach was applied by the researcher and by the CIO participants engaged in the identification and interpretation of the constructs (Charmaz, 2006). This study, consistent with constructivist grounded theory, acknowledges that the results from the analysis are relevant to time, place, culture, and situation (Charmaz, 2006).

At this point, with the generally accepted procurement behavior theories in the marketing literature discussed, four subject matter experts were interviewed to assess their priorities in purchasing Web services and to determine which procurement behavior theories would be suitable to model this. Constructed grounded theory was selected because existing theory needed to be rati-

fied by participants according to their interpretation of the model (Creswell, 2009; Strang, 2011a).

A number of researchers have applied this formal research methodology to examine subject matter experts in order to validate and extend older theories (Creswell, 2009). For example, Pappu and Mundy (2002) applied this methodology to develop a model representing the strategic transportation buyer-seller relationships from an organizational learning perspective. The findings were that organizational learning theory was not new, but it was novel to uncover how practitioners were applying it to build relationships with buyers in the supply chain-transportation industry.

In another study using *Constructed Grounded Theory* Strang (2011a) applied this formal method on a cellular telecommunications development company based in Sydney, Australia. He interviewed participants and used the nominal brainstorming technique to help them build a model of their new product development procedures used for creating smart phone product features. He compared the cognitive domain learning theories used in education psychology from the *Taxonomy of Learning* (Anderson & Krathwohl, 2001). The findings were that the practitioners applied the *Taxonomy of Learning* cognitive domain stages for cellular phone new product development in an entirely different sequence.

The *Theory of Reasoned Action* (TRA) from Figure 2 was argued to be the most relevant model for assessing business procurement behavior for Web services, because it includes factors to address objective and subject norms, both of which could be anticipated to influence the process of group decision making. A number of researchers have applied TRA to examine consumer behavior (Didarloo et al., 2012; Diedrich, Terrados, Arroyo, & Balaguer, 2013; Erden & Von Krogh, 2012; Hansen & Risborg, 2012; Hsu & Huang, 2012; Middlestadt, 2012; Ramayah, Yeap, & Ignatius, 2013; Shin & Choo, 2012; Trongmateerut & Sweeney, 2013; Vu & Leez, 2013; Xiao, 2012; Yau & Wu, 2012). However, only a few of these studies were relevant to business decision making behavior and none of them directly referenced Web services procurement.

Trongmateerut and Sweeney (2013) applied TRA to study the behavior of business people blowing the whistle on one another in a corporate setting. They validated scales measuring whistle-blowing subjective norms, attitudes, and intentions using the TRA construct across two contrasting cultures: collectivist Thai and individualistic American employees. Not surprisingly, they found subjective norm influences were stronger in the collectivist Thai culture. Their validated instrument may be of use in future studies of Web service procurement behavior.

Erden and Von Krogh (2012) published a fascinating study of collaborative organizational learning in a university context, using the TRA to measure the behavioral intentions of the faculty. They were able to find some support for the TRA construct to explain why faculty intended to learn new procedures. This shows the TRA model is very flexible in its potential application across disciplines.

Groen and Wouters (2012) applied TRA in an organizational setting to discover why employees took more initiative to improve their performance after using a management by objectives goal setting process. They found that performance measurements stimulated employee initiatives to improve operational performance, especially when employees participated in the writing of their own departmental performance measures. In essence they replicated the TRA model, showing that employees who worked together on goals had higher perceived social pressure and higher perceived capability take action (behave). This may be useful in studies where there are performance repercussions on Web services procurement decisions.

Zhang, Yang and Bi (2013) conducted a study at the organizational level of analysis using the TRA. They explored why employees in departments at a Chinese company were willing to accept cleaner production technologies. Their study did not reveal

new information about TRA but the situation of adapting to new production technologies could be somewhat similar to meeting in groups to discuss procurement alternatives.

Richetin, Perugini, Conner, Adjali, Hurling, Sengupta and Greetham (2012) investigated the behaviors of employees at a large university towards reducing their resource consumption. Although their study appeared to be motivated by institutional environment conservation goals, their use of the TRA at the organizational level of analysis was innovative. They integrated attitude measures along with consumption economic factors in their analysis. They found that the subjective norm factors of the TRA model were influential in predicting employee behavior towards pro-environmental actions. This study was relevant to the current chapter in as far as it was used in a procurement related situation of not buying (not consuming).

Finally, Jin, Chai and Tan (2012) applied the TRA to evaluate new service development tools to improve organizational process quality at two financial institutions in Singapore and Taiwan. They found that employee attitude and subjective norms predicted behavior intention. Perceived usefulness and perceived ease of use impacted their attitudes while the feeling of competitive pressure influenced subjective norms. Although they noted it was a small sample size and a focus on only financial services, their implementation of TRA at the organizational level of analysis was fruitful. Since the context was related to process, it may be similar enough to Web service procurement to suggest TRA would be successful to achieve this research chapter mandate.

Solutions and Recommendations

The four participants were interviewed individually and given a summary of the literature review. They were asked questions concerning their procurement procedures for Web services. Specifically they were asked to explain their decision making processes. The purpose of this was to construct the participant's meaning of Web service procurement behavior and to validate or extend the TRA model to explain this.

The first participant was a Chief Information Officer (CIO) at a hospital in Texas. He responded to the procurement decision making process interview question: "to satisfy our growth, we have to tackle problems common to large medical organizations accumulating and generating massive volumes of data."

We have 63 specialty and subspecialty areas, 600 patient-related databases (that we know about), plus many links to other hospitals and research labs. To get an idea of the data requirements, think about the implications of this — our researchers need to store genetic markers; cataloging a single 1 × 3 inch slide requires a million data points. How do you architect security to be open and closed at the same time? By that I mean we want to share data with Baylor, for example, but we can't put them as just another user group on our network. We often need a view of data but not necessarily a single database to provide that view. Finally, on top of all these technical, governance, and regulatory issues, we have to continually circle back to the doctors, nurses, research scientists, and business administration users and ask the question are we giving you what you need to do your job. We use their requirements in a procurement matrix to make the decisions together with end users.

The second participant was a CIO at an electricity generation company in Florida. He stated that they make Web service related buying decisions based on their "business plan, with a great deal of communication with the business units."

Because demand is potentially infinite, projects must be prioritized, with enough granularity to enable the decision-making process. We do not use a formal chargeback system but, based on the

situation, some specific projects may be charged back. Balancing company-wide IT spending with specific needs of business units is an ongoing task if you're going to avoid suboptimization.

The CIO stated that they used a prioritized list of requirements, weighted by departmental importance (for example power transmission to existing customers has higher weight than new meter system development).

The third participant was a CIO at a higher education institution in California. He commented that they collaborate on procurement decisions using predetermined priorities weighted by business plan objectives.

We need Web services with strong IP platforms to help us remotely manage campuses in the United States and Mexico — most of the updates are to software development platforms used to deliver information technology courses, eliminating the need for physical site visits by a technician. Our ability to remotely manage technology is helped by smarter software, which reduces training time. We're also moving steadily away from proprietary systems." He also pointed out it was [less expensive for license costs] to use Moodle for a Learning Management System (LMS) as an open software Web service rather than hire advanced programmers in-house to build a LMS or to purchase a commercial LMS like Blackboard.

The fourth participant interview was with a CIO of a Credit Union (bank) in Virginia. He mentioned that they also outsource their ATM maintenance as well as their banking Web services.

When it comes time for Web services procurement decisions, they base them on key performance indicators (KPIs). Every decision must be linked to what it can return on investment. There is also a weight towards compatibility with our existing technology, which is SAP R/3.

During the discussions, the CIO pointed out that all of their applications were online. Their Web service procurement decisions are collaborative, involving key stakeholders from various business units located throughout the United States, in five European Union countries, and in Australia. The KPI's could be considered attributes and the proportion of business unit revenue contribution would be considered objective norm weights. Subject norm weights are generally influence by personal experience.

The four participants were invited to a brief online Web conference in order to empirically test out a constructed TRA model using their respective personal experience, knowledge, and attitudes. Since it was deemed too onerous to ask the organizational stakeholders to interact in this experiment, the participants were required to offer subject norm beliefs that they felt would be typical of their own end users. The participants were invited to form a simulated project to make a procurement decision for a Web services product which would likely be relevant to all of their organizations. Their unanimous choice was to select a new online (hosted) ERP system.

First the participants were asked to individually write down and prioritize the ten likely requirements of their stakeholders for this ERP system, based on what they truly believed their end users would say. These were then combined, with help from the researcher, to reword some requirements, and to eliminate those which were identical. From this a list of 18 unique core requirements were produced. Together the participants were then asked to prioritize this list, with the help of the researcher serving as a proxy advocate of the stakeholders so as to interject subject norm weights. The researcher guided the participants through this using an integer scale of -3 (lowest, negative, not wanted) to +3 (highest, essential). Each participant wrote down a weight (using the -3 to +3 scale), then the researcher took the median of their values, without casting a vote.

In a similar fashion, the participants were then asked to individually write down up to ten attitudes they held about important features of ERP systems, either positive or negative, based on their experience, moral ethics, and job accountabilities from their respective industries. The researcher worked with the participants to develop a unique list of 11 attitudes. The participants were then asked to develop weights for their attitudes toward the ERP requirements, using an integer scale of -3 (lowest, negative, not wanted) to +3 (highest, essential). Each participant wrote down a weight (using the -3 to +3 scale), then the researcher took the median of their values, without casting a vote. The rationale for doing this in reverse fashion, subject norms first then personal attitudes second, was to avoid bias in trying to develop objective requirements for their stakeholders. Based on the results this technique seemed to have worked.

Then the researcher asked each participant to indicate the ratio of how much each CIO would be willing to let their stakeholders influence the procurement decision, on a scale of 0% to 100% where 100% meant the end users were in total control. They were told that the stakeholders would be using this constructed model so as to interject objectivity into the decision making process. The mean was taken which was 40% (N=4), thus the subject norm weight was 60%.

The researcher selected three personal attitudes towards the Web services ERP requirements were taken, along with three stakeholder requirements (of 18), so as to demonstrate a scaled down model in this chapter. The result of this was coded into the constructed Web services procurement decision making model illustrated in Table 3. On the left, each of the decision maker's overall top three attitudes toward ERP systems was listed. For example, the researcher selected 'low cost…', 'automated backup…', and customizable security' as the three personal decision maker attitudes toward the ERP requirements for this scaled down model. He selected 'Internet access…', 'online

... training..', and '... reports..' as representative stakeholder subject norm requirements. The term 'attitudes' were used to describe beliefs for the decision makers while 'criteria' was chosen as the caption for the subject norm beliefs. The label 'priorities' was given to both person decision maker importance weights as well we the stakeholder importance wrights. The researcher then asked the participants to provide the most likely ERP Web service providers (which generated a list of 12 e-business ERP hosted software provider companies).

Next the researcher filled out the model (in Table 3) with the requirements, attitudes, criteria and priorities. He gave this to the four participants as an attachment and then asked them to email him back a completed score for the ERP Web service alternatives which the researcher theoretically-selected to ensure that the common choices of all participants were reflected (which ended up to be three; SAP, Oracle, and Manugistics). The participants were asked to complete the matrix by scoring each intersecting cell between the ERP alternative and requirement, using the same -3 to +3 scale they had practiced using earlier (thus they would be somewhat familiar with it). They were told to do this individually but were welcome to ask the advice of their staff if needed. The research took the median of the four responses from each participant and entered this value into the final matrix, which is reflected in Table 3.

The model in Table 3 was developed in Google Open Calc. Equation 1 was implemented in the 'weighted score' cells. This was done to fit the data into the conceptual model of Figure 2. For example, the weighted score of "2.80" was calculated by multiplying the attitudes and criteria by the 'ratings' for SAP, respectively. Then the priority of 30% for the personal decision maker importance weight was multiplied by the intermediate total of the personal attitudes rated for SAP. In this case, the calculation would be: $((3 * -3) + (-1 * -1) + (2 * -3)) * 30\% = -4.2$ (where "*" means multiply). Next the organizational stakeholder beliefs toward the requires were multiplied by the stakeholder importance weight of 70%, as follows: $((2 * 2) + (1 * 3) + (3 * 1)) * 70\% = 7$. The weighted score for SAP was -4.2 + 7 = 2.8 which was the lowest score (higher means better in this model). Based on the results in Table 3, the simulated ERP Web services procurement decision was to select Manugistics, with the score of 11.4 (highest).

Table 3. ERP Web service procurement decision making fitted model (N=4, author)

		ERP Web Service Alternatives		
Personal decision maker attitude toward requirements	*Attitudes*	SAP R/3	Oracle	Manugistics
Low cost per concurrent online user license	3	-3	-2	2
Automated backup through hosted vendor site	-1	-1	3	2
Customizable security authentication using AJAX API	2	-3	-2	3
Organizational stakeholder beliefs toward requirements	*Criteria*			
Internet access from all browsers (Mac, PC, PDA)	2	2	3	2
Online context-sensitive help/training modules	1	3	1	2
Customizable operational & executive reports	3	1	3	2
Decision making weights	*Priorities*			
Personal decision maker importance weight	30.00%			
Stakeholder importance weight (subjective norm)	70.00%	Scale -3=low, 0=medium, 3=high		
Weighted Score		**2.80**	**7.30**	**11.40**

The researcher emailed the fitted model in Table 3 to the four participants and invited their constructive feedback on the process as well as the simulated Web service procurement decision making results. All participants commented positively on both the process and the simulated results. In fact, all participants responded that they agreed with the final procurement decision predicted by this model, in as far as the factors and alternatives which were scaled into this exercise. They indicated they would likely implement this methodology into their Web service procurement decision making at their organizations. Furthermore, one of the participants suggested the model could easily be used for decision making beyond Web services, such as portfolio selection and even hiring competitions.

FUTURE RESEARCH DIRECTIONS

There seems to be emerging treads of studying Web services e-business consumer behavior using theories and models from outside the information technology field. In this chapter, marketing theories were used. It would be equally plausible to be able to explain organizational behavior using psychology or social-psychology theories (e.g., group decision making). These are suggested for further research.

Additionally, it is suggested that other researchers apply the marketing consumer behavior models outlined in this chapter in their own unique situations. Although only selected theories or models were discussed in detail (namely NPS and TRA), others were cited and could be explored to describe or explain other aspects of Web services. Suggested future topics are: leadership in Web service providers, project management of Web services deployment, multicultural perceptions of Web services design, factor analysis of Web service provisioning methods, and consumer behavior with social networking software.

It was also suggested that other researchers may wish to explore consumer behavior models similar to TRA such as TAM and others. The foundation for doing this was established by citing and applying TRA using empirical data collected from key practitioners in different industries.

CONCLUSION

The chapter proposed a state-of-the-art ontology and model for continued empirical research about organizational procurement decision making behavior for Web services or other products. This chapter was not about the uptake in organizational decision making behavior but rather an exploration of how four executives made Web services procurement decisions, by using an existing consumer behavior theories – the TRA model – derived the marketing discipline as described by CIO's as participants.

This chapter provided literature-grounded definitions of contemporary Web services and marketing theories which can model business demand through procurement decision making behavior.

The literature review addressed a number of disciplines, namely: information, behavior, psychology, political and social, economy, computing, education, business, gerontology, marketing and so on. The literature included manuscripts which could be categorized into journal papers, conference papers, and Web pages. The literature review cited 51 journal manuscripts and 26 conference papers. The following list summarizes the literature review by time:

- 2010-2013 (56 citations);
- 2005-2009 (10 citations);
- 2001-2004 (5 citations);
- 1975-1978 (3 citations);
- 1969-1974 (3 citations).

First, the literature was reviewed to identify contemporary Web 2.0 and Web service ontology alongside marketing theories which may describe organizational procurement behavior in the private, government and non-profit sectors. The Web services included cloud computing, social networking, data storage, security, and hosted applications.

Selected models were discussed for assessing procurement decision making behavior. The (constructivist) constructed grounded theory method was applied by interviewing Chief Information Officers (CIO) at large organizations across four industries in the USA: health care, higher education, energy creation, and banking. The purpose was to determine which marketing theories could effectively model their Web service procurement behavior. An empirical procurement decision making model was developed and fitted with data collected from the participants. The results indicated Web service procurement decision making behavior in businesses could easily be modeled, and this was ratified by the CIO's. The TRA model was useful as a construct to understand Web services procurement decision making behavior.

The implications of this model are important. Using TRA fitted to the data collected from participants (executives and stakeholders) provides a more objective and inclusive procurement decision making methodology for Web services. It also transforms qualitative beliefs into quantitative ratings which can be programmed into software. The software was open in that anyone can access it freely, from any platform which has a Google compliant browser, without having to purchase Microsoft Excel.

Theoretically, the model implemented TRA subject norms, using customizable weights (in this case it was 70% of the factors allocated to the stakeholders). Having a simple bidirectional scale from -3 to +3 allows negative attitudes to be voiced in the procurement decision making process. Furthermore, using the same scale for the Web service provider ratings allows bad performers to be differentiated from the best practice organizations, on each attribute individually. The method of using medians from all raters (decision makers and end users) in the organization applies nonparametric statistical principles to develop a reasonable rating which fairly represents the beliefs of all stakeholders.

REFERENCES

Ajzen, I. (1974). Effects of information on interpersonal attraction: Similarity versus affective value. *Journal of Personality and Social Psychology*, *29*(3), 374–380. doi:10.1037/h0036002 PMID:4814127

Ajzen, I. (1976). Uniqueness of behavioral effects in causal attribution. *Journal of Personality*, *44*(1), 98. doi:10.1111/j.1467-6494.1976.tb00586.x

Ajzen, I. (1977). Intuitive theories of events and the effects of base-rate information on prediction. *Journal of Personality and Social Psychology*, *35*(5), 303–314. doi:10.1037/0022-3514.35.5.303

Ajzen, I. (1978). Use and misuse of Bayes' theorem in causal attribution: Don't attribute it to Ajzen and Fishbein either. *Psychological Bulletin*, *85*(2), 244. doi:10.1037/0033-2909.85.2.244

Ajzen, I. (2012). Martin Fishbein legacy: The reasoned action approach. *The Annals of the American Academy of Political and Social Science*, *640*(1), 11–27. doi:10.1177/0002716211423363

Ajzen, I., & Fishbein, M. (1969). The prediction o f behavioral intentions in a choice situation. *Journal of Experimental Social Psychology*, *5*(1), 400–416. doi:10.1016/0022-1031(69)90033-X

Ajzen, I., & Fishbein, M. (1973). Attitudinal and normative variables as predictors of specific behaviors. *Journal of Personality and Social Psychology*, *27*(1), 41. doi:10.1037/h0034440

Ajzen, I., & Fishbein, M. (2004). Questions raised by a reasoned action approach: Comment on Ogden (2003). *Health Psychology, 23*(4), 431–434. doi:10.1037/0278-6133.23.4.431 PMID:15264981

Ajzen, I., & Fishbein, M. (2008). Scaling and testing multiplicative combinations in the expectancy value model of attitudes. *Journal of Applied Social Psychology, 38*(9), 2222–2247. doi:10.1111/j.1559-1816.2008.00389.x

Anderson, L., & Krathwohl, D. (2001). *A taxonomy for learning, teaching and assessing: A revision of Bloom's taxonomy of educational objectives.* New York, NY: Longman.

Ante, S. (2012, January 7). Avoiding innovation's terrible toll. *Wall Street Journal,* 3-4.

Barbot, C. (2013). A model of consumer choice with vertically differentiated goods: Reassessing the traditional demand theory and an application to tourism. *Journal of Transport Literature, 7*(1), 52–64. doi:10.1590/S2238-10312013000100003

Behavioural Precursors and HIV Testing Behaviour among African American Women. (2012). *Health Education Journal, 71*(1), 102-114.

Buera, F. J., & Kaboski, J. P. (2012). The rise of the service economy. *The American Economic Review, 102*(6), 2540. doi:10.1257/aer.102.6.2540

Buti, A. L., Eakins, D., Fussell, H., Kunkel, L. E., Kudura, A., & Mccarty, D. (2013). Clinician attitudes, social norms and intentions to use a computer-assisted intervention. *Journal of Substance Abuse Treatment, 44*(4), 433. doi:10.1016/j.jsat.2012.08.220 PMID:23021495

Buyya, R., Broberg, J., & Goscinski, A. M. (2011). *Cloud computing: Principles and paradigms.* New York: Wiley. doi:10.1002/9780470940105

Carrera, P., & Caballero, A., & Muã'Oz, D. (2012). Futureâ€ oriented emotions in the prediction of bingeâ€ drinking intention and expectation: the role of anticipated and anticipatory emotions. *Scandinavian Journal of Psychology, 53*(3), 273–279. doi:10.1111/j.1467-9450.2012.00948.x PMID:22448916

Charmaz, K. (2006). *Constructing grounded theory: A practical guide* (2nd ed.). London, UK: Sage.

Cheng, H.-H., & Huang, S.-W. (2013). Exploring antecedents and consequence of online group-buying intention: An extended perspective on theory of planned behavior. *International Journal of Information Management, 33*(1), 185–198. doi:10.1016/j.ijinfomgt.2012.09.003

Cheng, P.-Y., Hsu, P.-K., & Chiou, W.-B. (2012). Undergraduates' intentions to take examinations for professional certification: Examinations of four competing models. *Asia Pacific Education Review, 13*(4), 691–700. doi:10.1007/s12564-012-9229-6

Chorlton, K., Conner, M., & Jamson, S. (2012). Identifying the psychological determinants of risky riding: An application of an extended theory of planned behaviour. *Accident; Analysis and Prevention, 49*, 142. doi:10.1016/j.aap.2011.07.003 PMID:23036391

Creswell, J. W. (2009). *Research design: Qualitative, quantitative, and mixed methods approaches* (3rd ed.). Thousand Oaks, CA: Sage. doi:10.1037/e599802009-001

Davis, F. D. (1989). Perceived usefulness, perceived ease of use, and user acceptance of information technology. *Management Information Systems Quarterly, 13*(1), 319–340. doi:10.2307/249008

Didarloo, A. R., Shojaeizadeh, D., Gharaaghaji, R., Habibzadeh, H., Niknami, S., & Pourali, R. (2012). Prediction of self-management behavior among Iranian women with type 2 diabetes: Application of the theory of reasoned action along with self-efficacy (ETRA). *Iranian Red Crescent Medical Journal*, *14*(2), 86–95. PMID:22737561

Diedrich, A., Terrados, J., Arroyo, N. L., & Balaguer, P. (2013). Modeling the influence of attitudes and beliefs on recreational boaters' use of buoys in the Balearic Islands. *Ocean and Coastal Management*, *78*, 112. doi:10.1016/j.ocecoaman.2013.02.027

Diewert, W. E. (2012). Afriat's theorem and some extensions to choice under uncertainty. *The Economic Journal*, *122*(560), 305–331. doi:10.1111/j.1468-0297.2012.02504.x

Erden, Z., & Von Krogh, G. (2012). Knowledge sharing in an online community of volunteers: The role of community munificence. *European Management Review*, *9*(4), 213–227. doi:10.1111/j.1740-4762.2012.01039.x

Estrin, J. (2009). *Closing the innovation gap: Reigniting the spark of creativity in a global economy*. New York: McGraw-Hill.

Foxall, G. R., Yan, J., Oliveira-Castro, J. M., & Wells, V. K. (2011). Brand-related and situational influences on demand elasticity. *Journal of Business Research*, *66*(1), 73. doi:10.1016/j.jbusres.2011.07.025

Glaser, B. G., & Holton, J. (2005). Basic social processes, the grounded theory review. *International Journal of Grounded Theory Review*, *4*(3), 1–27.

Golicic, S. L., & Smith, C. D. (2013). A meta-analysis of environmentally sustainable supply chain management practices and firm performance. *Journal of Supply Chain Management*, *49*(2), 78–95. doi:10.1111/jscm.12006

Google. (2013). *Traveling made simpler in 3D Google earth and maps*. Paper presented at the Google IO Developers Conference. San Francisco, CA.

Gould, R., & Lee, K.-I. (2012). Predicting congregate meal program participation: Applying the extended theory of planned behavior. *International Journal of Hospitality Management*, *31*(3), 828–836. doi:10.1016/j.ijhm.2011.09.019

Griepentrog, B. K., Harold, C. M., Holtz, B. C., Klimoski, R. J., & Marsh, S. M. (2012). Integrating social identity and the theory of planned behavior: Predicting withdrawal from an organizational recruitment process. *Personnel Psychology*, *65*(4), 723–753. doi:10.1111/peps.12000

Groen, B. A. C., & Wouters, M. J. F. (2012). Why do employees take more initiatives to improve their performance after co-developing performance measures? A field study. *Management Accounting Research*, *23*(2), 120–141. doi:10.1016/j.mar.2012.01.001

Hagger, M. S., Lonsdale, A. J., Hein, V., Koka, A., Lintunen, T., & Pasi, H. et al. (2012). Predicting alcohol consumption and binge drinking in company employees: An application of planned behaviour and self-determination theories. *British Journal of Health Psychology*, *17*(2), 379. doi:10.1111/j.2044-8287.2011.02043.x PMID:22106875

Hansen, T., & Risborg, M. S. N. (2012). Understanding consumer purchase of free-of cosmetics: A value-driven TRA approach. *Journal of Consumer Behaviour*, *11*(6), 477–486. doi:10.1002/cb.1397

Hsu, C. H. C., & Huang, S. (2012). An extension of the theory of planned behavior model for tourists. *Journal of Hospitality & Tourism Research (Washington, D.C.)*, *36*(3), 390–417. doi:10.1177/1096348010390817

Huang, H.-C. (2012). Factors influencing intention to move into senior housing. *Journal of Applied Gerontology, 31*(4), 488–509. doi:10.1177/0733464810392225

Hyland, P. E., Mclaughlin, C. G., Boduszek, D., & Prentice, G. R. (2012). Intentions to participate in counselling among front-line, at-risk irish government employees: An application of the theory of planned behaviour. *British Journal of Guidance & Counselling, 40*(3), 279–299. doi:10.1080/03 069885.2012.681769

Jin, D., Chai, K.-H., & Tan, K.-C. (2012). Organizational adoption of new service development tools. *Managing Service Quality, 22*(3), 233–259. doi:10.1108/09604521211230978

Kotabe, M., & Helsen, K. (2010). *Global marketing management* (5th ed.). Newark, NJ: John Wiley & Sons.

Kotler, P., & Keller, K. (2009). *A framework for marketing management* (4th ed.). Upper Saddle River, NJ: Prentice-Hall.

Mausbach, B. T., Moore, R. C., Davine, T., Cardenas, V., Bowie, C. R., & Ho, J. et al. (2013). The use of the theory of planned behavior to predict engagement in functional behaviors in schizophrenia. *Psychiatry Research, 205*(1-2), 36. doi:10.1016/j. psychres.2012.09.016 PMID:23031803

Middlestadt, S. E. (2012). Beliefs underlying eating better and moving more: Lessons learned from comparative salient belief elicitations with adults and youths. *The Annals of the American Academy of Political and Social Science, 640*(1), 81–100. doi:10.1177/0002716211425015

Newton, J. D., Ewing, M. T., Burney, S., & Hay, M. (2011). Resolving the theory of planned behaviour's â€˜expectancy-value muddleâ€™ using dimensional salience. *Psychology & Health*, 1–15.

Pappu, M., & Mundy, R. A. (2002). Understanding strategic transportation buyer-seller relationships from an organizational learning perspective: A grounded theory approach. *Transportation Journal, 4*(41).

Ramayah, T., Yeap, J. A. L., & Ignatius, J. (2013). An empirical inquiry on knowledge sharing among academicians in higher learning institutions. *Minerva: A Review of Science. Learning and Policy, 51*(2), 131–154.

Reichheld, F. (2013). *Net promoter score™ (NPS) measuring overall satisfaction with the customer experience, and predicting customer loyalty*. Satmatrix Corporation, Bain & Company.

Richetin, J., Perugini, M., Conner, M., Adjali, I., Hurling, R., Sengupta, A., & Greetham, D. (2012). To reduce and not to reduce resource consumption? That is two questions. *Journal of Environmental Psychology, 32*(2), 112–122. doi:10.1016/j.jenvp.2012.01.003

Ruscitti, F. (2012). On the boundary behavior of the excess demand function. *Research in Economics, 66*(4), 371. doi:10.1016/j.rie.2012.05.001

Shin, D.-H., & Choo, H. (2012). Exploring cross-cultural value structures with smartphones. *Journal of Global Information Management, 20*(2), 67–93. doi:10.4018/jgim.2012040104

Spink, K. S., Wilson, K. S., & Bostick, J. M. (2012). Theory of planned behavior and intention to exercise: Effects of setting. *American Journal of Health Behavior, 36*(2), 254. doi:10.5993/ AJHB.36.2.10 PMID:22370262

Strang, K. D. (Ed.). (2008). *Collaborative synergy and leadership in e-business*. Hershey, PA: IGI Global.

Strang, K. D. (2009). Assessing team member interpersonal competencies in new product development e-projects. *International Journal of Project Organisation and Management, 1*(4), 335–357. doi:10.1504/IJPOM.2009.029105

Strang, K. D. (2010a). Comparing learning and knowledge management theories in an Australian telecommunications practice. *Asian Journal of Management Cases, 7*(1), 33–54. doi:10.1177/097282011000700104

Strang, K. D. (2010b). *Effectively teach professionals online: Explaining and testing educational psychology theories* (2nd ed.). Saarbruecken, Germany: VDM Publishing.

Strang, K. D. (2011a). A grounded theory study of cellular phone new product development. *International Journal of Internet and Enterprise Management, 7*(4), 366–387. doi:10.1504/IJIEM.2011.045112

Strang, K. D. (2011b). Leadership substitutes and personality impact on time and quality in virtual new product development. *Project Management Journal, 42*(1), 73–90. doi:10.1002/pmj.20208

Strang, K. D. (2012a, January 26). *Evaluating marketing investment projects in the uranium mining industry.* Paper presented at the System of Systems Conference. El Paso, TX.

Strang, K. D. (2012b). Group cohesion, personality and leadership effect on networked marketing staff performance. *International Journal of Networking and Virtual Organisations, 10*(2), 187–209. doi:10.1504/IJNVO.2012.045734

Strang, K. D. (2012c). Investment selection in complex multinational projects. *International Journal of Information Technology Project Management, 3*(2), 1–13.

Strang, K. D. (2012d). Nonparametric correspondence analysis of global risk management techniques. *International Journal of Risk and Contingency Management, 1*(3), 1–24. doi:10.4018/ijrcm.2012070101

Strang, K. D. (2012e). Prioritization and supply chain logistics as a marketing function in a mining company. *Journal of Marketing Channels, 19*(2), 1–15. doi:10.1080/1046669X.2012.667763

Strang, K. D. (2013a). Homeowner behavioral intent to evacuate after flood warnings. *International Journal of Risk and Contingency Management, 2*(3), 1–28. doi:10.4018/ijrcm.2013070101

Strang, K. D. (2013b). Risk management research design ideologies, strategies, methods and techniques. *International Journal of Risk and Contingency Management, 2*(2), 1–26. doi:10.4018/ijrcm.2013040101

Strang, K. D., & Chan, C. E. L. (2010). Simulating e-business innovation process improvement with virtual teams across Europe and Asia. *International Journal of E-Entrepreneurship and Innovation, 1*(1), 22–41. doi:10.4018/jeei.2010010102

Sun, Z., Zhang, P., Dong, D., Kajan, E., Dorloff, F.-D., & Bedini, I. (2012). Customer decision making in web services. In *Handbook of research on e-business standards and protocols: Documents, data, and advanced web technologies.* Hershey, PA: IGI Global. doi:10.4018/978-1-4666-0146-8.ch010

Trongmateerut, P., & Sweeney, J. T. (2013). The influence of subjective norms on whistle-blowing: A cross-cultural investigation. *Journal of Business Ethics, 112*(3), 437–451. doi:10.1007/s10551-012-1270-1

Turchik, J. A., & Gidycz, C. A. (2012). Prediction of sexual risk behaviors in college students using the theory of planned behavior: A prospective analysis. *Journal of Social and Clinical Psychology*, *31*(1), 1. doi:10.1521/jscp.2012.31.1.1

Usdod. (2013). *History of the ARPAnet*. Washington, DC: United States Department of Defense (USDOD).

Vu, H. T., & Leez, T.-T. (2013). Soap operas as a matchmaker: A cultivation analysis of the effects of South Korean TV dramas on Vietnamese women's marital intentions. *Journalism & Mass Communication Quarterly*, *90*(2), 308–330. doi:10.1177/1077699013482912

Weber, A., Dwyer, T., & Mummery, K. (2012). Morphine administration by paramedics: An application of the theory of planned behaviour. *Injury*, *43*(9), 1393. doi:10.1016/j.injury.2010.12.006 PMID:21215396

Wolf, G. (2004, September). Steve Jobs: The next insanely great thing. *Wired Magazine*, 1-5.

Xiao, Z. (2012). Correlates of condom use among Chinese college students in Hunan province. *AIDS Education and Prevention*, *24*(5), 469–482. doi:10.1521/aeap.2012.24.5.469 PMID:23016507

Yan, L. (2008). *The internet of things: From RFID to the next-generation pervasive networked systems*. New York: Auerbach. doi:10.1201/9781420052824

Yang, J. (2012). Predicting cheating behavior: A longitudinal study with Chinese business students. *Social Behavior and Personality*, *40*(6), 933. doi:10.2224/sbp.2012.40.6.933

Yau, O. H. M., & Wu, W.-Y. (2012). Feng Shui principles in residential housing selection. *Psychology and Marketing*, *29*(7), 502–518. doi:10.1002/mar.20538

Yeo, C. S. (2008). *Market-oriented cloud computing: Vision, hype, and reality for delivering IT services as computing utilities*. Paper presented at the High Performance Computing and Communications. Melbourne, Australia.

Zhang, B., Yang, S., & Bi, J. (2013). Enterprises' willingness to adopt/develop cleaner production technologies: An empirical study in Changshu, China. *Journal of Cleaner Production*, *40*, 62. doi:10.1016/j.jclepro.2010.12.009

Zoellner, J., Krzeski, E., Harden, S., Cook, E., Allen, K., & Estabrooks, P. A. (2012). Qualitative application of the theory of planned behavior to understand beverage consumption behaviors among adults. *Journal of the Academy of Nutrition and Dietetics*, *112*(11), 1774. doi:10.1016/j.jand.2012.06.368 PMID:23102176

ADDITIONAL READING

Ajzen, I. (1991). The theory of planned behavior. *Organizational Behavior and Human Decision Processes*, *50*(1), 179–211. doi:10.1016/0749-5978(91)90020-T

Ajzen, I., & Fishbein, M. (1980). *Understanding attitudes and predicting social behavior*. Englewood Cliffs, NJ: Prentice-Hall.

Gomes, L. F. A. M., Moshkovich, H., & Torres, A. (2010). Marketing decisions in small businesses: how verbal decision analysis can help. *International Journal of Management and Decision Making*, *11*(1), 19–36. doi:10.1504/IJMDM.2010.033641

Hale, J. L., Householder, B. J., & Greene, K. L. (2003). The theory of reasoned action. In J. P. Dillard, & M. Pfau (Eds.), *The persuasion handbook: Developments in theory and practice* (pp. 259–286). Thousand Oaks, CA: Sage.

Hemetsberger, A., & Godula, G. (2007). Integrating expert customers in new product dvelopment in industrial business - virtual routes to success. *Innovative Marketing*, *3*(3), 28.

Macquarie, E. F. (2006). *The marketing research toolbox: A concise guide for beginners* (2nd ed.). London, UK: Sage.

Miller, K. (2005). *Communications theories: perspectives, processes, and contexts*. New York: McGraw-Hill.

Sawhney, M., Verona, G., & Prandelli, E. (2005). Collaborating to create: The Internet as a platform for customer engagement in product innovation. *Journal of Interactive Marketing*, *19*(4), 4–17. doi:10.1002/dir.20046

Song, M., & Noh, J. (2006). Best new product development and management practices in the Korean high-tech industry. *Industrial Marketing Management*, *35*(3), 262–278. doi:10.1016/j.indmarman.2005.04.007

Strang, K. D. (2009). Using recursive regression to explore nonlinear relationships and interactions: A tutorial applied to a multicultural education study. *Practical Assessment, Research & Evaluation*, *14*(3), 1–13. Available http://pareonline.net/getvn.asp?v=14&n=3

Strang, K. D. (2010). Radiology manufacturing projects and politics: Scientist and politician normalized risk decision processes. *International Journal of Management and Decision Making*, *11*(3/4), 231–248. doi:10.1504/IJMDM.2011.040701

Strang, K. D. (2011). Applying multidisciplinary logistic techniques to improve operations productivity at a mine. *Logistics Research Journal*, *3*(4), 207–219. doi:10.1007/s12159-011-0058-5

Strang, K. D. (2011). Articulating knowledge sharing processes in multinational e-business product designing. *International Journal of Collaborative Enterprise*, *2*(2/3), 203–224. doi:10.1504/IJCENT.2011.042968

Strang, K. D. (2011). Portfolio selection methodology for a nuclear project. *Project Management Journal*, *42*(2), 81–93.

Strang, K. D. (2012a). Applied financial nonlinear programming models for decision making. *International Journal of Applied Decision Sciences*, *5*(4), 370–395. doi:10.1504/IJADS.2012.050023

Strang, K. D. (2012b). Group cohesion, personality and leadership effect on networked marketing staff performance. *International Journal of Networking and Virtual Organisations*, *10*(2), 187–209. doi:10.1504/IJNVO.2012.045734

Strang, K. D. (2012c). Importance of verifying queue model assumptions before planning with simulation software. *European Journal of Operational Research*, *218*(2), 493–504. doi:10.1016/j.ejor.2011.10.054

Strang, K. D. (2012d). Investment selection in complex multinational projects. *International Journal of Information Technology Project Management*, *3*(2), 1–13.

Strang, K. D. (2012e). Logistic planning with nonlinear goal programming models in spreadsheets. *International Journal of Applied Logistics*, *2*(4), 1–14. doi:10.4018/jal.2012100101

Strang, K. D. (2012f). Man versus math: Behaviorist exploration of post-crisis non-banking asset management. *Journal of Asset Management*, *13*(5), 348–467. doi:10.1057/jam.2012.14

Strang, K. D. (2012g). Nonparametric correspondence analysis of global risk management techniques. *International Journal of Risk and Contingency Management*, *1*(3), 1–24. doi:10.4018/ijrcm.2012070101

Swink, M., & Song, M. (2007). Effects of marketing-manufacturing integration on new product development time and competitive advantage. *Journal of Operations Management*, *25*(1), 203–217. doi:10.1016/j.jom.2006.03.001

Wagner, S. M., & Hoegl, M. (2006). Involving suppliers in product development: Insights from R&D directors and project managers. *Industrial Marketing Management*, *35*(8), 936–943. doi:10.1016/j.indmarman.2005.10.009

Weber, K., Sun, J., Sun, Z., Kliewer, G., Grothklags, S., & Jung, N. (2003). Systems integration for revenue-creating control processes. *Journal of Revenue and Pricing Management*, *2*(2), 120–137. doi:10.1057/palgrave.rpm.5170057

Whipple, J. S., & Gentry, J. J. (2000). A Network Comparison of Alliance Motives and Achievements. *Journal of Business and Industrial Marketing*, *15*(5), 301–322. doi:10.1108/08858620010345460

KEY TERMS AND DEFINITIONS

Cloud Computing: A public forum where Internet developers can provide powerful datacenters which allow other users to transform or update their data, as well as to contribute data or processes of interest to others (such as printing, data storage and language/code conversion).

Consumer Behavior: A set of interdisciplinary theories in the marketing field which are which integrate psychology, anthropology (culture), sociology, economics and statistics.

Enterprise Resource Planning (ERP): Server-based or Internet-hosted end-to-end business processing software developed as a mature best-practice, that is built on a core chart of accounts in a general ledger, with applications for all relevant operational processes linked together, usually with specialized modules for certain industry-specific functions link manufacturing bill-of-materials, warehouse inventory distribution, transportation logistics optimization, and others.

Net Promoter Score (NPS): One of the best-known models for measuring customer perception of satisfaction and to predict customer repurchase loyalty, particularly for services rather than products, using a validated survey instrument, which asks customers to rate their perceptions of satisfaction for 10 attributes, using a Likert scale where 0 is lowest and 10 is highest; benchmarks are published for NPS in various industries which facilitate organizational comparisons.

Procurement Decision Making: A subset of consumer behavior which applies to businesses (profit, government, and non-profits), which covers the buying process cycle from specification through selection and acquisition; the emphasis is generally on the group decision making methodology and behavior which occur at the end of the cycle to select the best service or product to acquire.

Social Networking: Internet sites which provide a platform for publicly-shared knowledge sharing through the generally using micro-blogging in communities of interest or practice, whereby user share information, ideas, personal messages, and other content such as videos; popular examples include Facebook, Twitter, Youtube and MySpace.

Theory of Reasoned Action (TRA): A validated model and marketing theory with three factor components: (1) personal attitude, subjective norm, and behavioral intention (planned behavior); whereby a person's behavioral intention depends on the person's attitude about the behavior (multiplied by or 'weighted' by their evaluation of the outcome likelihood of that behavior) plus subjective norm beliefs (social peer pressure) corresponding to what they believe others would like (multiplied by the importance attributed to peer beliefs), which has been proven to be a reliable predictor of actual behavior.

Web 2.0: Emerged in the 21st century from the World Wide Web Consortium to refer to collaborative applications, or software linked together over the WWW where end-users may contribute both data and processes. Web services are the commercial applications offered to individuals and organizations, such as social networking, cloud computing, data storage, hosted ERP's, security, and others.

Web Services: Synonymous with hosted-applications, it refers to Internet-based applications include: mashups, blogs, wikis, feeds, tagging systems, user-created publication systems, and social networking applications. Several Web 2.0 interaction methods are available to the individual and business consumer market. The most popular include, Software as a Service (SaaS), Gleaning Resource Descriptions from Dialects of Languages (GRDDL), Really Simple Syndication (RSS), Asynchronous JavaScript and XML (AJAX), micro formats, and Representational State Transfer (Buyya et al., 2011). Interaction methods are used for managing process and data flow.

Chapter 3
Co–Creation of Innovations in ICT–Based Service Encounters

Jannick Kirk Sørensen
Aalborg University – Copenhagen, Denmark

Anders Henten
Aalborg University – Copenhagen, Denmark

ABSTRACT

Innovations in services often emanate from service encounters (i.e. the touch points between the service producers and the customers). Two different types of service encounters are dealt with: face-to-face and ICT-based service encounters. The aim of the chapter is to examine the specific conditions for innovations from ICT-based service encounters. The service encounter research tradition is mostly concerned with customer satisfaction. The perspective of the present chapter is on innovations in the service encounter. The specific contribution of the chapter is to establish a conceptual foundation for innovations in ICT-based service encounters.

INTRODUCTION

When customers meet service producers in a face-to-face service encounter, the possibility exists for co-creation of innovations of service products and processes. When the service encounter is mediated via the Web, important properties are changed since the direct face-to-face contact is replaced

with keyboards, graphical interfaces, cameras, microphones, etc. The assumption of this paper is, therefore, that the conditions for co-creation of innovations in service encounters also are changed. The aim of the paper is to discuss this hypothesis and, thereby, improve the theoretical understanding of the processes of co-creation of innovations in ICT-based service encounters.

DOI: 10.4018/978-1-4666-5884-4.ch003

This is done by combining three different approaches: First, the characteristics of ICT-based services as opposed to face-to-face based services are discussed. Thereafter, the advantages and disadvantages with respect to interactions between users and producers regarding ICT and face-to-face based services are examined. Thirdly, theories concerning user involvement in ICT service development, which do not have their explicit point of departure in ICT service encounters, are discussed. The idea is that the relatively new field of service encounter based innovation can learn from existing theories from other adjoining fields.

The persons who receive or use a service can be termed in many ways, e.g. 'customers', 'consumers', or 'users'. Each of these terms carries connotations which refer to a specific role, but as McLaughlin (2009) in the context of social work studies notices, the terms are also embedded in specific discourses. In this paper, we will primarily apply the term 'customer'. This term signifies the specific individual who is selecting (and possibly buying) a service delivered either in a face-to-face encounter, via ICT, or in a combination of both. The term 'consumer' is an abstraction denoting the role of a person buying something. Finally, the term 'user' gives emphasis to the role of somebody using something without reference to any economic relations between the different agents in the market.

The focus is on the co-creation of ideas for innovations or impulses for or sparks of ideas emanating from ICT-based service encounters. The realization of the actual innovations often requires much longer and complex processes, where the ideas for innovations are considered and dealt with inside the service producing entities before they result in new services or production processes. The emphasis of this paper is on the moments or time frames in which service users encounter the services in question and where these encounters possibly result in sparks of ideas later to be considered for realization.

The Web is, presently, a well-known interface for end-user access to ICT-based services. In the paper, we will, however, use the broader term 'ICT-based service encounters'. Our focal point is the customer's perspective regarding the change from face-to-face to interface-based service encounters, not the questions of how the ICT-based service is produced technically. The term 'ICT-based service encounters' allows us to include self-services like airline-check-in kiosks, ticket dispensers, and ATMs, as well as app-based mobile services and other Internet-based services that are not presented in a Web browser but have a specifically designed interface. The theories, hypotheses, and conclusions presented in the paper cover Web-based services as well as other ICT-based services.

Three concepts need initially to be briefly discussed in order to approach the issue: Co-creation, service encounter, and innovation. Co-creation is a term often used in connection with the topic of co-creation of value (e.g. Normann and Ramirez, 1993; Fiat et al., 1995). However, in our context, the focus is on co-creation of innovations. Such co-created innovation activities may include different cooperating producers as well as the customers of the services, but our focus is on the interplay between producers and customers. This is why the emphasis is on service encounters.

The concept of service encounters has mostly been examined in connection with customer satisfaction analyses (e.g. Czepiel, 1990; Bitner et al., 2000; Meuter et al., 2000; Massad et al., 2006). However, in this paper and the research project (Innovation in the Customer Encounter, ICE), which has been the starting point for the paper,[1] the interest has been on service encounters as the basis for innovations. What a service encounter is can be discussed and is subject to different interpretations of the concept (Grönroos, 1990; Lusch and Vargo, 2006). In the context of this paper, we will understand the concept of service encounters as the different touch points, where the customers of services get in contact with the service providers and/or products including search, ordering, delivery, and other possible instances of service encounters.

Service encounters are, obviously, of a very varied character. Some service encounters are B2B-based, others are B2C. Some encounters are short, and others have a longer duration or are repetitive. In some cases, the producing companies are large and in other cases, they are small or medium sized. Some producing entities are public and others private. And, some service encounters are based on face-to-face-meetings, while others are ICT-based or a combination thereof. In the present paper, we will only concentrate on the differentiation between face-to-face based encounters and ICT-based encounters and will examine theoretical aspects of the conditions for innovations to emanate from ICT-based encounters.

The last mentioned concept to briefly discuss is innovation. This is a concept that has been subject to much debate and definition (Gallouj, 2002; Drejer, 2004; Fuglsang, 2010). In this paper, we will suffice to take our point of departure in the Schumpeterian conceptualization including different types of innovation encompassing product innovations, process innovations, new sources of supply, new markets, and organizational innovations. As our emphasis is on innovations from the service encounters, the two most relevant types of innovations are product and process innovations. Moreover, a differentiation between radical innovations and incremental innovations is relevant. Later in the paper, it will be discussed whether innovations coming out of service encounters will primarily be radical or incremental.

The basic claim of the paper is that many innovations in services emanate from the service encounters, i.e. the touch points between the service producers and the service customers – in the case of face-to-face service encounters – or the meeting between the ICT-based services and the customers – in the case of an ICT-based service encounters. In the case of the production of goods in manufacturing, the producers and customers are generally separated in time and distance and seldom meet, and innovative ideas from customers only reach the producers indirectly. In the case of services, the stylized pattern is that production and consumption are closely related if not taking place simultaneously, and that innovative impulses or ideas can be transferred directly between the customers and producers. This constitutes the basis for an important source of innovations in services, namely the co-creation of innovative ideas or impulses from the encounters between the customers and the producers. A broader examination of these issues can be found in a paper by Sundbo et al. (2013), which summarizes central conclusions from the abovementioned ICE-project.

However, the direct and unmediated encounter or interaction between the customers and producers only takes place in face-to-face service encounters. If the encounter is mediated by ICT, as is the case with Web-based services, the question is how this affects the service encounter with respect to the co-creation of innovations. This is what this paper aims at examining with the purpose of improving the understanding of the processes of co-creation of innovations in ICT-based service encounters.

This topic has already been discussed, e.g., in a paper by Henten (2012) entitled 'Innovation from the ICT-based service encounter'. However, in the present paper, we examine the topic more thoroughly in theoretical terms, first by characterizing more precisely what ICT-based service encounters are, secondly by discussing more deeply the conditions for innovations to emanate from ICT-based service encounters, and thirdly by reviewing theories from other fields that can shed light on the processes of co-creation of innovative ideas in ICT-based service encounters. The paper is thus a conceptual contribution and does not refer to any set of coherent empirical evidence. An empirically based examination of innovations from service encounters can be found in Sundbo, et al. (2013).

The section following the introduction presents three different research traditions, which can contribute to the conceptualization of innovations from ICT-based service encounters. In the first sub-section, there is a discussion of how ICT-based services can be characterized. They can neither clearly be seen as goods, nor can they unambiguously be classified as services. They are something else. In the section, different conceptualizations of goods and services are discussed and ICT-based services are situated in relation to the goods/services dichotomy.

In the second sub-section, a differentiation is made between different kinds of ICT-based services and the conditions for innovative ideas to be initiated in the encounters between the services provided and the customers are examined. Two different approaches are investigated. One approach is concerned with media richness (Daft, et al., 1987), and the other approach is media choice theory (Fulk and Steinfield, 1990). Each of these approaches contributes to a structure for discussing the innovations in ICT-based service encounters.

The third sub-section provides a review of theories that in other ways focus on customers or users as sources of innovation. Inspiration is sought in human-computer interaction research, and in design research, particularly methods developed within interaction design.

In the last section before the summary and conclusion, the conceptualizations of ICT-based services, the approaches to understanding the conditions for innovations in ICT-based service encounters, and theories with implications for the development of innovations in customer/producer interactions are put together in order to discuss possible directions for an improved understanding of innovations in ICT-based service encounters.

THREE RESEARCH TRADITIONS

Service Research Tradition

The aim of the paper is to discuss the conditions for co-creation of innovations in ICT-based service encounters. In order to do this, a conceptualization of what ICT-based services are is obviously important. Two foundational aspects of such a conceptualization are examined in the present section. First, the concept of ICT-based services is discussed in relation to the dichotomy between goods and services. Secondly, a differentiation between different types of ICT-based services is made.

The stylized service encounter is a face-to-face encounter between a customer and an employee, and this encounter is the basis for many innovative sparks and ideas. The question is whether ICT-based services share (some of) the same characteristics as face-to-face-based services in terms of innovation patterns or whether they, to a larger extent, resemble goods. The innovation of goods will, of course, also be inspired by the reactions of customers. However, the contacts between the producers and users of goods are more indirect than in the case of services, and innovations will, therefore, primarily be based on other kinds of inspirations and sources than the ones coming out of the customer encounters.

The differences traditionally mentioned between goods and services revolve around the ideas of simultaneousness in production and consumption in the case of services and immateriality of services (Henten, 2012). These claims are not always right, but do hold true in many cases. A fundamental reason for the differentiation between goods and services is, in reality, historical. The differentiation is a consequence of the capitalist mode of production. Before the capitalist mode of production became prevalent, a differentiation was not often essential, as most relations between producers and users would have – what we today would call – a service character. Shoes or furniture that we today would consider as goods would most often be produced directly for specific users. It was only with the industrialization, which developed in connection with the capitalist mode of production, that the goods produced, to a larger extent, would be separated from their immediate producers and marketed on an anonymous market. However, in those areas of production, which did not result in any physical products, it was not possible to separate the immediate producers from the results of production and not either to sell the products on an anonymous market.

This does not mean that the production of services would not be subsumed under the capitalist mode of production. The laborers in the service industries are also subject to the capitalist conditions. However, the production of goods remains the arch-typical kind of production of the capitalist mode of production. Under these conditions, the goods produced are separated from their immediate producers and are marketed on anonymous markets. And, this does not apply to services. Face-to-face services cannot be separated from their immediate producers and they cannot be marketed on anonymous markets. The question is now how ICT-based services are situated in this kind of dichotomy.

In order to address this question, a differentiation between different kinds of ICT-based services is necessary. First of all, practically all services include ICT-based elements today. When ordering, for instance, a service requiring a face-to-face encounter, this will often be done digitally. There are thus elements (touch points) in the service processes, which are most often digitized. However, the kinds of ICT-based services that we are interested in here are the services, which are all digitized – either communicational services or informational (content) services (Scupola et al., 2009).

In the paper by Scupola et al. (2009), the idea of a convergence between communicational and informational goods and services is presented. Informational services, which formerly would require a face-to-face encounter can presently be entered on digital media and can, therefore, be separated from their immediate producers and be marketed on anonymous markets. They thus obtain a goods-like character. In other cases, digital products, which hitherto have been sold

as goods, for instance software, can be sold as services via communication networks. Among these two converging developments trends, far the most important is the one, where informational services acquire a goods-like character by being entered on digital media and exchanged on communication networks.

In a broader context than informational and communicational goods and services, it is also possible to talk about a degree of convergence between goods and services. Indeed, the dividing line between goods and services has never been clear-cut. However, a certain convergence between goods and services can increasingly be witnessed, for example with the growing 'servitization' (Vandermerwe and Rada, 1988) of manufacturing companies. Companies, which formerly would concentrate on selling their goods to customers (or intermediaries) and no more, will increasingly add service elements to their products.

In an instructive paper by Hofacker et al. (2007), a distinction between goods, services, and e-services is made – where the concept of e-services is similar to the concept of ICT-based services in the present paper. 10 different criteria are depicted, showing that e-services to a large extent have characteristics similar to goods, but also on some criteria resemble services but on other criteria neither resemble goods nor services. The most important criterion in our context is that while services are said to have inseparable consumption (simultaneousness of production and consumption), goods as well as e-services are considered to have separable consumption. The point is that ICT-based services (e-services) have some of the same characteristics as goods, while maintaining some of the characteristics of services. ICT-based services are something 'in between', which has implications for the innovations emanating for the service encounters in ICT-based services.

A similar discussion has taken place around the concept of 'service-dominant logic' put forward by Lusch and Vargo (2006). An intensive discussion has arisen around this concept (e.g. Lusch and Vargo, 2011; O'Shaughnessy and O'Shaughnessy, 2011), which emphasizes the differences between a goods-dominant logic and a service-dominant logic. Instead of the persistent debates on absolute differences between goods and services, Lusch and Vargo (2006, 2011) promote the idea that products are produced and marketed according to a combination of goods-dominant logics and service-dominant logics. This 'softens up' the often rigid discussions concerning goods and services and points to the fact that different products have different combinations of goods- and service-dominant logics. For our purpose, this means that ICT-based services have a strong element of goods-dominant logics.

In an examination of ICT-based informational and communicational services, a distinction can be made between infrastructural and super-structural services, where the infrastructural services are those that are 'invisible' to the user, while the super-structural are those that the user encounters in terms of informational (content) services and/or communicational services.

One could argue that until infrastructural services break down, the receiver of the services takes them for granted. They are invisible most of the time. The service itself should not occupy the receiver's attention, but rather support the receiver's activities. A typical example would be the different computers and servers involved in an online purchase. For the end-user, this organization of the system architecture is mostly invisible, except in the case where the Web-browser re-directs or re-loads the webpage, e.g. to authenticate the payment (Connell, 2008; Kodali, 2005). Since this kind of service only seldom and indirectly makes itself visible to the end user, it can be categorized on the same level as other 'invisible' services like water supply and electricity services. Only when they fail, the customers or users are reminded of their existence (Dreyfus, 1991).

In such cases, it is difficult to argue that the service is created in a service encounter; it is black-boxed. Tentatively, we could categorize services (both face-to-face and ICT-based) according to whether they purposely attempt to catch the receiver's attention or not. The reason for catching the attention could either be an intention to add extra value to the service, e.g. to differentiate it from competitors' services, to create a brand experience, or because the receiver's active participation increases the value of the service for the service provider and/or the receiver, or in worst cases prevents the service delivered from becoming useless and worthless.

Media and Communication Tradition

The relationship between providers and customers of services is also the focal point in Bordewijk and van Kaam's (1986) early classification of 'tele-information services', i.e. the super-structural informational and communicational services. Their examination of the power balance in the ICT service encounter is based on a discussion of the social and democratic perspectives of the introduction of ICT. Bordewijk and van Kaam (1986) identify four categories of information traffic between the 'information services provider' and the 'information services consumer', namely: 1) *allocution* – addressing an audience in a one-way distribution of information without talk-back, 2) *conversation* – where the ownership as well of the handling of information is distributed among the participants, 3) *consultation* – where the consumer requests a specific piece of information, and 4) *registration* – where the consumer is delivering the information, possibly without his or her knowledge (surveillance).

In the first category, the information flows only in one direction: 'allocution' – a word that is derived from the Roman word 'allocutio', meaning 'the address of a Roman general to his troops' (Bordewijk & van Kaam, 1986). It implies that there is no direct talk-back taking place in the situation. Broadcast media like traditional radio and TV could be examples of this type. We can add to Bordewijk and van Kaam (1986) that the feedback might take place later through other channels of communication than the one which was used in the first place to deliver the service, e.g. as 'letters to the editor' in the case of radio- and TV programs. It could thus be argued that innovation is impeded by a slow, filtered, and delayed feedback.

In Bordewijk and van Kaam's last category – registration – the information also only flows in one direction, in this case from the customer to the service provider. This can take place with or without the customer's awareness or knowledge, in the latter case as 'surveillance'. In light of the increase of data-mining and other methods for identification of information patterns in large amounts of heterogeneous data (so-called 'big data'), one could argue that innovation can very well emanate in this type of ICT-service encounter without the knowledge of the customer e.g. through methods of data mining (Barry & Linoff, 2004) via latent sematic analysis (Sarwar, Karypis, Konstan and Riedl, 2000). Hereby, information useful for a broad range of purposes, ranging from person- alized advertisements and media content recom- mendation to the discovery of rare illnesses, for instance, can be revealed. Again, like in the case of 'allocution', the customers only have an indirect influence on the interpretation of their 'feedback' or 'information'. This lack of influence has been criticized as 'de-individualization' of the person requesting a service (Vedder, 1999).

The two other categories of tele-information services, consultation and conversation, offer more explicit similarities to encounters of a face-to-face character. In Bordewijk and van Kaam's 'conversa- tion' category, all nodes possess the same level of power, providing a quite equal service encounter. In reality, a service provider might facilitate the conversation through an infrastructure, thereby also being the relevant actor for innovation in the service encounter. Today's social network services could be mentioned in the conversation category.

In the last category, consultation, the customer requests specific information from a service pro- vider. This situation also offers a high potential for innovation in the service encounter if the service provider or the customer gets the opportunity to contextualize and motivate the request. By looking at the customer's wider motive for the consultation the customer might be served better, but again this requires that this knowledge is not lost in the service encounter or afterwards

When the service encounter is Web-based, the communicative properties of the media used (e.g. text, voice, pictures, and video) play an important role for the potential innovation in the service encounter: Which media are made available to customers to express ideas to the service provider? What can be communicated through these media, and what cannot? In the context of organizational studies, determinants for employees' and manag- ers' choice of medium (e.g. face-to-face, telephone, email) in different situations have been studied, resulting in two different theories: Media richness theory (Daft, Lengel, & Treviño, 1987) and media choice theory (Fulk & Steinfield, 1990).

Media richness theory is often used to apply a technical understanding of media as a mere conveyer of information, focusing on the ability of different media to transport different amounts of information. It is often assumed that the face- to-face meeting is the richest type of media since the 'bandwidth' is the broadest (Treviño, Daft, & Lengel, 1990). This tradition can be opposed to media choice theories that are oriented towards the symbolic and social meaning of different media, cf. Fulk and Steinfield (1990). The 'richest' media may not always be the most suitable, since the sender's choice of media also carries a message in itself. Webster and Treviño (1995), however, suggest that the two traditions should be seen as complementary.

For the study of innovation in the ICT-based service encounter, the media richness theory as well as the media choice theory has deficits: First of all, focusing on media use inside organizations, they are less suitable for the study of communication between an organization and individual customers or users. In the more ephemeral B2C service encounters, one must assume a weaker and shorter relationship compared to the organization context of media choice and media richness theories.

From another perspective, the differences between media richness theory and media choice theory are helpful: In purely ICT-based communications, a limited choice of media, e.g. online forms, text input fields, email, chat-functions, telephone hotline etc., is offered. The lack of richness in the communication between customer and service provider is with the media richness theory assumed to affect the innovativeness in the service encounter negatively. In contrast, with media choice theory the absence of the richness may not influence the innovativeness, or might even contribute to the innovativeness.

If ICT-based service encounters are understood as a less rich variant of the face-to-face service encounter, the lack of media richness can easily be depicted as a weakness for innovation in the service encounter. With media choice theory, we can instead argue that the less rich media also have properties that are attractive or suitable for innovation in the customer encounter: E.g. by offering users templates or categories, the communication may be more structured, by using written text instead of spoken words, arguments may be further developed, by asynchronous communication, the customer or the service provider might avoid embarrassing answers. Focusing on the symbolic meaning of media choice would here provide a sounder basis. An open question is, however, how the media chosen relates to the quality of the innovation. A hypothesis would be that incremental innovations would be easier to communicate than more radical innovations, and that a closer and longer collaboration between customers and providers would produce more informed innovations.

In a more recent contribution on technology-enabled value co-creation processes, Breidbach, Kolb, and Srinivasan (2013) aim to avoid the differentiation between social 'human touch' and technology by using the overarching concept of 'connectivity', borrowed from Giddens (1984). The connectivity concept adds a time-dimension to the customer encounter, focusing on the touch points. The focal point of Breidbach et al., (2013) is thus 'connectivity gaps'. The empirical background for their study is the consulting industry. The B2B context means that the service encounters take place over long time and that, in their case, it is typically the customers, not the service providers who choose the ICT solution, e.g. video conference systems. For the study of shorter-term service encounters, the connectivity concept should be approached with care since the customers of these encounters typically have less or no free choice of communication channels and since the exchange of information is more formalized.

As we notice above, the ICT-based service encounter is a designed situation in the sense that a Web-designer or interface designer has been involved in shaping the interface and procedures in the service organization have been established to handle the incoming customer feedback. The communication is typically rectified in the sense that the service provider already in the design of the service has decided which media channels should be offered for customer feedback. Customers' ability to communicate with the service provider is thus shaped by the options provided in the interface.

Human-Computer Interaction

Theories on ICTs as platforms for customer encounters can be said to come from different research traditions/academic fields that apparently have very few intersections. As we touched upon earlier in the paper, one group of research contributions has grown out of service research. From this perspective, ICT based service encounters are perceived as a certain category of and variation over the classic face-to-face service encounter. Subsequently, it is named "self-service technologies" in the literature. The customer's interaction with interfaces is researched with classic service concepts such as satisfaction, efficiency and service recovery (Meuter et al., 2000; Bitner et al., 2000). In this research, ICT is looked at as the new element entering the established customer-provider relationship.

Parallel but independent, with a different starting point and with different methods, the research fields of human-computer interaction (HCI), usability and interaction design are also occupied with ICT encounters. For the study of innovations in ICT-based service encounters, the HCI tradition provides a very valuable source of inspiration both on a methodological and on a theoretical level. The HCI research tradition has for decades been studying the relationship between users and ICT systems in order to facilitate this relationship, particularly by developing methods and techniques to involve users in the ICT design process. However, if one looks for the word 'customer' in the research fields of Human Computer Interaction and Interaction Design, not many papers are found. A search, conducted August 2012 across all issues of the journal "Interactions," returns just eight articles out of 346869 that include the keyword "customer".[2] Similarly, a search in "ACM Transactions on Computer-Human Interaction" returns only three articles and the conference proceedings of the SIGCHI conference on Human Factors in computing systems, only two papers. None of the articles concern innovation in the ICT-based customer encounter. The "customer" in these texts is often a black-boxed and opaque entity, which is external to the proposed solution or research question.

The absence of the customer does, however, not imply that the research is irrelevant to the question of innovation in the ICT customer encounter. In the HCI literature, the perspective is seldom that of purchase, but that of the use. The starting

point for the HCI research was computer science's recognition of the 'human factors' of computer programming (Salzer, 1960). In the early era of fragile mainframe computers placed in labs, the human factor should be taken into account to prevent cumbersome time-consuming errors and misunderstandings. The early human-centered ICT innovation, therefore, had error prevention, not customer satisfaction, as its primary goal. As computers and computer interfaces became an integrated part of work place contexts, the research focus shifted from understanding the human as part of the machine to a social, semantic and contextual focus on the relationships between humans and ICT-systems. This shift means also other opportunities. The re-occurring use and contact between the service and the user should offer ample possibilities for innovation.

To transfer knowledge, important for the innovation, from the actual users to the designers of the ICT-systems, a number of user-centered design methods were developed. They differ in the way they involve the actual users in term of active participation or subjects under observation, how they construct the users, as well in the means of documentation as in the length of this 'staged' customer encounter. In any case, the user and the use-situation are seen as resources for ICT innovation.

Methods with little or no actual involvement of users includes 'scenarios' and 'personas' (Cooper, 1999; Pruitt & Grudin, 2003; Djajadiningrat, Gaver & Fres, 2000), where fictitious users and stories involving the use of the planned ICT system are constructed on the basis of research, e.g. ethnographically inspired observations of and interviews with users (Holtzblatt, 2005; Ylirisku & Buur, 2007). Other more involving methods include the testing of prototypes with users, e.g. an interface or a system flow (Wright & Monk, 1991; Monk et al., 1993). This can take place in several phases, gradually presenting users with more detailed and finished systems. A special and entirely ICT-based type of this is the so-called 'beta testing' (Duncan,

1996), where core customers, e.g. in a community, are invited to test not yet finished Web services or software and provide their comments via, for instance, blogs. The registration and analysis of use patterns and software performance constitutes an indirect source for innovation in the ICT-based service encounter, e.g. through the optimization of websites (Weischedel & Huizingh, 2006). In the last case, users may only notice their contribution to innovation, if at all, in the moment when they give their consent to the registration.

An entirely different approach to users can be found in the participatory design tradition, originally emerging from Scandinavia. Here, workers and other employees were mobilized in extensive workshops that not only constructed them as very valuable resources of knowledge in the work place context, but also insisted on a workers' emancipation agenda (Ehn, 1988). When ICT would be introduced in the work place context, those directly affected should influence the design decisions. In Ehn's early work, which is partly influenced by Marxist theory, customers do not appear at all.[3]

Participatory design never really found its way to the industry (Gregory, 2003), but a very important research outcome was the observation of the ICT-design process as a dialogical process that necessarily must involve all stakeholders (Ehn, 1988; Ehn & Kyng, 1991). Ehn (1988) uses Wittgenstein's (1953) concept of language games to describe how a shared understanding of the ICT artifact must emerge in a design process. As the development of this shared language is an explorative process based on mutual acknowledgement, a formalized approach to ICT development is discarded in favor of an iterative process (Ehn, 1988; Ehn & Kyng, 1991). However, since the knowledge, language, and experiences are different for the different stakeholders, and since experience-based tacit knowing (Polanyi, 1983) is difficult to represent without any representation of the context, the research turned towards the means and conditions for finding or creating a shared language among the participants also covering non-verbal experiences and tacit knowledge (Brandt, 2007). Typically, the participatory design involves relatively many workshops and methodological considerations of how non-designers (e.g. the users) can be facilitated in their examination and expression of design possibilities, without expecting users to become professional designers or conversely just observers (Bredies, Chow, and Joost, 2010).

What still distinguishes the HCI and interaction design research from the service research is its roots in technology. The user-centered design, particularly participatory design have nevertheless still something to offer to the study of ICT innovation in the customer encounter: Not only does this tradition introduce end-users as co-designers on an equal footing with system developers, it also points at an important observation, namely the communicative gaps between professional system developers and normal users, which implies that the system developers not always understand the users' needs, and that users not always know of or understands the potentials in the technology.

The tradition of participatory design can be said to be continued in the practice of co-creation and co-design. An example of this are collective design platforms (Paulini, Murty & Maher, 2012), where Internet communities are engaged in joint innovation projects. Although the innovation process is open to everyone, it is not necessarily the end-users or customers who participate (Paulini et al., 2012). Another example is the inclusion of ideas developed by lead-users in the innovation process (Lilien, Morrison, Searls, Sonnack & Von Hippel, 2002; von Hippel, 2005). Compared to the original mission and findings from the participatory design tradition, these newer practices have another scope: The aim is seldom emancipation but rather a bigger diversity of ideas and a better articulation of the user context. Also, it is questionable to which extent the Web-based platforms for collaboration and exchange of ideas actually address the 'language-game' problem identified by Ehn (1989). In an empirical study of online co-creative activities, Füller et al. (2009) notice that the quality of the interface tools provided for the co-creation are important for users' feeling of empowerment or lack of empowerment. We can, with Ehn (1989) and Brandt (2007), critically ask whether online platforms, with their limited array of communication possibilities (compared to the face-to-face participatory design workshops), actually are able to convey all innovative ideas or, conversely, whether ideas that can be expressed well in the online media have better chances.

None of the above-mentioned methods and practices has the moment of the ICT-based service encounter as focal point. The only methods that could claim to use the ICT service encounter as source for innovation are the usage statistics, telemetry and error-reporting (Weischedel & Huizingh, 2006). However, since dialogue with the customer very seldom takes place in these cases they fall outside the category of customer-driven service encounter innovation. If an error-reporting application is launched automatically when another application crashes, prompting the user for permission to send a report to the software developer, we can hardly term this an innovation in the ICT-service encounter.

DISCUSSION

In the previous sections, we have characterized different elements in the ICT-based service encounter that might determine the possibility for and quality of innovation in this kind of customer encounter. We have noticed that the ICT-based service encounter has some elements of a goods-dominant logic, since customers – or users – of the ICT service seldom have much contact with the provider of the service. The characteristic of a service being inseparable from the moment where it is produced does not hold in the case of ICT services. Furthermore, due to the computer code producing the ICT service, users are presented

with industrialized service encounters. The small variations that can be obtained via customizable or personalized interfaces do not result in significantly different services (Sørensen, 2011). On the other hand, due to their immateriality and focus on process, ICT-services share some characteristics with face-to-face services.

However, since the service encounter is mediated through an interface, the communicative properties of this interface, in terms of media channels offered for the communication between customer and service provider, move into the foreground. On a theoretical basis, it is difficult to determine whether the lack of richness in the ICT-based customer encounter inhibits, impedes, or conversely nurtures the innovation-oriented contact between customer and service provider. With the starting point in Ehn's observation of the language game taking place in the design situation, it is difficult to imagine that a less rich media would be better for innovation. Conversely, with the starting point in the media choice theory, it can be theorized that at least some users find it more convenient to communicate innovative ideas in this way: They may remain more anonymous, they may avoid a rejection of their idea, and they may have time to unfold and describe it better. The question of the choice between different strategies for facilitating innovation is located on a more general level.

Harris and Henderson (1999) observe that the rule-based information structures of ICT systems lend themselves naturally to bureaucratic workflows with their focus on regularities and predictability. The irregularities and particularities of users' real life are seen as exceptions. Typically, computer systems force users to adapt their goals and intentions, regardless of how irregular they are, to the structure of the system. This also applies to interfaces and workflows of ICT services. It could be argued that computer mediated innovation (as is the case with innovation in the Web-based service encounter) leads to less richness in the diversity of ideas. If we assume that radical innovation takes place not in areas of the predictable, but in the areas where communication is difficult or is about to break down, a less rich media than face-to-face encounters may be problematic.

The hypothesis is, therefore, that the ICT-based service encounter only can contribute with incremental innovations and corrections of errors. The question is, however, whether the purpose of innovation in the ICT-based service encounter necessarily should be to generate radical innovation? If rather incremental innovation, testing, and confirmation are the purposes, a communication design, which rectifies customer feedback, may be more efficient. By re-interpreting the media richness term to encompass the different interactive options offered in ICT-based service encounters, it could, with Harris and Henderson (1999), be argued that media richness not only should be defined through different categories of media, but also through the degree of formalization of the communication. In this sense, Web services are often examples of very poor possibilities for the user to provide rich feedback that can be useful for innovation. It could be argued that it is not the richness of different (interactive) media that determines the potential for innovation in the service encounter, but the degree of formalizing the communication.

In the beginning of this paper, we observed an ambiguity of ICT-based services, as services with a strong element of goods-dominant logics. Now, in order to escape this ambiguity, a strategy could be to look at goods as well as services and ICT interfaces as results of design work and design decisions. The previous section's discussion of different ways of involving users and users' knowledge in the design and innovation of ICT services already points in this direction, as well as the observation that the question of media choice rather concerns the communication options that the service provider offers for feedback related to the service encounter than the customer's free choice of media. Innovation in the ICT-based service encounter is framed by and defined through the capabilities and properties of the media channels offered.

In the search for a scientific basis for the role of designers in society, Krippendorff (2006) provides an interesting input to the discussion of the characteristics of ICT services. By placing different types of design work on a 'trajectory of artificiality' (Krippendorff, 2006), he draws attention to the complexity of the work of designers that goes beyond providing nice shapes and pleasant aesthetics to industrially produced artifacts. The trajectory starts with the design of physical products. At the next level, Krippendorff places goods, services and identities on the same level. This contrasts with the classic distinction between goods and services. It is the common property of something to be marketed and sold that unites goods and services in one category: "[g]oods are manufactured to be traded and sold, not merely used [like products]. Functions are secondary to their role in the marketplace and serve at best as sales arguments" (Krippendorff, 2006). Krippendorff points at the transformation of practices to services through institutionalization. They "need to be designed to be recognized and trustworthy so that customers return and develop loyalties to the service providers." Krippendorff's focal point is thus the customer's purchase of a service, not the use. In the same vein, still focusing on marketability, he places 'identities' on the same level as goods and services, defined through their symbolic qualities. Being objects for sale or institutionalized procedures, designers focus on their marketability, their symbolic qualities, and the identity they provide. They have already become detached from simple use.

Important for the discussion of ICT services, Krippendorff distinguishes 'interfaces' from 'services' at the next level of artificiality. Interfaces are seen as "a human-technological symbiosis" (Krippendorff, 2006) that makes technological complexity inside the machine understandable for users. Without interfaces, most modern technology like computers, airplanes, and atomic power plants would be impossible to operate. In this way they present abstractions of processes and actions. Krippendorff's position of interfaces as something more abstract challenges the traditional notion of ICT services. A higher degree of artificiality means an additional layer of design decisions being added, thereby limiting the space for natural variation, spontaneity, and improvisation. The service delivery becomes easier to reproduce and control, but does that impede innovation? The following levels of artificiality are 'multiuser systems/networks', 'projects' and finally 'discourses' (Krippendorff, 2006). At these levels it is even more difficult to imagine user-driven (or user-controlled) innovation, at least on an equal footing.

Depending on how design and artificiality is understood in practice, the question is whether innovation in service encounters that are highly formalized, either due to the interface of an ICT-system or due to a rigid script for the face-to-face service encounter, is possible. Are the organizational thresholds so high that they scare most customers away from contributing? Or is it a matter of encouraging the involved staff and customers, respectively provide ample feedback channels at the interface of the ICT-based service? Another question open for research is to which extent the experiences in the service encounter animate customers to contribute, or whether the impulses and ideas emanating from the ICT-service encounter in reality are rooted in the customer's general goal with the service. In the latter case, ICT is just a tool that could be replaced with a face-to-face encounter while the innovation would focus on the larger goals and conditions for the service. In the first case the communicative properties of the ICT encounter, e.g. the interface, information architecture, and workflow stand as objects for the innovation. Possibly, we can identify two types of innovation: One type that operates on a meta-level of the service, searching broadly for alternative innovative ways of achieving the result that the intended service normally would deliver, and another type that is concerned with optimizing the communication and work-flow.

The observation of the elements of a goods-dominant logic in ICT-services and the observation of the higher degree of artificiality of interfaces produce the assumption that ICT-based services are not very open for encounter based innovation. Their design and functionality are determined not only by technology but also by the organizational interests of cost-saving through the use of ICT-based services.

FUTURE RESEARCH DIRECTION

A wide range of initiatives to assemble innovative input from customers is called for including interactive and experiential customer interfaces. Although an outcome of this paper is the conclusion that ICT services often are relatively rigid and not open to customer input, the rigidity of ICT services are also an expression of the rigidity of the organizations behind the ICT interfaces. This is an issue that needs further examination.

Moreover, on the basis of the theoretical assumptions that have been discussed in this paper, a next step is to analyze concrete examples of ICT-based service encounters in order to study the innovativeness of these service encounters. The possible transposition of positive examples from specific cases and specific technological set-ups can be examined. But, not only can ICT-based service encounters learn from other ICT-based encounters. It is also important to study the possibility for transferring positive experiences from face-to-face encounters to ICT-based encounters, and how ICT-based encounters can be combined with face-to-face encounters.

SUMMARY AND CONCLUSION

The paper has discussed different research fields that can contribute to the conceptualization of innovations in ICT-based service encounters. The three research fields are: The service research tradition, research on media and communication, and the human-computer interaction field. Table 1 provides a summary of research fields and contributions.

From a theoretical perspective it seems that there is little space in the ICT-based service encounter for innovation. With Krippendorff, we observe that since ICT-services are based on human-computer interfaces, an extra layer of artificiality and design is added to the one that already transformed practices to services by institutionalizing them and making them objects for economic transactions. With the help of media richness theory we observe that the ICT-based customer encounter is less rich and more formalized than the face-to-face encounter potentially is. The service encounter must to a higher degree

be anticipated correctly in the interface and the ICT service structure cannot as human service encounters be adjusted to the situation.

This does not exclude the possibility that encounter based innovation can take place in the ICT-based service encounter, but it is assumed that the barriers are higher: If the innovation should be encounter-driven, a specific infrastructure must be offered that can encourage customers to contribute, and this infrastructure must be capable of stimulating, capturing, and conveying in a loss-less form the richness of the customer input. If these inputs are not well articulated in a way that is suitable for the media offered by the service provider for customer 'feedback', they are lost. Furthermore, in order to be 'understood', a shared

Table 1. Summary of contributing research fields

Field	Sub-Field	Contribution
Service research	Characteristics of ICT services: Goods vs. service dominant logics	ICT services have both elements of goods dominant logics and service dominant logics, potentially making them less sensitive to innovation in service encounter.
	Innovation in the service encounter	The absence or reduced occurrence of the face-to-face service encounter changes the conditions for innovation in the service encounter.
	Co-creation	ICT services enable large-scale co-creation, but poses limitations on the richness of the communication.
	Infra-structural vs. super-structural services	As targets for innovation in service encounter, super-structural services are more relevant, since the customer is more aware of the service delivered.
Media and communication	Media richness – Media choice	The two theories lead to different predictions concerning innovation in the service encounter.
	Shared language between users and designers/language game	The language game theory highlights the necessity of a shared language between customers, service providers, and designers for innovation to take place.
	Classification of tele-information services	Highlights the possibility of innovation in the service encounter to take place without the customers' knowledge (surveillance). Highlights the importance of dialogue in the service encounter.
Human Computer Interaction	Participatory design	Provides an early method for innovation in the service encounter. Highlights stakeholder interests.
	Focus on the user, not the customer	Highlights the two competing focal points: The single moment of purchase versus the re-occurring moments of use of the ICT-service.
	Rigid computer systems versus diverging user needs	Highlights the tension in innovation and design of ICT services between the necessity of a coherent system and the diverging user needs: The limits of customer-driven innovation.
	Interaction design methods and techniques	Provide alternative means to facilitate innovation in the service encounter. Highlights the relationship between choice of empirical method and outcome of the customer-driven innovation

language must first be developed between the innovative users and the programmers/interaction designers. But since the communication channel service encounter is ICT-based, the conditions for this language game to take place are limited. Since the language is limited, the result will be ideas with a predictable scope. The innovations to take place in the ICT-service encounter will to a higher degree be limited to what programmers, managers, and interaction designers can deduce from indirect observations. If not supplemented with other initiatives to gather innovative ideas from a broad array of customers, the risk exists that the user-driven innovation will only will be an echo of the organizational view.

REFERENCES

Berry, M. J. A., & Linoff, G. S. (2004). *Data mining techniques: For marketing, sales, and customer relationship management* (2nd ed.). Indianapolis, IN: Wiley Publishing.

Bitner, M. J., Brown, S. W., & Meuter, M. L. (2000). Technology infusion in service encounters. *Journal of the Academy of Marketing Services, 28*(1), 138–149. doi:10.1177/0092070300281013

Brandt, E. (2007). How tangible mock-ups support design collaboration. *Knowledge, Technology & Policy, 20*(3), 179–192. doi:10.1007/s12130-007-9021-9

Bredies, K., Chow, R., & Joost, G. (2010). Addressing use as design: A comparison of constructivist design approaches. *The Design Journal, 13*(2), 156–179. doi:10.2752/175470710X12735884220853

Breidbach, C. F., Kolb, D. G., & Srinivasan, A. (2013). Connectivity in service systems: Does technology-enablement impact the ability of a service system to co-create value? *Journal of Service Research*. doi:10.1177/1094670512470869

Connell, B. (2008). What is service-oriented architecture (SOA)? *SearchSOA*. Retrieved April 30, 2013, from http://searchsoa.techtarget.com/definition/service-oriented-architecture

Cooper, A. (1999). *The inmates are running the asylum: Why high tech products drive us crazy and how to restore the sanity*. Indianapolis, IN: SAMS. doi:10.1007/978-3-322-99786-9_1

Czepiel, J. A. (1990). Service encounters and service relationships: Implications for research. *Journal of Business Research, 20*(1), 13–21. doi:10.1016/0148-2963(90)90038-F

Daft, R. L., Lengel, R. H., & Trevino, L. K. (1987). Message equivocality, media selection, and manager performance: Implications for information systems. *Management Information Systems Quarterly, 11*(3), 355. doi:10.2307/248682

Djajadiningrat, J. P., Gaver, W. W., & Fres, J. W. (2000). Interaction relabeling and extreme characters. In *Proceedings of the Conference on Designing Interactive Systems Processes, Practices, Methods, and Techniques - DIS '00* (pp. 66–71). New York: ACM Press.

Drejer, I. (2004). Indentifying innovation in surveys of services: A Schumpeterian perspective. *Research Policy, 33*, 551–652. doi:10.1016/j.respol.2003.07.004

Dreyfus, H. L. (1991). *Being-in-the-world : A commentary on Heidegger's Being and Time, division I*. Cambridge, MA: MIT Press.

Duncan, G. (1996). Waiting with Beta'd breath. *TidBITS, 328*.

Ehn, P. (1988). *Work-oriented design of computer artifacts*. Stockholm: Arbejdslivscentrum.

Ehn, P., & Kyng, M. (1991). Cardboard computers: Mocking-it-up or hands-on the future. In J. M. Greenbaum, & M. Kyng (Eds.), *Design at work: Cooperative design of computer systems* (pp. 169–195). Hoboken, NJ: Lawrence Erlbaum Associates.

Firat, A. F., & Venkatesh, A. (1995). Liberatory postmodernism and the reenchantment of consumption. *The Journal of Consumer Research*, (3): 239–267. doi:10.1086/209448

Fuglsang, L. (2010). Bricolage and invisible innovation in public service innovation. *Journal of Innovation Economics*, 5(1), 67. doi:10.3917/jie.005.0067

Fulk, J., & Steinfield, C. W. (1990). *Organizations and communication technology*. Newbury Park, CA: Sage Publications.

Füller, J., Mühlbacher, H., Matzler, K., & Jawecki, G. (2009). Consumer empowerment through internet-based co-creation. *Journal of Management Information Systems*, 26(3), 71–102. doi:10.2753/MIS0742-1222260303

Gallouj, F. (2002). *Innovation in the service economy*. Cheltenham, UK: Edward Elgar. doi:10.4337/9781843765370

Giddens, A. (1984). *The constitution of society: Outline of the theory of structuration*. Berkeley, CA: University of California Press.

Gregory, J. (2003). Scandinavian approaches to participatory design. *International Journal of Engineering Education*, 19(1), 62–74.

Grönroos, C. (1990). *Service management and marketing: Managing the moments of truth in service competition*. Lexington, MA: Lexington Books.

Harris, J., & Henderson, A. (1999). A better mythology for system design. In *Proceedings of the SIGCHI Conference on Human Factors in Computing Systems the CHI is the Limit - CHI '99* (pp. 88–95). New York: ACM Press.

Heidegger, M. (1967). *Sein und zeit*. Tübingen, Germany: M. Niemeyer.

Henten, A. (2012). Innovations from the ICT-based service encounter. *Info*, 14(2), 42–56. doi:10.1108/14636691211204851

Hofacker, C. F., Goldsmith, R. E., Bridges, E., & Swilley, E. (2007). E-services: A synthesis and research agenda. In H. Evanschitzky, & R. I. Gopalkrishnan (Eds.), *E-services: Opportunities and threats* (pp. 13–44). DUV. doi:10.1007/978-3-8350-9614-1_3

Holtzblatt, K. (2005). Customer-centered design for mobile applications. *Personal and Ubiquitous Computing*, 9(4), 227–237. doi:10.1007/s00779-004-0324-5

Kodali, R. R. (2005). What is service-oriented architecture? *JavaWorld*. Retrieved April 30, 2013, from http://www.javaworld.com/javaworld/jw-06-2005/jw-0613-soa.html

Lilien, G. L., Morrison, P. D., Searls, K., Sonnack, M., & von Hippel, E. (2002). Performance assessment of the lead user idea-generation process for new product development. *Management Science*, 48(8), 1042–1059. doi:10.1287/mnsc.48.8.1042.171

Lusch, R. F., & Vargo, S. (2006). *The service-dominant logic of marketing: Dialog, debate, and directions*. Armonk, NY: M.E. Sharpe.

Massad, N., Heckman, R., & Crowston, K. (2006). Customer satisfaction with electronic service encounters. *International Journal of Electronic Commerce*, 10(4), 73–104. doi:10.2753/JEC1086-4415100403

McLaughlin, H. (2009). What's in a name: Client, patient, customer, consumer, expert by experience, service user--What's next? *British Journal of Social Work*, 39(6), 1101–1117. doi:10.1093/bjsw/bcm155

Meuter, M. L., Ostrom, A. L., Roundtree, R. I., & Bitner, M. J. (2000). Self-service technologies: Understanding customer satisfaction with technology-based service encounters. *Journal of Marketing, 64*, 50–64. doi:10.1509/jmkg.64.3.50.18024

Monk, A., Wright, P., Haber, J., & Davenport, L. (1993). *Improving your human - computer interface: A practical technique.* Upper Saddle River, NJ: Prentice Hall International.

Normann, R., & Ramírez, R. (1993, July-August). From value chain to value constellation: Designing interactive strategy. *Harvard Business Review*, 65–77. PMID:10127040

O'Shaughnessy, J., & O'Shaughnessy, N. J. (2011). Service-dominant logic: a rejoinder to Lusch and Vargo's reply. *European Journal of Marketing, 45*(7/8), 1310–1318. doi:10.1108/03090561111137732

Paulini, M., Murty, P., & Maher, M. L. (2012). Design processes in collective innovation communities: A study of communication. *CoDesign*, 1–24.

Polanyi, M. (1983). *The tacit dimension.* Gloucester, MA: Peter Smith.

Pruitt, J., & Grudin, J. (2003). Personas. In *Proceedings of the 2003 Conference on Designing for User Experiences - DUX '03* (pp. 1–15). New York: ACM Press.

Salzer, J. M. (1960). Data processing. In *Papers presented at the May 3-5, 1960, western joint IRE-AIEE-ACM computer conference on - IRE-AIEE-ACM '60 (western).* New York: ACM Press.

Sarwar, B. M., Karypis, G., Konstan, J. A., & Riedl, J. T. (2000). Application of dimensionality reduction in recommender system -- A case study. In *Proceedings of ACM WEBKDD Workshop.* ACM.

Scupola, A., Henten, A., & Westh Nicolajsen, H. (2009). E-services: Characteristics, scope and conceptual strengths. *International Journal of E-Services and Mobile Applications, 1*(3), 1–16. doi:10.4018/jesma.2009070101

Sørensen, J. K. (2011). *The paradox of personalisation: Public service broadcasters' approaches to media personalisation technologies. University of Southern Denmark.* SDU.

Sundbo, J., Sundbo, D., & Henten, A. (2013). Service co-innovation service encounters as basis for innovation. In *Proceedings of RESER 2013.* RESER.

Tang, J. C. (2007). Approaching and leave-taking. [–es.]. *ACM Transactions on Computer-Human Interaction, 14*(1), 5. doi:10.1145/1229855.1229860

Trevino, L. K., Daft, R. L., & Lengel, R. H. (1990). Understanding managers' media choices: A symbolic interactionist perspective. In C. W. Steinfield, & J. Fulk (Eds.), *Organizations and communcation technology* (pp. 71–94). Newbury Park, CA: Sage Publications.

Treviño, L. K., Webster, J., & Stein, E. W. (2000). Making connections: Complementary influences on communication media choices, attitudes, and use. *Organization Science, 11*(2), 163–182. doi:10.1287/orsc.11.2.163.12510

Vandermerwe, S., & Rada, J. (1988). Servitization of business: Adding value by adding services. *European Management Journal, 6*(4), 314–324. doi:10.1016/0263-2373(88)90033-3

Vedder, A. (1999). KDD: The challenge to individualism. *Ethics and Information Technology, 1*(4), 275–281. doi:10.1023/A:1010016102284

Webster, J., & Treviño, L. K. (1995). Rational and social theories as complementary explanations of communication media choices: Two policy-capturing studies. *Academy of Management Journal, 38*(6), 1544–1572. doi:10.2307/256843

Weischedel, B., & Huizingh, E. K. R. E. (2006). Website optimization with web metrics. In *Proceedings of the 8th International Conference on Electronic Commerce the New E-Commerce: Innovations for Conquering Current Barriers, Obstacles and Limitations to Conducting Successful Business on the Internet - ICEC '06* (pp. 463–470). New York: ACM Press.

Wittgenstein, L. (1953). *Philosophical investigations*. Oxford, UK: B. Blackwell.

Wright, P. C., & Monk, A. F. (1991). A cost-effective evaluation method for use by designers. *International Journal of Man-Machine Studies, 35*(6), 891–912. doi:10.1016/S0020-7373(05)80167-1

Ylirisku, S., & Buur, J. (2007). *Designing with video*. London: Springer London.

ADDITIONAL READING

Alam, I. (2006). Removing the fuzziness from the fuzzy front-end of service innovations through customer interactions. *Industrial Marketing Management, 35*(4), 468–480. doi:10.1016/j.indmarman.2005.04.004

Au, A. K. C., & Chan, D. K.-S. (2013). Organizational media choice in performance feedback: a multifaceted. *Journal of Applied Social Psychology, 43*(2), 397–407. doi:10.1111/j.1559-1816.2013.01009.x

Bogers, M., Afuah, A., & Bastian, B. (2010). Users as Innovators: A Review, Critique, and Future Research Directions. *Journal of Management, 36*(4), 857–875. doi:10.1177/0149206309353944

Buur, J., & Bagger, K. (1999). Replacing Usability Testing with User Dialogue. *Communications of the ACM, 42*(5), 63–66. doi:10.1145/301353.301417

Buur, J., & Bødker, S. (2000). From usability lab to design collaboratorium. In D. Boyarski & W. A. Kellogg (Eds.), *Proceedings of the conference on Designing interactive systems processes, practices, methods, and techniques - DIS '00* (pp. 297–307). New York, New York, USA: ACM Press.

Clatworthy, S. D. (2011). Service Innovation Through Touch-points: Development of an Innovation Toolkit for the First Stages of New Service Development. *International Journal of Design, 5*(2). Retrieved from http://www.ijdesign.org/ojs/index.php/IJDesign/article/view/939

Coelho, P. S., & Henseler, J. (2012). Creating customer loyalty through service customization. *European Journal of Marketing, 46*(3/4), 331–356. doi:10.1108/03090561211202503

Demirkan, H., Kauffman, R. J., Vayghan, J. A., Fill, H.-G., Karagiannis, D., & Maglio, P. P. (2008). Service-oriented technology and management: Perspectives on research and practice for the coming decade. *Electronic Commerce Research and Applications, 7*(4), 356–376. doi:10.1016/j.elerap.2008.07.002

Durugbo, C., Riedel, J., & Pawar, K. (2011). Towards a unified model of co-creation. *2011 17th International Conference on Concurrent Enterprising*, 1–8.

Gelderman, C. J., Ghijsen, P. W. T., & van Diemen, R. (2011). Choosing self-service technologies or interpersonal services—The impact of situational factors and technology-related attitudes. *Journal of Retailing and Consumer Services, 18*(5), 414–421. doi:10.1016/j.jretconser.2011.06.003

Hassenzahl, M., & Tractinsky, N. (2006). User experience - a research agenda. *Behaviour & Information Technology, 25*(2), 91–97. doi:10.1080/01449290500330331

Hoyer, W. D., Chandy, R., Dorotic, M., Krafft, M., & Singh, S. S. (2010). Consumer Cocreation in New Product Development. *Journal of Service Research*, *13*(3), 283–296. doi:10.1177/1094670510375604

Keh, H. T., & Pang, J. (2010). Customer Reactions to Service Separation. *Journal of Marketing*, *74*(2), 55–70. doi:10.1509/jmkg.74.2.55

Keinonen, T. K. (2010). Protect and Appreciate - Notes on the Justification of User-Centered Design. *International Journal of Design*, *4*(1). Retrieved from http://www.ijdesign.org/ojs/index.php/IJDesign/article/view/561

Matthing, J., Sandén, B., & Edvardsson, B. (2004). New service development: learning from and with customers. *International Journal of Service Industry Management*, *15*(5), 479–498. doi:10.1108/09564230410564948

McHardy, J. (2009). Make-Shift Ciopfaspovs: an Exploration of Users in Design. In G. Anceschi (Ed.), Multiple Ways to Design Research (pp. 181 – 194). Et al. Edizioni.

Michel, S., Brown, S. W., & Gallan, A. S. (2008). Service-Logic Innovations: HOW TO INNOVATE CUSTOMERS, NOT PRODUCTS. *California Management Review*, *50*, 49–65. doi:10.2307/41166445

Patricio, L., Fisk, R. P., & Falcao e Cunha, J. (2008). Designing Multi-Interface Service Experiences: The Service Experience Blueprint. *Journal of Service Research*, *10*(4), 318–334. doi:10.1177/1094670508314264

Schumann, J. H., Wünderlich, N. V., & Wangenheim, F. (2012). Technology mediation in service delivery: A new typology and an agenda for managers and academics. *Technovation*, *32*(2), 133–143. doi:10.1016/j.technovation.2011.10.002

Scupola, A., Nicolajsen, H. W., & Falch, M. (2009). Investigating the role of customers in service innovation. In *Proceedings of the First International Conference on Service Science and Innovation*.

Simester, D. (2011). When You Shouldn't Listen To Your Critics. *Harvard Business Review*, *89*, 42. PMID:22111429

Spinuzzi, C. (2002). A Scandinavian challenge, a US response: methodological assumptions in Scandinavian and US prototyping approaches. In *SIGDOC '02 - 20th Annual international Conference on Computer Documentation* (pp. 208–215). Toronto, Ontario, Canada, October 20 - 23, 2002: ACM Press, New York, NY.

Teixeira, J., Patrício, L., Nunes, N. J., & Nóbrega, L. (2011). Customer experience modeling: designing interactions for service systems. *HUMAN-COMPUTER INTERACTION – INTERACT 2011. Lecture Notes in Computer Science*, *6949*, 136–143. doi:10.1007/978-3-642-23768-3_11

Treiblmaier, H., & Strebinger, A. (2008). The effect of e-commerce on the integration of IT structure and brand architecture. *Information Systems Journal*, *18*(5), 479–498. doi:10.1111/j.1365-2575.2007.00288.x

Van Rijnsoever, F. J., Faber, J., Brinkman, M. L. J., & van Weele, M. A. (n.d.). User-producer interaction in Web site development: Motives, modes, and misfits. *Journal of the American Society for Information Science & Technology*, *61*(3), 495–504.

Zysman, J., Feldman, S., Kushida, K. E., Murray, J., & Nielsen, N. C. (2013). Services with Everything: The ICT-Enabled Digital Transformation of Services. In D. Breznitz, & J. Zysman (Eds.), *The Third Globalization : Can Wealthy Nations Stay Rich in the Twenty-First Century?* (pp. 99–129). New York: Oxford University Press. doi:10.1093/acprof:oso/9780199917822.003.0006

KEY TERMS AND DEFINITIONS

Co-Creation: The term co-creation is most often used in connection with co-creation of value, i.e. either the co-creation of value by producers and users or by different collaborating producers. In the context of the present paper, there is focus on the co-creation of innovations by producers and customers.

Customer Encounter: The customer encounter is the meeting between the producers and customers of a service. It is, therefore, sometimes called service encounter. As opposed to the production of goods in manufacturing, where the immediate producers of the goods do not meet the customers of the goods, there is a direct encounter between the producer and the customer of a service – either face-to-face or ICT-based.

Goods-Dominant Logic: The terms goods-dominant vs. service-dominant logics are associated with the writings of Lusch and Vargo (e.g. 2006), where the point is that there can be goods-like characteristics of services and services-like characteristics of goods. Instead of merely characterizing a product as either a good or a service, it is important to examine the combined characteristics of a product.

Human-Computer Interaction: HCI is a research tradition concerned with the interfaces between humans and computers. This may be either the humans producing or using the hardware and software. In the context of the present paper, the purpose of including the HCI tradition is that research from this tradition can shade new light on ICT-based service encounters.

ICT-Based Services: Services have traditionally been conceived as face-to-face-services, where the producer and the user of a service meet when the service is delivered. In the case of ICT-based services, information and communication technologies constitute the interface between the service provider and the service user.

Innovation: In accordance with the Schumpeterian differentiation between invention, innovation and diffusion, innovations are defined by new products, processes, and organizational modes of production being taken to market. This resonates well with use of the term in this paper, as it is concerned with new products, processes, and organizations forms emanating from the meeting between producers and customers.

Media Choice: Media choice can be seen as based on the (opposing) view that the most appropriate forms of communication differ with the aim of the communication. E-mail can be a better form of communication for some purposes than a telephone call or a face-to-face meeting.

Media Richness: Media richness is a concept signifying how 'rich' the communication between different parties is. Richness denotes the quality and quantity of the different elements being part of the communication. It is traditionally assumed that face-to-face communication is the richest form of communication and a kind of 'gold standard' for communication, while the different forms of electronic communications have different lower degrees of richness.

ENDNOTES

[1]   ICE (Innovation in the Customer Encounter) was a Danish research project (2008-2012) funded by the Danish Strategic Research Council conducted by researchers from Roskilde University and Aalborg University Copenhagen. The project was on innovations in the service encounter.

[2]   Using a free-text search for the word "customer" creates more results: "Interactions" 493 articles, "ACM Transactions on Computer-Human Interaction" 57, "SIGCHI conference on Human Factors": 131.

3   Ehn, 1988 p. 86:"We must relate the design of computer artifacts to all three aspects of practice: In *practice as work*, this is to the transformation of a given labor process and to the users' participation in the design process. In *practice as language*, it is to the professional language and the interaction in a given labor process as well as the associated design process. In *practice as morals*, it is to the politics and power of the different groups and classes involved in a given labor process as well as in the associated design process." (original emphasis)

Chapter 4
Multi–Agent Active Services for Online Social Networks

Enrico Franchi
University of Parma, Italy

Agostino Poggi
University of Parma, Italy

Michele Tomaiuolo
University of Parma, Italy

ABSTRACT

This chapter has the goal of showing how multi-agent systems can be a suitable means for supporting the development and the composition of services in dynamic and complex environments. In particular, the chapter copes with the problem of developing services in the field of social networks. After an introduction on the relationships between multi-agent systems, services, and social networks, the chapter describes how multi-agent systems can support the interaction and the collaboration among the members of a social network through a set of active services.

INTRODUCTION

One of the main challenge of multi-agent systems was to become the main means to support legacy systems interoperability and to facilitate the realization of scalable distributed systems (Genesereth, 1997; FIPA, 2013). However, in the last decades, service-oriented technologies had an impressive progress and seem to have good chances to compete with multi-agent systems as main means for the development of scalable and interoperable systems. The problem of such technologies is that they cannot provide the autonomy of agents together with their social and proactive capabilities of agents. As a result, the realization of flexible adaptive distributed systems may be difficult.

DOI: 10.4018/978-1-4666-5884-4.ch004

An integration of multi-agent systems with service-oriented technologies seems be the most suitable solution for the realization of scalable and interoperable distributed applications (see, for example, Greenwood & Calisti, 2004; Huhns et al., 2005).

However, in some application areas, multi-agent systems can be considered a suitable means for directly providing services. Social networks represent one of these areas. Indeed, social networks and multi-agent systems have many similarities and the members of a social network often interact with the other members as agents in a multi-agent system. Hence, it is possible to envisage, for the next future, networks of humans and agents, where agents provide services aimed at improving the exchange of information and the collaboration among members.

This chapter describes the relationships between multi-agent and service oriented systems and shows how multi-agent systems can be the means for providing dynamic and customizable services in social networks.

BACKGROUND

Agent, software agent and multi-agent system are terms that find their way in a number of research areas, including artificial intelligence, databases, operating systems and computer networks literature, as well as in several application areas, including business process management, network management, power systems control and space exploration (Pěchouček & Mařík, 2008; Bordini, 2009). Although there is no universally accepted definition for the term agent (Genesereth & Ketchpel, 1994; Wooldridge & Jennings, 1995; Russell & Norvig, 2003), all definitions agree that an agent is essentially a special software component that is:

- **Autonomous:** As it should operate without the direct intervention of humans or others and should have control over its actions and internal state.
- **Social:** As it should cooperate with humans or other agents in order to achieve its tasks.
- **Reactive:** Because it should perceive its environment and respond in a timely fashion to changes that occur in the environment.
- **Pro-Active:** As it should not simply act in response to its environment, but should also be able to exhibit goal-directed behavior by taking the initiative.

Moreover, some definitions assert that if necessary an agent can be:

- **Mobile:** Showing the ability to travel between different nodes in a computer network.
- **Truthful:** Providing the certainty that it will not deliberately communicate false information.
- **Benevolent:** Always trying to perform what is asked to it.
- **Rational:** Always acting in order to achieve its goals, and never to prevent its goals being achieved.
- **Able to Learn:** Adapting itself to fit its environment and to the desires of its users.

Agents may operate in dynamic and uncertain environments, making decisions at run-time. Moreover, agents take advantage of their social ability to exhibit a flexible coordination that makes them able to cooperate in the achievement of a global goal and compete in the distribution of resources and tasks. Coordination among agents can be handled with a variety of approaches, including negotiation, contracting, organizational structuring and multi-agent planning.

Negotiation is the communication process of a group of agents in order to reach a mutually accepted agreement on some matter (Jennings, 2001). Negotiation can be competitive or cooperative, depending on the behavior of the agents involved. Competitive negotiation is used in situations where agents have independent goals that interact with each other. They are not a priori cooperative, sharing information or willing to back down for the greater good; namely they are competitive. Cooperative negotiation is used in situations where agents have a common goal to achieve or a single task to execute. Among the negotiation techniques, contracting is probably the best way for searching the most appropriate task that satisfy a specific contract. Contracting is a negotiation technique based on a decentralized market structure where agents can take on two roles, manager or contractor, with managers trying to assign tasks to the most appropriate contractors (Smith & Davis, 1980).

Contracting solves the problems of assigning the execution of a task to a suitable contractor. However, it does not give any help in the identification of the contracts that a set of tasks must satisfy and in the definition of the way in which they must executed to obtain the solution of a problem. To cope with these two issues, agents can take advantage of multi-agent planning techniques. Multi-agent techniques allow agents to define plans for advancing towards their common/individual goal, preventing any possible interference among the actions of the different agents (Tonino et al., 2002). In order to avoid inconsistent or conflicting actions and interactions, agents build a multi-agent plan that details all the future actions and interactions required to achieve their goals, and interleave execution with more planning and re-planning. Multi-agent planning can be either centralized or distributed (Rosenschein, 1982; Le Pape, 1990; Durfee, 1999). In centralized multi-agent planning, a coordinating agent receives all partial or local plans from individual agents, analyses them in order to identify potential inconsistencies and conflicting interactions (e.g., conflicts between agents over limited resources). The coordinating agent then attempts to modify these partial plans and combines them into a multi-agent plan without conflicts. In distributed multi-agent planning, the idea is to provide each agent with a model of other agents plans. Agents communicate in order to build and update their individual plans and the models of other agents until all the plans have not conflicts.

Multi-agent planning and contracting techniques can be combined for the solution of complex problems, where it is necessary to identify both the agents able to perform the tasks and the way in which to combine their execution. Moreover, different works demonstrated that the quality of the results often depends on the way in which the agents of the systems are organized. Organizational structuring defines some coordination techniques that allow the design of the organization that govern the interaction among the agents of a system by defining the information, communication, and control relationships among its agents (Ferber et al., 2004; Horling & Lesser, 2005).

From the technological point of view, a lot of work has been done in the last decades for spreading the use of agents for the realization of software applications. Several software systems and technological specifications are the results of such work. Among them, the main results are the definition of FIPA specifications (FIPA, 2000), a set of specifications oriented to support the interoperability between heterogeneous agent systems, and an agent development framework, called JADE (Bellifemine et al., 2008, JADE, 2013), that implements such specifications and supports the interoperability between agents and the most common technologies currently used for realizing software applications.

MULTI-AGENT SYSTEMS AND WEB SERVICES

While Web services may be used in an isolated way to accomplish a specific business task, the need to aggregate multiple services in a new single meaningful composite service or to integrate them as part of workflow processes is more and more felt. In particular, a lot of work needs to be done in order to develop true flexible, adaptive intelligent service-oriented systems. Several researchers and companies have envisages as strategic the use and the improvement of semantic Web technologies (Vitvar et al, 2007). Others have turned their attention on multi-agent systems and their integration with semantic Web technologies as the main support for developing real adaptive intelligent service-oriented systems (Huhns, 2005).

In fact, the ability of agents of operating in dynamic and uncertain environments allows coping with the usual problems of failures or unavailability of services and the consequent need of finding substitute services and/or backtracking the system in a state where an alternative workflow can be executed. Moreover, the capabilities of some kinds of agent of learning from their experience make them able to improve their performance over the time, avoiding untrusted and unreliable providers and reusing successful solutions. Even more important is the agents' ability in coordinating themselves, as it can be the main ingredient for the development of flexible, intelligent and automatic Web services composition solutions. Negotiation is applicable with success for automating some operations in both the design and the execution phases of the provision of a composite service. In fact, in the design phase, negotiation techniques help customers in selecting the most appropriate component services and in reaching an agreement about all the issues characterizing the provision of such services. In the execution phase, negotiation can be useful for the redistribution of the component services among the different servers of a provider and even among the servers of different

providers. Finally, the use of multi-agent planning techniques allows the combination of the different component services and the control of their execution to provide the required composite service.

However, the integration between Web services and multi-agent technologies is quite difficult, as their communication patterns are quite different from a semantic point of view. Indeed, communication between agents is based on the exchange of messages defined though the speech act theory and its main goal is to update the knowledge and environment of the receiver as well as the sender agent, rather than to request the execution of a service. Furthermore, the language that defines the messages and the effects of their exchange on the agents is described by using formal semantics based on the modal logic. Therefore, large parts of the proposed solutions for their integration required high cost for the implementation (i.e., Web services must be encapsulated into agents) and low performances (i.e., an important part of the computation derives from the interaction of the agents that control the Web services).

Several researchers belonging to the agent community have dealt with the issues concerning the interconnection of agent systems with W3C compliant Web services, with the aim of allowing each technology to discover and invoke instances of the other. The proposed integration approaches (Greenwood & Calisti, 2004; Nguyen, 2005; Shafiq et al., 2005) denote different shades of meaning of the same idea, i.e. a wrapper or an adapter module playing the role of mediator between the two technologies. Most of them have adopted the gateway approach, providing a translation of WSDL descriptions and UDDI entries to and from FIPA specifications, thereby limiting the communication to simple request-response interactions. One approach (Soto, 2006), which differentiates quite substantially from the others, realizes a FIPA compliant JADE Message Transport System for Web Services enabling agents to interact through the Web with Web services preserving the FIPA compliant communication framework. It only provides a solution for an integration at a low level, leaving a number of issues at higher levels still unresolved.

The most significant of these approaches is WSIGS (Web Services Integration Gateway Service), a standalone, encapsulated application that provides transparent, bidirectional transformations between JADE agent services and Web services (Greenwood & Calisti, 2004). WSIG supports registration and discovery of JADE agents and agent services by Web service clients, automatic cross-translation of DF directory entries into UDDI directory entries and invocation of JADE Agent services by Web services. Moreover, when an agent needs to invoke a Web service, then WSIG creates the SOAP message and sends it to the provider. However, WSIG supports only simple WSDL description of Web services, without taking into account the possible semantic annotation that can be associated with the description of a Web service. Moreover, it does not provide any means that agents can use for directly composing Web services, but is able to support an indirect composition, though the composition of the tasks of some agents that are built on the tasks provided by Web services.

Several works proposed the use of semantic information to support a more effective use and composition of Web services in multi-agent systems.

Paulucci et al. (2002) present a matching engine that is able to identify Web services based on semantic information. In particular, they propose the use of DAML-S as language for the description of the Web services and describe the algorithm used for matching the service lookup requests to the DAML-S descriptions of the Web services. Wu et al. (2003) propose the use of a hierarchical task network planner for compositing Web services called SHOP2. In particular, they also use DAML-S as means for the description of Web services, but a translator has the duty of transforming such descriptions into representations usable by SHOP2 for defining the plan that describes the execution of the composite service. DACA is a distributed agent coalition algorithm for autonomic Web service composition (Tong et al., 2009). In particular, such an algorithm works on the relations among service agents. Such relations identifies the possible dependencies among the tasks performed by the services associated with the agents and the coalition algorithm manages the definition of a composite service as a graph search problem on the relations among service agents. SWSCPA is a multi-agent system based on JADE that solves the problem of composing Web services as a planning problem (Pan & Mao, 2013). In particular, SWSCPA is able to build an optimized plan for the execution of Web services based on a set of OWL-S descriptions. It associates an OWL-S description with each Web service that contains the functional information necessary for the composition with other Web services, and the information providing a measure of the quality of service that should provide the service. Such information about quality of service is built from the data obtained through the previous executions of the service.

SOCIAL NETWORKS

A social network is typically defined as a finite set or sets of actors and the relation or relations defined on them (Wasserman & Faust, 1994). The presence of relational information is critical and defining of social networks. In this context, an actor is essentially any social entity, such as a discrete individual, a corporate, or collective social unit. The use of the term "actor" does not imply that the entities have the volition or the ability to act. The relationships among the actors can be any kind of social tie and establish a linkage between a pair of actorslkj. If the two actors have the same role in the relationship, then the relationship is undirected else is directed. A network with only directed relationships is called a directed network; a network with only undirected relationships is called an undirected network. Typical examples of relationships are (i) evaluations, such as friendship, respect or trust, (ii) transfers of material or immaterial resources, such as information, money or diseases, (iii) behavioral interaction, e.g., sending messages, (iv) formal or biological relationships, such as marriage, employment or kinship.

Much research has been performed in the framework of social networks, or, more in general, of complex networks since the first half of the twentieth century, stemming from the seminal works of Moreno (1934) and Lewin (1936,1952), and, later of Fisher (1977), Wellman (1979), Wellman & Berkowitz (1988) and Milgram (1967).

Independently from social network analysis, other kinds of networks were studied in the context of Complex Network Theory (CNT). A complex network can be tentatively defined as a network with non-trivial topological features, i.e., features that are not present in regular lattices or simpler network structures such as Erdos-Rényi graphs. Among these features, typical examples are heavy-tailed degree distributions, high transitivity or, more in general, unusual structural patterns.

The discipline has drawn a lot of attention in the late nineties, because among the networks studied there were samples from the Web graph, which was an extremely popular subject at the time, and it did not take long before network scientists directed their attention towards social networks as well.

Among the most cited papers in the field, there are the seminal works by Watts and Strogatz (1998) and Barabási and Albert (1999). Watts and Strogatz studied both social and non-social networks and provided a unifying model for the so-called "small-worlds," i.e., networks where no pairs or nodes are really "distant" and where triangle-shaped paths are frequent. On the other hand, Barábasi and Albert's paper introduced a model for scale-free networks, i.e., networks with power-law degree distribution, starting the investigation from a network of Web links and a citation graph.

In the last decade, a new kind of software closely related to social networks emerged. In these Web platforms, users not only put or read content, but are also linked with relationships, so that, in essence, a social network is formed.

These online social networks (OSN), often also called social networking sites, have revolutionized how people interact. In fact, OSN allows them to stay in touch with their acquaintances, reconnect with old friends, and establish new relationships with other people based on hobbies, interests, and friendship circles. Online social networks are based on a set of Web-based services that allow people to define a profile. Such a profile can be made accessible to the other users of the network, to maintain a list of users with whom they share a connection, to publish resources and to make them available to other users and to use such connections for interact with new users and for making visible their social networks (Boyd and Ellison, 2007). Online social networks involve people from the entire world, of any age and with any kind of education; however, a recent study identified in females and in the persons aged 18-34 and with a high education as the majority of their visitors (Nielsen, 2011).

Although privacy should be of paramount importance in online social networks, users have little awareness for the issue, which is especially troubling, since the improper use of users' private information can cause undesirable or damaging consequences in their lives because such information can kick start a plethora of more sophisticated attacks. For example, apparently harmless information such as name, location and age can be used to connect a profile to a real-world identity for more than half of the residents in the USA (Irani et al., 2011). Such information is typically not hard to gather, especially if a person has profiles in multiple online social networks.

Regardless of the privacy settings among users, the service provider point of view on privacy is that privacy mostly regards privacy among users; however, it is hard to generalize, because of the ample number of different systems, whose creators are expected to have radically different ideas on the subject. Privacy is almost never considered as a right that users have against the service provider itself, which is rather natural as the sheer amount of personal information made available by the users is invaluable for the service providers, being the foundation for the targeted advertisement that is, in most cases, the principal source of income for said providers. It is worth noting that since there is no privacy from the service provider, an attacker gaining access to the system can acquire huge amounts of information.

SOCIAL NETWORKS AND MULTI-AGENT SYSTEMS

Understanding the intrinsic computational properties of social networks is necessary to grasp the relationship between multi-agent systems and social networks: indeed, without such an understanding, multi-agent approach could not be used to build software systems supporting social networking.

Milgram pioneered the study of these properties performing the experiment, which led to the investigation of the so-called small world phenomenon (Milgram, 1967). In Milgram's experiment, a group of randomly chosen people received the name and address of another randomly chosen person living in a distant city; then, people were asked to route a mail message toward the target person chosen only among their friends or close acquaintances. The experiment pointed out that: i) people are connected through very short chains of acquaintances, with a 5-6 links length, in average and ii) people are able to route the messages to the target person using mostly local information and performing local actions.

A result of the Milgram's experiment is that people behavior was similar to that of rational autonomous agents. In fact, every person choses his/her successor in his/her list of acquaintances

considering elements like geographical proximity or profession similarity, which is essentially using only local and elementary information to pursue a global complex goal, with no need to use their "humanity". From our point of view, this is a particularly relevant conclusion, since it points to the emergence of a global behavior from local strategies, feature that is one of the key properties of multi-agent systems.

More recently, the studies on the small world problem led to two computationally-based approaches to search for people within social networks. The Milgram's original experiment led to a machine-based approach, consisting in the problem of looking for a remote agent given its name/id. Adamic & Adar (2005) presented a comprehensive review of the different algorithms and their performance. The second approach deals with finding a specific agent who matches some criterion, such as having a given capability or expertise. This is quite similar to the problem of navigating one's social network in search for someone with a given expertise or for an answer to a specific question. In an enterprise setting, this is the problem of looking inside the organization for someone able to solve a specific problem or answer to a specific question. When solved with agent-based techniques, this problem resembles the "collaborative filtering" one and is usually termed as "expert finding"; therefore, some authors use these definitions interchangeably.

The expert finding problem is similar to Milgram's original problem in that the social network of each node is the search space in which the request is processed. It should be emphasized that, both problems strongly rely on the local search ability and the occurrence of the small world phenomenon, i.e., on the fact that two random individuals are preferably, mostly connected by short chains of acquaintanceships. If social networks were not searchable, it would be impossible to find efficiently a person matching some criteria unless personally known and, then, the Milgram's experiment would have failed. On the other hand, if the chains were very long, the search would be not feasible.

Kautz, Selman, & Shah (1997) have done a pioneering work on this subject; their papers describe ReferralWeb, which is an agent based interactive system for reconstructing, visualizing, and searching social networks on the World-Wide Web, whose main focus is selecting an expert of a given field in one's (extended) social network.

In ReferralWeb a social network is modelled by a graph consisting of the nodes which represent individuals, and of edges between nodes which indicate the direct relationships between the individuals. When the names of individuals are in close proximity in any documents publicly available on the Web, such as home pages, co-authorships in published papers or organization charts in institutional websites, then, ReferralWeb deduces the existence of direct relationships. As the ReferralWeb proposers thought that "experts" would never find time to fill their own profile, ReferralWeb does not require its users to fill a user profile describing their skills.

The search for people or documents is based on the following types of action:

- Asking to find the chain connecting himself/herself to a named individual.
- Searching for an expert in a given topic and providing a maximum social radius (the number of "links" in the chain connecting the person performing the query with the expert).
- Requesting a list of documents written by people "close" to a given expert.

ReferralWeb is not meant to be a tool to create social networks, i.e., to help people socializing. Rather, it is based on the idea of using the social network to make searches more focused and effective. ReferralWeb also emphasizes the importance of the referral chains themselves as means to build trust on the selected expert.

Yu et al. describe in detail a working "expert finding" algorithm; the authors also performed comprehensive simulations to test their approach and implemented a prototype called MARS (Yu & Singh, 2003). Each user is assigned an agent who: (i) learns the user's preferences and interests and (ii) maintains a view of its user's acquaintances, which are used to prioritize incoming queries, possibly issuing referrals when others might be more suitable to answer a given query. Each agent first rates, according to the user's feedback, those who provided an answer and those who referred to them, and then, it modifies its neighbors accordingly. Consequently, the referral system evolves to reflect the changes in the social network.

A response to a query specifying what information is being sought, if given, may consist of an answer or a referral, depending on the query and on the expertise of the answering agent. If an agent is reasonably confident that its expertise matches the query, it directly answers; otherwise, it yields referrals to other supposedly expert agents.

Each agent maintains models of its acquaintances. An agent sends its query initially only to some of its neighbors, which are the individuals with the closest acquaintances. The agent who receives a referral may pursue it even if the referred party is not already an acquaintance; "good" acquaintances are going to be promoted to neighbors on an intuitive basis. When new neighbors are considered (included) some of previous ones will be discarded, since the number of neighbors is bounded. The authors decided that reputation should increase slowly, but fall quickly and that rewards and penalties are greater for agents nearer to the answering agent. This implies that a bad decision results in bad reputation, but if agents just started a chain of referrals leading to a bad agent, then the penalty is modest.

The expertise model is captured through a classical vector space model (Salton & McGill, 1983). Term vectors are used to express both the profile of the user and the acquaintance model for each of its acquaintances. Since a term vector also models the required expertise, the cosine of the angle between the user vectors with the subject vector yields the competence of a user in a given subject. Intuitively, when there are two agents with expertise in the same direction, the one with the greater expertise is more desirable

Each agent learns its user's profile and its acquaintance models based on an evaluation of the answers received as well as on the referrals that led to them. A referral graph, which is local to each agent, encodes how the computation spreads as a query originates from an agent and referrals or answers are sent back to this agent.

Foner et al. describe a slightly different point of view that was implemented in Yenta, a prototype contemporary to ReferralWeb (Foner, 1997). Yenta is not a referral tool, but a full-fledged matchmaking system, that is a system to help people with similar interests to get in touch. Both matchmakers and referral tools make it possible to find experts, but matchmakers are less efficient in searching than the traditional referral tools.

Yenta agents do not get information from the Web; instead, they scan user's emails, Usenet posts and (possibly) documents in order to discover their users' interests and hobbies. The advantage is that many potentially interesting people do not publicly write and are consequently invisible to tools relying on public data. Collected data are then used to introduce users to each other. Since in the nineties Web communities were built around the idea of common interests rather than of personal acquaintances, the system was a truly distributed social networking system for the time.

Franchi and Poggi (2011) presented an algorithm allowing agents to expand their social network using their acquaintances as broker. The algorithm is the kernel of a multi-agent system implementing a fully distributed Social Network System based on user provided profiles. The system is based on the notion that users should be the sole owners of the information they provide (either consciously or unconsciously). Hence, the

system addresses privacy issues by design and the amount of information users have to disclose in order to make new friends is minimized. Users are represented by agents that in order to extend their user's social network both mediate access to private data and proactively negotiate with other agents.

The basic idea is that agents are not allowed to communicate unless they have mutually established a connection; this is the reason why a mutually known agent must act as a broker in the first stages of communication. As an example, let agent *A* represents a particular user and has the task to expand her/his social networks with some former fellow students that graduated in the same year and school. Suppose that an agent *B*, known to *A*, represents one of those former schoolmates. In order to contact other schoolmates, *A* gives permission to *B* to tell every agent it knows to represent one of their schoolmates about *A*. Let *C* and *D* be two of those agents. Both *C* and *D* are known to *B*, but not to *A*. Suppose *C* accepts to be connected with *A*: then it gives permission to *B* to inform *A* about *C*. Eventually, *A* knows about *C* and they can temporarily communicate and decide to establish a link and possibly share more information. On the other hand, for example, *D* may refuse to connect with *A*. Then it forbids *B* to inform *A* about *D* and in this case, *A* will not be able to communicate with *D*. Although the algorithm is created with privacy concerns in mind, some information must be shared in order for links to be established; at least the receiver of the proposal must be aware of the proposal itself and of the existence of the proponent

MULTI-AGENT SERVICES FOR SOCIAL NETWORKS

The diffusion of social networks is opening new scenarios for realizing different kinds of applications, either to support new social networking activities, or to exploit established relationships among users and offer higher-level services. One promising direction is the use of a social network as a sort of grid platform for accessing and composing services, to realize a rich virtual computing environment (Chard et al., 2010). However, such scenarios would require highly adaptive services, to react to potentially very differentiated and dynamic environments.

The situation becomes even more interesting and promising, in the event that location-based communities and services are taken into consideration. In all those cases, software agents are a natural fit, for mediating access to local software- or hardware-based services, including access to data, sensors, monitors, printers and various kinds of actuators. Given their ability to negotiate and plan in a dynamic social context, software agents are also fit for composing locally available services and resources, following existing trust relationships with other persons and agents located in the user's proximity area. New trust relationships can also be created, on the basis of reputation and mutual acknowledgement, through the incremental and controlled exchange of profile data.

Especially in the case of completely distributed or federated social networking platforms, multi-agent systems can play an important role. Indeed, one of the very specific features of multi-agent systems is the sociality of agents, i.e. their ability to communicate in a semantic way and develop trust relationships among them. Moreover, agents can express their communication acts by means of acknowledged standards, like FIPA, for interoperability among diverse systems, and exchange messages directly, in a peer-to-peer way. Therefore, it is not surprising that these two technologies are often applied together for developing advanced social platforms. In particular, multi-agent systems have been used as (i) an underlying layer or a middleware for developing social networking platforms, and (ii) a technology to increase the autonomous and intelligent behavior of existing systems.

For the first type of solutions, many of the distinguishing features of multi-agent systems can be fully exploited. Indeed, multi-agent systems provide semantic communication among agents, which is handy for expressing all the different actions that users can perform on a social platform. The different types of messages can be understood according to their pragmatics meaning, and applied according to existing trust relations among the users and their respective agents. In addition, complex negotiation protocols can help creating acknowledgements and trust among users, in an automatic or assisted way, without exposing sensitive data. Mobility can also be useful for moving the computation closer to data, if massive analysis has to be performed, but can also be handy for adding functionality to a node of a distributed social platform or to a user's client application.

In the second case, agents are mainly exploited because of their proactive and reactive behaviors, for providing recommendations of both users and content and for providing personalization of results. Reactive abilities are particularly important in a social networking environment, where events happen continuously and users can be easily distracted by the huge information overflow, which is associated with richly interconnected social networks. Sensing the environment and executing automatic tasks can reduce this overload significantly. Goal-oriented behaviors, on the other hand, can support users in persecuting their long term objectives about friend and content discovery, i.e. finding known persons registered in the network, making new acquaintances with users with common interests, finding interesting content from new sources or hidden among other less relevant data.

A CASE STUDY: BLOGRACY

As an example of use of the described services, we present a distributed social networking system, named Blogracy, whose goal is to provide adaptive and composite services on top of its core features. At the lower level, Blogracy uses widespread and stable peer-to-peer technologies, such as distributed hash tables and the BitTorrent protocol, for coping with intrinsic defects of centralized architectures and for being the basis of solid distributed social networking platforms. At the higher level, it takes advantage of multi-agent systems for simplifying the implementation of social network services in a decentralized setting.

The architecture of the application is modular and composed of two basic components: (i) an underlying module for basic file sharing and DHT operations, realized as an extension over existing implementations, and (ii) an OpenSocial container, i.e., a module providing the services of the social platform to the local user through a Web interface. Additionally, the system supports autonomous agents for providing (i) recommendations of both users and content, (ii) personalization of results, (iii) trust negotiation mechanisms.

The Blogracy system itself relies only on users' nodes for its operation. Therefore, users need to perform background tasks on their own, in a distributed way. A layer of autonomous agents takes charge of assisting the user in finding new interesting content and connections and for pushing the local user's activities to followers.

In particular, a personal assistant (PA) monitors the local user's actions in the platform and learns the user's profile, beyond information provided explicitly. The PA receives the user's queries, forwards them to the available information finders (IF) and presents the results to the user. Moreover, a PA provides the local user with recommendations about possibly interesting content and connections available in the network. Another task performed by the PA is the personalization of results. Indeed, as a social network becomes larger and more richly interconnected, users unavoidably face some form of information overflow. A personal agent, using user's profile, can arrange presented data in a way to give evidence to the most interesting bits.

An IF is an agent that searches information on the repository contained into the node where it lives, through an automatic TF-IDF indexing and explicit hashtags associated with local posts. It provides this information both to its user and to other trusted users. An IF agent receives users' queries, finds appropriate results and filters them by using its user's access policies. An information pusher (IP) is an agent that monitors the changes in the local repository and pushes the new information to the PA agent of interested subscribers who are currently connected. An IP agent can forward content produced by the local user and by her/his remote acquaintances to other contacts, according to privacy preserving policies and to recent queries made by other users.

Over the OpenSocial container, Blogracy can also provide functionalities for pervasive online social networking, specifically for realizing locality and proximity groups. In this case, the system has to rely on highly adaptive services both to sustain the basic operations of the location-based social networking and to provide advanced functionalities. For this purpose, each node of the social network has to host multiple agents, with different levels of agency. Some of the more important agents are (i) the neighborhood manager (NM) agent, which cooperates with lower level agents to discover the users in its neighborhood; (ii) the trust negotiator (TN) agent, which is involved in the decisions regarding privacy and access rules, and (iii) the OpenSocial agent, which provides a bridge towards the underlying Blogracy modules.

A user may own multiple nodes (e.g., an instance on the smart-phone and an instance on his home computer) and, since the actual location of the user is important for our application, the nodes in the different devices negotiate which should be considered active (i.e., which one determines the user location). In fact, the nodes can either determine the device that registered an explicit user action or can ask the user to select the device he is currently using.

Apart from the personal circles defined by each user, we also have two additional kinds of groups: (i) proximity groups and (ii) location groups. Proximity groups are centered on each member of the social networking system and represent physical closeness to such member. Proximity groups are extremely fluid, in the sense that users can physically move and consequently the set of users belonging to a proximity group varies in time. Each user configures the hysteresis, or sticky-ness, of his proximity group, i.e., how long the other users are considered part of it after they are no longer physically close to him. Although a proximity group may be entirely public, for privacy reasons it is safer to consider only proximity groups that are subset of other groups (or to the set union of all groups, i.e., only "friends" are part of a proximity group). The NM agent informs the OpenSocial agent when users enter and leave the Proximity group and the latter notifies the OpenSocial container about it.

On the other hand, a location group is associated with the users in the proximity of a given location (e.g., a classroom or a museum room) and has a host (i.e., a node) that both identifies and supports the group. Moreover, a location group is associated with a location profile maintained either on the central server or on its host. In fact, a location, although logically different from a regular user, works in the same way and a location group is essentially a proximity group for the location.

The availability of a generic TN agent is also important, since users joining a proximity or location group are not necessarily connected a priori in the social network, and they may need to acknowledge their profile attributes before practical social interaction. Such a negotiation requires the controlled exchange of credentials and policies, without disclosing unnecessary sensible information, yet establishing trust if possible. In (Bergenti et al., 2009), a generic library supporting zero-knowledge proof for attribute verifica-

tion is presented. The same mechanisms can also facilitate the creation of trust in social networks.

Agents present different degrees of autonomy and intelligence. For example, lower level agents are mostly reactive; e.g., they inform the NM agent when a new node is discovered. The NM agent itself has some degrees of autonomy and intelligence:

- It aggregates information from the agents that discover new peers.
- It informs the OpenSocial of the state of neighborhood.
- It tries to present a consistent view, merging the data from the different sources.
- It configures the discovering agents according to high-level criteria, such as battery consumption and hardware availability.

The OpenSocial agent is basically a gateway to the OpenSocial container translating the other agents requests for the OpenSocial container and a TN agent is a true agent that performs potentially complex negotiations on his user's behalf and depending from the configuration may work in entire autonomy.

FUTURE RESEARCH DIRECTIONS

In the previous sections, we showed how multi-agent systems could support service-oriented systems for providing composite services and how they can be the suitable means for supporting the actions of the members of a social network.

Multi-agent and service-oriented systems are still evolving towards a complete maturity. In particular, the evolution and the strengthening of the semantic Web technologies, as well as other related technologies for providing semantic services, should influence the evolution of multi-agent technologies. In fact, the use of agents for the composition of services is considered one of the most promising area where applying agents and improvements on the composition techniques will depend on the quality of the semantic information on the services available to the agents.

Moreover, multi-agent systems have the potential to become one of the most important means for the development of intelligent services for social networks and for automatize the execution of some tasks that currently their members perform manually. In fact, the coordination, knowledge management, and learning capabilities provided by multi-agent systems can already be used to help the members of a social network by making easy the execution of complex tasks and by acting in their behalf to perform tasks in collaboration with other members of the social network.

CONCLUSION

This chapter showed how multi-agent systems can be considered a suitable means for supporting the composition of services and for adapting them to the modifications of the environment where they act. Moreover, it showed how in some situations they could be used with success for directly providing adaptive services. It happens in social networks. Hence, this chapter described how multi-agent systems could support service-oriented systems for providing composite services and how they can be the suitable means for supporting the actions of the members of a social network.

REFERENCES

Adamic, L., & Adar, E. (2005). How to search a social network. *Social Networks*, *27*(3), 187–203. doi:10.1016/j.socnet.2005.01.007

Barabási, A. L., & Albert, R. (1999). Emergence of scaling in random networks. *Science*, *286*(5439), 509–512. doi:10.1126/science.286.5439.509 PMID:10521342

Bellifemine, F., Caire, G., Poggi, A., & Rimassa, G. (2008). JADE: A software framework for developing multi-agent applications: Lessons learned. *Information and Software Technology Journal*, *50*, 10–21. doi:10.1016/j.infsof.2007.10.008

Bergenti, F., Rossi, L., & Tomaiuolo, M. (2009). Towards automated trust negotiation in MAS. In *Proceedings of WOA 2009*. Parma, Italy: WOA.

Bordini, R. H. (2009). *Multi-agent programming: Languages, tools and applications*. Berlin, Germany: Springer.

Boyd, D. M., & Ellison, N. B. (2007). Social network sites: Definition, history, and scholarship. *Journal of Computer-Mediated Communication*, *13*(1), 210–230. doi:10.1111/j.1083-6101.2007.00393.x

Chard, K., Caton, S., Rana, O., & Bubendorfer, K. (2010). Social cloud: Cloud computing in social networks. In *Proceedings of 2010 IEEE 3rd International Conference on Cloud* Computing (pp. 99-106). Miami, FL: IEEE.

Durfee, E. H. (1999). Distributed problem solving and planning. In G. Weiss (Ed.), *Multiagent systems: A modern approach to distributed artificial intelligence* (pp. 121–164). Cambridge, MA: MIT Press.

Ferber, J., Gutknecht, O., & Michel, F. (2004). From agents to organizations: An organizational view of multi-agent systems. In *Agent-oriented software engineering IV* (pp. 214–230). Berlin, Germany: Springer. doi:10.1007/978-3-540-24620-6_15

FIPA. (2013). *FIPA specifications*. Retrieved November 18, 2013 from http:www.fipa.org

Fisher, C. S. (1977). *Networks and places: Social relations in the urban setting*. New York: Free Press.

Foner, L. (1997). Yenta: A multi-agent, referral-based matchmaking system. In *Proceedings of First International Conference on Autonomous Agents* (pp. 301-307). Marina del Rey, CA: ACM.

Franchi, E., & Poggi, A. (2011). Multi-agent systems and social networks. In M. Cruz-Cunha, G. D. Putnik, N. Lopes, P. Gonçalves, & E. Miranda (Eds.), *Business social networking: Organizational, managerial, and technological dimensions* (pp. 84–97). Hershey, PA: IGI Global. doi:10.4018/978-1-61350-168-9.ch005

Genesereth, M. R. (1997). An agent-based framework for interoperability. In J. M. Bradshaw (Ed.), *Software agents* (pp. 317–345). Cambridge, MA: MIT Press.

Genesereth, M. R., & Ketchpel, S. P. (1994). Software agents. *Communications of the ACM*, *37*(7), 48–53. doi:10.1145/176789.176794

Greenwood, D., & Calisti, M. (2004). Engineering web service-agent integration. In *Proceedings of 2004 IEEE International Conference on Systems, Man and Cybernetics* (Vol. 2, pp. 1918-1925). The Hague, The Netherlands: IEEE.

Horling, B., & Lesser, V. (2005). A survey of multi-agent organizational paradigms. *The Knowledge Engineering Review*, *19*(4), 281–316. doi:10.1017/S0269888905000317

Huhns, M. N., Singh, M. P., Burstein, M., Decker, K., & Durfee, K. E., Finin, … Zavafa, L. (2005). Research directions for service-oriented multiagent systems. *IEEE Internet Computing*, *9*(6), 65–70. doi:10.1109/MIC.2005.132

Irani, D. et al. (2011). Modeling unintended personal-information leakage from multiple online social networks. *Internet Computing*, *15*, 13–19. doi:10.1109/MIC.2011.25

JADE. (2013). *Jade software web site*. Retrieved November 18, 2013, from http://jade.tilab.com/

Jennings, N. R., Faratin, P., Lomuscio, A. R., Parsons, S., Sierra, C., & Wooldridge, M. (2001). Automated negotiation: Prospects, methods and challenges. *Group Decision and Negotiation*, *10*(2), 199–215. doi:10.1023/A:1008746126376

Kautz, H., Selman, B., & Shah, M. (1997a). Combining social networks and collaborative filtering. *Communications of the ACM*, *40*(3), 63–65. doi:10.1145/245108.245123

Le Pape, C. (1990). A combination of centralized and distributed methods for multi-agent planning and scheduling. In *Proceedings of 1990 IEEE International Conference on Robotics and Automation* (pp. 488-493). Cincinnati, OH: IEEE.

Lewin, K. (1936). *Principles of topological psychology*. New York: McGraw Hill. doi:10.1037/10019-000

Lewin, K. (1952). Field theory in social science. In D. Cartwright (Ed.), *Selected theoretical papers*. London, UK: Tavistock.

Milgram, S. (1967). The small world problem. *Psychology Today*, *1*(1), 61–67.

Moreno, J. L. (1934). *Who shall survive?* New York: Beacon Press.

Nguyen, X. T. (2005). Demonstration of WS-2JADE. In *Proceedings of Fourth International Joint Conference on Autonomous Agents and Multi-Agent Systems* (pp. 135–136). Utrecht, The Netherlands: ACM.

Pan, S., & Mao, Q. (2013). Case study on web service composition based on multi-agent system. *Journal of Software*, *8*(4), 900–907. doi:10.4304/jsw.8.4.900-907

Paolucci, M., Kawamura, T., Payne, T. R., & Sycara, K. (2002). Semantic matching of web services capabilities. In I. Horrocks, & J. Hendler (Eds.), *The semantic web - ISWC 2002, (LNCS)* (pp. 333–347). Berlin, Germany: Springer.

Pěchouček, M., & Mařík, V. (2008). Industrial deployment of multi-agent technologies: Review and selected case studies. *Autonomous Agents and Multi-Agent Systems*, *17*(3), 397–431. doi:10.1007/s10458-008-9050-0

Rosenschein, J. S. (1982). Synchronization of multi-agent plans. In *Proceedings of Second National Conference on Artificial Intelligence* (pp. 115–119). Pittsburgh, PA: AAAI Press.

Russell, S. J., & Norvig, P. (2010). *Artificial intelligence: A modern approach*. Englewood Cliffs, NJ: Prentice Hall.

Salton, G., & McGill, M. (1983). *Introduction to modern information retrieval*. New York: McGraw Hill.

Shafiq, M. O., Ali, A., Ahmad, H. F., & Suguri, H. (2005). AgentWeb gateway - A middleware for dynamic integration of multi agent system and web services framework. In *Proceedings of 14th IEEE International Workshops on Enabling Technologies: Infrastructure for Collaborative Enterprise* (pp. 267–270). Washington, DC: IEEE.

Smith, R., & Davis, R. (1980). The contract net protocol: High level communication and control in a distributed problem solver. *IEEE Transactions on Computers*, *29*(12), 1104–1113. doi:10.1109/TC.1980.1675516

Soto, E. L. (2006). FIPA agent messaging grounded on web services. In *Proceedings of 3rd International Conference on Grid Service Engineering and Management* (pp. 247-248). Erfurt, Germany: Academic Press.

Tong, H., Cao, J., Zhang, S., & Li, M. (2009). A distributed agent coalition algorithm for web service composition. In *Proceedings of 2009 World Conference on* Services (pp. 62-69). Los Angeles, CA: IEEE.

Tonino, H., Bos, A., de Weerdt, M., & Witteveen, C. (2002). Plan coordination by revision in collective agent based systems. *Artificial Intelligence*, *142*(2), 121–145. doi:10.1016/S0004-3702(02)00273-4

Vitvar, T., Mocan, A., Kerrigan, M., Zaremba, M., Zaremba, M., & Moran, M. et al. (2007). Semantically-enabled service oriented architecture: Concepts, technology and application. *Service Oriented Computing and Applications*, *1*(2), 129–154. doi:10.1007/s11761-007-0009-9

Wasserman, S., & Faust, K. (1994). *Social network analysis: Methods and applications*. Cambridge, UK: Cambridge University Press. doi:10.1017/CBO9780511815478

Wellman, B. (1979). The community question: The intimate networks of East Yorkers. *American Journal of Sociology*, *84*, 1201–1231. doi:10.1086/226906

Wellman, B., & Berkowitz, S. D. (1988). *Social structures: A network approach*. Cambridge, UK: Cambridge University Press.

Wooldridge, M. J., & Jennings, N. R. (1995). Intelligent agents: Theory and practice. *The Knowledge Engineering Review*, *10*(2), 115–152. doi:10.1017/S0269888900008122

Wu, D., Parsia, B., Sirin, E., Hendler, J., & Nau, D. (2003). Automating DAML-S web services composition using SHOP2. In D. Fensel, K. Sycara, & J. Mylopoulos (Eds.), *The semantic web - ISWC 2003, (LNCS)* (Vol. 2870, pp. 195–210). Berlin, Germany: Springer. doi:10.1007/978-3-540-39718-2_13

Yu, B., & Singh, M. (2003). Searching social networks. In Proceedings of Second International Joint Conference on Autonomous Agents and Multiagent Systems (pp. 65-72). New York: ACM.

ADDITIONAL READING

Alonso, G., Casati, F., Kuno, H., & Machiraju, V. (2004). *Web Services. Concepts, Architectures and Applications*. Berlin, Germany: Springer.

Androutsellis-Theotokis, S., & Spinellis, D. (2004). A survey of peer-to-peer content distribution technologies. *ACM Computing Surveys*, *36*(4), 335–371. doi:10.1145/1041680.1041681

Bordini, R., Dastani, M., Dix, J., & Fallah-Seghrouchni, A. (Eds.). (2005). *Multi-Agent Programming: Languages, Platforms and Applications. Multiagent Systems, Artificial Societies, and Simulated Organizations*. Berlin, Germany: Springer. doi:10.1007/b137449

Buhler, P. A., & Vidal, J. M. (2005). Towards Adaptive Workflow Enactment Using Multiagent Systems. *Information Technology Management*, *6*(1), 61–87. doi:10.1007/s10799-004-7775-2

Campbell, M. I., Cagan, J., & Kotovsky, K. (1999). A-Design: an agent-based approach to conceptual design in a dynamic environment. *Research in Engineering Design*, *11*, 172–192. doi:10.1007/s001630050013

Carrington, P. J., Scott, J., & Wasserman, S. (Eds.). (2005). *Models and methods in social network analysis*. Cambridge, UK: Cambridge University Press. doi:10.1017/CBO9780511811395

Dietrich, A. J., Kirn, S., & Sugumaran, V. (2007). A Service-Oriented Architecture for Mass Customization. A Shoe Industry Case Study. *IEEE Transactions on Engineering Management*, *54*(1), 190–204. doi:10.1109/TEM.2006.889076

Dustdar, S., & Schreiner, W. (2005). A survey on Web services composition. *International Journal on Web and Grid Services*, *1*(1), 1–30. doi:10.1504/IJWGS.2005.007545

Epstein, J. (1999). Agent-based computational models and generative social science. *Complexity*, *4*(5), 41–60. doi:10.1002/(SICI)1099-0526(199905/06)4:5<41::AID-CPLX9>3.0.CO;2-F

Ferber, J. (1999). *Multi-agent systems: an introduction to distributed artificial intelligence*. Reading, MA, USA: Addison-Wesley.

Franchi, E., & Poggi, A. (2012). Multi-Agent Systems and Social Networks. In M. M. Cruz-Cunha, G. D. Putnik, N. Lopes, P. Gonçalves, & E. Miranda (Eds.), *Handbook of Research on Business Social Networking: Organizational, Managerial, and Technological Dimensions* (pp. 84–97). Hershey, PA, USA: Information Science Reference.

Hummon, N. (2000). Utility and dynamic social networks. *Social Networks*, *22*(3), 221–249. doi:10.1016/S0378-8733(00)00024-1

Jennings, N., Corera, J., & Laresgoiti, I. (1995). Developing industrial multi-agent systems. In *First International Conference on Multi-Agent Systems* (pp. 423–430). San Francisco, CA, USA: Kluwer.

Liu, S., Küngas, P., & Matskin, M. (2006). Agent-Based Web Service Composition with JADE and JXTA. In *2006 International Conference on Semantic Web and Web Services* (pp. 110-116). Las Vegas, NV, USA.

Martinez, E., & Lespérance, Y. (2004). IG-JADE-PKSlib: An Agent-Based Framework for Advanced Web Ser-vice Composition and Provisioning. In *AAMAS 2004 Workshop on Web-services and Agent-based Engineering* (pp. 2-10). New York, NY, USA.

Mika, P. (2005). Flink: Semantic Web technology for the extraction and analysis of social networks. *Web Semantics: Science. Services and Agents on the World Wide Web*, *3*(2-3), 211–223. doi:10.1016/j.websem.2005.05.006

Muller, J. (1998). Architectures and applications of intelligent agents: A survey. *The Knowledge Engineering Review, 13*(4), 353–380. doi:10.1017/S0269888998004020

Negri, A., Poggi, A., Tomaiuolo, M., & Turci, P. (2006). Dynamic Grid tasks composition and distribution through agents. *Concurrency and Computation, 18*(8), 875–885. doi:10.1002/cpe.982

Newman, M.E.J.(2010). *Networks: An Introduction.* Oxford, UK: Oxford University Press. doi:10.1093/acprof:oso/9780199206650.001.0001

Paolucci, M., & Sycara, K. (2003). Autonomous Semantic Web Services. *IEEE Internet Computing, 7*(5), 34–41. doi:10.1109/MIC.2003.1232516

Poggi, A., Tomaiuolo, M., & Turci, P. (2007). *An Agent-Based Service Oriented Architecture* (pp. 157–165). Genoa, Italy: WOA.

Shen, W., Norrie, D. H., & Barthès, J. P. (2001). *Multi-agent systems for concurrent intelligent design and manufacturing.* London, UK: Taylor and Francis. doi:10.4324/9780203305607

Stroud, D. (2008). Social networking: An age-neutral commodity - Social networking becomes a mature Web application. *Journal of Direct. Data and Digital Marketing Practice, 9*(3), 278–292. doi:10.1057/palgrave.dddmp.4350099

Tomaiuolo, M., Turci, P., Bergenti, F., & Poggi, A. (2006). An Ontology Support for Semantic Aware Agents. In *M. Kolp, P. Bresciani, B. Henderson-Sellers, M. Winikoff, Agent-Oriented Information Systems III* (pp. 140–153). Lecture Notes in Computer Science Berlin, Germany: Springer. doi:10.1007/11916291_10

Wang, F., Moreno, Y., & Sun, Y. (2006). Structure of peer-to-peer social networks. *Physical Review E: Statistical, Nonlinear, and Soft Matter Physics, 73*(3), 1–8. doi:10.1103/PhysRevE.73.036123

KEY TERMS AND DEFINITIONS

Contracting: A process where agents can assume the role of manager and contractor and where managers tries to assign tasks to the most appropriate contractors.

Coordination: A process in which a group of agents engages in order to ensure that each of them acts in a coherent manner.

Expert Finding: The problem of distributed searching someone with a given set of skills and a given level of trust using a social network.

Multi-Agent Planning: A process that can involve agents plan for a common goal, agents coordinating the plan of others, or agents refining their own plans while negotiating over tasks or resources.

Multi-Agent System: A multi-agent system (MAS) is a loosely coupled network of software agents that interact to solve problems that are beyond the individual capacities or knowledge of each software agent.

Negotiation: A process by which a group of agents come to a mutually acceptable agreement on some matter.

Social Network: social structure made of agents (individuals) which are connected by one or more different relationships.

Software Agent: A software agent is a computer program that is situated in some environment and capable of autonomous action in order to meet its design objectives.

Section 2
Technologies of Demand–Driven Web Services

Chapter 5
Generalized Demand–Driven Web Services

Mihai Horia Zaharia
"Gheorghe Asachi" Technical University, Romania

ABSTRACT

Highly developed economies are based on the knowledge society. A variety of software tools are used in almost every aspect of human life. Service-oriented architectures are limited to corporate-related business solutions. This chapter proposes a novel approach aimed to overcome the differences between real life services and software services. Using the design approaches for the current service-oriented architecture, a solution that can be implemented in open source systems has been proposed. As a result, a new approach to creating an agent for service composition is introduced. The agent itself is created by service composition too. The proposed approach might facilitate the research and development of Web services, service-oriented architectures, and intelligent agents.

INTRODUCTION

Globalization and the information based society have begun to modify all business processes, beginning with resource identification and finishing with product delivery. Rainey (2012) presents a new sustainable adoption model in the context of globalization. He considers that innovation will play a key role in the future global system.

The main directions of research are related to the improvement of technologies, business models, and leadership.

There is a corporatist approach that neglects the impact of small and medium enterprises (SMEs) on the global market (OECD, 2012). The motives may be related to the decreased chances to create new knowledge due to an insufficient amount of funding regarding their own research and develop-

DOI: 10.4018/978-1-4666-5884-4.ch005

ment (R&D) departments. Also a small company that really identifies a free corner in the market can quickly increase in power and influence. Anyhow, the most dynamic part of the advanced economies is still based on SMEs. The globalization process is already based on using a high level of information technologies communication (ICT). Further global cyberspace development will be a common goal for all involved actors.

The idea of shifting business mostly in cyberspace is not new. The experts predicted that this might be a valuable approach a decade ago (Lowson, King, & Hunter, 1999). They also expressed some concerns related to the control of the very complex infrastructure that was expected to emerge. Their fears have proved to be partially correct, especially from the security related point of view. As for the rest, reality proves that the people have begun to increase the activity over Internet, but in most cases, they just replicate real life procedures. So the problems are similar in both approaches. The e-business concept offers almost equal chances for anyone who wants to develop and deliver various services for the society (Hong, Nag, & Yao, 2009). There are initiatives like the Android market or Apple store that give access to anyone who wants to publish their application and be paid for it. Moreover, it is the open source initiative that has begun to be more attractive due to the global economic crisis.

Various software packages like Systems Applications and Products in Data Processing (SAP) are already seen as evolving into an interface layer between preexisting technologies for business management and the new cyberspace related procedures (Anderson, 2011). The new concept of Web service begins to offer a first solution in this direction.

Services may be delivered by a person or by any kind of economical agent, beginning with small companies and ending with transnational corporations. Due to the generalization of electronic payment in advanced economies, the entire business cycle can be virtualized, excepting pro-

duction and delivery. Even the production can be considered as virtualized if we look at the SCADA based systems (Galloway & Hancke, 2012). The distribution can also be seen as virtualized in the case of software products delivery. This economic model is already in place and its adoption is continuously increasing because of lowering costs.

In the near future, the main problem will be the identification, classification and evaluation of performance and costs of cyberspace services. The importance of cyberspace services will increase (Peppard & Rylander, 2005). As a result, the implementation differences between the services produced in the real world and the virtual ones will disappear from the user's point of view. Human services, production services, business services and computing services are still treated separately. The business world demands more and more complex instruments for computer aided decision support (Sauter, 2011). The next step will be to find an integrated approach in presenting and using all services. The concept of service, no matter if it is virtual (e.g. Web service) or real (e.g. goods transportation or face-to-face), must be reviewed in the context of globalization and future cyber-infrastructure.

In the following sections, a new approach in designing and implementing demand driven services based on intelligent agents and service oriented architecture is presented. After analyzing the current meaning of terms, such as service, electronic service and demand driven Web services, several new approaches in solving their problems have emerged. The concept of demand driven Web service was enlarged to encompass the classical service providers. This was required by the accelerated integration of classic business models in the present information based society. Those traditional processes are still managed with various software solutions. Within this chapter, a simple solution based on open source approaches, such as LDAP, was proposed for service metadata indexing. A new concept of implementing intelligent agents, without a dedicated framework, is used for designing the concept of generalized demand driven Web services. In order to accomplish that, an architectural design pattern, used by IBM in developing service oriented architectures, was modified. The main idea is to recreate intelligent agents as a service composition. Finally, the conclusions and future work are presented, as well.

BACKGROUND

Competition pressure is continuously increasing due to the process of globalization, which determines all business involved actors to adopt the most efficient approaches. Any highly competitive environment proves that one of the key points in surviving is the ability to quickly adapt and react to any changes that appear within the market. As a result, in the last decades, the so called "agile" models of development have been adopted at various levels in their production and distribution chain (Karakostas & Kardaras, 2012). The business models have also begun to use this pattern. The demand driven paradigm is closely related to the agile models, and begins to be more and more important in the market. The business flow can be adapted, virtually in any point, according to the demands of the client. Changes can be made at the production level. Most of the goods production is automated. As a result, personalized services or demand driven services can be deployed if the customer accepts that; in some cases the price may substantially increase.

The term of electronic service is related to the concept of electronic commerce and emerged when companies began to use the Internet for interfacing with their customers. The first functional implementation of the concept was presented in 1979 by Michael Aldrich who used the TV and the telephone to sell goods on line. (Aldrich, 2011).

In Europe, the first implementation on a larger scale took place in France, in 1982 (OECD, 1999), when the national telephone company used this solution for on line payment.

After a larger adoption of the new IT related technologies, business models have begun to change to a degree that depend upon the adoption IT within companies. The emergence of corporations has made new concepts such as e-government and decision support system viable. Due to this process of changes in the business paradigm, new terms like electronic service have been created. In the USA, the first official adoption of such terms appeared in 2002 within the E-Government Act (USA Gov., 2002) where the term of electronic government services was used. The meaning was the same with the original term (service), but the implementation was done by using IT related technologies. This is probably the main reason to avoid defining the term of electronic service as a new concept. On the other hand, the term service is widely used in software engineering. As a result, confusion may appear between the two meanings.

Since Web services emerged and began to be directly fitted to the economic flows, the confusion seemed to diminish because it was the first time when the two meanings began to naturally emerge in the context of electronic business.

For example, the EU Commission accepts the idea that, due to the rapid changes in informational society, the definition for e-service may support continuous changes. Yet, there are some elements that are essential in defining the concept such as:

- The service is delivered using the Internet;
- The service is provided automatically or with minimal human intervention;
- The service is closely related to IT (Borec, 2012).

So, the current meaning of e-service may be: any type of classic service that can be offered only using IT available tools.

Due to the complexity of business economic flows, basic services were composed to deliver more complex ones. The idea is not new, only the implementation form differs. The transactional systems were the first distributed implementations of complex business flows.

The interaction between the common user and the society is increasing due to availability of the high band Internet and also due to the generalized use of mobile devices. As a result, the concept of electronically offered demand driven services has begun to be feasible.

There is a difference between what the user expects and what he/she might obtain. In most cases the changes apply to new service development, software service customization (Cummins, 2009). If money and time are not a problem, than almost anything can be done, if the provider limits permit. Those restrictions are looser for real life business service providers, and tighter for virtual service providers. Virtual service represents a real life business related service that was transferred into the cyberspace. In fact the associated business workflow is modeled. The problem is solved nowadays using SOA.

The main reason for the discrepancy between client expectations and what the market offers is that the user does not have a very good representation either of company workflows or the limitations of the virtual service provider. The problem is usually solved either by using a human consultant, or electronically, by presenting an interactive form that offers all the possible variations and terms of acquiring these features or modification to the initial structure of the service.

The concept of demand-driven services tries to rethink a way of using information infrastructure in terms of increasing its services dynamics until at least it reaches the demands of the business environment. There are some guidelines in designing a demand-driven service system (Mosher, Helmbock, Hogan, McCarthy, & O'Mara, 2006). The first procedure regards the demand control by trying to educate internal and external customers. This also refers to the ability of handling automated workflow systems, and the need to explain what can be done in the informational system. Then, a diversified offer of services for the same demand is required in order to improve quality and decrease the client's costs. If typical business flows are analyzed, it can be observed that they are basically unchanged. As a result, the continuous changes, which also must be applied to IT services of the business model can be easily followed if fine grain architecture is used for the service system. So, increasing the number of service based tiers in the multilayer multitier approach is required.

If ERP related demand-driven services are analyzed, it can be concluded that most of the software companies' efforts are related to dedicated software products that support this feature (Agarwal, Kenkre, Pandit, & Sengupta, 2011; Ross, 2011). A customer-centric approach is needed because it helps the client to decrease their internal costs. So implementing a demand driven solution will be an asset for the organization (Mosher, Helmbock, Hogan, McCarthy, & O'Mara, 2006).

A NEW APPROACH IN DEMAND DRIVEN WEB SERVICES

The new economical paradigm (of an information based society) is usually adopted superficially, but it is quickly adjusted according to the local culture (Weissenberger-Eibl & Spieth, 2006). As a consequence, in many cases the economic efficiency may decrease in comparison with the previously adopted economical models. The social memory needs at least two generations in order to partially acquire the new concepts (Anastasio, Ehrenberger, Watson, & Zhang, 2012). Within a democratic society, reliable assistance is provided to people while implementing the change. Unfortunately, using only human resources is not economically feasible. This leaves only one possibility: to use complex information systems that will provide people with assistance and training. At the same time, these systems will provide additional functionality to the society. So, the increase of IT adoption at the business workflow level will not only escalate the economic efficiency of the business itself, but will also help the society to quickly adopt, on every level, new economic models. To obtain this, the concept of demand driven service must be extended.

So, the time has come for integrating virtual and real business services (traditional ones) under a unique presentation. In this context a new form of demand-driven service will appear. It can be named *generalized demand driven Web services* (GDDWS). This is because the presentation and the combination using the producer to consumer (P2C) approach of those services will be made from the Internet by using distributed applications. Another synonym may be a *generalized demand driven service,* if we analyze the problem from an economic point of view, because the instrument for implementing this concept can be neglected. Cyberspace related terminology it can be also named *cyber-production services.*

Let us clarify the meaning of *provided services* and *service provider* in the context of the newly proposed approach. There are two types of services: virtual (computing related services) and real (an entity from real life). In the case of real services an electronic representation will be created. The *service provider* may be any person that is able to perform a well-defined job or set of jobs according to a standard classification. Another situation is when the service provider is represented by a small business. Another set of service providers can be represented by medium and large businesses, transnational corporations and public administration systems.

Provided services are the traditional ones but with a supplementary software layer. This plays the role of an adapter so it hides the various differences as much as possible.

To integrate the human service provider (freelancer) in the proposed system some steps are needed. First, a search of the existing human providers who have information about their offered services on the Web must be made. Here there are two distinct possibilities. One is to use the semantic Web approach in combination with natural language processing, in order to retrieve the desired information from the Internet. This approach is not so feasible due to the great dispersion of data type and coding.

The other way (that is most efficient) is to use a dedicated agent that crawls through the Internet (Şah & Wade, 2012). The agent will retrieve a minimal metadata, basic information about service providers, like address, contact information, especially electronic if possible, and the type of service. Each agent will have its electronic certificate that will uniquely identify its owner. This is required for security reasons, but also because some time the agent will pay for some used services. Another possibility is to use external search providers.

In the second stage of the process, an electronic form will be presented directly, by using an agent, if possible, or by e-mail. This will guarantee that an efficient catalogue of all service providers can be created. If a small business provides the services, the approach used for a freelancer can also be implemented. For rest of cases the agent will perform some information retrieval procedures over the company's Web site and will generate the first metadata. In most situations, prices of the services are not available on the Web. For these situations a dedicated application must be deployed in order to create a secure communication channel with the system and retrieve the cost related information needed to properly maintain updated information about the business.

Obtaining a common presentation for any type of service is still difficult. Contracts like Web Services Description Language (WSDL) are not yet able to capture the diversity of information required to use a service. This refers especially to handling failures and certain legal aspects. There are other approaches, like Electronic Business using eXtensible Markup Language (EBXML) that try to offer an open infrastructure (Quin, 2012). There is also the universal description, discovery and integration (UDDI) specification that is very complex. An extension of UDDI (UDDIe) was created and incorporates service leasing and replication (ShaikhAli, Rana, Al-Ali, & Walker, 2003). So, the additional information about the real users is easily integrated in any required standard.

Another problem is related to the fact that the response time needed to process a request may vary due to the distributed nature of many transactions (Daigneau, 2011). But these are common problems of distributed systems and can be solved in time, with some additional costs.

SERVICE BASED INTELLIGENT AGENTS (SBIA)

The problem of creating a common representation for the service is also related to covering the differences of the heterogeneous system that is created over the Internet. Connecting various information systems is a complex but common task nowadays. The database federating systems have already solved this problem (Hsiao, 1992). There are differences between the closed system solutions and the Internet based one in terms of control distribution and increased security risks.

The semantic Web may offer some solutions (Fabian, Kunz, Konnegen, MüLler, & GüNther, 2012) but, in most cases, they are too complicated. One possibility in using semantic Web and also making a quick integration into a real distributed environment is to use intelligent agents. This approach was used in a primitive form when the first database federating systems were created. Efficient models that use the experience from semantic Web, federated systems and intelligent agents have already been proposed (Thomas, Yoon, & Redmond, 2009).

There are many agent based frameworks (Weiss, 2013) that cover all the possible uses of agents. Yet, the rate of software industry adoption is slower. There are some frameworks like JACK (Howden, Rönnquist, Hodgson, & Lucas, 2001) in the software industry or Retsina (Paolucci,

Shehory, Sycara, Kalp, & A., 2000) for Internet searches that prove that the adoption is possible. The need to use agents in industry is a reality (Almeida, Terra, Dias, & Gonçalves, 2010). Their applications in cyberspace is virtually endless. In the manufacturing industry, the holonic systems are already in place (Botti & Boggino, 2008). So, the use of agents based framework is at the stage of a dedicated solution for specific situations. But this is not the full potential of the approach. It can be widely used in cyberspace, with or without the collaboration of humans.

The use of intelligent agents in industry is limited. That is because they are partially standardized, the frameworks are not yet very scalable and they present significant security risks (Ugurlu & Erdogan, 2005). Other reasons are related to the need for a dedicated execution environment, and to the complexity of programming that requires highly qualified people.

The potential of this approach is still very important. In order to solve the security risks, the most common solution will be to use the existing public key infrastructure (PKI) (Aye, et al., 2013). This may solve the problem of a unique identification user interface agent and can act in its owner's name even by making payments for some services. Unfortunately, the remaining problem concerns the code of the agent that must be executed on the host machine. The source code certification is unfeasible from an economical point of view (Contos, Hunt, & Derodeff, 2007).

So, a new approach in designing intelligent agents systems must be adopted in order to use their potential in the future cyberspace. There are two possible solutions for executing the foreign code into a host computer. One is to virtualize it into a secure environment that gives access only to the needed computing resources, and guarantees good isolation from the user data (Payer & Gross, 2011). This method is already used by several Internet security solutions available on the market like Comodo (Comodo Group, 2013) or Avast (Avast, 2013).

In most cases, when an agent arrives into a new host, it will need various information about the local machine or about the surrounding environment. The modern approach is to access dedicated services. If the service oriented architectures (SOA) seem to represent the immediate future of the Internet (Sun, Dong, & Yearwood, 2011) then a paradigm shift in designing intelligent agents support or frameworks is needed. The other approach is to eliminate framework dependency by creating an agent as an independent service.

In the traditional artificial intelligence approach, the intelligent agent is seen as an entity that performs the following tasks (Weiss, 2000):

- Gathers information about the nearby environment using some form of sensors.
- Uses some reasoning procedures in order to analyze the existent and newly acquired information about the environment, and it finally decides if some actions must be taken or not in accordance with its goals.
- Can act in various manners using some effectors to induce changes at the environment level or to produce new data.

As a result, some basic mechanisms used in agent development can be identified (Weiss, 2013):

- **Persistence:** The agent may have a generic adaptor to common types of persistence systems.
- **Communication:** The agent will have the possibility of initiating any number of bidirectional communication channels, without concerns related to security and other aspects of quality of service.
- **Computing:** The agent will use either the local available computing services, or the cloud based services where any demand can be satisfied with a reasonable price.
- **Translators:** Various translator services are available to be used when the agent must interface with any desired entity.

- **Reasoning:** Various services of inference engines that can be used to execute the reasoning programs of the agents.
- **Effectors:** Various services that will solve certain problems for the agent.
- **Mobile:** The agent will be created or recreated at its destination.
- **Autonomous:** The degree of autonomy will depend on the creator's needs.

Each of these mechanisms may be found as services in the open systems or in the closed corporate systems. There is a problem related only to agent creation. The agent maker service must be able to analyze multiple charts and abstractions that define the agent. A feasible approach is to use Unified Modeling Language (UML) and use case analysis in agent description with the help of a tool (Bauer & Odell, 2005). This allows the designer to fully concentrate on the agents' roles and actions, without knowing too much about the details needed to make functional agents. In the beginning, a scripting based approach will be used. This is suitable due to high granularity of the problem. The number of mechanisms used to create an agent is small and their interactions are clear.

In Figure 1 the life cycle of the agent is presented. This is a typical agent cycle (FIPA, 2000) with some details needed due to service implementation. The system will provide two repositories: one for the service code and the other for service knowledge. There are three classes of agents. There is a standard implementation of the agent that comes with the system, such as the library. The user can write his/hers own agents or they can be demand driven generated. Finally, there are the agents that temporarily come into the system to solve some jobs.

If the agents are standard they will use the code from the library but they may come with their own knowledge. In the other case their code will also come from outside the system and will be stored in the external code section too. If the

Figure 1. Agent as service life cycle

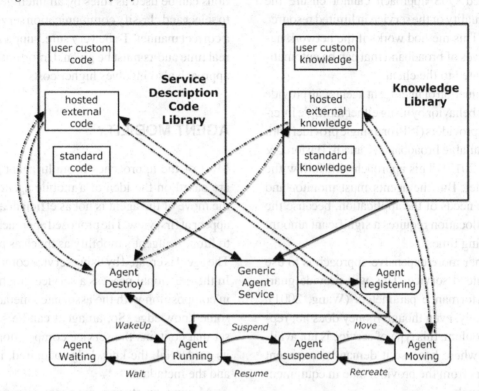

user or the system decides that some of the visiting agents are interested, a separate negotiation must be conducted to see if a fair price can be obtained from the user or the system that owns the agents in question. Any intelligent agent uses some knowledge that can be inherited or gathered during its life. It will be the system or the agent's decision if their knowledge must be stored temporarily or permanently in the knowledge library.

Some clarifications regarding agent moving are depicted in Figure 1. The agent is not frozen during the current operation phase. Instead, the agent is suspended and then destroyed on its current location. Before suspending it, a snapshot of its current code and knowledge is made. A special request with the agent owner's credential is sent to the destination system. The request encloses the agent code, knowledge and a request for new agent creation. The rest of the agent states are traditional.

In the case of agent waiting state, if the agent implementation uses only asynchronous procedure calls and multithreaded design, then this state can be ignored because only portions of the agent will really wait.

In the case of the demand driven agent implementation this cycle will be completed with the states presented by Sun (Sun, Finnie, & Yearwood, 2010).

AGENT COMMUNICATION

From communication networks point of view the concept of demand driven service had been implemented using differentiated services (DS), the traffic being divided into a small number of groups called forwarding classes (Kulkarni, Nazeeruddin, & McClean, 2006). Unfortunately, it seems that this approach (Wang, 2001) or any personalized QoS approach cannot ensure the expected quality of the service in limited resource networks. This method works if the network has large reserves of broadband that can be automatically allocated to the client.

A combination of intelligent agents can provide this type of behavior by using either multiple Internet service providers (ISP) or a single provider with enough available broadband (Canadi, Barford, & Sommers, 2012). This approach will follow the cloud model. But the agents must monitor and predict the needs of the application, because the resource allocation requires a significant amount of computing time.

The other more expensive approach is to use the guaranteed service. This will provide guaranteed performance parameters (Wang, 2001). Unfortunately, even though money does not represent a problem, this type of service is not available everywhere because it demands consistent investments from the provider side in equipment and personnel.

In the Internet, communication services may also encounter problems even when the guaranteed services are selected. This is due to the fact that peer-to-peer (P2P) applications emerge. When a P2P sub-network is created, all the initial estimations regarding network throughput, data flood dimension and magnitudes of the network designers prove to be underestimated. In most cases, common users of an ISP share a common communication channel. So, this unexpected imbalance (sudden uplink high demands during a long period of time) can drive to large variations in QoS.

The P2P traffic is difficult to be detected due to its unpredictable nature, when the design of communication network is made (Barreiros & Lundqvist, 2011). As a result, only a dedicated physical communication channel can assure good performance. The other possibility is to over design the communication network, but the cost is higher compared to the previous solution. These observations can be used as rules by an intelligent agent to select and classify communication services into a correct manner. To be very sure, supplementary real time audits must be given. Unfortunately this approach also involves higher costs.

AGENT MOBILITY

Most of the approaches in multi agent systems are based on the idea of a mobile agent. In fact the move of the agent is not as efficient as it may appear at first view. The proposed approach prefers to limit the agent's mobility as much as possible. The agent is created by using service composition. In the creational process a service graph is used in composition with the associated metadata and some knowledge. So, an agent can be seen as a set that contains the service composition graph, its credential, the knowledge acquired, if exists, and the metadata.

Moving or storing an agent is resumed to handling the required agent description set. In order to move an agent, a lot of parameters must be analyzed. This is necessary because otherwise, at the global level, there will be too many agents that will permanently move. This may drive the system to have local bottlenecks at the computing and at the communication level. The agents will eventually escape from the bottlenecked zone but in terms of availability their activity will come too late for the other agents involved in the process.

The decision of moving or not moving a newly created agent or an existent one may depend on the following aspects:

- The localization of most available needed services. If there are no available services within a small neighborhood, the decision may be to move the agent to the next location that fulfills this requirement.
- A good QoS of nearby or needed communication channels.

- Available computing power. It may be neglected if a cloud service is chosen for computational tasks.
- Data to be processed may be available locally or not.
- The total costs for the agent's execution must be reasonable.
- Other supplementary user requests.

There is the possibility of automatic relocation or letting the user choose the algorithm or the set of rules used in the moving decision.

Agent collaboration will be accomplished by the use of communication services, and any translation between various standards can be made by using the proper translation services. The problem that remains is choosing the best communication service in accordance with user's basic specifications. For instance, either cost, or execution speed may be alternatively selected as the dominant optimum factor in service selection.

In terms of agent reasoning the proposed solution has the great advantage that the inference engine service is selected in accordance with its creator needs. Because the classic AI algorithms also have an open source version, the composition of some basic behavior instructions is possible.

Since autonomy is related to the degree of freedom in moving and in decisional acts (Nguyen, Perini, Tonella, Miles, Harman, & Luck, 2009) the degree of an agent's autonomy will depend on its primary role in the system. The availability of a service also refers to the instantaneous server load, so new requests must be rejected when a high load is encountered. This approach must be used even when the server is located into a cloud, because there is a delay between the new resource demand and the cloud answer.

TRUST OF SERVICE

If the agent is implemented as a service, there is a problem of trust. Trust is related to the security evaluation that the agent must perform before using the services offered by another agent. It can be defined as a measurable level of risk (Gambetta, 2000).

An efficient trust model is one that is dynamically updated with external information. The problem is not really solved because a question appears: what is the trust that can be attributed to the entity that provides information concerning the reputation of something? The PKI breaks this logical cycle by introducing the concept of a third party that provides trust, commonly known as certification authority (CA) (Coronado-Garcia & Perez-Leguizamo, 2011).

From the point of view of the current approach, it is enough to impose the use of digital certificates within any interaction to solve the problem of trust. In uncertain cases when not all the used services have a well-known reputation, trust can be computed as a simple probability analysis. That can be computed over the tree created from the trust of component services in order to compute the trust for newly created service. This approach works for both types of services: real and virtual.

The case of the human trust problems are different through. Real life situations are sometimes more illogical that may be expected. This is due to the fact that human behavior is only partially predictable. For example, the stock exchange panics based on an injection of false information, which proves that the business environment can easily be destabilized. The system must have a predictable behavior from a businessman's point of view. As a result the systems that will support GDDWS must also use the trust evaluation techniques based on peer opinion in order to avoid rejection from their business related users.

Due to the complexity of human relations, the trust and reputation of the same individual can be very different depending on the group level where the analysis is done. As a consequence, various models for measuring these parameters have emerged. Three types of trust models are proposed: basic, general and situational (Marsh,

1994). The basic trust model uses the previous experience of the agent. The general trust model refers to the trust between two agents, and the situational trust model is related to a trust that depends on the specific situation.

The trust for a service is also related to incident handling. In this case a classification system that indicates the importance of the event may be used. This can be computed by using some special tables that contain information related to the impact that service failures may have over the business and also the urgency of solving the incident (Taylor, 2012).

USER SATISFACTION

This is a very complicated issue because human users have an irrational component that influences their decisions. As a result, a mean of the responses of human users will represent good approximation. More sophisticated methods such as fuzzy operators may be used, but in this case it is not clear if the computing effort is justified. A short set of service parameters must be evaluated by using closed ended questions. Usually, three to five possible answers to every question will give a good separation of the answers. This kind of analysis may be conducted only if the final destination of a service in the graph is a human user.

Because a complex service may include in its components multiple sub-domains of services, an assessment of user satisfaction should be conducted within each of the sub-domains if possible. For example, if the user buys something from an electronic market, the minimum test will demand answers on: transportation costs, speed and quality, product description, presentation and also about the seller's behavior, if a human seller has been also involved.

The evaluation at the composing services level can be obtained without performing it explicitly all the time. This will speed up the system without ignoring user satisfaction. If a Web service is running, user satisfaction can be neglected because the evaluation of trust will embed some quality evaluation parameters. The trust factor must also be computed if a human user is at the other end of the line.

REPUTATION

The reputation refers to the information received from third parties by agents regarding the behavior of their partners (Buskens, 1995). The definition does not specify how reputation is quantified. There are two possibilities for evaluating service reputation. One is to use an anonymous evaluation. The method seems to be better but, unfortunately, it has a weak point. A campaign of disinformation can easily be conducted. The other possibility is to use well known service providers. This may be more susceptible of control, but being known gives them a reputation factor that can be easily decreased. A classic example refers to the Standard and Poor's problems of credibility that appears when all the market players begin to criticize their evaluations (Jaffe & Shine, 2011).

These service providers can be chosen by using a third party reputation provider like in the PKI approach, but the demands will be so great, that it is possible for this to be economically unfeasible. As a result, a mixed solution should be chosen. To create the reputation market, some general accepted providers must be used. For anything else, local providers will be selected. They may be certified by a general entity but after that, they control, at the local level, the problem of service reputation. Finally the agent may combine its own reputation rating with one that is received from the local or general provider.

Any service, real or virtual, should have one or more reputation fields that may be automatically filled by the system/user that consumes it, after each use of the service. These fields will represent customer satisfaction, service profitability, service revenue, service support and cost (Dutta & Pinder, 2011). This approach will guarantee transparent QoS computing.

USING SBIA IN SOA

Using automated paid services in business consultancy that is offered by decision support systems (DSS) can open new possibilities for anyone who wants to do business. This type of system is usually available only in transnational corporations or governmental structures. Most of the complex software products have the stage of private use followed in time by the public availability of the product in the lifecycle. So, in the next decade there are chances that these types of systems will operate with lower costs, affordable to the general public. This will give a boost to the local economy, but it will also help in overlapping the national and organizational cultural differences that still raise problems in economic collaboration.

Another service provided by SOA based applications may include offering automated insurance. In the automatic evaluation of insurance risk and its associated costs, the protocols are already functional and, in most situations, an AI based service is used to estimate them. A strong resistance before the large adoption of automated insurance is expected to appear on the market because the service virtualization will decrease the number of jobs for the people in the insurance field. But when more and more services will be provided by using cyberspace automated insurance will be the only rational step because it is already a part of the current business model.

In Figure 2 the general case of SOA based service for GDDWS's life cycle is presented. As it can be seen each problem is first analyzed from the domain's point of view. The IBM business modeling process can be used at various levels of analysis (Ng, Fung, Chan, & Mak, 2010). Then the

needed services are searched. In case of multiple offerings some selection rules will be used. After that the service is planned and its QoS is established. Then the service model must be approved. This can be made automatically for simple jobs and manually for very complex problems. Then the service will enter in a phase of development and testing. Finally the service will be published and added to the repository (see Figure 1). The demand driven part is activated only when an existent service demands some adjustments to fit to the user's request. Otherwise it is more efficient to reconstruct the service from scratch. This last decision can be changed if the costs of creating a new service are higher than those generated by creating a demand driven one.

As it can be seen in Figure 2, there are some branches that appear to be incorrectly handled. This is due to the complexity of the presented problem. Most of business software use the transactional model governed by the ACID set of rules (Haerder & Reuter, 1983). Due to the inherent specifics of a business transaction, it may be recursively composed from other transactions. When the main transaction that encompasses all internal transactions, is aborted, each internal transaction must also be aborted and the system must be restored to its original state. The same approach will be used in the generation of a GDDWS. Because the system was designed to also support mobile nodes, the implementation of transactional support must be based on a journalized execution approach. In this case, the main computing effort will be done at the level of service provider computing infrastructure, without significant overload at the node level. In Figure 2 the subset of operations marked with dotted lines will be considered as an atomic operation so any failure will be automatically handled. The whole system must be designed having the transactional approach in mind.

A generic SOA for demand driven services has the following actors: brokers, requestors and

Figure 2. GDDWS SOA service life cycle

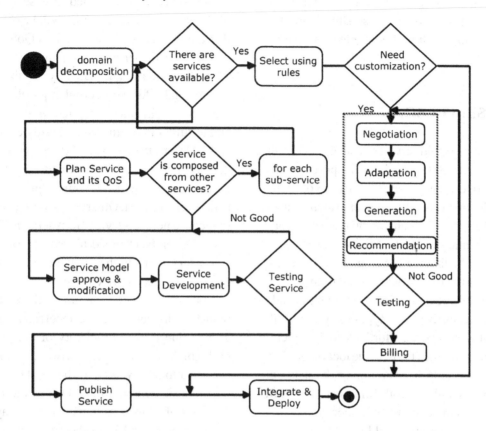

providers. Their interactions are similar with the ones from real life business (Sun, Dong, & Yearwood, 2011).

THE DESIGN OF A SBIA SOA BASED SYSTEM

The creation of distributed applications has become nowadays easier than in the past. There are design patterns, meta-programming models and visual tools that help in designing and implementing good and reliable applications (Pautasso & Alonso, 2005).

Systems that are so complex like the ones oriented in managing business workflows need a systematic approach in design. As a result, on each level of the architecture, a software architect will use various types of architectural model and

design patterns. In the case of the proposed system a composition between the standard multi-layer multi-tier model and a design pattern oriented on the SOA specificity will be used. To be more precise, the basic design pattern used is the integrator pattern that is presented in Table 1 (Arsanjani, Zhang, Ellis, Allam, & Channabasavaiah, 2007) with some modifications.

Table 1. Architectural design of the proposed SBIA system

Presentation Layer		
Business Process Choreography	Architecture Integrator	Business Performance Management
Services/Business Layer		
[Enterprise Components]		
Persistence Related Systems		

© 2007 IBM. Used with permission.

This system was designed for small and medium enterprises. As a result, the effort of deploying a GDDWS into a small or medium company will be acceptable.

The design using service based intelligent agents will provide two advantages.

One advantage consists in using a design similar to the one of Java beans technologies. The agents will be created, and they will provide customizable parts not only in terms of template view (if the implicit ones are not enough), but also in terms of business logic where supplementary computations required by the client can easily be deployed. The rest of needed operations can be done by describing in a graphical manner (if needed) the required service composition. This can be done either from scratch, or by customizing a generic business flow that is already provided using a library.

The other advantage is cost related in terms of the needed computing infrastructure. The economic model is similar to the one used in the cloud approach. It is unfeasible for a small or medium enterprise to create or buy and deploy the complex software and hardware systems required to implement an SOA, but it will be feasible to buy these services from a third party. This will give a great advantage in terms of cost efficiency, because the involved costs will fit with the current needs of the company without having the supplementary costs related to maintaining and developing the main software and hardware infrastructure.

It is difficult to briefly present the details regarding the complexity of the new proposed application, because this will require the presentation and detailed analyses at the level of a complex multi-layer, multi-tier application. To further clarify the concept, each layer and tier, even if it is seen as a black box, will require a clear specification at the interface level with the rest of system's components at least by the use of design patterns, but this is not the aim of this chapter.

In the following paragraphs we will discuss about each layer of the system architecture of the SBIA by presenting its functionality and the proposed solution.

The Presentation Layer

It represents the interface between the client and the system's layer. Due to its nature, the language, graphical or not, used to interact with users is business oriented in most cases. Access, interaction, process choreography, business function service, common service and information management services are all accessible from here (Zimmermann, Doubrovski, Grundler, & Hogg, 2005).

The proposed approach has a higher level of generality. In the presentation layer there is an interface agent that can have general or personalized use. With the map of user choices and abstract factory design pattern, the presentation agent can choose the needed form of graphic and text representation in accordance with the type of originating device of the agent (Ahmadi & Kong, 2012).

In terms of visual service composition tools, the research has just begun. The technologies used in service development have encouraged their own different models on the market. Probably the most important problem in developing a visual tool useful in performing an activity is the need for standardizing the visual language. Nowadays each business school or company that produces related software solutions tries to use its own visual language when it comes to describing the business workflows. Most of the languages have consistent similarities. So, the process of adopting a common solution will be easy. The new language must encompass the specific symbols for business workflow (Arlbjern & Haug, 2010) but also higher class symbols and representations specific to data mining (Vercellis, 2009) or to information retrieval (Büttcher, Clarke, & Cormack, 2010). Visual language components are already being used in IT governance (Marks, 2008).

All related visual languages or collections have entities that begin with executive staff related representations and finish with detailed operators and actors specific to basic workflows. This is due to the manner in which business is conducted. Each staff layer will have its own image about the organization and it will also have proper visual representation. The variety of the used representations may represent a problem because, in most cases, it represents different points of view over the same issue. As an example, we have the feature tree (Taylor, 2012) or the traceability matrix or the organizational charts. The most probable approach is to adopt all these solutions at the highest layer of representation, but to use common representations when middle or lower levels in the organization are defined.

Using SOA will become the dominant solution because the complexity and the dimension of relations needed to do business will continuously increase at middle and top management levels (Mathis & Jackson, 2009; Anthony, 1965). The decision will be actively assisted by intelligent agents that will help the user when working with the system. Measuring the individual or departmental efficiency will also be improved by the use of the software instruments.

The user designs a business workflow and demands an analysis from the system of intelligent agents. Then the system will search for the needed services. The required service set may include human services, integrated production facilities; places to buy some components, transport and anything else that is required. Then the system will evaluate what is available and will present more options to the user.

In the background, complex analyses related to various performance factors will be made. The user will accept or modify the business flow and the process is repeated. The user will activate the business using the automatic composition or will have all the information needed to proceed to the manual activation of the business flow.

Business Process Choreography

In this layer various types of choreographer services are implemented. The selected service choreographer (business modeling language) will create a particular operation that is checked. Then, the final destination of the internal or external service is accessed.

Service Composition

The main application of service composition refers (Blake, Cummings, Bansal, & Bansal, 2012) to the economic activities. There are a number of approaches regarding the service composition problem. Most of them are based on various applications of AI (Sun, Finnie, & Yearwood, 2010). Usually, the most widely known solutions are proposed by the top companies with a large amount of experience in business related applications. Each company tries to persuade the market to adopt its vision on the subject. Due to the large distribution of the solutions available in the market it is hard to say that a unique standard will be soon adopted. Anyhow, this is necessary because the lack of standards is another difficulty in creating the common cyberspace economic layer, which is the next logical step in developing information based societies (Luo, Li, Liu, Zheng, & Dong, 2010).

The most used solutions for service composition are based on Business Process Execution Language (BPEL) or its variants, such as Business Process Execution Language for Web Services (BPEL4WS). The Microsoft Corporation uses a global approach called the Enterprise Service Bus (ESB). This is very efficient in the corporatist well controlled and designed computing environment, but it may encounter problems in other contexts. The proposed system must have dedicated interfaces needed to accept any existent provider in the market. The services can be created manually or automatically. Usually the automatic solution can be better used in situations where the manner of problem solving doesn't change too quickly. In the situations when custom combinations are required interventions from the human operator are needed. The magnitude of this involvement depends on the accumulated experience in solving the problem.

Artificial intelligence can be useful in assisting human decision as much as possible (Medjahed & Bouguettaya, 2011). The demand driven services must be offered to users directly according to their specific needs. The main problem is that creating a new service driven by demand or not, may require the adaptation of the existing services. The feature to dynamically create new services during automatic creation time is required. This will imply different costs for each newly created service in accordance with the supplementary costs induced by the services that compose it. This is the reason a dedicated pay per service type is needed. The existing infrastructure can handle this method. Due to the unique certification of the agent, these payments can be issued on the user's name. In closed environments the problem of price can appear only if outside services are required.

Because the service presentation and metadata are not globally standardized the researchers were forced to come with highly complicated approaches that try to handle the large variation of input parameters. In most of the cases various AI related techniques are used (Rao & Su, 2005).

In the proposed SBIA the dynamic or static creation of a new service such as service composition is based on a task graph (Fujii & Suda, 2005). It will be recursively decomposed until a service composition graph emerges. To create a service graph, it is enough to use several patterns that describe how a task can be created using standards or demand driven services. The rest of the constraints in the service selection have already been done in the basic service selection phase. So, after the graph validation, one or more translator services will be used in order to obtain the service graph. The translator services will

check the input and output compatibility with the pre- and post-services before inserting a service in the graph. If some small mismatches are found in the service description, then a request for a demand driven service is issued to the system. Otherwise, the search for the service is extended at global levels by the agents used in the process. Due to the use of an interface agent, the SBIA will learn in time the ways and needs of the user, so the degree of automation in the business flow creation will be increased.

When a credit approval process is needed, the system's SBIA will take some steps. The final product will be an agent that will search for the best offer from the market using the user rules and then will automatically create the credit form that is accepted by the selected bank. The needed base services will be as follows:

- **An Inference Engine:** Used to process the user rules.
- **A Crawler Service:** Used to retrieve the existing credit offers from the Internet.
- **A Translator Service:** Needed for various forms of interpretation both to read or to write depending on the case.
- **And Persistence Service:** To store all temporary produced data, and eventually, if the user decides not to destroy everything, the agent after its job completion.
- **A Communication Service:** That will use the user's credential to pay for the communication if it is required.
- **A Human Computer Interface:** This will increase the number of users from various social layers.

In these conditions the agent will have the ability to fulfill its goals. Unfortunately a common user will not have the knowledge to create something like that from a scratch. Instead, the user can buy a demand driven service from the market. In this case the base service will have all the previously mentioned abilities, and the user will remain to make modifications only in the set of rules of the agent. This approach will give common people access to complex business instruments by hiding all the processes that do not concern them.

Service Publishing

There are many already adopted standards or in the early stages of adoption regarding publishing the service on the Internet. The idea of self-discoverable services is not new and it was developed in close relation with improving the e-commerce paradigm (McGovern, Tyagi, Stevens, & Mathew, 2003). Some authors are centered on refining protocols that increase the efficiency of cooperation among different services (Denaro, Pezze, Tosi, & Schilling, 2006). Most approaches are related to the particular optimization of services based infrastructure depending on the problem type (Daigneau, 2011). The problem is very important because the user must know that a service exists in order to see if it is useful or not for his/her needs. All proposed solutions have various approaches, but they are based on the need:

- To be compatible with business specifications.
- To be easily found on the Internet.
- To have a well-defined manner of structuring the information.

All the approaches based on SOA use a service broker to maintain a list of the available services. When a service is created it must be published in that list. The solutions used to implement those systems may vary from fully distributed approaches to fully centralized ones. There is not enough information to choose the best market approach. This complexity is probably due to the business pressure, which sometimes disregards simpler approaches because of the inherent limitation to business flow. In most cases the solution is selected according to the already existing software ecosystem.

In fact, there is a normal but extremely complex database with information about services that must be available on the Internet as fast and as widely as possible. Most implementations neglect the fact that the number of new types of service creations per time unit is smaller than the number of searches in the database. As a result, the classical approach that offers the same speed in database read or write operations is not mandatory (Losee & Church, 2004).

Indexing in global distributed applications may become a real problem. There is a functional example of unique worldwide indexing on the market. This is the International Standard Book Number - ISBN. The system is implemented using a directory approach, but the information updating is slow and under human control in initial processing stages. So, a directory based approach may work. Unfortunately the UDDI proposal was partially rejected by the market so other solutions must be analyzed (SAP, 2005). Lightweight Directory Access Protocol (LDAP) is also a database, but not a relational one (Sermersheim, 2006). Keeping information organized in directories offers a solution that provides high performance in reading information but with the cost of slow writes. This is exactly the situation of using the service broker database. Implementing this solution may present a series of advantages like portability. A solution can be based on an open source approach or, if it is needed, a database management system (DBMS) with a LDAP interface can be used. The last approach is not suitable for the proposed solution. Because the LDAP supports PKI, no supplementary security measures are needed in most cases. If the scalability seems to be a problem products that solve all the related problems are already in the market (Radware, 2012).

The metadata of a service must contain the already classical standardized information, but also the service availability, trust, reputation, user satisfaction, communication network QoS, number of hopes, channel availability, the communication channel cost, the time to complete as well the insurance cost. Because a cyber-service is a piece of business insurance, it is required (Dong & Tomlin, 2012). It can be global or per service type.

There are many business related ontologies nowadays on the market. As we have previously argued, the maturity has not yet been achieved in this area. The main reasons are related to the high complexity of the ontologies, lack of standardization at the global level and to the fact that most of them are property of the corporations that develop them in close relationship with their proprietary complex software solutions. The main problem is not related to choosing the ontology but to finding a unitary and quick manner of making it available to all the partners in the business process. Due to the importance of this issue, standardization of the ontology must be done between proprietary solutions and the open source ones. In this context, the proposed use of a system that is derived from LDAP for indexing all metadata specific to business flow can provide a cheap and independent solution in the market.

Service Selection

In the proposed solution the general architecture structure remains unchanged, but the degree of distribution is significantly increased. In fact, a temporary assembly of services may be created in order to analyze the offer at a global level. The service selection is based on the efficiency and supplementary user rules.

A distributed approach must be used. Service selection can be defined or maintained by a dedicated agent. It can be located at the host or at the cluster level. If the node and its vicinity have enough available computing power, and if the needed services are available the agent can be deployed. Then it is recommended that each agent tries to define its neighborhood. Otherwise it sends out requests to the dedicated agent in order

to define its vicinity. The vicinity will enclose nearby systems that can provide the agent with what it needs.

Working with a static defined neighborhood may appear a better solution due to its simplicity. Unfortunately, it can be used under a very restrictive set of assumptions that will maintain the possible set of nodes, from where a selection is done, restricted at a LAN level. The reason is that only at this level can the behavior of servers be predictable (Hamburg & Zaharia, 2000) and also a high quality communication network is guaranteed. This can be accomplished where there is a unique control of the computing environment, such as a corporate LAN. This approach is not feasible when any available service on the Internet is chosen. In this case, the neighborhood is dynamically defined as a function of a series of factors, such as: the overload of some systems, the number of hop, the availability and performances of the communication channel and the communication costs.

The service search will be done in a distributed fashion. When the agent has just arrived into a place it has two options. One is to assume a broker's role, if this is not found. The other possibility is to look for the broker outside its vicinity. If one or more agents are found, than the agent may choose to interrogate them or the broker in order to retrieve a list of available services. If the agent does not find any required service then the agent must move to another location. Before doing that, it will try to look for other agents located in possible destination places and ask them information about their local environments.

The agent will try to solve its task at the place of creation. Migration is decided only if most of the required services are in other places with slow or unreliable communication channels. For instance a job may be initiated from the mobile phone, and it will migrate at the personal or external cloud level where it is executed. After the agent gets the locations of needed services a supplementary choice is made. In a closed corporatist environment, this is not needed because the agent will have access to resources in accordance with its credentials, and the QoS infrastructure is very good. Unfortunately, into an open system with multiple offers, some selection must be done. If we have a number of providers that offer the same needed solution, a cost based function will be computed to properly select the best of them. In the computing process some supplementary factors, as reputation, are taken into account.

There are some parameters of services that must be analyzed, such as service availability, trust, reputation, user satisfaction, communication network, QoS, number of hop, channel availability, the communication channel costs, the time to complete and the insurance costs.

The best way to select services is to use a multi-criteria algorithm (Skroch, 2010). This is always a complex task. Unfortunately, in most of cases, a user has no experience in prioritizing the parameters that are taken into account in selecting the proper service. Because most of the parameters are also obtained as estimations, a method that provides a good estimation is needed instead of one that will use high precision calculus. Using fuzzy based multi-criteria selection will be a good idea. The DEMATEL method is usually suitable when it comes to resolving a group decision-making problem. Fuzzy Integral and Gray Relation may also be a proper approach (Tzeng & Huang, 2011).

Services/Business Layer

In this case the semantic layer is presented using various forms of basic services. Here are various rule engines, complex look tables, workflow integration, utility business service, service level automation, and resource virtualization which have been implemented. Also it is the level where general operations like credit authorization, queries and reservations are executed.

Yet semantic service oriented architectures (SSOA) are difficult to use because of their in-

credible complexity (Oberle, Barros, Kylau, & Heinzl, 2013). The main reason is the insufficient standardization at the service level, especially at the presentation one. The semantic Web has tried to solve the problem during the last decades. But the complexity of the proposed solutions still makes it unfeasible for large scale adoption. In federated information systems the problems are solved using complex scripts and pieces of software (Betz, 2007). One of the approaches that may prove feasible in the semantic Web field is using intelligent agents.

SSOA includes as its main actors: the SSOA components, the stakeholders, the semantic modeling and Web service providers (Vitvar, 2007; Vitvar, Zaremba, Moran, & Mocan, 2008). This approach has the disadvantage of installing the most parts of the needed infrastructure on the same computing node.

The SSOA component model (Moran, 2011) is used in this proposal. Each component may also be decomposed by using the same approach. This will continue recursively until the lower layer services, which are implemented or are easy to be implemented, are reached. This makes the approach reliable. The medium granularity of the solution offers enough flexibility, but also the ability to use automated tools in order to quickly compose and create any demand driven service that is needed. Implementation must be asynchronous in order to assure good fault tolerance to communication failures. Also, a design based on an event driven paradigm is recommended (Hornsby & Leppanen, 2011).

At the higher layer, a demand driven service composition is very similar with the dataflow model. Any change in the event will trigger the composition of the new service procedures with the new specifications. When a GDDWS is created, the price can be automatically generated by adding the price of supplementary resources used to customize it to the original service price. If the server that offers various services is being deployed on the cloud, then the price calculation must take into account the price of the cloud that is dynamic when large variations in computing resource demands appear.

Enterprise Components

At this level the basic support for the workflow, lookup tables and ERP integration can be found. The differences between virtual and real services are covered by dedicated but different pieces of software that have connectors offered at this level. The layer is optional, and it is specific only to the medium and large companies that adopt centralized solutions like ESB. In the resting cases some primitive roots for services in upper layers may appear.

Persistence Related Systems

Within the persistence related systems layer the data persistence services can be found. Autonomous services are used to assure data persistence in the system. These services can have any type of implementation beginning from a simple local centralized storage and reaching to full distributed file systems or cloud storage.

Due to the loose coupling, services with different implementation may cooperate to solve a temporary demand. At this level, the services are orchestrated using the rules-based logic and the workflow from the upper layer. Either operation system or data warehouses can be used in each type of persistence related operations, such as the ones used for temporary business process flow or permanent ones.

Business Performance Management

The layer of business performance management contains service interaction, security, QoS, message processing, modeling, management, intelligence, integration and communication. As it can be seen in Table 1, this layer is represented as crossing the layers. This means that we have supplementary tiers between each layer, which will provide the referred functionalities. The workload management system can be used to measure service efficiency (Dan, et al., 2004).

Communication Network Security

The current development of Internet infrastructure passes the network communication QoS problem to be solved at the level of the Internet service provider. Anyhow within highly developed economies this problem may be neglected due to the high availability of the Internet related services at affordable costs. The presented approach will not overload the communication network more than a classical application for electronic commerce. This is possible because the core of the agent is composed of a knowledge database (set of rules) and a part of business logic. Even a specific object dimension can be significantly reduced if zipped communication is used when it is transferred. The overload induced by this approach is supported by the new processors no matter if the system is designed for devices that are mobile or not. The communications between agents may be higher and sometimes complex, but this is hidden by the fact that most of the execution will be done at the service provider's level (where the computing power and the communication network availability do not represent a problem). Because the service provider has great economic power, it can negotiate in other terms with the Internet service provider to obtain lower costs. Also, the efficiency in using its hardware and software infrastructure will be higher than the rest of operators in the market. This will drive the provider to offer decent prices to its users. The same economic model is already used by the datacenters that offer services within the market.

QoS for the Communication Network

The QoS for communication networks is specified usually by a service-level agreement (SLA) (Ledoux & Kouki, 2012). In cases when the communication variable speed or other types of glitches are not a concern, supplementary analysis is not required. Usually, the economic constraints dictate to avoid too high demands at the communication network QoS level if this is not critical. Otherwise, the cost may strongly increase.

Another problem is related to service availability. This concerns mostly the wireless communication channels. In developed countries the wired networks service availability does not represent a problem because rates of failures are negligible. Because the proposed system is highly distributed and has a fine to medium granularity, the communication demands in terms of QoS will be in normal limits and most Internet Service Providers (ISPs) can comply with them.

In wireless communication based ambient there are no supplementary problems regarding the intelligent agents. To assure problem avoidance a caching mechanism for temporary dataflow disturbance control may be used. When communications are down the application will store all the required operations, and information that must be transmitted as well as the data request instruction, until the communication channels are available again (Popi & Festor, 2009). Possible delays in some workflows of process construction due to network failure, will trigger the restart of some workflow processes when the communication channel is available again.

Usually only the user and its interface agent are located on mobile devices. In most cases a continuous connection between the mobile terminal and the rest of the system is not required. It will be a good idea to use a supplementary reputation factor that will be computed, by the agent's system, about the known or new encountered ISPs.

Agent Security System

The security of the classical agent systems that are based on using a dedicated environment for agents is related only to analyzing the code execution of an incoming agent. In this case, the foreign code and its data are analyzed for possible tampering or malicious behavior. Sometimes the code is executed into a virtual machine. Anyhow complex mechanisms are required without gaining full trust in the code's safeness (Basak, Toshniwal, Maskalik, & Sequeira, 2010).

The security of the agent is handled in a traditional manner by using the existing tools and technologies. The service oriented architecture used in agent creation, was designed by also taking into account the market of mobile devices, and by using the public key infrastructure (PKI). Nowadays, multiple security risks have emerged at global level due to various political and economic factors. From the design architect's point of view, the use of security related design patterns in refining the main architecture will provide enough strength for any application that is designed from scratch. If PKI and security design patterns are used, there will be no supplementary security related problems. Analyzing the service trust will further decrease the probability of security risks. This is probably the main asset of the approach, because it will increase the chance of transferring the existing agent related know-how to the industry. Furthermore, special agents that will analyze each message can be used to increase the security (Pinzón, Francisco de Paz, Tapia, Bajo, & Corchado, 2012; Tapia, Rodríguez, Bajo, & Corchado, 2009).

Quality of Service for GDDWS

Quality of service for GDDWS can be viewed as having two subsets. One is related to technical aspects of QoS, and the other is related to user perception or satisfaction. The software or virtual service QoS evaluation is a resource related problem (Belzarena, Bermolen, & Casas, 2010). In the virtual case, we refer to one or more Web services of the same type that are connected at the input or output of the analyzed service. By contrast, the evaluation of services offered by real users may be difficult. In fact the situation can be quickly solved by enclosing the parameters used for the human client into the larger list used for the virtual client evaluation.

Technical QoS is strongly dependent on the type of service that does not need to be analyzed. In most situations it refers to technical specification. And it must originate from a human expert for both types of services, either real or virtual ones. The QoS, in terms of technical parameters, can be certified directly by the customers but also by a third party. The creation of new dedicated certification bodies is not a solution in the short term. It may emerge in time, if the market really needs it. Until then, the ISO style certification can be extended over the electronic services (American Global Standards, 2013).

One of the problems is related to the Service Level Agreement (SLA). The concept of a free market is based on different offers that give the client the possibility to even find services based on its demands. As a result, it is almost impossible to fully standardize a SLA and the minimal standard is given by the set of laws issued by a state. Probably the most difficult problem in generalized service automatic selection would be the compliance with the same SLA's (Redl, Breskovic, Brandic, & Dustdar, 2012).

In most situations some rules will be given by the management in basic SLA selection, but final approval may be made by a human operator. The solution is unfeasible because it reinserts the human link in the chain, with supplementary costs in terms of time and money.

Another possibility is to create special juridical services that will issue a certificate about a SLA, in order to certify that there are no legal traps or other misjudgments or intentional omissions that may cause problems in the future. Anyhow, this type of service is clearly defined in the market, so the fully automated generalized service composition may require time.

Architecture Integrator

As in the previous case, it involves tiers at each intersection layer on both sides. It will provide the possibility of having a common point to access the services related to integration, monitoring and managing the whole infrastructure (Keen, et al., 2004).

This concept is simple but the implementation can prove very difficult. The interconnection between two or more complex IT infrastructures involves creating compatibility at each software layer or organizational type. There are two problems here. One is to create compatibility among existing software infrastructures that must be interconnected now (Gold-Bernstein & Ruh, 2004). This is a complex task but can be managed if enough resources are available. The second problem is related to the design of the integrator system to assure a minimal effort in the future when new components must be connected to the system using the integrator.

When the design begins, both of the problems must be addressed because otherwise future integration is compromised from the start. The explanation is related to the cost optimization that is inherent when something is designed. So the implementation only for basic integration will be a particular solution, depending on interconnected systems specifications. Even so, a general adapter is almost impossible to obtain because all possible variations cannot be predicted. Instead of focusing on creating the best adapter, the market has already found an alternate solution with similar effects based on plugins. The best thing to do is to minimize the adaptation effort.

For services, the mechanism used in service composition can be adapted to provide compatibility. As for the rest, special designed plugins may intermediate any kind of information transfer. So, the adapter architecture will be based on a standard set of rules that must be complied by each service that joins the system. When a service must be integrated a demand driven mechanism will be used to adapt the service using the general set of rules provided by the integrator layer. Choosing a plugin based approach may be considered dangerous because this approach has the disadvantage of the second system syndrome (Brooks, 1995). This problem can be avoided if a very strict set of rules is enforced when the plugin system is designed. In this case there is no problem because the integrator layer is well defined in the paradigm used in the system's design. When this approach is used, there are two possible solutions. The most common and cheap one is to design the integrator as optimized as possible related to the existing knowledge about the systems that must be integrated and to provide a separate plugin space that will create the adaptation for further systems that will join later.

Making the integrator act like some form of generalized proxy will have advantages and disadvantages. The disadvantage will be the need for more resources in deployment of the solution because of the centralized approach. Nowadays, a cluster or cloud based solution may solve the problem at acceptable costs. There is also a big advantage. This is related to the control and security of the system. Even if each organization has its own internal security system, the integration makes everything more sensitive to man in the middle based types of attack. Therefore a centralized approach may have a supplementary layer of security eventually based on the use of an inference engine to detect suspicious behavior in communication between the organizations, may be an asset.

The interface with top management must also be placed at this level. The main motif is related both to the security and to fault tolerance. The information and knowledge database of top man-

agement may remain available to them if, from some reason, a part of the system is temporary unavailable.

New organization integration is very difficult. The integration must be made on each business related level. The process is called a multi-sourcing service integrator (DIR:Texas, 2012; NCOIC, 2013; Stoneseed, 2013). As already presented, a similar solution was given by our proposed system too. There is a conceptual difference because multi-sourcing is seen as providing a centralized access point for services and billing and the proposed approach is mostly distributed.

Using this solution gives the local level of interconnected organization enough liberty to benefit from the advantages of the distributed approach but at the same time may benefit from the advantages of the centralized one.

The efficiency of the model can be achieved only when the market will adopt it at large scale. Otherwise, the involved costs will make it unfeasible for most of the targeted clients. There are two possible scenarios in acquiring economic efficiency depending on the policies adopted by the corporations or government. One possibility, which is the most feasible one, is that a corporation will choose to support the short term economic inefficiency of the approach in order to extend, on long term, its market. The other consists of a governmental level decision that will do the same with the aim of accelerating the adoption of IT at a national level.

The reliability of the proposed solution is acquired because in the design phase typical methods and patterns for modern distributed applications were used. The reliability of the system will be determined by the reliability of the chosen technologies. Because these technologies are feasible and already used at the corporate level, there are good chances that this problem will be overcome without major problems. Because in the design phase a classical approach based on multi-layer multi-tier model and design patterns was used, the solution is very flexible regarding possible technology changes, by a simple replacement of some parts with the new required ones.

FUTURE RESEARCH DIRECTIONS

In future work, a standard for the service representation and interface will be proposed. Then, the design proposed for each layer of the application can be implemented and tested. After this is done, the next logical step is the implementation of various needed services. The idea is to produce buckets of services with various implementations in different technologies, but with the same common interface and associated metadata. A method for service composition will finally be chosen or developed from scratch. After that, the first test of the proposed architecture may begin

CONCLUSION

This chapter has presented a novel approach to design and implement SOA as a base for the virtual business environment into an open system based market. The market has a weak representation in terms of open source full solution related to business virtualization existence. The current solutions provided by market leading companies are designed as having corporate or governmental targets in mind.

A new concept of generalized demand driven Web services has been proposed here in an effort to create a service based layer that will hide, at the cyberspace level, the differences between virtual and real service providers. This encapsulation will decrease the design effort of future business related SOA architecture. The solution is technologically independent, so that any mix of technologies can be used in the implementation phase. A new way of indexing the service metadata based on LDAP was proposed. The solution may represent a cheap and fast alternative to classical broker solution.

Because one of the problems specific to an open market is service selection, an analysis has also been made in this chapter. The minimal sets of supplementary service parameters required for analysis in order to make a good choice, in accordance with user constraints, were presented. Another approach in designing the integrator for these types of systems is presented. The plugin based approach is not the cheapest solution, but it may be the best compromise between costs and scalability during the system's life cycle. The solution is independent of the granularity of the implemented business system, so it can be used for small unique services, but also for managing large businesses. This approach will give the client the possibility to efficiently access services that are fitted to its needs, and for the businessman to easily initiate or destroy business flows as needed.

The main social welfare of this approach is related to the following aspects:

- Increase and support the adoption of information technology at the level of small and medium businesses.
- Increase the economic efficiency for small and medium businesses by providing an efficient way of offering demand driven services in the same manner as the corporations do.
- Increase the diversity of the offers and their prices in the market which is the key for any healthy competition based economy.

Until now, there was a clear separation between the complex systems used in corporations to handle modern solutions, such as demand driven services and the ones used in the rest of the market. Unfortunately, within small and medium business few improvements in this area are affordable. Cloud computing is the first concept that opens the service market for small and medium affairs. So creating new architecture and infrastructure that will help them enter into fair competition with corporations will be an important asset, not only for the businessman but also for the economy in general, because it will maintain healthy competition in the market.

By creating agents through software services composition, the large areas of know how that are mostly used and developed only at an academic level now, can be finally used in the business environment with good results.

One of the advantages of the proposed system is related to the extension of the concept in order to help the traditional way of doing business so it can be integrated into the informational society. Nowadays, in the best case, simple tools for Web presence that are similar with ones used in electronic commerce are being used.

The proposed system will provide not only a quicker and may be a more graphical manner to define the agents used in client interface, but it will also provide implementation of some parts of the needed business logic. It will also help to optimize maintenance and development costs that may vary depending on the current business needs.

This approach is feasible because it will conduct to a generalization of using these complex business tools. As a result, the number of electronic service providers will increase on the market and prices will became affordable for small and medium enterprises.

REFERENCES

Agarwal, S., Kenkre, S., Pandit, V., & Sengupta, B. (2011). Studying the evolution of skill profiles in distributed, specialization driven service delivery systems through work orchestration. In *Proceedings of the 2011 Annual SRII Global Conference* (pp. 201-213). Washington, DC: IEEE Computer Society.

Ahmadi, H., & Kong, J. (2012). User-centric adaptation of web information for small screens. *Journal of Visual Languages and Computing*, *23*(1), 13–28. doi:10.1016/j.jvlc.2011.09.002

Aldrich, M. (2011). *Inventor's story*. Retrieved from http://www.aldricharchive.com/inventors_story.html

Almeida, F., Terra, B. M., Dias, P. A., & Gonçalves, G. (2010). Adoption issues of multi-agent systems in manufacturing industry. In *Proceedings of Fifth International Multi-Conference on Computing in the Global Information Technology* (pp. 238–244). Valencia, CA: Conference Publishing Services - IEEE. doi:10.1109/ICCGI.2010.48

American Global Standards. (2013). *Virtual Cert™ program - American global standards*. Retrieved April 25, 2013, from http://www.americanglobal.org/process/virtual-cert/

Anastasio, T. J., Ehrenberger, K. A., Watson, P., & Zhang, W. (2012). *Individual and collective memory consolidation - Analogous processes on different levels*. Cambridge, MA: MIT Press.

Anderson, G. W. (2011). *Sams teach yourself SAP in 24 hours*. Indianapolis, IN: Pearson Education, Inc.

Anthony, R. N. (1965). *Planning and control systems: A framework for analysis*. Boston: Division of Research, Graduate School of Business Administration, Harvard University.

Arlbjern, J. S., & Haug, A. (2010). *Business process optimization*. Aarhus, Denmark: Academica.

Arsanjani, A., Zhang, L.-J., Ellis, M., Allam, A., & Channabasavaiah, K. (2007, March 28). *Design an SOA solution using a reference architecture*. Retrieved april 18, 2013, from http://www.ibm.com/developerworks/library/ar-archtemp/

Avast. (2013). *Virtualization parameters*. Retrieved April 22, 2013, from http://avast.helpmax. net/en/additional-protection/sandbox/expert-settings/virtualization-parameters/

Aye, N., Khin, H. S., & Win, T. T. KoKo, T., Than, M. Z., Hattori, F., & Kuwabara, K. (2013). Multi-domain public key infrastructure for information security with use of a multi-agent system. In *Proceedings of the 5th Asian Conference on Intelligent Information and Database Systems* - (pp. 365-374). Heidelberg, Germany: Springer-Verlag.

Barreiros, M., & Lundqvist, P. (2011). *QOS-enabled networks*. West Sussex, UK: John Wiley & Sons, Ltd. doi:10.1002/9780470976814

Basak, D., Toshniwal, R., Maskalik, S., & Sequeira, A. (2010). Virtualizing networking and security in the cloud. *SIGOPS Operating Systems Review*, 86-94.

Bauer, B., & Odell, J. (2005). UML 2.0 and agents: How to build agent-based systems with the new UML standard. *Engineering Applications of Artificial Intelligence*, *18*(2), 141–157. doi:10.1016/j. engappai.2004.11.016

Belzarena, P., Bermolen, P., & Casas, P. (2010). End-to-end quality of service-based admission control using the fictitious network analysis. *Computer Communications*, *33*, S157–S166. doi:10.1016/j.comcom.2010.04.024

Betz, C. T. (2007). *Architecture and patterns for IT service management, resource planning, and governance: Making shoes for the cobbler's children: Making shoes for the cobbler's children.* San Francisco: Morgan Kaufmann Publishers Inc.

Blake, M. B., Cummings, D. J., Bansal, A., & Bansal, S. K. (2012). Workflow composition of service level agreements for web services. Elsevier Science Publishers B. V., 234-244.

Borec, T. (2012, October 2). *EU: What are eservices?* Retrieved November 4, 2013, from http:// ebiz.pwc.com/2012/10/eu-what-are-eservices/

Botti, V., & Boggino, A. C. (2008). *ANEMONA - A multi-agent methodology for holonic manufacturing systems*. London: Springer-Verlag.

Brooks, J. F. (1995). *The mythical man-month: Essays on software engineering* (2nd ed.). Chicago: Addison Wesley Longman, Inc.

Buskens, V. (1995). *Social networks and the effect of reputation on cooperation*. The ISCORE discussion papers. Retrieved April 1, 2013, from http://www.uu.nl/SiteCollectionImages/Fac_SW/ SOC/Iscore%20Papers/IscorePaper42_Buskens1995.pdf

Büttcher, S., Clarke, C. L., & Cormack, G. V. (2010). *Information retrieval: Implementing and evaluating search engines*. Cambridge, MA: MIT Press.

Canadi, I., Barford, P., & Sommers, J. (2012). Revisiting broadband performance. In *Proceedings of the 2012 ACM Conference on Internet Measurement Conference* (pp. 273-286). New York: ACM.

Comodo Group. (2013). *The virtual kiosk*. Retrieved April 26, 2013, from http://help.comodo. com/topic-72-1-451-4738-The--Virtual-Kiosk. html

Contos, B. T., Hunt, S., & Derodeff, C. (2007). *Physical and logical security convergence: Powered by enterprise security management*. Burlington, MA: Syngress Publishing.

Coronado-Garcia, L. C., & Perez-Leguizamo, C. (2011). A mission-critical certification authority architecture for high reliability and response time. *International Journal of Critical Computer-Based Systems*, 6-24.

Cummins, F. A. (2009). *Building the agile enterprise: With SOA, BPM and MBM*. San Francisco: Morgan Kaufmann Publishers Inc.

Daigneau, R. (2011). *Service design patterns - Fundamental design solutions for SOAP/WSDL and RESTful web services*. Reading, MA: Addison-Wesley Professional.

Dan, A., Davis, D., Kearney, R., Keller, A., King, R., Kuebler, D., & Youssef, A. (2004). Web services on demand: WSLA-driven automated management. *IBM Systems Journal, 43*(1), 136–158. doi:10.1147/sj.431.0136

Denaro, G., Pezze, M., Tosi, D., & Schilling, D. (2006). Towards self-adaptive service-oriented architectures. In *Proceedings of 2006 workshop on Testing, Analysis, and Verification of Web Services and Applications* (pp. 10 – 16). New York: ACM.

DIR. Texas. (2012). *Datacenter service: Capgemini contract*. Retrieved 25 June, 2013, from http://www.dir.texas.gov/SiteCollectionDocuments/DCS/_CAP/Exhibit%202/CAP_Exhibit%202.1_Multisourcing%20Service%20Integrator%20SOW_20111228.pdf

Dong, L., & Tomlin, B. (2012). Managing disruption risk: The interplay between operations and insurance. *Management Science, 58*(10), 1898–1915. doi:10.1287/mnsc.1120.1524

Dutta, S., & Pinder, A. J. (2011). *Service intelligence and performance management - Moving beyond the rearview mirror*. Retrieved Mars 19, 2013, from http://www.mercedsystems.com/m2/resource_library/Aberdeen%20Group%20Whitepaper%20-%20Service%20Intelligence%20and%20Performance%20Management.pdf

Fabian, B., Kunz, S., & Konnegen, M., MüLler, S., & GüNther, O. (2012). Access control for semantic data federations in industrial product-lifecycle management. *Computers in Industry, 63*(9), 930–940. doi:10.1016/j.compind.2012.08.015

FIPA. (2000, August 28). *FIPA agent management specification*. Retrieved May 15, 2013, from http://www.fipa.org: http://www.fipa.org/specs/fipa00023/XC00023H.html

Fujii, K., & Suda, T. (2005). Semantics-based dynamic service composition. *IEEE Journal on Selected Areas in Communications, 23*(12), 2361–2372. doi:10.1109/JSAC.2005.857202

Galloway, B., & Hancke, G. P. (2012). Introduction to industrial control networks. *Introduction to Industrial Control Networks, 15*(2), 860–880.

Gambetta, D. (2000). Can we trust trust? In D. Gambetta (Ed.), *Trust: Making and breaking cooperative relations* (pp. 213–237). Oxford, UK: Department of Sociology, University of Oxford.

Gold-Bernstein, B., & Ruh, W. (2004). *Enterprise integration: The essential guide to integration solutions*. Reading, MA: Addison-Wesley Professional.

Gov, U. S. A. (2002, December 17). *LAW 107–347*. Retrieved from http://frwebgate.access.gpo.gov/cgi-bin/getdoc.cgi?dbname=107_cong_public_laws&docid=f:publ347.107.pdf

Haerder, T., & Reuter, A. (1983). Principles of transaction-oriented database recovery. *ACM Computing Surveys*, (15): 287–317. doi:10.1145/289.291

Hamburg, I., & Zaharia, M. H. (2000). Tools for a participative computer aided modeling of flows in production. [Goshen, KY: Integrated Technology Systems.]. *Proceedings of, EDA2000*, 627–632.

Hong, S., Nag, B. N., & Yao, D. Q. (2009). Improving e-trade auction volume by consortium. In V. Sugumaran (Ed.), *Distributed artificial intelligence, agent technology, and collaborative applications* (pp. 91–115). Hershey, PA: IGI Global.

Hornsby, A., & Leppanen, T. (2011). event.Hub: An event-driven information hub for mobile devices. In *Proceedings of the 8th International Conference on Ubiquitous Intelligence and Computing* (pp. 209-223). Banff, Canada: Springer-Verlag.

Howden, N., Rönnquist, R., Hodgson, A., & Lucas, A. (2001). JACK intelligent agents – Summary of an agent infrastructure. In *Proceedings of 5th International Conference on Autonomous Agents*. Montreal, Canada: ACM.

Hsiao, D. K. (1992). Federated databases and systems: Part II --- A tutorial on their resource consolidation. *The VLDB Journal*, 285–310. doi:10.1007/BF01231702

Jaffe, M., & Shine, T. (2011, April 19). *S&P's credibility under fire as agency issues US debt warning.* Retrieved Mars 25, 2013, from http://abcnews.go.com/Politics/standard-poors-credibility-fire-us-debt-warning/story?id=13407823

Karakostas, B., & Kardaras, D. (2012). *Services customization using web technologies.* Hershey, PA: IGI Global.

Keen, M., Acharya, A., Bishop, S., Hopkins, A., Milinski, S., Nott, C., & Verschueren, P. (2004). *Patterns: Implementing an SOA using an enterprise service bus the business process/services layer.* Boulder, CO: IBM.

Kulkarni, P., Nazeeruddin, M., & McClean, S. (2006). Building a controlled delay assured forwarding class in differentiated services network. In *Proceedings of the 2006 SIGCOMM Workshop on Internet Network Management* (pp. 11-16). New York: ACM.

Ledoux, T., & Kouki, Y. (2012). SLA-driven capacity planning for Cloud applications. In *Proceedings of the 2012 IEEE 4th International Conference on Cloud Computing Technology and Science (CloudCom)* (pp. 135-140). Washington, DC: IEEE Computer Society.

Losee, R., & Church, L. J. (2004). Information retrieval with distributed databases: Analytic models of performance. *IEEE Transactions on Parallel and Distributed Systems*, 18–27. doi:10.1109/TPDS.2004.1264782

Lowson, B., King, R., & Hunter, A. (1999). *Quick response managing the supply chain to meet consumer demand.* West Sussex, UK: John Wiley & Sons Ltd.

Luo, J., Li, W., Liu, B., Zheng, X., & Dong, F. (2010). Multi-agent coordination for service composition. In *Agent-based service-oriented computing. series: Advanced information and knowledge processing, XIII* (pp. 47–79). London: Springer-Verlag Limited. doi:10.1007/978-1-84996-041-0_3

Marks, E. A. (2008). *Service-oriented architecture governance for the services driven enterprise.* Hoboken, NJ: John Wiley & Sons, Inc.

Marsh, S. P. (1994). *Formalising trust as a computational concept.* (Unpublished doctoral dissertation). Stirling, UK.

Mathis, R. L., & Jackson, J. H. (2009). *Human resource management.* Mason, GA: Cengage Learning.

McGovern, J., Tyagi, S., Stevens, M., & Mathew, S. (2003). *Java web services architecture.* San Francisco: Morgan Kaufmann.

Medjahed, B., & Bouguettaya, A. (2011). *Service composition for the semantic web.* New York: Springer Science Business Media. doi:10.1007/978-1-4419-8465-4

Moran, M. J. (2011). *Semantic service oriented architecture - Component model, reference architecture and evaluated prototype.* (Unpublished doctoral dissertation). Galway, Ireland.

Mosher, L., Helmbock, J., Hogan, J., McCarthy, C., & O'Mara, M. (2006, April 7). *Demand-driven IT service management through enterprise resource planning for IT: IBM IT service management strategy and vision*. Retrieved April 6, 2013, from http://www-935.ibm.com/services/fr/cio/optimise/optit_wp_gts_demanddriven.pdf

Musion. (2013, February 19). *Musion to present its futuristic holographic technology at international confex & live experience*. Retrieved April 14, 2013, from http://www.it-analysis.com/business/innovation/news_release.php?rel=36660

NCOIC. (2013). *Design phase service integration capability pattern*. Retrieved June 28, 2013, from https://www.ncoic.org/apps/group_public/document.php?document_id=15964

Ng, T., Fung, J., Chan, L., & Mak, V. (2010). *Understanding IBM SOA foundation suite - Learning visually with examples*. Crawfordsville: IBM Press, Pearson plc.

Nguyen, C. D., Perini, A., Tonella, P., Miles, S., Harman, M., & Luck, M. (2009). Evolutionary testing of autonomous software agents. In *Proceedings of the 8th International Conference on Autonomous Agents and Multiagent Systems* (vol. 1, pp. 521-528). Richland: International Foundation for Autonomous Agents and Multiagent Systems.

Oberle, D., Barros, A., Kylau, U., & Heinzl, S. (2013). A unified description language for human to automated services. *Information Systems, 38*(1), 155–181. doi:10.1016/j.is.2012.06.004

OECD. (1999). *Economic and social impact of e-commerce: Preliminary findings and research agenda (OECD Digital Economy Papers, No. 40)*. Paris: OECD Publishing.

OECD. (2012, April 30). *Procedural fairness and transparency 2012 - Key points*. Retrieved April 20, 2013, from www.oecd.org: http://www.oecd.org/daf/competition/mergers/50235955.pdf

Paolucci, M., Shehory, O., Sycara, K., Kalp, D., & A., P. (2000). A planning component for RETSINA agents. In N. Jennings & Y. Lesperance (Eds.), *Lecture Notes in Computer Science (LNCS)*, (vol. 1757, pp. 147-161). Heidelberg, Germany: Springer-Verlag.

Pautasso, C., & Alonso, G. (2005). From web service composition to megaprogramming. In M. Shan, U. Dayal, & M. Hsu (Eds.), *Technologies for e-services (LNCS)* (pp. 39–53). Heidelberg, Germany: Springer. doi:10.1007/978-3-540-31811-8_4

Payer, M., & Gross, T. R. (2011). Fine-grained user-space security through virtualization. *ACM SIGPLAN Notices, 46*(7), 157–168. doi:10.1145/2007477.1952703

Peppard, J., & Rylander, A. (2005). Products and services in cyberspace. *International Journal of Information Management, 25*, 335–345. doi:10.1016/j.ijinfomgt.2005.04.005

Pinzón, C., Francisco de Paz, J., Tapia, D. I., Bajo, J., & Corchado, J. M. (2012). Improving the security level of the FUSION@ multi-agent architecture. *Expert System Application, 39*(8), 7536–7545. doi:10.1016/j.eswa.2012.01.127

Popi, C., & Festor, O. (2009). Flow monitoring in wireless MESH networks. In *Proceedings of the 3rd International Conference on Autonomous Infrastructure, Management and Security: Scalability of Networks and Services* (pp. 134-146). Enschede, The Netherlands: Springer-Verlag.

Quin, L. (2012, January 24). *Extensible markup language (XML)*. Retrieved April 5, 2013, from www.w3.org: http://www.w3.org/XML/

Radware. (2012). *LDAP network challenges: Radware carrier solutions*. Retrieved April 5, 2013, from http://www.radware.com/: http://www.radware.com/

Rainey, D. L. (2012). A model for improving the adoption of sustainability in the context of globalization and innovation. In F. Nobre, D. Walker, & R. Harris (Eds.), *Technological, managerial and organizational core competencies: Dynamic innovation and sustainable development* (pp. 18–39). Hershey, PA: IGI Global. doi:10.4018/978-1-4666-0882-5.ch306

Rao, J., & Su, X. (2005). A survey of automated web service composition methods. In *Proceedings of the First International Conference on Semantic Web Services and Web Process Composition* (pp. 43-54). Heidelberg, Germany: Springer-Verlag.

Redl, C., Breskovic, I., Brandic, I., & Dustdar, S. (2012). Automatic SLA matching and provider selection in grid and cloud computing markets. In *Proceedings of the 2012 ACM/IEEE 13th International Conference on Grid Computing* (pp. 85-94). Washington, DC: IEEE Computer Society.

Robbins, S. P., & Judge, T. A. (2012). *Organizational behavior*. Upper Saddle River, NJ: Pearson Education.

Ross, D. F. (2011). *Introduction to supply chain management technologies* (2nd ed.). Boca Raton, FL: CRC Press.

Şah, M., & Wade, V. (2012). Automatic metadata mining from multilingual enterprise content. *Web Semantics: Science. Services and Agents on the World Wide Web*, *11*, 41–62. doi:10.1016/j.websem.2011.11.001

SAP. (2005, December 18). *Microsoft, IBM, SAP to discontinue UDDI web services registry effort*. Retrieved from http://soa.sys-con.com/node/164624

Sauter, V. L. (2011). *Decision support systems for business intelligence*. Hoboken, NJ: John Wiley & Sons. doi:10.1002/9780470634431

Sermersheim, J. (2006, June 1). *Lightweight directory access protocol (LDAP), the protocol*. Retrieved April 9, 2013, from http://tools.ietf.org/html/rfc4511

ShaikhAli. A., Rana, O., Al-Ali, R., & Walker, D. (2003). UDDIe: An extended registry for web services. In *Proceedings of the 2003 Symposium on Applications and the Internet Workshops* (pp. 85-89). San Leandro, CA: IEEE Computer Society.

Shenker, S., & Wroclawski, J. (1997, September 1). *General characterization parameters for integrated service network elements*. Retrieved April 6, 2013, from https://tools.ietf.org/rfc/rfc2215.txt

Skroch, O. (2010). Multi-criteria service selection with optimal stopping in dynamic service-oriented systems. In *Proceedings of the 6th International Conference on Distributed Computing and Internet Technology* (pp. 110-121). Berlin: Springer-Verlag.

Stoneseed. (2013). *You can download our multisourcing whitepaper here*. Retrieved June 24, 2013, from http://stoneseed.co.uk: http://stoneseed.co.uk/blog/wp-content/themes/vulcan/download.php

Sun, Z., Dong, D., & Yearwood, J. (2011). Demand driven web services. In H.-F. Leung, D. K. Chiu, & P. C. Hung (Eds.), *Service intelligence and service science: Evolutionary technologies and challenges* (pp. 35–55). Hershey, PA: Information Science Reference.

Sun, Z., Finnie, G., & Yearwood, J. (2010). Case based web services. In I. Lee (Ed.), *Encyclopedia of e-business development and management in the global economy* (pp. 871–882). Hershey, PA: Business Science Reference. doi:10.4018/978-1-61520-611-7.ch087

Tapia, D. I., Rodríguez, S., Bajo, J., & Corchado, J. (2009). FUSION@, a SOA-based multi-agent. In J. M. Corchado, S. Rodríguez, J. Llinas, & J. Molina (Eds.), *International symposium on distributed computing and artificial intelligence 2008, advances in soft computing architecture,* (vol. 50, pp. 99-107). Heidelberg, Germany: Springer.

Taylor, S. (2012). *Service intelligence, improving your bottom line with the power of IT service management.* Crawfordsville: Pearson Education.

Thomas, M., Yoon, V., & Redmond, R. (2009). Extending loosely coupled federated information systems using agent technology. In V. Sugumaran (Ed.), *Distributed artificial intelligence, agent technology, and collaborative applications* (pp. 116–131). Hershey, PA: IGI Global.

Tzeng, G. H., & Huang, J. J. (2011). *Multiple attribute decision making: Methods and applications.* Boca Raton, FL: CRC Press, Taylor & Francis Group.

Ugurlu, S., & Erdogan, N. (2005). A secure communication framework for mobile agents. In *Proceedings of the 20th International Conference on Computer and Information Sciences* (pp. 412-421). Heidelberg, Germany: Springer-Verlag.

Vercellis, C. (2009). *Business intelligence, data mining and optimization for decision making.* Cornwall, UK: John Wiley & Sons.

Vitvar, T. (2007). SESA: Emerging technology for service-centric environments. *IEEE Software, 24*(6), 56–67. doi:10.1109/MS.2007.178

Vitvar, T., Zaremba, M., Moran, M., & Mocan, A. (2008). Mediation using WSMO, WSML and WSMX. In C. Petrie, H. Lausen, M. Zaremba, & T. Margaria-Steen (Eds.), *Semantic web services challenge: Results from the first year (semantic web and beyond)* (pp. 72–83). Heidelberg, Germany: Springer.

Wang, Z. (2001). *Internet QoS - Architectures and mechanisms for quality of service.* San Francisco: Morgan Kaufmann.

Weiss, G. (2000). *Multiagent systems: A modern approach to distributed artificial intelligence.* Cambridge, MA: MIT Press.

Weiss, G. (2013). *Multiagent systems* (2nd ed.). Cambridge, MA: MIT Press.

Weissenberger-Eibl, M. A., & Spieth, P. (2006). Knowledge transfer: Affected by organisational culture? In K. Tochtermann & H. Maurer (Eds.), *Proceedings of I-KNOW'06, 6th International Conference on KnowledgeManagement* (pp. 68-75). Hedelberg, Germany: Springer.

Wikipedia. (2013, May 6). *Comparison of agent-based modeling software.* Retrieved May 13, 2013, from http://en.wikipedia.org/wiki/Comparison_of_agent-based_modeling_software

Yeo, C. S., Venugopal, S., Chu, X., & Buyya, R. (2010). Autonomic metered pricing for a utility computing service. *Future Generation Computer Systems, 26*(8), 1368–1380. doi:10.1016/j.future.2009.05.024

Zimmermann, O., Doubrovski, V., Grundler, J., & Hogg, K. (2005). Service-oriented architecture and business process choreography in an order management scenario: Rationale, concepts, lessons learned. In *Companion to the 20th annual ACM SIGPLAN conference on object-oriented programming, systems, languages, and applications* (pp. 301-312). New York: ACM.

ADITIONAL READING

Albers, M. J. (2011). *Usability of Complex Information Systems Evaluation of User Interaction.* Boca Raton: CRC Press, Taylor & Francis Group.

Aubin, J. P. (2009). *Viability Theory*. Boston: Birkhäuser, Springer Science. doi:10.1007/978-0-8176-4910-4

Baunl, C., Kunzel, M., Nimis, J., & Tai, S. (2011). *Cloud Computing Web-Based Dynamic IT Services*. Heidelberg: Springer-Verlag.

Beatty, J., & Chen, A. (2012). *Visual models for software requirements visual models for software requirements best practices*. Redmond: Microsoft Press.

Buyya, R., & Bubendorfer, K. (2010). *Market-oriented grid and utility computing*. Hoboken: John Wiley & Sons, Inc.

Cao, L. P. (2010). Domain driven data mining. New York: Springer Science+Business Media.

Castelfranchi, C. (2010). *Trust theory a socio-cognitive and computational model*. Singapore: John Wiley & Sons Ltd.

Craig, T., & Ludloff, M. E. (2011). *Privacy and Big Data. Gravenstein*. O'Reilly Media, Inc.

Davis, J. (2009). *Open Source SOA*. Greenwich: Manning Publications Co.

Deforche, K. (2012). *Effectively use services with Dynamics AX 2012 and create your own services*. Birmingham: Packt Publishing Ltd.

Elisa Bertino, E. M. (2010). *Security for Web Services and Service-Oriented Architectures*. Heidelberg: Springer-Verlag. doi:10.1007/978-3-540-87742-4

Eriksson, H., & Penker, M. (2000). *Business modeling with UML: business patterns at work*. Hoboken: John Wiley & Sons, Inc.

Erl, T. (2005). *Service-Oriented Architecture: Concepts, Technology, and Design*. Crawfordsville: Prentice Hall PTR.

Feldman, R. (2006). *The text mining handbook*. Cambridge: Cambridge University Press. doi:10.1017/CBO9780511546914

Fensel, D. (2011). *Foundations for the WEB of information and services - a review of 20 years of semantic WEB research*. Berlin: Springer-Verlag. doi:10.1007/978-3-642-19797-0

Han, J., Kamber, M., & J., P. (2012). *Data Mining, Concepts and Techniques*. Waltham: Morgan Kaufmann, Elsevie.

Ishikawa, A. (2007). *Knowledge management and risk strategies*. Singapore: Stallion Press.

Ivanov, I. V. (2012). *Cloud Computing and Services Science*. New York: Springer. doi:10.1007/978-1-4614-2326-3

Johnson, C. (2006). *Intelligent Business*. Essex: Pearson Education Limited.

Kouvelis, P. D. (2012). *The handbook of integrated Risk Management in Global Supply Chains*. Hoboken: John Wiley & Sons.

Krum, C. (2010). *Mobile marketing - finding your customers no matter where they are*. Indianapolis: Pearson Education, Inc.

Lightstone, T. T., Nadeau, S., T., & Jagadish, H. V. (2011). Database modeling and design. Burlington: Morgan Kaufmann, Elsevier.

Linthicum, D. S. (2010). *Cloud Computing and SOA Convergence in Your Enterprise*. Boston: Pearson Education, Inc.

Michelini, L. (2012). *Social Innovation and New Business Models*. New York: Springer. doi:10.1007/978-3-642-32150-4

Neumann, D. B. M. (2010). Economic Models and Algorithms for Distributed Systems. Basel: Birkhäuser Verlag AG.

Pazos Arias, J., Fernandez Vilas, A., & Diaz Redondo, R. (2012). *Recommender Systems for the SocialWeb*. Berlin, Heidelberg: Springer-Verlag. doi:10.1007/978-3-642-25694-3

Praeg, C. P., & Spath, D. (2011). *Quality Management for IT Services: Perspectives on Business and Process Performance*. Hershey: IGI Global.

Swagatam Das, S., Abraham, A., & Konar, A. (2009). *Metaheuristic Clustering*. Berlin, Heidelberg: Springer-Verlag.

Wilder, B. (2012). *Cloud Architecture Patterns. Gravenstein*. O'Reilly Media, Inc.

KEY TERMS AND DEFINITIONS

Availability: The percent of time that a system is in functioning condition. The referred time is the expected working time. Scheduled shutdowns are ignored in parameter calculation.

Business Logic: A component from the multilayer multitier approach used in designing distributed applications. It captures most of the supplementary processing related to business dataflow that are not implemented in database layer.

Demand Driven Services: New services created by deriving existing ones by applying minor to medium modification over the initial functionality and interface.

Distributed Artificial Intelligence: Application of multi-agent intelligent system. Main differences appear due to the techniques used in the concept implementation. Some are simulators, other are dedicated frameworks and only a few are framework independent.

Distributed Systems: loosely coupled software architectures mapped onto a real distributed heterogeneous infrastructure that offer support for node collaboration on each magnitude necessary to fulfill the programmer's need. The basics are offered by the operating system that may have various degrees of support for distributed application, but the core of a distributed system is usually in the market related applications given by the distributed software that is running on the distributed infrastructure.

Intelligent Agents: Pieces of software with variable complexity that usually need a support framework that may emulate in various degrees some intelligent behaviors.

Reliability: The capacity of a system or component to fulfill its goals according to the design specification.

Serviceability: The supplementary design measures that will make the system maintenance much easier and with lower costs.

Service-Oriented Computing: Particular case of distributed computing that uses a service as base for designing an application. The services can be composed and the design is very flexible.

Web-Based Services: Native or not services with a Web interface that hides the implementation and execution differences.

Web Service Discovery: Searching the desired service using its metadata and some semantic rules to acquire, at least, a similar match that may be derived into a demand driven service that perfectly fits the initial need.

Web Service Life Cycle: Finite state machine that describes all possible stable states within which the agents exists or interact.

Chapter 6
Social Web Services Management

Zakaria Maamar
Zayed University, UAE

Ejub Kajan
State University of Novi Pazar, Serbia

Noura Faci
Claude Bernard Lyon 1 University, France

Emir Ugljanin
State University of Novi Pazar, Serbia

ABSTRACT

As part of our ongoing work on social-intensive Web services, also referred to as social Web services, different types of networks that connect them together are developed. These networks include collaboration, substitution, and competition, and permit the addressing of specific issues related to Web service use such as composition, discovery, and high-availability. "Social" is embraced because of the similarities of situations that Web services run into at run time with situations that people experience daily. Indeed, Web services compete, collaborate, and substitute. This is typical to what people do. This chapter sheds light on some criteria that support Web service selection of a certain network to sign up over another. These criteria are driven by the security means that each network deploys to ensure the safety and privacy of its members from potential attacks. When a Web service signs up in a network, it becomes exposed to both the authority of the network and the existing members in the network as well. These two can check and alter the Web service's credentials, which may jeopardize its reputation and correctness levels.

INTRODUCTION

As part of our ongoing research work on blending social computing with service-oriented computing we developed three types of social networks having Web services as members (Maamar et al., 2011a). These networks address specific issues related to

composition of Web services namely discovery and high-availability. The development of these networks is strictly dependent on the functionalities that Web services offer. checkWeatherForecast and convertExchangeRate are examples of functionalities. We refer to these networks as collaboration, substitution, and competition. In a collaboration

DOI: 10.4018/978-1-4666-5884-4.ch006

network, the functionalities of Web services are different and sometimes complement each other, e.g., checkWeatherForecast and bookOutdoorVenue. Contrarily, in substitution and competition networks the functionalities are semantically similar, e.g., bookTrainSeat and reserveTrainTicket. There exist different techniques and approaches to compare Web services' functionalities in term of either difference or similarity (Di Martino, 2009), but this is outside this chapter's scope.

Compared to (regular) Web services, social Web services establish and maintain networks of contacts; count on their (privileged) contacts when needed; form with other peers strong and long lasting collaborative social groups; and, know with whom to partner so that ontology reconciliation is minimized (Maamar et al., 2011a; Maamar et al., 2011b; Maamar et al., 2011d). Collaboration, substitution, and competition networks support a social Web service, respectively, recommend the peers that it likes to work with in the case of composition, recommend the peers that can substitute for it in the case of failure, and be aware of the peers that compete against it in the case of selection.

Like persons who sign up in social networks (e.g., Facebook and Linked) after assessing criteria such as services offered, reputation, and reliability, we advocate that Web services should do the same. Indeed when a social Web service joins a network, it becomes exposed to the authority responsible for managing the network and also the existing members in the network. Both can check its credentials with the risk of altering them, which may jeopardize its reputation and correctness levels. This risk could be tackled subject to setting up appropriate means. For this purpose we define *privacy, trust, fairness,* and, *traceability* criteria that back the sign-up decision of a Web service in a network. To identify these criteria we look at how existing Web-based social networks such as Facebook and LinkedIn "control" the exposure of their members' profiles through a list of rights and responsibilities. We define similar rights and responsibilities in response to the particular needs, requirements, and characteristics of Web services.

After a brief overview of social Web services the next sections of the chapter introduce the criteria that assess the quality-of-service of social networks, the policies for managing these networks, the relationships between these criteria and policies, and last but not least the commitments that enforce the compliance with these policies. A set of future research directions are listed and then concluding remarks are drawn.

SOCIAL WEB SERVICES

Social Web services are at the cross-road of two main disciplines: social computing (exemplified by Web 2.0) and service-oriented computing (exemplified by Web services). Existing research work either adopts Web services to assist in developing social networks of users or develops social networks of Web services to address certain issues such as Web services discovery. In this chapter the focus is on the latter type of social networks.

In the first category of social networks of users, we cite the following works. Maaradji et al. propose a social composer that advises users on the next actions they can take in response to events such as Web services selection (Maaradji et al., 2010). Xie et al. (2008) introduce a framework for semantic service composition based on social networks. Wu et al. rank Web services using non-functional properties and invocation requests at run-time (Wu et al., 2009). A Web service's popularity as analyzed by users is the social element that is considered during the ranking. Last but not least, Nam Ko et al. discuss the social Web in which "social-networks connect services" help third-party in developing social applications without having to build social networks (Nam Ko et al., 2010).

In the second category of social networks of Web services, we cite our works by Maamar et al. (2011c, 2011e). In the first work we suggest a method to engineer social Web services. Questions that are addressed in this method include what relationships exist between Web services, what social networks correspond to these relationships, how to build social networks of Web services, and what social behaviors can Web services exhibit. In the second work we use social networks to address the specific problem of Web services discovery. Different social networks permit to describe the situations in which Web services engage for instance collaboration and recommendation. We emphasize that Web services are not isolated components that respond to user queries, only. Contrarily, Web services compete against other, similar Web services during selection, collaborate with other, different Web services during composition, and may replace other, similar Web services during failure despite the competition.

SOCIAL NETWORK SIGN-UP CRITERIA

Competition, substitution, and collaboration are the networks in which Web services can sign up (after signing up they are referred to as social Web services). To support the sign-up decision privacy, trust, fairness, and traceability criteria are evaluated per network. We recall that a network is led by an authority (sn_{auth}) that connects new Web services to existing members, assesses the weights of edges in the network, and enforces the management policies of the network. Policies are discussed a little bit later.

Competition Network

By being part of a competition network, a social Web service (sws_i) is exposed to its competitors and *vice-versa*, which makes them all aware of each other.

1. **Privacy:** A social Web service needs to ensure that appropriate means in this network guarantee the protection of its sensitive de-

tails (e.g., non-functional properties (QoS)) from unauthorized accesses of competing members in the network. If some members get hold of these details they could use them, for instance to beef up their capabilities and hence, become better competitors. We measure the privacy level of a competition network ($Privacy_{Comp}$) by:

$$Privacy_{Comp} = min_{i \in [1,n]} \left(\frac{\left| failedAttacks_{sws_i} \right|}{Attacks_{sws_i}} \right)$$

where |*failedAttacks*| represents the total number of attacks that sws_i was subject to but failed, |*Attacks*| is the total number of attacks on sws_i, and n is the number of social Web services in the network. A lower value of $Privacy_{Comp}$ indicates a poor privacy level in the network.

2. **Trust:** A social Web service needs to be ensured about the trustworthiness of the authority of this network, i.e., it does not leak private details to other members in the network. Some of these details might have been requested by the authority to approve the membership request of the Web service in the network. We measure the trust level of a competition network ($Trust_{Comp}$) by:

$$Trust_{Comp} = 1 - \frac{1}{n} * \sum_{i=1}^{n} \sum_{j=1}^{m} \alpha_{sws_{i,j}} * LeakProb\left(privateDetail_{sws_{i,j}} \right)$$

where *LeakProb*() is a function that returns the probability that the authority reveals sws_i's *privateDetail$_j$* to other peers, $\alpha_{sws_{i,j}}$ is a weight factor reflecting the importance of a private detail (the sum of all α is equal to 1), and m is the number of private details per social Web service.

137

3. **Fairness:** A social Web service needs to be sure that the authority of this network treats all the members equally by for instance, allowing them to avail of the same benefits (or "services"), e.g., knowing the members that join or leave the network. In the network community, Jain et al. propose a well-known fairness index (Jain et al. 1998) that we adopt to measure the fairness level of a competition network (*Fair*$_{Comp}$) as follows:

$$Fair_{Comp} = \frac{\left(\sum_{i=1}^{n} Benefits_{sws_i} \right)^2}{n * \sum_{i=1}^{n} \left(Benefits_{sws_i} \right)^2}$$

where $Benefits_{sws_i}$ represents the number of "services" made available by the authority to sws_i. $Fair_{Comp}$ equals to 1 corresponds to the best case where all social Web services avail of the same benefits. $Fair_{Comp}$ equals to $\frac{k}{n}$ corresponds to the case where k social Web services, only, avail of the same benefits, and the rest (i.e., n-k) do not avail of any benefit.

4. **Traceability:** It permits to keep track of the social Web services' operations and interactions so that the authority can hold them accountable for the outcomes of these operations and interactions in the case of conflicts (e.g., exchanging contradicting details) or irregularities (e.g., flooding the network with unnecessary details). The authority can also analyze these outcomes to verify the quality of social Web services' self-details. This would increase the confidence level of the authority in the social Web services in the network as well as the trust among the social Web services. Traceability runs according to a certain frequency and

for a certain duration over operations (*op*) and/or interactions (*int*). We measure the traceability level of a competition network (*Trace*$_{Comp}$) by:

$$Trace_{Comp} = \frac{1}{2} * \left(\beta_{op} * freq_{op} + \beta_{int} * freq_{int} \right) * d$$

where $\beta \in \{0,1\}$, $\beta_{op} + \beta_{int} = 1$, and *freq* and d are frequency and duration parameters, respectively. Traceability value can be ranked as low, average, or high with respect to some min and max values. For instance high traceability means that a social Web service relies on the authority to generate an accurate trace of the operations that were executed. When the authority detects irregularities, traceability permits for instance, to pin down the responsible social Web services.

Substitution Network

By being part of a substitution network, a social Web service knows the peers that it can count on when it fails so that the completion of the business processes that this social Web service implements is not stopped. Moreover the social Web service can compare its non-functional properties to other peers' similar properties so that a successful substitution is achieved.

1. **Privacy:** A social Web service needs to ensure that negotiations with other peers in this network regarding substitution details (e.g., compensation and penalties in case of no-compliance) are kept confidential. Some of these details can be used by malicious social Web services to be selected instead of appropriate substitutes. We measure the privacy level of a substitution network (*Privacy*$_{Subs}$) as *Privacy*$_{Comp}$ with focus on negotiation:

$Privacy_{Subs}$

$$= min_{i \in [i,n]} \left(\frac{\sum_{j=1}^{n} \left| failedAttacks_{sws_i,sws_j} \right|}{\left| Attacks_{sws_i,sws_j} \right|} \right)$$

where |*failedAttacks*| represents the total number of attacks on the negotiation details involving sws_i and sws_j but failed, and |*Attacks*| is the total number of attacks targeting these two social Web services.

2. **Trust:** Since business-process execution continuity is critical, a social Web service needs to be sure that the members in this network will take over the completion of these processes as expected. We measure the trust level of a substitution network ($Trust_{Subs}$) by:

$$Trust_{Subs} = min_{i \in [1,n]} \left(\frac{successfulSubs_{sws_i}}{Subs_{sws_i}} \right)$$

where $successfulSubs_{sws_i}$ represents the total number of substitutions requested by sws_i and that were complete and $Subs_{sws_i}$ is the total number of substitution requests.

3. **Fairness:** Social Web services need to be sure that the authority of this network allows them all to act as substitutes without favoring some over others. We measure the fairness level of a substitution network ($Fair_{Subs}$) by:

$$Fair_{Subs} = \left(\sqrt{\frac{1}{n} \sum_{i=1}^{n} \left(rf_{sws_i} - \mu \right)^2} \right)^{-1}$$

where $rf_{sws_i} = \frac{ass_{sws_i}}{ass}$ (relative frequency of substituting sws_i), $\mu = \frac{1}{n} * \sum_{i=1}^{n} rf_{sws_i}$ (mean of all relative frequencies), ass_{sws_i} is the number of substitution assignments to other peers in case of sws_i's failures, and *ass* is the total number of substitution assignments in the network.

4. **Traceability:** ($Trace_{Subs}$) interpretation is similar to the interpretation in the competition network ($Trace_{Comp}$). A social Web service can rely on the authority to generate an accurate trace of the interactions that took place before, during, and after substitution.

Collaboration Network

By being part of a collaboration network, a social Web service knows the peers that it likes to work with when building compositions.

1. **Privacy:** A social Web service needs to ensure that appropriate means in this network permit to secure its private details (e.g., non-functional properties (QoS)) since some of these details can be revealed by some untrustworthy members in the network. This puts the social Web service in a vulnerable position when these details are revealed to other (competing) peers by these members. We measure the privacy level of a collaboration network ($Privacy_{Col}$) by:

$Privacy_{Col}$

$$= min_{i \in [1,n]} \left(1 - \frac{\left| focussedRevelations_{sws_i} \right|}{\left| Revelations \right|} \right)$$

where |*FocussedRevelations*| represents the total number of revelations that sws_i was subject to and |*Revelations*| is the total number of revelations affecting the network.

2. **Trust:** A social Web service needs to make sure that the peers it recommends for appending into under-development compositions behave and operate as expected. We measure the trust level of a collaboration network ($Trust_{Col}$) by:

$$Trust_{Col} = min_{i \in [1,n]} \left(\frac{successfulRec_{sws_i}}{Rec_{sws_i}} \right)$$

where *successfulRec* represents the number of recommendations that sws_i made for other peers that accepted and behaved as expected and *Rec* is the total number of recommendations by sws_i.

3. **Fairness:** is not relevant in this network since social Web services are complementary; i.e., they don't compete.

4. **Traceability:** ($Trace_{Col}$) interpretation is similar to the interpretation in competition ($TraceComp$) and substitution ($Trace_{Subs}$) networks. A social Web service can rely on the authority to generate an accurate trace of the recommendation actions that were issued. When the authority detects for instance, regular unsuccessful recommendations, it can look for the reasons.

SOCIAL NETWORKS' MANAGEMENT POLICIES

We briefly mentioned the role of a network's authority in enforcing the implementation of this network's management policies. This enforcement requires making the social Web services aware of the policies so that they can avail of the network's

benefits and also comply with the policies to avoid violations and hence, penalties. We propose some policies per type of network and criterion. We also show that policy compliance happens through a set of commitments.

Competition-Driven Policies

1. **Privacy (*priComp*):** It aims at restricting access to the social Web services' details. The following policies propose ways to achieve this aim.
   a. $P_{priComp,1}$: A social Web service should label its details (e.g., self like ID and nonfunctional like reputation level) as either private, protected, or public.
   b. $P_{priComp,2}$: A social Web service should announce its credentials (e.g., ID and reputation level) to a peer prior to requesting details from this peer. The announcement is done regardless of these details' access levels whether private, protected, or public.

2. **Trust (*truComp*):** It aims at encouraging the social Web services to share their details with the authority (or other peers) upon request. The following policies propose ways to achieve this aim.
   a. $P_{truComp,1}$: A social Web service should expect requests from the authority on its details including private.
   b. $P_{truComp,2}$: A social Web service should send the authority valid non-functional details so that its competitiveness level to other peers is properly assessed.

3. **Fairness (*faiComp*):** It aims at making the social Web services "feel" that they are all treated equally. The following policies propose ways to achieve this aim.
   a. $P_{faiComp,1}$: A social Web service should be kept informed about any detail shared by the authority with other members in the network.

b. $P_{faiComp,2}$: A social Web service should ensure that it shares the same details with all peers in the network.

4. **Traceability (*traComp*):** It aims at tracking the social Web services' operations for quality assurance purposes. The following policies propose ways to achieve this aim.

a. $P_{traComp,1}$: A social Web service should be probed regularly by the authority as part of the monitoring operations that this authority performs.

b. $P_{traComp,2}$: A socialWeb service should be informed by the authority about any necessary action that it has to take in response to this probe.

Substitution-Driven Policies

1. **Privacy (*priSubs*):** It aims at keeping substitution details between the social Web services confidential. The following policies propose ways to achieve this aim.

a. $P_{priSubs,1}$: A social Web service that may be subject to failure should agree with the authority on the substitution details that need to be labeled as either protected or private; public details are not subject to privacy restrictions. Examples of details include compensations and penalties in the case of no-compliance.

b. $P_{priSubs,2}$: A (substitute) socialWeb service should inform the failing socialWeb service about its performance details that need to be labeled as either public, protected, or private.

c. $P_{priSubs,3}$: A social Web service should check the credentials of a peer before it lets this peer act as a substitute.

2. **Trust (*truSubs*):** It aims at ensuring that the social Web services have full confidence in the potential substitutes so that execution process continuity is achieved. The following policies propose ways to achieve this aim.

a. $P_{truSubs,1}$: A social Web service should share with the substitute peer all the necessary details that guarantee execution-process continuity.

b. $P_{truSubs,2}$: A (substitute) social Web service should replace the failing peer as agreed upon between this social Web service, this peer, and the authority.

3. **Fairness (*faiSubs*):** It aims at making the social Web services "feel" that they are given the opportunity to act as substitutes equally. The following policies propose ways to achieve this aim.

a. $P_{faiSubs,1}$: A (substitute) social Web service will be evaluated by the authority with the same criteria used for other peers.

b. $P_{faiSubs,2}$: A social Web service will be kept informed by the authority on all substitution opportunities.

4. **Traceability (*traSubs*):** The aim of traceability and corresponding policies is similar in all networks.

Collaboration-Driven Policies

1. **Privacy (*priCol*):** It aims at protecting the social Web services from the collaborator peers that attempt to collect their details in order to share them with unauthorized peers. The following policies propose ways to achieve this aim.

a. $P_{priCol,1}$: A social Web service should label its details (e.g., with whom it collaborates heavily) as either private, protected, or public.

b. $P_{priCol,2}$: A social Web service should only share the details that the collaborator peer needs before this peer is appended into a composition.

c. $P_{priCol,3}$: A social Web service is penalized by the network's authority when it reveals details to non-members of this network.

2. **Trust (*truCol*):** It aims at ensuring that the social Web services have full confidence in the peers that they recommend to append into ongoing compositions. The following policies propose ways to achieve this aim.

   a. $P_{truCol,1}$: A (collaborator) social Web service should take part in a composition as agreed upon between the recommending peer, this social Web service, and the authority.

   b. $P_{truCol,2}$: A (collaborator) social Web service should operate properly as expected by the recommending peer and authority.

3. **Fairness (*faiCol*):** As fairness is not important in collaboration networks, policies are not required.

4. **Traceability (*traCol*):** The aim of traceability and corresponding policies is similar in all networks.

LINKING SELECTION CRITERIA TO MANAGEMENT POLICIES

The purpose of linking network selection-criteria to network management-policies is to monitor and assess the adoption and efficiency of these policies with respect to the values that these criteria take. Indeed a low value of a certain criterion in a certain network can indicate the inappropriateness of some policies or the limited compliance with some policies. Corrective actions are deemed appropriate such as reviewing existing policies or developing new ones. In the following we discuss the links between criteria and policies per type of network.

Competition Network

1. Privacy criterion is associated with two policies that refer to labeling social Web services' details and checking social Web services' credentials, respectively. A poor privacy level (i.e., $Privacy_{Comp}$ close to zero) raises concerns about the efficiency of the means that assess these credentials as stated in $P_{priComp,2}$. To improve the privacy level corrective actions consist of checking the currently used assessment means or using better, new means so that attacks on social Web services' details are prevented or at least reduced.

2. Trust criterion is associated with two policies that both refer to exchanging details between social Web services and the network's authority. A poor trust level (i.e., $Trust_{Comp}$ close to zero) raises concerns about the credibility of the authority as these social Web services can become reluctant to sending their details as stated in $P_{truComp,1}$. To improve the trust level corrective actions consist of addressing the deficiencies of the authority by for instance, examining this authority's motives in revealing private details and identifying the beneficiaries of these details.

3. Fairness criterion is associated with two policies that both refer to sharing details between social Web services and between social Web services and the network's authority. A poor fairness level (i.e., $Fair_{Comp}$ close to zero and $\frac{k}{n}$ less than a threshold) raises concerns about the efficiency of the means that inform these socialWeb services of the available benefits as stated in $P_{faiComp,1}$ and $P_{faiComp,2}$. To improve the fairness level corrective actions consist of identifying the social Web services that had limited access to the benefits and improving the communication means so that, all social Web services are informed of the benefits.

4. Traceability criterion is associated with two policies that refer to probing and advising social Web services by the network's authority. A poor traceability level (i.e., $Trace_{Comp}$ close to zero) raises concerns about the quality

of the monitoring means that this authority deploys as stated in $P_{traComp,1}$ as well as the willingness of these social Web services in implementing the advices of this authority as stated in $P_{traComp,2}$. To improve the traceability level corrective actions consist of improving the monitoring means and warning the social Web services. We define two additional policies for penalizing and promoting social Web services, respectively, as follows:

a. $P_{traComp,3}$: A social Web service is penalized by the authority when the corrective actions (or advices) that it recommends are not implemented by this social Web service.

b. $P_{traComp,4}$: A social Web service is rewarded by the authority when the corrective actions (or advices) that it recommends are implemented by this social Web service.

Substitution Network

1. Privacy criterion is associated with three policies that refer to labeling substitution details, reporting performance details following substitution, and checking substitutes' credentials. A poor privacy level (i.e., $Privacy_{Subs}$ close to zero) raises concerns about the efficiency of the means used first, to protect these details as stated in $P_{priSubs,1}$ and $P_{priSubs,2}$ and second, to assess these credentials as stated in $P_{priSubs,3}$. To improve the privacy level corrective actions consist of improving the protection and credential check means so that, unauthorized requests over substitution and performance details can be prevented.

2. Trust criterion is associated with two policies that refer to sharing details between failing and substitute social Web services and guaranteeing execution process continuity, respectively. A poor trust level (i.e., $Trust_{Subs}$ close to zero) raises concerns about the ap-

propriateness of these details as stated in $P_{truSubs,1}$ and the confidence that these failing social Web services have in these substitute peers as stated in $P_{truSubs,2}$. To improve the trust level corrective actions include reviewing the means to select substitute social Web services. We define an additional policy for penalizing the substitutes as follows:

a. $P_{truSubs,3}$: A (substitute) social Web service is penalized by the authority when it does not take over the pending operations of a failing peer as agreed initially.

3. Fairness criterion is associated with two policies that refer to evaluating substitute social Web services and sharing substitution opportunities between failing and substitute social Web services and the network's authority. A poor fairness level (i.e., $Fair_{Subs}$ close to zero) raises concerns about the disparity in the criteria used for evaluating these substitute social Web services as stated in $P_{faiSubs,1}$ and the efficiency of the means that inform these substitute social Web services about the substitution opportunities as stated in $P_{faiSubs,2}$. To improve the fairness level corrective actions include revising these evaluation criteria and improving the communication means so that, all social Web services are informed of the substitution opportunities.

4. Traceability criterion is similar in all networks.

Collaboration Network

1. Privacy criterion is associated with three policies that refer to labeling social Web services' collaboration details, sharing these details between recommending and recommended (collaborator) social Web services, and penalizing recommended (collaborator) social Web services. A poor privacy level (i.e., $Privacy_{Col}$ close to zero) raises concerns about the appropriateness of these details

for not disturbing the composition progress as stated in $P_{priCol,2}$ and the efficiency of the means that prevent revealing these details as stated in $P_{priCol,3}$. To improve the privacy level corrective actions consist of identifying the necessary details to share and guaranteeing that recommended peers are trustworthy.

2. Trust criterion is associated with two policies that refer to confirming the participation of recommended social Web services in compositions and guaranteeing the proper functioning of these recommended social Web services. A poor trust level (i.e., $Trust_{Subs}$ close to zero) raises concerns about the confidence that the recommending social Web services have in the recommended peers as stated in $P_{truCol,1}$. To improve this level corrective actions consist of checking the trustworthiness of the recommended peers. We define two additional policies for penalizing the collaborators as follows:

   a. $P_{truCol,3}$: A (collaborator) social Web service is penalized by the authority when it deviates from its expected functioning.

   b. $P_{truCol,4}$: A (collaborator) social Web service is penalized by the authority when it does not take part in a composition as expected.

3. Fairness criterion is not related to any policy.

4. Traceability criterion is similar in all networks.

CONTROLING SOCIAL WEB SERVICES' ACTIONS IN NETWORKS

When a social Web service signs up in a social network, it becomes exposed to the authority of this network and the existing members in this network. This social Web service also avails of the benefits of being a member of the network such as contacting other potential members based on their profile. Because social Web services can now take different actions whose outcomes might ``harm'' peers in the same network (e.g., revealing their private details), or even slowdown the operation of this network (e.g., broadcasting irrelevant details), we hold the social Web services accountable for their actions so that monitoring who did what and when is deemed necessary. In (Maamar et al., 2013b) we suggest commitments as a means to guarantee the compliance of social Web services with the social networks' regulations and detect any violation of these regulations. These commitments reinforce the value-added of management policies to the proper functioning of social networks.

Singh et al. (2009) are the first of few who advocate for examining Service-Oriented Architecture (SOA) principles from a commitment perspective. The traditional SOA is built upon low-level abstractions that are inappropriate for capturing the intrinsic and complex characteristics of business services such as autonomy, complexity, and adaptability. Contrarily a commitment-based SOA allows to judge the correctness of a service enactment as long as the commitments are not violated and to support business compliance without dictating specific operationalization. To identify appropriate commitments for social Web services, we looked at how users' rights and responsibilities are specified in some online social applications like Facebook (www.facebook.com/legal/terms) and LinkedIn (www.linkedin.com/static?key=privacy_policy&trk=hb_ft_priv). Moreover, in preparation for linking responsibilities to commitments, we represent a Responsibility (Resp) with three elements: obligation or permission, actions to perform, and possible conditions that authorize the execution of actions. Some of our proposed responsibilities are listed below:

- **Resp-1:** Collecting any detail (d) in a social network would require indicating the purpose (p) of this collection to this detail's owner (o), represented as Permission(Collect(d, o, valid(p))).

- **Resp-2:** Posting any detail (d) on a social network should be correct, represented as Obligation(Post(d, true)).

- **Resp-3:** Collecting any detail (d) from a social network should not be tampered afterwards, represented as Obligation(not-Tamper(d, o, collection(d))).

The commitments built upon the aforementioned responsibilities are structured using the formalism of Fornara and Colombetti (Fornara and Colombetti, 2002): C-Resp-i(debtor, creditor, content([|condition]) where C-Resp-i is a commitment associated with Resp-i and [] means optional.

- **C-Resp-1:** (sws_i, sws_j, Collect(d, sws_j)|valid(p-d)) is a conditional commitment by sws_i to sws_j, that if valid(p-d) holds then Collect(d, sws_j) will be satisfied.

- **C-Resp-2:** (sws_i, sn-auth, Post(d-self)) is a commitment by sws_i to sn-auth, that Post(d-self) will be satisfied. Self refers to sws_i.

- **C-Resp-3:** (sws_i, sws_j, not-Tamper(d-public, sws_j)|collection(d-public)) is a conditional commitment by sws_i to sws_j, that if collection(d-public) holds then not-Tamper(d-public, sws_j) will be satisfied.

It is possible that social Web services do not honor the commitments that they bind to for reasons such as being malicious or temporary shortage of computation resources. Detecting violations is possible using monitoring (Modgil et al., 2009) which can be coupled to compensation in order to take corrective actions. Besides commitment violation, social Web services can carry out actions that are prohibited. This raises the importance of setting sanctions like decrementing their reputation levels and/or revoking some access privileges.

- **C-Resp-1:** Violation arises when collection occurs over a non-public detail, and prohibition arises when the purpose of a detail collection is neither composition nor substitution.
  - Violation monitoring requires that sws_j reports to sn-auth recurrent, tentative accesses to its non-public details from sws_i. If these tentatives are confirmed using logs for example, this will be a violation to accessing non-public details on sws_j. Sanctions consist of reviewing the trust/reputation levels of sws_i if first time. Otherwise, eject sws_i from the social network if these levels go below a threshold.

- **C-Resp-2:** Violation arises when incorrect details are posted on a social network.
  - Violation monitoring requires that sn-auth checks the veracity of the self-details that sws_i posts. To this end it tracks sws_is operations over time. If this veracity is not confirmed, this will be a violation to posting valid details. Compensations include forcing sws_i to review its details.

- **C-Resp-3:** Violation arises when a collected detail is tampered, and prohibition arises when a detail is collected without approval.
  - Violation monitoring requires that sn-auth checks how sws_i uses the details it has collected from sws_j. If the integrity of these details is not maintained, this will be a violation to collecting details on sws_j. Compensations include either posting/refreshing new/existing details on sws_j.

RELATED WORK

Establishing criteria to assist Web services decide whether or not they sign up in a social network should lead into developing a Quality of Social Network (QoSN) model. Similar models exist in other fields through the use of Quality of Service (QoS) that is built upon non-functional properties. Our literature review did not reveal explicit works on QoSN but aspects related to quality social network, software quality assessment using social networks, and relationship between quality of social networks and investment decisions.

Perego et al. (2009) discuss the quality social network as part of a collaborative environment to personalize Web access. The notion of quality social network is quite different from the suggested model in this chapter. The authors use social tagging to evaluate the quality of Web resources based on users' preferences and opinions. The safety and trustworthiness are among the aspects that the quality social network addresses. According to Perego et al., "...the Web as a whole is still considered by many as a source of unreliable and untrustworthy information, thus preventing the exploitation of its full potentialities". The quality social network provides end-users the possibility of associating labels with Web resources as well as using rates to express their disagreement on existing labels.

Tawileh et al. (2008) propose a social networking approach to assess the quality of Free and Open Source Software (FOSS). The increasing number of available FOSS does not ease the job of users who have to select the most suitable ones in response to specific needs and requirements. The social networking approach is built upon a trust-aware recommendation system that promotes different types of users including expert reviewers, users with profiles, and users without profiles.

Tonchev and Tonchev (2010) look at social networks, e.g., Facebook and Twitter, from a quality perspective, which is in line with the proposed model in this chapter. They insist that the popular-ity of social networks can sustain business growth subject to maintaining a good service quality. They raise the question of what a social network quality is and how it can be measured. A set of criteria for assessing this quality is listed including conformance to specifications, features and content, safety and security, privacy, and access.

Dasgupta and Dasgupta (2010) shed the light on the obstacles that users have to wrestle with when they sign up simultaneously in different social networks. Duplicate information, privacy loss, and redundant information flow result from this simultaneous sign up. Today's social networks applications are almost the same in terms of features provided to users. To alleviate these obstacles Dasgupta and Dasgupta propose the Social Network as a Service (SNaaS) model. It is kind of single counter that offers specialized services such as blogging, mentoring, and community management. These services will then give access to specific social networks applications, e.g., LinkedIn that concentrates on corporate social network aspects.

FUTURE RESEARCH DIRECTIONS

We have looked into some future research opportunities associated with social Web services (Maamar et al., 2013a) and here we summarize three of them.

Labeling Communities with Social Qualities: Efforts put into assigning social qualities (e.g., selfishness, fairness, and trustworthiness) to Web services are described in (Yahyaoui et al., 2013). For instance, a selfish Web service continuously receives positive response from peers when it seeks their assistance for substitution, but it continuously declines others' assistance requests. The identification of these social qualities took into account the fact that Web services offering similar functionalities are grouped together into communities. Communities are pockets of expertise (with reference to the functionalities of Web services) that, among other things, ease the discovery of necessary Web services during users' requests satisfaction. Analyzing communities from a social perspective will require identifying possible social relations between communities, building social networks of communities using these relations, and assigning social qualities to communities after mining into these networks. The following relations are expected to exist between communities: competition, collaboration delegation (or sub-contracting), and coopetition (simultaneous competition and delegation).

Incentives for Social Web Services: A social Web service needs to evaluate the impact of signing up in networks, e.g., collaboration and substitution, using the rewards that it receives back, for example. Social Web services will accept to recommend or replace a peer only if the generated incentive is at least equal or higher to what it could acquire without being a member of these networks. Incentive mechanisms have been studied using cooperative game theory in the multi-agent context. However, this raises other questions such as: what are the adaptations required for social Web services' incentive analysis; how the incentives influence reasoning about trust and reputation of these social Web services; and what is the link between argumentation and incentives.

Realizing an Ecosystem of Social Web Services: The success in Web services goes well beyond the building of loosely coupled, interoperable software components. Nowadays, large-scale collaboration through social media (e.g., social networks) and new generation of service-oriented software have spurred the growth of Web service ecosystems. An ecosystem of social Web services is required in order to define first, the necessary actors that take part in this ecosystem formation and second, the interactions that occur between these actors during this ecosystem management. Such ecosystem permits to track who does what and where and when it is done. The actors in the ecosystem are referred to as providers of Web services, providers of social networks of social Web services, consumers of Web services, and providers of social networks of consumers. They all engage in different types of interactions like making Web services sign up in social networks of social Web services, supporting users seek advices from existing members in a social network of consumers, and combining social networks of consumers and of Web services to achieve users' requests.

CONCLUSION

This chapter discussed the assessment of social networks populated with Web services. These networks are referred to as collaboration, substitution, and competition and allow Web services to recommend the collaborator and substitute peers as well as to be aware of the competitor peers. The assessment was built upon four criteria that are privacy, trust, fairness, and traceability. Besides these criteria, policies that guarantee the proper management of the social networks were defined. Upon signing up in a social network, social Web services have to fully comply with these policies. The connection between the selection criteria of social networks and the policies for social networks management was also discussed in the chapter. This connection permitted to review the efficiency of the existing policies calling for new policy definition in some cases. Last but not least, ensuring the good ``behavior'' of social Web services in networks was established through commitments that reinforce the value-added of policies to a proper management of social networks. Any violation of these commitments detected through monitoring requires taking corrective actions and imposing sanctions on the faulty social Web services. Prior to concluding the chapter a set of future research directions were identified.

REFERENCES

Dasgupta, D., & Dasgupta, R. (2010). *Social networks using web 2.0, part 2: Social network as a service (SNaaS)*. Retrieved from http://www.ibm.com/developerworks/webservices/library/ws-socialpart2/index.html?ca=drs

Di Martino, B. (2009). Semantic web services discovery based on structural ontology matching. *International Journal of Web and Grid Services*, *5*(1), 46–65. doi:10.1504/IJWGS.2009.023868

Fornara, N., & Colombetti, M. (2002). Operational specification of a commitment- based agent communication language. In *Proceedings of the 1st International Joint Conference on Autonomous Agents & MultiAgent Systems (AAMAS'2002)*, (pp. 536-542). Bologna, Italy: AAMAS.

Jain, R., Chiu, D.-M., & Hawe, W. (1998). A quantitative measure of fairness and discrimination for resource allocation in shared computer systems. In *Proceedings of CoRR*. CoRR.

Maamar, Z., Bentahar, D., Faci, N., & Thiran, P. (2013a). Social web services research roadmap: Present & future. In *Distributed computing innovations for business, engineering, and science*. Hershey, PA: IGI Global Publishing.

Maamar, Z., Faci, N., Badr, Y., Krug Wives, L., Bispo dos Santos, P., Benslimane, D., & Palazzo Moreira de Oliveira, J. (2011a). Towards a framework for weaving social networks principles into web services discovery. In *Proceedings of the International Conference on Web Intelligence, Mining, and Semantics (WIMS'2011)*. Sogndal, Norway: WIMS.

Maamar, Z., Faci, N., Boukadi, K., Sheng, Q. Z., & Yao, L. (2013b). *Commitments to regulate social web services operation*. IEEE Transactions on Services Computing.

Maamar, Z., Faci, N., Krug Wives, L., Badr, Y., Bispo dos Santos, P., & Palazzo Moreira de Oliveira, J. (2011b). Using social networks to web services discovery. *IEEE Internet Computing*, *15*(4), 48–54. doi:10.1109/MIC.2011.27

Maamar, Z., Faci, N., Krug Wives, L., Yahyaoui, H., & Hacid, H. (2011c). Towards a method for engineering social web services. In *Proceedings of the IFIP WG8.1 Working Conference on Method Engineering (ME'2011)*. Paris, France: IFIP.

Maamar, Z., Hacid, H., & Hunhs, M. N. (2011d). Why web services need social networks. *IEEE Internet Computing*, *15*(2), 90–94. doi:10.1109/MIC.2011.49

Maamar, Z., Krug Wives, L., Badr, Y., Elnaffar, S., Boukadi, K., & Faci, N. (2011e). LinkedWS: A novel web services discovery model based on the metaphor of social networks. *Simulation Modelling Practice and Theory*, *19*(10), 121–132. doi:10.1016/j.simpat.2010.06.018

Maaradji, A., Hacid, H., Daigremont, J., & Crespi, N. (2010). Towards a social network based approach for services composition. In *Proceedings of the 2010 IEEE International Conference on Communications (ICC'2010)*. Cape Town, South Africa: IEEE.

Modgil, S., Faci, N., Rech Meneguzzi, F., Oren, N., Miles, S., & Luck, M. (2009). A framework for monitoring agent-based normative systems. In *Proceedings of the 8th International Conference on Autonomous Agents and MultiAgent Systems (AAMAS'2009)*. Budapest, Hungary: AAMAS.

Nam Ko, M., Cheek, G. P., Shehab, M., & Sandhu, R. (2010). Social-networks connect services. *IEEE Computer*, *43*(8), 37–43. doi:10.1109/MC.2010.239

Perego, A., Carminati, B., & Ferrari, E. (2009). The quality of social network: A collaborative environment for personalizing web access. In *Proceedings of the International Conference on Collaborative Computing: Networking, Applications, and Worksharing (CollaborateCom'2009)*. Washington, DC: CollaborateCom.

Singh, M. P., Chopra, A. K., & Desai, N. (2009). Commitment-based service- oriented architecture. *Computer, 42*(11), 72–79. doi:10.1109/MC.2009.347

Tawileh, A., Rana, O., & Mcintosh, S. (2008). A social networking approach to F/OSS quality assessment. In *Proceedings of the International Conference on Computer Mediated Social Networking (ICCMSN' 2008)*. Dunedin, New Zealand: ICCMSN.

Tonchev, A., & Tonchev, C. (2010). *Social networks: A quality perspective*. The Big Q Blog. Retrieved from http://www.juran.com/blog/?p=127

Wu, Q., Iyengar, A., Subramanian, R., Rouvellou, I., Silva-Lepe, I., & Mikalsen, T. (2009). Combining quality of service and social information for ranking services. In *Proceedings of ServiceWave 2009 Workshops held in Conjunction with the 7th International Conference on Service Service-Oriented Computing (ICSOC'2009)*. Stockholm, Sweden: ICSOC.

Xie, X., Du, B., & Zhang, Z. (2008). Semantic service composition based on social network. In *Proceedings of the 17ᵗʰ International World Wide Web Conference (WWW'2008)*. Beijing, China: WWW.

Yahyaoui, H., Maamar, Z., Lim, E., & Thiran, P. (2013). Towards a community-based, social network-driven framework for web services management. *Future Generation Computer Systems, 29*(6), 1363–1377. doi:10.1016/j.future.2013.02.003

ADDITIONAL READING

Badr, Y., & Maamar, Z. (2009). Can Enterprises Capitalize on Their Social Networks? *Cutter IT Journal, 22*(10), 10–14.

Bansal, S., Bansal, A., & Blake, M. B. (2010). Trust-based Dynamic Web Service Composition Using Social Network Analysis. In *Proceedings of the International Workshop on Business Applications for Social Network Analysis (BASNA'2010) held in conjunction with the Fourth International Conference on Internet Multimedia Systems Architecture and Applications (IM-SAA'2010)*, Bangalore, India, pp. 1–8.

Castelfranchi, C. (1995). Commitments: From Individual Intentions to Groups and Organizations. In *Proceedings of the International Conference on MultiAgent Systems (ICMAS'1995)*, San Francisco, California, USA, pp. 41–48.

Chard, K., Caton, S., Rana, O., & Bubendorfer, K. (2010). Social Cloud: Cloud Computing in Social Networks. In *Proceedings of the 3rd IEEE International Conference on Cloud Computing (CLOUD'2010)*, Miami, Florida, USA, pp.99–106.

Khosravifar, B., Bentahar, J., Moazin, A., & Thiran, P. (2010). Analyzing Communities of Web Services Using Incentives. *International Journal of Web Services Research, 7*(3), 30–51. doi:10.4018/jwsr.2010070102

McDonald, D. W. (2003). Recommending Collaboration with Social Networks: A Comparative Evaluation. In *Proceedings of the SIGCHI Conference on Human Factors in Computing Systems (CHI'2003)*, pp. 593–600, Ft. Lauderdale, Florida, USA, pp. 593–600.

Min, L., Weiming, S., Qi, H., & Junwei, Y. (2009). A Weighted Ontology-based Semantic Similarity Algorithm for Web Services. *Expert Systems with Applications, 36*(10), 12480–12490. doi:10.1016/j.eswa.2009.04.034

Moody, J., & White, D. R. (2003). Structural Cohesion and Embeddedness: A Hierarchical Concept of Social Groups. *American Sociological Review*, *68*(1), 103–127. doi:10.2307/3088904

Obreiter, P., & Nimis, J. (2003). A Taxonomy of Incentive Patterns - The Design Space of Incentives for Cooperation. In *Proceedings of Second International Workshop on Agents and Peer-to-Peer Computing (AP2PC'2003)*, Melbourne, Australia, pp. 89–100.

Pujol, J. M., Sanguesa, R., & Delgado, J. (2002). Extracting Reputation in Multi Agent Systems by Means of Social Network Topology. In *Proceedings of the First International Joint Conference on Autonomous Agents & Multi-Agent Systems (AAMAS'2002)*, Bologna, Italy, pp. 467–474.

Vossen, G. (2009). Web 2.0: A Buzzword, a Serious Development, just Fun, or What? In *Proceedings of the International Conference on Security and Cryptography (SECRYPT'2009)*, Milan, Italy, 33–40.

Xiao, Z., Zhang, Q., Shi, Y., & Gao, Y. (2012). How Much to Share: A Repeated Game Model for Peer-to-Peer Streaming under Service Differentiation Incentives. *IEEE Transactions on Parallel and Distributed Systems*, *23*(2), 288–295. doi:10.1109/TPDS.2011.167

KEY TERMS AND DEFINITIONS

Composite Web Service: Composition targets users' requests that cannot be satisfied by any single, available Web service. A composite Web service obtained by combining available Web services may be used. Several specification languages to compose Web services exist for example WS-BPEL (de facto standard), WSCDL, and XLANG. A composite Web service could be built either proactively or reactively. The former is an off-line process that gathers available component Web services in-advance to form a composite Web service. This one is pre-compiled and ready for execution upon users' requests. The latter creates a composite Web service on-the-fly upon users' requests. Because of the on-the fly property, a dedicated module is in charge of identifying the needed component Web services, making them collaborate, tracking their execution, and resolving their conflicts if they arise.

Ecosystem of Social Web Services: It consists of a set of actors namely providers of Web Services, providers of social networks of social Web services, consumers of Web services), and providers of social networks of consumers. They all engage in different types of interactions like making Web services sign up in social networks of social Web services, supporting users seek advices from existing members in a social network of consumers, and combining social networks of consumers and of Web services to achieve users' requests.

SOA (Service-Oriented Architecture): SOA is an architecture style that builds on loosely coupled, interoperable and composable components or software agents called services. Services have well-defined interfaces based standard protocols (usually Web-services but most definitions mention that it is not the only possible implementation) as well as Quality of Service (QoS) attributes (or policies) on how these interfaces can be used by Service Consumers. SOA definitions mentions the basic communication pattern for SOA is request/reply but many definitions also talk about asynchronous communications as well.

Social Computing: Social computing is related to applications that support collaborative work (GroupWare) and techniques for modeling, simulating, studying, and analyzing the society (i.e., study the social behavior). Examples of applications include on-line communities and tools, and interactive entertainment and training. Another definition sees social computing as an emerging paradigm that involves a multi-disciplinary approach for analyzing and modeling social behaviors on different media and platforms to produce intelligent applications. Main characteristics of social computing are connectivity, collaboration, and community.

Web Service: It is "a software application identified by a URI, whose interfaces and binding are capable of being defined, described, and discovered by XML artifacts, and supports direct interactions with other software applications using XML-based messages via Internet-based applications" (W3C). A Web service implements a functionality (e.g., Book Order and Forecast Weather) that users and other peers invoke by submitting appropriate messages to this Web service. The life cycle of a Web service could be summarized with five stages namely description, publication, discovery, invocation, and composition. Briefly, providers describe their Web services and publish them on dedicated registries. Potential consumers (i.e., requesters) interact with these registries to discover relevant Web services, so they could invoke them. In case the discovery fails, i.e., requests cannot be satisfied by any single Web service, the available Web services may be composed to satisfy the consumer's request.

Chapter 7
Declarative Service Modeling through Adaptive Case Management

Evan Morrison
University of Wollongong, Australia

Hoa Dam
University of Wollongong, Australia

Aditya Ghose
University of Wollongong, Australia

Alex Menzies
Expert and Decision Support Systems Institute, Australia

Katayoun Khodaei
University of Wollongong, Australia

ABSTRACT

Adaptive case management addresses the shift away from the prescriptive process-centric view of operations towards a declarative framework for operational descriptions that promotes dynamic task selection in knowledge-intensive operations. A key difference between prescriptive services and declarative services is the way by which control flow is defined. Repeatable and straight-thru processes have been successfully used to model and optimise simple activity-based value chains. Increasingly, traditional process modeling techniques are being applied to knowledge intensive activities with often poor outcomes. By taking an adaptive case management approach to knowledge-intensive services, it is possible to model and execute workflows such as medical protocols that have previously been too difficult to describe with typical BPM frameworks. In this chapter, the authors describe an approach to design-level adaptive case management leveraging off existing repositories' semantically annotated business process models.

DOI: 10.4018/978-1-4666-5884-4.ch007

1 INTRODUCTION

Research in business process management (BPM) has recently been heavily focused on the operational activities of organisations. One crucial research challenge in the space is that of activity fulfilment in dynamic environments. Recently, there has been an increasing drive for the examination of case handling and management as an alternative to traditional straight-thru processing (Zhu et al., 2013). Straight-thru processing deals with the construction and operation of repeatable workflow and process designs, whereas, case management investigates roles, life cycle, and activity implementation from a more consumer or interactional point of view (Ly, Rinderle-Ma, Göser, & Dadam, 2012). This chapter addresses the shift away from the prescriptive process centric view of operations toward a declarative framework for operational descriptions. This movement promotes intelligent task diversity in knowledge intensive operations. A key difference between prescriptive processes and declarative process is the definition of control flow. Repeatable and straight-thru processes allow easy modeling and optimisation of basic activity based value chains (Morrison, Ghose, Dam, Hinge, & Hoesch-Klohe, 2012). Poor outcomes typically result from the application of process modeling techniques to knowledge intensive activities (Zhu et al., 2013). An adaptive case management (ACM) approach to process management makes it possible to create knowledge intensive workflows that are not possible to model using traditional BPM systems.

"Case management is built around the concept of processing a case, a collection of information and coordinated activities, by organisational knowledge workers" (Zhu et al., 2013). Typically, a case is a focused view of an interaction with a business unit or organisation by an external entity (customer). A customer, driven through some desire or need, engages with an organisation. These engagements typically result in mutual exchange for services and resources. Through these interactions, various processes compositions and choreographies appear to create a semi coherent procedure aimed at satisfying the customer's primary goals or desires. This differs from traditional workflows, which make personalised customer transactions and narrative based progressions impossible. Prescriptive processes also typically mean that a customer engaging at multiple touch points will need to repeat activities, such as explaining goals several times for each process context. Within a case management framework, a customer engagement case contains all details of the customer's goals and past interactions, sharing case details throughout the execution cycle. As such, all relevant data and information are available from within the processes and also for the composition engine.

During the creation of workflow systems, process designers strive to create process models and designs that benefit many varying use cases (Bleistein, Cox, & Verner, 2006; Edirisuriya & Johannesson, 2009; Wang & Ghose, 2010). The problem for these activities is in defining processes that can be used in varying contexts based on customer demands and intentions (Koliadis, Ghose, & Padmanabhuni, 2008; Wang & Ghose, 2010; Gordijn, Soetendal, & Paalvast, 2005). Being able to dynamically construct a process that effectively works to satisfy consumer goals as well as business goals taking into consideration operational and historic context is necessary in a business setting (Koliadis & Ghose, 2006; Koliadis et al., 2008; Gordijn et al., 2005). To ensure that enterprise context is realised we presuppose that process models contribute to some part of an organizational strategy and also satisfy customer desires.

In this chapter, we describe the use of adaptive case management (Khomyakov & Bider, 2000; Mundbrod, Kolb, & Reichert, 2012; Strijbosch, 2011; Hildebrandt, Mukkamala, & Slaats, 2011a, 2011b) and strategic alignment (Morrison et al., 2012) to model task composition and choreography that will provides declarative support to organizations with existing process management solutions. This work leverages research into semantically annotated tasks for meaningful business process modeling.

Using the declarative case management framework presented in this chapter, organization will be able to leverage their existing process management systems to begin to transition and support new knowledge intensive services in an adaptive case management context.

This chapter is broken into the following order. In § 2, we have provided an example scenario that describes a generic complaint handling process, this process is used to demonstrate a scenario where declarative service modeling is beneficial and is also used throughout the chapter to provide details on key concepts. In § 3, we provide a background of the language that form the basis of this framework. In § 4 we provide the key chapter contributions. First, we describe a mechanism for computing end-to-end scenarios using existing organisational process definitions. Secondly, we show how to compute the semantic state of new constructed case management sequence flows. We compare our work to existing literature in § 7, then conclude and position our future work in § 8.

2 MOTIVATING EXAMPLE

Throughout this chapter, we will use a fictionalised motivating example for telephone company *VirgaFone* to introduce the conceptual building

blocks and finally a framework of dynamic and declarative service composition. The knowledge systems that we work with are shown in the overview of VirgaFone in Figure 1. These are the strategic landscape, process repository, business rules and knowledge base. The strategic landscape includes details of the rationale and desires that VirgaFone wishes to achieve with it's call centre. A process repository is used to maintain all operational activities that VirgaFone is capable of performing. Business rules are integrated into processes to maintain application logic across the operational elements of VirgaFone. A knowledge base of key definition and logical correlations is used to support decision making between strategic and operational levels.

Process Repository: The example case for the company *VirgaFone* described here is of a *complaint handling process*. The complaint handling process is a commonly servitised process that is deployed across in most telecom customer call centres. The process has been depicted in Figure 2 using the business process modeling notation (the notation is discussed in § 3).

The process flows as follows, if a customer is upset at any point in time with the level of service or products that they have received through a transaction with *VirgaFone*, they will call the call centre and make a complaint. The first stage of a complaint handling process is to ensure that the customer details are recorded, and as such verifying customer details is the first task completed by the call centre agent. In the event that a customer

Figure 1. VirgaFone Call Centre overview

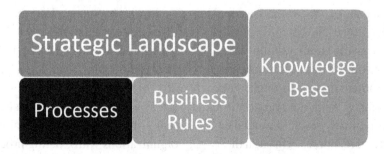

Figure 2. VirgaFone complaints handling process

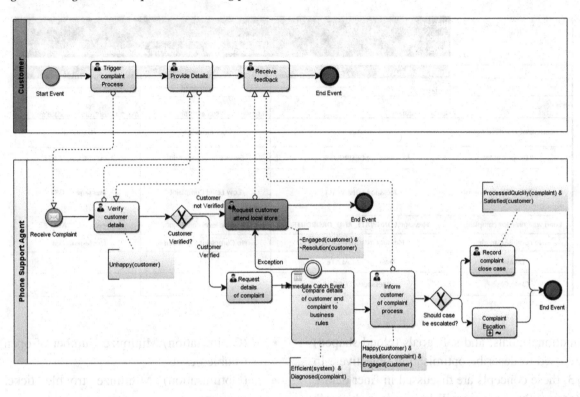

can not be verified over the phone then they will be directed to make their complaint in person at the closest local store or business kiosk. This is marked in the model as an orange task, as it is a *non-intentional* or *exceptional* task (discussed in § 3).

Business Rules: After a customer has been verified, then the complaint is recorded and assessed against a collection of business rules. Business rules can be represented in any number of formations, including through SBVR (Semantics of Business Vocabulary and Business Rules), plain text and processable rules formats (for example drools rules language). To avoid confusion we are using a Drools spreadsheet encoding of a set of simple decision rules. These are shown in Figure 3, the first section describes the rule namespace and reference classes, the second section describes a set of mapping from state to conditions for the process flow. Currently, the rules state that if a

complain is made about long waits, that the process should be directed to the close case task, otherwise if the customer is experiencing call drop outs that their case should be escalated for further customer satisfaction management.

When the process has been completed, either the customers will have been directed to a business centre/kiosk, the customers complaint will have been recorded or the customers complaint will have been escalated for further processing by a customer engagement officer.

Strategic Landscape: A strategic landscape is a list of strategic goals that describe core values that the call centre wants to realize. We have used an *i** styled goal notation to model strategies. A goal model, describes the organisational desires and intentions, they guide specific process deployments with purpose and reason. A goal model describes the *why* of operations. Notational hard goals (rounded ellipses) are used to describe

Figure 3. Decision rules for VirgaFone complaints handling process

	RuleSet	au.edu.uow.dsl	
	Import	au.edu.uow.dsl.DecisionTable.Message	
	Notes	This decision table is used for complaint handling escalations	
	RuleTable VirgaFone		
	CONDITION	ACTION	ACTION
	m:Message		
	status == $param	m.setMessage("$param");update(m);	m.setStatus($param);update(m);
Complaint Handling Rules	**Status**	**Set message**	**Set status**
Call Drops out lots	Message.DROPOUTS	Service level complaint	Message.ESCALATE
Long wait time for complaints	Message.LONGWAIT	Low Level Complaint	Message.CLOSE
Long wait time for complaints	Message.LONGWAIT_AND_DROPOUTS	Service level complaint	Message.ESCALATE
No complaint made	Message.NOCOMPLAINT	No Complaint Recorded	Message.CLOSE
Escalate	Message.ESCALATE		
Close Case	Message.CLOSE		

functional goals, and soft goals (cloud shaped) are used to describe optimisation objectives. In §3, these concepts are discussed in finer detail. Because this process will be run in a dynamic environment, where call load and exceptional scenarios highly possible to occur, a goal model of VirgaFone's aims and objectives can be used to inform decision makers when process improvement activities are performed. In Figure 4, a goal model of the call centre has been provided and describes the heirarchy of soft / hard goals for the call centre.

Each functional goal usually has an included predicate description that can help during strategic alignment. The strategies of the VirgaFone call centre are as follows:

- (Optimisation) Minimize call centre staffing costs
- (Optimisation) Minimize complaint escalations
- (Optimisation) Minimize trouble report rates
- (Optimisation) Maximize Trouble tickets cleared

- (Optimisation) Minimize Number of open trouble tickets
- (Optimisation) Minimize trouble ticket volume
- (Optimisation) Maximize number of trouble tickets closed
- (Optimisation) Minimize average time duration between trouble ticket creation to clear
- (Optimisation) Minimize diagnosis to complete
- (Optimisation) Minimize time Spent in Pending/Holding State
- (Optimisation) Minimize time spent on Diagnosis
- (Goal) Maintain efficient complaint handling systems
- (Goal) Maintain High Resolution speeds
- (Goal) Achieve high satisfaction amongst customers
- (Goal) Achieve high customer engagement

Knowledge Base: Artefacts from different levels of abstraction generally are described in different languages and with differing levels of

Figure 4. Goal model for VirgaFone Call Centre

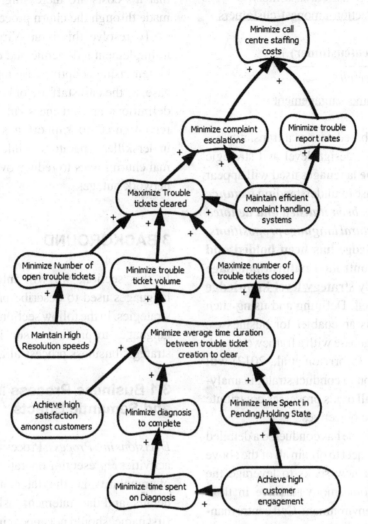

coarseness, it is essential to maintain a data dictionary and knowledge base that describes key concepts and can be used to translate between the concepts. A domain specific knowledge base that describes the call centre is provided below as a set of rules are written as a knowledge dictionary i.e. $A \Rightarrow B$. Whenever A is observable then B exists.

Resolution(complaint) $\wedge$
(Execution(time) < 10min**)**
$\Rightarrow$ **Resolution(complaint, highspeed)**

$$\frac{|\ instance(\textbf{Resolution(complaint, highspeed)})\ |}{|\ instance(all)\ |} \geq .55 \Rightarrow$$

Maintain-High-Resolution-speeds

$$\frac{|\ instance(Resolution(complaint))\ |}{|\ instance(all)\ |} \geq .75 \Rightarrow$$

Efficient(ComplaintSystem)

Efficient(ComplaintSystem) $\Rightarrow$ Maintain-efficient-complaint-handling-systems

Processed(case) $\land$ Satisfied(customer) $\Rightarrow$
<u>Achieve-high-satisfaction-amongst-customers</u>

$$\frac{|\ instance(\ \mathbf{Engaged(customer)}\ )\ |}{|\ instance(all)\ |} \geq .75 \Rightarrow$$

<u>Achieve-high-customer-engagement</u>

The knowledge based acts as a translator between instance level, design level and strategic level, and as such the languages used will appear non-standard, for ease of understanding *instance level knowledge has been italisied and denoted using controlled natural language propositions*, **design level knowledge has been bolded and is denoted using controlled natural language propositions**, finally <u>strategy level knowledge has been underlined</u>. Defining and using such a knowledge base is an enabler for businesses. Using this knowledgebase with a framework such as that described in (Morrison et al., 2012) will allow an organisation to conduct strategic analysis, to determine if all of it's processes contribute towards it's strategic objectives.

Scenario: VirgaFone has conducted a detailed business analysis project to obtain all of the above BPM artefacts, and now seeks to leverage the information to become more adaptive in their dynamic operating environment. Call centre managers have observed that in the event that there is a large network outage in a particular area, their customers begin to complain heavily. When this happens, VirgaFone's normal customers have high wait times and become disgruntled with a high churn rate (a customer churns from a network by switching carriers). VirgaFone would like to lower these churn occurrences and has invested heavily in a scalable call centre (during peak demands, the call centre requests resources from external call centres or other call departments); however, the additional call centre team are not as flexible or knowledgeable about the complaints process as existing staff members. Though has now found that by simply throwing more bodies at it's problem

that it's costs are increasing beyond the losses made through the churn process.

To resolve this issue VirgaFone has begun to implement a dynamic and declarative service system using adaptive case management. In this case, as the call staff are onboarded, the process definitions and business rules are dynamically reconfigured to support a smaller number of underskilled operators, while maintaining optimal churn losses to reduce overall losses during network outages.

3 BACKGROUND

In this section, we will introduce the set of languages used to describe process models and strategies. In the follow sections, we will use these languages to produce a succinct description of strategic business process alignment.

3.1 Business Process Models and Semantic Effects

Decisions in a Process: Processes are created using activities representing operations at the same level of granularity, i.e. the statement 'verify customer details' and the statement 'ask the user for their first name' should not appear in the same process. Each process may itself become an activity in a more abstract process model, i.e. the activity 'ask the user for their first name' may occur in a process 'verify customer details'. The Business Process Modeling Notation, BPMN (Dijkman & Van Gorp, 2011), is a standardized notation for process models, by which a process model can be viewed as a representation of a set of activities, and decision rules. The purpose of process modeling is to show the activities that actors or systems perform. Each process should represent a specific, repeatable set of steps. Generally process models are created from a combination of activities, decisions and sequence flow. An activity is a single unit of operation and describes a specific step that can be completed. A decision is a point where the model splits. Depending on environmental state or a user choice, only one path is generally chosen to follow during the execution of a process. Sequence flow is the transition between two activities. Sequence gives order to the activities and creating process models, used to represent business specific process models. It is formed using a collection of activities, gateways, events, sequence flows, pools, swim lanes, and message flows. In this work, whenever a process model is referred to, we mean it to have the qualities and elements of a BPMN process model. A set of business process models is referred to as a process portfolio. In much the same way as an investment portfolio, a process portfolio is representative of an organizations process assets based on their existing needs and functional requirements.

In a process model, gateways can be used to describe choices and other types of process decisions. XOR gateways can be used to represent exclusive choice and branches the execution of a process model depending on either user choice, or environmental variables. AND gateways represent a parallel sequence splitting. When a process model splits via an AND gateway, activities of all outgoing branches of the gateway are run independently of the other branches. The sequence between activities on the same branch is still maintained. There are other types of gateways; the reader is referred to (Dijkman & Van Gorp, 2011) for complete executional semantics.

An event in a process model, is a triggering object, and can be used to instantiate or cease execution through the process, they can also be used to handle intermediate events, such as timer alarms when a process is taking too long. Typically all process models have both a start and an end event. A start event is used as the execution entry point in the process model. An end event is used as the execution termination point of the process model. Once an execution sequence reaches an end event then the instance of the process model has come to an end. It is possible to have more

than one starting event and more than one end event in a given model, though for more than one start event the process needs to clearly define a default start point.

Sequence flow in a process model generally goes from one starting event through a series of activities and gateways to the end event. However it is also very possible to have multiple start events and multiple and end events, signifying different triggering or entry points in the model and different ending points in the model.

An effect scenario describes the result of executing an instance of an activity or part of a process model. The effect scenarios of activities in a process model are given with semantic annotations that describe the resulting changes of state brought about by executing the activity. In this paper we represent each effect as a prime implicant proposition and consider a set of effects as a sentence constructed by the conjunction of the propositions in the set. Through a mechanism of accumulation of effect scenarios, the effects of a process model can be found. Hinge (Hinge, Ghose, & Koliadis, 2009), has described a function for accumulation that takes two effect scenarios and returns a consistent set of effect scenarios called an accumulated effect scenario. This accumulation can be done in a pairwise manner across a process model to find the effect scenarios of the process.

In a similar fashion, Hoesch-Klohe's (Hoesch-Klohe, Ghose, & Le., 2010) framework Abnoba, can be used to annotate QoS capabilities to activities in a process model. These activities can then be pairwise accumulated, to show capabilities for the process.

There are various encodings of process models. Typically, the encodings either find a basis in the space of Petri-net's or graphs. The most common encoding for process models is a WF-net (workflow network) described by van der Aalst (Van Der Aalst, 1998), however, is not suitable for this work because of the nature of execution traces. For this article, a directed graph process model has been used; however, the authors contend that the definitions of alignment will fit the process encodings definitions of Dijkman et. al. (Dijkman & Van Gorp, 2011). Dijkman et. al. have described an extensive BPMN graph encoding including the execution semantic of a large selection of BPMN elements, which is by far too detailed to describe in the space allowed. A process model as a graph is a strongly connected directed graph, where activities events and gateways are nodes in the graph and sequence flow are the edges. Each node in the graph is labelled with a type, a name, and extra attributes such as QoS values and semantic effects.

3.2 Strategy Modeling Language

When thinking at an organizational level, it is common to focus on the notion of a strategic plan. Generally, a strategic plan can be broken down into the following headings:

- Organizational description that includes, its structure, vision and mission statement.
- Context, describing the industry scope as trends, advances, opportunities, and weaknesses. The organizational context will also include information about governance and distinctive competencies that make the organization unique.
- Risks including both new and existing. The strategy should list ways that the organization has identified to mitigate these risks.
- A strategy model is a hierarchical definition of strategies that the organization believes will help move it forward while also addressing contextual issues and identified risks. Each strategy usually has an aim, purpose, constraints and stakeholders.
- Processes/Programs are lists of the operational mechanisms that an organization will use to realize strategies in the strategy model.

In previous work (Ghose, Lê, K, & Morrison, 2010), we have proposed a language that can be used by senior executives for describing organizational strategies as part of the strategy model in a strategic plan. This language is the strategy modeling language (SML). The core modeling elements of SML are: Functional Goals, Plans, and Optimization Objectives. These elements can be used in combination to describe a typical strategy model.

There has been a vast amount of work describing strategy modeling such as that done in (Ghose et al., 2010). A strategy model in the strategy modeling language (SML) can be constructed to describe an organization's strategies. SML was developed to provide analysts with a crisp language for describing organization strategies using Goals, and Plans, Optimization Objectives. Using SML we have established an alignment function that maps cumulative effects to strategic goals.

For the most part, goals are the building block of strategy description languages. When describing a goal, various requirements are encoded (as part of the goal description) to the goal. When the goal's requirements are achieved the goal is realized. For an introduction to goals and methodologies that exist for goal interpretation the reader is referred to (van Lamsweerde, 2001). Functional Goals describe outcomes that organizations would like to achieve. When written in SML, these can be evaluated as either fulfilled or not fulfilled. Functional goals are used to reflect internal and external realities that an organization wishes to achieve, and generally address strengths, weaknesses and opportunities that have been identified in a SWOT analysis.

In most strategic plans, it is common to identify functional goals that for the short, medium and long terms. When these goals are explicitly ordered then they become part of a strategic plan. Each plan in SML describes milestones in an organizational strategy. A plan is an ordered sequence of functional goals. Plans may follow tactical decisions that describe a means to realize higher-level goals.

An optimization objective in SML is used to discriminate over preferences for strategic outcomes. An optimization objective is typically either the maximization or minimization of a function on a set of given QoS capabilities.

A strategy is either a plan or a functional goal or an optimization objective. A strategy model is a set of all strategies that are to be analysed.

4 TASK COMPOSITION AND CHOREOGRAPHY

Recall our example scenario § 2, where *VirgaFone* wishes to recompute their operational stack to meet the demands of their changing environment. In the first instance, it would be ideal to be able to recompute the process model that they follow, to better manage their workforce. To recompute a process model, it's graph encoding needs to be mathematically analysed. In the following section we provide a method for structuring process models in graph form and then algorithmically reconstruct the model into new compositions and choreography's to meet the requirements of a dynamic end-to-end customer engagement.

A process model as a graph is a strongly connected directed graph, where activities events and gateways are nodes in the graph and sequence flow are the edges. Each node in the graph is labelled with a type, a name, and extra attributes such as QoS values and semantic effects.

Definition 1: Semantically Annotated Process Model

A process model is a labeled directed graph $p = \langle N, F, l, \Omega, \psi, \phi \rangle$ with the following properties:

1. N is a finite non-empty set of nodes. ψ, ϕ are the start and end nodes respectively and $\psi, \phi \in N$.
2. F a set of control flow links, $F \subseteq N \times N$.
3. Ω is a set of labels, each label ω is of the form $\langle type, name, \langle v, \varepsilon, \gamma \rangle \rangle$. Where type is the type of element, i.e. event, activity, gateway, task. Name is the name of the element. $\langle v, \varepsilon, \gamma \rangle$ is a tuple representing the QoS capabilities for the element, effect scenario and customer state of the node respectively.
4. $l : N \rightarrow \Omega$ is a labeling function that assigns labels to nodes of the process model.
5. $\forall n \in N, (n, \psi) \notin F \wedge (\phi, n) \notin F$ i.e., the start node has no incoming edges and the end node has no outgoing edges.

From our example, in Figure 2, each activity, event, pool, and gateway will be encoded as a node in a graph. Sequence and message arrows will be encoded as edges connecting two nodes, and annotations such as *'efficient(system)'* will be encoded as the effect scenario ε for the labeled node *'compare details of customer and complaint to business rules'*.

A process model $p = \langle N, F, l, \Omega, \psi, \phi \rangle$ is *well formed* if a strongly connected graph can be formed from its nodes and edges, i.e., $(N, F \cup (\phi, \psi))$ is a strongly connected graph. A well formed process model p is a well formed decision free process if there are no XOR gateways in the process model. There are procedures that can be used to construct a collection of well formed decision free process models from a given well formed process model[1]. In this work, we assume that all processes are well formed decision free process models. We denote a process portfolio of well formed decision free process models P.

An example of a decision free version of the complaint handling process is $\langle \, \{$ [Receive complaint], [verify customer details], [customer verified?], [request customer attend local store], [end event] }, {⟨ [Receive complaint], [verify customer details] ⟩, ⟨ [verify customer details, customer verified?] ⟩, ⟨ [customer verified?, request customer attend local store] ⟩, ⟨ [request customer attend local store], [end event] ⟩}, Ω, [Receive complaint], [end event] ⟩, where Ω is the set of labels and associated effects, i.e. {⟨ *Activity, [Verify customer details], ⟨∅,* unhappy(customer), *∅⟩⟩,⟨* Activity, [Request customer attend local store], ⟨∅,¬ engaged(customer) ∧¬ resolution(customer), ∅⟩⟩}.

The result of accumulating effect scenarios and QoS capabilities in process models is a set of effect scenarios and QoS capabilities that describe the entire process model. There are occasions when it is beneficial to find the effect scenarios or QoS capabilities of a particular instance (or trace) of a process model. A trace is a sequence of activities showing a possible execution instance of the given process. Each trace begins at the start of the process model and continues along to activities in the process until a given point within the process model. To find these traces, either sequential paths, parallel paths, or a combination of the two must be used to describe the instance of the process model of interest.

Given a process model $p = \langle N, F, l, \Omega, \psi, \phi \rangle$, a path through the model is:

$$\langle (n_1, n_2), (n_2, n_3), \ldots, (n_{j-1}, n_j) \rangle$$

where elements of the path are control flow links and each (n_x, n_y) in the path is distinct. We shall say $n_i \prec n_j$, or n_i precedes n_j, iff there exists a path $\langle (n_i, n_{i+1}), \ldots, (n_{j-1}, n_j) \rangle$.

Definition 2: Neighbor Function

Let $Neighbor_p(n_i) : N \to 2^N$ be a function that returns the neighbor of any node n_i *in a process* p.

$$Neighbor_p(n_i) = \left\{ \begin{matrix} n_j | n_j \neq n_i \wedge \\ \left(\left((n_i, n_j) \in F \right) \vee \\ \left(n_i \nprec n_j \wedge n_j \nprec n_i \right) \right) \end{matrix} \right\}$$

Definition 3: Trace

Given a process model $p = \langle N, F, l, \Omega, \psi, \phi \rangle$, *a trace is a sequence*

$$\sigma = n_1, n_2, \ldots, n_m,$$

where:

- $|N| = |\sigma|$.
- For each pair n_i, n_{i+1} in σ, $n_{i+1} \in Neighbor_p(n_i)$ for $1 \leq i \leq m$.
- For any two nodes $n_i, n_j \in \sigma$, where $i < j$, and $n_j \nprec n_i$.

The set of all traces of the process model p is £$_p$.

For any two nodes n_i and n_j in a trace σ, if $\sigma = \langle \ldots, n_i, \ldots, n_j, \ldots \rangle$ we say n_i **precedes** n_j. If for all traces $\sigma \in \Sigma_p$ of a given process model n_i precedes n_j then we say that n_i **always precedes** n_j and denote $n_i =_\Sigma n_j$.

Cumulative effects and QoS values are computable over process traces. Accumulation of effects and QoS values have been discussed in previous work (Morrison et al., 2012; Hinge et al., 2009; Hoesch-Klohe et al., 2010; Koliadis & Ghose, 2006), the result of which is a consistent set of effects and QoS values that give a semantic meaning to a process model. An accumulation function *accumulate*() takes as input a trace σ and returns a tuple $\langle \Upsilon, \mathcal{E}, \Gamma \rangle$ which are the set of cumulative QoS values, the set of cumulative effects and the cumulative customer state respectively. For details of accumulation the reader is referred to (Morrison et al., 2012; Hinge et al., 2009; Hoesch-Klohe et al., 2010; Koliadis & Ghose, 2006). The accumulation of the decision free process, from *[Receive complaint]* to *[end event]*

A process model with traces, accumulated effects and QoS values is represented with a case sequence.

Definition 4: Case Sequence (See Box 1)

For any case sequence C, if all $p \in M$ are in a process portfolio **P**, then we say that C belongs to **P**, denoted $C \mapsto \mathbf{P}$. To compute the accumulated effects and QoS capabilities for a case sequence, each sequential pair of traces $\langle \sigma_i, \sigma_j \rangle \in \Sigma$,

where $\langle \Upsilon_i, \mathcal{E}_i, \Gamma_i \rangle$ are the cumulative QoS, effect values and customer states for trace σ_i and $\langle \upsilon_{j_\psi}, \varepsilon_{j_\psi}, \gamma_{j_\psi} \rangle$ are the QoS, effects and statess for the start node of σ_j first *pairwise-accumulate* $\langle \Upsilon_i, \mathcal{E}_i, \Gamma_i \rangle$ and $\langle \upsilon_{j_\psi}, \varepsilon_{j_\psi}, \gamma_{j_\psi} \rangle$ then accumulate across the remains of the trace σ_j, the reader is referred to (Hinge et al., 2009) for methods of pairwise-accumulating cumulative effects with effects. The result of this process is a cumulative effect $\langle \Upsilon_P, \mathcal{E}_P, \Gamma_P \rangle$.

Returning to our example, were to we to wish to determine the case wide effect for a customer who had phoned VirgaFone to make a complaint but due to staffing issues was unable to be verified. We would first create a decision free process of the path that the customer had taken through the process. Then compose the process with any other processes that the customer may have followed as part of their engagement with VirgaFone.

Box 1.

A case sequence C is a tuple:

$$\langle \mathcal{M}, \Pi, \mathcal{A}, N, F, l, a, \Omega, \psi, \varphi \rangle$$

Where:

1. *$\mathcal{M}$ is a set of processes that are part of the case sequence.*
2. *Π is a sequence of traces $\Sigma_p \in \mathcal{M}$.*
3. *$\mathcal{A}$ is a set of tuples $\langle \Upsilon, \mathcal{E}, \Gamma \rangle$ of QoS values, accumulated effects, and customer environment.*
4. *N is a finite non-empty set of nodes. ψ, φ are the start and end nodes respectively and $\psi, \varphi \in N$.*
5. *F a set of control flow links, $F \subseteq N \times N$.*
6. *Ω is a set of labels, each label ω is of the form $\langle type, name, \langle \upsilon, \epsilon, \gamma \rangle \rangle$. Where type is the type of element. name is the name of the element. $\langle \upsilon, \epsilon, \gamma \rangle$ is a tuple representing the QoS capabilities for the element, effect scenario of the element and customer state respectively.*
7. *$a : \Pi \to \mathcal{A}$ is function that maps trace sequences to accumulation tuples.*
8. *$l : N \to \Omega$ is a labelling function that assigns labels to nodes of the case sequence.*
9. *$\forall n \in N, (n, \psi) \notin F \wedge (\varphi, n) \notin F$ i.e., the start node has no incoming edges and the end node has no outgoing edges*

A cumulative semantic effect of {*unhappy(customer)*, ⌐ engaged(customer), ¬ resolution(customer)} can be found. By computing QoS based artefacts such as engagement time we can compute the QoS effect, e.g. {*10min, $-10 staffing*}. Finally a case based effect could also be carried through {*80% churnRisk, -$50 goodwill*}

When describing an adaptive case management system an a difficulty exists of describing cases and caseflow across differing levels of abstraction (between perennial non-operational soft workflows and transient processes). In this framework, we propose that composing processes to correct the degree of abstraction is the best way to address this issue. Composition has been choosen here because the decomposition requires a pool of potential predefined sub-processes or atomic tasks (or requires extensive insightful thoughts by an analyst). Further to this, in the event of an organizational change, or in a change of understanding, transforming the purpose of multiple layers of processes and their decomposition becomes cumbersome and expensive. An unrefined process is compound, and due to this that it is often necessary to consider the sequencing of processes or parallel execution of processes. When fused together, these composed processes may create a complex enough expression to consider the expression a case.

Given any number of process models with the purpose of investigating the consequences of running them in sequence or parallel, it becomes necessary to understand both the QoS value and semantic effect of the composed processes to gain insights. We compute accumulation over the composed process by manipulating processes and case sequences using a sequential combination operator and a parallel combination operator which both translate the composed processes into case sequences which we have already shown an accumulation procedure for. We will denote pairwise case sequence composition accumulation as $C_i \uplus C_j$. Sequential process composition, requires the selection of a trace from the set of possible traces for both of the processes. The end event of the first process is then converted to an intermediate event and joined to the start (converted to an intermediate event) of the selected trace from the next process in a series. Each new sequence of nodes shows an end-to-end arrangement of a composed process. Using pairwise accumulation along each sequence it is possible to compute the of effects and QoS values for the composed process. The joining of two processes in sequence is denoted by the operator $\otimes$.

To find parallel traces, we essentially join two processes into a parallel design. Converting the start and end events from each into intermediate events and placing the processes between parallel gateways. Using the methods in definition 3 to compute the set of traces for the composed process it is easy to find the end-to-end arrangement of the composed process. The joining of two processes in parallel is denoted by the operator $\oplus$.

Due to the nature of the sequential composition, in a case sequence composition description $\oplus$ has precedence over $\otimes$, i.e. $p_1 \otimes p_2 \oplus p_3 = p_1 \otimes (p_2 \oplus p_3) \neq (p_1 \otimes p_2) \oplus p_3$. The composed models generated through these procedures is a case sequence.

Given a process portfolio P, we assume there exists a number of case sequences $C_1, C_2, \ldots$ that can be constructed by composing various processes and case sequences together. An accumulation function *accumulate* provides a method for semantic definition from each C_i to some tuple $a = \langle \Upsilon, \mathcal{E}, \Gamma \rangle$, i.e. *accumulate(C) = a* where a is a closed well formed formula, and due to the nature of effect accumulation Th(accumulate(C)) *accumulate(C)*.

Let a *base case sequence* B_P for a particular process portfolio P, be any case sequence $C \sqsubseteq \mathcal{P}$ with $U = \{p \mid p \in M_C\}$ where there does not exist another case sequence $C' \sqsubseteq \mathcal{P}$ with $V = \{p \mid p \in M_{C'}\}$ where $V \subset U$.

Given a set of base case sequences $\{B, B' \ldots \in B_P\}$, an *extension case sequence* of a base case sequence B with $W = \{p \mid p \in M_B\}$, is any case sequence $C \sqsubset \mathcal{P}$ and $C \notin B_C$ with $U = \{p \mid p \in M_C\}$ where $W \subset U$ and there does not exist another case sequence $C' \sqsubset \mathcal{P}$ and $C' \notin B_P$ with $V = \{p \mid p \in M_{C'}\}$ where $V \subset U$ and $W \subset V$ and there exists an operator $\oplus$ or $\otimes$ where $B \oplus B' = C$ or $B \otimes B' = C$. A child extension is some case sequence C'^* that can be found by forming a chain of extension case sequences, i.e. if C is a base case sequence and C' is an extension case sequence for C, and C'' is an extension case sequence for C' etc., until C'^*

Definition 5: Case Sequence Accumulation (Box 2)

By finding case sequences, and then using an accumulation function, it is easy to describe the effect scenarios or QoS capabilities of a multiple processes instance, i.e., if multiple processes were used to handle a particular case, then a QoS capabilities like time taken can be computed. It is also possible to use semantic effect annotations to provide contextual information on the state of a case at any given point during the processing of the case across any number of processes.

5 CORRELATING CASES AND STRATEGIES

By having existing process models that describe the capabilities of an organization it is assumed that the organization intends to use the processes to achieve its strategies. Realization of functional goals in this context is done by defining functional goals in operational terms. The way that we define functional goals in operational terms is by correlating them to processes. If a correlation between functional goals and processes is made, then this is a demonstration of goal realization.

Goal realization can be undertaken in various ways as shown by Letier and Ponsard (Ponsard et al., 2007; Letier & van Lamsweerde, 2002). In this work, we use entailment to represent the realization of strategies.

Our framework will be presented using a finitely propositional language LANG over a set of propositional letters $A = \{\alpha, \beta, \gamma\}$, truth-functional connectives $\neg, \wedge, \vee, \rightarrow, \leftrightarrow$, and the truth-functional constants $T, \bot$. An interpretation of LANG is a function from A to $\{T, F\}$; Ω is the set of interpretations of LANG. A model of a well formed formula X is an interpretation that makes X true.

In classic propositional logic entailment is a relation between two well formed formulas X and Y. Each formula we will use to demonstrate realization is a prime implicate. Let Γ be a theory,

Box 2.

Let $q = \langle \Upsilon, \mathcal{E}, \Gamma \rangle$ be a tuple describing some set of QoS and effect scenarios and C be a case sequence. Let some base case sequence C_0 have an associated q', where $q' \not\models q$ and for each $i \geq 0$ where C_{i+1} is an extension case sequence of C_i:

$accumulate(C_{i+1}) = Th(accumulate(C_i)) \biguplus C_{i+1}$

Then q is the semantic description and cumulative effect of C iff: $q = \biguplus_{i=0}^{\infty}(C_i)$ and C is a child extension of C_n.

X and Y be wffs, then the antecedent formula X entails the consequent formula Y iff $X \neq \varnothing$ and every model of X under Γ is a model of Y, denoted $\Gamma, X Y$. A functional goal is realizable if a set of effect scenario entails it and if the set of effect scenarios is consistent.

Definition 6: Goal Realization (Letier & van Lamsweerde, 2002; Ponsard et al., 2007) (See Box 3)

By showing that each functional goal in a strategy model has a process or a case sequence that realizes it, we are able to demonstrate that there is synergy between the operational and strategic sides of the organization.

5.1 Satisfaction of Optimization Objectives

An optimization objective in a strategy model is a optimization function that provides an ordering over a set of case sequences given a QoS preference. A c-semiring framework (Bistarelli, Montanari, & Rossi, 1997) can be used to adequately model such preference orderings. In (Hoesch-Klohe et al., 2010), a number of instances for green QoS were described using this framework.

Given a set of case sequences $\{C_1, C_2, ..., C_n\}$ where each case sequence has a pair $\langle \Upsilon_{C_i}, \mathcal{E}_{C_i}, \Gamma_{C_i} \rangle$ of QoS capabilities and semantic effect scenarios. The set of possible QoS capabilities for a process portfolio Υ_p is $\{\Upsilon_{Ci} \mid C_i \sqsubset P\}$.

For example, consider two case sequences C_i and C_j each with one instance of QoS Capability described in Table 1.

The capabilties for C_i are $\{[cost_{C_1}]\$1.00, [time_{C_1}]10min\}$ and the capabilties for C_2 are $\{[cost_{C_2}]\$1.50, [time_{C_2}]5min\}$. The set of possible QoS capabilties for the process portfolio are then:

$$\Upsilon_p = \{[cost_{C_1}]\$1.00, [time_{C_1}]$$
$$10min, [cost_{C_2}]\$1.50, [time_{C_2}]5min\}$$

Definition 7: Optimal Case Sequence (See Box 4)

Continuing our example, to find the optimal case sequence with respect to *time*, we would compute the *minimal time* capabiltiy $v_{C_i}^{*time}$ $= [time_{C_2}]5min$. An aggregation of objectives may be substituted into the optimization type.

Table 1. Case C_i and C_j considered

Case Sequence	Cost	Time
C_1	$1.00	10 *minutes*
C_2	$1.50	5 *minutes*

Box 3.

Given background knowledgebase Γ, a set $\{\epsilon_1, ..., \epsilon_n\}$ of effects scenarios, and a goal G, then the goal is definable in terms of the effect scenarios and realizable in terms of the case sequences where the effect scenarios come from if:

1. $\Gamma, \epsilon_1 \wedge \cdots \wedge \epsilon_n \models G$ (completeness)
2. $\Gamma, \epsilon_1 \wedge \cdots \wedge \epsilon_n \not\models \bot$ (consistency)

Box 4.

> Given a set of case sequences $\{C_i, \ldots, C_j\}$ with a set of capabilities Υ made of all of the case sequence QoS values where $\forall v_{C_l} \in \Upsilon_{C_l}, v_{C_l} \in \Upsilon$ and a c-semiring $O_{type} = \langle A, \oplus, \otimes, \perp, \top \rangle$ describing a particular QoS preference type and preference ordering $\leq_{O_{type}}$, and a set of cumulative QoS capabilities $\Upsilon \subseteq A$, we denote more preferred QoS capabilities v_k^{*type} (with resp. to the preference ordering $\leq_{O_{type}}$). An optimal case sequences C_k^{*type} is a case sequences with the best QoS value.

6 ALIGNMENT BETWEEN CASES AND STRATEGIES

Alignment between cases and strategies follows from the previous section discussing the realisation between cases and strategies. Alignment is the correlation of cases sequences to strategies and provides a system level understanding of how effective the case management systems choreographing the business operations is. An alignment framework previously described in detail in (Morrison et al., 2012) can be used to establish correlations between the case sequences of our system and the strategic landscape of the business as a whole.

Definition 8: Alignment of case sequence with goals (See Box 5)

Consider a set of case sequences $\{C_1, \ldots, C_n\}$ where $C_i \sqsubset P$. Given a goal G, we want to determine if the process portfolio P is aligned to the goal G. We can use the following basic test: if $\exists C_i \sqsubset P$ s.t. ALN_C^G then, P is aligned to G.

Definition 9: Alignment with Plans (See Box 6)

Given a description of goal and plan alignment to business processes, if a business wishes to find which process models are optimally aligned to the strategies then optimization objectives must be used. To compute optimal alignment scenarios, given a functional goal G, and two case sequences C and C' with alignment relationships ALN_C^G and $ALN_{C'}^G$.

For example, consider an organizational optimization objective O: *'minimize cycle time'* applied to a functional goal encouraging the use of vacation time. Case C may be a manual case sequence that requires the employee to submit leave request forms and find their own replacements, and case sequence C' may be an automated process that automatically selects replacement employees and stream lines the approval process. A QoS execution description for case sequence C may be *Time < 2 days*, and the QoS execution description for case sequence C' may be *Time < 2 hours*. Provided that there are no alternative QoS objectives, then the selection function will select process C' as being the optimal process to satisfy the goal.

Definition 10: Alignment with optimization objectives (See Box 7)

Box 5.

> A case sequence C with a set of effect scenarios $\mathcal{E}_C$ realizes a goal G, iff $\exists \epsilon_i \in \mathcal{E}_C$ where $\epsilon_i \models G$ and $\forall \epsilon_j \in \mathcal{E}_C, \epsilon_j \wedge G \not\models \perp$. We will write: $\mathcal{ALN}_C^G$, if this is the case.

Box 6.

Let a plan L be a sequence of goals $\langle G_1, \ldots, G_n \rangle$. For the plan to be completely realized by a process model (or process models) each pair of consecutive goals $\langle G_i, G_j \rangle$ in the plan must be realized. A plan is realized and aligned to a set of processes if all consecutive goal pairs in the plan are realized. Pairs of goals are realizable in the following ways:

1. *Let C_k be a case sequence with process $p_k \in \mathcal{M}_k$, and C_l be a case sequence with a process $p_l \in \mathcal{M}_l$, s.t. $\mathcal{M}_k / \{p_k\} = \{\emptyset\}$ and $\mathcal{M}_l / \{p_l\} = \{\emptyset\}$. Given a case sequence C_m with $p_k, p_l \in \mathcal{M}_m$ where for all $n_k \in N_k$ and $n_l \in N_l$, $n_k \ll_{\Sigma_C} n_l$, if C_k realizes G_i (but not G_j) and C_m realizes $G_i \wedge G_j$ then the case sequence C_m realizes the goal pair.*
2. *Given a base case sequence C_n, where there is an activity a with effect scenario ϵ_a, an activity b with effect scenario ϵ_b and $a \ll_{\Sigma_n} b$, if $\epsilon_a \models G_i$, $\epsilon_a \not\models G_i \wedge G_j$, $\epsilon_b \models G_i \wedge G_j$ and there is an end effect scenario of case sequence C_n that entails $G_i \wedge G_j$ then the case sequence C_n realizes the goal pair.*

If a plan L is realizable by a case sequence C then the case sequence is aligned to the plan, denoted $\mathcal{ALN}_C^L$. Consider a set case sequences $\{C_1, \ldots, C_n\}$ constructed from process models in a process portfolio $\mathcal{P}$. Given a plan $L = \langle G_1, \ldots, G_n \rangle$, the process portfolio $\mathcal{P}$ is aligned to the plan L if $\exists C \sqsubset \mathcal{P}$ s.t. $\mathcal{ALN}_C^L$ then, $\mathcal{P}$ is aligned to L.

Box 7.

Given a functonal goal G, an optimization objective $\mathcal{O}$, and two alignment scenarios $\mathcal{ALN}_C^G$ and $\mathcal{ALN}_{C'}^G$ where $C, C' \sqsubset \mathcal{P}$, then the optimal case sequence is the case sequence that is optimal with respect to the optimization objective $C \Uparrow_{\mathcal{P}}^G \mathcal{O}$. This is the process aligned to the goal that is more preferred based on the optimization objective.

Similarly, given a plan L, where $\mathcal{ALN}_C^L$ and $\mathcal{ALN}_{C'}^L$ the optimal case sequence is the case sequence aligned to the plan that optimizes the optimization objective, denoted, $C \Uparrow_{\mathcal{P}}^L \mathcal{O}$.

Using the above definitions we are able to define a notion of strategic alignment of business processes.

Definition 11: Strategic alignment (See Box 8)

To then compute optimal case sequences that achieve strategic requirements we define optimal strategic alignment.

Definition 12: Optimal Strategic Alignment (See Box 9)

6.1 Application of AI Techniques to Automate Alignment

Diagnosis is often described as an abduction problem in AI. It's idea is to produce an explanation that best accounts for a set of observable symptoms. More precisely, a diagnostic conclusion should plausible enough to explain the symptoms and it should be significantly better than any other explanations. Abductive reasoning is used in many AI problems as a reasoning paradigm. Abduction, or Abductive inference is a form of

Box 8.

Let $\mathcal{P}$ be a process portfolio, S be a set of strategies, made up of a set of goals $\mathcal{G}$, a set of plans $\mathcal{L}$, and a set of optimization objectives $\mathcal{O}$. We say that $\mathcal{ALN}_{\mathcal{P}}^{S}$ iff:

1. For each $G \in \mathcal{G}$, $\mathcal{ALN}_{\mathcal{P}}^{G}$ and
   $\forall C \sqsubset \mathcal{P} \cdot (\epsilon_C \wedge G \not\models \perp | \epsilon_C \in \mathcal{E}_C)$
2. For each $L \in \mathcal{L}$, $\mathcal{ALN}_{\mathcal{P}}^{L}$ and
   $\forall C \sqsubset \mathcal{C} \cdot (\epsilon_C \wedge L \not\models \perp | (\epsilon_C \in \mathcal{E}_C))$

Box 9.

Given a set of case sequences $\mathrm{OPT} = \{C | C \sqsubset \mathcal{P}\}$ is aligned optimally to the set of strategies, denoted $\mathcal{ALN}*_{\mathrm{OPT}}^{S}$ iff:

1. $\mathcal{ALN}_{\mathcal{P}}^{S}$
2. For each $G \in \mathcal{G}$, there is a case sequence $C \in \mathrm{OPT}$ s.t. $\mathcal{ALN}_{C}^{G}$ and $C \Updownarrow_{\mathcal{P}}^{G} \mathcal{O}$
3. For each $L \in \mathcal{L}$, there is a case sequence $C \in \mathrm{OPT}$ s.t. $\mathcal{ALN}_{C}^{L}$ and $C \Updownarrow_{\mathcal{P}}^{L} \mathcal{O}$
4. There is no smaller set of case sequences that are optimal with respect to S.

---

inference that takes a set of observations, a set of possible events that could have occurred and then returns the most likely explanation for the observation (Josephson, 1994). It can be best described as a kind of interpreting inference. The role of abduction has been demonstrated in various applications, most commonly in problems that require diagnosis. It has been proposed as a reasoning paradigm in AI for planning, default reasoning and diagnosis (Kakas & Sadri, 2002). Abduction within the realm of first order logic can be defined with the following schema: For any given observation O, given T, a collection of facts, E is an explanation for T such that no other E' can explains T better than E does. Therefore E is the most likely explanation of events that led to O (Josephson, 1994).

Using an alignment framework as shown above, along with an abductive reasoner, it is possible to find potential best set of processes to run together dynamically, using the organisational strategies, existing semantically annotated processes and execution level case state information.

7 RELATED WORK

In (Khomyakov & Bider, 2000) Khomyakov and Bider propose a reverse approach to achieving case flexibility by first describing a set of workflow states and then using restrictions of obligations, prohibitions and recommendations a theoretical hybrid automata machinery is able to constructively create all combinations of states and hence describing all that is possible given a set of process and a set of constraints. In (Mundbrod et al., 2012) Mundbrod has presented a lifecycle methodology and framework for supporting collaborative knowledge work. Mundbrod has identified a large number of elements that can be used to describe large scale and complex systems including complex financial services and criminal investigation scenarios, which involve highly trained knowledge workrs.

Hildebrandt (Hildebrandt et al., 2011a, 2011b) has approached the creation of a dynamic and declarative case management system with a system of Dynamic Condition Response Graphs that provide state transition modeling for case systems. In particular their work focuses on the execution level store of case models and have provided a rigorous and formal model of case management systems. We believe that their condition response graphs are complementary to our Case Sequence models. Using our framework a case management system can be designed at a broad overviewing level; and then the Dynamic Condition Response Graph can be used to model and assess case behaviour at execution time. In future work we would like to provide further evaluation of our framework under design usage to compare with the execution support of the Hildebrandt model.

In previous work (Van Der Aalst, 1998; Dijkman & Van Gorp, 2011; Bose & van der Aalst, 2010; Rinderle-Ma, Reichert, & Weber, 2008; Ly et al., 2012), many researchers have described formal models for graph encoding specific process model types. In our work we provide a general summary for process model formulation (based loosely on the work of our peers); however, we draw attention to the fact that all automation and computation in our framework is done at the design level rather than at the execution level and as such various elements of some graph encodings do not fit with the definitions we've provided. By maintaining a process and task definition at the design level, reconfiguration can be computed without the need for execution, so that new adaptive task sequences can be constructed without an example execution trace. For example, in (Bose & van der Aalst, 2010), Bose and van der Aalst et. al. have described an execution trace over the state space of unbounded logs for a workflow net, where their notion of an ordering relation is a sequence of possible state transitions. Our notion differs as it is done at a design level. Further to this, each trace dealt with in this paper through a semantically annotated process model is one of the many possible interleaving executional designs that exists in the process model. In (Rinderle-Ma et al., 2008; Ly et al., 2012) Rinderle-Ma et. al.

have described a notion of executional event trace that is similar to the executional traces of van der Aalst, this notion of trace like those in (Bose & van der Aalst, 2010) requires dropping from design into the domain of execution artifacts.

8 CONCLUSION

In this chapter, we have provided a method to compute case sequences from a collection of process models. Elements on the system described have been developed into a prototype library[2]. The result and benefit of using a case management system formed from existing legacy process management systems is that transition and change costs will be dramatically reduced for the organisation. The results of moving towards adaptive case management using our framework will provide organizational case managers an apparatus to understand the current case state of affairs across the entire operational context. The framework that we have presented contributes to a better understanding of adaptive case management and further tool support will equipped decision makers with a device to understand sustainability of this technology in an operational context.

ACKNOWLEDGMENT

The authors would like to thank Yingzhi Gou from the University of Wollongong for their contribution in reviewing the presented chapter and tireless work and assistance in the evaluation of the systems described herein.

REFERENCES

(2002). Abduction in logic programming, computational logic. In Kakas, A. C., & Sadri, F. (Eds.), *Logic programming and beyond*. Berlin: Springer.

Bistarelli, S., Montanari, U., & Rossi, F. (1997). Semiring-based constraint satisfaction and optimization. *Journal of the ACM, 44*(2), 201–236. doi:10.1145/256303.256306

Bleistein, S. J., Cox, K., & Verner, J. (2006). Validating strategic alignment of organizational IT requirements using goal modeling and problem diagrams. *Journal of Systems and Software, 79*(3), 362–378. doi:10.1016/j.jss.2005.04.033

Bose, R. J. C., & van der Aalst, W. (2010). Trace alignment in process mining: Opportunities for process diagnostics. In *Business process management* (pp. 227–242). Berlin: Springer. doi:10.1007/978-3-642-15618-2_17

Dijkman, R., & Van Gorp, P. (2011). BPMN 2.0 execution semantics formalized as graph rewrite rules. In *Business process modeling notation* (pp. 16–30). Berlin: Springer. doi:10.1007/978-3-642-25160-3

Edirisuriya, A., & Johannesson, P. (2009). On the alignment of business models and process models. In *Business process management workshops* (Vol. 17, pp. 68–79). Berlin: Springer. doi:10.1007/978-3-642-00328-8_7

Ghose, A. K., & Lê, L. K, H.-K., & Morrison, E. D. (2010). The business service representation language: A preliminary report. In Service modelling and representation techniques. Academic Press.

Gordijn, J., Soetendal, J., & Paalvast, E. (2005). VA3: Governance selection in value webs. In *Challenges of expanding internet: E-commerce, e-business, and e-government* (Vol. 189, pp. 17–31). Academic Press. doi:10.1007/0-387-29773-1_2

Hildebrandt, T., Mukkamala, R. R., & Slaats, T. (2011a). Declarative modelling and safe distribution of healthcare workflows. In *Proceedings of First International Symposium*. FHIES.

Hildebrandt, T., Mukkamala, R. R., & Slaats, T. (2011b). Designing a cross-organizational case management system using dynamic condition response graphs. In *Proceedings of 15th International Enterprise Distributed Object Computing Conference*. Academic Press.

Hinge, K., Ghose, A. K., & Koliadis, G. (2009). Process seer: A tool for semantic effect annotation of business process models. In *Proceedings of 13th IEEE International eDoc Conference*. IEEE.

Hoesch-Klohe, K., Ghose, A. K., & Le, L.-S. (2010). Towards green business process management. In *Proceedings of the IEEE International Services Computing Conference*. IEEE.

Josephson, S. G. (1994). *Abductive inference: Computation, philosophy, technology*. Cambridge, UK: Cambridge University Press. doi:10.1017/CBO9780511530128

Khomyakov, M., & Bider, I. (2000). Achieving workflow flexibility through taming the chaos. In *Proceedings of 6th International Conference on Object Oriented Information Systems*. Academic Press.

Koliadis, G., & Ghose, A. (2006). Relating business process models to goal-oriented requirements models in kaos. In *Advances in knowledge acquisition and management* (Vol. 4303, pp. 25–39). Berlin: Springer. doi:10.1007/11961239_3

Koliadis, G., Ghose, A., & Padmanabhuni, S. (2008). Towards an enterprise business process architecture standard. In *Proceedings of IEEE Congress on Services* (pp. 239-246). IEEE.

Letier, E., & van Lamsweerde, A. (2002). Deriving operational software specifications from system goals. *SIGSOFT Softw. Eng. Notes, 27*(6), 119–128. doi:10.1145/605466.605485

Ly, L., Rinderle-Ma, S., Göser, K., & Dadam, P. (2012). On enabling integrated process compliance with semantic constraints in process management systems. *Information Systems Frontiers, 14*(2), 195–219. doi:10.1007/s10796-009-9185-9

Morrison, E. D., Ghose, A. K., Dam, H. K., Hinge, K. G., & Hoesch-Klohe, K. (2012). Strategic alignment of business processes. In Proceedings of Service-Oriented Computing, ICSOC 2011 Workshops (pp. 9-21). ICSOC.

Mundbrod, N., Kolb, J., & Reichert, M. (2012). Towards a system support of collaborative knowledge work. In *Proceedings of 1st International Workshop on Adaptive Case Management*. Academic Press.

Ponsard, C., Massonet, P., Molderez, J., Rifaut, A., Lamsweerde, A., & Van, H. (2007). Early verification and validation of mission critical systems. *Formal Methods in System Design, 30*, 233–247. doi:10.1007/s10703-006-0028-8

Rinderle-Ma, S., Reichert, M., & Weber, B. (2008). Relaxed compliance notions in adaptive process management systems. In *Proceedings of Conceptual Modeling - ER Conference* (Vol. 5231, pp. 232-247). Berlin: Springer.

Strijbosch, K. (2011). *Adaptive case management: A new way of supporting knowledge work.* (Unpublished Doctoral Dissertation). Radboud Universiteit Nijmegen.

Van Der Aalst, W. M. P. (1998). The application of petrinets to workflow management. *Journal of Circuits. Systems and Computers, 8*(1), 21–66.

Van Lamsweerde, A. (2001). Goal-oriented requirements engineering: A guided tour. In *Proceedings of Requirements Engineering Conference* (pp. 249-262). Academic Press.

Wang, H., & Ghose, A. K. (2010). Green strategic alignment: Aligning business strategies with sustainability objectives. In B. Unhelkar (Ed.), *Handbook of research in green ICT* (pp. 29–41). Academic Press. doi:10.4018/978-1-61692-834-6.ch002

Zhu, W.-D., Kirchner, M., Ko, T., Oland, M., Prasad, B., Prentice, M., & Ruggiero, M. A. (2013). *Advanced case management with ibm case manager.* IBM Redbooks.

ADDITIONAL READING

Adams, M. Arthur H M ter Hofstede, David Edmond, and Wil M P van der Aalst. Facilitating Flexibility and Dynamic Exception Handling in Workflows through Worklets. In CAiSE 2005, 2005.

Aime, M. D., Lioy, A., & Paolo, C. (2011). Pomi. Automatic (Re) Configuration of IT Systems for Dependability. *IEEE Transactions on Services Computing, 4*(2), 110–124. doi:10.1109/TSC.2010.31

Armistead, C., Pritchard, J.-P., & Machin, S. (1999). Strategic Business Process Management for Organisational Effectiveness. *Long Range Planning, 32*(1), 96–106. doi:10.1016/S0024-6301(98)00130-7

Benjamin, C. M. (2012). Fung, Thomas Trojer, Patrick C.K. Hung, Li Xiong, Khalil Al-Hussaeni, and Rachida Dssouli. Service-Oriented Architecture for High-Dimensional Private Data Mashup. *IEEE Transactions on Services Computing, 5*(3), 373–386.

Carine, S. C. R., & Ben Achour, C. (1998). Guiding Goal Modeling Using Scenarios. *IEEE Transactions on Software Engineering, 24*(12), 1055–1071. doi:10.1109/32.738339

Cherbakov, L., Galambos, G., Harishankar, R., Kalyana, S., & Rackham, G. (2005). Impact of service orientation at the business level. *IBM Systems Journal*, *44*(4), 653–668. doi:10.1147/sj.444.0653

Desai, N., Bhamidipaty, A., Sharma, B., Varshneya, V. K., Vasa, M., & Nagar, S. Process Trace Identification from Unstructured Execution Logs. In *2010 IEEE International Conference on Services Computing*, pages 17–24. IEEE, July 2010.

Dewan, R., Seidmann, A., & Walter, Z. Workflow optimization through task redesign in business information processes. In *Proceedings of the Thirty-First Hawaii International Conference on System Sciences*, volume 1, pages 240–252. IEEE Comput. Soc, 1998.

Hendler, J., Tate, A., & Drummond, M. (1990). AI Planning: Systems and Techniques. *AI Magazine*, *11*(2), 61–77.

John, C. (1991). Henderson and N Venkatraman. Understanding Strategic Alignment. *Business Quarterly*, *55*(3), 72–78.

Khomyakov, M., & Bider, I. Achieving Workflow Flexibility through Taming the Chaos. In *OOIS'00 - 6th International Conference on Object Oriented Information Systems*, pages 85–92. Springer-Verlag, Berlin, 2000.

Korhonen, J. J., Hiekkanen, K., & Heiskala, M. Map to Service-Oriented Business and IT: A Stratified Approach. In *Proceedings of the 16th Americas Conference on Information Systems, Lima, Peru*, 2010.

Linda, I. (2013). Terlouw and Antonia Albani. An Enterprise Ontology-Based Approach to Service Specification. *IEEE Transactions on Services Computing*, *6*(1), 89–101.

Lu, R., & Sadiq, S. Managing Process Variants as and Information Resource. In *Proceedings of the Fourth International Conference on Business Process Management (BPM'06)*, 2006. L T Ly, S Rinderle, and P Dadam. Semantic Correctness in Adaptive Process Management Systems. In *Proceedings of the 4th International Conference on Business Process Management (BPM'06)*, 2006. Keith D Swenson, Nathaniel Palmer, Max J Pucher, Charles Webster MD, and Alberto Manuel. *How Knowledge Workers Get Things Done*. Future Strategies Inc., 2012.

Philipp. Leitner, Schahram Dustdar, Branimir Wetzstein, and Frank Leymann. Cost-based prevention of violations of service level agreements in composed services using self-adaptation. In *2012 First International Workshop on European Software Services and Systems Research - Results and Challenges (S-Cube)*, pages 34–35. IEEE, June 2012.

(2013, April). Philipp. Leitner, Waldemar Hummer, and Schahram Dustdar. Cost-Based Optimization of Service Compositions. *IEEE Transactions on Services Computing*, *6*(2), 239–251.

Steven, J. (2006). Bleistein, Karl Cox, and June Verner. Validating strategic alignment of organizational IT requirements using goal modeling and problem diagrams. *Journal of Systems and Software*, *79*(3), 362–378. doi:10.1016/j.jss.2005.04.033

Thomas, R. (1989). Gruber. Automated Knowledge Acquisition for Strategic Knowledge. *Machine Learning*, *4*, 293–336. doi:10.1007/BF00130716

Wang, H.-L., & Ghose, A. K. On the foundations of strategic alignment. In *Proc. of the 2006 Australia and New Zealand Academy of Management Conference*, 2006.

Wang, M., & Wang, H. Intelligent Agent Supported Business Process Management. In *Proceedings of the 38th Annual Hawaii International Conference on System Sciences (HICSS'05)*, page p. 71b, 2005.

Wynn, D., Eckert, C., & Clarkson, P. J. Planning Business Processes in Product Development Organisation s. In *REBPS'03 - Workshop on Requirements Engineering for Busines s Process Support*, Klagenfurt/Veldern, Austria, 2003.

Zielinnski, K., Szydlo, T., Szymacha, R., Kosinski, J., Kosinska, J., & Jarzab, M. (2012, April). Adaptive SOA Solution Stack. *IEEE Transactions on Services Computing*, 5(2), 149–163. doi:10.1109/TSC.2011.8

KEY TERMS AND DEFINITIONS

Case Management: Method of managing customer interactions, storing information on the customer history for decision making.

Case Sequence: An instance of a customer's engagement with an organisation.

Effect Scenario: The semantic result of executing a process model to a certain point.

Execution Scenario: A series of activities from a service design that can be executed by a workflow engine without any further sequence information.

Execution Trace: An execution scenario instance complete with execution log.

Process Model: A graphical representation of an operational artefact consisting of events, activities and flow arcs showing logical sequence.

Process Repository: A collection of related process models.

Semantic Annotation: A description of the world state change directly linked to the execution of an activity.

Service Composition: Merger of execution scenarios from one or more service designs. These can be in parallel or in sequence.

Strategic Alignment: A state where operations correlate to strategic intent in an optimal manner.

ENDNOTES

[1] A supporting toolkit of libraries implementing most functions described here can be downloaded from http://www.dsl.uow.edu.au/edm92/textseer/, including a procedure to create decision free process models.

[2] The source code for the framework can be found online at http://www.dsl.uow.edu.au/edm92/textseer

Chapter 8
Design of Web Services for Mobile Monitoring and Access to Measurements

Evelina Pencheva
Technical University of Sofia, Bulgaria

ABSTRACT

Provisioning of applications and value-added services for mobile (remote) monitoring and access to measurements data is supported by advanced communication models such as Internet of Things (IoT). IoT provides ubiquitous connectivity anytime and with anything. IoT applications are able to communicate with the environment, to receive information about its status, to exchange and use the information. Identification of generic functions for monitoring management, data acquisition, and access to information provides capabilities to define abstraction of transport technology and control protocols. This chapter presents an approach to design Web Services Application Programming Interfaces (API) for mobile monitoring and database access. Aspects of the Web Services implementation are discussed. A traffic model of Web Services application server is described formally. The Web Services application server handles traffic of different priorities generated by third party applications and by processes at the database server's side. The traffic model takes into account the distributed structure of the Web Services application server and applies mechanisms for adaptive admission control and load balancing to prevent overload. The utilization of Web Services application server is evaluated through simulation.

INTRODUCTION

The advance of Internet from a network of interconnected computers and mobile terminals, to a network of interconnected objects (things) enables provisioning of applications and value added services for mobile monitoring. Within the paradigm of Internet of things (IoT), the objects have their own IP addresses and identifiers, may be embedded in complex systems and use sensors (ITU, 2005; INFSO, 2008). These "smart" objects are able to recognize each other, communicate

DOI: 10.4018/978-1-4666-5884-4.ch008

with the environment, receive information about its status, exchange and use the information. The communication between objects may be limited to particular areas (Intranet of things) or may be publicly accessible (Galluccio, 2011; Li, 2012; Wang, 2013). The ubiquitous connectivity of objects requires integration between heterogeneous sensors as sources of information. Usually in IoT applications, sensors provide information from physically distributed dynamic processes and their interoperability appears to be a real challenge.

Extending IoT with the Web Services technology is a way to achieve interoperable communications between objects (Castellani, 2011). Web Services feature automated service discovery and composition as well as the ability to deal with heterogeneous sources of information. Embedding Web Services into IoT objects eases the integration of distributed dynamic processes. Embedded Web Services may be regarded as physical information servers in constrained nodes. They follow the REpresentational State Transfer (REST) style of software architecture for distributed systems. The usage of efficient payload encoding and Web linking format for constrained Web servers improves the performance of embedded Web Services (Shelby, 2012).

A lot of academic research has been conducted in the field of mobile monitoring services. However, most of the research studies different ways to collect and evaluate data, and different privacy issues that are related to data collecting but the distribution of data to third parties has had less attention. Fox, Kamburugamuve and Hartman (2012) suggest architecture of IoT system, where Web Services Application Programming Interfaces (APIs) are defined between sensors and a central controlling unit, and between the central controlling unit and applications. Works related to embedded Web services for IoT applications consider different application domains (Elgazzr, 2012; Agarwal, 2010, Ryu, 2012). Design of Web Services for IoT applications requires identification of generic functions for monitoring management, data acquisition and data transfer, and

access to information. The synthesis of generic functionality allows definition of abstraction that is independent of transport technology and control protocols.

Web Service technology is used for smart objects because of the expressiveness of the underlying principles. The usage of Web Services for resource constrained environment in which smart objects exist is a true challenge. There is a vast quantity of use cases for embedded Web Services in the area of mobile monitoring. The potential of mobile monitoring applications based on Web Services spans over different remote measurements and machine-to-machine communications. Telemetry is used in distant weather stations (Al-Ali, 2010; Schmutzler, 2008; Ciancetta, 2007) to transmit information about current temperature, humidity, wind, and green gasses concentration. Telemetry is also used in tracking systems (Kyusakov, 2011; Maciá-Pérez, 2007) to transmit fuel consumption data in order to optimize the routes and to save fuel costs, and as a consequence to reduce the pollution. Embedded Web Services for machine to machine communications and telemetry may be efficiently implemented in healthcare applications such as remote patient monitoring, ageing independently, personal fitness or disease management (De Capua, 2010; Ramos, 2011; Stoicu-Tivadar, 2012). By examining the results from the studies by Priyantha (2008) and Schmeltzer (2008), it is clear that the Web services are intended reasonably for smart objects and that the performance is suitable for the constrained resources.

The unified communication between databases such as DB2, MySQL, PostgreSQL, Oracle, SQLite, and application is provided by so called database abstraction layer. If an application programmer wishes to implement code for all database interfaces in order to provide flexibility and portability, then he or she has to tailor the code to the vendor-specific interfaces of the different products. The significant amount of work regarding the code implementation and tests might be reduced by a consistent API which forms the database abstraction layers and lowers the complexity of the task as much as possible. Any vendor-agnostic abstraction layer and its APIs should be designed in a way that the power of the database language is accompanied by easy support of multiple database servers, complex functionality like transactions, dynamic construction of queries and security functions. An effective information encapsulation layer provides benefits such as coupling between the object schema and data schema, an ability to evolve either one, provisioning of a common place to implement data-oriented business rules, and increasing application performance (Kim, 2006).

There are a number of approaches that industries have employed when exposing their databases as Web Services (Kang, 2009; Ambler, 2012). The diversity of abstraction layers with different interfaces in numerous programming languages such as Drupal 7 Database API, Java API for XML Web Services, SOAP with Attachments API for Java, Java DB, Java Data Objects, and News-Knowledge Web Service API provide a standard, vendor-agnostic abstraction layer for accessing database servers. In parallel, intensive research is conducted on applying advanced technologies for the information abstraction layer. Yang, Zhang and Zhao (2010) analyze database connection mechanism of a Web application system based on three-tier architecture, and the corresponding relationship between main steps and auto-generated code used to achieve database access in the Dreamweaver development environment. Qu, Feng and Sun (2008) analyze the difficulties of the united access of the distributed and heterogeneous biological information database and present an approach based on Web service and multi-agents, which add intelligence to the united access. In (Selis, 2008), efforts towards database integration and interoperability, based on Web Services and ontologies are described. Haselmann, Thies and Vossen (2010) introduce a concept for a "universal" API for Database-as-a-Service systems which is aimed to be suitable for systems ranging from those that allow storage of schema-less data to systems with capabilities of a traditional relational database system. While the research studies the abstraction of traditional database operations, subscriptions to and notifications about events on data stored in the database may be required. For example, a third party application may be interested in events about achieved thresholds in the stored measurements.

This chapter proposes an approach to design Web Services APIs for mobile monitoring and third party's access to data. Any application that uses the measurements is considered as a third party. Implementation aspects are considered and the Web Service performance is evaluated.

There exist different methods for evaluation of Service-Oriented Architecture (SOA) application servers (Yang, 2008). The traffic model of SOA application server presented in the chapter considers traffic of different priorities generated by applications and by the database-side processes. It takes into account the distributed structure of a SOA application server and applies mechanisms for adaptive admission control and load balancing to prevent overload.

The chapter is structured as follows. First, generic architecture based on Web Services that may be used for mobile monitoring and third party access to measurements is described. Next, an approach to design APIs for mobile monitoring and database access is presented based on identification of generic functions that have to be supported. Implementation of Web Services APIs that provide third party access to measurements requires deployment of SOA application server. The chapter discusses the communication protocols supported by the SOA application server and the mapping of Web Services operations onto communication protocol messages. Further, a traffic model of SOA application server is proposed. The model considers the distributed nature of the SOA application server and applies access control in order to prevent from overload. At the end of the chapter, some simulation results for the utilization of the SOA application server are presented.

ARCHITECTURE OF MOBILE MONITORING SYSTEM BASED ON WEB SERVICES

Mobile monitoring is a form of machine to machine communications where information from the environment is captured by mobile objects and transmitted in order to be centrally processed. A system for mobile monitoring based on IoT usually consists of objects representing a central control unit and a set of mobile agents. The central unit (CU) provides the overall control of the measurement process and it is responsible for gathering information from mobile agents. Mobile Agents (MAs) perform measurements and report on acquired data. The central unit is also in charge of mobile agents' registration, measurement mode management, local data processing and submission to database. To allow interworking between diverse sensors and the control unit, the interface between the mobile agents and the central unit may be based on Web Services APIs. The access to measurements database must be secured and restricted to authorized applications. The access of third party to database measurements allows external application to use stored data and it also may be provided through Web Services. The Web Services gateway is responsible for the secured and managed access to measurements and it makes the translation between Web Services interfaces and database operations.

Figure 1 shows the generic architecture of IoT system for mobile monitoring and third party access to measurements based on Web Services. The definition of Web Services for mobile monitoring and database access provides system scalability and technological independency.

System scalability may be achieved by deployment of several Central Control Units and a mediation Proxy server that is used for communication with the Database Management System (not shown in Figure 1). The Proxy server may concentrate data received from different Central Control Units and may abstract the Central Control Unit implementation from the Database Management System platform. Further, authentication, authorization and accounting functions may be provided by an AAA server. The AAA server may be involved in verification of mobile agent and control unit identities, as well as in the authentication and authorization of third party applications.

CORE FUNCTIONS FOR MOBILE MONITORING

The design of Web Services APIs for mobile monitoring is based on identification of generic functions. The core mobile monitoring functions in IoT environment include: MA registration, management of operation mode, and reporting

Figure 1. Generic architecture for mobile monitoring and third party access to measurements based on Web Services

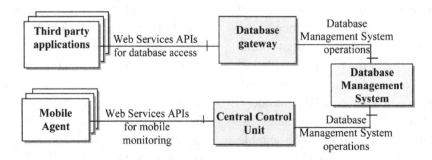

of measurement data. In order to recognize each other the mobile agents and the central unit need to have identifications.

Identification

The MA is an embedded device equipped with sensor(s), positioning module, data transmission module and power supply module. Each MA and the CU have unique identities (IDs). The temporary identities protect the confidentiality of the MA identity against passive eavesdroppers. New temporary identity (TID) is allocated when the MA performs registration procedure, when the CU configures and modifies the MA's operation mode, or the CU sends notifications to the MA (e.g. when the MS needs to be deregistered). As far as the part of the system related to mobile monitoring is a specific application, the initial values of security related parameters may be pre-configured in both the MA and CU. The security related parameters include the following: unique ID of the MA (ID_M), unique ID of the CU (ID_C), initial temporary identity of MA (TID_M), and a shared secret.

Registration

Registration is performed initially after the MA is switched on or after change of its IP address. The aim is to bind the IP address that is currently used by the MA and MA identity. Prior to registration which allows the MA to operate in the mobile monitoring system e.g. to perform measurements and to send reports, the MA must obtain IP connectivity. The registration is based on successful authentication. The authentication is to assert that both MA and CU are who they pretend to be and uses the unique IDs and the shared secret. In addition, in order to protect the unique ID_M, as a part of registration a new TID_M is assigned to the MA.

Mobile Monitoring

The MA may be configured to operate in different operation modes. Periodic monitoring and reporting require the MA to make measurements and to send reports at given rates. Triggered reporting operation mode requires monitoring for certain criteria and submitting reports on their occurrences. CU may start and stop periodic and triggered monitoring. The third mode of operation is reporting on demand, where the CU induced reporting requires MA to perform measurements and to send reports on demand. MAs report the measurement data that have been collected according to the configured monitoring mode periodically, on event occurrence, or on demand.

CORE FUNCTIONS FOR THIRD PARTY ACCESS TO MEASUREMENT DATA

The design of Web Services interfaces that allow third party to access measurements data is based on identification of generic functions for database access.

Secured Service Discovery

Service security is essential for IoT service access and resolution service. Resolution is a service by which a given identification is associated with a set of addresses of information services and interaction services. Resolution is based on a priori knowledge achieved by service discovery. Discovery is a service to find unknown services based on a rough specification of the desired result. It may be utilized by a human or another service. The discovery execution considers credentials for authorization. The security related functional components provide secure discovery of an IoT service and restricted discovery.

Secured discovery restricts the discovery of service to those third party applications that are authorized to know about it. Secured service discovery includes the following functional components: authentication of third party application, assertion and authorization. Authorization allows general access to discovery, service discovery based on service specification and filtering of discovery results. In some case, service authentication is also a matter of concern, for example, how to authenticate requests coming from other Web Services. So, where appropriate, authentication must be mutual including both third party application and service authentication. Moreover, if the third party needs to be charged for access to measurements, there is a need for the authenticated application to confirm its intention to use the discovered Web Service by signing a service agreement. The signing of service agreement is to ensure non-repudiation, or in other words to prevent the third party application from denying it has used the service. Typical service agreement presentation and signing is done by digital signature.

Information Services

Information services allow querying, adding and deleting data, as well as subscription and notifications about specific events in measurements dataset. Query function may be used by third party application to retrieve specific data from the database. Authorized applications may be allowed to add or delete data. Subscription function may be used by third party application to request notifications about changes in the measurements data. Un-subscription function may be used by the applications to cancel one or several existing subscriptions. Notification function is required when data that was identified upon subscription changes or when the invoked Subscription function requested submission of all the initial values of the referenced data.

DESCRIPTION OF WEB SERVICE INTERFACES FOR MONITORING MANAGEMENT

The Web Service for monitoring management provides APIs supported by both MA and CU.

The RegistrationCU interface allows the MA to initiate registration/deregistration from the CU. It supports the following operations:

- Register() operation is used by the MA to request registration by using its temporary identity TID_M. The registration may have duration. It is the responsibility of the MA to keep the registration active by periodically refreshing it. If the MA does not refresh its registration, the CU will silently remove the registration when the registration timer expires. The MA can perform re-registration at any time by invoking this operation.
- ChallengeCU() operation is used by the MA to request authentication of the CU. The CU must respond with the correct response to the challenges. The invocation of this operation may be interleaved by with challenge calls by the CU on the RegistrationMA interface.
- AllocateTemporaryIdentity() operation is used by the MA to request allocation of a new temporary identity. The CU assigns the TID_M and returns it to the MA after successful authentication.
- Deregister() operation is used by the MA to request deregistration by using its temporary identity TID_M.

The RegistrationMA interface allows the CU to initiate new registration or deregistration of the MA. The supported operations include the following:

- SupportedAuthenticationMechanism() operation queries the MA about the supported authentication mechanisms. Based on the MA response, the CU will select one of the suggested authentication mechanisms and that mechanism is to be used for authentication by both CU and MA.
- ReRegister() operation is used by the CU to initiate re-authentication due to certain conditions.
- ChallengeMA() operation is used by the CU to request authentication of the MA. The MA must respond with the correct response to the challenge. The invocation of this operation may be interleaved by with challenge calls by the MA on the RegistrationCU interface. The MA will respond immediately to authentication challenge from the CU, and would not wait until the CU has responded to any challenge the MA may issue.

- CUNotitification() operation is used by the CU to deregister the MA for administrative reasons.

Figure 2 depicts the sequence diagram for MA registration.

The MobileMonitoring interface allows the CU to request reports on measurements. It supports the following operations:

- GetMeasurements() operation is intended to retrieve the measurement on demand along with the MA's location. The accuracy requested is the desired accuracy for the response. The acceptable accuracy is the limit acceptable to the requester. If the accuracy requested cannot be supported policy or service exception would be returned.
- GetLocation() operation is intended to retrieved the location of the MA.

Figure 2. Scenario of MA registration

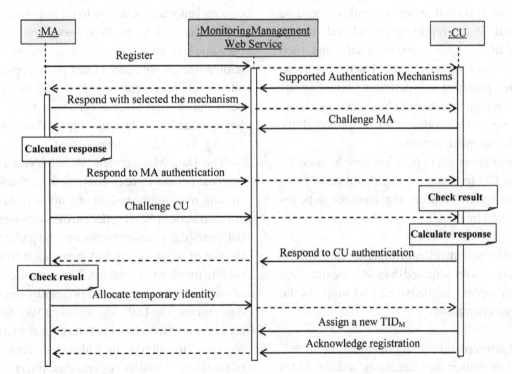

The MeasurementReportingManager interface allows the CU to configure the MA monitoring mode. The CU uses the interface to setup reporting for measurements events and supports the following operations:

- StartPeriodicReporting() is intended to configure periodic reporting of measurements at a CU defined interval. The accuracy requested is the desired accuracy for the response. If the accuracy requested is not supported by the MA, a policy exception will be returned to the CU.

- StartTriggeredReporting() is intended to request monitoring for certain criteria and submitting reports on their occurrences. The operation sets the reporting criteria, i.e. timestamp, location, threshold values etc. The number and duration of reporting may be requested as part of the setup of reporting or may be governed by service policies, or combination of the two. If the frequency or duration requested is greater than allowed by the service policy, then the value specified in service policy would be used. If the reporting period ends before all of the reports have been delivered, then the reporting terminates. The tracing accuracy provided will determine how fine the measurements have to be. Service policies govern what values can be provided for measurement accuracy.

- EndReporting() operation may be used by the CU to end reporting. Until this operation returns, reports may continue to be received by the CU.

The MeasurementReporting() interfaces allow the MA to deliver acquired data. It is the interface to which reports are delivered and supports the following operations:

- MeasurementReport() operation is intended to deliver measurements and the MA's

location to the CU. The operation indicates the met criteria when sending the report.

- LocationNotification() operation is used to notify the CU about the MA's location.

- MeasurementError() operation is sent to the CU to indicate that reporting has been cancelled due to some reason.

- LocationError() operation is sent to the CU to indicate that notification about MA's location cannot be delivered due to some reason.

- MeasurementEnd() operation indicates that the reporting has completed. This message will be submitted when the duration for reporting has been completed, but not in case of an error reporting.

DESCRIPTION OF WEB SERVICE INTERFACES FOR THIRD PARTY ACCESS TO MEASUREMENT DATA

Two Web Services are proposed for third party access to measurement data, one for service access and another for access to measurement data.

The Secured Access Web Service provides application level security functions including mutual authentication between a third party application and the Database gateway. It also allows a third party application to discover the available Web Services and to select the appropriate ones by signing a service level agreement.

The Data Management Web Service allows external access to data content. It enables consuming measurement data and up to third party authorization uploading data in the measurements database (e.g. measurements may be gathered by the use of other means which are apart from the mobile monitoring system). The supported APIs allow submission, modification and deletion of data entries. The Data Management Web Service provides also interfaces to query for data matching specific criteria. In addition to abstraction of traditional database operations, interfaces for subscription to and notification for events related to measurements of interest are defined.

The architecture of third party access to measurement data is shown in Figure 3.

The Secured Access Web Service APIs may be used for Initial Access, Application Level Authentication, Service Discovery and Service Selection, as shown in Figure 4.

Before using services, the third party application and the Database gateway authenticate each other. Authentication prevents from unauthorized access. Once authenticated, the third party application selects the service interface to be used. To ensure non-repudiation, the Database gateway can request signing of a service agreement before allowing the Data Management Web Service to be used. Only after the authentication, service selection, and signing of the service agreement have been done the third party application can start using the actual Data Management service. Apart from providing security, the authentication and service selection process also allows IoT service providers to define permission profiles for different users. The level of privileges can be made to depend on the level of trust awarded to the third party applications.

Figure 4. Use cases for secure service access

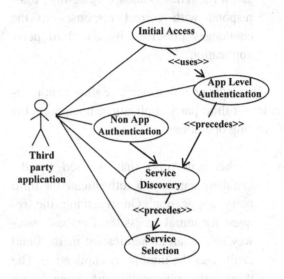

The Initial Access interface allows a third party application to request service access. It supports the following operations:

- InitiateAuthentication3rdParty() is used by a third party application at initial contact to request authentication indicating the supported authentication operations.
- AuthenticateDG() is used by a third party application to authenticate the Database

Figure 3. Architecture for third party access to databases

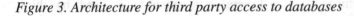

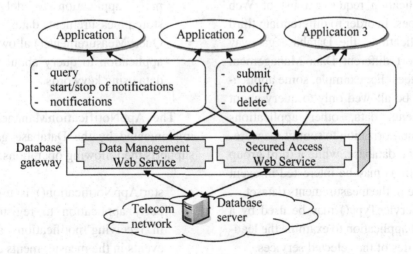

gateway. The Database gateway must respond with correct responses to the challenges presented by the third party application.

The Authentication interface allows authentication of third party application. It supports the following operations:

- AuthenticateApp() that is used by the Database gateway to authenticate the third party application. On receiving the request for initial access the Database gateway selects an authentication method and challenges the third party application. The third party application must respond with the correct responses to the challenges made by the Database gateway.

The ServiceDiscovery interface allows a third party application to discover Measurement data services supported by the Database gateway. The interface defines the following operations:

- SelectSigningAlgorithm() is used to agree on algorithm for signed exchanges.
- ListServiceTypes() is used by a third party application to become aware of the available services. By this operation, a third party application requests a list of Web service types. In order to differentiate third party applications, the Database gateway may support different Data Management Web Services. For example, some applications may be allowed only to query about measurements data, other applications may have authorization to submit measurements to the database, while a third group of applications may be interested in event occurrence in the measurements dataset.
- DescribeServiceType() may be used by a third party application to examine the leading properties of the selected services.

- DiscoverService() is a mean by which a third party application can retrieved a specific set of Web Services showing the service type name and the service property list. The Database gateway returns a list of services meeting the requirements and their service properties.
- SelectService() is intended to inform the Database gateway about the Web service selected by the third party application.
- SignServiceAgreement() is used to sign a service agreement electronically. The third party application invokes the operation indicating that it has signed the agreement. The response returns indication that Database gateway has signed the agreement too.

The DataAccess interface is implemented by the Database gateway and it supports the following operations:

- SubmitData() allows an authorized third party application to submit data to the measurements database.
- ModifyMeasurements() is used by third party application to update previously submitted measurements data.
- DeleteMeasurements() is used by third party application to delete previously stored measurements data.
- QueryMeasurements() allows a third party application to query about measurements data using keywords.

The AppNotificationManager interface is implemented by the Database gateway and it supports the following operations:

- startAppNotification() is used by a third party application to register its interest in receiving notifications about specific events in the measurements dataset.

- endAppNotification() is used by the third party application to indicate that it is no longer interested in receiving notifications.

The AppNotification interface has to be implemented by the third party application and supports the following operation:

- notifyAppMeasurements() operation allows to receive notifications after specific events defined by startAppNotification() operation have occurred in the dataset.

WEB SERVICES IMPLEMENTATION ASPECTS

Deployment of Web Services in a telecommunication network requires implementation of interface between the Database gateway and the Database server.

One of the alternatives for the communication between Database gateway and the Database server is to use Transmission Control Protocol (TCP) connections for database operation, e.g. for Structural Query Language (SQL) operations.

Another alternative is based on Lightweight Data Access Protocol (LDAP) using the Query, Create, Delete and Update messages (RFC 4511). Query request messages are coded as LDAP SearchRequest messages, while Query result messages are coded as LDAP SearchResultEntry, SearchResultReference, and SearchResultDone messages. Delete request messages are coded as LDAP DelRequest messages or as LDAP ModifyRequest messages with the 'operation' field set to 'delete', depending on the data to be deleted, while Delete result messages are coded as LDAP DelResponse messages or as LDAP ModifyResponse messages, depending on the used LDAP request message. Update request messages are coded as LDAP ModifyRequest messages with 'operation' field set to 'replace'. Update result messages are coded as LDAP ModifyResponse messages.

Subscribe request messages use the HTTP Post method and contain a SOAP message envelope. Subscribe response messages are coded as HTTP response message. Subscribe request and response messages contain a SOAP message envelope header with a header block containing a message identifier and a connection identifier. The message identifier uniquely identifies the Subscribe message request-response pair within a connection. The Database gateway allocates the value and uses it together with the connection identifier to correlate a received subscribe response with already sent subscribe request. The connection identifier identifies the connection between the Database gateway and the Database server. The Database server copies the SOAP Envelope Header received in the Subscribe request and sends it unmodified in the Subscribe response. Subscribe request messages contain a SOAP message envelope body formatted according to specific XML schema. Subscribe response messages contain an empty SOAP message envelope body. Only the HTTP status code in the Subscribe response message is used to indicate success or failure.

Notify request messages use the HTTP Post method and contain a SOAP message envelope. Notify response messages are coded as HTTP response message. Notify request and response messages contain a SOAP message envelope header with a header block containing an optional service identifier, a message identifier and a connection identifier. The service identifier points the service in the Database gateway. Its value is copied from the Subscribe message or preconfigured in the Database server. The message identifier uniquely identifies the Notify message request-response pair within a connection. The Database gateway copies the SOAP Envelope Header received in the Notify request message and sends it unmodified in the Notify response message. Notify request messages contain a SOAP message envelope body formatted according to specific XML schema. The

185

HTTP status code in the Notify response message indicates success or failure.

Figure 5 shows the protocol stacks in the interface between the Database gateway and the Database server.

TRAFFIC MODEL OF WEB SERVICES GATEWAY

In the architecture for mobile monitoring based on Web Services, the Database gateway is a special type of application server that provides Web Services APIs for third party applications and communication protocols for the Measurements Database server. To provide open access for third party applications to measurements dataset a Database gateway has to be deployed. This gateway translates the SOAP request to Database Management System operations and vice versa.

Service-oriented architecture is a contract driven architecture. There have to be contracts between the Database gateway and the Service Providers (SPs) hosting third party applications. The contract (Service Level Agreement – SLA) includes constraints and restrictions (De, 2010). The most important parameters, from the performance point of view, include the guaranteed number and maximum number of application calls from a certain SP per time unit, and also guaranteed number and maximum number of notification from the Database server to each SP per time unit. In order to prevent the Database gateway from overload, admission control is applied for each SP which considers the restrictions included in the contract. The admission control makes the decision whether an incoming message from SP or Database server is to be accepted or rejected. It applies the mechanism of Token bucket (TB) (Park, 2003).

Usually, a Database gateway has a distributed architecture with several converters, which translate the SOAP request from applications to Database Management System operations and vice versa. It is important to distribute the accepted messages between different converter and that is why the load balancing mechanism is applied. In the suggested traffic model of the Database gateway, the well known Round Robin mechanism is applied for load balancing (Liu, 2002).

A typical message exchange template includes traffic from third party applications and from the database server. The traffic from the third party applications consists of requests for access to measurements data (denoted by 'query'), subscriptions to notifications (denoted by 'start'), and subscription cancelations (denoted by 'stop'). The traffic from the database server includes notifications about events in the measurements data (denoted by 'notify'). Different messages are of different priority classes. From the highest to the lowest priority these classes are as follows: 'stop', 'notify', 'query', 'start'. The 'stop' messages are with the highest priority because they indicate that the notifications from the database server must be terminated. If a certain subscription to

Figure 5. Protocol stacks for the interface between Database gateway and Database server

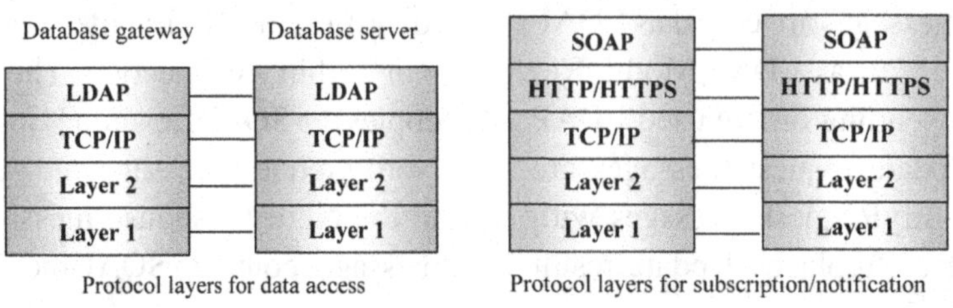

Database gateway	Database server
LDAP	**LDAP**
TCP/IP	**TCP/IP**
Layer 2	**Layer 2**
Layer 1	**Layer 1**

Protocol layers for data access

Database gateway	Database server
SOAP	**SOAP**
HTTP/HTTPS	**HTTP/HTTPS**
TCP/IP	**TCP/IP**
Layer 2	**Layer 2**
Layer 1	**Layer 1**

Protocol layers for subscription/notification

notifications is accepted then notifications have to be forwarded to the applications. Any query for access to the database may be regarded separately from the others, as far as a subscription is expected to force a number of notifications.

Figure 6 shows the model of the i-th Access controller. To protect the Database gateway from overload a rough admission control is used (TB1). If a message is rejected, filter F6 passes only rejected 'stop' messages. If a 'stop' message is rejected, the application has to be informed. The filter F1 passes 'notify' messages which are forwarded to TB2 that prevents the Database gateway from overload caused by database server initiated notifications. The conforming notifications are forwarded to the application. The filter F2 passes 'query' messages which are forwarded to TB3 that prevents the Database gateway from overload caused by application's requests. The conforming requests are forwarded to the load balancer (LB). If the accepted message is neither notification nor query message it is filtered by F3 which passes 'start' messages. The 'start' messages are forwarded to TB3 which controls that the constraint of accepted number of 'start' mes-

sages is fulfilled. The accepted 'start' message is forwarded for load balancing. The messages that do not pass filter F3 are forwarded to filter F4. In case of 'stop' message, filter F5 is used to correlate the 'stop' message with the corresponding 'start' message.

The message traffic is observed at regular time intervals $[t_{k-1}, t_k)$. The model of the j-th converter is shown in Figure 7 where $Z_j(t_k)$ is the number of all notifications sent by the database within the interval $[t_{k-1}, t_k)$. Each of the converters is modeled as a single FIFO buffer (Q) with limited size. The message is fetched out of the queue, translated by the processing unit (PU) and forwarded either to the Database server or to the application.

Token Bucket Model

The token bucket model $TB(T, \rho, \mu)$ is characterized by volume T, rate ρ and level μ. The Equation (1) represents the initial token level.

$$\mu(t_0) = T. \tag{1}$$

Figure 6. Model of i-th access controller

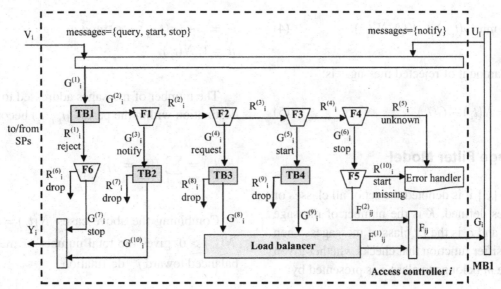

Figure 7. Model of jth converter

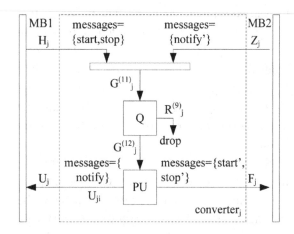

The token level at the end of the time interval $[t_{k-1}, t_k)$ is:

$$\mu(t_k) = \mu(t_{k-1}) + A(t_k) - G(t_k). \qquad (2)$$

where $A(t_k)$ is the amount of tokens arrived within $[t_{k-1}, t_k)$, and $G(t_k)$ is the amount of tokens given in $[t_{k-1}, t_k)$.

By $N(t_k)$ it is denoted the number of messages arrived to the TB within $[t_{k-1}, t_k)$. Then

$$A(t_k) = \min(T - \mu(t_{k-1}), \rho.(t_k - t_{k-1})). \qquad (3)$$

$$G(t_k) = \min(\mu(t_{k-1}) + A(t_k), N(t_k)). \qquad (4)$$

The amount of rejected messages is:

$$R(t_k) = N(t_k) - G(t_k). \qquad (5)$$

Message Filter Model

By $C = \{c_j\}$ it is denoted the set of all classes of messages defined, K is the number of message classes, and c_j is the jth class of messages. Then the classifier function that checks whether given message m belongs to class c_j is presented by:

$$d(m, c_j) = j.I(m \in c_j) \qquad (6)$$

where I is an indicator function i.e. $I(s)=1$ if s is true, and $I(s)=0$ otherwise. The number of messages belonging to class c_j and passed by a filter is:

$$F(c_j, N(t_k)) = I(N(t_k) > 0).\sum_{n=1}^{N(t_k)} I(j = d(m_n \in c_j)) \qquad (7)$$

The number of messages rejected by the filter is:

$$R(c_j, N(t_k)) = N(t_k) - F(c_j, N(t_k)) \qquad (8)$$

Load Balancer Model

The load balancer model $LB(\sigma, M)$ is characterized by its internal state σ and the set of destinations M that LB is going to distribute the load to. Then the LB initial state is $\sigma(t_0) = random(m)$ where m is the power of set M and $random(m)$ is uniform distribution between $0..m-1$.

If $N(t_k) = 0$ then $\sigma(t_k) = \sigma(t_{k-1})$ and the number of messages distributed to the jth element of M is $F_i(t_k) = 0$. If $N(t_k) > 0$ then the index of the element of M that is going to be the destination for the nth message within $[t_{k-1}, t_k)$ is:

$$b_n = 1 + (\sigma(t_{k-1}) + n) \bmod m,$$
$$n = 1..N(t_k) \qquad (9)$$

The number of messages addressed to the jth destination within the period $[t_{k-1}, t_k)$ becomes:

$$F_j(t_k) = \sum_{n=1}^{N(t_k)} I(b_n = j) \qquad (10)$$

Combining the above cases $N(t_k) = 0$ and $N(t_k) > 0$ gives the total number of messages balanced toward j^{th} destination

$$F_j(t_k) = I(N(t_k) > 0) \cdot \sum_{n=1}^{N(t_k)} I(b_n = j) \qquad (11)$$

Converter Model

Let any message of class c_j requires $w^{(j)}$ amount of service provided by the converter it is dispatched to. Then the state of the buffer can be recurrently presented as

$$q(t_k) = q(t_{k-1}) - G(t_k) + A(t_k) \qquad (12)$$

where $G(t_k)$ is the amount of messages fetched out of the buffer and $A(t_k)$ is the amount of the placed ones and $q(t_0) = 0$. Having ζ of the total converter's capacity dedicated to message conversion and a hard limit set on the length of the buffer, denoted by Q_{max}, it is easy to define for $G(t_k)$ and $A(t_k)$ the following

$$G(t_k) = I(q(t_{k-1}) + N(t_k) > 0) \times \max_m \left(\zeta \cdot (t_k - t_{k-1}) \geq \sum_{l=1}^{m} \sum_{j=1}^{K} w^{(j)} \cdot I(q[l] \in c_j) \right) \qquad (13)$$

$$A(t_k) = \min \begin{pmatrix} N(t_k), G(t_k) \\ + Q_{max} - q(t_{k-1}) \end{pmatrix} \qquad (14)$$

It is trivial to observe that the amount of losses caused by finite buffer in the converter within $[t_{k-1}, t_k)$ is

$$R(t_k) = N(t_k) - A(t_k) \qquad (15)$$

Database Gateway Utilization Model

Using the Token Bucket model, Filter model and Load Balancer model as component models it becomes feasible to express all the message flows shown in Figure 6 and Figure 7, and more specifically between i-th access controller and j-th converter. The following notations are used:

- N: Number of SPs, respectively access controllers
- M: Number of converters
- κ_i: Capacity of i-th access controller dedicated to access control function
- κ_j: Capacity of j-th converter dedicated to conversion.

The gateway utilization and throughput in $[t_{k-1}, t_k)$ are given by Equations (16) and (17) respectively.

$$\eta(t_k) = \frac{\sum_{i=1}^{N} Y_i(t_k) + \sum_{j=1}^{M} F_j(t_k)}{(t_k - t_{k-1}) \cdot \left(\sum_{j=1}^{M} \kappa_j + \sum_{i=1}^{N} \kappa_i \right)}. \qquad (16)$$

$$\gamma(t_k) = \eta(t_k) \cdot \left(\sum_{j=1}^{M} \kappa_j + \sum_{i=1}^{N} \kappa_i \right). \qquad (17)$$

Adaptive Control Strategy

The loss function for the Database gateway is given by:

$$L = \sum_{k=1}^{K} \left(\sum_{i=1}^{N} (\alpha_i(t_k) \sum_{p=4}^{8} R_i^{(p)}.(t_k)) + \sum_{j=1}^{M} \beta_j(t_k).R_j^9(t_k) \right), \qquad (18)$$

where K is the number of observed intervals.

The parameters $\{ \alpha_i, \beta_j, i = 1... N, j = 1...M \}$ are nonnegative functions of time assigning relative weights given to various losses. The first parameter imposes a penalty on lost traffic at the admission control for the i-th TB and the second parameter imposes penalty on losses in the j-th converter. The problem is to find a control policy that minimizes this function.

By $\rho_{g_i}^{(2)}$ it is denoted the guaranteed rate of notification from the SLA between i-th SP and the Database server. The focus is set on the losses of notifications as far as the converters had spent part of their capacity to perform conversion. Thus the control policy is on the actual rate of tokens for i-th TB2 as follows:

$$
\rho_i^{(2)}(t_k) = \rho_{g_i}^{(2)}(t_k) + \left| \begin{array}{c} \max(\kappa_i(t_k - t_{k-1}) \\ -G_i^{(1)}(t_k), 0) \cdot \dfrac{U_i(t_k)}{V_i(t_k) + U_i(t_k)} \end{array} \right|. \tag{19}
$$

The left side of Equation (19) presents the rate of tokens that will be granted to i-th SP for the interval $[t_k, t_{k+1})$ especially for messages of notification type. The first component on the right side is the guaranteed rate of tokens from SLA, and the second component represents the part of available resources of i-th access controller that are proportionally engaged with the notifications flow of messages.

EVALUATION OF DATABASE GATEWAY UTILIZATION

The evaluation of the Database gateway utilization is done by simulation. The simulation is done on a simplified model with four classes of messages and four converters.

Simulation Parameters

The capacity of the gateway is 800 requests per second which is distributed between the converters. The behavior of each SP is modeled by Mar-

kov Modulated Poisson Process (MMPP). New application requests are generated according to three-state MMPP, where each state is featured by its rate i.e. requests per second respectively 0, 60, and 120 (Matur, 2009). Transitions between different states are uniformly distributed and occurred according to Poisson process with mean 5s. The time intervals between 'query' messages generated by each SP are exponentially distributed as the arrival process in the context of Web services with mean 120 s (Muscariello, 2005). The number of generated subscription request is a normally distributed random variable and its mean constitutes about one third of all requests per state. During an application session the time intervals between 'notify' messages generated by the network are exponentially distributed with mean 60 s. The SPs traffic is policed by access controllers whose conforming outputs are multiplexed between 4 converters. The token rate is equal to the guaranteed rate and the bucket size is determined by the peak rate. Initially, $\mu_i(t_0) = T_0$, $q_i(t_0) = 0$. The length of the interval for observation $[t_k - t_{k-1})$ is set to 100 ms. The processing time for a single request/response in a converter is 5 ms.

Numerical Results

The aim of simulation is to evaluate the Database gateway utilization setting different values of guaranteed rates and fixed peak rates. The guaranteed rates for a certain SP define the constraints for preventing the Database gateway from overload (GR_1), constraints for the rates of 'notify' messages (GR_2), 'query' messages (GR_3), and 'start' messages (GR_4). The processing capacity of the Database gateway must be distributed between different types of messages, where the overall message peak rate (PR_1) must be spread between 'notify' messages (PR_2), 'query' messages (PR_3), 'start' messages (PR_4), and 'stop' messages.

The simulation is run in a space of SLAs where each contract is consisted of tuple (PR_i, GR_i) for every TB_i of given access controller. Table 1 summarizes the outcome of the simulation. The Database gateway utilization is evaluated as a function of the number of SPs and guaranteed rates. The guaranteed rates of messages per second are included into four different SLAs. The values of peak rates are limited by the converter capacity.

The simulation results are summarized in Table 1.

The simulation results show that the utilization depends on both the number of SPs and the specific values of rates in SLAs. In case for the Database gateway the congestion threshold value is set to 80%, it is most likely that the appropriate choice is to have 22 SPs applying second type or third type of SLA. The application of adaptive control leads to higher utilization than the case without one. The average throughput gain is about 8%.

CONCLUSION

The chapter presents a new structural approach to definition of APIs for mobile monitoring that may be used in IoT applications. Derived from generic functions the APIs provide an abstraction of mobile monitoring that is independent of the protocols used for implementation.

The open access to measurements data allows third party applications to access measurement data in a secured manner. In addition to traditional database operations, the APIs define operations for subscription about and notifications for events concerning measurements stored in the database. The designed functions for mutual authentication and Web service selection increase security and allow differentiation of applications. The proposed Web Services for open access to measurements data accelerate the development of new attractive third party applications and shorten time to market.

The suggested solution for internal access to measurements database through Web Services interfaces provides an abstraction of Database Management System operations which is an additional level of flexibility e.g. in case of change of the storage technology. The application areas encompass healthcare, transport and logistics, smart home, smart city, retail, environment etc.

The traffic model of the Database gateway which is the mediator between third party applications and the measurements database describes typical communications involving messages of different priority. The applied adaptive access control distributes the Database gateway's resources between the Service Providers according to their current needs. The Database gateway performance is evaluated and constraints in SLA are identified.

The future work concerning the presented results is planned to elaborate the simulation model, in order to reflect the length of each message i.e. to include details regarding the operation parameters types, return types and exceptions.

Table 1. Summary of the database gateway utilization

SPs	SLA₁{40,18, 6,10}	SLA₂{60, 27, 9,15}	SLA₃{80,36, 12, 20}	SLA₄{90,42,14, 20}
16	0,48117	0,55989	0,64582	0,67225
18	0,56003	0,63892	0,71052	0,75730
20	0,61485	0,71056	0,79056	0,83024
22	0,67582	0,78321	0,87061	0,90745
24	0,73712	0,84809	0,94226	0,99487

REFERENCES

Agarwal, S. (2010). Remote health monitoring using mobile, phones and web services. *Telemedicine Journal and e-Health*, 16(5), 603–607. doi:10.1089/tmj.2009.0165 PMID:20575728

Al-Ali, A., Zualkernan, I., & Aloul, F. (2010). A mobile GPRS-sensors array for air pollution monitoring. *IEEE Sensors Journal*, 10(10), 1666–1671. doi:10.1109/JSEN.2010.2045890

Ambler, S. (2012). *Encapsulating database access: An agile best practice*. Retrieved from http://www.agiledata.org/essays/implementationStrategies.html

Castellani, A. P., Gheda, M., Bui, N., & Rossi, M. (2011). Web services for the internet of things through CoAP and EXI. In *Proceedings of IEEE International Conference on Communications Workshops*. IEEE.

Ciancetta, F., D'Apice, B., Landi, C., & Pelvio, A. (2007). *Mobile sensor network architecture for environmental monitoring*. Retrieved from http://www.imeko.org/publications/tc19-2007/IMEKO-TC19-2007-064.pdf

De, P., Chodhury, P., & Choudhury, S. (2010). A framework for performance analysis of client/server based SOA and P2P SOA. In *Proceeedings of International Conference on Computer and Network Technology ICCNT'10*, (pp. 79-83). ICCNT.

De Capua, C., Meduri, A., & Morello, R. (2010). Smart ECG measurement system based on web-service-oriented architecture for telemedicine applications. *IEEE Transactions on Instrumentation and Measurement*, 59(10), 2530–2538. doi:10.1109/TIM.2010.2057652

Elgazzar, K., Aboelfotoh, M., Martin, P., & Hassanein, H. (2012). Ubiquitous health monitoring using mobile web services. *Procedia Computer Science*, 10, 332–339. doi:10.1016/j.procs.2012.06.044

Fox, G. C., Kamburugamuve, S., & Hartman, R. (2012). Architecture and measured characteristics of a cloud based internet of things API. In *Proceedings of International Conference on Collaboration Technologies and Systems CTS' 2012*, (pp. 6-12). CTS.

Galluccio, L., Morabito, G., & Palazzo, S. (2011). On the potentials of object group localization in the internet of things. In *Proceedings of IEEE International Symposium on World of Wireless, Mobile and Multimedia Networks WoWMoM'2011*, (pp. 1-9). IEEE.

Haselmann, T., Thies, G., & Vossen, G. (2010). Looking into a REST-based universal API for database-as-a-service systems. In *Proceedings of IEEE Conf. on Commerce and Enterprise Computing CEC'10*, (pp. 17-20). IEEE.

INFSO D.4 Networked Enterprise & RFID INFSO G.2 Micro & Nanosystems. (2008). Internet of things in 2020. *Roadmap for the Future, 1*, 1-27.

ITU-T. (2005). *ITU internet reports 2005: The internet of things*. Retrieved from http://www.itu.int/osg/spu/publications/internetofthings/

Kang, W., Son, S. H., & Stankovic, J. (2009). PRIDE: A data abstraction layer for large-scale 2-tier sensor networks. In *Proceedings of IEEE Communications Society Conf. on Sensor, Mesh and Ad Hoc Communications and Networks, SECON'09*. IEEE.

Kim, D., Squyres, J., & Lumsdaine, A. (2006). The introduction of the OSCAR database API (ODA). In *Proceedings of International Conference on High-Performance Computing in an Advanced Collaborative Environment*. Academic Press.

Kim, Y., Ryu, Y., & Yoo, J. (2012). Cloud services based mobile monitoring for photovoltaic systems. In *Proceedings of IEEE International Conference on Cloud Computing Technology and Science CloudCom'2012*, (pp. 578 – 580). IEEE.

Kyusakov, R., Eliasson, J., Delsing, J., van Deventer, J., & Gustafsson, J. (2011). Integration of wireless sensor and actuator nodes with IT infrastructure using service-oriented architecture. *IEEE Transactions on Industrial Informatics, 6*(1), 1–9.

Liu, J., Kit, H. C., Hambi, M., & Tsui, C. Y. (2002). Stable round-robin scheduling algorithms for high-performance input queued switches. In *Proceedings of Symposium on High Performance Interconnects*, (pp. 43-51). Academic Press.

Lyytikainen, H. (2012). *Designing web services for location-aware mobile devices, case: Traffic monitoring service*. Retrieved from http://lib.tkk.fi/Dipl/2012/urn100645.pdf

Maciá-Pérez, F., Marcos-Jorquera, D., & Gilart-Iglesias, V. (2007). Embedded web services for industrial TCP/IP services monitoring. In *Proceedings of IEEE Conference on Emerging Technologies and Factory Automation,* (pp. 1115-1122). IEEE.

Matur, V., Dhopesshwarkar, S., & Apte, V. (2009). MASTH proxy: An extensible platform for web overload control. In *Proceedings of the International Conference on World Wide Web*, (pp. 1113-1114). WWW.

Muscariello, M., Mellia, M., Meo, M., Marsan, A., & Cigno, R. (2005). Markov models of internet traffic and a new hierarchical MMPP model. *Computer Communications, 28*(16), 1835–1851. doi:10.1016/j.comcom.2005.02.012

Park, E. C., & Choi, C. H. (2003). Adaptive token bucket algorithm for fair bandwidth allocation in DiffServ networks. In *Proceedings of IEEE Clobal Telecommunications Conference GLOBECOM'03*, (pp. 3176-3180). IEEE.

Pryyantha, B., Kansal, A., Goraczko, M., & Zhao, F. (2008). Tiny web services: Design and implementation of interoperable and evolvable sensor networks. In *Proceedings of 6th ACM Conference on Embedded Network Sensor Systems*, (pp. 253-266). ACM.

Qu, X., Feng, J., & Sun, W. (2008). United access of distributed biological information database based on web service and multi-agent. In *Proceedings of Conf. Control and Decision*, (pp. 4257–4260). Academic Press.

Ramos, V., Delamer, I., & Lastra, J. (2011). Embedded service oriented monitoring, diagnostics and control: Towards the asset-aware and self-recovery factor. In *Proceedings of IEEE International Conference on Industrial Informatics*, (pp. 497 – 502). IEEE.

Schmutzler, J., Wolff, A., & Wietfeld, C. (2008). Comparative performance evaluation of web services and JXTA for embedded environmental monitoring systems. In *Proceedings of Conference on Enterprise Distributed Object Computing*, (pp. 369-376). Academic Press.

Sellis, T., Skoutas, D., & Staikos, K. (2008). Database interoperability through web services and ontologies. In *Proceedings of International Conference on BioInformatics and BioEngineering*. BIBE.

Shelby, Z. (2010). Embedded web services. *IEEE Wireless Communications, 17*(6), 52–57. doi:10.1109/MWC.2010.5675778

Stoicu-Tivadar, V., Stoicu-Tivadar, L., Puscoci, S., Berian, D., & Topac, V. (2012). WebService-based solution for an intelligent telecare system. In *Recent advances in intelligent engineering systems*. Berlin: Springer. doi:10.1007/978-3-642-23229-9_18

Yang, J., & Park, H. (2008). A design of open service access gateway for converged web service. In *Proceedings of International Conference on Advanced Communication Technology*, (pp. 1807-1810). Academic Press.

Yang, J., Zhang, Z., & Zhao, Y. (2010). Analysis on database connection mechanism of web application system in dreamweaver. In *Proceedings of International Conference on Internet Technology and Applications*, (pp. 1- 4). Academic Press.

ADDITIONAL READING

Associati, C. (2011). The Evolution of Internet of Things, Retrieved from: http://www.casaleggio. it/ pubblicazioni /Focus_Internet_of_things_v1.81%20-%20eng.pdf

Botero, O., & Chaouchi, H. (2010). RFID Applications and Related Research Issues. In H. Chaouchi (Ed.), *The Internet of things. Connecting Objects to the Web*. Wiley.

Broustis, I., Sundaram, G., Mizikovsly, S., & Viswanathan, H. (2012). M2M Security. In D. Boswarthich, O. Elloumi, & O. Hersent (Eds.), *M2M Communications A System Approach*. Wiley. doi:10.1002/9781119974031.ch8

Buckl, C. wt.al. (2009). Services to the field: an approach for resource constrained sensor/actor networks, Proc. of WAINA'09, Bradford, United Kingdom.

Carcelle, X., & Bourgeau, T. (2010). Power Line Communication Technology Overview. In H. Chaouchi (Ed.), *The Internet of things. Connecting Objects to the Web*. Wiley.

Castellani, P., et al. (2011). Web Services for the Internet of Things through CoAP and EXI, Proc. of IEEE International Conference on Communications Workshops, pp.1-6.

Chaouchi, H. (2010). Introduction to the Internet of Things. In H. Chaouchi (Ed.), *The Internet of things. Connecting Objects to the Web*. Wiley.

Duffy, P., S. Chakrabarti, R. Cragie, Y. Ohba, A. Yegin. (2011). Protocol for Carrying Authentication for Network Access (PANA) Relay Element, draft-ohba-pana-relay- 03 (Work in progress).

Elloumi, O., & Forlivesi, C. (2012). ETSI M2M Services Architecture. In D. Boswarthich, O. Elloumi, & O. Hersent (Eds.), *M2M Communications A System Approach*. Wiley. doi:10.1002/9781119974031.ch5

Elloumi, O., & Scholler, F. (2012). M2M Requirements and High-Level Architectural Principles. In D. Boswarthich, O. Elloumi, & O. Hersent (Eds.), *M2M Communications A System Approach*. Wiley. doi:10.1002/9781119974031.ch4

Ennesser, F. (2012). Smart Cards in M2M Communications. In D. Boswarthich, O. Elloumi, & O. Hersent (Eds.), *M2M Communications A System Approach*. Wiley. doi:10.1002/9781119974031. ch10

Harish, A. (2010). Radio frequency Identification Technology Overview. In H. Chaouchi (Ed.), *The Internet of things. Connecting Objects to the Web*. Wiley.

Hersent, O., Boswarthick, D., Elloumi, O. (2102). *The Internet of Things. Key Applications and Protocols*. Wiley.

Mainwaring, K., & Srivastava, L. (2010). The Internet of Things – Setting the Standards. In H. Chaouchi (Ed.), *The Internet of things. Connecting Objects to the Web*. Wiley.

Norp, T., & Landais, B. (2012). M2M Optimizations in Public Mobile Networks. In D. Boswarthich, O. Elloumi, & O. Hersent (Eds.), *M2M Communications A System Approach*. Wiley. doi:10.1002/9781119974031.ch6

Papapostolou, A., & Chaouchi, H. (2010). RFID Deployment for Location and Mobility Management on the Internet. In H. Chaouchi (Ed.), *The Internet of things. Connecting Objects to the Web*. Wiley.

Pascual-Espada, J. (2012). Service Orchestration on the Internet of Things, *International Journal of Interactive Multimedia and Artificial Intelligence*.

Serbanati, A., Medaglia, C., & Ceipidor, U. (2011). Building Blocks of the Internet of Things: State of the Art and Beyond. In Turcu, C. Deploying RFID - Challenges, Solutions, and Open Issues, CCBY-NC-SA

Shelby Z., et. al. (2012). Constrained Application Protocol (CoAP), Internet Draft, 2012.

Shelby. Z. (2012). Constrained RESTful Environments (CoRE) Link Format, RFC 6690.

Toutain, L., & Minaburo, A. (2012). The role of IP in M2M. In D. Boswarthich, O. Elloumi, & O. Hersent (Eds.), *M2M Communications A System Approach*. Wiley. doi:10.1002/9781119974031. ch7

Vasseur, J., & Dunkels, A. (2010). *Interconnecting Smart Objects with IP. The Next Internet*. Morgan Kaufmann.

Viswanathan, H. (2012). The Business of M2M. In D. Boswarthich, O. Elloumi, & O. Hersent (Eds.), *M2M Communications A System Approach*. Wiley. doi:10.1002/9781119974031.ch2

Vos, G. (2012). M2M Terminals and Modules. In D. Boswarthich, O. Elloumi, & O. Hersent (Eds.), *M2M Communications A System Approach*. Wiley. doi:10.1002/9781119974031.ch9

Watteyne, T., & Pister, K. (2010). Wireless Sensor Networks: Technology Overview. In H. Chaouchi (Ed.), *The Internet of things. Connecting Objects to the Web*. Wiley.

Weber, R. (2010). Governance of the Internet of Things. In H. Chaouchi (Ed.), *The Internet of things. Connecting Objects to the Web*. Wiley.

KEY TERMS AND DEFINITIONS

Application Programming Interface (API): An application programming interface (API) specifies how the software components interact. An API may be regarded as a software library that describes the expected behavior in an implementation-independent way.

Authentication: Authentication is the process of identifying an individual, aiming to assure that one is who or what pretended to be.

Authorization: Authorization is the process of granting or denying access to resources and it is used to verify if the individual requesting or initiating an action has the right to do so.

Central Unit (CU): Central unit (CU) provides the overall control of the measurement process and it is responsible for gathering information from mobile agents.

Database Management System: Database Management System (DBMS) is a software system designed to allow the definition, creation, querying, update, and administration of databases.

Embedded Web Services: Embedded Web services are integrated in distributed embedded systems composed of many different nodes which communicate with each other.

Internet of Things (IoT): Internet of things is referred as a network of smart objects interconnected using Internet Protocol. Each of the smart objects has a unique identifier and may communicate with the other ones.

Machine-to-Machine Communications: Machine to machine communications is a generalization of remote monitoring that applies autonomic communications between devices.

Mobile Agent (MA): Mobile agent is a smart object that performs measurements and report on acquired data. It is equipped with sensor, actuator, microprocessor, communication module and power supply.

Mobile Monitoring: Mobile monitoring is related to remote measurements made by mobile units and send to a central unit. For example, tt is used to transmit information about current temperature, humidity, concentration of green gasses etc.

Markov Modulated Poisson Process (MMPP): Is a mathematical model for the time between job arrivals to a system. The simplest such process is a Poisson process where the time between each arrival is exponentially distributed.

Operation Mode: Operation mode is the configured mode of operation of mobile agents.

Mobile agent may perform measurements periodically, on occurrence of specific criteria, and on demand.

Service Level Agreement (SLA): A Service-Level Agreement (SLA) is a part of a service contract where a service is formally defined. In practice, the term *SLA* is sometimes used to refer to the contracted delivery time (of the service or performance).

Service Security: Service security describes mechanisms that guarantee that only trusted instances of an application can communicate with each other or access resources, while illegitimates instances cannot.

Third Party: A party that offers applications and that is different from a network operator or service provider.

Chapter 9
Developing a New Revenue Business Model in Social Network:
A Case Study of Facebook

Te Fu Chen
Lunghwa University of Science and Technology, Taiwan

ABSTRACT

This chapter focuses on a new business model in social networking, uses platform strategy to discuss possible business models, evaluates the optimal model for partnering with social networking service providers. This research develops a new revenue business model in social networking with a case study and discusses its potential monetization business model. The chapter reviews five business models including: 1) social media startups; 2) challenges social networks face: must monetize or die; 3) a case study of the new effective social business model – Facebook; 4) monetization: Facebook revenue and business model; and 5) a discussion of monetizing social networks: the four dominant business models and how you should implement them in the future. Through a comprehensive review, the chapter proposes a social media monetization model as the reference for firms to implement new business models of social networking.

DOI: 10.4018/978-1-4666-5884-4.ch009

INTRODUCTION

Backgrounds and Motivations

Social networking sites like Facebook have emerged recently as one of the hottest names on the Internet, with daily news reports of new partnerships, advertising initiatives and acquisition activity. Indeed, several of the top six social networking sites – Twitter, MySpace, Facebook, Hi5, Orkut and Friendster - rank among the top 10 most-visited websites globally. Unsurprisingly, the growth in interest in social networking has led to a number of important deals by major online brands and media firms. These include News Corp's July 2005 acquisition of MySpace for US$580m and more recently Microsoft's purchase of a 1.6% stake in Facebook for $240m, a purchase price that values the entire company, which has annual revenue of some $100-150m, at an impressive $15bn.

A social networking service (SNS) is a platform to build social networks or social relations among people who, for example, share interests, activities, backgrounds, or real-life connections. A social network service consists of a representation of each user (often a profile), his/her social links, and a variety of additional services. Most social network services are Web-based and provide means for users to interact over the Internet, such as e-mail and instant messaging. Online community services are sometimes considered as a social network service, though in a broader sense, social network service usually means an individual-centered service whereas online community services are group-centered. Social networking sites allow users to share ideas, pictures, posts, activities, events, and interests with people in their network. The main types of social networking services are those that contain category places (such as former school year or classmates), means to connect with friends (usually with self-description pages), and a recommendation system linked to trust. Popular methods now combine many of these, with American-based services such as Facebook, Google+, Tumblr and Twitter widely used worldwide. SNS has been a popular field of research for years. Through interacting with others, many people find social network interesting and log in regularly. The explosive growth of social network sites accounts for not only the popularity of Web 2.0, but also the gradual change of online social behaviors through these SNS. The research looks at the social networking business model and analyzes its future, including forecasting the number of social networking members expected globally.

Problems

In this research five problems can be raised:

1. How do social networking services fit into the larger online media landscape today?
2. How are social networking services spreading across the globe?
3. Will advertising, subscription fees or premium, "extra" services dominate the social networking business model?
4. How large is the revenue opportunity?
5. Where and what's the potential of new business model in a social network? Any potential business model derived?

Objectives

The objective of this research is to:

1. Find out the potential of new business model in social network, and its potential business model. To derive potential business model, the research uses platform strategy[1] to discuss possible business model.
2. Quantify the opportunity in social networking services, and assess your strengths in building an effective strategy to create or expand your social networking-based revenue streams.

3. Evaluate the optimal model for partnering with social networking service providers.
4. Develop a revenue model for social networking services that fits into you larger Web data revenue strategy, examining advertising, subscription fees and premium services.
5. Devise tactics to counter social networking moves by competitors.

BACKGROUND

Business Model

The "Harvard Business Review on Business Model Innovation" charts four basic tenets of a business model: how the company creates and delivers value to its customers, the ways in which the company will earn a profit, which key components will be utilized and which key processes the company will incorporate. Key components include staff and human resources, machinery and technology as well as branding efforts. Business operations such as manufacturing and training make up the business's key processes. Each business model differs depending on the organization's size, industry and expectations. A business model describes the rationale of how an organization creates, delivers, and captures value (Osterwalder et al., 2010) (economic, social, cultural, or other forms of value). The process of business model construction is part of business strategy. In theory and practice, the term business model is used for a broad range of informal and formal descriptions to represent core aspects of a business, including purpose, target customers, offerings, strategies, infrastructure, organizational structures, trading practices, and operational processes and policies. The literature has provided very diverse interpretations and definitions of a business model. A systematic review and analysis of manager responses to a survey defines business models as the design of organizational structures to enact a commercial opportunity (George and Bock, 2011). Further

extensions to this design logic emphasize the use of narrative or coherence in business model descriptions as mechanisms by which entrepreneurs create extraordinarily successful growth firms (George and Bock, 2012).

BUSINESS MODELS AND INNOVATION

Osterwalder (2005) indicated before, it used to be sufficient to say in what industry you where in, for somebody to understand what your company was doing. All players had more or less the same business model. Today it is not sufficient to choose a lucrative industry, but you must also design a competitive business model. In addition, increased competition and rapid copying of successful business models forces all players to continuously innovate and adapt their business model to gain and/or sustain a competitive edge. The business model topic is very popular among business people today because in various industries we can see a proliferation of new and innovative business models (i.e. new ways of making money). In several industries new business models are threatening or even replacing established companies and conventional ways of doing business. The business model concept helps executives as well as entrepreneurs increase their capacity to manage continuous change and constantly adapt to rapidly changing business environments by injecting new ideas into their business model. Therefore, the interest in business models comes from two opposing sides: Established companies have to find new and innovative business models to compete against growing competition and to fend off insurgents. Entrepreneurs want to find new and innovative business models to carve out their space in the marketplace (Osterwalder, 2005).

Moreover, based on an extensive literature research and real-world experience Osterwalder (2005) defined a business model as consisting of 9 building blocks that constitute the business model canvas (Figure 1). It has the characteristics of any other type of model (e.g. in architecture or engineering). Like other models it is a simplified description and representation of a complex real world object. It describes the original in a way that we understand its essence without having to deal with all its characteristics and complexities. In the same line of thought we can define a business model as a simplified description of how a company does business and makes (or intends to make) money without having to go into the complex details of all its strategy, processes, units, rules, hierarchies, workflows, and systems.

1. The value proposition of what is offered to the market;
2. The segment(s) of clients that are addressed by the value proposition;
3. The communication and distribution channels to reach clients and offer them the value proposition;
4. The relationships established with clients;
5. The key resources needed to make the business model possible;
6. The key activities necessary to implement the business model;
7. The key partners and their motivations to participate in the business model;

8. The revenue streams generated by the business model (constituting the revenue model);
9. The cost structure resulting from the business model.

Companies that thoroughly understand their business model and know how the building blocks relate to each other will be able to constantly rethink and redesign these blocks and their relationship to innovate before their business model is copied. The term business model is also closely related to innovation. The business model concept is related to a whole new range of business design opportunities. There are examples of business model innovations in each of the 9 building blocks described. The most obvious is innovating in the value proposition (Osterwalder, 2005).

Social Network

Wasserman, Faust (1994) indicated a social network is a social structure made up of a set of social actors (such as individuals or organizations) and a set of the dyadic ties between these actors. The social network perspective provides a set of methods for analyzing the structure of whole social entities as well as a variety of theories explaining the patterns observed in these structures. Boyd, Ellison (2007) defined social network: social

Figure 1. Business model canvas
Source: Osterwalder (2005)

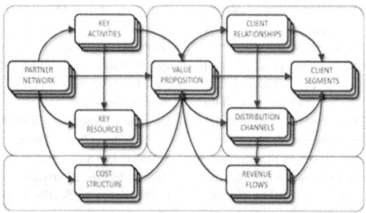

network service sites as: "Web-based services that allow individuals to (1) construct a public or semi-public profile within a bounded system, (2) articulate a list of other users with whom they share a connection, and (3) view and traverse their list of connections and those made by others within the system". Common examples include Facebook, MySpace, Twitter, Orkut, etc.

Social network service could be divided into four categories: social, information, multimedia and gaming (Mikolaj Jan Piskorski, Masaru Nomura, Kanako Miyoshi, mixi, 2008). It is however, not commonly seen in the social network currently. As with the growth of social networks and gradual acceptance of "social media" (Charlene Li and Josh Bernoff, 2008), it is possible that collaboration in the social network won't be uncommon in the future. Note here that the context between collaboration in social network and business network is different. In fact, the scenarios, interaction and purpose of use as well as its potential applications in a social network vs. a business network are fundamentally different, too. Social network platforms are avenues for distribution, and application developers should be taking advantage of all of them.

FIVE BUSINESS MODELS FOR SOCIAL MEDIA STARTUPS

Loayza (2009) indicated during the first Internet boom, the most common business model was probably, "get a ton of traffic, then figure out how to make money" — which savvy readers will note isn't a very good business model. Often, the way those businesses attempted to make money on that traffic was to use display or text advertising. Making money from advertising is still possible, but it's no longer as easy as building a site and putting some ads on it. Fortunately, there are a number of business models to choose from. Today's social media startups are finding unique ways of generating revenue from the very beginning. Loayza (2009) indicated there are a few of

the revenue models that they're using and how you can apply them to your company (Table 1).

Social Networks Face Challenging

Robert Andrews, Paidcontent (2009) indicated social networks face a tough time in 2009, when the twin realities of disappointing ad sales and the worsening economy will dawn on the sector. Deloitte analyst Paul Lee's insightful forecast says the networks have quickly gathered, but failed to profit from, of millions of users: "Average revenue per user for some of the largest new media sites are measured in just pennies per month, not pounds. This compares with a typical average revenue per user of tens of dollars for a cable subscriber, a regular newspaper reader or a movie fan. Social networks may need at least 100 users to generate the equivalent revenues of every traditional media customer they compete with."

Lee says a liberal ethos that the monetisation angle will eventually get figured out farther down the line has been "accepted, even encouraged, through 2008" - but "a fundamentally harsher financial outlook in 2009 and beyond, combined with an expected contraction in online advertising" will force the networks to focus more on making money from existing subscribers than continuing to add new users.

Other downbeat warnings:

1. Social networks whose future looks uncertain may suffer a debilitating outflow of senior management."
2. The book value of some social networks may be written down; some companies may fail altogether if funding dries up."
3. The risk of audiences falling as hard-pressed users focus on things like paying utility bills instead of broadband entertainment.

As one network, Wasabi, adds a white-label offering, Lee said courting business customers in such a way may be "too little, too late". So the social sites absolutely have to "articulate and

Table 1. Five business models for social media startups

Models	Descriptions and Examples
1. Freemium Model	This business model works by offering a basic service for free, while charging for a premium service with advanced features to paying members. Examples of the Freemium Model: UserVoice, Flickr, Vimeo, LinkedIn, and PollDaddy. The biggest challenge for businesses using the freemium model is figuring how much to give away for free so that users will still need and want to upgrade to a paying plan. If most users can get by with the basic free plan, they won't have a need to upgrade. For example, I'll probably never upgrade my LinkedIn account and because I don't shoot high definition videos, I'll never need a Premium Vimeo account either.
2. Affiliate Model	This is a model in which a business makes money by driving traffic, leads, or sales to another, affiliated company's website. Businesses that sell a product, meanwhile, rely on affiliated sites to send them the traffic or leads they need to make sales. Examples of the Affiliate Model: Illuminated Mind, ShoeMoney, DIY Themes. Like businesses that rely on advertising, high traffic sites predictably have a much easier time making money using affiliate links than sites that are just starting out. High traffic means that even low conversion numbers can equal big bucks. However, in just a year since starting his blog, Jonathan Mead from the Illuminated Mind generates enough income from affiliate links that he has been able to leave his full-time job.
3. Subscription Model	Sites using the subscription model require users to pay a fee (generally monthly or yearly) to access a product or service. Examples of the Subscription Model: Label 2.0, Scrooge Strategy, Netflix. What are the biggest obstacles in the subscription-based model? 1. Price – Musicians are used to free. MySpace is free, YouTube() is free, there is free information everywhere and musicians would rather spend $500 on a new guitar pedal than invest $50 into something that can find them hundreds of fans with which they can begin to make a living on. 2. Stereotypes – Musicians do not think of themselves as marketers. They feel like that is what a manager, record label or promoter is supposed to do. We are helping them turn that stereotype upside down by teaching them how to market themselves to create better relationships with their fans which is going to help their business in the long haul. 3. Monthly membership sites have a high attrition rate – The reason is after their 1st or second time they login, they forget about it and never come back. We are doing everything that we can to ensure that there is always something going on, from new lessons to trainings to calls and webinars to activity in the forums to leveraging the community to make everyone stronger.
4. Virtual Goods Model	Users pay for virtual goods, such as weapons, upgrades, points, or gifts, on a website or in a game. Examples of the Virtual Goods Model: Acclaim Games, Meez, Weeworld, Facebook Gifts. Virtual Goods come in all shapes and sizes. Hot or Not was one of the pioneers of virtual good in the online dating industry by allowing users to send virtual roses to other users that cost from $2 to $10. The beauty of virtual goods is that margins are high, since goods essentially only cost as much as the bandwidth required to serve them, which is generally almost zero.
5. Advertising Model	Description: Sites that rely on advertising, sell advertisements against their traffic. In basic terms: the more traffic you have, the more you can charge for ads (additional demographics about your site's visitors, such as age, gender, location, or interests, also affects the amount you can charge advertisers to place ads on your site). Examples of the Advertising Model: Yahoo!, MySpace, Tweet Later

Source: Loayza (2009)

deliver on a clear, credible route to revenues" - profiting from aggregate social-site behaviour if advertising to individuals proves hard.

MAIN FOCUS OF THE CHAPTER

A New Business Model for Facebook

Facebook is an online social networking service. Its name comes from a colloquialism for the directory given to American university students (Eldon, Eric, 2008). Facebook was founded in February 2004 by Mark Zuckerberg with his col-lege roommates and fellow Harvard University students Eduardo Saverin, Andrew McCollum, Dustin Moskovitz and Chris Hughes (Carlson, Nicholas, 2010). The founders had initially limited the website's membership to students of the University of Harvard, but later expanded it to colleges in the Boston area, the Ivy League, and Stanford University. It gradually added support for students at various other universities before it opened to high-school students, and eventually to anyone aged 13 and over. Facebook now allows anyone who claims to be at least 13 years old to become a registered user of the website (Facebook, 2011).

New Business Models: Failing for Free

Future Summit Blog (May 2008) indicated a powerful business model that has emerged on the Web is opening up your product or service to allow others to do the innovating for you. Examples abound, Facebook and the iPhone, have had over 50,000 applications each developed for them by people outside their organisations. Amazon, Google, eBay and YouTube have for years provided access to developers to take their data or content and use it how they see fit. "Developers" or sometimes "API" (Application Programming Interface). An example of an innovation from an API which provides a visual search interface over Amazon, eBay and YouTube and deployed the same interface in Facebook called "Friendly Search".

In effect this business model leverages lessons learn't from the Open Source Movement and the concept of "Crowdsourcing". Developing new products or services that they need to adopt the concept of "porosity," or make your product porous so others can take things and add to them. Clay Shirky, the US Internet luminary, talks about "Failing for Free". Effectively many of the applications developed will not set the world on fire but some take off and are picked up by millions of users. This has also seen with iPhone apps and Games. If you can get 50,000 adaptations to your product for free you will out innovate your competitors. This model move into the physical product world with organisations like Lego building the "Mindstorms Developer Community". Effectively you get you product designs and market research for free and only produce products that will sell.

Facebook and Business Model 2.0

Business Model 2.0

Stephens (2007) indicated, if you back up and look at your business model, then you will see that your current information systems don't handle every aspect of your model. Maybe you do have a project management system or a system to procure network addresses but you don't have systems in place that manage your customer relationships, your cost tracking, or simple communications within the group. Here is where Collaborative and Social Solutions can fill in the gap. With 25,000 sites within the enterprise, there is no limit to what is currently being automated. There is a learning curve on how these tools can be setup, configured and even programmed to some level. Over the next few years, we will continually be asked to deliver more value, faster delivery, and utilize fewer resources. The only way to accomplish this is to automate as many of the small tasks as possible and you have the Business 2.0 tools within your own company. Allaire (2009) indicated, Internet Business Models 2.0 on the Horizon. Many of new online businesses models, in fact, are driving new ideas in overall business models, and opening up entire new economies. Broadly coined' Affiliate and Syndication Networks', these models enable any Web site (theoretically) to leverage the assets of other Web sites to create new value. A great example of this was pioneered by Amazon.com, who introduced an "affiliate" program years ago. But the idea expands radically once one realizes that this model could be at the core of a broader revolution in how we view the Web. Based on Metcalfe's Law, which states that the value of a network (the Internet) increases exponentially for every n-node added to the network, this is the basis for a shift in how we develop online businesses. In this new worldview, every Web site out there is a potential asset for your own Web site. Instead of viewing the Web as islands of content linked together merely by surface-level hyperlinks, it views the Web as an interconnected network of value, with sub-surface-level links between the content, commerce and customer assets of every Web site. In short, it is an entirely new economy built out of the Web. Taking your Web business to the next level requires Web syndication and affiliate networks. Getting there requires introspection on what aspects of your business support this model.

Tapsns.com (2009) indicated Tim O'Reilly probably meant no more than to market his omnipresent conferences when he coined the term "Web 2.0," but the results have included giving some kind of ill-conceived business model faith to tens of thousands of hapless would-be entrepreneurs, and a smaller number of even more at-risk investors. As though the Ferris Wheel (or, more aptly, the Great Mandala), had not already spun this way before, the idea of creating jillions of companies with no business model, no profits, and only some kind of ginned-up success metric (like eyeballs, remember?) was already proven to be a terminally bad one. To put it bluntly, when business models and profits are ignored, everybody gets hurt. There were only seven customers in the Web 2.0 world, and today, if anything, that number may be shrinking. In lieu of being bought by one of these acquirers, what do these metric-heavy, cash-light companies do? This week, a "new" analysis of Facebook has everyone talking: burning cash at gargantuan rates (perhaps $50-80MM per year), with the original investor money nearly gone, and the hoped-for Mystery Model not yet arrived, it may suddenly be Ox Sxxx time for the poster child of the 2.0 group. One could be empathetic and note that online ad dollar growth has slowed into reverse thanks to the current economic woes, but guess what? That's called business. It isn't clear that matters would be enough different without this blip to matter.

How many companies are out there, just as there were in 1999 and early 2000, with a single lonely revenue line in the business model called Online Ads, for which the spreadsheet numbers will never get into the same room as the accounting figures? Is there any light at the end of this tunnel? One answer is subscriptions, but these are generally reserved for content that no one else has, that has value for the purchaser (like the SNS newsletter, one hopes). But if Facebook, with its many challengers in socnet country, is that

irreplaceable, or has customers in a demographic willing to pay – for anything. What happens to Facebook, and those thousands of other companies, if there are no ads, and no subscribers? Their bills will continue to pile up for storage, electricity, bandwidth, support. Not so long ago giving advice to technology startups, and helping them create alliances. One of non-obvious suggestions to new CEOs was this: Never launch a business in which success creates the greatest risk of failure. Enter Facebook. The more popular it is, the more expenses it has (Tapsns.com, 2009).

Facebook and the "Duke Nukem Forever" of Business Models

John Paczkowski (2008) indicated Microsoft (MSFT) must be so proud. The company's $240 million investment in Facebook, one that implicitly valued the social network at $15 billion, hasn't yet paid off. But it will. In three years or so when Facebook finally settles on a business model. Assuming, of course, that it's a viable one. And that it doesn't send privacy advocates into paroxysms of angry status updates.

In an interview with Frankfurter Allgemeine Zeitung this week, Facebook CEO Mark Zuckerberg trotted out the old "growth over profits" cliché as explanation for the company's long-absent business model. "… what every great Internet company has done is to figure out a way to make money that has to match to what they are doing on the site," Zuckerberg said. "I don't think social networks can be monetized in the same way that search did. But on both sites people find information valuable. I'm pretty sure that we will find an analogous business model. But we are experimenting already. One group is very focused on targeting; another part is focused on social recommendation from your friends. In three years from now we have to figure out what the optimum model is. But that is not our primary focus today, growth is primary, revenue is secondary." (John Paczkowski, 2008)

Facebook Squeezes Digg into a New Business Model

Nick O'Neill (2010) indicated while Digg is in the process of rolling out a new version of their site, Facebook's decision to release a "like button for the Internet" could significantly impact Digg. Combine that with their previously released share analytics and share button, and you can see how Digg is getting squeezed into a new business model.

Digg Abandons their Community

Digg is preparing to roll out a new version of their site and this time around they could end up abandoning their extremely active community. While people doubt that Digg would completely remove the importance of their user base, it's hard for Digg to argue that they are an effective aggregator when their demographics skew heavily toward 18 to 25 year old males. That's why the company is preparing to unleash a new version of the site with a back-end that's powered by Facebook's open source database solution: Cassandra. The company's new architecture is driven by the need to track data coming in from sources around the Web. For example, rather than simply using the community as the basis of what's popular, the company will now take into consideration the number of shares on Facebook as well as tweets on Twitter (Nick O'Neill, 2010).

Facebook can't take all the credit for Digg's new found strategy. Twitter was the first company to completely open the stream, giving rise to a mini-industry of aggregators. Right now however, Twitter is still a fraction of the size of Facebook and when Facebook first opened up share analytics, it became clear that the company was dead set on having its own industry of aggregators built around the service. While Digg has been regularly criticized for reflecting a small segment of the population, it has become increasingly difficult for the company to publicly state otherwise. With

Twitter initially giving rise to a global network of public content distributors (the people sharing) it's become clear that sharing is the new basis for relevance. After seeing Twitter's success and an entire ecosystem of aggregators and search services, Facebook realized the need to give developers access to more data. We sat back and watched Facebook's Twitterfication take place last year, culminating with the launch of new privacy settings. Now Facebook plans to continue expanding their opening of the platform and the aggregation of information through their global like button. While it wasn't Facebook's intention to lessen Digg's relevance, Twitter and Facebook have made it clear that Digg's community cannot control the future of timely information (Nick O'Neill, 2010).

Digg Adapts and Reinvents Itself

Dealing with the realities of the real-time Web Digg is adapting and in the near future will unleash a new version of the site which is truly powered by the real-time Web. While the community will have their say in the new algorithm, sites like Facebook and Twitter will become much more important. It's critical timing for Digg. Over the weekend I was reading the article, "5 Creepy Ways Video Games Are Trying To Get You Addicted" when I noticed the share count on Digg and Facebook (pictured below). The article had over 18,000 shares on Facebook and only 24 on Digg, preventing it from reaching the coveted homepage. While this isn't exactly a rare occurrence (AddThis.com has told us that Facebook continues to rise while Digg is down 3 percent), what made this so significant was that Cracked.com (the site where this article was published) is a Digg.com community favorite. It's so popular within Digg that the site has entire box within the sidebar dedicated to content that's currently trending on Digg. If Cracked.com recognizes that more of their traffic begins coming from Facebook and not from Digg, it's only natural that they'll reduce their emphasis on "Diggable content". Fortunately for Digg, all is not lost as they are adapting rapidly. However as domestic traffic continues to drop according to Compete.com, the importance of the Digg redesign could not be any clearer. Only time will tell what happens to Digg but shifting business models has been necessitated by a more open Facebook (Nick O'Neill, 2010).

Facebook Shows Off Polls in Davos: New Business Model or Just Cool Toy?

Robert Andrews, paidContent.org (2009) indicated, as expected, Telegraph.co.uk got it wrong. A Facebook spokesperson told us: "The polls run at the World Economic Forum were not part of a commercially available product for advertisers and should not be confused with Facebook's Engagement Ads ... Nothing has changed in our approach."

Original: Facebook's demonstration of some polling technology to luminaries at the World Economic Forum this weekend is causing some to wonder whether the social network isn't trying out yet another monetization model. The company's founder's sister Randi Zuckerberg introduced the online public polls to 12 forums in Davos, generating real-time feedback for panel speakers. Now Telegraph.co.uk, which interviewed Zuckerberg, says Facebook is to offer the tool to companies who could conduct market research on potential new products by polling Facebook users. Randi Zuckerberg, Facebook's global markets director, said: "I had tons of people saying 'this could be so incredible for our business'. It takes a very long time to do a focus group, and businesses often don't have the luxury of time. I think they liked the instant responses. Davos is really a key place to launch an instant tool like this. It's beneficial for everyone to see us as a global community of 150 million users. The vast majority are not just college students in the U.S. talking about things in their bedrooms. We are showing how we are

a serious and insightful community." (Robert Andrews, paidContent.org, 2009)

And now Telegraph.co.uk is calling it "an attempt to finally monetize the social-networking site by creating one of the world's largest market-research databases". There was no announcement at Davos about a new market-research platform strategy for Facebook, so it's unclear whether this is Telegraph.co.uk jumping the gun or a potential new business model drawn up as instantaneously as the poll results Zuckerberg's new toy received in Switzerland. It's true, though, that Facebook, with this year forecast to be crunch time for social networks, should be looking for as many ways to make money as possible, after erring with its controversial Beacon last year and now trying to build enthusiasm for its Engagement Ads. Though Facebook revoked users' ability to create polls late last year, it's retained the underlying functionality for itself (Robert Andrews, paidContent.org, 2009).

The New Effective Social Business Model – Facebook Wins

Organizations that have adopted the social business model utilize social media tools and social networking behavioral standards across functional areas for communicating and engaging with external audiences, including customers, prospective customers, prospective employees, suppliers, and partners. Combining social networking etiquette (Brogan, 2011) (being helpful, transparent and authentic) with business engagement on LinkedIn (for one-to-one interaction), Twitter (for immediacy) and Facebook (for content sharing) more fully involves employees in the organization and increases customer intimacy and trust (Burgess, 2012). Social.advantages (2009) indicated, "It's too early to say". "The jury is still out" and "It's difficult to tell" because things are not so easy. But in the running popularity wars of Facebook and Twitter, while Twitter catches up on its share of traffic, it has to be said that Facebook is reflecting maturity. Notwithstanding a lot of bull from personal users who have been long time Facebook fans, Facebook managed to roll out changes which reduced the functionality gap between itself and twitter and while both have now made their pages more manageable by tweaking 'lists' and other such, Facebook's early advertising revenues have also given it some 'moral strength' and some 'freshness of ideas'.

Facebook has kicked off the non advertising led era of brand reputation management, product launches and the knowledge era for brands and products everywhere with a very simple proposition. It is going to cost you a packet and you are doing it because you are getting what you want. In effect, you choose your specific segments of Facebook users from healthcare users to premium hotel services user or even mother care and feminine hygiene product users and instead of just paying for banal advertising, you pay for engaging the consumers. First off, you would pay $10K and $30K for holding contests and while basic pages remain free, Facebook will control both look and performance. More details here Also, all these launches coming without fanfare is a step in the right direction as information economy holds and knowledge is at a premium. Also, as more than 40 million users spend 30 minutes and more on the site, they will soon start allocating more time to stay in touch. All in all, another far thinking proposition which seems to have outlasted its detractors in the last 2-3 years. Are things looking up for Twitter? P&G, Pepsi and even those with primarily domestic markets in the USA like Kraft and the sports brands will definitely find this a paying proposition and not to denigrate advertising but at a much more premium and effective brand value than two-bit clicks and CTRs. This is not a part of the FACEBOOK VS. TWITTER series 19/800 esp. not the part where "Facebook wins," just one of those things we started, socially (Social.advantages, 2009)!

MONETIZING SOCIAL NETWORKS

The Four Dominant Business Models and How You Should Implement Them in Future

VentureDig (2010) indicated the business models within the social media realm are much different than traditional businesses. In social networking, they're ever-changing, backed by eye-opening revenue and have very little documentation.

Reason: as soon as someone sits down to outline ways social networks can be monetized, another model emerges, and another model ceases. For this reason, this piece will be routinely updated with new models and new feedback from your comments. Below are the Four Primary Business Models in the social networking space that VentureDig (2010) has experienced–they primarily are concerned with Facebook Applications. There may be others, or extensions of these, or even ideas out there that have yet to be tested yet are profoundly viable.

1. Display Ads

This is your bread and butter business model. It centers on showing Display/Context Ads. The two major forms of this are CPC (cost per click) and CPA (cost per action or acquisition). Example: with the ad above, the user clicks the ad, they take a quiz, and usually they fill out their email address or phone number. The advertiser (IQ Quiz) will pay the Facebook developer (you) each time a user fills out their email address or phone number. Usually, there's a middle man involved. The middle man is called an ad network. These types of ads can pay out a CPM of $0.05 – $0.80 (*Depending on Country*) Say you serve 1 million impressions of these per day, at a $0.20 CPM, you can expect to make $200 per day, or $6,000 a month (VentureDig, 2010).

2. Branding Certain Elements within an Application

This business model is rather new, and personally, my favorite. This model centers on branding a certain element within your application. For instance, LivingSocial is an application where users can make a list of their favorite things. Big brands, like Porsche, may want to get in front of their audience and have users speak about their brand in a viral, social networking space. Therefore, Porsche will pay LivingSocial for each exposure to their audience. By exposure, VentureDig (2010) means hitting the newsfeed of the user on Facebook: I like to think of this model as a Cost Per Share (CPS).

Using the above example, let's say you have 1 million impressions of a certain application. For each person that shares Porsche with their friends via Newsfeed, Porsche will pay $5 because these users are loyal and will argue why the Porsche is the best car via comments. Of those 1 million daily impressions or exposures to the app, 0.01% (or 100) users are into Porsches and post their Porsche list to their news feed. With 100 users sharing on their newsfeed per day, at a price of $5 CPS, your app will be making $500 per day, or $15,000 a month. This is much better than the Banner Ad payouts of $6,000/month; additionally, the user experience isn't as bland. By this, VentureDig (2010) means, the user doesn't feel like he or she is getting hammered with ads.

The only cons with using the CPS model is, (i) As of this past week, Facebook is hiding and disabling application news to be blasted on the home feed; thus, this business model could be dead in a couple weeks; (ii) second, the CPS model requires someone who's creative and persistent on your team. Because social media is so new, and this model is so new, it's much easier to setup a business model based on banner ads (all you do is sign up with an ad network and place the creative ad code on your site). With CPS models, you must identify specific elements within your application that are valuable, and you must then find big brands (like Coca Cola) to buy it. When you're a small startup, this is nearly impossible. Thus, in place of this void, companies like Appsavvy, come into the picture (VentureDig, 2010).

3. Virtual Currency

This business model is astonishing. The concept of virtual currency is profoundly simple, however, the numbers and revenue this churns out is eye-opening. In order to advance in virtual games, you need to invest either (i) Your own Time, or (ii) Your own Money. Being that most people don't have the time to invest into building a virtual farm, they spend real money in order to save them time. Who's profiting from this? The game developers. And they're profiting big-time. With this powerful element, alternative monetization methods have emerged. For instance, instead of investing your own money in a game, you can take a survey instead–likely, you'll have to provide your email address. This practice has stirred up some controversy recently with some offers being ambiguous. So, now the model looks more like this: You invest either (i) Your own Time, (ii) Your own Money, or (iii) Alternative Method: Take a survey (in which a small fraction are misleading) Prediction: The virtual currency model will likely experience a minor shake-out of the ambiguous offers; this shake-out will benefit both the consumer and Facebook application ecosystem. I'm predicting that Facebook will outline certain practices that these alternative offers must follow. This is a long-term business model, and once Facebook outlines specific policies that outlaw some of the misleading offers that have crept through, the cash will start rolling in for these developers without eyebrows being raised (VentureDig, 2010).

4. Virtual Gifts

Virtual gifts may be even more astonishing than virtual currency. Giving a virtual gift is the same thing as giving someone a gift in real life; except one thing: they're not real. Surprisingly this hasn't deterred anyone, people are snatching up virtual gifts at an incredible rate. How incredible? Well, Virtual Gifts are expected to surpass $1 billion for U.S. users in 2009. That's right, $1 billion. Read more here. The most important element of virtual gifts centers on its use within Southeast Asian countries. In Southeast Asia, specifically countries like Indonesia, Facebook is in hyper-growth mode…right now. The only problem is that the traditional monetization model (I. Display Ads), simply do not scale or work in Southeast Asian countries. The only thing that works is virtual gifts–and they work–a lot. Unfortunately, though, Facebook Developers don't have access to this monetization model because Facebook has their own Virtual Gift Marketplace (VentureDig, 2010).

5. The Numbers

From TechCrunch, here's a summary of how much Facebook apps are raking in:

1. **Zynga:** Farmville-61M Mafia Wars-25.8M Yoville-19.8M Texas Hold Em' Poker-18.3M Total Estimated Revenue For Year: $200 million.
2. **Playfish:** Pet Society- 20.5M Restaurant City-17.3M Country Story- 8M 135 million total installs for all games Total Estimated Revenue For Year: $75 million.
3. **Playdom:** Mobsters-14M Bumper Stickers-11.7M Own Your Friends-10.1M; Sorority Life-7.1M Mobsters 2-3.5M Poker Palace-1.5M Total Estimated Revenue For Year: $60m.

Wrapping Up: What Business Model Should You Go With? With Banner Ads, specifically CPA-based ads, it's only a matter of time before the revenue stream becomes less dominant. You're going to have to get more creative. The user will cap out at a certain point because there's only so many times you can see a quiz ads, or game ads. Though you can control this with frequency

caps, after a while the revenues will plateau and quickly decline. Additionally, Southeast Asia is in hyper-growth mode. However, it's essentially un-monetizable at this stage (besides serving Admax ads, which face a limited ad supply); thus leading to the next point: the most viable way to monetize Southeast Asia and other international countries is through virtual gifts for now (VentureDig, 2010).

VentureDig (2010) indicated how you should implement these models going into 2010: display ads:

1. Allocate about 60% of your ad space to high-quality brand ad networks (you'll need traffic, and a lot of applying)
2. Allocate about 20% of your ad space to CPA-based Ad Networks
3. Allocate about 10% of your ad space to Job Listing Ad Networks
4. Allocate about 10% of your ad space to product/widget based ad networks (Amazon Affiliates, Widgetbucks)

Brand Certain Elements within Your Application for CPS (Cost Per Share): Get creative with your application and business model by identifying the major value for your users, and evaluating whether or not you can brand pieces of value without hurting the user experience, but enhancing it. Virtual Currency: Build virtual currency extensions into your application, but be sure to conduct due diligence on who you're partnering with. Keep an eye on this arena, as VentureDig (2010) has a feeling some players in this realm are going to be called out and chastised if the recent allegations about misleading users are indeed true. As a Facebook developer, Facebook made it clear that it's your job to understand what types of offers are being presented to your users. Have someone on your team routinely click the offers and investigate each ad creative (VentureDig, 2010).

Virtual Gifts: Virtual gifts are going to continue to be a cash cow well into 2010. It's critical that you somehow find a way to implement Virtual

Gifts into your application. Why? Because this will be the primary way to monetize International countries; you don't want to find yourself with millions of users that make nothing for your application because they'll end up costing you money in terms of support costs, as well as other expenses. For now Facebook has the monopoly on this monetization route; however, it seems as if they'll soon be granting developer's access to this revenue stream (VentureDig, 2010).

SOCIAL MEDIA MONETIZATION AND REVENUE

Laurel Papworth (2008) indicated about the various social media monetization strategies shows some case studies and examples, including social network size, the revenue streams, valuations and profits in Social Media Monetization Models (Figure 2).

Revenue Source: The X Axis (the horizontal one) is whether the money comes to you (you are the social network host or provider) from the members in the community or from external clients such as advertisers or sponsorship from companies. REVENUE FLOW: The Y Axis (vertical one) asks if the money flows in a traditional way i.e. host simply sets a fee to members or external companies. Or whether it's a Customer to Customer (C2C) or Business 2 Business (B2B) social network economy. Also known as a peer to peer economy. In these cases, the host gets a "clip of the sale" – a percentage for enabling the transactions to take place. Oh I should mention – B2C works as well. This is where the revenue generated traditionally, says from Advertising, and is shared back to the member who uploads the content (creates the page). Like AdSense sharing back to the community (Laurel Papworth, 2008).

Quadrants: Pretty well break up into member pays host. External companies pay host. host pays members, members pay members, and ones that are hard to show on a chart -heh – such as external companies APIs directly empowering members to sell to other members user generated products on demand (e.g. CafePress) (Laurel Papworth, 2008).

Therefore, the list is:

Figure 2. Social media monetization models: revenues for social networks
Source: Laurel Papworth (2008)

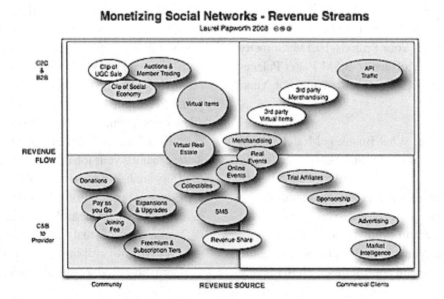

Donations: Wikipedia needs about 4 mills each year. In March they got a donation of 3 million. Open Source has always worked this way. And Shareware. The new widgets that can be added to anything from blog posts to Facebook profiles to wordpress plugins will increase how we show gratitude and value from donated products and services. Joining fee (one-off), Pay as you go (each time or per minute), subscription (weekly or monthly) are fairly obvious. High subscription charges or joining fees offer a high barrier to entry and therefore can reflect luxury or exclusivity. Expect to see more. Blizzard has spent $200 million since 2004 (altogether, not yearly) on World of Warcraft and make $1.1 billion per year on their communities. Expansions and upgrades work mostly with 'downloaded software' based communities such as World of Warcraft 'Burning Crusade' expansion and the gazillion that came from Everquest and Ultima online communities. A way of refreshing content and charging for it. In 2D networks it's more like to be a premium service (either one off fee or tiered subs) (Laurel Papworth, 2008).

Merchandising of real life products through say, CafePress gives either the host or the member, or both, an opportunity to gain revenue from user customizable products on demand. Think of eBay but for new, user created products such as cups and t-shirts. Zazzle is a similar service – here's the Zazzle Create a Product API. API based sales – eBay allowed members to trade on their own sites rather than forcing them to eBay to trade. Revenues increased by 86% for eBay. 40% of Salesforce revenue comes from external sites (API), not their own website. $490 million per quarter comes from Amazon API, not visiting their site. Not bad. (Thank goodness for Progammable Web) Along with Merchandising, empowering event management (Upcoming.org, Eventfull) and the taking of ticket purchase can lead to a clip of the ticket sale from the network back to the host. Online Events such as poker games that have an entry free or admission fee.

These are viral spiked network activities (Laurel Papworth, 2008).

Freemium: sign up for free, get more if you pay tiered subscriptions. LinkedIn makes around $75 million – 100 million (2008). 1/4 of that is advertising, 3/4 tiered subscriptions including corporate services with job search. SMS – offering other viral events (Idol SMS voting) or simply text messaging amongst members. Very profitable at the moment, in Australia, for a number of under the radar companies. Virtual Goods – 2 billion dollar industry in 2007. Gives Habbo a revenue of $17 per month from 10% of their members adding up to $200million per year. Collectible add a scarcity and (sometimes) a whole sub ecosystem to your virtual or real world products. Think Webkinz or some other fluffy pixel toys. Facebook gifts (only 250, 000 available!). Advertising – makes MySpace $2.17 per member per year. TechCrunch about $2.5 million revenue a year. Sucks when it is intrusive.

Social Network Ad Spending: A Brighter Outlook

2009 is turning into a year of major shifts in the social network business. Facebook, once a distant No. 2, has outperformed MySpace in nearly every measure of usage and is on track to surpass its rival in ad spending by 2011. The Social Network Ad Spending report asks—and answers—the critical question: Is the experimental phase of social network marketing drawing to an end? Paid online social network advertising is expected to fall 3% this year, as a result of the poor economy and difficulties at MySpace. However, eMarketer projects that US marketers will increase their spending 13.2% in 2010, to $1.3 billion (Table 2) (eMarketer, 2009).

Key questions the "Social Network Ad Spending report answers:

1. How much are marketers spending to advertise on social networks?

Table 2. US online social network advertising spending 2008-2011 (millions and % change)

2008	$1,175 (32.9%)
2009	$1,140 (-3.0%)
2010	$1,290 (13.2%)
2011	$1,395 (8.2%)

Source: eMarketer, July 2009

2.   What is driving Facebook's growth as an advertising venue?
3.   What percentage of companies market via social networks—and is their spending growing?
4.   What is the future of delivering targeted ads based on the social graph?
5.   And many others…

eMarketer Reports: On Target and Up to Date

The Social Network Ad Spending report aggregates the latest data from marketing and communications researchers with eMarketer analysis to provide the information you need to make timely, well-informed business decisions. Facebook, once a distant No. 2, has outperformed MySpace in nearly every measure of usage and is on track to surpass its rival in ad spending by 2011. And while paid advertising on online social networks is expected to fall 3% in 2009—a result of the poor economy and the difficulties at MySpace—

eMarketer projects that US marketers will increase their spending 13.2% in 2010, to $1.29 billion. The expected rebound in spending will come as more companies focus on creating and implementing an overall social marketing strategy. This foundation will be essential to the development of social network advertising because it will signal that the experimental phase may finally be ending. Spending is expected to grow 8.2% in 2011 to reach $1.4 billion. Although 2009 will see an estimated 3% spending decline, mostly due to the recession and difficulties at MySpace, the good news is that the rest of the business is still growing. eMarketer believes much of the increase in social network ad spending in the next two years will take place on Facebook (eMarketer, 2009).

US spending at MySpace is expected to fall 15% in 2009, to $495 million, while US spending at Facebook is projected to rise 9%, to $230 million. Consequently, MySpace's share of US spending is projected to fall to 43.4% in 2009, while Facebook and other social network venues will increase their share (Table 3).

While the US accounts for the majority of ad spending on MySpace and Facebook, non-US spending is growing rapidly at Facebook. eMarketer estimates that marketers will spend a total of $520 million to advertise on MySpace worldwide in 2009, down 14% from 2008. Worldwide spending on Facebook, by contrast, is expected to grow 20%, to $300 million, in 2009 (Table 4).

Table 3. US online social network advertising spending, by Venue, 2008 & 2009 (millions and % of total)

	2008	2008% of Total	2009	2009% of Total
My space	$585	49.8%	$495	43.4%
Facebook	$210	17.9%	$230	20.2%
Other destination social networks	$340	28.9%	$345	30.3%
Widgets and applications	$40	3.4%	$70	6.1%
Total	$1,175	100%	$1,140	100%

Source: eMarketer, May 2009

Table 4. US, non-US and worldwide online advertising spending on Myspace and Facebook, 2008 & 2009

	2008	2009
My space		
US	$585	$495
Non-US	$20	$25
Worldwide	$605	$520
Facebook		
US	$210	$230
Non-US	$40	$70
Worldwide	$250	$300

Source: eMarketer, May 2009

As a percentage of total US online ad spending, advertising on social networks is expected to remain relatively flat at 4.7% to 4.8% over the next few years. Marketers continue to innovate in social network advertising, and one development to watch in the second half of 2009 is the ability to target advertising based on the social graph—the network of online connections between consumers. This advertising will appear not only within social networks, but on other Websites as well. Near-term spending on this form of advertising is limited, due to consumer privacy concerns and the potential for legislation regarding targeted advertising. But the concept of using people's social connections to deliver targeted advertising across the Web is exciting territory to explore (eMarketer, 2009).

Trial Affiliates – if you watch an ad, they give you a product for free or discounted, and the advertised company pays them. Also look at $uper Rewards – social network advertising affiliates that place ads in your Facebook games and earn you revenue. Mobwars makes $22k per day for the kids err developers that made it. $uper Rewards said that one (Facebook) application made $1 million in a week. Virtual real estate – this will finally start to move as the Web3D takes off, Google Lively and the new layered social virtual worlds

(avatars on standard Web pages) are figuring it out but it's already a nice earner for Linden Labs who make $4 million per month from Second Life real estate sales ($8m each month altogether). Here's RocketOn showing how to customers use avatars to throw advertising around your webpages. Revenue share is where the host gives the member a slice of advertising revenue. A la Foneros. User generated content sales can mean the host takes a clip. So too, auction of real world content – anything member to member. Peer to peer economies – host takes a clip of loans, jobs and other (non media) based economic activity between members. Peer to peer banking will be 10.6 billion dollar industry by 2009. Some networks make money by selling psychographic and demographic information. Market Intelligence may also be customer community discussions around a brand or product/service (Laurel Papworth, 2008).

Social Networks Monetized Revenue

Laurel Papworth (2008) indicated "Know your own value": one company charges for video uploads, another (Tube Mogul, YouTube) does it for free, another pays you (Metacafe). Pick a revenue stream, stick to it. If they are giving it away, you charge a fee and raise the entry barrier. Make it a luxury brand. We pay for what we value. Caveat: of course that won't work for the majority of crappy Facebook wannabe networks. Follow the network's values. Currency is a medium of exchange, a store of value, and a standard of value. We monetize where we add one of these values. Even donations simply show a standard of value (we valued at $x amount).

Watch for new industries. Virtual Goods was a 2 billion dollar industry in 2007, peer to peer banking will be a $10.6 billion dollar industry by next year. Don't just focus on how much Linden Labs is making per minute on virtual goods in Second Life, look at the long tail (lots of small companies making small amounts). Watch the money – marketers are learning how to engage with networks for the soft returns (brand recall 5x higher in SNs, people return to your website 5x more often, stay 9x as long) but once companies figure out this can be a big revenue earner, everyone will be grabbing their slice of the pie. Allow for ecosystems. If you can open APIs, encourage external blogs and forums and wiki databases, and have members trading on eBay your pixel products, premium memberships or some other feature, you have got it made. And don't let me catch you saying there are no proven business models for social networks and social media. Exit strategies (flipping networks is a busy little industry) aren't really revenue but still, its social media money (Laurel Papworth, 2008).

Monetization: Facebook Revenue and Business Model

A revenue model is a subset component of a business model. The revenue model focuses on answering the question of how the business will generate revenue and, ultimately, how the company will be profitable. The revenue model depends on the industry. For example, a website might employ a contextual advertising model, which means the business generates money by users clicking on third-party ads within the page content. A baseball stadium, on the other hand, may have a revenue model that includes raising money from ancillary goods such as team apparel and dining outlets (Catherine, 2013). Laurel Papworth (2009) indicated social media monetization is a funny thing – most people don't understand that where there are people, there is money. It is highly improbable that the day will come when millions of people together will not mean money. Why? Because money = value systems. We use money – or some form of currency – to show what we value. Here's speculation by The Business Insider on Facebook's revenue streams: Earlier this week (July 2nd 2009) we spoke to several sources that each have some insight into Facebook's financials (none of them know precisely).

Taking the sources' input together, we'd estimate the company's expected 2009 revenue this way:

- $125 million from brand ads
- $150 million from Facebook's ad deal with Microsoft
- $75 million from virtual goods
- $200 million from self-service ads
- Total: $550 Million

The trick is figuring out what bits are valued and how much, and by whom, and in what way. That's the thing…In this case, the virtual goods (Facebook birthday cake for $1 anyone?) and the self-service ads (Facebooks answer to Google's Adsense, or Adwords or whatever it's called) are surprisingly high, no? Compared to the traditional deals…Nick Roshon asks why Facebook revenue is so low compared to MySpace. MySpace Google ad deal is included in their $2.17 per member per year – that's a nice chunk of change. MySpace also run event management - such as product launches and album launches for major labels, so they have additional revenue streams. Also MySpace is a more mature organisation… though cutting back their staff (450 international staff to 100) is going to severely limit growth (Laurel Papworth, 2009).

FUTURE RESEARCH DIRECTIONS

How Facebook is Changing Business Models, Shaping Brand Identity

Evelyn Rusli (2010) said although far from perfect in their social media efforts, Virgin America, Comcast and Cisco have all employed parts of Owyang's rules. They were also (relatively speaking) early movers on blogs, Twitter and Facebook. Each of course represents a very different sector, but there were several shared threads (Table 5):

The chapter suggests future research opportunities as the follows:

Table 5. How Facebook is changing business models, shaping brand identity

Course	Shared Threads
1. Expansion	These companies are increasing the number of employees dedicated to social media. Cisco's Brill currently manages a team of 7, she predicts that will rise to 20 to 30 by 2011. Comcast's Eliason says he's adding two more to his ten-person staff this year. The rising headcount naturally reflects the companies' growing online initiatives— Cisco already has 25 blogs and more than 100 Twitter accounts (sometimes there is such a thing as too much of a good thing).
2. Identity	Within corporations, social media is also breaking out of its silo. Companies may be building out specialized teams for social media, but many are also encouraging other employees to use social CRM tools and to become active external agents. For the last few years we've been focused on how companies should push out their content and interact with the market, the less apparent power of social media is how it will disrupt the mechanics of business. Eliason says that it has the potential to completely restructure companies, flatten organizations, and democratize the workplace: "We're going to see a real big shift with employees, whether it is employees talking externally or even talking internally...it's going to be a new way of having a little bit more power than they did before. And so companies are going to have to figure out a whole new game plan and change their culture... Companies are going to be a smaller place." Eliason's boss, Comcast CEO Brian Roberts has also acknowledged the power of Twitter, saying in late 2009 that it has "changed the culture of our company." The expansion of social media also has the power to reshape the very guts of a company: its brand identity. According to Brill, Cisco's social media initiative has softened the company's image, making it less formal and more human (a nice complement to the company's "human network" campaign). "We basically have to relearn how we do things, how we communicate, and it's no longer the polished marketing brochure, the polished website— conversations are happening," she says. Of course with that power comes risk-— the increase in dialogue and brand ambassadors reduces the control a company has over its message. Cisco's solution was to accept that risk and try to minimize it by education and offering a "social media certification program" to all employees.
3. Stay Focused On Your Business Objectives	This is related to Owyang's first (oddly phrased) rule, "don't fondle the hammer." The executives warned that companies shouldn't be caught up in specific platforms or rough metrics. Everything should be done in the context of your businesses' objectives and broader strategy. For example, when it comes to return on investment, Eliason says "The real approach to ROI in this space, is to get all these groups together, PR, marketing, HR IT, and talk through what's important to you. So we get huge return on investment when we listen to these things and then we act or fix things because we're listening. The dollars are huge. You could have a 30 minute event that pays for my team for well over a year." Meanwhile, Virgin America's Payson says a flexible model will help you meet your objectives and stay responsive, he balances flexibility with structure by working in three-month cycles. The team plans for developments and initiatives on a three-month time line, but will constantly readjust according to buzz activity and user feedback.
4.Facebook, It's Complicated	I couldn't let them go without a parting question on Facebook. Conclusion (not a big surprise): it's complicated. The companies were all grateful for the platform, but they also highlighted some serious concerns. Brill was upset by the company's recent launch of Community Pages, which are pseudo-Wiki pages regulated by the Facebook community. She says a page on Cisco was frequently confused with the company's official profile: "I'm surprised that they would even do something like this without consulting the brands...It looked a lot like our corporate fan page and I think it's hard for the users to determine what's official and what Facebook created." Virgin's Payson was more upset by what he described as a lack of transparency, calling on Facebook to follow Twitter's lead and give companies more access to analytical tools/data.

1. Companies may be building out specialized teams for social media, and encouraging other employees to use social CRM tools and to become active external agents.
2. The expansion of social media also has the power to reshape the very guts of a company: its brand identity.
3. A flexible social media model will help companies meet their objectives and stay responsive, balance flexibility with structure.

CONCLUSION

Before companies launch their startup, the need to make sure that they have a clear business model in mind. Companies will most likely have to change and tweak their business model as their startup progresses, but at least they will be focused on cash generation from the start, which means they'll be ahead of the game. This chapter covered many business models available to Web startups.

2010 was the year of social networking monetization. There was a significant amount of changes, and more players are soon to enter the space. As soon as revenue is released to the public and that revenue is significant, Fortune 500 companies salivating at the chance to get in on the game. This would likely be met with acquisitions, as well as in-house spinoffs launched to capture some of the pie (think of Hulu's launch in order to respond to YouTube). If there's one thing to take away from all of this, it's simply: Be creative with your business model in 2013, be flexible and make sure it aligns itself with the well-being and interest of your users.

There are many opportunities for making money on the Facebook Platform, but most of that opportunity is for Facebook, Inc. rather than for the brains that are developing on their platform. For those who want to develop for Facebook, hope you are comfortable having the rules of the game dictated to you, because for true innovators, that's not a comfortable situation to invest yourself into.

According to Evelyn Rusli (2010), many corporations have mastered the tricky art of signing up for a Facebook account, the next step is leveraging social media tools in a meaningful way that impacts your brand and your bottom line. While some have found varying degrees of success, the vast majority could use a crash course stat. There are four laws of social business: 1.don't fondle the hammer (don't focus on the specific tools, think about your broader marketing agenda), 2.live the 80% rule (get your company ready for social media, that's "80% of success"), 3.customers don't care what department you're in, and 4.real time is not fast enough (Jeremiah Owyang, 2010).

REFERENCES

Allaire, J. (2009). *Building new business models on the web*. SYS-CON Media Inc.

Andrews, A. (2009a). *Social networks face challenging 2009, must monetise or die*. Retrieved July 1, 2012, from http://paidcontent.co.uk/article/419-social-networks-face-challenging-2009-must-monetise-or-die/

Andrews, A. (2009b). *Facebook shows off polls in davos, new business model or just cool toy?* Retrieved July 1, 2012, from http://www.washingtonpost.com/wp-dyn/content/article/2009/02/02/AR2009020200876.html

Boyd, m., & Ellison, N. B. (2007). Social network sites: Definition, history, and scholarship. *Journal of Computer-Mediated Communication, 13*(1). doi:10.1111/j.1083-6101.2007.00393.x

Brogan, C. (2011). *An insider's guide to social media etiquette*. Retrieved July 1, 2012, from http://www.chrisbrogan.com/socialmediaetiquette/, ChrisBrogan.com. 24 February.

Burgess, C. (2012). *The rise of the employee brand*. Retrieved July 1, 2012, from http://www.business2community.com/branding/the-rise-of-the-employee-brand-0140637

Capozzi, C. (2013). *Business model vs. revenue model*. Retrieved July 1, 2012, from http://www.ehow.com/info_7760925_business-model-vs-revenue-model.html

Carlson, N. (2010, March 5). At last – The full story of how Facebook was founded. *Business Insider*.

Eldon, E. (2008). *2008 growth puts Facebook in better position to make money*. San Francisco: VentureBeat.

Future Summit Blog. (2008). *New business models: Get the world innovating for you for free*. Retrieved July 1, 2012, from http://www.futuresummit.org/blog/new-business-models-get-the-world-innovating-for-you-for-free/

George, G., & Bock, A. J. (2011). The business model in practice and its implications for entrepreneurship research. *Entrepreneurship Theory and Practice, 35*(1), 83–111. doi:10.1111/j.1540-6520.2010.00424.x

George, G., & Bock, A. J. (2012). *Models of opportunity: How entrepreneurs design firms to achieve the unexpected.* Cambridge, UK: Cambridge University Press. doi:10.1017/CBO9780511984815

Jun, L. (2009). *Five business models for social media start-ups.* Retrieved July 1, 2012, from http://mashable.com/2009/07/14/social-media-business-models/

Laurel, P. (2008). *Social media monetization and revenue, under Australia, featured, featured articles, monetization, money, online communities, ROI, consumer economy, digital economy, peer-2peer, revenue, web 2.0 presentation at PANPA (part) and web directions 2008 (full).* Retrieved July 1, 2012, from http://laurelpapworth.com/social-media-monetization-and-revenue/

Laurel, P. (2009). *Monetization: Facebook revenue and business model, under featured, metrics, monetization, money, business, revenue.* Retrieved July 1, 2012, from http://laurelpapworth.com/monetization-facebook-revenue-and-business-model/

Li, C., & Bernoff, J. (2008). *Groundswell: Winning in a world transformed by social technologies.* Cambridge, MA: Harvard Business Press.

O'Neill, N. (2010). *Facebook squeezes digg into a new business model.* Retrieved July 1, 2012, from http://www.allfacebook.com/2010/03/facebook-digg-business/

Osterwalder, A. (2005). *What is a business model?* Retrieved July 1, 2012, from http://business-model-design.blogspot.com/2005/11/what-is-business-model.html

Osterwalder, A., Pigneur, Y., & Smith, A. (2010). *Business model generation.* Hoboken, NJ: John Wiley & Sons Inc.

Paczkowski, J. (2008). *Facebook and the Duke Nukem Forever of business models.* Retrieved July 1, 2012, from http://digitaldaily.allthingsd.com/20081010/facebook-and-the-duke-nukem-forever-of-business-models/

Review, H. B. (2009). *Harvard business review on business model innovation.* Cambridge, MA: Harvard Business School Press.

Rusli, E. (2010). *How Facebook and Twitter are changing business models, shaping brand identity.* Retrieved July 1, 2012, from http://techcrunch.com/2010/05/13/how-facebook-and-twitter-are-changing-business-models-shaping-brand-identity-video/?utm_source=feedburner&utm_medium=feed&utm_campaign=Feed:+Techcrunch+(TechCrunch)

Social.advantages. (2009). *The new effective social business model – Facebook wins.* Retrieved July 1, 2012, from http://social.advantages.us/2009/11/15/the-new-effective-social-business-model-facebook-wins/

Stephens, T. R. (2007). *Business model 2.0.* Retrieved July 1, 2012, from http://www.rtodd.com/collaborage/2007/10/ business_model_20.html

Tapsns.com. (2009). *Facebook and business model 2.0.* Retrieved July 1, 2012, from http://www.tapsns.com/blog/index.php/2009/01/facebook-and-business-model-20/

VentureDig. (2010). *Monetizing social networks: The four dominant business models and how you should implement them in 2010.* Retrieved July 1, 2012, from http://venturedig.com/tech/monetizing-social-networks-the-four-dominant-business-models-and-how-you-should-implement-them-in-2010/

Wasserman, S., & Faust, K. (1994). Social network analysis in the social and behavioral sciences. In *Social network analysis: Methods and applications*. Cambridge, UK: Cambridge University Press. doi:10.1017/CBO9780511815478

ADDITIONAL READING

Alemán, A. M. M., & Wartman, K. L. (2009). *Online social networking on campus: understanding what matters in student culture* (1st ed.). New York, London: Routledge.

Aneja, N., & Gambhir, S. (2013). Ad-hoc-Social-Network-A-Comprehensive-Survey. Retrieved October 1, 2012, from http://www.ijser.org/researchpaper%5CAd-hoc-Social-Network-A-Comprehensive-Survey.pdf

Armano, D. (2012), Social Business: Where It's Been & Where It's Going, Retrieved October 1, 2012, from http://darmano.typepad.com/logic_emotion/2012/05/social_biz.html.

Arrington, M. (April 25, 2012). The Age Of Facebook. TechCrunch.

Barabási, A. (2003). *Linked: How everything is connected to everything else and what it means for business, science, and everyday life*. New York, NY: Plum.

Barham, N. (2004). *Disconnected: Why our kids are turning their backs on everything we thought we knew* (1st ed.). Ebury Press.

Baron, N. S. (2008). *Always on: language in an online and mobile world*. Oxford, New York: Oxford University Press. doi:10.1093/acprof:oso/9780195313055.001.0001

Benioff, M. (2012), Welcome to the Social Media Revolution, BBC News. 10 May.

Brito, M. (2012), 8 Cultural Indicators of social Business Transformation, Social Business News. 14 May.

Brogan, C. (2011), An Insider's Guide to Social Media Etiquette Retrieved October 1, 2012, from http://www.chrisbrogan.com/socialmediaetiquette/, ChrisBrogan.com. 24 February.

Burgess, C. (2012), The Rise of the Employee Brand Retrieved October 1, 2012, from http://www.business2community.com/branding/the-rise-of-the-employee-brand-0140637.

Burkhart, T., Krumeich, J., Werth, D., & Loos, P. (2011), Analyzing the Business Model Concept — A Comprehensive Classification of Literature, Proceedings of the International Conference on Information Systems (ICIS 2011). Paper 12. Retrieved October 1, 2012, from http://aisel.aisnet.org/icis2011/proceedings/generaltopics/12

Canales, B. (2011), What is Social Business? Hula Hub magazine. 30 November.

Carr, D. F. (2012), How to Design a Social Business, InformationWeek. 8 May.

Cass, J. (2010), General Motors Brands Use Immerse & Disperse To Adopt Social Media Retrieved October 1, 2012, from http://pr.typepad.com/pr_communications/2010/03/general-motors-brands-use-immerse-disperse-to-adopt-social-media.html.

Chesbrough, H., & Rosenbloom, R. S. (2002). *The Role of the Business Model in capturing value from Innovation: Evidence from XEROX Corporation's Technology Spinoff Companies*. Boston, Massachusetts: Harvard Business School.

Cockrell, C., Plumbing the mysterious practices of 'digital youth': In first public report from a 'seminal' study, UC Berkeley scholars shed light on kids' use of Web 2.0 tools, UC Berkeley News, University of California, Berkeley, News Center, 28 April.

Davis, D.C. (2007), MySpace Isn't Your Space: Expanding the Fair Credit Reporting Act to Ensure Accountability and Fairness in Employer Searches of Online Social Networking Services, 16 Kan. J.L., & Pub. Pol'y 237.

Else, L., & Turkle, S. (2006), Living online: I'll have to ask my friends, New Scientist, issue 2569, 20 September.

Estrada, E. (2011). *The Structure of Complex Networks: Theory and Applications*. Oxford University Press. doi:10.1093/acprof:o so/9780199591756.001.0001

Freeman, L. C. (2004). *The Development of Social Network Analysis: A Study in the Sociology of Science*. Empirical Press.

George, A. B. (2011). *Encyclopedia of Social Networks*. CA: SAGE Publications, Inc.

George, G., & Bock, A. J. (2012). *Models of opportunity: How entrepreneurs design firms to achieve the unexpected*. Cambridge University Press. doi:10.1017/CBO9780511984815

Glaser, M. (2007), Your Guide to Social Networking Online, PBS Media Shift, August.

Hamel, G. (2000). *Leading the revolution*. Boston: Harvard Business School Press.

Hardaway, F. (2012), Forget Social Media -- Here Comes Social Business, Phoenix Business Journal. 8 May.

Kadushin, C. (2012). *Understanding Social Networks: Theories, Concepts, and Findings*. Oxford University Press.

Kelsey, T. (2010). Social Networking Spaces: From Facebook to Twitter and Everything. In *Between*. Springer-Verlag.

Kirkpatrick, D. (2006). Why Facebook matters: It's not just for arranging dates., & it's not just another social network. Facebook offers sophisticated tools for maintaining social relationships. *Fortune*, (October): 6.

Lee, N. (2012), Facebook Nation: Total Information Awareness, New York, NY: Springer Science+ Business Media.

Linder, J., & Cantrell, S. (2000). *Changing Business Models: Surveying the Landscape*. Accenture Institute for Strategic Change.

Marsh, K. (2012), South Africa: How Social Business is Creating Changes, All Africa. 10 May.

Miller, D. (2011), Tales from Facebook, Polity press: 1 Ed.

Muegge, S. (2012). *Business Model Discovery by Technology Entrepreneurs* (pp. 5–16). Technology Innovation Management Review.

Muegge S., Haw C., & Matthews Sir T. (2013), Business Models for Entrepreneurs and Startups: Best of TIM Review, Talent First Network press, Book 2.

Powers, W. (2010). *Hamlet's Blackberry: a practical philosophy for building a good life in the digital age* (1st ed.). New York: Harper.

Rainie, L., & Wellman, B. (2012). *Networked: The New Social Operating System*. MIT Press.

Santiago Restrepo Barrera. Colombia (2012), Business model tool, Business life model, Retrieved October 1, 2012, from http://www.imaginatunegocio.com/#!business-life-model/c1o75.

Scott, J. (1991). *Social Network Analysis: a handbook*. CA: SAGE Publications, Inc.

Timmers, P. (1998). Business Models for Electronic Markets. *Electronic Markets*, 8(2), 3–8. doi:10.1080/10196789800000016

Wasserman, S., & Faust, K. (1994). *Social Network Analysis: Methods and Applications. Structural Analysis in the Social Sciences*. Cambridge University Press. doi:10.1017/CBO9780511815478

Wellman, B., & Berkowitz, S. D. (1988). *Social Structures: A Network Approach. Structural Analysis in the Social Sciences*. Cambridge University Press.

Zott, C., Amit, R., & Massa, L. (2010), The Business Model: Theoretical Roots, Recent Developments, and Future Research, Spain: IESE Business School, University of Navarra press, WP-862.

KEY TERMS AND DEFINITIONS

Business Model: The "Harvard Business Review on Business Model Innovation" charts four basic tenets of a business model: how the company creates and delivers value to its customers, the ways in which the company will earn a profit, which key components will be utilized and which key processes the company will incorporate. Key components include staff and human resources, machinery and technology as well as branding efforts. Each business model differs depending on the organization's size, industry and expectations. A business model describes the rationale of how an organization creates, delivers, and captures value (Osterwalder et al., 2010) (economic, social, cultural, or other forms of value).

Business Model 2.0: Allaire (2009) indicated, Internet Business Models 2.0 on the Horizon. Many of new online businesses models, in fact, are driving new ideas in overall business models, and opening up entire new economies. Broadly coined' Affiliate and Syndication Networks', these models enable any Web site (theoretically) to leverage the assets of other Web sites to create new value. In short, it is an entirely new economy built out of the Web. Taking your Web business to the next level requires Web syndication and affiliate networks. Getting there requires introspection on what aspects of your business support this model.

Facebook: Facebook is an online social networking service. Its name comes from a colloquialism for the directory given to American university students (Eldon, Eric, 2008). Facebook was founded in February 2004 by Mark Zuckerberg with his college roommates and fellow Harvard University students Eduardo Saverin, Andrew McCollum, Dustin Moskovitz and Chris Hughes (Carlson, Nicholas, 2010).

Monetization: Monetization is the process of converting or establishing something into legal tender. It usually refers to the coining of currency or the printing of banknotes by central banks. The currency promises to deliver a given amount of a recognized commodity of a universally (globally) agreed to rarity and value, providing the currency with the foundation of legitimacy or value.

SNS: A social networking service (SNS) is a platform to build social networks or social relations among people who, for example, share interests, activities, backgrounds, or real-life connections. A social network service consists of a representation of each user (often a profile), his/her social links, and a variety of additional services. Most social network services are Web-based and provide means for users to interact over the Internet, such as e-mail and instant messaging.

Social Business Model: Organizations that have adopted the social business model utilize social media tools and social networking behavioral standards across functional areas for communicating and engaging with external audiences, including customers, prospective customers, prospective employees, suppliers, and partners. Combining social networking etiquette (Brogan, 2011) (being helpful, transparent and authentic) with business engagement on LinkedIn (for one-to-one interaction), Twitter (for immediacy) and Facebook (for content sharing) more fully involves employees in the organization and increases customer intimacy and trust (Burgess, 2012).

Social Network: Wasserman, Faust (1994) indicated a social network is a social structure made up of a set of social actors (such as individuals or organizations) and a set of the dyadic ties between these actors. The social network perspective provides a set of methods for analyzing the structure of whole social entities as well as a variety of theories explaining the patterns observed in these structures.

Revenue Business Model: A revenue model is a subset component of a business model. The revenue model focuses on answering the question of how the business will generate revenue and, ultimately, how the company will be profitable. The revenue model depends on the industry. For example, a website might employ a contextual advertising model, which means the business generates money by users clicking on third-party ads within the page content. A baseball stadium, on the other hand, may have a revenue model that includes raising money from ancillary goods such as team apparel and dining outlets (Catherine, 2013).

ENDNOTES

[1]   David Evans, Richard Schmalensee (2007)

Chapter 10
Secure Network Solutions for Enterprise Cloud Services

Chengcheng Huang
University of Ballarat, Australia

Phil Smith
University of Ballarat, Australia

Zhaohao Sun
University of Ballarat, Australia

ABSTRACT

Securing a cloud network is an important challenge for delivering cloud services to enterprise clouds. There are a number of secure network protocols, such as VPN protocols, currently available, to provide different secure network solutions for enterprise clouds. For example, PPTP, IPSec, and SSL/TLS are the most widely used VPN protocols in today's securing network solutions. However, there are some significant challenges in the implementation stage. For example, which VPN solution is easy to deploy in delivering cloud services? Which VPN solution is most user-friendly in enterprise clouds? This chapter explores these issues by implementing different VPNs in a virtual cloud network environment using open source software and tools. This chapter also reviews cloud computing and cloud services and looks at their relationships. The results not only provide experimental evidence but also facilitate the network implementers in deployment of secure network solutions for enterprise cloud services.

INTRODUCTION

Cloud computing is one of the most significant developments in information technology (Bauer & Adams, 2012). Ried (2011) predicted that the cloud computing market will grow from $40.7 billion in 2011 to $240 billion in 2020. Cloud computing has been recognized as the fifth generation of computing after mainframe computing, personal computing, client-server computing and the Web (Khmelevsky & Voytenko, 2010).

Cloud computing has two meanings. It can refer to either the applications delivered as services over the Internet or the hardware and systems software

DOI: 10.4018/978-1-4666-5884-4.ch010

in the data centers that provide those services (Yang, Tan, Dai, & Guo, 2009). Cloud computing provides its services based on the service model. Examples of the service model are infrastructure as a Service (IaaS), Platform as a Service (PaaS) and Software as a Service (SaaS) (Buyya, Broberg, & Goscinski, 2010). Cloud services can be developed in different cloud environments, such as private cloud, public cloud, community cloud and hybrid Cloud, according to the deployment models (Sitaram & Manjunath, 2011). Enterprise cloud is developed on the service model and deployment model according to the business requirements and demands of the enterprise.

One of the challenges facing enterprise clouds and cloud services is cloud security. In particular, the problem of how to secure the cloud service connections, especially in a large geographic area without interference from unauthorized parties, has drawn considerable attention from cloud developers. One of the popular solutions is to deploy Virtual Private Network (VPN) technologies.

VPN is a network technology that establishes a connection through a public network utilizing encryption technology to privatize and secure data for transmission between two enterprises (Gentry, 2001). There are a number of VPN protocols which provide different solutions to VPN deployment and guarantee the efficient delivery of cloud services from different areas. Popular VPN technologies include: PPTP (Point-to-Point Tunneling Protocol), L2TP (Layer Two Tunneling Protocol), MPLS (Multiprotocol Label Switching), GRE (Generic Routing Encapsulation), IPsec (Internet Protocol Security), and TLS/SSL (Transport Layer Security/Secure Sockets Layer) based on RFC (Request For Comments) (RFC, 2012). Recent studies indicate that VPN technologies play an important role in cloud computing and bring significant advantages to enterprises in securing cloud connections. For instance, Hao et al (2010) indicated that L2TP or IPSec can be utilized to provide connectivity and security to access the cloud network for enterprises. Jamil and Zaki (2011) stated that enterprises can use VPN connections to increase the cloud security and minimize network attacks such as DDoS (Distributed Denial of Service) attacks and network sniffing. Gupta and Verma (2012) concluded that dynamic IP-VPN can improve the security of an enterprise. However, different VPN solutions result in significant differences due to the weaknesses, strengths and vulnerabilities of deploying VPN protocols (Jaha, Shatwan, & Ashibani, 2008). Hence, implementing a suitable and secure VPN solution for the enterprise cloud is a significant challenge for network implementers and enterprises. Important questions faced by the cloud network developers include: Which VPN solution is easy to deploy in delivering cloud services? Which VPN solution is most user-friendly in enterprise cloud? This chapter addresses these issues by evaluating the most popular VPN solutions in a virtual cloud network environment.

The remainder of this chapter is organized as follows. Firstly, a review of cloud computing, enterprise cloud, and cloud services and their relationships are given in this chapter. Secondly, this chapter explores each securing network solution, describes the test bed setup, deployment process, and evaluates the experiment results and discusses related work. Finally some future research directions and some concluding remarks are provided.

CLOUD COMPUTING AND CLOUD SERVICES

This section reviews the definition of cloud computing, basic characteristics of cloud computing and discusses the cloud deployment models and cloud services. This section also illustrates the relationship between cloud computing and cloud services and introduces the enterprise cloud services. The section concludes by reviewing the benefits and challenges of cloud services.

Cloud Computing

There are many definitions of cloud computing and no definition is accepted by all scholars in the field (Thomas, 2012). Nonetheless, one of the most accepted definitions for cloud computing, provided by U.S. National Institute of Standards and Technology (NIST), is "a model for enabling convenient, on demand network access to a shared pool of configurable computing resources (e.g., networks, servers, storage, applications, and services) that can be rapidly provisioned and released with minimal management effort or service provider interaction" (Mell & Grance, 2011, p. 6).

The concept of cloud computing dates back to the 1950s when large-scale mainframe computers became available in academia and corporations (Strachey, 1959). Large-scale mainframes as a service became popular at that time, that is, many institutions rented large-scale mainframes rather than purchased them subject to paying renting fees. However, cloud computing only became popular in the past several years, and is still in its infancy today (Thomas, 2012).

Based on the definition, cloud computing is composed of five essential functional characteristics:

- **On-Demand Self-Service:** Which means that resources are "instantly" available to the user requests via a service or provisioning website (Bauer & Adams, 2012).
- **Broad Network Access** Which means that users intend to access the cloud services anywhere through any kinds of wire line or wireless network device they wish to use over whatever IP access network is most suitable (Bauer & Adams, 2012).
- **Resource Pooling:** Which means that service providers deploy a pool of different physical and virtual resources such as servers, storage devices, and other data centre resources that are shared across multiple

consumers to reduce costs to the service providers (Mell & Grance, 2011).

- **Rapid Elasticity:** Which means the ability of a user to acquire computing resources quickly so that they can commence work within a short period of time and improve the efficiency, as well as enable application group to respond to business conditions extremely rapidly (Carstensen, Morgentha, & Golden, 2012).
- **Measured Servicing:** Which means that measuring resource consumption and suitably pricing to cloud users for their cloud resource consumption inspires the consumer to release unneeded resources so that they can be used by other cloud consumers rather than squandering the resources (Bauer & Adams, 2012).

Unlike other types of Internet-based computing, cloud computing provides computing resources and services such as network infrastructure, hardware and software based on the demand of users. Users only pay for the computing resources and services they use. Cloud services are provided by independent organizations or by cloud service providers to facilitate the cloud migration and the cloud management for the customers (Sosinsky, 2010). Shifting from the traditional computing network to cloud computing network helps enterprises to reduce the network administration costs and improve the efficiency of the services (Buyya, et al., 2010), because the enterprises do not have to invest upfront on expensive IT infrastructure. They can simply use the computing resources or services provided by cloud providers with agreements. The providers deal with all the maintenance tasks.

Cloud Deployment Models

There are a number of different ways to deploy cloud services depending upon factors such as security requirements, partnership with other organization, private or public accessibility, and type of network access. These deployment models provide different solutions to the way in which customers can control their resources, and the scale, cost, and availability of resources (Badger, Grance, Patt-Corner, & Voas, 2012). There are four different deployment models defined by the National Institute of Standards and Technology (NIST) and accepted by the majority of cloud stakeholders today: private cloud, public cloud, community cloud, and hybrid cloud (Buyya, et al., 2010).

Private Cloud

Private cloud, also called internal cloud, provides the cloud services built in a private network with existing resources provided by an internal enterprise for use in other internal enterprises (Halpert, 2011). A private cloud might be managed by the enterprise's IT department or a third party cloud provider. One of the advantages of a private cloud is that the enterprise can style the structure of cloud and modify the infrastructures or configurations any time to meet exactly what it needs (Finn, Vredevoort, Lownds, & Flynn, 2012). Private cloud is one of the popular solutions for public, private, and government organizations worldwide to exploit cloud benefits such as flexibility, cost reduction, agility etc. (Buyya, et al., 2010). Furthermore, private cloud is the best solution when the data security and privacy are of top priority to the enterprise (Thomas, 2012).

An enterprise deploying a private cloud may not benefit from the same degree of savings on up-front capital costs as using public cloud because the enterprise still needs to purchase, install, and manage the cloud infrastructure (Thomas, 2012). Nonetheless, private clouds provide better flexibility, greater operational efficiency, high reliability and high data security and the capability to deliver other benefits of cloud computing while minimizing some of its shortcomings (Sosinsky, 2010).

Public Cloud

A public cloud, also called external cloud, is one in which the cloud infrastructure is provisioned for open use by the general public while being owned, managed, operated by an organization (Mell & Grance, 2011). In other words, a third party owned and operated hardware, networking, storage, services, application and interfaces can be used by not only individuals, but also other enterprises (Hurwitz, Kaufman, Halper, & Kirsch, 2012). Moreover, a public cloud is based on the standard cloud computing model. It might be provided on a free or pay-per-usage basis.

One of the advantages of a public cloud is that the service is always ready for use by the end users and they only need to pay if they access to those services (Hurwitz, et al., 2012). Enterprises can implement a new business application in a short time instead of investing significant resources in advance to set up and run the solution. The enterprise has no control of the cloud services and data when the services are external (Thomas, 2012).

Community Cloud

A community cloud is a cloud in which groups of individuals and organizations with similar IT requirements share an infrastructure provided by a single service provider (BCS The Chartered Institute for IT, 2012). The groups could be an industry consortium, an awareness group, or another group altogether (Halpert, 2011). Community clouds could be managed by the organizations or a third party and may exist on premise or off premise. A community cloud is less expensive than a private cloud but more expensive than a public cloud, and it may provide a higher level of privacy, security and policy compliance than a public cloud (Williams, 2009).

One of the benefits of community clouds is that the costs of the cloud services are spread between all the customers which make it more economical than a single tenant arrangement with the service provider. Moreover, community cloud users usually benefit from better security and privacy (Halpert, 2011). An example of community cloud is OpenCirrus formed by HP, Intel, Yahoo, etc (Buyya, et al., 2010).

Hybrid Cloud

A hybrid cloud is a composition of two or more clouds such as private, community or public clouds where those clouds remain their unique entities, but are bound together as a unit (Sosinsky, 2010). Hybrid cloud environments are usually implemented where a customer requires for a mix of cloud services (BCS The Chartered Institute for IT, 2012). For instance, an enterprise may store the sensitive data on its local dedicated server and less sensitive data in the cloud. The services are maintained by both internal and external providers (Thomas, 2012).

One of the advantages of hybrid cloud is that it allows enterprises to take advantage of the scalability and cost-effectiveness that a public cloud computing environment provides without exposing important applications and data to the third party vulnerabilities (Thomas, 2012). Some examples of offering hybrid cloud solutions include Amazon Virtual Private Cloud, Skytap Virtual Lab, and CohesiveFT VPN-Cubed (Buyya, et al., 2010).

Cloud Services

Cloud services are one of the critical components of cloud computing. A cloud service is any computing resource provided by the cloud computing providers over the Internet (Rouse, Cloud services, 2011). Cloud services are designed to be flexible, scalable to applications, resources and services, and fully managed by a cloud services provider. Therefore, a cloud service can dynamically scale to meet the needs of its customers so that the customers do not need to deploy their own resources

for the service nor allocate IT staff to manage the service. Examples of cloud services can be online data storage and backup solutions, Web-based e-mail services.

Cloud services broadly comprise three different types of service: Infrastructure as a Service (IaaS), Platform as a Service (PaaS) and Software as a Service (SaaS) (Buyya, et al., 2010). In each case the services reside remotely and are accessed over a network, usually the Internet, through a user's Web browser, rather than being deployed locally on a user's computer. Each service focuses on a specific layer in a computer's runtime stack such as hardware, system software (or platform) and application respectively (Sitaram & Manjunath, 2011). The Figure 1 illustrates the relationship among these three cloud services.

Infrastructure as a Service (IaaS)

IaaS corresponds to the bottom layer of cloud computing systems (Buyya, et al., 2010). IaaS allows users to gain access to different kinds of infrastructure. Typically, different services are provided by dividing a very large physical infrastructure resource into smaller virtual resources (Halpert, 2011). For instance, the service can be a virtual machine with an operating system, application platforms, middleware, database servers, enterprise service busses, third-party components

Figure 1. The relationships among Cloud services. Adapted from Bauer and Adams (2012)

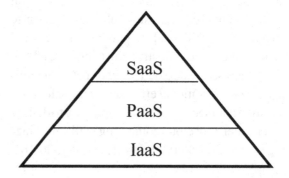

and frameworks, and management and monitoring software (Kommalapati, 2010). The IT professionals who manage the infrastructure have full control of all the infrastructures and configurations, and they have responsibilities for maintaining all the facilities of the infrastructure.

Platform as a Service (PaaS)

PaaS is a higher level of cloud computing services which makes a cloud easily programmable (Buyya, et al., 2010). For example, PaaS allows users to create the applications using programming languages, libraries, and tools from the provider. In this form of cloud services, the users control the software deployment and configuration settings (Mell & Grance, 2011). PaaS also provides necessary supporting services such as storage, security, and integration infrastructure for a complete platform.

Software as a Service (SaaS)

SaaS resides on top of the cloud stack and provides a rich Web-based interface to consumers (Halpert, 2011). Consumers can obtain the same software services and functionality on-line as locally installed computer program (Buyya, et al., 2010) SaaS is a pay-as-you-go paradigm so users only need to pay for the services provided when they access the resources. There are no upfront commitments or any long-term contracts for the end users. There are many free SaaS such as Internet email communication software.

SaaS is one of the best solutions for enterprises or organizations to deal with the shortage of skilled resources for managing their IT systems (Thomas, 2012). The possible cloud resources such as Gmail, Google Docs, and Facebook can be installed at the back-end to deliver the cloud services to the customers. SaaS is meant for all the end customers.

Other Cloud Services

Network as a service (NaaS) is one of the latest cloud services. NaaS was proposed in 2012 (Costa, Migliavacca, Pietzuch, & Wolf, 2012). The concept of NaaS is to outsource to the cloud networking service providers in order to limit the cost of data communications for the cloud consumers, as well as to improve network flexibility (Costa, et al., 2012). NaaS enable the cloud consumers to use network connectivity services and/or inter-cloud network connectivity services. It includes flexible and extended VPN, and bandwidth on demand (Focus Group, 2012).

Storage as a Service (StaaS) has drawn an increasing attention from some enterprises recently. StaaS is a business model that a giant enterprise leases or rents its storage infrastructure to a small company or individual to store data (Rouse, 2009). StaaS is also being recognized as an alternative way to mitigate risks in disaster recovery, as well as offering long-term preservation for records for businesses, which improves both in business continuity and availability.

Additionally, the number of cloud based services increased rapidly in recent years. Shan (2009) published a comprehensive taxonomy model includes latest cloud services such as Strategy-as-a-Service, Collaboration-as-a-Service, Business Process-as-a-Service, Database-as-a-Service, etc. Besides, ITU (International Telecommunication Union) (2012) officially announced that Network as a service (NaaS), Communications as a Service (CaaS), Desktop as a Service (DaaS), Service Delivery Platform as a Service (SDPaaS) become a part of the essential cloud computing models, recognized service categories of a tele-communication-centric cloud ecosystem. Along with the rapid development of cloud computing, more and more cloud services will be proposed and implemented to satisfy the cloud consumers.

Enterprise Cloud Services

Generally, an enterprise could be the cloud service provider or cloud service consumer. On one hand, an enterprise as a service provider benefits by providing different cloud services to various cloud consumers. For example, Amazon, one of the most famous cloud enterprises, provides access to a virtual computing environment and allows customers' applications run on a "virtual CPU". The cloud consumers pay 10 cents per clock hour to the enterprise and they can get as many "virtual CPUs" as they need (Barr, Varia, & Wood, 2006). Therefore, the enterprise earns income from providing cloud services to the cloud consumers. In Australia, the most well-known cloud service providers include Dimension Data, Fujitsu, Wipro, Emantra, Telstra, Melbourne IT (Carr, May, & Stewart, 2012).

An enterprise as a service consumer, can acquire cloud services from different cloud providers all over world. For instance, an enterprise can acquire a hosted application server, data storage, computing and networking infrastructure for building and running Windows applications from Microsoft cloud computing platform called Windows Azure (Kommalapati, 2010). Enterprises can obtain most of the services from different cloud service providers so that they can focus on their business without paying too much attention to IT infrastructure and services.

Benefits and Challenges of Cloud Services

Cloud services have a number of benefits. Firstly, cloud users only pay for what they use because most of the pricing models are consumption-based. Secondly, cloud services are easy to use because cloud services allow you to avoid the hardware and software procurement and capital expenditure stage and to concentrate on implementation. Thirdly, cloud users can enjoy the up-to-date cloud services without worrying about extra costs

because the cloud services providers constantly update their services (BCS The Chartered Institute for IT, 2012). Fourthly, the flexibility and scalability of cloud services enable to increase the needed infrastructure and services according to the need of the clients, and also it will reduce the precious time needed to offer a new service (Al-Masah & Al-Sharafi, 2013). Fifthly, the mobility of cloud services allows cloud users access to the services from mobile workforce (BCS The Chartered Institute for IT, 2012).

However, there are some challenges of cloud services including privacy, reliability, and the possibility of being locked into one cloud service provider. There are also questions on the ability to seamlessly convert to cloud without interfering with the existing in-house systems and information resources (Harding, 2011). Some enterprises might hesitate to take advantage of cloud services due to these challenges and concerns. Moreover, experts indicate that the biggest challenge about cloud services is data security (Thomas, 2012). In other words, secure network solution is one of the critical components in offering high quality cloud services to the cloud users, especially the secure and reliable connection for the remote users. The following sections will look more deeply into secure network solutions.

SECURE NETWORK SOLUTIONS

Secure network solutions provide an assurance that a network performs its critical functions correctly without any harmful side effects (Joshi, 2008). Virtual Private Network (VPN) is one of the popular solutions in securing the cloud connections, and has been utilized extensively in enterprise cloud deployment. Moreover, VPN technology provides secure and seamless solutions to link cloud and enterprise infrastructure, as well as offering secure connection between consumers and the enterprise cloud, in order to protect the communication without meddling by unauthorized users (Wood, Ramakrishnan, Shenoy, & Merwe, 2012).

VPN solutions can be deployed by using different protocols, such as PPTP, IPSec and SSL/TLS protocol. The following subsection reviews the fundamental of VPN and its protocols.

VPN Fundamentals

VPN dates back to the 1990s. It allows an organization to share private network services over a public or shared infrastructure such as the Internet or service provider backbone network (Lewis, 2006). Although VPN technologies have been widely used for more than two decades at different times, it still plays an important role in enterprise cloud development. The various types of VPNs provide different solutions to enterprises to meet different needs.

Definition of VPN

VPN is a network technology that is usually used to establish a connection though a public network such as Internet utilizing encryption technology to privatize data for transmission between two trusted parties (Gentry, 2001). A VPN connection can be simply described as a VPN tunnel that is built between the Branch Office and Corporate Hub across the Internet so that both sides of the enterprise can access each other privately (Lewis, 2006). VPN can also be utilized to access the cloud services remotely by establishing a VPN tunnel between cloud users and the cloud. There are many recognized and acknowledged definitions of VPN. One of the popular definitions of VPN is:

A virtual private network is a combination of tunneling encryption, authentication and access control used to carry traffic over the Internet (or a managed Internet protocol (IP) network or a provider's backbone) (Younglove, 2000, pp. 260-262).

Based on this definition, a VPN utilizes three different technologies to secure its connections, encryption, authentication and access control. Encryption is the process of converting plain text to cipher text in such a way that only authorized entities can read it (Goldreich, 2004). Examples include 3DES, the RC series (RC2/4/5/6) and RSA etc. Authentication is the process of confirming the identities of the message originator (Ferguson, 2012). Examples include hash functions and digital signatures. Access control is the process of verifying the user who has been given the permission or keys to access the information or resources (Strebe, 2006). If the user is not in the permission list, access is denied.

Types of VPN

VPNs can be classified into various types based on the construction of the VPN and the goals they are constructed to achieve. Generally, based on the OSI (Open Systems Interconnection) model, VPNs can be classified as: Data Link Layer VPNs, Network Layer VPNs, and Application Layer VPNs (Malik, 2002). Data Link Layer VPNs connect two private networks using a shared network infrastructure which is based on switched link layer technology such as Frame Relay or Asynchronous Transfer Mode (ATM) (Gleeson, Lin, Heinanen, Armitage, & Malis, 2000). Network Layer VPNs are constructed by using Layer 3 tunneling and/or encryption techniques such as IPSec tunneling and encryption protocol to create VPNs (Malik, 2002). The tunnel connects two points of a VPN across the public network infrastructure (Venkateswaran, 2001). Application Layer VPNs are developed to work particularly with specific applications (Malik, 2002). One of famous examples is SSL/TLS based VPNs. SSL/TLS based VPNs offer encryption between Web browsers and servers in SSL connections.

VPN Protocols

A VPN protocol is one of the essential and critical components in developing VPNs. Each protocol has its own strengths, weaknesses as well as distinctive deployment method. The most popular VPN protocols for enterprise cloud deployment include PPTP, IPSec and SSL/TLS.

PPTP

PPTP (Point-to-Point Tunneling Protocol) was developed by a vendor consortium including Microsoft, Ascend Communications (today part of Alcatel-Lucent), and 3Com, and published in 1999 (Hamzeh, Pall, Verthein, Taarud, Little, & Zorn, 1999). It is one of the most popular dial-in protocols and it operates at the Data Link layer (Layer 2) of the OSI model (Cisco, 2003). PPTP is an extension of point-to-point protocol (PPP) (Narayan, et al., 2009). PPTP uses TCP for its control channel and improved GRE tunnel for data transportation (Cisco, 2003). Basically, PPTP encapsulates PPP frames in IP datagrams for transmission over an IP network. Specifically, creating communication between two sites using PPTP involves three stages and each stage has to be completed prior to the next (Narayan, et al., 2009). Firstly, a PPTP client will establish a link through IP network from the source to the destination using PPP type connection. Secondly, the PPTP protocol creates a control connection, using TCP, from the client to the PPTP server after the link has been established. Thirdly, PPTP protocol creates IP datagrams containing encrypted PPP packets which are transported through the tunnel.

Additionally, PPTP always combines with additional security methods to guarantee the integrity of the messages and the security of the tunnel (Cisco, 2003). The standard PPP authentication methods such as Password Authentication Protocol (PAP) and Challenge Handshake Authentication Protocol (CHAP) can be utilized in PPTP deploy-

ment. Besides, MS-CHAP, an enhanced version of the CHAP authentication method developed by Microsoft provides ability to use the security information. Moreover, Microsoft uses a stronger encryption, Microsoft Point-to-Point Encryption (MPPE), for use with PPTP instead of utilizing PPP to encrypt data.

IPSec

IPSec (Internet Protocol Security or IP security) was developed by Internet Engineering Task Force (IETF) in early 1990s (Ioannidis, 2011). IPSec is a collection of protocols, conventions, and mechanisms in order to ensure the authenticity and guarantee the confidentiality of the content of the IP packets (Bantoft & Wouters, 2006). From a security aspect, IPSec ensures the confidentiality, integrity and authenticity of data communication by providing a mechanism for secure data transmission over unprotected networks such as the Internet. From the deployment point of view, IPSec allows to construct a VPN tunnel between two private networks by using encryption algorithms. It also allows the authentication taking place at the both ends of the tunnel.

IPSec consists of three distinctive components to create a security framework: Internet Key Exchange (IKE), Encapsulating Security Protocol (ESP), and Authentication Header (AH) (Malik, 2002). IKE provides a framework that allows IPSec peers negotiating security parameters and creating authenticated key. In general, it is used to negotiate the parameters between two IPSec peers for constructing a tunnel. ESP and AH provides a framework for authenticating and securing of data (Bantoft & Wouters, 2006). On one hand, ESP provides encryption while AH does not. Specifically, ESP is the protocol utilized for encapsulating the original IP packet and providing encryption and authentication for the data. 3DES or AES is the most famous algorithm used in ESP which provides data confidentiality by encrypting the packet's contents. On the other hand, AH is the protocol utilized for authenticating the data as well as the IP header. Instead of providing encrypting the data, it provides a hash which allows the data and the packet's IP header to be checked to ensure that the data was not altered with in transit. Although AH is an important component of the IPSec protocol suite, it is not being deployed as often as ESP (Malik, 2002). Mostly, IKE and ESP are implemented together.

IPSec operates in two ways: Transport mode and Tunnel mode (Ioannidis, 2011). In transport mode, only the payload of the IP packet is encrypted (Malik, 2002). An extra ESP or AH header will be inserted between the payload and its IP header once the ESP or AH is used. Transport mode requires the original IP header including addresses which can be routed over the public network. Transport mode is typically used for end-to-end communications. For example, transport mode can be used when an encrypted telnet or remote desktop session from a workstation to a server. In tunnel mode, a new IP header is generated and inserted in front of the ESP or AH header (Bantoft & Wouters, 2006). This new IP header includes the source and destination IP addresses of the two IPSec peers rather than the original host's IP addresses and the destination host's IP addresses. In general, tunnel mode is the most widely used mode in IPSec deployments especially in network-to-network communications (e.g. between routers to link sites), host-to-network communications (e.g. remote access) and host-to-host communication (e.g. private chat).

SSL/TLS

Secure Sockets Layer (SSL) was originally developed by Netscape Communications as a way to provide communication security over the Internet (Davies, 2011). SSL has been implemented in the major Web browsers such as Internet Explorer, Netscape, and Firefox. SSL protocol is a client/ server protocol that provides basic security services to the communicating peers such as authentication, connection confidentiality services, and connection integrity services (Oppliger, 2009). SSL protocol evolved in three versions: SSL 1.0, SSL 2.0, and SSL 3.0. The TLS (Transport Layer Security) is structurally identical to the SSL protocol. TLS was developed based on the SSL 3.0. Usually, TLS 1.0 can be recognized as SSL 3.1 (Chou, 2002). The latest version of TLS is TLS 1.2, which is specified in RFC 5246 (Dierks & Rescorla, 2008). TLS operates in the same general manner as SSL. However, TLS uses stronger authentication and encryption protocols (Stewart & Chapple, 2011). Moreover, TLS is able to encrypt UDP and Session Initiation Protocol (SIP, which is a protocol associated with VoIP) connections.

SSL/TLS VPN is another secure solution for the enterprise cloud in securing end-to-end communication over the Internet (Park & Park, 2011). It establishes connectivity using SSL/TLS, which operates at Level 4-5 (Transport Layer and Session Layer). Information is encapsulated at Level 6-7 (Presentation Layer and Application Layer). Hence, SSL/TLS VPN communicates at the highest levels in the OSI model (Fortinet, 2013). Moreover, SSL 3.0 operates in two stages: one is connection establishment; the other is data transfer (Weaver, 2006). In connection establishment state, authentication is required from users before allowing access so that only the authorized peers can establish the SSL/TLS VPN tunnel. To do so, SSL/TLS will encrypt the section between peers so that applications can exchange and authenticate user names and passwords without interfering by the eavesdroppers (Steinberg & Speed, 2005). In data transfer stage, the SSL/TLS tunnel will be activated and all the data will be encrypted before transmitting. SSL/TLS supports different encryption algorithms within each SSL/TLS session and only the SSL/TLS peers are able to read and understand the messages (Steinberg & Speed, 2005).

Besides, SSL/TLS VPN delivers three modes of SSL/TLS VPN access: clientless, thin client and tunnel mode (Cisco, 2012). Clientless mode provides secure connection to private Web resources and Web content. This mode is significantly useful for visiting most contents that you would like to access in a Web browser such as Internet access, databases, and online tools that employ a Web interface. Thin client mode enhances the abilities of the cryptographic functions of the Web browser to access remotely to TCP-based applications such as Post Office Protocol version 3 (POP3), Simple Mail Transfer Protocol (SMTP), Internet Message Access protocol (IMAP), Telnet, and Secure Shell (SSH) (Cisco, 2012). Tunnel mode enables remote users to connect to the internal network freely from anywhere by utilizing traditionally means of Web-based access from computers or other terminal devices (Fortinet, 2013). This mode supports most IP-based applications, such as Microsoft Outlook, Microsoft Exchange, and Lotus Notes E-mail.

SECURE NETWORK SOLUTIONS DEPLOYMENT FOR ENTERPRISE CLOUD

As discussed above, VPN is one of the popular solutions used in enterprise cloud deployment in securing the cloud connections. It has also been discussed that Data link layer VPNs can be developed using PPTP protocol. Network Layer VPNs can be implemented by IPSec protocol. Application Layer VPNs can be constructed by SSL/TLS protocol. Each solution has its own deployment method and corresponding connection method to connect to the cloud from the consumer's end. Moreover, the complexity of each implementation is different as well as the user experiences.

The following section explores these differences by implementing each solution in a test bed environment in an attempt to answer questions such as which VPN solution is easy to deploy in

delivering cloud services, which VPN solution is most user-friendly in cloud computing? Open source software and tools will be utilized in the experiment. The enterprise inter-cloud architecture, test bed environment, and deployment processes as well as the simulation software used in the experiment are also described.

Enterprise Inter-Cloud Architecture

Dayananda and Kumar (2012) proposed an enterprise inter-cloud architecture as shown in Figure 2. This enterprise inter-cloud computing architecture consists of three critical components: corporate cloud network, Internet and cloud network (Cloud A and Cloud B). Both corporate cloud network and cloud networks are linked to the Internet. Each network can communicate to each other only if a proper solution has been implemented on each side of the network because Cloud A, Cloud B and Corporate network are private networks which cannot be accessed from the outside of the enterprise. VPN is one of the popular solutions in this scenario because it is more economical than leased line and is secure and scalable (Cohen & Kaempfer, 2000). In this case, we decided to develop a test bed environment based on this architecture using open source software and tools.

Test Bed Setup and Deployment Process

According to the aforementioned enterprise inter-cloud computing architecture, we propose our own network architecture for our experiment, as shown in Figure 3. The architecture is composed of three critical components: Enterprise, Internet and Cloud. Enterprise acts as the cloud consumer in this architecture and Cloud plays the role of cloud provider. Suppose all the cloud services are stored on the cloud server, a VPN tunnel needs to be set up between each edge router so that the users from the enterprise network can access to the cloud services on the cloud side. The test bed

Figure 2. An Enterprise Inter-cloud architecture. Adapted from Dayananda and Kumar (2012)

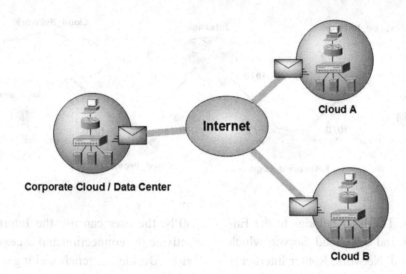

Figure 3. VPN Construction for Inter-cloud architecture

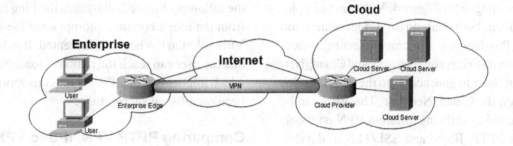

environment was created based on this architecture with the help of two open source software called GNS3 and VirtualBox.

GNS3 (Graphical Network Simulator version 3) is an open source software that simulates complex networks while being as close as possible to the way real networks perform, without having dedicated network hardware such as routers and switches (GNS3, 2013). GNS3 is an excellent simulation tool for network engineers to measure experiment features and to check configurations that need to be deployed later on real devices. VirtualBox is one of the powerful virtualization products for enterprises to run different virtual operating systems such Windows, Linux individually or simultaneously on an existing com-

puter (Oracle Corporation, 2009). It is freely available as an open source software (VirtualBox, 2009). Hence, the combination of GNS3 with VirtualBox is one of the best solutions for establishing the test bed environment.

In our experiment, a window 7 based computer was used as the physical PC. Both GNS3 and VirtualBox were running on this physical PC. GNS3 was used to create three Cisco7200 routers to simulate Enterprise Edge, Internet and Cloud Provider respectively with c7200-advipservicesk9_li-mz.124-11.t IOS (operating system for Cisco router). VirtualBox was used to emulate Windows XP operating system for the user and Windows 2003 for the Cloud Server. Furthermore, Figure 4 illustrates the test bed

Figure 4. Test bed environment in GNS3

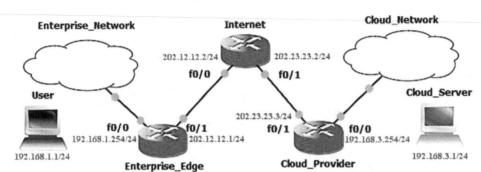

created in GNS3. The User belongs to the Enterprise_Network and the Cloud_Server, which is part of the Cloud_Network. Router Internet is used to simulate the Internet. Additionally, for experimental purposes, we assigned an IP address to each interface.

According to the Figure 4, VPN can be implemented on both Enterprise_Edge router and Cloud_Provider router to provide secure connection between Enterprise_Network and Cloud_Network, in order to gain access to the cloud service stored on the Cloud_Network. The VPN can be constructed by utilizing different VPN protocols such as PPTP, IPSec and SSL/TLS to develop Data link layer VPNs, Network Layer VPNs and Application Layer VPNs respectively. Table 1 summarizes the critical configurations of each VPN solution on Enterprise_Edge router and/or Cloud_Provider router.

A Cisco SSL VPN Client needs to be installed on the router in advance for SSL/TLS VPN development.

After deploying the configurations correctly on the routers, the user needs to use different methods to connect to the cloud Cloud_Network. For instance, with PPTP VPN, the user needs to create a Virtual Private Network Connection to connect to the cloud, as shown in Figure 5. Moreover, with IPSec VPN, the connection turns on automatically once the router identifies the network traffic met the access criteria. Additionally, with SSL/TLS

VPN, the user can use the Internet browser to activate the connection and access the cloud services. Besides, in general, a Ping service provided by Windows operating system will be used to test the reachability in order to verify the connectivity between the user and Cloud Server. For instance, the following Figure 6 illustrates the Ping results from the user's common prompt once the IPSec VPN solution has been implemented. It indicates that the user can reach the remote Cloud_Server, which implies that the IPSec VPN connection has been established successfully.

Comparing PPTP VPN, IPSec VPN and SSL/TLS VPN

After successfully deploying each VPN solution on the test bed environment, the configurations of those solutions were compared against the criteria laid out in Table 2 in order to answer the questions: which VPN solution is most user-friendly in cloud computing? Which VPN solution is easy to deploy in delivering cloud services?

For the question: which VPN solution is easy to deploy in delivering cloud services? It can be observed that PPTP VPN and SSL/TLS VPN are easier than IPSec VPN in deployment because the enterprise edge router is not necessary to support VPN and it does not need any configuration requirements based on the Table 2. All the configurations only need to be deployed on the Cloud

Table 1. VPN Configurations on Enterprise_Edge Router and/or Cloud_Provider Router

	PPTP VPN	IPSec VPN	SSL/TLS VPN
Enterprise_Edge Router	No configuration	crypto isakmp policy 10 encr 3des hash md5 authentication pre-share group 2 crypto isakmp key cisco address 202.23.23.3 ! crypto ipsec transform-set MYSET esp-des esp-md5-hmac ! crypto map MYMAP 10 ipsec-isakmp set peer 202.23.23.3 set transform-set MYSET match address VPN ! interface FastEthernet0/1 crypto map MYMAP ! ip access-list extended VPN permit ip 192.168.1.0 0.0.0.255 192.168.3.0 0.0.0.255	No configuration
Cloud_Provider Router	vpdn enable ! vpdn-group 1 ! Default PPTP VPDN group accept-dialin protocol pptp virtual-template 1 ! username test privilege 15 password 0 test ! interface Virtual-Template1 ip unnumbered FastEthernet0/1 peer default ip address pool test no keepalive ppp encrypt mppe auto ppp authentication pap chap ms-chap ! ip local pool test 192.168.3.100 192.168.3.200	crypto isakmp policy 10 encr 3des hash md5 authentication pre-share group 2 crypto isakmp key cisco address 202.12.12.1 ! crypto ipsec transform-set MYSET esp-des esp-md5-hmac ! crypto map MYMAP 10 ipsec-isakmp set peer 202.12.12.1 set transform-set MYSET match address VPN ! interface FastEthernet0/1 crypto map MYMAP ! ip access-list extended VPN permit ip 192.168.3.0 0.0.0.255 192.168.1.0 0.0.0.255	aaa new-model aaa authentication login webvpn local ! username test privilege 15 password 0 test ! ip local pool sslvpn-pool 192.168.3.100 192.168.3.200 ! webvpn gateway VPNGW ip address 202.23.23.3 port 443 ssl trustpoint TP-self-signed-4279256517 inservice ! webvpn install svc disk0:/webvpn/svc.pkg ! webvpn context WEBTEXT ssl authenticate verify all ! policy group SSLVPN-POLICY functions svc-enabled banner "This is Cisco IOS SSL VPN" svc address-pool "sslvpn-pool" svc split include 192.168.1.0 255.255.255.0 default-group-policy SSLVPN-POLICY aaa authentication list webvpn gateway VPNGW inservice

side. Besides, deploying PPTP VPN is relatively simpler than SSL/TLS VPN to the Cloud Provider because SSL/TLS VPN needs to install Cisco SSL VPN Client on the Cisco router in advance to provide authentication and it requires a higher level router and IOS. For example, Cisco 2500 series router supported PPTP VPN but did not support SSL/TLS VPN (Cisco, 2007). Then, PPTP VPN is the easiest and simplest to deploy based on this experiments.

Figure 5. PPTP VPN connection in user

Connect Virtual Private Network Connection
User name:
test
Password:
[To change the saved password, click here]
Save this user name and password for the following users:
Me only
Anyone who uses this computer
Connect
Cancel
Properties
Help

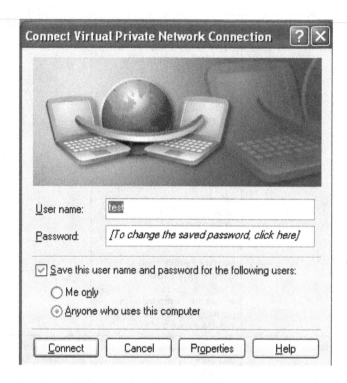

Figure 6. Ping results from user to Cloud_Server in IPSec VPN

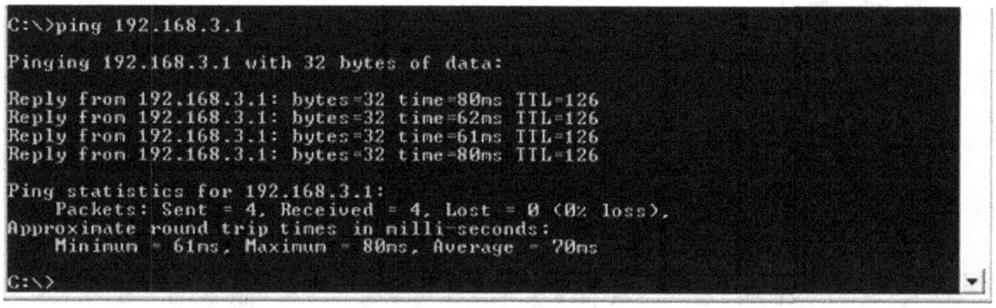

C:\>ping 192.168.3.1
Pinging 192.168.3.1 with 32 bytes of data:
Reply from 192.168.3.1: bytes=32 time=80ms TTL=126
Reply from 192.168.3.1: bytes=32 time=62ms TTL=126
Reply from 192.168.3.1: bytes=32 time=61ms TTL=126
Reply from 192.168.3.1: bytes=32 time=80ms TTL=126
Ping statistics for 192.168.3.1:
Packets: Sent = 4, Received = 4, Lost = 0 (0% loss),
Approximate round trip times in milli-seconds:
Minimum = 61ms, Maximum = 80ms, Average = 70ms
C:\>

Table 2. VPNs comparison

	PPTP VPN	IPSec VPN	SSL/TLS VPN
What is the type of the VPN?	Data link layer VPNs	Network Layer VPNs	Application Layer VPNs
How easy to use to the "User"?	Medium	Difficult	Easy
How difficult to deploy?	Easy	Difficult	Medium
Does enterprise edge router need to be configured?	NO	YES	NO
Does enterprise edge router need to be VPN capable?	NO	YES	NO
Is VPN specific configuration on the enterprise router required?	NO	YES	NO

For the question: which VPN solution is most user-friendly in cloud computing? It can be observed that PPTP VPN and SSL/TLS VPN do not need to deploy on the enterprise edge router. In other words, these two solutions do not highly depend on the router to establish VPN connections based on Table 2. Therefore, the user can access to the cloud services anywhere, even outside of the enterprise, as long as the Internet access is available. Unlike IPSec VPN, it highly relies on the router and the User only can access to the cloud services inside the enterprise network based on this experiment. Moreover, SSL/TLS VPN is more user-friendly than PPTP VPN because users only need to use a Web browser to access to the cloud services instead of creating a new VPN connection. So, users can enjoy the cloud services even on a smart TV (it has integration of the Internet and Web 2.0 features) (Vidyarthi, 2010). SSL/TLS VPN is relatively more flexible than PPTP VPN. Hence, SSL/TLS VPN solution is more user-friendly than the other two solutions based on this experiment.

DISCUSSION AND RELATED WORK

We have mentioned some of the researches related to this field, in particular those associated with cloud computing, cloud services and enterprise cloud services. We now discuss some related work in terms of secure network solution, VPN comparison, VPN for enterprise cloud.

Chen, Nepal, and Liu (2011) focused on performance observation by comparing with or without application layer VPN for intra-cloud and inter-cloud communication and proposed an electronic contract based solution that provides a secure connectivity as a service (CaaS) for intra-cloud and inter-cloud communications. They completed two tests to evaluate the performance cost of using the proposed secure connectivity service for intra-cloud and inter-cloud communication. The first test evaluated the overhead

of using and without using VPN for intra-cloud communication. The second test evaluated the cost of using and without using VPN for inter-cloud communication by comparing the latencies and throughput. In contrast, our research focuses on user experience such as cloud users and cloud implementers by comparing different VPN solutions in enterprise cloud network. Therefore, our research, to the best of our knowledge, is the first attempt to look at the user side in enterprise cloud services by implementing different secure network solutions.

Narayan, Brooking, and Vere (2009) evaluate the VPN performance by implementing IPSec, PPTP and SSL on three different operating systems such as Windows Vista, Windows Server 2003 and Linux Fedora Core 6. Kotuliak, Rybár, and Trúchly (2011) evaluate the VPN performance on two computers running the Linux Debian Operating System with IPSec and SSL. These two studies mainly focus on performance evaluation by creating different VPNs using operating system(s). This means that their experiments are conducted at the operating system level, whereas our work is undertaken at the router level, especially using Cisco routers and in the cloud environment. Therefore our research is a new attempt in the field of secure network solutions and their comparisons.

Gou and Liu (2012) examined dynamic IPsec VPN architecture for private cloud services. Liao and Su (2011) looked at a dynamic VPN architecture for private cloud computing. Hiroaki et al (2010) explored dynamic IP-VPN architecture for cloud computing. Although these three papers discuss the dynamic VPN in the cloud, they mainly pay attention to the dynamic VPN architecture in the cloud environment. In contrast, our research focuses on secure network solutions for enterprise cloud services.

To sum up, to the best of our knowledge, our research appears to be the first attempt to look at the secure network solutions for enterprise cloud services. More specifically, we evaluated three different VPN solutions in the enterprise cloud environment by implementing the VPN protocols on Cisco routers. The evaluation focused on the user experience on both cloud users and cloud implementers.

FUTURE RESEARCH DIRECTIONS

This chapter discussed the popular secure network solutions for enterprise cloud services. The discussions and the experiments provided in this chapter present an early stage of our research into secure network solutions for enterprise cloud services. Further research will focus on two possible directions based on this study:

- Secure network performance evaluation for enterprise cloud services,
- VPN as a Service for enterprise cloud services.

In what follows, we expound each of these areas in some detail.

There are a number of VPN protocols such as PPTP, L2TP, MPLS, GRE, IPsec, and TLS/SSL currently used to develop VPN networks (Lewis, 2006). Selecting the most appropriate solution(s) for the enterprise cloud network can provide enormous challenges to the network designer. Thus it is important to investigate the performance distinctions such as bandwidth utilization, latency between different VPN solutions in enterprise cloud network. The outcomes of this future work might provide some experimental reference for cloud network designers and implementers.

VPN as a Service is one of the subsets of the Network as a service (NaaS). NaaS is one of the latest cloud services (Costa, et al., 2012).NaaS brings huge attraction to the enterprises and industries nowadays because it limits the cost of data communications for the cloud consumers as well as improves network flexibility. It is important to thoroughly investigate the benefits and shortcomings of NaaS, taking into account the influence and impact on enterprise network as well as the security issues. This might improve the understanding of NaaS in terms of the demands of an enterprise cloud computing network.

CONCLUSION

After reviewing cloud computing and cloud services and their relationships, this chapter examined the secure network solutions for enterprise cloud services. A test bed environment was developed by utilizing different open software and tools for the purpose of experiencing the distinction of each solution. An inter-cloud network architecture was proposed which demonstrated the process of the experiments. The experiment shows that a PPTP VPN solution is easier and simpler than IPSec VPN solution and SSL/TLS VPN solution in deployment. However, SSL/TLS VPN solution is more user-friendly than PPTP VPN solution and IPSec VPN solution based on our experiment. This chapter also looked at one of the popular secure network solutions by using VPN technologies for securing the cloud connections between cloud consumers and the cloud network.This provides experimental reference of secure network solution deployment to the cloud network developers.

Although the experiment has reached its aim, there were some unavoidable limitations and shortcomings. First of all, the experiments only contain three different VPN solutions. A number of well-known technologies can be utilized in securing the cloud connections for the enterprise cloud services. Those technologies that did not include in this chapter will be explored in the future study. Second, the experiments were performed in the virtual test bed environment created by open source software and tools. So, the complexity of the cloud network has been minimized compared to the real cloud network environment. Therefore, the configurations might be different in a complex enterprise network if additional network techniques have been deployed. Third, the outcome and discussion were only based on the experiments and the configurations. The results purposed in this chapter could be different in various scenarios. Those results will be improved in future investigation in order to minimize the potential mistakes.

REFERENCES

Al-Masah, A. S., & Al-Sharafi, A. M. (2013). Benefits of cloud computing for network infrastructure monitoring service. *International Journal of Advances in Engineering and Technology*, 46-51.

Badger, L., Grance, T., Patt-Corner, R., & Voas, J. (2012). *Draft cloud computing synopsis and recommendations*. Gaithersburg, MD: NIST.

Bantoft, K., & Wouters, P. (2006). *Openswan building and integrating virtual private networks*. Birmingham, UK: Packt Publishing.

Barr, J., Varia, J., & Wood, M. (2006). *Amazon EC2 beta*. Retrieved November 27, 2012, from http://aws.typepad.com/aws/2006/08/amazon_ec2_beta.html

Bauer, E., & Adams, R. (2012). *Reliability and availability of cloud computing*. New York: John Wiley & Sons. doi:10.1002/9781118393994

BCS The Chartered Institute for IT. (2012). *Cloud computing: Moving IT out of the office*. Swindon, UK: British Informatics Society Limited.

Buyya, R., Broberg, J., & Goscinski, A. M. (2010). *Cloud computing principles and paradigms*. Hoboken, NJ: John Wiley & Sons, Inc.

Carr, P., May, T., & Stewart, S. (2012). *Australia's trusted infrastructure-as-a-service cloud provider market 2012*. Retrieved November 28, 2012, from http://www.longhausshop.com/reports/single-user-online-version-1.html

Carstensen, J., Morgentha, J., & Golden, B. (2012). *Cloud computing assessing the risks*. Ely: IT Governance Publishing.

Chen, S., Nepal, S., & Liu, R. (2011). Secure connectivity for intra-cloud and inter-cloud communication. In *Proceedings of International Conference on Parallel Processing Workshops* (pp. 154 - 159). Taipei, Taiwan: Elsevier.

Chou, W. (2002). Inside SSL: The secure sockets layer protocol. *IT Professional*, 4(4), 47–52. doi:10.1109/MITP.2002.1046644

Cisco. (2003). *Designing VPN security*. Cisco Press.

Cisco. (2007). *Cisco router and security device manager*. Retrieved July 30, 2013, from http://www.cisco.com/en/US/prod/collateral/routers/ps5318/product_data_sheet0900aecd800fd118.html

Cisco. (2012). *SSL VPN configuration guide* (Cisco IOS release 15M&T). Cisco Press.

Cohen, R., & Kaempfer, G. (2000). On the cost of virtual private networks. *IEEE/ACM Transactions on Networking*, 8(6), 775–784. doi:10.1109/90.893873

Costa, P., Migliavacca, M., Pietzuch, P., & Wolf, A. L. (2012). NaaS: Network-as-a-service in the cloud. In *Proceedings of the 2nd USENIX Conference on Hot Topics in Management of Internet, Cloud, and Enterprise Networks and Services, Hot-ICE*. Berkeley, CA: USENIX Association.

Davies, J. (2011). *Implementing SSL / TLS using cryptography and PKI*. Hoboken, NJ: John Wiley & Sons.

Dayananda, S. M., & Kumar, A. (2012). Architecture for inter-cloud services using IPSec VPN. In *Proceedings of Advanced Computing & Communication Technologies (ACCT), 2012 Second International Conference* (pp. 463-467). Rohtak: IEEE Computer Society.

Dierks, T., & Rescorla, E. (2008). *The transport layer security (TLS) protocol version 1.2*. Retrieved June 18, 2013, from http://datatracker.ietf.org/doc/rfc5246/?include_text=1

Ferguson, B. (2012). *CompTIA network+ review guide exam: N10-005*. Hoboken, NJ: John Wiley & Sons.

Finn, A., Vredevoort, H., Lownds, P., & Flynn, D. (2012). *Microsoft private cloud computing*. Hoboken, NJ: John Wiley & Sons.

Focus Group. (2012). *Focus group on cloud computing technical report part 1*. Geneva: International Telecommunication Union.

Fortinet. (2013). *FortiOS™ handbook SSL VPN for FortiOS 5.0*. Fortinet.

Gentry, P. B. (2001). What is a VPN? *Information Security Technical Report*, *6*(1), 15–22. doi:10.1016/S1363-4127(01)00103-0

Gleeson, B., Lin, A., Heinanen, J., Armitage, G., & Malis, A. (2000). *A framework for IP based virtual private networks*. Retrieved March 26, 2013, from http://www.rfc-editor.org/rfc/rfc2764.txt

GNS3. (2013). *What is GNS3?* Retrieved June 5, 2013, from http://www.gns3.net/

Goldreich, O. (2004). Foundations of cryptography: Volume 2, basic applications. Cambridge, UK: Cambridge University Press.

Gou, Q.-D., & Liu, Y.-H. (2012). Dynamic IPsec VPN architecture for private cloud services. In *Proceedings of 2012 International Conference on Wavelet Active Media Technology and Information Processing* (pp. 250-253). Sichuan, Canada: IEEE Xplore.

Gupta, P., & Verma, A. (2012). Concept of VPN on cloud computing for elasticity by simple load balancing technique. *International Journal of Engineering and Innovative Technology*, 274-278.

Halpert, B. (2011). *Auditing cloud computing a security and privacy guide*. Toronto, Canada: John Wiley & Sons, Inc. doi:10.1002/9781118269091

Hamzeh, K., Pall, G. S., Verthein, W., Taarud, J., Little, W. A., & Zorn, G. (1999). *Point-to-point tunneling protocol (PPTP)*. The Internet Society.

Hao, F., Lakshman, T. V., Mukherjee, S., & Song, H. (2010). Secure cloud computing with a virtualized network infrastructure. In *Proceedings of 2nd USENIX Conference on Hot Topics in Cloud Computing* (pp. 16-16). Boston, MA: USENIX.

Harding, C. (2011). *Cloud computing for business -The open group guide. Zaltbommel*. Van Haren Publishing.

Hata, H., Kamizuru, Y., Honda, A., Hashimoto, T., Shimizu, K., & Yao, H. (2010). Dynamic IP-VPN architecture for cloud computing. In *Proceedings of 8th Asia-Pacific Symposium on Information and Telecommunication Technologies* (pp. 1-5). Kuching: NTT Communications.

Hurwitz, J., Kaufman, M., Halper, F., & Kirsch, D. (2012). *Hybrid cloud for dummies*. Hoboken, NJ: John Wiley & Sons.

Ioannidis, J. (2011). IPsec. In H. C. Tilborg, & S. Jajodia (Eds.), *Encyclopedia of cryptography and security* (pp. 635–638). New York: Springer US.

Jaha, A. A., Shatwan, F. B., & Ashibani, M. (2008). Proper virtual private network (VPN) solution. In *Proceedings of the Second International Conference on Next Generation Mobile Applications, Services and Technologies* (pp. 309-314). IEEE Computer Society.

Jamil, D., & Zaki, H. (2011). Cloud computing security. *International Journal of Engineering Science and Technology*, *3*, 4.

Joshi, J. (2008). *Network security*. Burlington, MA: Elsevier.

Khmelevsky, Y., & Voytenko, V. (2010). Cloud computing infrastructure prototype for university education and research. In *Proceedings of the 15th Western Canadian Conference on Computing Education*. Kelowna: WCCCE.

Kommalapati, H. (2010). *Windows Azure for enterprises*. Retrieved November 28, 2012, from http://msdn.microsoft.com/en-us/magazine/ee309870.aspx

Kotuliak, I., Rybár, P., & Trúchly, P. (2011). Performance comparison of IPsec and TLS based VPN technologies. In *Proceedings of 9th International Conference on Emerging eLearning Technologies and Applications* (pp. 217-221). IEEE.

Lewis, M. (2006). *Comparing, designing, and deploying VPNs*. Cisco Press.

Liao, W., & Su, S. (2011). A dynamic VPN architecture for private cloud computing. In *Proceedings of 4th IEEE/ACM International Conference on Cloud and Utility Computing* (pp. 409-414). Melbourne, Australia: IEEE.

Malik, S. (2002). *Network security principles and practices*. Cisco Press.

Mell, P., & Grance, T. (2011). *The NIST definition of cloud computing*. Washington, DC: National Institute of Standards and Technology.

Narayan, S., Brooking, K., & Vere, S. D. (2009). Network performance analysis of VPN protocols: An empirical comparison on different operating systems. In *Proceedings of 2009 International Conference on Networks Security, Wireless Communications and Trusted Computing*. IEEE Computer Society.

Oppliger, R. (2009). *SSL and TLS: Theory and practice*. Norwood, NJ: Artech House.

Oracle Corporation. (2009). *Documentation*. Retrieved June 5, 2013, from https://www.virtualbox.org/wiki/Documentation

Park, K.-W., & Park, K. H. (2011). ACCENT: Cognitive cryptography plugged compression for SSL/TLS-based cloud computing services. *ACM Transactions on Internet Technology, 11*(2), 1–30. doi:10.1145/2049656.2049659

RFC. (2012). *RFC editor*. Retrieved Nov 15, 2013, from http://www.rfc-editor.org/

Ried, S. (2011). *Sizing the cloud*. Washington, DC: Forrester.

Rouse, M. (2009). *Storage as a service (SaaS)*. Retrieved July 11, 2013, from http://searchstorage.techtarget.com/definition/Storage-as-a-Service-SaaS

Rouse, M. (2011). *Cloud services*. Retrieved July 03, 2013, from http://searchcloudprovider.techtarget.com/definition/cloud-services

Shan, T. (2009). *Cloud taxonomy and ontology*. Retrieved August 1, 2013, from http://tonyshan.ulitzer.com/node/1469454

Sitaram, D., & Manjunath, G. (2011). *Moving to the cloud developing apps in the new world of cloud computing*. Burlington, MA: Elsevier Science.

Sosinsky, B. (2010). *Cloud computing bible*. Hoboken, NJ: John Wiley & Sons.

Steinberg, J., & Speed, T. (2005). *SSL VPN understanding, evaluating and planning secure, web-based remote access*. Birmingham, AL: Packt Publishing.

Stewart, J. M., & Chapple, M. (2011). *CISSP certified information systems security professional study guide*. Hoboken, NJ: John Wiley & Sons.

Strachey, C. (1959). Time sharing in large fast computers. In *Proceedings of International Conference on Information Processing Congress* (pp. 336–341). Paris: UNESCO.

Strebe, M. (2006). *Network security foundations: Technology fundamentals for IT success*. Hoboken, NJ: John Wiley & Sons, Inc.

Thomas, P. Y. (2012). Harnessing the potential of cloud computing to transform higher education. In L. Chao (Ed.), *Cloud computing for teaching and learning strategies for design and implementation* (pp. 147–158). Hershey, PA: IGI Global. doi:10.4018/978-1-4666-0957-0.ch010

Venkateswaran, R. (2001). Virtual private networks. *IEEE Potentials, (1)*, 11-15.

Vidyarthi, N. (2010). *Opinion: Will Google's smart TV finally bring apps and web browsing to the living room?* Retrieved August 09, 2013, from http://socialtimes.com/opinion-will-googles-smart-tv-finally-bring-apps-and-Web-browsing-to-the-living-room_b13046

VirtualBox. (2009). *Welcome to VirtualBox. org.* Retrieved June 5, 2013, from https://www. virtualbox.org/

Weaver, A. C. (2006). Secure sockets layer. *Computer*, 88–90. doi:10.1109/MC.2006.138

Williams, A. (2009). *The feds, not forrester, are developing better definitions for cloud computing.* Retrieved July 03, 2013, from http://readwrite.com/2009/10/13/forrrester-says-we-need-better#awesm=~oav2lHYSPRCOcG

Wood, T., Ramakrishnan, K. K., Shenoy, P., & Merwe, J. V. (2012). Enterprise-ready virtual cloud pools: Vision, opportunities and challenges. In *Special focus on security and performance of networks and clouds* (pp. 995–1004). Academic Press. doi:10.1093/comjnl/bxs060

Yang, B., Tan, F., Dai, Y.-S., & Guo, S. (2009). Performance evaluation of cloud service considering fault recovery. In M. G. Jaatun, G. Zhao, & C. Rong (Eds.), *Cloud computing* (pp. 571–576). Berlin: Springer. doi:10.1007/978-3-642-10665-1_54

Younglove, R. W. (2000). Virtual private networks - How they work. *Computing & Control Engineering Journal*, *11*(6), 260–262. doi:10.1049/cce:20000602

ADDITIONAL READING

Chang, W. Y., Abu-Amara, H., & Sanford, J. F. (2010). Transforming enterprise cloud services. Dordrecht: Springer Science+Business Media B.V.

Chee, B. J., & Jr., C. F. (2010). *Cloud computing: Technologies and strategies of the ubiquitous data center.* USA: CRC Press.

Chorafas, D. N. (2010). *Cloud computing strategies.* Hoboken: CRC Press. doi:10.1201/9781439834541

Csico System. (2004). *Comparing MPLS-based VPNs, IPSec-based VPNs, and a combined approach* Retrieved April 19, 2013, from http://www.cisco.com/warp/public/cc/so/neso/vpn/vpnsp/solmk_wp.pdf

Dasgupta, D., & Rahman, M. (2011). Estimating security coverage for cloud services. 2011 IEEE Third International *Conference on Privacy, Security, Risk and Trust and 2011 IEEE Third International Conference on Social Computing* (pp. 1064-1071). Boston: IEEE Xplore.

Deal, R. (2005). *The complete Cisco VPN configuration guide.* USA: Cisco Press.

Feilner, M. (2006). *OpenVPN building and integrating virtual private networks.* Birmingham: Packt Publishing.

Ferguson, N., Schneier, B., & Kohno, T. (2012). *Cryptography engineering: Design principles and practical applications.* Canada: WILEY.

Furht, B., & Escalante, A. (2010). *Handbook of cloud computing.* New York: Springer. doi:10.1007/978-1-4419-6524-0

Hartpence, B. (2011). *Packet guide to routing and switching.* Sebastopol: O'Reilly Media.

Head, M. R., Sailer, A., Shaikh, H., & Shea, D. G. (2010). Towards self-assisted troubleshooting for the deployment of private clouds. *2010 IEEE 3rd International Conference on Cloud Computing* (pp. 156-163). Miami: IEEE.

Held, G. (2004). *Virtual private networking: A construction, operation and utilization guide.* Chichester: John Wiley & Sons, Ltd. doi:10.1002/0470020342

Hoang, T.-T.-M. (2012). *Computer networks, the Internet and next generation networks: A protocol-based and architecture-based perspective.* Frankfurt: Lang, Peter, GmbH, Internationaler Verlag der Wissenschaften.

Ivanov, I., Sinderen, M. v., & Shishkov, B. (2012). *Cloud computing and services science.* New York, NY: Springer New York. doi:10.1007/978-1-4614-2326-3

Jennings, R. (2009). *Cloud computing with the windows azure platform.* Hoboken: John Wiley & Sons, Inc.

Krutz, R. L., & Vines, R. D. (2010). *Cloud security a comprehensive guide to secure cloud computing.* Hoboken: John Wiley & Sons.

Mather, T., Kumaraswamy, S., & Latif, S. (2009). *Cloud security and privacy an enterprise perspective on risks and compliance.* Sebastopol: O'Reilly Media, Inc.

McDonald, K. T. (2010). *Above the clouds: Managing risk in the world of cloud computing.* Ely: IT Governance Publishing.

McGrath, M. (2012). *Understanding PaaS.* Sebastopol: O'Reilly Media.

Miller, M. (2009). *Cloud computing: Web-based applications that change the way you work and collaborate online.* USA: Que Publishing.

Newcombe, L. (2012). *Securing cloud services a pragmatic approach to security architecture in the cloud.* Ely: IT Governance Publishing.

Oki, E., Rojas-Cessa, R., Tatipamula, M., & Vogt, C. (2012). *Advanced Internet protocols, services, and applications.* Hoboken: John Wiley & Sons. doi:10.1002/9781118180822

Raj, P. (2013). *Cloud enterprise architecture.* USA: CRC Press.

Shroff, G. (2010). *Enterprise cloud computing: Technology, architecture, applications.* New York: Cambridge University Press. doi:10.1017/CBO9780511778476

Tang, L., Dong, J., Zhao, Y., & Zhang, L.-J. (2010). Enterprise cloud service architecture. Cloud Computing (CLOUD) (pp. 27 - 34). USA: IEEEXplore.

Yuricik, W., & Doss, D. (2001). A planning framework for implementing virtual private networks. [USA: IEEEXplore.]. *IT Professional, 3*(3), 41–44. doi:10.1109/6294.939974

KEY ITEMS AND DEFINITIONS

Cloud Computing: It refers to applications and services that run on a distributed network using virtualized resources and accessed via a computer network such as Internet.

Enterprise Cloud: It is the cloud that provides private access and is controlled by either a single enterprise or consortium of businesses.

Internet Protocol Security (IPSec): It is a collection of protocols, conventions, and mechanisms used for ensure the authenticity and guarantee the confidentiality of the content of the IP packets. It operates at the Network layer (Layer 3) of the OSI model.

Point-to-Point Tunneling Protocol (PPTP): It is one of the most popular dial-in protocols operates at the Data Link layer (Layer 2) of the OSI model.

Private Cloud: Cloud infrastructures are controlled solely for a single organization. Cloud infrastructures can be managed internally or by a third-party and hosted internally or externally.

Public Cloud: Cloud infrastructure is open for public use and it can be owned, managed, operated by an organization.

Secure Sockets Layer/Transport Layer Security (SSL/TLS): It is one of the most popular protocols provides communication security over the Internet. It has been classified as one of the Transport Layer Protocols (Layer 4) according to the OSI model.

Security: It refers to a broad set of policies, technologies, and controls implemented to protect data, applications and infrastructure.

Software as a Service (SaaS): It is one of the most important cloud services that makes the application software available to the cloud customers.

Virtual Private Network (VPN): One of the most popular solutions in establishing a connection though a public network utilizing encryption technology to privatize data for transmission between two trusted parties.

Chapter 11
A Practical Approach to Enhancement of Accuracy of Similarity Model Using WordNet towards Semantic Service Discovery

Chellammal Surianarayanan
Bharathidasan University, India

Gopinath Ganapathy
Bharathidasan University, India

Manikandan Sethunarayanan Ramasamy
Bharathidasan University Constituent College, India

ABSTRACT

Semantic Web service discovery provides high retrieval accuracy. However, it imposes an implicit constraint to service clients that the clients must express their queries with the same domain ontologies as used by the service providers. Fulfilling this criterion is very tedious. Hence, a WordNet (general ontology)-based similarity model is proposed for service discovery, and its accuracy is enhanced to a level comparable to the accuracy of computing similarity using service specific ontologies. This is done by optimizing similarity threshold, which refers to a minimum similarity that is required to decide whether a given pair of services is similar or not. The proposed model is implemented and results are presented. The approach warrants clients to express their queries without specifying any ontology and alleviates the problem of maintaining complex domain ontologies. Moreover, the computation time of WordNet-based model is very low when compared to specific ontology-based model.

DOI: 10.4018/978-1-4666-5884-4.ch011

INTRODUCTION

Automation in service discovery is an inevitable requirement of applications which have service composition in real time. Very frequently complex business applications are fulfilled by discovering and combining several services from different domains in a relatively short time. The central requirement of service composition is automatic service discovery with high retrieval accuracy and low computation time. Conventional Universal Description, Discovery and Integration (UDDI) based discovery is keyword based (Sohali & Zamanifar, 2009) and it does not support automatic discovery. Web Service Description Language (WSDL) based discovery has no explicit semantics and limits the discovery to manual methods (Sivashanmugam, Miller, Sheth, & Verma, 2005), Syeda-Mahmood, Shah, Akkiraju, Ivan, & Goodwin, 2005). Semantic service description languages such as (Guo, Le, & Xia, 2005), (Klusch & Kaufer, 2009), (Kopecky, Vitvar, Bournez, & Farrell, 2007) allow service providers to express their intended semantics using formal concepts in ontologies. The formal semantics of services makes services machine interpretable which leads to automatic discovery without human intervention.

Though semantic service discovery brought high accuracy and maximal automation into service discovery (Sycara, Paolucci, Ankolekar, & Srinivasan, 2003), it suffers from the following serious issues. Firstly, semantic service discovery imposes an implicit constraint that while querying, service clients should express their requirements using the same domain ontologies as used by the service providers. In practice service providers may develop their own domain ontologies to express their semantics but for service clients it is very different to express their queries using the same ontologies. Moreover, in Business to Consumer (B2C) environment, the service clients are human users and they are not very clear about even what they need and most of the times they are

unable to express their requirements in the same ontology as that of advertisement (Gopinath & Chellammal, 2010). Secondly, the creation and maintenance of domain ontologies are costly and require special expertise. Thirdly, semantic service discovery is time consuming (Lv, Zhou, & Cao, 2009), (Mokhtar, Kaul, Georgantas, & Issarny, 2006).

To alleviate the above issues we propose a new model for computing similarity between services using WordNet, a generic ontology with a special focus to enhance the accuracy of WordNet based similarity model to a level comparable to the accuracy achieved with similarity based on service specific ontologies. Comparing the efficiency of WordNet (generic approach) based similarity computation against similarity computation based on service specific ontologies is an important issue and existing literature has given little focus to address this issue. The proposed approach is supported by the following aspects.

The functional characteristics of a service are expressed through its input and output parameters. While finding matched services for a given query, the input and output parameters of services are the chief factors in deciding whether a query and an advertised service are similar. With a detailed survey on service descriptions, it is found that service providers tend to give meaningful English words such as *Author, Price, Book, Publication, Title, Film, ComedyFilm, RecommendedPrice, TaxedPrice, PreparedFood, Destination, Hospital, Hotel, WheeledCar, Duration, University, Lecturer_In_Academia, Postal_Address,* etc., to name the parameters. Almost each service tends to use meaningful words to name the parameters. As long as the input and output parameters of services are named using meaningful English words, WordNet, a generic ontology(rather than service specific ontologies), may be used to find the semantic similarity between words. WordNet (Miller, Beckwith, Fellbaum, Gross, & Miller 1990) is a lexical database for English which groups nouns, verbs, adverbs and adjectives into *synsets* through various semantic relations such as hypernyms, hyponyms, meronyms, troponyms, antonyms, etc. WordNet groups words into synsets by meaning or semantic similarity. It is proposed to use this semantic similarity in WordNet for finding similarity among Web services.

The main objectives of this work is to propose a method of computing similarity between services using WordNet ontology and to enhance the accuracy of the proposed model to a level comparable to the accuracy of similarity computation using the semantics of services expressed in specific ontologies (.owl files). So, the proposed model can replace the specific ontology based model. In the proposed approach, a parameter called *similarity threshold* is defined to represent a minimum similarity score that should exist between two services to infer those services as similar services. The accuracy of the proposed model is enhanced by adjusting this parameter. Appropriate value for this parameter is empirically arrived and recommended. For simplicity, we denote the proposed method of computing similarity among services using WordNet ontology as *WordNet Model* and method of computing similarity among services using service specific ontologies as *Service Specific Ontology Model*. With this approach, the service clients are assured to express their queries without specifying any ontology. Employing WordNet for finding similarity alleviates the problem of maintaining complex domain ontologies. The computation time of the proposed approach is very low when compared to that of Service Specific Ontology Model. The above features make the method more applicable to real time service based applications.

Literature related to the proposed theme of research are reviewed and discussed as follows. WordNet ontology is primarily used for expanding queries and extending Vector Space Model(VSM) during service matching. To handle the inadequacy of VSM which considers words only at syntactic level, the method (Kokash, 2006) expands the query and concept descriptions in WSDL using

their synonyms from WordNet. However, the experimentation of (Kokash, 2006) shows that the use of WordNet in query expansion did not help much to improve the precision or recall of service matching. To avoid excessive sparsity of feature vector that arises while expanding a query, a novel WordNet powered feature vector extraction is presented in (Chen, Yang, Wang, & Zhang, 2010). Though this method reduces the dimension and sparsity of feature vectors, it achieves only 2% increase in precision when compared to VSM model. Another approach presented in (Nayak & Lee, 2007) transforms WSDL services into a richer semantic representation language, Web Ontology Language for Services (OWL-S) and it enhances the semantics of the terms of WSDL and OWL-S using their synonyms from WordNet. Similarly the approach (Chukmol, Benharkat, & Amghar, 2008) presents a collaborative tagging-based environment for service discovery. In this approach, users are allowed to tag or annotate a service with a keyword or a tag for which synonym sets are obtained using WordNet. Another method (Wu & Wu, 2005) classifies the properties of services into four types, namely, Common Properties, Service Properties, Service Interface and Quality of Service (QoS) and uses WordNet and HowNet powered similarity measure to find similarity of strings which describe the Common Properties such as service name, service key, service description, service owner, etc. A suite of methods, namely, WordNet-powered VSM, WSDL structure matching, similarity among WSDL terms based on semantic distance in WordNet (called semantic structure matching), a combination of WordNet-powered VSM and semantic structure matching are discussed for service discovery in (Stroulia & Wang, 2005) and among the four methods, combination of WordNet-powered VSM and semantic structure matching is found to be more precise.

There are some methods which use WordNet semantic similarity for service discovery. A technique that combines WordNet with WSDL is presented in (Ren, Chen, Xiao, Song, & Li, 2008) for service composition. In this method, senses of parameter names from WSDL services are obtained from WordNet and the senses are expanded using synonyms, hyponyms, hypernyms, meronyms and holonyms. In another work (Karimpour & Taghiyareh, 2009), the *message* parts of WSDL are annotated with synsets from WordNet and matched services for a given query are discovered using different WordNet similarities. WordNet similarity proposed by Claudia & Martin(1998) is used in (Qu, Sun, Li, Liu, & Lin, 2009) to cluster similar services. Though the methods (Ren et al., 2008), (Karimpour & Taghiyareh, 2009), (Qu et al., 2009) use WordNet similarity for finding similarity among services, they did not address comparing the efficiency of WordNet Model with Service Specific Ontology Model. Further, they did not study the impact of similarity threshold on the accuracy of similarity computation.

In this work, we fix a minimum similarity called *similarity threshold* while finding similarity between any two services. Two services will be considered as similar only when similarity score between them is at least the similarity threshold. We analyze the impact of similarity threshold on accuracy of WordNet Model. We enhance the accuracy of WordNet Model to a level comparable to that of Service Specific Ontology Model by optimizing the value of similarity threshold so that WordNet Model can well be applied in service composition based applications instead of Service Specific Ontology Model in which creation and maintenance of domain ontologies is costly and needs special expertise.

The chapter is organized as follows. Section 1 presents the practical issues with the method of finding similarity among services using service specific ontologies and introduces a more practical model, WordNet ontology based model for finding similarity among services. Further, literature related to the proposed theme is reviewed and discussed. Section 2 describes the proposed

similarity models, namely, WordNet Model and Service Specific Ontology Model in detail. Section 3 describes the experimentation carried out to test the proposed models with a typical test collection. Section 4 presents the discussion on the results obtained and Section 5 concludes the chapter.

SIMILARITY MODELS

As the functional characteristics of a service are mainly expressed using input and output parameters, the similarity between any two services say, A and B denoted by $Sim(A, B)$ is computed as the average of input and output similarities between A and B as given in

$$Sim(A, B) = 0.5 \times (InputSim(A, B) + OutputSim(A, B)) \qquad (1)$$

In Equation (1), $InputSim(A, B)$ refers to input similarity between A and B which is computed from the individual similarity values of all input parameters of A with respect to each input parameter of B. $OutputSim(A, B)$ refers to output similarity between A and B which is computed from the individual similarity values of all output parameters of A with respect to each output parameter of B. The computation of $InputSim(A, B)$ is similar to that of $OutputSim(A, B)$. The computation of $OutputSim(A, B)$ according to WordNet Model and the Standard Service Specific Ontology Model is discussed as follows.

WordNet Model

Let us consider two services A and B. Let m and n denote the number of output parameters of A and B respectively. Let $p_1^a, p_2^a, ..., p_m^a$ denote the *1st, 2nd, 3rd, ..., mth* output parameters of service A. Let $p_1^b, p_2^b, ..., p_n^b$ denote the *1st, 2nd, 3rd, ..., nth* output parameters of service B. The output parameters of A and B are given in Figure 1.

Figure 1. Output parameters of service A and B

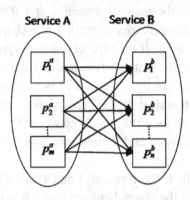

The output similarity among A and B denoted by *OutputSim(A, B)* is computed using

$$OutputSim(A,B) =$$
$$\frac{1}{m}\sum_i \max\{paramSim(p_i^a, p_j^b) \big| j = 1,2,...,n\}$$
(2)

In Equation (2), $paramSim(p_i^a, p_j^b)$ denote the similarity between i^{th} output parameter of service A and j^{th} output parameter of service B. The computation of similarity between any two parameters whether inputs or outputs is same and it is given as follows.

With an investigation of service description files, it is found that the names of parameters generally consist of single meaningful words such as *author, price, title, book, film, cola, coffee, destination, hotel, address, researcher, food, photograph, icon, drinks, dvd, vhs, funding*, etc. Also, sometimes, the names of parameters are composed of more than one word as in, *taxedprice, recommendedpriceindollar, preparedfood, academic_support_staff, comedyfilm, postaladdress, professor_in_academia*, etc.

Let us consider two parameters A and B. Let l and k denote the number of words of A and B respectively. Let $w_1^a, w_2^a, ..., w_l^a$ denote the *1st, 2nd, 3rd, ..., l^{th}* words of parameter A. Let $w_1^b, w_2^b, ..., w_k^b$ denote the *1st, 2nd, 3rd, ..., k^{th}* words

of parameter B. The similarity between any two parameters A and B, *paramSim(A, B)* is computed using

$$paramSim(A,B) =$$
$$\frac{1}{l}\sum_l \max\{wordSim(w_l^a, w_j^b) \big| j = 1,2,...,k\}$$
(3)

In Equation (3) $wordSim(w_l^a, w_j^b)$ denotes the similarity between l^{th} word of parameter A and j^{th} word of parameter B. In general, the similarity between any two words A and B is computed using WordNet based semantic similarity. There are two types of WordNet similarity measures, namely, information content based measures proposed by Jiang & Conrath (1997), Lin (1998), Resnik(1999) and path length based measures proposed by Banerjee & Pedersen (2002), Leacock & Chodorow (1998), Wu & Palmer(1994). In our work, Wu-Palmer similarity measure (Wu & Palmer, 1994) is chosen for finding similarity between words as it is faster than the other methods (Karimpour & Taghiyareh, 2009).

Let us consider two words A and B. Let r and t denote the number of senses of A and B respectively. Let $s_1^a, s_2^a, ..., s_r^a$ denote the *1st, 2nd, 3rd, ..., r^{th}* senses of word A. Let $s_1^b, s_2^b, ..., s_t^b$ denote the *1st, 2nd, 3rd, ..., t^{th}* senses of word B. Now, the similarity between the words A and B is computed using

$$wordSim(A,B) =$$
$$\frac{1}{r}\sum_r \max\{WuPalmerSim(s_r^a, s_j^b) \big| j = 1,2,...,t\}$$
(4)

In Equation (4) $WuPalmerSim(s_r^a, s_t^b)$ denote the similarity between r^{th} synset/sense of word A and t^{th} synset/sense of word B. Similarity between two synsets, say A and B is computed using

$$WuPalmerSim(A, B) =$$
$$2 \times depth(LCS) \, / \, (depth(A) + depth(B))$$

$$(5)$$

In Equation (5) *depth(LCS)* denotes the depth of Least Common Subsumer of synset *A* and synset *B*, *depth(A)* denotes the depth of synset *A* and *depth(B)* denotes the depth of synset *B*. Here, depth of a synset refers to the distance of the synset to the root.

Service Specific Ontology Model

In this model, services are assumed to be described using OWL-S ('.owls' files) with their semantics described using specific ontologies ('.owl' files). The similarity between any two services *A* and *B* is computed using (1). The computation of *InputSim(A, B)* is similar to *OutputSim(A, B)* which is computed using

$$OutputSim(A, B) =$$
$$\frac{1}{m} \sum_i \max\{DoM(p_i^a, p_j^b) \big| j = 1, 2, ..., n\}$$

$$(6)$$

In Equation (6) $DoM(p_i^a, p_j^b)$ denotes the Degree of Match between i^{th} output parameter of service *A* and j^{th} output parameter of service *B*. The *DoM* between two parameters, say, *A* and *B* is computed as follows. Let the parameter *A* be a concept *Novel* described in *books* ontology as http://127.0.0.1/ontology/books.owl#Novel. Let the parameter *B* be a concept *Book* described in the same *books* ontology as, http://127.0.0.1/ontology/books.owl#Book. Now, the value of *DoM* between *A* and *B* is computed using the following semantic relationships. Also, a similarity score ranging from 0 to 1 is assigned to the *DoM* based on the semantic relationship.

- **Exact:** If the type of both *A* and *B* are same, then the match between *A* and *B* is *exact* and a similarity score of 1 is assigned.
- **Plug-In:** If the type of *A* is sub type of *B*, then the match between *A* and *B* is *plug-in*. A similarity score of 0.75 is assigned.
- **Subsumes:** If the type of *B* is sub type of *A*, then the match between *A* and *B* is *subsumes* and a similarity score of 0.5 is assigned.
- **Fail:** If the types of *A* and *B* are different, then the match between *A* and *B* is *fail* and a similarity score of 0 is assigned.

The Service Specific Ontology Model is used as a standard or reference while enhancing the accuracy of WordNet Model.

EXPERIMENTATION

There are two objectives of experimentation. The first objective is to compute the precision of Word-Net Model and Service Specific Ontology Model for various queries by varying similarity threshold and analyze the results. Based on the analysis, an appropriate value for similarity threshold has to be recommended. The second objective is to find the time taken by both the models for various queries and compare the results. Towards these objectives, the proposed similarity models are implemented using the experimental set up given in Figure 2.

The WordNet Model is implemented using Pederson Similarity Library(Pederson, Patwardhan, & Michelizzi, 2004), WordNet QueryData API and WordNet. The Service Specific Ontology Model is implemented using OWL-S API which consists of in-built Pellet reasoner. The reasoner is used to find various semantic relations, namely, equivalent, plug-in, subsumes and fail among the parameters of concerned services. The models are tested on a Laptop with Intel Pentium(R) Dual-Core, 2.20GHz CPU, 3.0 GB

Figure 2. Experimental setup

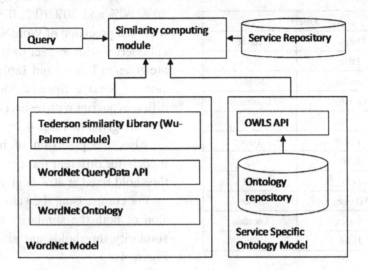

memory and Windows 7 Ultimate Operating System. A test collection of 100 services from different domains such as communication, medical, education, food, travel, and film has been prepared using *OWL-S Service Retrieval TC, Version 3.0.* The test collection includes a variety of services such as services having one output and one input (most common type), services having two inputs, services having two outputs, services having only inputs, services having only outputs and services with parameters containing short words or acronyms. The test collection is given in Appendix 1 for reference.

The performance of the models is evaluated using precision and recall. For a query, let P_w and P_o denote the precision of WordNet and Service Specific Ontology Models respectively. For a query, let R_w and R_o denote the recall of WordNet and Service Specific Ontology Models respectively. Further, for a query let N_{rr}^w and N_r^w denote the number of relevant services retrieved and the number of services retrieved using Word-Net Model. Similarly, for a query let N_{rr}^o and N_r^o denote the number of relevant services retrieved and the number of services retrieved using Service Specific Ontology Model. For a query,

let N_{tr} denote the actual number of relevant services present in the test collection. The values of P_w, R_w, P_o and R_o are computed using

$$P_w = \frac{N_{rr}^w}{N_r^w} \tag{7}$$

$$R_w = \frac{N_{rr}^w}{N_{tr}} \tag{8}$$

$$P_o = \frac{N_{rr}^o}{N_r^o} \tag{9}$$

$$R_o = \frac{N_{rr}^o}{N_{tr}} \tag{10}$$

Different queries are chosen as test queries. The query IDs, inputs and outputs of test queries are given in Table 1.

The similarity between two services given by (1) ranges from 0 to 1. We assign a minimum value for similarity between services called *similarity threshold*. A service will be considered

Table 1. Test queries

Query ID	Query	
	Output	Input
1	Price	Book
2	Funding	Missile
3	Lecturer	University
4	Drinks	Price
5	Author	book
6	Film	Title
7	Vhs	Titl
8	Whiskey	Price
9	Photograph	Location
10	Hotel	City

as similar to a query only when it has similarity at least equal to the similarity threshold with the query. To study the impact of similarity threshold on the accuracy of similarity models, the values of P_w, R_w, P_o and R_o are computed for different

similarity thresholds, namely, 20%, 30%, 40%, 50%, 60% and 70% (0.2, 0.3, 0.4, 0.5, 0.6 and 0.7). The precision of WordNet Model for different queries with respect to similarity thresholds are given in Table 2 and Table 3. Also, the precision of Service Specific Ontology Model for different queries with respect to similarity thresholds are given in Table 4.

Also, the precision of both the similarity models for different test queries with similarity threshold fixed at 40% is given Figure 3.

For comparison, the values of average precision of both the similarity models for various similarity thresholds are given in Table 5 and Figure 4.

From Table 5 and Figure 4, the precision of WordNet Model is found to increase with similarity threshold and it becomes almost equal to the precision of Service Specific Ontology Model when the similarity threshold is fixed at 70%.

Table 2. Precision of WordNet Model for different queries with respect to similarity threshold (20%, 30%, 40% and 50%)

Query ID	Similarity Threshold = 20%			Similarity Threshold = 30%			Similarity Threshold=40%			Similarity Threshold=50%		
	N_r^w	N_{rr}^w	P_w	N_r^w	N_{rr}^w	P_w	N_r^w	N_{rr}^w	N_r^w	N_r^w	N_{rr}^w	P_w
1	39	3	7.69	36	3	8.33	32	3	9.38	24	3	12.5
2	22	7	31.8	18	7	38.8	7	7	100.	7	7	100.
3	22	3	13.6	13	3	23.0	18	3	16.6	13	3	23.0
4	42	7	16.6	34	7	20.5	13	7	53.8	13	7	53.8
5	37	5	13.5	30	5	16.6	22	5	22.7	6	5	83.3
6	45	12	26.6	45	12	26.6	22	12	54.5	17	12	70.5
7	30	12	40.0	30	12	40.0	22	12	54.5	17	12	70.5
8	36	7	19.4	35	7	20.0	7	7	100.	7	7	100.
9	24	2	8.33	23	2	8.70	2	2	100.	2	2	100.
10	31	4	12.9	18	4	22.2	4	4	100.	4	4	100.

Table 3. Precision of WordNet Model for different queries with respect to similarity threshold (60% and 70%)

Query ID	Similarity Threshold=60%			Similarity Threshold= 70%		
	N_r^w	N_{rr}^w	P_w	N_r^w	N_{rr}^w	P_w
1	12	3	25.00	9	3	33.33
2	7	7	100	7	7	100
3	12	3	25.00	5	3	60
4	12	7	58.33	12	7	58.33
5	6	5	83.33	5	5	100
6	16	12	75.00	16	12	75
7	16	12	75.00	16	12	75
8	7	7	100	7	7	100
9	2	2	100	2	2	100
10	4	4	100	4	4	100

Table 4. Precision of Service Specific Ontology Model for different queries with respect to similarity threshold

Query ID	Similarity Threshold=20%			Similarity Threshold=30% or 40% or 50% or 60% or 70%		
	N_r^o	N_{rr}^o	P_o	N_r^o	N_{rr}^o	P_o
1	13	3	23.0	8	3	37.5
2	7	7	100.	7	7	100.
3	8	3	37.5	5	3	60.0
4	9	7	77.7	7	7	100.
5	7	5	71.4	5	5	100.
6	16	12	75.0	16	12	75.0
7	16	12	75.0	16	12	75.0
8	7	7	100.	7	7	100.
9	6	2	33.3	2	2	100.
10	6	4	66.6	4	4	100.

Figure 3. Precision of similarity models (with similarity threshold=40%)

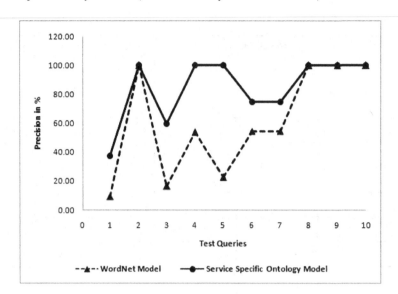

Table 5. Average precision of similarity models for various similarity thresholds

S.No.	Similarity Threshold	Average Precision in %	
		WordNet Model	Service Specific Ontology Model
1	20%	19.0	65.98
2	30%	22.5	84.75
3	40%	61.1	84.75
4	50%	71.3	84.75
5	60%	74.1	84.75
6	70%	80.1%	84.75

Figure 4. Average Precision of similarity models with respect to similarity threshold

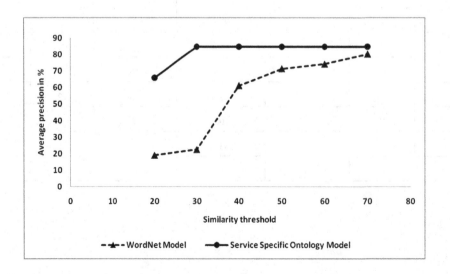

Further, regarding recall, the recall of both models is found to be 100% for all queries.

Towards the second objective two tests are carried out. The computation time of WordNet Model is affected by number of senses of words. So, an experiment is carried out to find how the computation of WordNet Model changes with respect to number of senses and the results are given in Table 6.

From Table 6, it is seen that the computation time of WordNet Model increases with increase

in number of senses. The average computation time taken by WordNet Model for matching a single parameter is found to be 608 milli seconds.

Further, the time taken by WordNet Model and Service Specific Ontology Model for performing a single service match in case of different test queries is computed and given in Table 7 and Figure 5.

From Table 7 and Figure 5, it is understood that the average computation time involved in WordNet Model (1064.2 milli seconds) is less when compared to Service Specific Ontology Model (5131.2 milli seconds).

Table 6. Computation time of WordNet Model with respect to number of senses

Number of Senses	Computation Time in Milliseconds
1	112
2	257
3	454
4	595
5	615
6	678
7	885
10	1265

Table 7. Computation time of single service match using WordNet Model and Service Specific Ontology Model

Query ID	Computation Time in Milliseconds	
	WordNet Model	Service Specific Ontology Model
1	1919	5088
2	545	5664
3	773	5568
4	1231	4944
5	1503	4848
6	1669	4848
7	1045	4800
8	987	4848
9	376	5520
10	594	5184

DISCUSSION

From Table 2 and Table 3, it is found that the precision of WordNet Model is influenced much by the value of similarity threshold. For example, consider that the similarity threshold is fixed as 20%. WordNet Model retrieves 39 services for query 1 (Output: Price and Input: Book) whereas the actual number of relevant services is only 3. While finding output similarity between the query and available services, for query-output, 'price', the WordNet Model finds exact match (price and price, in service, S_1). But the model also finds similarity score of at least or more than 0.2(or 20%) among the other output pairs, (price and book), (price and film), (price and dollar) and (price and author). Similarly, for the query-input, 'book', the model finds similarity for other input pairs (book and price), (book and university), (book and title), (book and novel), (book and publication) and (book and missile). For query 2, the model retrieves extra (irrelevant) services (15) other than expected services (7) due to the similarity among the input pairs, (missile and university) and (missile and book) for the query-input, 'missile'.

For query 3, the model detects irrelevant services due to the similarity among the output pairs, (lecturer and author) and input pairs (university and book), (university and publication)

Figure 5. Computation time taken by similarity models for single service match

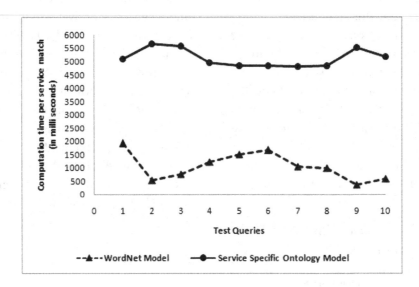

and (university and city). For query 4, the model detects extra services (35) due to similarity among the output pair (drink and food) and input pairs (price and book), (price and title) and (price and novel). Similarly, for query 5, extra services are retrieved due to the similarity among the output pairs (author and price), (author and film), (author and researcher), (author and lecturer) and (author and professor) and input pairs (book and price), (book and university), (book and missile), (book and title) and (book and publication). For query 6, the retrieval of extra services is due to the similarity among the output pairs (film and price), (film and book), (film and author), (film and videomedia), (film and dvd), (film and address) and (film and hotel) and input pairs (title and book), (title and food), (title and price) and (title and novel). For query 7, the output term 'vhs' is not found in WordNet database and WordNet Model retrieves services based on Input similarity as in query 6. For query 8, the model finds irrelevant services due to similarity among the output pair (whiskey and food) and input pairs (price and book), (price and title) and (price and novel). For query 9, the retrieval of irrelevant services is due to the similarity among the output pairs (photograph and

film), (photograph and book), (photograph and videomedia) and (photograph and hotel) and input pairs (location and person), (location and vehicle) and (location and city). For query 10, the retrieval of irrelevant services is due the similarity among the output pair (hotel and book) and input pairs (city and university), (city and location), (city and country) and (city and village).

From Table 4, it is found that with similarity threshold 0.2, the Service Specific Ontology Model detects irrelevant services (for example, for query 1, the model retrieves 13 services whereas only 3 services are relevant) due to similarity among services that have normalized plug-in score of around 0.2. Further, the precision of Service Specific Ontology Model is good when compared with WordNet Model. Because Service Specific Ontology Model uses the semantics from ontologies specific to services but WordNet Model uses semantics from the general ontology WordNet.

From Table 5, it is found that the average precision of WordNet Model with similarity threshold 20% is very less of 19.07% whereas the precision of Service Specific Ontology Model is found to be 65.98% (here the irrelevancy is due to normalized plug-in matching among services but of different domains). To improve the precision, the threshold is increased from 20% to 30%. Now, the precision of both the models is found to be increasing. With similarity thresholds 0.4, 0.5, 0.6 and 0.7 the precision of WordNet Model is significantly improved to 61.17%, 71.39%, 74.16% and 80.17% respectively. Also, with similarity thresholds, 30%, 40%, 50%, 60% and 70%, the average precision of Service Specific Ontology Model is found to be 84.75%. When we increase the similarity threshold still to 75% (0.75), the precision of WordNet and Service Specific Ontology Models is found to be 82.4% and 96.6% respectively. But with similarity threshold 75%, the recall of the models is found to decrease to 96.6%.

Further, the computation time of single service match for different queries is computed using both the models. From Table 7, the average value of time taken to complete a single service match for WordNet Model and Service Specific Ontology Model is found to be 1.06 seconds and 5.13 seconds respectively.

Ultimately in the case of Service Specific Ontology Model, though the model provides high accuracy, the model is useful only when the clients are capable of expressing their queries with specific ontologies. In practice fulfilling this requirement is very difficult. Clients tend to express their queries *Input: book; Output: Price* rather than *Input:* http://127.0.0.1/ontology/books.owl#_book; *output:* http://127.0.0.1/ontology/concept.owl#_price. This difficulty is resolved in WordNet Model where users are not required to specify any ontology while querying. WordNet Model is found to be of more practical importance and it is based on the implicit feature that parameters are named using meaningful English words. At times developers may tend to use acronyms while naming parameters as in the services S_{78} and S_{79} (Please refer: Annexure A). The input of S_{78} contains the acronym 'EMA' and the input of S_{79} contains 'GPS'. As WordNet does not support acronyms it is suggested to preprocess the acronyms before finding semantic similarity

using WordNet. Also, occasionally developers tend to use short words such as 'max' instead of 'maximum' as in service S_{68}(input: maxprice). Now, consider query 4. The service S_{68} is found to be one of the relevant services for query 4. The precision and recall of query 4 is not affected though the service S_{68} contains short word 'max' which is not available in WordNet, because in this case the other word 'price' alone is sufficient in finding the all relevant matches. Though the occurrence of acronyms and short words are not very frequent, a separate mapping for acronyms and short words with their expanded values may be used to provide better results.

CONCLUSION

In this paper, two models, namely, WordNet Model and Service Specific Ontology Model are proposed to compute similarity among services. The average recall of both the models is found to be 100% for different test queries posted to a test collection of 100 services. The average precision of WordNet Model is significantly improved when the similarity threshold is fixed at 40% or 50%. Further, the computation time taken to complete a single service match is found as 1.06 seconds and 5.13 seconds for WordNet and Service Specific Ontology Models. Based on the results, the accuracy of WordNet Model (80.17%) becomes almost same as the accuracy of Service Specific Ontology Model (84.75%) with similarity threshold fixed at 70%. Based on observations we recommend WordNet Model with similarity threshold of 0.75 (75%) for applications which require stringent similarity requirements. For applications which can tolerate comparatively less accuracy, WordNet Model with similarity threshold around 60% to 70% is suggested.

The proposed approach can achieve high retrieval accuracy while avoiding the cost involved in specific ontology based solutions. The approach assures the service clients to express their queries without specifying any domain specific ontologies. This approach is not only applicable to B2C environment but also to service composition based applications in various domains. Further, the proposed approach is more preferred to domain specific ontology based solutions and it is found to be more practical to service composition based applications due to the following reasons. It provides sufficient accuracy. Its computation time is low. In this model, there are no constraints for clients to specify relevant ontologies during querying. It avoids the creation and maintenance of domain specific ontologies which is a challenge and requires special expertise.

REFERENCES

Banerjee, S., & Pedersen, T. (2002). An adapted Lesk algorithm for word sense disambiguation using WordNet. In *Computational linguistics and intelligent text processing* (pp. 136–145). Berlin: Springer. doi:10.1007/3-540-45715-1_11

Chen, L., Yang, G., Wang, D., & Zhang, Y. (2010). WordNet-powered web services discovery using kernel-based similarity matching mechanism. In *Proceedings of Service Oriented System Engineering (SOSE), 2010 Fifth IEEE International Symposium on* (pp. 64-68). IEEE.

Chukmol, U., Benharkat, A. N., & Amghar, Y. (2008). Enhancing web service discovery by using collaborative tagging system. In *Proceedings of Next Generation Web Services Practices* (pp. 54–59). IEEE. doi:10.1109/NWeSP.2008.29

Gopinath, G., & Chellammal, S. (2010). An approach to identify candidate services for semantic web service discovery. In Proceedings of Service-Oriented Computing and Applications (SOCA), (pp. 321-324). IEEE.

Guo, R., Le, J., & Xia, X. (2005). Capability matching of web services based on OWL-S. In *Proceedings of Database and Expert Systems Applications* (pp. 653–657). IEEE.

Jiang, J. J., & Conrath, D. W. (1997). Semantic similarity based on corpus statistics and lexical taxonomy. In *Proceedings of International Conference on Research in Computational Linguistics* (pp. 19-33). Academic Press.

Karimpour, R., & Taghiyareh, F. (2009). Conceptual discovery of web services using WordNet. In *Proceedings of Services Computing Conference,* (pp. 440-444). IEEE.

Klusch, M., & Kaufer, F. (2009). WSMO-MX: A hybrid semantic web service matchmaker. *Web Intelligence and Agent Systems*, *7*(1), 23–42.

Kokash, N. (2006). A comparison of web service interface similarity measures. *Frontiers in Artificial Intelligence and Applications*, *142*, 220–231.

Kopecky, J., Vitvar, T., Bournez, C., & Farrell, J. (2007). Sawsdl: Semantic annotations for WSDL and XML schema. *IEEE Internet Computing*, *11*(6), 60–67. doi:10.1109/MIC.2007.134

Leacock, C., & Chodorow, M. (1998). Combining local context and WordNet similarity for word sense identification. *WordNet: An Electronic Lexical Database*, *49*(2), 265–283.

Lin, D. (1998). An information-theoretic definition of similarity. In *Proceedings of ICML* (Vol. 98, pp. 296-304). ICML.

Lv, Q., Zhou, J., & Cao, Q. (2009). Service matching mechanisms in pervasive computing environments. In *Proceedings of Intelligent Systems and Applications* (pp. 1–4). IEEE. doi:10.1109/IWISA.2009.5073110

Miller, G. A., Beckwith, R., Fellbaum, C., Gross, D., & Miller, K. J. (1990). Introduction to wordnet: An on-line lexical database. *International Journal of Lexicography*, *3*(4), 235–244. doi:10.1093/ijl/3.4.235

Mokhtar, S. B., Kaul, A., Georgantas, N., & Issarny, V. (2006). Towards efficient matching of semantic web service capabilities. In *Proceedings of International Workshop on Web Services–Modeling and Testing (WS-MaTe 2006)* (pp. 137-152). WS-MaTe.

Nayak, R., & Lee, B. (2007). Web service discovery with additional semantics and clustering. In *Proceedings of Web Intelligence* (pp. 555–558). IEEE. doi:10.1109/WI.2007.82

Pedersen, T., Patwardhan, S., & Michelizzi, J. (2004). WordNet: Similarity: Measuring the relatedness of concepts. In Demonstration papers at HLT-NAACL 2004 (pp. 38-41). Association for Computational Linguistics.

Qu, X., Sun, H., Li, X., Liu, X., & Lin, W. (2009). WSSM: A WordNet-based web services similarity mining mechanism. In Proceedings of Future Computing, Service Computation, Cognitive, Adaptive, Content, Patterns, (pp. 339-345). IEEE.

Ren, K., Chen, J., Xiao, N., Song, J., & Li, J. (2008). Building quick service query list using wordnet for automated service composition. In *Proceedings of Asia-Pacific Services Computing Conference,* (pp. 297-302). IEEE.

Resnik, P. (1999). Semantic similarity in a taxonomy: An information-based measure and its application to problems of ambiguity in natural language. *Journal of Artificial Intelligence Research*, *11*, 95–130.

Sivashanmugam, K., Miller, J. A., Sheth, A. P., & Verma, K. (2005). Framework for semantic web process composition. *International Journal of Electronic Commerce*, *9*(2), 71–106.

Sohali, A., & Zamanifar, K. (2009). Matching model for semantic web services discovery. *Journal of Theoretical and Applied Information Technology*, *7*(2), 139–144.

Stroulia, E., & Wang, Y. (2005). Structural and semantic matching for assessing web-service similarity. *International Journal of Cooperative Information Systems*, *14*(4), 407–437. doi:10.1142/S0218843005001213

Sycara, K., Paolucci, M., Ankolekar, A., & Srinivasan, N. (2003). Automated discovery, interaction and composition of semantic web services. *Web Semantics: Science. Services and Agents on the World Wide Web*, *1*(1), 27–46. doi:10.1016/j.websem.2003.07.002

Syeda-Mahmood, T., Shah, G., Akkiraju, R., Ivan, A. A., & Goodwin, R. (2005). Searching service repositories by combining semantic and ontological matching. In *Proceedings of Web Services* (pp. 13–20). IEEE. doi:10.1109/ICWS.2005.102

Wu, J., & Wu, Z. (2005). Similarity-based web service matchmaking. [). IEEE.]. *Proceedings of Services Computing*, *1*, 287–294.

Wu, Z., & Palmer, M. (1994). Verbs semantics and lexical selection. In *Proceedings of the 32nd Annual Meeting on Association for Computational Linguistics* (pp. 133-138). Association for Computational Linguistics.

ADDITIONAL READING

Bianchini, D., De Antonellis, V., & Melchiori, M. (2008). Flexible semantic-based service matchmaking and discovery. *World Wide Web (Bussum)*, *11*(2), 227–251. doi:10.1007/s11280-007-0040-y

Birukou, A., Blanzieri, E., D'Andrea, V., Giorgini, P., & Kokash, N. (2007). Improving Web service discovery with usage data. *Software, IEEE*, *24*(6), 47–54. doi:10.1109/MS.2007.169

Calado, I., Barros, H., & Bittencourt, I. I. (2009, March). An approach for semantic Web services automatic discovery and composition with similarity metrics. In *Proceedings of the 2009 ACM symposium on Applied Computing* (pp. 694-695). ACM.

Chen, L., Song, Z. L., Zhang, Y., & Miao, Z. (2011). WordNet-Enhanced Dynamic Semantic Web Services Discovery. In *Emerging Research in Artificial Intelligence and Computational Intelligence* (pp. 529–536). Springer Berlin Heidelberg. doi:10.1007/978-3-642-24282-3_73

Di Martino, B. (2009). Semantic Web services discovery based on structural ontology matching. *International Journal of Web and Grid Services*, 5(1), 46–65. doi:10.1504/IJWGS.2009.023868

Dong, X., Halevy, A., Madhavan, J., Nemes, E., & Zhang, J. (2004, August). Similarity search for Web services. In *Proceedings of the Thirtieth international conference on Very large data bases-Volume 30* (pp. 372-383). VLDB Endowment.

Dong, X., Madhavan, J., & Halevy, A. (2004). Mining structures for semantics. *ACM SIGKDD Explorations Newsletter*, 6(2), 53–60. doi:10.1145/1046456.1046463

Fellbaum, C. (1990). English verbs as a semantic net. *International Journal of Lexicography*, 3(4), 278–301. doi:10.1093/ijl/3.4.278

Fellbaum, C. (2010). WordNet. In R. Poli et al. (Eds.), *Theory and Applications of Ontology: Computer Applications* (pp. 231–243). Springer Netherlands. doi:10.1007/978-90-481-8847-5_10

Hearst, M. A. (1998). Automated discovery of WordNet relations. *WordNet: an electronic lexical database*, 131-151.

Klusch, M., Fries, B., & Sycara, K. (2009). OWLS-MX: A hybrid Semantic Web service matchmaker for OWL-S services. *Web Semantics: Science. Services and Agents on the World Wide Web*, 7(2), 121–133. doi:10.1016/j.websem.2008.10.001

Kokash, N., van den Heuvel, W. J., & D'Andrea, V. (2006). Leveraging Web services discovery with customizable hybrid matching. In *Service-Oriented Computing–ICSOC 2006* (pp. 522–528). Springer Berlin Heidelberg. doi:10.1007/11948148_50

Konduri, A., & Chan, C. C. (2010). Predicting Similarity of Web Services Using WordNet. *Intelligent Soft Computation and Evolving Data Mining: Integrating Advanced Technologies*, 354-369

Liu, F., Shi, Y., Yu, J., Wang, T., & Wu, J. (2010, July). Measuring similarity of Web services based on wsdl. In *Web Services (ICWS), 2010 IEEE International Conference on* (pp. 155-162). IEEE.

Miller, G. A. (1990). Nouns in WordNet: a lexical inheritance system. *International journal of Lexicography*, 3(4), 245-264.

Miller, G. A. (1995). WordNet: a lexical database for English. *Communications of the ACM*, 38(11), 39–41. doi:10.1145/219717.219748

Paolucci, M., Kawamura, T., Payne, T. R., & Sycara, K. (2002). Semantic matching of Web services capabilities. In The Semantic Web—ISWC 2002 (pp. 333-347). Springer Berlin Heidelberg.

Papazoglou, M. P. (2008). Web Services: Principles and Technology. Pearson – Prentice Hall, 782 pages.

Paulraj, D., & Swamynathan, S. (2012). Content based service discovery in semantic Web services using wordnet. In Advanced Computing, Networking and Security (pp. 48-56). Springer Berlin Heidelberg.

Shu, G., Rana, O. F., Avis, N. J., & Dingfang, C. (2007). Ontology-based semantic match-making approach. *Advances in Engineering Software*, *38*(1), 59–67. doi:10.1016/j.advengsoft.2006.05.004

Sotolongo, R., Kobashikawa, C., Dong, F., & Hirota, K. (2008). Algorithm for Web Service Discovery Based on Information Retrieval Using WordNet and Linear Discriminant Functions. *Journal of Advanced Computational Intelligence and Intelligent Informatics*, *12*(2), 182–189.

Talantikite, H. N., Aissani, D., & Boudjlida, N. (2009). Semantic annotations for Web services discovery and composition. *Computer Standards & Interfaces*, *31*(6), 1108–1117. doi:10.1016/j.csi.2008.09.041

Toch, E., Gal, A., Reinhartz-Berger, I., & Dori, D. (2007). A semantic approach to approximate service retrieval. *ACM Transactions on Internet Technology*, *8*(1), 2. doi:10.1145/1294148.1294150

Wang, T., & Hirst, G. (2011, July). Refining the notions of depth and density in WordNet-based semantic similarity measures. In *Proceedings of the Conference on Empirical Methods in Natural Language Processing* (pp. 1003-1011). Association for Computational Linguistics.

Wang, Y., & Stroulia, E. (2003, December). Flexible interface matching for Web-service discovery. In *Web Information Systems Engineering, 2003. WISE 2003. Proceedings of the Fourth International Conference on* (pp. 147-156). IEEE.

KEY TERMS AND DEFINITIONS

Precision: It is the ratio of number of services retrieved relevant to the number of services retrieved.

Recall: It is the ratio of number of services retrieved relevant to the actual number of relevant services.

Service Discovery: The process of retrieving matched services for a query by computing similarity between query and functional characteristics of advertised services.

Semantic Service Discovery: The process of finding matched services for a query according to semantics of services expressed through ontologies.

Service Specific Ontologies: These ontologies represent the ontologies used by service providers to describe the semantics of concepts of services.

Similarity Threshold: It represents the minimum value for similarity that should exist between a query and an advertised service to consider that the service is similar to the query.

WordNet: It is a lexical database of English. It is domain independent ontology which organizes English words as a network of semantically related words and concepts.

WordNet Similarity: It represents the semantic similarity or relatedness between words computed using path length or information content based measures from the WordNet database.

APPENDIX

Table 8. Test collection

Service ID	Service URL	Outputs	Inputs
S$_1$	http://127.0.0.1/services/1.1/BookPrice.owls	#_Price	#_book
S$_2$	http://127.0.0.1/services/1.1/EntranceFee_service.owls	#_Taxedprice	#_person
S$_3$	http://127.0.0.1/services/1.1/4wheeledcar_price_service.owls	#_Price	#_4wheeledcar
S$_4$	http://127.0.0.1/services/1.1/4wheeledcarbicycle_price_service.owls	#_Price	#_bicycle
S$_5$	http://127.0.0.1/services/1.1/title_comedyfilm_service.owls	#_Comedyfilm	#_title
S$_6$	http://127.0.0.1/services/1.1/title_comedyfilm_Megaservice.owls	#_Comedyfilm	#_title
S$_7$	http://127.0.0.1/services/1.1/title_comedyfilm_BFservice.owls	#_Comedyfilm	#_title
S$_8$	http://127.0.0.1/services/1.1/AcademicBookNumberSearch.owls	#_Book	#_academic-item-number
S$_9$	http://127.0.0.1/services/1.1/BookFinder.owls	#_Book	#_title
S$_{10}$	http://127.0.0.1/services/1.1/vehicle_price_service.owls	#_Price	#_vehicle
S$_{11}$	http://127.0.0.1/services/1.1/title_pricebook_service.owls	#_Price	#_title
S$_{12}$	http://127.0.0.1/services/1.1/preparedfood_price_service.owls	#_Price	#_preparedfood
S$_{13}$	http://127.0.0.1/services/1.1/agent_price_MianMarktservice.owls	#_Price	#_agent
S$_{14}$	http://127.0.0.1/services/1.1/apple_price_service.owls	#_Price	#_apple
S$_{15}$	http://127.0.0.1/services/1.1/AcademicBookNumberOrISBNSearch.owls	#_Book	#_publication-number
S$_{16}$	http://127.0.0.1/services/1.1/EntranceFeeindollar_service.owls	#_Taxedpriceindollar	#_person
S$_{17}$	http://127.0.0.1/services/1.1/BookSearchService.owls	#_Book	#_title
S$_{18}$	http://127.0.0.1/services/1.1/missile_financing_USservice.owls	#_Financing	#_missile
S$_{19}$	http://127.0.0.1/services/1.1/missile_financing_Chinaservice.owls	#_Financing	#_missile
S$_{20}$	http://127.0.0.1/services/1.1/missile_financing_Russianservice.owls	#_Financing	#_missile
S$_{21}$	http://127.0.0.1/services/1.1/publication_author_service.owls	#_Author	#_publication
S$_{22}$	http://127.0.0.1/services/1.1/book_authorprice_Novelservice.owls	#_Author	#_book
S$_{23}$	http://127.0.0.1/services/1.1/missile_funding_NKoreaservice.owls	#_Funding	#_missile
S$_{24}$	http://127.0.0.1/services/1.1/missile_funding_Pakservice.owls	#_Funding	#_missile
S$_{25}$	http://127.0.0.1/services/1.1/novel_author_service.owls	#_Author	#_novel
S$_{26}$	http://127.0.0.1/services/1.1/missile_funding_Asianservice.owls	#_Funding	#_missile
S$_{27}$	http://127.0.0.1/services/1.1/missile_funding_Indiaservice.owls	#_Funding	#_missile
S$_{28}$	http://127.0.0.1/services/1.1/book_author_EncSSservice.owls	#_Author	#_book
S$_{29}$	http://127.0.0.1/services/1.1/book_author_service.owls	#_Author	#_book
S$_{30}$	http://127.0.0.1/services/1.1/title_lowcomedyfilm_service.owls	#_Lowcomedyfilm	#_title
S$_{31}$	http://127.0.0.1/services/1.1/title_highcomedyfilmreport_service.owls	#_Highcomedyfilm	#_title
S$_{32}$	http://127.0.0.1/services/1.1/title_film_service.owls	#_Film	#_title

continued on following page

Table 8. Continued

Service ID	Service URL	Outputs	Inputs
S_{33}	http://127.0.0.1/services/1.1/title_filmP2P_service.owls	#_Film	#_title
S_{34}	http://127.0.0.1/services/1.1/title_filmActionComedy_service.owls	#_Film	#_title
S_{35}	http://127.0.0.1/services/1.1/title_videomediarecommendedprice_service.owls	#_Videomedia	#_title
S_{36}	http://127.0.0.1/services/1.1/title_videomedia_service.owls	#_Videomedia	#_title
S_{37}	http://127.0.0.1/services/1.1/title_videomediaMM_service.owls	#_Videomedia	#_title
S_{38}	http://127.0.0.1/services/1.1/title_vhs_service.owls	#_Vhs	#_title
S_{39}	http://127.0.0.1/services/1.1/surfing_destination_AUSservice.owls	#_Destination	#_surfing
S_{40}	http://127.0.0.1/services/1.1/surfing_destination_Alwaysservice.owls	#_Destination	#_surfing
S_{41}	http://127.0.0.1/services/1.1/surfing_destination_SOHservice.owls	#_Destination	#_surfing
S_{42}	http://127.0.0.1/services/1.1/surfing_destination_service.owls	#_Destination	#_surfing
S_{43}	http://127.0.0.1/services/1.1/university_lecturer-in-academia_service.owls	#_Lecturer-in-academia	#_university
S_{44}	http://127.0.0.1/services/1.1/price_coffeewhiskey_Thebestservice.owls	#_Coffee, #_Whiskey	#_price
S_{45}	http://127.0.0.1/services/1.1/price_coffeewhiskey_service.owls	#_Coffee, #_Whiskey	#_price
S_{46}	http://127.0.0.1/services/1.1/price_cola_Gudduservice.owls	#_Cola	#_price
S_{47}	http://127.0.0.1/services/1.1/price_cola_Hallo2service.owls	#_Cola	#_price
S_{48}	http://127.0.0.1/services/1.1/price_cola_Halloservice.owls	#_Cola	#_price
S_{49}	http://127.0.0.1/services/1.1/university_lecturer-in-academia_Recommendservice.owls	#_Lecturer-in-academia	#_university
S_{50}	http://127.0.0.1/services/1.1/university_professor-in-academia_service.owls	#_Professor-in-academia	#_university
S_{51}	http://127.0.0.1/services/1.1/price_whiskeycoffee_service.owls	#_Whiskey, #_Coffee	#_price
S_{52}	http://127.0.0.1/services/1.1/store_preparedfood_service.owls	#_Preparedfood	#_store
S_{53}	http://127.0.0.1/services/1.1/store_preparedfood_Merchantservice.owls	#_Preparedfood	#_store
S_{54}	http://127.0.0.1/services/1.1/Available_preparedfoodquantity_service.owls	#_Preparedfood	#_grocerystore
S_{55}	http://127.0.0.1/services/1.1/Required_preparedfoodquantity_service.owls	#_Preparedfood	#_grocerystore
S_{56}	http://127.0.0.1/services/1.1/wholesalestore_preparedfood_service.owls	#_Preparedfood	#_wholesalestore
S_{57}	http://127.0.0.1/services/1.1/retailstore_preparedfood_service.owls	#_Preparedfood	#_retailstore
S_{58}	http://127.0.0.1/services/1.1/visiting-researcher_address_service.owls	#_Address	#_visiting-researcher
S_{59}	http://127.0.0.1/services/1.1/researcher_postal-address_service.owls	#_Postal-address	#_researcher
S_{60}	http://127.0.0.1/services/1.1/researcher_address_service.owls	#_Address	#_researcher
S_{61}	http://127.0.0.1/services/1.1/researcher_address_HOM2service.owls	#_Address	#_researcher

continued on following page

Table 8. Continued

Service ID	Service URL	Outputs	Inputs
S_{62}	http://127.0.0.1/services/1.1/village_hotel_service.owls	#_Hotel	#_village
S_{63}	http://127.0.0.1/services/1.1/towncountry_hotel_service.owls	#_Hotel	#_country
S_{64}	http://127.0.0.1/services/1.1/city_hotel_Germanservice.owls	#_Hotel	#_city
S_{65}	http://127.0.0.1/services/1.1/city_hotel_Saarlandservice.owls	#_Hotel	#_city
S_{66}	http://127.0.0.1/services/1.1/university_academic-support-staff_service.owls	#_Academic-support-staff	#_university
S_{67}	http://127.0.0.1/services/1.1/university_lecturer-in-academiaCurrentSemmester_service.owls	#_Lecturer-in-academia	#_university
S_{68}	http://127.0.0.1/services/1.0/maxprice_drinks_service.owls	#_Drinks	#_maxprice
S_{69}	http://127.0.0.1/services/1.1/novel_price_service.owls	#_Price	#_novel
S_{70}	http://127.0.0.1/services/1.1/location_icon_service.owls	#_Icon	#_location
S_{71}	http://127.0.0.1/services/1.1/location_photograph_service.owls	#_Photograph	#_location
S_{72}	http://127.0.0.1/services/1.1/university_research-fellow-in-academia_service.owls	#_Research-fellow-in-academia	#_university
S_{73}	http://127.0.0.1/services/1.1/university_researcher_service.owls	#_Researcher	#_university
S_{74}	http://127.0.0.1/services/1.1/university_senior-lecturer-in-academia_service.owls	#_Senior-lecturer-in-academia	#_university
S_{75}	http://127.0.0.1/services/1.1/title_dvd_service.owls	#_dvd	#_title
S_{76}	http://127.0.0.1/services/1.1/municipal-unit_drought_service.owls	#_municipal-unit	#_drought
S_{77}	http://127.0.0.1/services/1.1/#government_scholarship_service.owls	#_government	#_scholarship
S_{78}	http://127.0.0.1/services/1.1/#SendEMAPhoneNumberService	#_sendEMA phonenumber_EMAphonenumber	#_ SendEMAPhone Number _PatientGPSPosition
S_{79}	http://127.0.0.1/services/1.1/#PatientTransportService.owls	#_PatientTransport_Acknowledgement	#_PatientTransport_PatientGPSPosition
S_{80}	http://127.0.0.1/services/1.1/#sports_beach_service.owls	#_Beach	#_Sports
S_{81}	http://127.0.0.1/services/1.1/#surfinghiking_nationalpark_service.owls	#_NationalPark	#_Hiking, #_Surfing
S_{82}	http://127.0.0.1/services/1.1/#SetUpCostAndHealingPlan_service.owls	#_SetUpCostAnd Healing Plan_CostAnd HealingPlan	#_SetUpCostAndHealing Plan_RequiredDrugs
S_{83}	http://127.0.0.1/services/1.1#project_skilledoccupation_service.owls	#_skilledoccupation	#_project
S_{84}	http://127.0.0.1/services/1.1#SelectFlightService.owls	#_SelectFlight_Flight Number	#_SelectFlight_LiftofFlights
S_{85}	http://127.0.0.1/services/1.1/InformHospital_service.owls	#_InformHospital_Acknowledgement Response	#InformHospital_Diagnosed Symptoms
S_{86}	http://127.0.0.1/services/1.1/hospital_biopsy_service.owls	#_biopsy	#_hospital
S_{87}	http://127.0.0.1/services/1.1/hospital_predicting_service.owls	#_predicting	#_hospital
S_{88}	http://127.0.0.1/services/1.1/medicalclinic_predicting_service.owls	#_predicting	#_medicalclinic

continued on following page

Table 8. Continued

Service ID	Service URL	Outputs	Inputs
S_{89}	http://127.0.0.1/services/1.0/country_skilledoccupation_jobsservice.owls	#_skilledoccupation	#_country
S_{90}	http://127.0.0.1/services/1.0/country_sportsposition_service.owls	#_sportsposition	#_country
S_{91}	http://127.0.0.1/services/1.0/country_profession_service.owls	#_profession	#_country
S_{92}	http://127.0.0.1/services/1.0/governmentdegree_givingback_service.owls	#_givingback	#_degree, #_Government
S_{93}	http://127.0.0.1/services/1.0/questionhospital_diagnosticprocess_service.owls	#_diagnosticprocess	#_hospital, #_question
S_{94}	http://127.0.0.1/services/1.0/nationalgovernment_scholarshipquantity_service.owls	#_Quantity	#_nationalgovernment, #_schorlarship
S_{95}	http://127.0.0.1/services/1.0/AddLinks__service.owls	----	#_geopolitical-entity
S_{96}	http://127.0.0.1/services/1.0/_mapGerman_service.owls	#_map	------
S_{97}	http://127.0.0.1/services/1.0/item-number_letter_service.owls	#_letter	#_item-number
S_{98}	http://127.0.0.1/services/1.0/_medicaldoctor_UNOservice.owls	#_medicaldoctor	------
S_{99}	http://127.0.0.1/services/1.0/objectperson__service.owls	-----------	#_object, #_person
S_{100}	http://127.0.0.1/services/1.0/KLM-Login_service.owls	-----	_linguisticexpression

Section 3
Applications of Demand–Driven Web Services

Chapter 12
Web Services in China

Dong Dong
Hebei Normal University, China

Lizhe Sun
Boston Consulting Group, Australia

Zhaohao Sun
University of Ballarat, Australia & Hebei Normal University, China

ABSTRACT

This chapter examines Web services in China. More specifically, it examines the state-of-the-art of China's Web services in terms of cloud services, mobile services, and social networking services through exploring several leading Web service providers in the ICT industry, including Alibaba, Tencent, China Mobile, and Huawei. This research reveals that the Chinese culture has played an important role in the success of China's Web services. The trade-off ideology and communication conventions from Chinese traditional culture, as well as Mao Zedong thought, greatly influenced the development of China's Web services. The findings of this chapter might facilitate the research and development of Web services and better understanding of the growth in China's ICT industry, as well as future trends.

INTRODUCTION

Generally speaking, a Web service is a service on the Web. The fundamental philosophy of Web services is to meet the needs of users precisely through providing Web services and thereby increase market share and revenue (Sun, Wang, & Dong, 2010). Similar to other countries, the development of Web services in China also encountered similar challenges such as how to meet the customer's demands, how to attract more customers as well as how to improve traditional services using Web services. The demand from markets and societies has been the driving force of the rapid development of the Web services in China.

There are many researches examining China's Web services. For example, Ai and Wang (2007) examine China Mobile's service model evolution.

DOI: 10.4018/978-1-4666-5884-4.ch012

Yang and Liu (2009) analyze the successful strategies of Taobao's e-commerce platform services. Ou and Davison (2009) look at why eBay lost to TaoBao in China. Yan (2011) expound Huawei's cloud computing. Fu and Shi (2007) compare electronic services in China to the U.S. China Academy of Telecommunicatoin Research of MIIT (2012) publishes the *Cloud Computing White Paper* to look at the state of art of China's cloud computing and cloud services. However, there are not systematic investigations into China's Web services in terms of cloud service, mobile service, and social networking service (SNS) in a unified way. This chapter addresses this issue by examining Web services in China. More specifically, this chapter examines the state of the art of China's Web services in terms of cloud services, mobile service, and SNS through exploring several leading Web service providers in the ICT industry including Alibaba, Tencent, China Mobile, and Huawei. This research reveals that Chinese culture has played an important role in the progress of China's Web services. The approach in this research might facilitate the research and development of Web services and the better understanding of China's ICT progress along with the dramatic development of China's economy in the past few decades. The finding can also help international e-service firms develop effective marketing policies to gain competitive advantages in the Web service marketplace.

The rest of this chapter is organized as follows: We analyze the fundamentals of Web services including the various understanding about Web services, and players in Web services, Chinese culture, and the relationship between culture and the Web services. We also look at China's answers to Web services, and examine Alibaba as the leader of Web services, Tencent as the leader of social networking services, Huawei as the leader of cloud services, China Mobile as the leader of mobile services from a cultural perspective. Finally, we end this chapter with concluding remarks and future research directions.

FUNDAMENTALS OF WEB SERVICES

This section first reviews Web services and then looks at Web services in terms of cloud services, mobile services, and social networking services.

Web Services

Web services can be defined from both a technological perspective and from a commercial perspective. From a technological perspective, a Web service is a communication approach between two electronic devices over the Web. That is, a Web service is a software system that can be accessed by other applications with widely available protocols and transports (Gartner, 2013). In other words, a Web service is a software system provided at a network address over the Web or in the cloud. Web-based applications are one of the critical components of Web services. They are composed of coarse-grained business functions accessed over the Web or in the cloud (Chung, Lin, & Mathieu, 2003). With the dramatic development of the Internet and mobile technology in the past decade, Web services have been flourished in e-commerce and e-business. They have also offered a number of strategic advantages such as mobility, flexibility, interactivity, and interchangeability in comparison with traditional services..

From a commercial perspective, a Web service is a collection of business activities within a business process and it is available over a network to internal and/or external business partners to achieve commercial goals. A Web service consists of Web service entities, Web service platforms, and Web service transactions (Yang, 2008). A Web service entity is an objective object engaged in e-services, such as an enterprise, a bank, a shop, a certification center, a government agent or an individual. Web service entities consist of service providers, service requestors, and service brokers (Sun & Lau, 2007; Singh & Huhns, 2005). Among them, there are three kinds of flows to complete services: information flow, capital flow, and logistics flow. A Web service platform is a website where e-service entities engaged in the exchange of goods or services. A Web service transaction is a set of specific exchange activities between Web service entities, including inquiry, quotation, negotiation, transfer payments, advertising, recommendation, etc. (Sun, Dong, & Yearwood, 2011). Web services are referred to as a new digitalized business model that service entities using various electronic networks to perform tasks or transaction processes partially or completely. Web services encompass computing services, storage services, data services, information services, knowledge services, remote device sharing services, software services and other services on the Web (Yang, 2008). In what follows, we look at cloud services, mobile services, and SNS in some detail.

Cloud Services

A cloud service is a Web service that is available to users on demand via the Internet from a cloud computing provider's servers. Cloud service providers present customers fast, easy and scalable accesses to applications and resources hosted on the Web. According to their value and visibility to the end users, cloud services are usually classified into three primary categories: Infrastructure as a Service (IaaS), Platform as a Service (PaaS), and Software as a Service (SaaS) (China Academy of Telecommunicatoin Research of MIIT, 2012). IaaS makes available computing resources (storage, processing and networking) as a service (Rimal, Choi, & Lumb, 2010). PaaS providers offer a managed higher-level software infrastructure, where customers can build and deploy particular classes of applications and services using the tools, environments, and programming languages supported by the cloud provider (Höfer & Karagiannis, 2011). SaaS is a model of software deployment where an application as a service is provided to customers across the Internet (Kulkarni, Gambhir, & Palwe, 2011). The key feature of SaaS is the separation

of the possession and ownership of software from its use. Delivering software's functionality as a set of distributed services that can be configured and bound at delivery time can overcome many current limitations constraining software use, deployment, and evolution (Turner, Budgen, & Brereton, 2003).

Mobile Services

A mobile service is also a Web service that allows users to consume at anytime, anywhere via mobile terminals such as smart phones and tablets. Basic mobile services include domestic and international call services, data roaming services and Internet services (Schneider, 2013). The value added mobile services include SMS, multimedia message (MMS), caller forwarding, call waiting, multi-party calls, and video voice mail (China Mobile, 2013). From a technology viewpoint, mobile services fall into four categories: voice services, message services, Internet connection and application services (Chen, Deng, & Lu, 2007). From a customer perspective, mobile services can be classified into individual-level services and enterprise-level services (Chen, Deng, & Lu, 2007). Individual-level services consist of communication and messaging services (Fetion, mobile blog, SMS, mobile navigation, etc.), business services (mobile payment, mobile banking, etc.), and entertainment services (music services, video services, gaming, etc.). Enterprise-level services include wireless broadband access, conference call, video conference, etc.

Mobile services can be delivered through mobile and wireless networks. Compared to other e-services that are bound to a fixed location, mobile services assume mobility on the part of the user of the services, the devices, the sessions or applications. Another difference is the location sensibility. Most mobile devices are equipped with the Global Positioning System (GPS) (Schneider, 2013). Real-time user-related contextual information, including location, can make mobile services more useful and relevant. Contextual information can be any information relevant to the use of a service. In addition to location-based information, which is typically generated through the GPS or network triangulation, air temperature, device battery power, tasks in the user's agenda, social contacts, or even blood pressure and heart rate can be utilized by mobile service providers. Contextual information allows automatic service delivery at the relevant time and place, the tagging of user-generated content and a more efficient use of the service (De Reuver, 2009).

Social Networking Services

A social networking service (SNS) is a kind of Web services that provides a platform to build social networks or social relations among people who share interests, activities, backgrounds, real-life connections, etc. (Turban & Volonino, 2011). SNS has six basic functions: identity management, expert finding, context awareness, contact management, network awareness and exchange (Richter & Koch, 2008). SNS can be classified into three categories from a market point of view (Wang, 2009). The first category is leisure and entertainment-oriented SNS. Kaixin (www.kaixin001.com) and 51 (www.51.com) fall into this category. They provide SNS for family members, friends, classmates, colleagues in a relaxed and interactive fashion to maintain closer contacts such as diaries, photo albums, dynamic records, repasts and social games. Registered Kaixin users have exceeded 140 million (as of the end of November 2013), which makes it as one of the China's leading and most influential real name social networking sites (Wang, 2009). The second category is campus SNS and marriage dating sites including Renren (www.renren.com), QQ, and Baihe (www.baihe.com). These websites help to connect users by sharing information, ideas and resources. The third category is business-oriented SNS such as Tianji (www.tianji.com), which per-

forms similar functions to LinkedIn. They provide a platform for business people and professionals to create, manage, and develop their professional relationships.

WEB SERVICES IN CHINA

In this section, we will look at China's answer to the Web services through case studies. These case studies are carried out on Alibaba, Tencent, Huawei, China Mobile in terms of cloud services, mobile services, and social networking services taking into account Chinese culture's influence on each of them.

Alibaba: The Leader of China's Web Services Providers

Alibaba is an Internet-based business platform for anyone/any company to buy/sell services or products online, developed by Alibaba Group which was founded in 1999 by 18 people led by Jack (Yun) Ma. Alibaba is now the leading Web services provider in both B2B and B2C e-commerce (Turban & Volonino, 2011). Alibaba consists of 25 business units and focuses on developing the e-commerce ecosystem. Alibaba employs more than 24,000 people around the world and has a global footprint of more than 70 offices covering China, India, the United Kingdom, and the United States. Table 1 summarizes the major businesses and affiliated entities of the Alibaba Group:

Alibaba's profit tripled in the first quarter of 2013 with rising expectations for the company's much anticipated IPO, which could value the company at $70 billion (China Internet Watch, 2013), The result reflects the Group's on-going platform enhancement activities, which are set to improve the user experience, supplier quality and trust and safety measures.

How does Chinese culture influence the success of Alibaba Group? Alibaba has established

Table 1. Alibaba Group's affiliated entities

Affiliated Entities	Businesses
Alibaba.com International	Leading global e-commerce platform for SMBs
Alibaba.com China	Leading domestic e-commerce platform for Chinese SMBs
AliExpress	Leading global e-commerce marketplace for consumers
Taobao(www. taobao.com)	China's most popular C2C online shopping destination
Tmall.com	China's leading B2C shopping destination for quality, brand-name goods
Juhuasuan.com	Comprehensive group shopping platform in China
eTao	Comprehensive shopping search engine in China
Alibaba Cloud Computing	Developer of platforms for cloud computing and data management
Alipay (www. alipay.com)	Most widely used third-party online payment platform in China

a strong enterprise culture based on the shared mission, vision, value system (Alibaba Group, 2013). Its business success and rapid growth are based on the spirit of entrepreneurship, innovation, and an unwavering focus on meeting the needs of its customers. Furthermore, the success of Alibaba dues to the establishment of a healthy trust system based on a trade-off between reality and virtuality, a trade-off between the obtained and the lost (*de shi*) in the completely free-of-charge model, and a trade-off between competition and cooperation. All these trade-offs reflects a kind of Chinese culture, because trade-off is one of

the core philosophies of Chinese culture (Tang, 1995). In what follows, we examine each of them in some detail.

A Trust System: A Trade-Off between Reality and Virtuality

Although credit card-based payment systems have been successful in North America and Europe, the popularizing rate of credit card in China remained low, and credit card-based payment systems were ineffective in China when Alibaba was founded in 1999. Moreover, it is hard to build trusting relationships between buyers and sellers in the traditional Chinese business cultural environment, particularly for e-commerce. Therefore, individual relationships (friendships) and cash-based transactions have been the basic method for making successful business deals in China. AliPay, an affiliated entity of Alibaba (see Table 1), is designed to address the issue of the trust mechanism in e-commerce environment. There are four steps to do a transaction using AliPay, as shown in Figure 1. The order of the activities in a business transaction is identified as the numeric labels in Figure 1. After studying the information about the interesting products on the Web, an online buyer decides to buy products such as clothes or shoes, which is the first step. 2. The online buyer first sends his payment to an AliPay account, which is an escrow account (Schneider, 2013). 3. Once the buyer indicates that s/he has received the product ordered, the buyer's money is then transferred from AliPay to the seller's account.

Figure 1. AliPay as a trustworthy service broker and Taobao as trust rating system

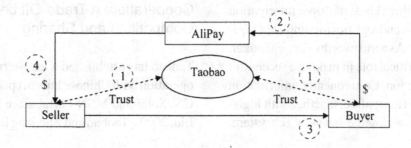

Taobao, another affiliated entity of Alibaba, encourages members to evaluate the credit of the transaction partner after each transaction (Liang & Song, 2008), which is the 4th step. The evaluation of credit forms the foundation of the trust system of Taobao. There are three comments for evaluation: positive, neutral, and negative. A "positive" comment increases the partner's credit by one point; "neutral" makes zero point; "negative" decreases the partner's credit by one point. Both online buyers and sellers care about credits which signals the degree of trust to the next potential buyer. The total credits are classified into 20 ranks with particular marks on each rank, and these marks are automatically displayed on sellers' profiles. A member with higher total credits is viewed as more trustworthy. Therefore, the more trustworthy seller has a greater potentiality to attract a buyer. Combined with Alipay as a trustworthy agent and Taobao's trust rating systems for registered members, Alibaba successfully provides online buyers and sellers with a comprehensive trust relationship solution. Perceived user trust is a much stronger determinant of user satisfaction than perceived platform functionality (Lu, Wang, & Hayes, 2012).

From a viewpoint of the service-oriented architecture (SOA) (Gisolfi, 2001), AliPay is a trustworthy service broker, as shown in Figure 1. AliPay can be considered as a contribution of Alibaba to the extension of SOA.

As a Web service provider, Taobao provides e-business platform services such as product promotion and trust rating system for both sellers and buyers; As Web service providers and requestors, sellers and buyers make deals with the help of Taobao, the platform service provider. As mentioned above, there are three kinds of flows: information flow, capital flow, and logistics to complete a business transaction. As a trustworthy service broker, AliPay plays a critical role in making a successful business transaction. Consequently, information flow and capital flow online, together with logistics offline form a closed e-business ecosystem.

Alibaba group has been making more efforts to build and enhance the successful e-commerce service ecosystem (Liang & Song, 2008).

The trust rating system of Taobao and escrow service of AliPay made a trade-off between the reality and virtuality. In the real world, a trusting relationship is very hard to build between sellers and buyers (Schneider, 2013) whereas in the virtual cyber world, a trusting relationship between sellers and buyers can be easily built by the rating system and trusted escrow partner.

Completely Free of Charge: A Trade-Off between the Obtained and the Lost

The key to gather popularity and attract a huge amount of online sellers and buyers is the free services provided by Taobao.com. It is free to set up shops on Taobao and to become a merchant (Taobao, 2013). A shop consists of a business profile, 50 product descriptions (pictures included), and unlimited buyer trade lead posting. These services are offered with free-of-charge for an unlimited time. In order to make products known to numerous buyers, a seller needs to post high quality products with beautiful images. A seller can send offers to clients by checking buying leads frequently, or stay online to negotiate with buyers directly. For a buyer, there are only three steps to buy products or service: search products, contact suppliers, and check messages. As a result, Taobao has successfully become the biggest C2C retail market in China. Alibaba announced that Taobao would continue to be operated under the free-of-charge model (Li, Zhang, Lu, Niu, Hou, & Zhu, 2012).

Cooperation: A Trade-Off between Competition and Sharing

Taobao has established a long-term win-win cooperation with Chinese Internet portals such as 21 CN, Sohu and MSN Portal since 2004 (Yang & Liu, 2009). Taobao and Zhejiang Branch of ICBC (the Industrial and Commercial Bank of China) signed a comprehensive economic cooperation agreement on October 27, 2003, which puts the bank into the place of intermediary to connect with the network and e-commerce (Liang & Song, 2008). This kind of cooperation not only increases the confidence of customers on creditable payment and settlement provided by Taobao, but also gives a convenient way for online vendors to receive payment. Currently, Alibaba promotes an open platform architecture, and pays more efforts to cooperate with other companies for the technical standards development in order to make the e-business industry become more mature (Liang & Song, 2008). Alibaba is also dedicated to the development of an e-commerce service ecosystem through the cooperation of e-business enterprises, IT firms, and telecom operators. Alibaba will integrate the e-business platform with credit, authentication, payment, logistics, as well as talents and market to provide e-services globally. In the construction progress of the e-commerce ecosystem, Alibaba will keep the idea that something obtained implies something should be given up (*de shi*), to maintain a win-win relationship with partners (Liang & Song, 2008).

Tencent: The Leader of China's Social Networking Services Providers

Tencent, Inc. (tencent.com), founded in 1998, is now the leading China's social networking services provider (China Internet Watch, 2013). Tencent aims to provide one-stop online social networking services to tens of millions of Internet users in China and throughout the world to meet the users' needs for online social communication, information sharing, entertainment, and e-commerce. Tencent has established seven main social business services: IM (Instant Messaging) service, online media service, wireless Internet value-added service, interactive entertainment service, Internet value-added service, e-commerce

and online advertising service (Tencent, 2013). Tencent QQ is the most popular online social networking website in China with more than 800 million active QQ users in 2013 (PR Newswire, 2013). QQ supports comprehensive online communications including text messaging, video and voice chat as well as online/offline file transfer. QQ also supports cross platform communication between PC and wireless terminals. E-commerce is the key element in their "Online Life" strategy (Tencent, 2013). Paipai is Tencent's online trading platform. Tenpay is Tencent's integrated payment platform. Compared to telephone, SMS, email, and other communication tools, QQ made a trade-off in the contact efficiency, communication ability, and communication costs and achieved a subtle balance (Li & Gao, 2013). The success of QQ lies on that it satisfies the social demand from Chinese for simultaneous communication at anytime, anywhere in a cheap, convenient, and efficient way. Simultaneous communication is a central part of Chinese culture, because ordinary Chinese are still reluctant to meet others with a planned appointment, to communicate with others using emails. Particularly, Chinese people prefer meeting by a dinner arrangement for business talking.

WeChat is one of the most successful Tencent's mobile chat Apps. App is short for application software that is runnable on mobile terminals. With more than 300 million users in 2013, WeChat is considered the first Chinese mobile social network now (Li & Gao, 2013). WeChat uses many creative functions such as *Voice chatting*, *Texting*, *Video chat*, *Group chat*, *Moments (Social)*, *Look around* and *Shake* to connect with user's friends and family. In June 2013, we conducted a simple survey on a meeting. The participants consist of two professors, an IT engineer, a CIT, a researcher from an automation engineering institute, a manager from an IT company, and a coordinator working for a tendering company. There is only one question for them: why do you use WeChat? The coordinator said that it is free; the researcher said it is very convenient to talk with his son who is studying abroad; The manager said that he can do business effectively. With WeChat, communication has no longer to be texting. It also provides user-friendly options to communicate by multi-media with people such as voice, photos, and video call. Additionally, WeChat goes beyond conversation and sharing. With *Moments*, people can stay connected and share photos and location with anyone. The *Shake* feature connects anyone who is shaking the mobile phone with the WeChat app at the same time. The *Look Around* option searches the people around the user who has the same interest in meeting new friends. In response to netizens' complaints about the possibility of being charged for using the mobile chat application, Tencent promised that the company's popular software would remain free (Xinhua, 2013).

"Any user is treated as a person regardless of gender, age, region, education level attributes from WeChat services. A user is exactly an object, an abstraction of all users, a union of demand sets from all users." stated by Mr Zhang Xiaolong, the leader of WeChat development team and the vice president of Tencent (Li & Gao, 2013, p. 34). Originally, WeChat discourages text communication (Li & Gao, 2013), because writing a Chinese character is more difficult than sending a picture for the users. Sometimes, s/he has to compose a message carefully. This is actually a very difficult task. Moreover, the well-written users speak every day, while poor-written users will not dare to speak out. The success of WeChat lies on that it meets the demand rhythm from mobile users and the chance of the mobile Internet service market. First, the China domestic mobile Internet is just started, WeChat is born ahead of others in the market place, consequently it seizes a good opportunity. Second, the key advantage of WeChat is the quick capture of user requirements, rapid implementation of current user needs, short life cycle of product from design to deployment online. For example, the *Look Around* function is originated from real Chinese users experience in daily life. Chinese people like to look for a

person who is related to firstly, whenever s/he visits a new community. No matter how technology developed, there is still a subconsciousness of a strong demand for deep communication as a human being. However, with the faster pace of our lives, more and more frequent movements of persons, communication costs (including time costs) are still increasingly greater (Li & Gao, 2013). It is significantly changing the human behaviors in a subtle manner. The overall success of WeChat lies on the trade-off between inclusiveness and creativity resulting from a Chinese culture perspective. Therefore, "WeChat is a kind of life style."(weixin.qq.com)

The WeChat platform is developed from user's requirements and experiences. The WeChat team welcomes third-party co-operations to join the innovation and development of the Web service industry in order to build a healthy Internet ecosystem (Li & Gao, 2013). The development of WeChat applications is not going to harm the interests of the mobile telecom carriers. In this regard, WeChat hopes a win-win cooperation. For example, WeChat can help the mobile telecom carriers to foster customer loyalty and improve ARPU (Average Revenue Per User, an indicator used by telecom operators to measure carriers operating income). From a cultural viewpoint, this is also a trade-off between competition and cooperation as Alibaba does.

It should be noted that a deep communication is related to communication modes. The communication modes include text communication, video communication, audio communication, face-to-face communication, online chat communication, mobile chat communication, and so on. Different communication modes have different communication efficiencies, which have significant influence on the quantity and quality of communication and information sharing. Different persons prefer to use different communication modes to deepen the information exchange and sharing. Ordinary Chinese prefers to use face-to-face communication to realize simultaneous communication. WeChat platform has been very successful in providing a mobile chat communication platform for ordinary Chinese, who might have not laptop or desktop, but have a mobile phone connecting the Internet. The WeChat platform makes ordinary Chinese realize online chat communication and mobile chat communication. As a part of Chinese culture, the children in a Chinese family have always been and are still the predominant providers of supporting for their aging parents. On the one hand, the proportion of elder Chinese in China is increasing, but on the other hand, the traditional Chinese family structure is undergoing rapid transformation as young adults migrate to other regions even abroad seeking better employment opportunities or pursuing academic degrees. These ongoing societal changes are challenging the conventional family communication patterns such as visiting parents frequently and enjoying the traditional festival (Spring Festival and Mid-Fall Festival) with parents at hometown since children may not return home for the sake of cost or time. How to express love and devotion to parents from work or study place far away from hometown? WeChat successfully provides the answer to this social problem of the Chinese parents that cannot type any characters into their mobile phones.

China Mobile: The Leader of China's Mobile Services Providers

China Mobile is a Chinese state-owned telecommunication company that provides mobile voice and multimedia services through its nationwide mobile telecommunications network. As the leading mobile services provider in China, China Mobile has the world's largest mobile network and the world's largest mobile customer base (China Mobile, 2012). By May 31, 2013, the total customer base of China Mobile reached 735 million (China Mobile, 2013). Data services revenue reached RMB 166.3 billion, increased 19.4% from the previous year, and accounted for 29.7% of the operating revenue of China Mobile,

which was an increase of 3.3%. Wireless data traffic revenue reached RMB 68.3 billion, representing an increase of 53.6% from the previous year (China Mobile, 2013). In Chinese telecom market, China Mobile is one of the dominant mobile service providers.

China started the first generation mobile communication services in 1987, then adopted the Global System for Mobile Communications standard (GSM) in the early 1990s (Ma, 2011). 3G technologies that aim to meet the demands of advanced mobile data services for multimedia applications such as music and video, was launched by China Mobile in 2008 (Ma, 2011). China Mobile embraced three strategic transitions: developing Four-Network (GSM, TD-SCDMA, TD-LTE, and WLAN) Coordination, strengthening infrastructure resource consolidation, and expanding into the mobile Internet sector (China Mobile, 2012). At the end of 2012, 3G base reached 280 thousand, covering all large and medium cities, some towns and villages. WLAN access points counted to 3.83 million. WLAN traffic increased by 274.0% compared to the previous year. In 2012, "Wireless City" had 70 million cumulative customers (China Mobile, 2012).

At the end of June 2013, Chinese netizens reached 591 million, the Internet populating rates of 44.1%. Mobile phone netizens reached 464 million (China Internet Network Information Center, 2013). In the first half of 2013, 70.0% of new Internet users access the Internet by mobile devices. Mobile Internet users become the first source for the increment. Mobile Internet users increased to 78.5% proportion of all netizens, while the proportion desktop computer netizens declined slightly (China Internet Network Information Center, 2013). The proportion of Internet users in the use of mobile phones continues to increase, and mobile phone leads to more stability as the first major Internet terminal (Fu, Yu, Chen, & Qin, 2013).

For Chinese mobile Internet users, there are 70.3% chatting, 66.6% browsing news. Searching for information ranks the third position, more than half (50.9%). Followed by listening to music (47.9%), playing micro blog (47.9%), online shopping (47.0%), e-mail (45.5%), playing WeChat (43.3%), navigating (42.0%), and watching videos (41.8%) (China Internet Network Information Center, 2013). Each of the top 10 behaviors covers more than 40% proportion, while reading literatures ranks 11 and reaches 39.4%. By the EPRO pay and Taobao promotion, online payment has also made significant progress, with the ratio reached 37.7%. However, the mobile Internet services remain developing since terminal price and 3G traffic costs are still high and WiFi network coverage is still limited to big cities (Fu, Yu, Chen, & Qin, 2013).

Ai and Wang (2007) proposed a service model that consists of three service levels: market-oriented, group-oriented, and individual-oriented. The goal of market-oriented service is to serve the widest range of customers, focusing on creating large-scale service output by large-scale service infrastructure suitable for customer value or service demand in a relatively centralized environment. Market-oriented strategy ensures that customers in different times, different places consume standard services. Group-oriented customer service is aware of the differentiation from customer service groups and targets for service according to the value of group characteristics or demand characteristics subdivision. The individual-oriented customer service focuses on the customer base whose unit is individual through personalized services designed to create a combination of customer value. Individual-oriented service provides personalized service according to the customer's particular characteristics and requirements. China Mobile is still at the group-oriented service level (Ai & Wang, 2007).

By our observation, China Mobile's service follows a technology-driven top-down approach rather than a demand-driven bottom-up. China Mobile first satisfies the Chinese market as a whole, which is an equalitarianism ideology that

provides each individual the ability to call from anywhere, anytime. Recently, China Mobile made increasing efforts to meet the demands from individuals and offers voice value-added services such as caller identity display, caller restrictions, call waiting, call forwarding, voice mail, conference calls, data services, etc. Data services include SMS&MMS, wireless data traffic, applications and information services (China Mobile, 2013). SMS refers to services that employ the existing resources of telecommunications networks to deliver and receive text messages, including subscriber-to-subscriber messages. MMS is a service that allows users to send messages with graphics, sounds, texts and motion pictures over wireless networks. Applications and information services include mobile music, mobile paper, mobile reading, mobile video, mobile market, etc.

Fetion is another distinguishing comprehensive "integrated communications services" released by China Mobile in 2007 (Zhang, 2011). Fetion is a convergence of voice, GPRS, SMS and other means of communications by covering the three different user communication forms: full real-time voice service, quasi-real-time text communication service and the small amount of data, asynchronous communication service. Fetion is a seamless connection between the Internet and mobile network for communication services. Compared to other similar services, one of the greatest features of Fetion is that the text messages are free from PC to mobile phone. The data transfer, voice chat, secure communications, and other services are supplemented with the latest versions.

Huawei: The Leader of China's Cloud Services Providers

As a China's answer to the ICT infrastructure, Huawei Technologies Co. Ltd is a Chinese global vendor of networking and telecommunications equipment and services headquartered in Shenzhen, China. Huawei is one of the largest telecommunications equipment makers and vendors in the world. Huawei's products and services have been deployed in more than 140 countries and currently serve 45 of the world's 50 largest telecoms operators including British Telecom (BT) and T-Mobile (Silverstein, Singhi, Liao, & Michael, 2012, p. 243).

Huawei claims that cloud computing will change the information industry, just as electric power industry changes people's life by providing cheap and convenient lighting service. Cloud computing will enrich people's life with low cost and convenient information and communication services (Yang Y., 2011). The hardware and software in the cloud can be re-used at different times and shared at different places, as well as automatically identify service peaks and valleys. From this perspective, could services reduce the cost of consumers. Could service consumers do not need to purchase hardware components such as storage equipment, network equipment, and software components such as various office applications (Yang Y., 2011).

Huawei is now developing cloud computing and terminal strategies to form an integrated solution consisting of cloud computing, network, terminal based on the telecommunication network foundations (Yan, 2011). In the new expansion puzzle, the market architecture will be adjusted to four big business groups: carriers, enterprise business, terminal and others (Liu, 2012). Meanwhile, Huawei is also aggressively recruiting top talents from other top companies. In its current strategic investment phase, Huawei has 6,000 teams for the cloud production line and this number is aggressively expanded to 10,000 by the end of 2012 (Liu, 2012).

Huawei deployed desktop cloud for Shanghai Research institute to satisfy the needs of thousands of users. Compared to traditional PC system, the solution saves 40% of the investment, reduces 71% power consumption. The CPU utilization of the devices increased from 5% to 60%. By June 2012, Huawei has delivered 130,000 cloud desktop systems worldwide. Huawei's desktop

cloud productions have been maturer with great advantages compared to traditional PC in terms of security, management, cost, power consumption, etc. (Huang H., 2012).

The founder of Huawei, Mr Zhengfei Ren became the No. 1 of the 50 most influential business leaders of China in 2011 (Ren, 2013). Ren was born in 1944 from a very poor family residing in an impoverished part of a struggling province, Guizhou. His father always advised him "Remember that knowledge is power. You must study hard even though others do not". Such an advice made him enroll in a university in Qongqing as an undergraduate student to study engineering majored in electronic engineering and telecommunication at the age of 19 (1963). Such an experience made him always respect intellectuals for their knowledge, technology and expertise. For example, Huawei has 140,000 employees, around 46% of whom are engaged in research and development (R&D), At least 10% of the annual revenue of Huawei has been invested to its R&D. Because of hardship experience, Mr Ren believed that "Neither poverty or descent is worth being ashamed of. Wealthy without knowledge is not glorious". He always thinks about when Huawei will fail in the market rather than about the success of Huawei in the market (Ren, 2001). This is one of his viewpoints of values.

Ren always proactively takes risk and pursuits chances when he works. At the early stage of Huawei (1992), he and his colleagues successfully developed the China's first PBX (private branch exchange) switcher, C&C08, used in telecommunication sector broadly. The C&C08 was very successful in the market because it can deliver similar performance to its competitors at a third of the price.

Like many other Chinese in his generation, Mr Ren studied the Works of Chairman Mao (Four Volumes) carefully and repeatedly. He also applied the important ideas and methods (including military strategies and tactics) of Mao Zedong in his work for decades. In what follows, we have a look at how Mr Ren practices the thought of Mao Zedong in Huawei's strategies and daily operations (Silverstein, Singhi, Liao, & Michael, 2012).

In the 1990s, many multinational telecommunication giants such as Ericsson and Cisco Systems invested and segmented the telecommunication market of cities of China. As a small private company, Huawei could not compete with these multinational telecommunication giants in big cities of China. Mr Ren borrows the idea from Mao's military strategy "encircling the cities from rural areas" as his marketing strategy to sell telecommunication products to the low-end market of poor countryside, then expand from small towns and cities, middle-size cities and finally to metropolitan cities of China. Huawei was successful in this marketing strategy and became the No. 1 of the 100 strong electronics companies of China in 2000. In the mid-1990s, Huawei began to extend its business operations to overseas. Following the similar marketing strategy, Huawei first engaged the market of developing countries, then extended to the market of developed countries by friendly value, excellent service and fast response (Silverstein, Singhi, Liao, & Michael, 2012, pp. 243-4). Huawei established Huawei R&D Center and opened its business in the USA in 2001. Hence, Huawei accelerated the occupation of European and American telecommunication market since early 2000s.

Similar to the application of the abovementioned Mao's strategy of "encircling the cities from rural areas," Huawei's long-standing strategy is "inserting a fresh flower on a heap of cow-dung " (Yan, 2011). Huawei never leaves the tradition to pursue innovation blindly, that is, Huawei never goes up innovations without the basis of existence. After flowering phase, flowers become the new cow dung. Therefore, "Inserting a fresh flower on a heap of cow-dung" is a Chinese folk slang. It originally means a pretty and smart girl is married to an ugly and stupid husband. Here, a flower is a metaphor of Huawei's excellent products and services while the cow-dung is a metaphor of Huawei's marketing place. By this "flower and cow dung" strategy, Huawei captures the countryside first as an early stage business. Instead of competing with other international companies in metropolises such as Beijing, Shanghai and Guangzhou, Huawei focuses on smaller rural markets where the international companies rarely tread. Huawei has sent engineers to 2,800 counties of China (China has 2856 counties) to sell its products.

Another well-known military strategy of Mao Zedong is "fighting a battle of annihilation by an absolutely overwhelming force". Mr Ren applies this military strategy as a marketing strategy. He emphasizes that Huawei must gather the overwhelming resources over that of the major competitors, concentrate human resources, capital resources, materials, technological superiority and financial resources to achieve breakthroughs in key areas taking into account critical success factor and selected strategic growth points (Liu, 2012).

In the toughest time of him and his army in the early 1930s, Mao Zedong published his seminal article, *A single spark can start a prairie fire*, in order to answer the pessimistic sentiment in the Mao's army: "How long can the red flag wave exactly?" (Mao, 1966). Applying the idea in the Mao's article, Mr Ren always thinks about "How long can the red flag of Huawei wave exactly? " In the competitive market, any company today, regardless of small or large, might be bankrupt tomorrow (Ren, 2013).

Mr Ren always admires "self-criticism" and uses "self-criticism" from Mao to improve organizations and optimize management activities of Huawei to improve the competitive force of Huawei in the domestic and international market (Ren, 2001). Ren believe that self-criticism is an excellent tool for thought, character, quality, skills and innovation. In fact, "self-criticism" used to be one of most important treatises of Chinese Communist Party in the Mao's era. In addition, following Mao, Mr Ren emphasizes combining theory with practice. To practize this thought, senior managers at Huawei are regularly rotated upward and downward (Silverstein, Singhi, Liao, & Michael, 2012, p. 243).

Therefore, Mr Ren used the set of methods, thoughts and strategies from Mao Zedong to keep Huawei develop effectively and efficiently. Mr Ren has also practiced a number of so-called out-dated management methods which used to be prevalent in the era of Mao Zedong. For example, he persists in revolutionary solidarity and mobilization as well as collective action in Huawei to compete with the world-class telecommunication giants since the founding of Huawei. He admires Mao's "independence and self-reliance" and keeps in mind that "Only on the basis of independence and self-reliance, one will be granted equality with respect". As an example, Huawei independently developed its own special purpose IC chip (A-SIC) which was the technological breakthrough in the global telecommunication world in the early 2000s.

Mr Ren stated that those who have been in the forefront of the world-class companies create opportunities and guide consumption by research and development. They swept all profits quickly in the "window of opportunity" then create greater opportunities for investment. However, Chinese enterprises usually tend to lag behind in this regard and identify the chance after the opportunity arises. If they make a correct decision, they can grasp the opportunity to succeed. Huawei is an excellent example (Ren, 2003). This is the essential reason why the large international companies develop more quickly than Chinese enterprises. Grasping and creating opportunities are two different visions that determine an enterprise and a country's development path (Ren, 2003). Almost every great entrepreneur should be, first of all, a great thinker. There are no lacks of entrepreneurs and businessmen in China. However, China lacks great thinkers in business and market. Mr Ren is an exception. That is, Mr Ren is not only a great

entrepreneur but also a great thinker. He always thinks about management at a strategic level and tells his senior managers at Huawai how to realize his strategic intention through operations in technology and product development and marketing. For example, Mr Ren told his managers at Huawei that a compromise as a strategy is a kind of jungle wisdom that is very pragmatic, flexible. All of the wise men in the jungle of humanity accept the compromise of others at the right time, or propose a compromise to others (Ren, 2008). After all, people have to survive, relying on rationality rather than emotionality. A compromise is a consensus in solving a problem involving two or more parties under certain conditions. It may not be the best solution, but there is no better solution coming up. A compromise has a number of benefits. A compromise does not mean abandoning principles and blindly concessions. A smart compromise is an appropriate exchange. In order to achieve the most important goal, people should make the appropriate concessions on secondary targets. Only keeping compromises can people achieve "win-win". Otherwise, both sides would certainly suffer loss, because compromise eliminates conflicts. Refusing to compromise would be a prelude to confrontation (Ren, 2010).

Poverty and suffering are a kind charismatic wealth for a tough-minded person. Mr Ren took 13 years (1987-2000) to build the strongest ICT company in China, which is also one of the strongest companies in the world by adopting some of Mao's military strategies in the competitive business market. Mr Ren took another dozen years to make Huawei become the No. 1 telecommunication giant in the world. In this sense, Mr Ren is greater in terms of marketing of telecommunication.

Currently Mr Ren is leading Huwei to embrace cloud computing to build the ICT infrastructure for public services, private services and individual services by Huawei ICT technologies under the business vision of "delivering high customization, strong customer service and superior value to customers by a low-cost, efficient-work-ethic labor force" (Silverstein, Singhi, Liao, & Michael, 2012). We can predict that Huawei will soon become the global leader in cloud services and cloud computing.

FUTURE RESEARCH DIRECTIONS

China's Web services are still evolving towards diversity and integration (Chen D., 2012). The diversity means that more and more new Web services companies are emerging in China. The integration means that leading Web services companies develop an integrated Web platform to provide various Web services including cloud services, social networking services and mobile services. Therefore, an intelligent platform for integrated Web services is an important future research direction. The related research topics might include

- Intelligent techniques for developing smart platform for integrated Web services
- Intelligent platform for social mobile Web services
- Intelligent platform for mobile cloud services

Culture has been playing an important role in business and services. The human culture of pursing optimization of production process from individuals and organizations promotes the development of intelligent systems. The human culture of pursing pervasive convenience and communication promotes the development of the Internet. The human culture of pursing online transaction, wireless interaction, and online social interaction promotes the development of e-commerce, mobile services and online social networking services. Culture plays a core role in the Web services development. Web services can be considered as a product of computerized culture. Web services are built on the encapsulation of culture and computing. Chinese culture is one of the driving forces of China's Web services. Chinese culture's influences on computing technology and services adoption in China have been studied in interdisciplinary domain recently (Bell, 2006; Appadurai, 1998; Abbott, Zheng, Du, & Willcocks, 2013; Gregory, Prifling, & Beck, 2009; Huang & Trauth, 2007; Ou & Davison, 2009). For example, Ou & Davison (2009) concluded that the inability of eBay (China) compete with indigenous Chinese C2C platforms dues to conflicts in the way they interpreted the culture differences of doing business in China. Therefore, another future research direction for China's Web services is culture-informed Web services. The related research topics might include

- How can we deal with the culture-informed Web services?
- How can we measure the culture effects on different levels including national, organizational, and individual levels?
- How will changes in Chinese culture influence the future of Web services?
- How can Web services companies adapt and leverage Chinese culture to maximize return?

CONCLUSION

This chapter examined Web services in China. More specifically, this chapter examined the state-of-the-art of China's Web services in terms of cloud services, SNS and mobile services by exploring several leading Web service providers in the ICT industry including Alibaba, Tencent, China Mobile, and Huawei. This research also revealed that Chinese culture has played an important role in the success for China's Web services.

Web Services sector is assumed to be of particular relevance with culture especially in China since it has been dramatically impacted by the traditional business and e-commerce. Whatever service model, B2B, B2C, or C2C, Web services are especially sensitive to local cultural needs. There are many lessons throughout the world that have failed to successfully marketing e-service. Culture has been widely addressed as one of the key reasons (Chappell & Feindt, 2000; Merritt, 2000). This research implicates that cultural computing is likely to be highly useful to marketing practitioners, and researchers who are interested in Web services in China.

In the future work we will explore culture informed Web services in China in depth. We will also investigate Chinese cultures with their impacts on Web services through developing metrics and approaches for measuring the values of Chinese culture and their impact on China's Web services.

ACKNOWLEDGMENT

This research is partially supported by the Natural Science Foundation of Hebei under a key research Grant No.F2013205192 and other research grants provided by the College of Mathematics and Information Science, Hebei Normal University, China.

REFERENCES

Abbott, P., Zheng, Y., Du, R., & Willcocks, L. (2013). From boudary spanning to creolization: A study of Chinese software and services outsourcing vendors. *The Journal of Strategic Information Systems, 22*, 121–136. doi:10.1016/j.jsis.2013.02.002

Ai, F., & Wang, M. (2007). On China mobile's service model evolution. *Market Modernization,* (4), 346.

Alibaba Group. (2013). *Company overview*. Retrieved June 29, 2013, from http://news.alibaba.com/specials/aboutalibaba/aligroup/index.html

Appadurai, A. (1998). *The social life of things: Commodities in cultural perspective*. Cambridge, UK: Cambridge Uniersity Press.

Bell, G. (2006). The age of thumb: A culture reading of mobile technologies from Asia. *Knowledge, Technology & Policy, 19*(2), 41–57. doi:10.1007/s12130-006-1023-5

Chappell, C., & Feindt, S. (2000). Analysis of e-commerce practice in SMEs. *Communications and Strategies, 37*(1), 49–70.

Chen, D. (2012). Modern service industry calls for discipline construction services. *China University Teaching,* (6), 29-31.

Chen, Z., Deng, C., & Lu, Y. (2007). Classification and analysis of mobile services and adoption models. *Statistics and Decision,* (21), 57-60.

China Academy of Telecommunicatoin Research of MIIT. (2012). *Cloud computing white paper*. Beijing: China Academy of Telecommunicatoin Research of MIIT.

China Internet Network Information Center. (2013). *China mobile internet development survey report*. Retrieved July 19, 2013, from www.cnnic.cn

China Internet Network Information Center. (2013). *The 32nd China internet development statistics report*. Retrieved July 19, 2013, from www.cnnic.cn

China Internet Watch. (2013). *The story of China's biggest social network: Qzone*. Retrieved September 15, 2013, from http://www.chinainternetwatch.com/category/social-media/

China Mobile. (2012). *Annual report 2012.* Retrieved July 12, 2013, from http://www.chinamobileltd.com/en/global/home.php

China Mobile. (2013). *Business review.* Retrieved July 10, 2013, from http://www.chinamobileltd.com/en/business/business.php

Chung, J.-Y., Lin, K., & Mathieu, R. G. (2003). Guest editors' introduction: Web services computing—Advancing software interoperability. *Computer, 36*(10), 35–37. doi:10.1109/MC.2003.1236469

De Reuver, M. (2009). *Governing mobile service innovation in co-evolving value-network.* Infrastructure Systems & Services. Next Generation Infrastructures Foundation.

Fu, L., Yu, L., Chen, Y., & Qin, W. (2013). Overview on development trends of mobile internet 2012-2013. *China Internet,* (2), 1-7.

Fu, N., & Shi, Y. (2007). The comparative research on electronic services in China and the U.S. *Sci-Tech Information Development & Economy, 17* (36), 133-134.

Gartner. (2013). *Gartner IT glossary.* Retrieved September 14, 2013, from http://www.gartner.com/it-glossary/Web-services/

Gisolfi, D. (2001). *Web services architect: Part 1.* Retrieved 7 14, 2013, from http://www.ibm.com/developerworks/library/ws-arc1/

Gregory, R., Prifling, M., & Beck, R. (2009). The role of cultural intelligence for the emergence of negotialted culture in IT offshore outsourcing projects. *Information Technology & People, 22,* 223–241. doi:10.1108/09593840910981428

Höfer, C. N., & Karagiannis, G. (2011). Cloud computing services: Taxonomy and comparison. *Journal of Internet Services and Applications,* 81-94.

Huang, H. (2012). Push a variety of new ICT production for cloud computing. *Communications World Weekly, 9*(10), 33–34.

Huang, H., & Trauth, E. M. (2007). Cultural influences and globally distributed information systems development: Experience from Chinese IT professionals. In *Proceeding of the 2007 ACM SIGMIS CPR Conference on Computer Personnel Reaearch* (pp. 36-45). ACM.

Kulkarni, G., Gambhir, J., & Palwe, R. (2011). Cloud computing-Software as service. *International Journal of Computer Trends and Technology,* 178-182.

Li, L., & Gao, H. (2013). WeChat: 300 million users behind. *News and Writing,* 34-36.

Li, X., Zhang, B., Lu, T., Niu, H., Hou, Y., & Zhu, L. (2012). *E-commerce in China:Taobao.* Retrieved August 2, 2013, from http://www.dwastell.org/MSc/Group6.pdf

Liang, X., & Song, F. (2008). *E-businessman wins the most.* Beijing, China: CITIC Press.

Liu, Q. (2012). Huawei's cloud plan. *CEOCIO, 1*(5), 47–48.

Lu, J., Wang, Z. L., & Hayes, A. L. (2012). How do technology readiness platform functionality and trust influence C2C user satisfaction? *Journal of Electronic Commerce Research, 13*(1), 50–69.

Ma, H. (2011). On China mobile 3G business development strategy and its future trends. *Information & Communications, 113,* 113–114.

Mao, Z. (1966). *A single spark can start a prairie fire.* Beijing: Foreign Languages Press.

Merritt, A. (2000). Culture in the cockpit: Do Hofstede's dimensions replicate? *Journal of Cross-Cultural Psychology, 3,* 283–301. doi:10.1177/0022022100031003001 PMID:11543415

Newswire, P. R. (2013, March 20). *Tencent announces 2012 fourth quarter and annual results.* Retrieved September 14, 2013, from http://www.prnewswire.com/news-releases/tencent-announces-2012-fourth-quarter-and-annual-results-199130711.html

Ou, C. X., & Davison, M. R. (2009). Why ebay lost to TaoBao in China: The global advantage. *Communications of the ACM, 52,* 145–148. doi:10.1145/1435417.1435450

Ren, Z. (2001). *The winter of Huawei.* Retrieved 4 24, 2013, from http://blog.roodo.com/shanks02/archives/11641667.html

Ren, Z. (2003). What to learn from the American. *Chinese Entrepreneur,* (11), 34-35.

Ren, Z. (2008). Learn to think in grey. *Business Review (Federal Reserve Bank of Philadelphia),* 1–1.

Ren, Z. (2010). The right direction comes from compromise. *China Businessman,* 26-28.

Ren, Z. (2013). *Ren Zhengfei (任正非).* Retrieved from http://baike.baidu.com/view/23495.htm

Richter, A., & Koch, M. (2008). Functions of social networking services. In *Proc. Intl. Conf. on the Design of Cooperative Systems* (pp. 87-98). Berlin: Springer.

Rimal, B., Choi, E., & Lumb, I. (2010). A taxonomy, survey, and issues of cloud computing ecosystems. In *Cloud computing: Principles, systems and applications* (pp. 21–46). London: Springer. doi:10.1007/978-1-84996-241-4_2

Schneider, G. P. (2013). *Electornic commerce* (10th ed.). Australia: Coourse Technology CENGAGE Learning.

Silverstein, M. J., Singhi, A., Liao, C., & Michael, D. (2012). *The $10 trillion prize captivating the newly affluent in China and India.* Boston: Harvard Business Review Press.

Singh, P. M., & Huhns, N. M. (2005). *Service-oriented computing: Semantics, processes, and agents.* Chichester, UK: John Wiley & Sons, Ltd.

Sun, Z., Dong, D., & Yearwood, J. (2011). Demand driven web service. In H.-F. Leung, D. K. Chiu, & P. C. Hung (Eds.), *Service intelligence and service science: Evolutionary technologies and challenges* (pp. 35–54). Hershey, PA: IGI Global.

Sun, Z., & Lau, S. K. (2007). Customer experience management in e-services. In *E-service intelligence* (pp. 365–388). Berlin: Springer. doi:10.1007/978-3-540-37017-8_17

Sun, Z., Wang, M., & Dong, D. (2010). Decision making in multiagent web services based on soft computing. In J. Casillas, & F. J. Martínez-López (Eds.), *Marketing intelligent systems using soft computing* (pp. 389–415). Berlin: Springer. doi:10.1007/978-3-642-15606-9_22

Tang, Z. (1995). Confucianism, Chinese culture, and reproductive behavior. *Population and Environment, 16*(3), 269–284. doi:10.1007/BF02331921

Taobao. (2013). *Taobao English guide.* Retrieved August 1, 2013, from http://taobaofocus.com/faq

Tencent. (2013). *E-commerce.* Retrieved Aug. 29, 2013, from http://www.tencent.com/en-us/ps/ecommerce.shtml

Turban, E., & Volonino, L. (2011). *Information technology for management: Improving strategic and operational performance.* Hoboken, NJ: John Wiley & Sons, Inc.

Turner, M., Budgen, D., & Brereton, P. (2003). Turning software into a service. *Computer, 36*(10), 38–44. doi:10.1109/MC.2003.1236470

Wang, L. (2009). State of the art and trends of social networking sites. *Modern Science & Technology of Telecommunications,* (6), 9-13.

Xinhua. (2013). *Tencent president: Wechat will remain free.* Retrieved September 15, 2013, from http://news.xinhuanet.com/english/china/2013-04/07/c_132290364.htm

Yan, Q. (2011). Huawei's cloud computing. *China Internet Week*, 22-24.

Yang, J. (2008). The concept and connotation of e-service. *Information Studies: Theory & Application, 31*(5), 670–674.

Yang, L., & Liu, X. (2009). Analysis on the successful strategies of Taobao's e-commerce. In *Proceedings of the 2009 International*, (pp. 202-205). Academic Press.

Yang, Y. (2011). *How could computing leads us towards ICT.* Retrieved July 8, 2013, from http://www.ciotimes.com/cloud/cyy/43789.html

Zhang, M. (2011). Mobile VAS value analysis from user demands perspective. *Information Research, 166*(8), 7–9.

ADDITIONAL READING

Alonso, G., Casati, F., Kuno, H., & Machiraju, V. (2004). *Web Services Concepts, Architectures and Applications.* Berlin, Heidelberg: Springer Verlag.

Boutaba, R., Cheng, L., & Zhang, Q. (2012). 5). On cloud computational models and the heterogeneity challenge. *Journal of Internet Services and Applications, 3*(1), 77–86. doi:10.1007/s13174-011-0054-7

Chen, J., & Hu, X. (2013). Smartphone Market in China: Challenges, Opportunities, and Promises. In I. Lee (Ed.), *Mobile Services Industries, Technologies, and Applications in the Global Economy* (pp. 120–132). Hershey, PA: Information Science Reference.

Cook, N., Milojicic, D., & Talwar, V. (2012). 5). Cloud management. *Journal of Internet Services and Applications, 3*(1), 67–75. doi:10.1007/s13174-011-0053-8

D., D. M., Katsaros, D., Mehra, P., Pallis, G., & Vakali, A. (2009). Cloud computing: Distributed Internet computing for IT and scientific research. *Internet Computing, 3* (5), pp. 10-13.

Evanschitzky, H., & Iyer, G. R. (2007). *E-Services Opportunities and Threats.* Deutscher Universitäts-Verlag.

Fensel, D. (2011). *Foundations for the Web of Information and Services.* Berlin, Heidelberg: Springer Verlag. doi:10.1007/978-3-642-19797-0

Hanna, N. K., & Qiang, C. Z.-W. (2010). 6). China's Emerging Informatization Strategy. *Journal of the Knowledge Economy, 1*(2), 128–164. doi:10.1007/s13132-009-0001-z

Huang, H., & Trauth, E. M. (2007). Cultural influences and globally distributed information systems development: experiences from Chinese IT professionals. *Proceedings of the 2007 ACM SIGMIS CPR conference on Computer personnel research: The global information technology workforce* (pp. 36-45). ACM.

Jamakovic, A., Bohnert, T. M., & Karagiannis, G. (2013). Mobile Cloud Networking: Mobile Network, Compute, and Storage as One Service On-Demand. In A. Galis, & A. Gavras (Eds.), *The Future Internet* (Vol. 7858, pp. 356–358). Lecture Notes in Computer Science Berlin, Heidelberg: Springer. doi:10.1007/978-3-642-38082-2_33

Kang, Y., Zhou, Y., Zhen, Z., & Lyu, M. R. (2011). A User Experience-Based Cloud Service Redeployment Mechanism. *2011 IEEE International Conference on Cloud Computing (CLOUD)* (pp. 227-234). IEEE.

Liu, Y., & Li, H. (2010). Mobile Internet diffusion in China: an empirical study. *Industrial Management & Data Systems*, *110*(3), 309–324. doi:10.1108/02635571011030006

Lu, J., Ruan, D., & Zhang, G. (2006). *E-Service Intelligence Mothodologies, Technologies, and Applications*. Berlin, Heidelberg: Springer Verlag.

Mache, C. (2009). Cloud Computing: An Overview. *ACM Queue; Tomorrow's Computing Today*, *7*(5), 2.

Mark, S. (2006). Culture as an explanation of technology acceptance differences: an empirical investigation of Chinese and US users. *Australasian Journal of Information Systems*, *14*(1), 5–25.

Mladenow, A., Kryvinska, N., & Strauss, C. (2012). 12). Towards cloud-centric service environments. *Journal of Service Science Research*, *4*(2), 213–234. doi:10.1007/s12927-012-0009-y

Nysveen, H., Pedersen, P. E., & Thorbjørnsen, H. (2005). 7). Intentions to Use Mobile Services: Antecedents and Cross-Service Comparisons. *Journal of the Academy of Marketing Science*, *33*(3), 330–346. doi:10.1177/0092070305276149

Peng, J., Quan, J., & Zhang, S. (2013). Mobile phone customer retention strategies and chinese e-commerce. *Electronic Commerce Research*, *12*(5).

Qi, J., Li, L., Li, Y., & Shu, H. (2009). 5/6). An extension of technology acceptance model: Analysis of the adoption of mobile data services in China. *Systems Research and Behavioral Science*, *26*(3), 391–407. doi:10.1002/sres.964

Sean, M., Li, Z., Bandyopadhyay, S., Zhang, J., & Ghalsasi, A. (2011). Cloud computing-The business perspective. *Decision Support Systems*, *51*(1), 176–189. doi:10.1016/j.dss.2010.12.006

Sun, Z., Zhang, P., Dong, D., Kajan, E., Dorloff, F.-D., & Bedini, I. (2012). Customer Decision Making in Web Services. In *Handbook of Research on E-Business Standards and Protocls: Documents, Data, and Advanced Web Technologies*. Hershey: IGI. doi:10.4018/978-1-4666-0146-8.ch010

Weinhardt, C., Blau, B., Conte, T., Filipova-Neumann, L., Meinl, T., & Michalk, W. (2011). *Business Aspects of Web Services*. Berlin, Heidelberg: Springer. doi:10.1007/978-3-642-22447-8

KEY TERMS AND DEFINITIONS

Cloud Computing: Cloud computing is an Internet-based computing model that thousands or even millions of servers connected into a whole in a remote data center to offer users to experience powerful computing capacity, very large scaled storage, and various software applications. Users access to the data center via terminal devices such as laptops, mobile phones through the Internet, according to their respective needs for storage, computing and other services.

Mobile Services: Mobile service is a kind of e-service accessed by mobile devices. A mobile device is a portable, handheld communications device connected to a wireless network that allows users to make voice calls, send messages and run applications.

Modern Service Sector: Modern service sector is developed in the relatively developed stage of industrialization, mainly relying on information technology and modern ideas, information and knowledge relatively intensive service sector, and emphasizes the features of high-tech knowledge and technology-intensive, compared with the traditional service industries.

SOA: Service Oriented Architecture (SOA) is an abstract framework for understanding significant relationships among the entities of Web service environment. It is a paradigm for organizing and utilizing distributed functionalities that may be under the control of different ownership domains.

Social Networking Services: A social network service is an online platform service that focuses on building and reflecting of social connections or social relations among members by the shared profiles, interests and activities.

Web Services: Web services are all the services available via the Web or the Internet from a business perspective. Web services are Web-based application components published using standard interface description languages and universally available via uniform communication protocols from a technological perspective.

Chapter 13

Adoption of Social Media Services:
The Case of Local Government Organizations in Australia

Mohd Hisham Mohd Sharif
University of Adelaide, Australia

Indrit Troshani
University of Adelaide, Australia

Robyn Davidson
University of Adelaide, Australia

ABSTRACT

The increasing diffusion of social media is attracting government organizations worldwide, including local government. Social media can help local government improve the manner in which it is engaged with community and its responsiveness whilst offering cost savings and flexibility. Yet, there is paucity of research in relation to the adoption of social media Web services in local government organizations. The aim of this chapter is to investigate the factors that drive the adoption of social media Web services within Australian local government. Using qualitative evidence, the authors find technological, organizational, and environmental factors that drive the decisions of local government organizations to adopt social media Web services. In addition to extending the existing body of knowledge, this chapter offers insight concerning important managerial implications for helping local governments to better understand social media adoption in their organizations.

DOI: 10.4018/978-1-4666-5884-4.ch013

INTRODUCTION

The increasing diffusion of social media is attracting government organizations worldwide including local government (Anttiroiko, 2010). Social media can help local government to become more responsive to its citizens, engage with the community and promote both accountability and transparency (Accenture, 2009; Australian Government, 2009; Eggers, 2007). Social media can also offer cost savings and flexibility (Lim & Palacios-Marques, 2011) to both local government and citizens using it whilst providing opportunities for improving service delivery and obtaining community feedback effectively and efficiently (Chang & Kannan, 2008; Markova, 2009; Osimo, 2008). In fact, evidence is emerging on how local government in the United Kingdom, United States, Australia, Germany and New Zealand are using social media for improving their services to the public (Anttiroiko, 2010; Purser, 2012; State Services Commission, 2008; Towns, 2010).

There is general agreement in extant literature that social media can be defined as any interactive Web-based application based on Web 2.0 technology that offers Web services enabling interactions between or amongst Web users and enhances their ability to create and share information on the Web (Boyd & Ellison, 2007; O'Reilly, 2007). Although social media and Web 2.0 are distinct concepts they are used interchangeably in the literature. Web 2.0 represents a newer platform foundation of the Web which consists of a set of technologies (e.g. Adobe Flash and RSS) to enable richer content to be published on the Web (O'Reilly, 2007). By contrast, social media refers to Web services that enable user generated content (UGC), that is, various forms of media content created by Internet users and available on the Web based Web 2.0 (Kaplan & Haenlein, 2010). Examples of social media applications include blogs and micro blogs (e.g. Twitter), wikis (e.g. Wikipedia), social networking (e.g. Facebook, LinkedIn), multimedia sharing services (e.g. YouTube), content syndication (e.g. RSS feeds), podcasting (e.g. iTunes) and content tagging services (Anderson, 2007; Hansen, Shneiderman, & Smith, 2010).

Despite the growing number of local governments taking part in implementing social media and federal government investment in terms of financial and organizational resources to improve social media initiatives (Steward, 2012), the uptake by government organizations in Australia, including local government has been sluggish and not as good as the development in the corporate world (Samuel, 2009). In a survey conducted with 235 local governments across Australia (Purser, 2012), only 25 percent of the local government organizations were identified to use social media and only six percent of local government organizations were identified to use social media extensively. Another recent survey of 560 council websites found that many local government websites are still based on one-way interaction designs and only eighty-two councils had social media applications promoted on their websites (Howard, 2012).

Like other IT projects, investment into Web services such as social media by governments often requires organizational change to culture, people, structure and processes if effective results are to be accomplished (Dadashzadeh, 2010; de Kool & van Wamelen, 2008). According to Osimo (2008), government organizations need to have a clear social media strategy to ensure the success of social media initiatives. Thus, in order to utilize the full potential of social media, a systematic approach is needed to identify the key determinants that influence successful adoption. Although various studies (Chang & Kannan, 2008; Meijer & Thaens, 2010; Wigand, 2010) and reports (Howard, 2012; Osimo, 2008; Purser, 2012) exist concerning the use of social media to enhance service delivery and the many benefits they offer, there is agreement amongst scholars that their adoption across local government remains underresearched (Millard, 2010; Nam, 2011; Wigand, 2010). Specifically, only limited studies have been found that can improve the understanding of the factors that drive social media adoption. Notably, James & Clarke (2010) explored the factors for designing social media applications for Australian local government whilst Purser (2012) focused on exploring the benefits, risks and barriers of using social media in Australian local government and identified areas where social media could be used effectively. Samuel (2009) outlines a number of deterrents which may make government organizations in Australia unwilling to embrace social media. In Japan, Schellong (2008) explored the effect of social networking services in improving re-building communities during natural disasters, including emergency management during earthquakes. In Canada and the US, Wigand (2010) focused on exploring social media adoption in local government in delivering information and services. While these studies focused on the types and patterns of social media that can be used in local government including the benefits and challenges of using such technology, they have ignored the factors that can drive social media adoption across these organizations which represents a gap in the existing body of knowledge.

Given the unique nature of social media as a Web service (O'Reilly, 2007), its differences to ICTs and Web technologies generally (Cormode & Krishnamurthy, 2008), we argue that further research is required to enhance current understanding of the adoption of social media as a Web service. There is widespread agreement that factors that drive technology adoption depend on the nature and type of the technology itself and the domain in which adoption occurs. This suggests that no one-size-fits-all approach can be adopted across technologies and domains and that factors that drive the adoption of specific technologies, including Web services, require specific attention and clarification (Dewar and Dutton, 1986, Damanpour, 1987, Walker, 2006). This is consistent with criticism of existing technology adoption research according to which "[t] he search for a universalistic theory may be inappropriate given the fundamental differences that

exist across innovation types. Empirical support for this conclusion is accumulating" (Dewar & Dutton, 1986, p. 1422).

To address this shortcoming, this chapter aims to answer the following research questions: i) why is social media (as a Web service) important for local government organizations? and, ii) what factors influence the adoption of social media in local government organizations? In pursuit of our aim, we focus on local government in Australia because of the rapidly emerging trend of social media use amongst organizations operating in this sector and the growing attention and interest that social media research is attracting (Alam & Walker, 2011; Sensis, 2012). Specifically, 62 percent of Internet users in Australia have a social media presence, 97 percent of whom use social networking applications, with Facebook being the most popular (Sensis, 2012). The growth of social media use in Australia is changing the way people communicate and interact with each other and with both private and public sector organisations including local government (Howard, 2012; Purser, 2012). Recognising the growing trends of social media use amongst Australians and the advantages that it can offer, an increasing number of local government organisations in Australia, ranging from metropolitan, rural and remote councils, are beginning to engage with the public by using social media in different ways. This includes promoting events and activities, providing clarification on issues, issuing alerts, gaining community input and engaging with young adults (ACELG, 2011; Howard, 2012; Purser, 2012). Social media applications such as Twitter and Facebook were also used by local government to inform and update residents during the 2011 natural disasters, for example, the Queensland floods and cyclone Yassi (ACELG, 2011).

Furthermore, there are stark differences between public sector organizations (including local government) and private sector firms, which mean that extant technology adoption research may not be readily applicable for explaining social media adoption in local government organizations. These differences may affect the manner in which social media adoption unfolds in these organizations. First, public and private sector organizations have different strategic and operational goals. The primary goal of private sector firms is profit maximization while public sector organizations generally have multiple goals including providing better public services such as education, healthcare, transport and urban planning (Boyne, 2002). Additionally, unlike public organisations, those operating in the private sector are typically driven by market signals, feasibility and economic viability considerations, including profit taking (Kamal, 2006). Public sector organizations also operate in an environment with little or no competitive pressure relative to their private sector counterparts. Consequently, the former may face less pressure to be efficient than the latter. Managers in the private sector may be motivated by direct monetary incentives (e.g. performance-based end of financial year bonuses) which may not necessarily be provided to managers in public sector organizations (Boyne, 2002). Rocheleau and Wu (2002) have confirmed that private sector organizations invest more resources into ICTs compared to the public sector. This is because the private sector views ICT as an important enabler for enhancing their competitive advantage which may not be as critical for public sector organizations given they operate like a monopoly for most public services. In fact, unlike private sector organizations that are generally known to adopt innovations proactively, due to a bureaucratic culture, public sector organizations generally introduce innovations reactively, that is, they wait for evidence to become available to justify their adoption decisions. Additionally, due to budget timing restrictions, public sector organizations may be subject to the temporal constraints of public sector budgeting cycles which in turn may be dictated by political influences or periodic changes in program priorities and top-level management (Caudle et al., 1991, Themistocleous et al., 2004). Finally, there is evidence suggesting that technologies in the not-for-profit sector, including public sector, or those that contribute to the public good often "have greater diffusion difficulties" (McGrath & Zell, 2001, p. 388) which need to be addressed in future research. Taken together, these reasons suggest that adoption models developed for the private sector cannot be automatically applied to public sector organizations (Ahmad & Zink, 1998, Fountain, 2001, McGrath & Zell, 2001, Henriksen & Mahnke, 2005).

The remainder of this chapter first discusses the theoretical framework, before explaining the data collection and analysis considerations. The findings are subsequently presented before conclusions are drawn and managerial implications discussed.

THEORETICAL FRAMEWORK

Technology adoption literature suggests that various theories have been used for explaining adoption which can be divided into two broad categories, namely, those that attempt to explain technology adoption by individuals and those that attempt to explain technology adoption by organizations. The Technology Acceptance Model (TAM) by Davis (1989) and the Unified Theory of Acceptance and Use of Technology (UTAUT) models proposed by Venkatesh, Morris, Davis, and Davis (2003) have been used predominantly for explaining technology adoption by individuals (Saldanha & Krishnan, 2012). Drawn from social psychology these theories argue that factors such as perceived ease of use (or effort expectancy) and perceived usefulness (or performance expectancy) explain user's behavioral intention to adopt technology. The main advantages of these models include their simplicity and generalizability across different settings. In organizational contexts, most research is based on theories such as Diffusion of Innovation Theory (Rogers, 1995), Institutional Theory (Scott, 1987), Resource–based

Theory (Wernerfelt, 1984) and the Technology-Organization-Environment (TOE) framework (DePietro, Wiarda, & Fleischer, 1990). Based on sociology diffusion of innovation theory explains the process by way of which technological innovation is communicated to prospective adopters in a social system whereas institutional theory explains technology is created, adapted, diffused, and becomes taken for granted over time. The resource-based theory argues that combinations of tangible and intangible resources can help firms derive sustained competitive advantage. This study uses TOE, a prominent approach used to explain, analyze and distinguish the drivers that influence technology adoption decisions in organizations (DePietro et al., 1990). This framework is often used to describe the context in which adoption take places. It incorporates factors that can influence adoption by organizations based on the technological, organizational and environmental contexts (DePietro et al., 1990; Fichman, 2000; Jeyaraj, Rottman, & Lacity, 2006).

The technological context concerns the inherent characteristics of a technology that can influence its adoption within organizations (DePietro et al., 1990). For example, potential adopters assess the characteristics of the technology by evaluating its advantages over adoption costs (Premkumar, Ramamurthy, & Nilakanta, 1994). The organizational context includes factors that characterize organizations such as size, structure, resource availability, readiness and infrastructure (DePietro et al., 1990). A positive organizational atmosphere which includes having good management support and favorable policies can help organizations in their decisions to adopt new technologies (Premkumar et al., 1994; Saldanha & Krishnan, 2012). The environmental context consists of the characteristics of the arena where organizations operate that can have an impact on them. This includes interactions with government (e.g. by way of regulation) and competitors (DePietro et al., 1990). Environmental factors such as success stories can encourage potential adopters

to adopt technologies by raising awareness and creating bandwagon pressures (Troshani, Jerram, & Rao Hill, 2011).

The TOE framework has been consistently used by researchers to investigate technology adoption in various organizational contexts such as Web 2.0 (Saldanha & Krishnan, 2012), social media in the private sector (Parveen, 2012), cloud computing (Low, Chen, & Wu, 2011), e-business (Zhu, Kraemer, & Xu, 2003; Zhu & Kraemer, 2005), e-government (Pudjianto, Zo, Ciganek, & Rho, 2011) and EDI (Chwelos, Benbasat, & Dexter, 2001). Extant research has identified factors within the three contexts that operate in various domains and national contexts (Baker, 2012). Nevertheless, there are consistent and growing calls to extend the TOE framework to other domains and technologies (Low et al., 2011) due to the complex and context-sensitive nature of technology adoption (Wolfe, 1994). In this study, we adopt the TOE framework for two reasons. First, the nature of this study is exploratory. The broadness and the integrating nature of TOE can create opportunities for new relevant constructs to be identified (Li, Lai, & Wang, 2010; Parveen, 2012) whilst also minimizing bias in construct selection. Second, although specific factors may vary across specific contexts, the TOE framework has a solid and consistent theoretical basis, consistent empirical support and the potential to be applied to other IS innovation domains (Kuan & Chau, 2001; Oliveira & Martins, 2010; Xu, Zhu, & Gibbs, 2004). Thus, because this study is attempting to explore the factors behind the adoption of social media as a Web service in local government organizations, using the TOE framework as a guide is a reasonable proposition.

DATA COLLECTION AND ANALYSIS

This study is exploratory in nature. It uses qualitative data as the main evidence. Data were collected using semi-structured face-to-face and phone interviews. Interviewing can be a powerful data collection technique because of its flexibility and ability to help source in-depth and rich information for exploring and understanding respondents' viewpoints on research issues (Huberman & Miles, 1994). In this study, respondents from 21 local government organizations across Australia that have adopted or were in the process of adopting social media applications were interviewed. The interviews were conducted in 2012. Judgment sampling was used to select local government organizations in order to obtain a good representation and productive participation from across Australia including metropolitan and rural locations (Marshall, 1996). Innovative local government organizations that are using social media were identified by consultation with the Australian Centre of Local Government Excellence (ACELG) and by analyzing relevant Web sites. Selection of interviewees was based on their involvement with the development and implementation of social media Web services within their organization. Typically interviewees were knowledgeable about adoption decisions and were willing to participate in the study (Kumar, Stern, & Anderson, 1993). They fulfilled roles of public relations or social media officers and were highly involved in introducing and implementing social media Web services in their organization. Snowballing was also used to identify interviewees by asking for referrals from participants (Sekaran, 2003). Interviewees were asked to suggest other local government organizations that were known to have used social media Web services effectively. To honor confidentiality data are presented anonymously. Table 1 shows the location and identifier of the organizations that participated in the interviews.

The interview questions focused on topics such as current use of social media, objectives for adopting social media Web services, benefits of using social media, characteristics of social media applications used, organizational support, resources provided, community expectations and influence from other parties. During the interviews

Table 1. Local government organization participants

Australian State	Identifier
South Australia	SA 1-6
Victoria	VIC 7-12
Western Australia	WA 13-14
Queensland	QLD 15-18
New South Wales	NSW 19-20
Tasmania	TAS 21

additional questions were raised to gather more in-depth information. The TOE framework was used as a guide to analyze the interview transcripts.

Data analysis and interpretation were carried out in three stages, namely, (i) data reduction, (ii) data display, and (iii) conclusion drawing/ verification. With data reduction, data summaries, clusters, and codes were developed which provided the basis for data display, that is, data belonging to emerging themes were incrementally condensed in an assembly of information, including synopses and diagrams (Huberman & Miles, 1994). Subsequently, conclusions were drawn and verification undertaken. Consequently, to draw meanings and interpretations from the data, we moved back and forth hermeneutically between the data and the relevant literature, comparing, contrasting and triangulating the identified theme patterns. The structure and analysis of findings were amended until a thorough understanding of the phenomena represented in the data developed as it pertains to our research questions (Huberman & Miles, 1994).

Construct validity has been adequately addressed by using multiple sources of information (Yin, 2009). Primary data were collected from interviews and secondary data from local government organization websites and relevant white papers. Interviews were with employees that carry out different roles within the organizations thus giving a different perspective and providing further triangulation of qualitative information

(Huberman & Miles, 1994). Whilst one of the investigators carried out the interviews, all three participated in data analysis, thereby reducing the potential bias that is commonly cited as a limitation of qualitative information sources, thereby strengthening triangulation even further (Yin, 2009). The chain of evidence was also maintained which traces the collected data to the interview summaries and conclusions. Validity was further addressed by carrying out follow up interviews to clarify unclear issues and gain a more in-depth understanding to increase rigor in the findings. These measures have enhanced the reliability of this research, thereby improving its overall quality.

FINDINGS

The factors that influence the adoption of social media as a Web service in Australian local government organizations are discussed in this section.

Technological Context

Relative Advantage

Relative advantage of social media was consistently identified as one of the most important factors influencing the adoption of social media as a Web service. The advantages that were discussed in relation to this factor include ease of access, instant communication, low maintenance and operational costs and the ability to create two-way communication with the community. Ease of access and instant communication with the local community were perceived as being useful. Interactions with the community included promoting local activities, disseminating information for weather warnings and other emergency issues, correcting misinformation and engaging with the community on a range of issues which could be

done ubiquitously. These benefits were expected to help build better communication with the community including a wider reach, particularly with youth groups that are highly engaged with social media. For example:

Well basically it's an approach for the council [i.e. local government organization] to engage with as many communities as possible, to feed them with information that they seek and get feedback from them, so I think social media has the capabilities to deliver our messages quickly and it is also another means for us to get instant feedback. (QLD 15)

While there was a general agreement that social media was important for engaging with the community, there are also concerns that its potential benefits will be outweighed by the effort of monitoring social media applications.

Every question has to be responded to in a very timely manner. You have to do it quickly because it is a real time world. It is very labor intensive. This means that we must always have somebody to monitor all the conversations and information exchange happening in the site. (SA 1)

Perceived Security

Fear that negative comments would be aired publicly by unauthorized parties was perceived as a risk by the interviewees. They were concerned that individuals would be able to post negative remarks, such as racist comments or disparaging comments towards local government which may harm the organization's reputation.

… there is a lot of potential problems that we could see emerging, such as people misusing it. So, we don't know what's going to happen. (NSW 20).

Furthermore, fear of illegal breaches into the organization's network from spyware as well as from viruses and malicious software were also perceived as a potential security risk. The breach could also be caused by irresponsible use of social media by employees (e.g. malicious code through Facebook apps).

Organizational Context

Management Drive

Management drive was considered to be one of the key factors in driving adoption. Respondents were in agreement that a critical factor in ensuring effective social media adoption is for management to actively encourage staff to explore and use social media as well as provide appropriate supporting resources.

Our CEO also is very passionate in communicating online. When we get that support from the top and an expectation from the top that we keep up to speed with everybody, then that was the directive that we need to follow. (VIC 10).

Social Media Policies

Social media policies were stressed by many as a consideration affecting the adoption decisions in local government organizations. Social media policies, concerning issues such as the handling of legal issues and guidelines of usage practices for both staff and external users, can drive social media adoption by providing confidence before making the adoption decision. Some respondents indicated that without adequate policies, they may be unable to fully take advantage of social media benefits:

… the biggest challenge was the policies and guidelines in the organization and deciding how social media should be adopted and who should be able to use it; how strict we should be with it. (QLD 18).

Environmental Context

Community Demand

The influence of community demand was perceived to be a major driver of social media adoption. There was general agreement that the increasing use of social media by the community raises the need for local government organizations to also be able to communicate and respond by using social media. This requirement to respond to community demand to use social media as one of its communication channels was consistently raised by many interviewees:

The main thing from the council's [i.e. local government organization's] perspective is to be responsive to the needs of the community. The community these days expects to be able to communicate in a whole lot of different ways. (VIC 11)

Bandwagon Effect

Bandwagon effect refers to the impact of success stories from local government organizations that had adopted social media Web services on those that were contemplating to adopt these Web services. Those that had been successful in implementing social media and allowing their benefits to be observed can create a bandwagon effect that can influence adoption decisions by others:

We do see other councils [i.e. local government organizations] and how they are using it to reap benefits, so that impacted on why we should take it up. We also learn from other councils to not only use it for disasters but how to utilize it in day to day operations. (QLD 16).

DISCUSSION

Figure 1 summarizes the factors that can impact on the adoption of social media Web services in local government organizations in Australia.

Our analysis provides insight into the factors that influence social media adoption in Australian local government organizations. Technological factors featured prominently in explaining social media adoption while relative advantage was the major driver of adoption. Our findings indicate that active social media adopters are those who are aware of social media benefits. Many interviewees reported that as they become aware of social media benefits and understand how it can be used effectively, the adoption process become easier. This suggests a need for greater awareness on social media benefits by adoption champions is required in order to influence decision makers. While there was a general agreement that social media can promote better engagement with the community, there were also concerns regarding its potential lack of security. A major concern is negative comments that may damage the local government organizations' reputation. This is caused by a lack of understanding on how to use social media. In reality, negative statements about

local government organizations will exist regardless of whether or not social media is used. By using social media effectively, organizations can turn the fear and negative remarks to their advantage. By interacting with the community through social media, they can correct misinformation that is spread in the community and can have better control over messages rather than having statements misused by inappropriate parties. Perceived lack of security can reduce the willingness of local government organizations to trial social media applications. However this can be overcome if organizations have the correct information and a good understanding of how social media Web services can be used as an effective channel of communication.

Organizational factors that drive social media adoption include management drive and social media policies. Not surprisingly, management drive played an important role in driving the adoption. The reason is that as the adoption progresses, the role of management is critical for providing adequate human, financial and infrastructure resources. Management drive also ensured adoption by constantly monitoring adoption initiatives. Interviews with successful adopters of social media reveal how important it is for management

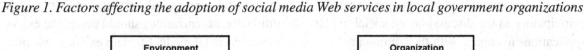

Figure 1. Factors affecting the adoption of social media Web services in local government organizations

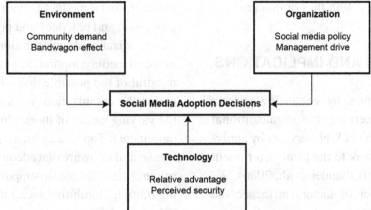

to become involved in social media adoption initiatives. When management support and drive social media adoption it positively influences that adoption across the organization.

The need for organizations to develop a policy before implementing social media Web services emerges as another important theme in the interviews. Social media policy outlines procedures and guidelines in relation to the use of social media. Our interviewees suggest that with no or incomplete policies the organization faced uncertainties in dealing with negative or offensive contributions or remarks, legal issues, security problems and even inappropriate use of social media by staff. Thus, in the early adoption stages, efforts should concentrate on developing a complete social media policy prior to embarking on adoption initiatives as a way of creating a suitable policy backing and framework for handling issues as they emerge.

The influence of bandwagon pressures was also an important determinant of social media adoption. Sharing success stories from local government organizations that have implemented social media applications creates bandwagon pressures by inspiring many organizations to follow in others' successful footsteps. Social media adoption also relies on community demand for daily interactions. Therefore, local government organizations need to go further than providing one-way information and become proactive and participatory in the discussions on social media applications to engage with the community.

CONTRIBUTION AND IMPLICATIONS

This study contributes by enhancing current understanding concerning the organizational adoption of social media Web services by applying the TOE framework to the local government context in Australia (Liljander et al., 2006). We found that a number of factors influence the decision of local government organizations for adopting social media Web services. These fac-

tors include technology factors (relative advantage and perceived security), organizational factors (social media policies and management drive), and environmental factors (community demand and bandwagon effects).

Although extant research has explored and investigated various adoption contexts of social media, limited studies exist concerning local government organizations. With this study, we attempt to fill this gap which is increasing given the growing use of social media services across local government. Specifically, it adds to literature by isolating specific factors and the manner in which these can jointly shape the motivation of local government organizations to adopt social media Web services. We have also extended and validated the TOE framework and confirmed its applicability and usefulness for exploring social media adoption.

This study offers important managerial implications concerning technology, organizational, and environmental considerations. In terms of technology, management should stress the relative advantage that social media can offer compared to alternatives. For example, management should demonstrate how social media benefits, including improved efficiency, communication, accessibility, and accountability, might outweigh obstacles encountered during adoption. Such obstacles may include perceptions of security concerns. Additionally, organizations should assess the extent to which social media fits with existing systems, processes, and practices and policy.

Organizational considerations are also relevant to social media adoption. Management should be mindful of the possible disparities that can exist across the organization in adoption rates due to the varying nature of its employees and their requirements. Top management support and drive is essential to ensure that adequate organizational resources are allocated to support adoption, including training. Inhibitive social media policies and cultural inertia may undermine adoption, suggesting that adequate policy changes may be necessary to improve adoption outcomes. Additionally, broader environment dimensions exist that can impact on the adoption of social media in local government. Demand from the community and successful adoption of social media by exemplar local government organizations may also foster adoption across organizations that are considering enhancing existing communication channels with citizens by using social media Web services.

Isolating relevant technology, organization and environment factors of social media adoption is crucial for managers to understand. Such understanding can help to shape the strategic position of their organizations and achieve effective relationships with all stakeholders. Furthermore, an improved understanding of local government adoption of social media could be useful to managers and IT/IS professionals as they design and implement novel social media Web services and even upgrade existing ones. Specifically, knowledge gained can be used to achieve greater efficiencies by developing actionable adoption tactics, strategies, and policies for improving the chances of achieving social media adoption success.

While this study uses the experiences from various local government organizations across Australia, the fact that the qualitative evidence was only drawn from twenty-one local government organizations suggests that the insights from this study may only be generalized to theory (Lee and Baskerville, 2003; Williams, 2000). Nevertheless, further qualitative and quantitative evidence is needed to address this limitation. Additionally, a deeper focus is required on the factors that inhibit social media adoption beyond the factors that drive it which is the focus of the present study. The model of social media adoption developed in this study could also be tested in other settings, in other countries for example, to further investigate and explore the adoption of social media Web services and implications as well as confirming and/or extending the developed model.

REFERENCES

Accenture. (2009). *Research & insights: Web 2.0 and the next generation of public service*. Retrieved from http://www.epractice.eu/en/library/309027

ACELG. (2011). *Local government and community engagement*. Sydney: Australian Centre of Excellence for Local Government, University of Technology, Sydney.

Ahmad, A. A., & Zink, S. D. (1998). Information technology adoption in Jordanian public sector organizations. *Journal of Government Information*, 25(2), 117–134. doi:10.1016/S1352-0237(97)00094-4

Alam, S., & Walker, D. (2011). The public Facebook: A case of Australian government Facebook pages and participation. In *Proceedings of ACIS 2011*. Sydney, Australia: ACIS.

Anderson, P. (2007, February). What is web 2.0? Ideas, technology and implications for education. *JISC Technology and Standards Watch*.

Anttiroiko, A. V. (2010). Innovation in democratic e-governance: Benefitting from web 2.0 applications in the public sector. *International Journal of Electronic Government Research*, 6(2), 18–36. doi:10.4018/jegr.2010040102

Australian Government. (2009). *Engage: Getting on with government 2.0, report of the government 2.0 taskforce*. ACT: Australian Government Information Management Office.

Baker, J. (2012). The technology–organization–environment framework. In *Information systems theory: Explaining and predicting our digital society* (Vol. 1, pp. 231–245). Springer Link. doi:10.1007/978-1-4419-6108-2_12

Boyd, D. M., & Ellison, N. B. (2007). Social network sites: Definition, history, and scholarship. *Journal of Computer-Mediated Communication*, 13(1), 210–230. doi:10.1111/j.1083-6101.2007.00393.x

Boyne, G. A. (2002). Public and private management: What's the difference? *Journal of Management Studies, 39*(1), 97–122. doi:10.1111/1467-6486.00284

Caudle, S. L., Gorr, W. L., & Newcomer, K. E. (1991). Key information systems management issues. *Management Information Systems Quarterly, 15*(2), 171–188. doi:10.2307/249378

Chang, A. M., & Kannan, P. (2008). *Leveraging web 2.0 in government.* IBM Centre for the Business of Government.

Chwelos, P., Benbasat, I., & Dexter, A. S. (2001). Empirical test of an EDI adoption model. *Information Systems Research, 12*(3), 304–321. doi:10.1287/isre.12.3.304.9708

Cormode, G., & Krishnamurthy, B. (2008). Key differences between web 1.0 and web 2.0. *First Monday, 13*(6), 2. doi:10.5210/fm.v13i6.2125

Dadashzadeh, M. (2010). Social media in government: From eGovernment to eGovernance. *Journal of Business & Economics Research, 8*(11), 81–86.

Damanpour, F. (1987). The adoption of technological, administrative, and ancillary innovations: Impact of organizational factors. *Journal of Management, 13*(4), 675–688. doi:10.1177/014920638701300408

Davis, F. D. (1989). Perceived usefulness, perceived ease of use, and user acceptance of information technology. *Management Information Systems Quarterly,* 319–340. doi:10.2307/249008

de Kool, D., & van Wamelen, J. (2008). Web 2.0: A new basis for e-government? In *Proceedings of the 3rd International Conference on Information & Communication Technologies: From Theory to Applications (ICTTA 2008).* ICTTA.

DePietro, R., Wiarda, E., & Fleischer, M. (1990). *The context for change: Organization, technology and environment.* Lexington, MA: Lexington Books.

Dewar, R. D., & Dutton, J. E. (1986). The adoption of radical and incremental innovations: An empirical analysis. *Management Science, 32*(11), 1422–1433. doi:10.1287/mnsc.32.11.1422

Eggers, W. D. (2007). *Government 2.0: Using technology to improve education, cut red tape, reduce gridlock, and enhance democracy.* Rowan & Littlefield Publishers, Manhattan Institute.

Fichman, R. G. (2000). The diffusion and assimilation of information technology innovations. In R. Zmud (Ed.), *Framing the domains of IT management: Projecting the future through the past.* Pinnaflex Publishing.

Fountain, J. (2001). Paradoxes of public sector customer service. *Governance: An International Journal of Policy, Administration and Institutions, 14*(1), 55–73. doi:10.1111/0952-1895.00151

Hansen, D., Shneiderman, B., & Smith, M. A. (2010). *Analyzing social media networks with NodeXL.* Morgan Kaufmann.

Henriksen, H. Z., & Mahnke, V. (2005). E-procurement adoption in the Danish public sector. *Scandinavian Journal of Information Systems, 17*(2), 85–106.

Howard, A. E. (2012). *Connecting with communities: How local government is using social media to engage with citizens.* ANZSOG Institute for Governance at the University of Canberra and Australian Centre of Excellence for Local Government.

Huberman, A. M., & Miles, M. B. (1994). Data management and analysis methods. In N. K. Denzin, & Y. S. Lincoln (Eds.), *Handbook of qualitative research* (pp. 428–444). Thousand Oaks, CA: Sage.

James, J., & Clarke, R. (2010). Transforming the relationship between citizens and local councils using web 2.0 technologies. In H. Yeatman (Ed.), *The SInet 2010 eBook: Proceedings of the SInet 2009 conference*. University of Wollongong.

Jeyaraj, A., Rottman, J. W., & Lacity, M. C. (2006). A review of the predictors, linkages, and biases in IT innovation adoption research. *Journal of Information Technology*, *21*(1), 1–23. doi:10.1057/palgrave.jit.2000056

Kamal, M. M. (2006). IT innovation adoption in the government sector: Identifying the critical success factors. *Journal of Enterprise Information Management*, *19*(2), 192–222. doi:10.1108/17410390610645085

Kaplan, A. M., & Haenlein, M. (2010). Users of the world, unite! The challenges and opportunities of social media. *Business Horizons*, *53*(1), 59–68. doi:10.1016/j.bushor.2009.09.003

Kuan, K. K. Y., & Chau, P. Y. K. (2001). A perception-based model for EDI adoption in small businesses using a technology-organization-environment framework. *Information & Management*, *38*(8), 507–512. doi:10.1016/S0378-7206(01)00073-8

Kumar, N., Stern, L. W., & Anderson, J. C. (1993). Conducting interorganizational research using key informants. *Academy of Management Journal*, *36*(6), 1633–1651. doi:10.2307/256824

Lee, A. S., & Baskerville, R. L. (2003). Generalizing generalizability in information systems research. *Information Systems Research*, *14*(3), 221–243. doi:10.1287/isre.14.3.221.16560

Li, D., Lai, F., & Wang, J. (2010). E-business assimilation in China's international trade firms: The technology-organization-environment framework. *Journal of Global Information Management*, *18*(1), 39–65. doi:10.4018/jgim.2010091103

Liljander, V., Gillberg, F., Gummerus, J., & van Riel, A. (2006). Technology readiness and the evaluation and adoption of self-service technologies. *Journal of Retailing and Consumer Services*, *13*(3), 177–191. doi:10.1016/j.jretconser.2005.08.004

Lim, S. B., & Palacios-Marques, D. (2011). Culture and purpose of web 2.0 service adoption: A study in the USA, Korea and Spain. *The Service Industries Journal*, *31*(1), 123–131. doi:10.1080/02642069.2010.485634

Low, C., Chen, Y., & Wu, M. (2011). Understanding the determinants of cloud computing adoption. *Industrial Management & Data Systems*, *111*(7), 1006–1023. doi:10.1108/02635571111161262

Markova, I. (2009). *Web 2.0 technology adoption by government departments*. Carleton University.

Marshall, M. N. (1996). Sampling for qualitative research. *Family Practice*, *13*(6), 522–526. doi:10.1093/fampra/13.6.522 PMID:9023528

McGrath, C., & Zell, D. (2001). The future of innovation diffusion research and its implications for management: A conversation with Everett Rogers. *Journal of Management Inquiry*, *10*(4), 386–391. doi:10.1177/1056492601104012

Meijer, A., & Thaens, M. (2010). Alignment 2.0: Strategic use of new internet technologies in government. *Government Information Quarterly*, *27*(2), 113–121. doi:10.1016/j.giq.2009.12.001

Millard, J. (2010). Government 1.5: Is the bottle half full or half empty. *European Journal of ePractice*, *9*(1), 35-50.

Nam, T. (2011). Towards the new phase of e-government: An empirical study on citizens' attitude about open government and government 2.0. In *Proceedings of the 11th Public Management Research Conference*. Maxwell School of Syracuse University.

O'Reilly, T. (2007). What is web 2.0: Design patterns and business models for the next generation of software. *Communications & Strategies*, *65*(1), 17–37.

Oliveira, T., & Martins, M. F. (2010). Understanding e-business adoption across industries in European countries. *Industrial Management & Data Systems*, *110*(9), 1337–1354. doi:10.1108/02635571011087428

Osimo, D. (2008). *Web 2.0 in government: Why and how?*. Institute for Prospective Technological Studies (IPTS), Joint Research Centre, European Commission, EUR No. *23358* EN.

Parveen, F. (2012). Impact of social media usage on organizations. In *Proceedings of the 16th Pacific Asia Conference on Information Systems (PACIS 2012)*. Ho Chi Minh City, Vietnam: PACIS.

Premkumar, G., Ramamurthy, K., & Nilakanta, S. (1994). Implementation of electronic data interchange: An innovation diffusion perspective. *Journal of Management Information Systems*, *11*(2), 157–186.

Pudjianto, B., Zo, H., Ciganek, A. P., & Rho, J. J. (2011). Determinants of e-government assimilation in Indonesia: An empirical investigation using a TOE framework. *Asia Pacific Journal of Information Systems*, *21*(1), 49–80.

Purser, K. (2012). Using social media in local government: 2011 survey report. Australian Centre of Excellence for Local Government, University of Technology.

Rocheleau, B., & Wu, L. (2002). Public versus private information systems. *American Review of Public Administration*, *32*(4), 379. doi:10.1177/027507402237866

Rogers, E. M. (1995). *Diffusion of innovations*. New York: Free Press.

Saldanha, T. J. V., & Krishnan, M. S. (2012). Organizational adoption of web 2.0 technologies: An empirical analysis. *Journal of Organizational Computing and Electronic Commerce*, *22*(4), 301–333. doi:10.1080/10919392.2012.723585

Samuel, A. (2009). Waiting for government 2.0: Why do public agencies take so long to embrace social media? In J. Gotze, & J. Bering Pedersen (Eds.), *State of the eUnion: Government 2.0 and onwards* (pp. 109–122). Academic Press.

Schellong, A. R. M. (2008). Government 2.0: An exploratory study of social networking services in Japanese local government. *Transforming Government: People. Process and Policy*, *2*(4), 225–242.

Scott, W. R. (1987). The adolescence of institutional theory. *Administrative Science Quarterly*, *32*(4), 493–511. doi:10.2307/2392880

Sekaran, U. (2003). *Research methods for business* (4th ed.). New York: John Wiley & Sons.

Sensis. (2012). *Yellow social media report*. Sensis Pty Ltd.

State Services Commission. (2008). *New Zealand e-government 2007: Progress towards transformation*. Wellington, New Zealand: New Zealand Government.

Steward, A. (2012). *Progress on government 2.0*. Retrieved from http://agimo.govspace.gov.au/2012/07/06/progress-on-government-2-0/#more-3982

Themistocleous, M., Irani, Z., Kuljis, J., & Love, P. E. D. (2004). Extending the information systems lifecycle through enterprise application intergration. In *Proceedings of the 37th Hawaii International Conference on System Sciences*. IEEE.

Towns, S. (2010). *Will Facebook replace traditional government websites*. Retrieved from http://www.govtech.com/e-government/Will-Facebook-Replace-Traditional-Government-Web.html

Troshani, I., Jerram, C., & Rao Hill, S. (2011). Exploring the public sector adoption of HRIS. *Industrial Management & Data Systems, 111*(3), 470–488. doi:10.1108/02635571111118314

Venkatesh, V., Morris, M. G., Davis, G. B., & Davis, F. D. (2003). User acceptance of information technology: Toward a unified view. *Management Information Systems Quarterly, 27*(3), 425–478.

Walker, R. M. (2006). Innovation type and diffusion: An empirical analysis of local government. *Public Administration, 84*(2), 311–335. doi:10.1111/j.1467-9299.2006.00004.x

Wernerfelt, B. (1984). A resource-based view of the firm. *Strategic Management Journal, 5*(2), 171–180. doi:10.1002/smj.4250050207

Wigand, F. D. L. (2010). Adoption of web 2.0 by Canadian and US governments. In *Comparative e-government*. New York: Springer. doi:10.1007/978-1-4419-6536-3_8

Williams, M. (2000). Interpretivism and generalization. *Sociology, 34*(2), 209–224. doi:10.1177/S0038038500000146

Wolfe, R. A. (1994). Organizational innovation: Review, critique and suggested research directions. *Journal of Management Studies, 31*(3), 405–431. doi:10.1111/j.1467-6486.1994.tb00624.x

Xu, S., Zhu, K., & Gibbs, J. (2004). Global technology, local adoption: A cross country investigation of internet adoption by companies in the United States and China. *Electronic Markets, 14*(1), 13–24. doi:10.1080/1019678042000175261

Yin, R. K. (2009). *Case study research: Design and methods*. Thousand Oaks, CA: Sage Publications.

Zhu, K., Kraemer, K., & Xu, S. (2003). Electronic business adoption by European firms: A cross-country assessment of the facilitators and inhibitors. *European Journal of Information Systems, 12*(4), 251–268. doi:10.1057/palgrave.ejis.3000475

Zhu, K., & Kraemer, K. L. (2005). Post-adoption variations in usage and value of e-business by organizations: Cross-country evidence from the retail industry. *Information Systems Research, 16*(1), 61–84. doi:10.1287/isre.1050.0045

ADDITIONAL READING

Acar, A., & Muraki, Y. (2011). Twitter for Crisis Communication: lessons learned from Japan's tsunami disaster. *International Journal of Web Based Communities, 7*(3), 392–402. doi:10.1504/IJWBC.2011.041206

Alkhateeb, F. M., Clauson, K. A., Khanfar, N. M., & Latif, D. A. (2008). Legal and Regulatory Risk Associated with Web 2.0 Adoption by Pharmaceutical Companies. *Journal of Medical Marketing: Device. Diagnostic and Pharmaceutical Marketing, 8*(4), 311–318. doi:10.1057/jmm.2008.20

Andriole, S. J. (2010). Business Impact of Web 2.0 Technologies. *Communications of the ACM, 53*(12), 67–79. doi:10.1145/1859204.1859225

Aula, P. (2010). Social Media, Reputation Risk and Ambient Publicity Management. *Strategy and Leadership, 38*(6), 43–49. doi:10.1108/10878571011088069

Briones, R. L., Kuch, B., Liu, B. F., & Jin, Y. (2011). Keeping Up With the Digital Age: how the American Red Cross uses social media to build relationships. *Public Relations Review, 37*(1), 37–43. doi:10.1016/j.pubrev.2010.12.006

Chikandiwa, S. T., Contogiannis, E., & Jembere, E. (2013). The Adoption of Social Media Mmarketing in South African Banks. *European Business Review, 25*(4), 365–381. doi:10.1108/EBR-02-2013-0013

Chua, A. Y., Goh, D. H., & Ang, R. P. (2012). Web 2.0 Applications in Government Web Sites: prevalence, use and correlations with perceived Web site quality. *Online Information Review*, *36*(2), 175–195. doi:10.1108/14684521211229020

Culnan, M. J., McHugh, P. J., & Zubillaga, J. I. (2010). How Large US Companies Can Use Twitter and Other Social Media to Gain Business Value. *MIS Quarterly Executive*, *9*(4), 243–259.

Gallaugher, J., & Ransbotham, S. (2010). Social Media and Customer Dialog Management at Starbucks. *MIS Quarterly Executive*, *9*(4), 197–212.

Hardey, M. (2007). The City in the Age of Web 2.0: a new synergistic relationship between place and people. *Information Communication and Society*, *10*(6), 867–884. doi:10.1080/13691180701751072

Hughes, A. L., & Palen, L. (2009). Twitter Adoption and Use in Mass Convergence and Emergency Events. *International Journal of Emergency Management*, *6*(3), 248–260. doi:10.1504/IJEM.2009.031564

Hui, G., & Hayllar, M. R. (2010). Creating Public Value in E-Government: a public-private-citizen collaboration framework in Web 2.0. *Australian Journal of Public Administration*, *69*(1), 120–131. doi:10.1111/j.1467-8500.2009.00662.x

Junco, R. (2012). Too Mmuch Face and Not Enough Books: the relationship between multiple indices of Facebook use and academic performance. *Computers in Human Behavior*, *28*(1), 187–198. doi:10.1016/j.chb.2011.08.026

Kietzmann, J. H., Hermkens, K., McCarthy, I. P., & Silvestre, B. S. (2011). Social Media? Get Serious! Understanding the Functional Building Blocks of Social Media. *Business Horizons*, *54*(3), 241–251. doi:10.1016/j.bushor.2011.01.005

Miller, A. R., & Tucker, C. (2013). Active Social Media Management: The case of health care. *Information Systems Research*, *24*(1), 52–70. doi:10.1287/isre.1120.0466

Molinari, F., & Ferro, E. (2009). Framing Web 2.0 in the Process of Public Sector Innovation: going down the participation ladder. *European Journal of ePractice*, *9*(1), 20-34.

Nair, M. (2011). Understanding and Measuring the Value of Social Media. *Journal of Corporate Accounting & Finance*, *22*(3), 45–51. doi:10.1002/jcaf.20674

Senadheera, V., Warren, M., & Leitch, S. (2011) A Study Into How Australian Banks Use Social Media. In proceedings of the 15th Pacific Asia Conference on Information Systems (PACIS 2011), The University of Queensland, pp. 1-12.

Usluel, Y. K., & Mazman, S. G. (2009). Adoption of Web 2.0 Tools in Distance Education. *Procedia-Social and Behavioral Sciences*, *1*(1), 818–823. doi:10.1016/j.sbspro.2009.01.146

Vuori, M. (2012). Exploring Uses of Social Media in a Global Corporation. *Journal of Systems and Information Technology*, *14*(2), 155–170. doi:10.1108/13287261211232171

Wagner, C., & Schroeder, A. (2010). Capabilities and Roles of Enterprise Wikis in Organizational Communication. *Technical Communication*, *57*(1), 68–89.

Wattal, S., Racherla, P., & Mandviwalla, M. (2010). Network Externalities and Technology Use: a quantitative analysis of intraorganizational blogs. *Journal of Management Information Systems*, *27*(1), 145–174. doi:10.2753/MIS0742-1222270107

Wattal, S., Schuff, D., Mandviwalla, M., & Williams, C. B. (2010). Web 2.0 and Politics: the 2008 US presidential election and an e-politics research agenda. *Management Information Systems Quarterly, 34*(4), 669–688.

Wilson, R. E., Gosling, S. D., & Graham, L. T. (2012). A Review of Facebook Research in the Social Sciences. *Perspectives on Psychological Science, 7*(3), 203–220. doi:10.1177/1745691612442904

Yates, D., Wagner, C., & Majchrzak, A. (2010). Factors Affecting Shapers of Organizational Wikis. *Journal of the American Society for Information Science and Technology, 61*(3), 543–554.

KEY TERMS AND DEFINITIONS

Bandwagon Effect: Refers to the impact of success stories from other organizations that had adopted social media Web services on those that were contemplating to adopt these Web services.

Chain of Evidence: Maintaining the chain of evidence concerns explaining how the evidence between/amongst various data processing phases is linked.

Construct Validity: Construct validity refers to the inference validity that observations in the collected data are in fact representative of the construct under investigation.

Interviewing: Interviewing is a data collection technique that can source in-depth and rich information by exploring and understanding respondents' viewpoints on research issues.

Local Government: In Australia, local government handles community needs including public relations, town planning, and waste collection. In Australia local governments are known by other names including councils, cities, shires, towns, or municipalities.

Social Media: Social media constitute any interactive Web-based application based on Web 2.0 that provides Web services enabling interactions between or amongst Web users and enhances their ability to create and share information on the Web.

Technology-Organization-Environment (TOE): Technology-Organization-Environment is a framework that can be used to explain, analyze and distinguish the drivers that influence technology adoption decisions in organizations.

Technology Adoption: Technology adoption represents acceptance of an innovation by organisations or individuals.

Web 2.0: Web 2.0 is a technology platform that consists of a set of technologies (e.g. Adobe Flash, RSS, wiki) that enable rich content to be published on the Web.

Web Service: A Web-service is a software function that enables interaction between devices over a network such as the World Wide Web (WEB).

Chapter 14
Approaching the Internet of Things through Integrating SOA and Complex Event Processing

Juan Boubeta-Puig
University of Cádiz, Spain

Guadalupe Ortiz
University of Cádiz, Spain

Inmaculada Medina-Bulo
University of Cádiz, Spain

ABSTRACT

The Internet of Things (IoT) provides a large amount of data, which can be shared or consumed by thousands of individuals and organizations around the world. These organizations can be connected using Service-Oriented Architectures (SOAs), which have emerged as an efficient solution for modular system implementation allowing easy communications among third-party applications; however, SOAs do not provide an efficient solution to consume IoT data for those systems requiring on-demand detection of significant or exceptional situations. In this regard, Complex Event Processing (CEP) technology continuously processes and correlates huge amounts of events to detect and respond to changing business processes. In this chapter, the authors propose the use of CEP to facilitate the demand-driven detection of relevant situations. This is achieved by aggregating simple events generated by an IoT platform in an event-driven SOA, which makes use of an enterprise service bus for the integration of IoT, CEP, and SOA. The authors illustrate this approach through the implementation of a case study. Results confirm that CEP provides a suitable solution for the case study problem statement.

DOI: 10.4018/978-1-4666-5884-4.ch014

INTRODUCTION

The *Internet of Things* (IoT) is defined by Haller et al. (2009) as a world where physical objects are integrated into the network, and where these objects can become active participants in business processes.

This huge amount of objects provided by IoT can be considered to produce simple events that need to be processed and correlated in real time. However, manually handling all of these events generated daily in heterogeneous systems is not feasible. On the other hand, *Service-Oriented Architectures* (SOAs) provide an efficient solution for the implementation of systems in which modularity and communication among third parties are key factors. This fact has led to the increasing development of distributed applications made up of reusable and sharable components (services). These components have well-defined platform-independent interfaces, which allow SOA-based systems to quickly and easily adapt to changing business conditions. However, these architectures are not suitable for environments where it is necessary to continuously analyze all the information flowing through the system, which might be a key factor for an automatic and early detection of critical situations for the business in question. Although some approaches allow this detection, they cannot be applied to different domains (Ye & Huang, 2011; Miori & Russo, 2012).

This limitation may be solved by the joint use of *Complex Event Processing* (CEP) (Etzion & Niblett, 2010) and SOA. CEP provides a set of techniques for helping to make an efficient use of an *Event-Driven Architecture* (EDA), enabling it to react to multiple events under multiple logical conditions (Taylor, Yochem, Les Phillips, & Martinez, 2009). In this regard, CEP can process and analyze large amounts of events and correlate them to detect and respond to critical business situations in real time; in this scope event patterns are used to infer new more complex and meaningful events. These events will help to make decisions when

necessary. Currently, the integration of EDA and SOA is known as *Event-Driven SOA* (ED-SOA) or SOA 2.0 (Sosinsky, 2011), an extension of SOA to respond to events that occur as a result of business processes. SOA 2.0 will ensure that services do not only exchange messages between them, but also publish events and receive events notifications from others. For this purpose, an *Enterprise Service Bus* (ESB) will be necessary to process, enrich and route messages between services of different applications. Thus, combining the use of CEP and SOA, we may detect relevant events in complex and heterogeneous systems, i.e., CEP will let us to analyze and correlate events in real time SOA 2.0.

The main contribution of this chapter is the definition and implementation of an architecture for integrating IoT, CEP and SOA 2.0 to facilitate an efficient detection of relevant situations in SOA scenarios. In order to illustrate our proposal, our architecture is applied to a case study of home automation. This case study is defined and implemented according to such technologies and is also evaluated. Technically, it consists of having various sources that collect sensor data across the globe, and then filtering, aggregating, transforming and detecting events patterns of interest (relevant situations) in real time. In particular, we use Xively (LogMeIn, 2013), a site to store, share and discover real time sensor, energy and environment data from objects, devices and buildings around the world.

The rest of the chapter is organized as follows. We define IoT, SOA, EDA, ED-SOA and the main features of CEP comparing them with SOA's features. Afterwards, we describe and implement our proposed architecture for the integration of IoT, CEP and SOA. Then, a home automation case study is explained, implemented and evaluated making use of our architecture. In addition, related approaches for the integration of CEP and SOA are summarized and compared to the one proposed in this chapter. Finally, future work and conclusions are highlighted.

BACKGROUND

Internet of Things

IoT establishes that all physical objects can be uniquely identified and represented in the on-line world, making use of *Radio-Frequency Identification* (RFID) technology, among others. IoT can have a high impact on several aspects of everyday-life and behavior of potential users (Atzori, Iera, & Morabito, 2010). According to these authors, some examples of possible scenarios where IoT can be applied are: home automation, assisted living, e-health, enhanced learning, automation and industrial manufacturing, logistics, business/process management, and intelligent transportation of people and goods.

Gubii et al. (2013) define the components required for IoT from a high level perspective: hardware (built with sensors, actuators, and embedded communication hardware), middleware (on demand storage and computing tools for data analytics), and presentation (tools which can be accessed on different platforms to provide visualization).

Xively is a real-time data infrastructure platform for the IoT, managing millions of data points per day from thousands of individuals, organizations and companies around the world. Thanks to its scalable infrastructure, Xively allows us to build IoT products and services, as well as storing, sharing and discovering real-time sensor, energy and environmental data from objects, devices and buildings around the world (LogMeIn, 2013).

Apart from enabling direct connections between any two devices, objects or environments, it can also be used to facilitate many-to-many connections. Therefore, heterogeneous systems can connect to each other in real time. Weather stations, air quality monitors, networked energy monitors, virtual worlds and mobile sensor devices may be some of such heterogeneous systems.

In addition, Xively provides a RESTful API that offers data as XML, CSV and JSON feeds. This API allows us to easily write applications which pull data from any number of feeds in real time.

Service-Oriented Architecture

"SOA is a logical way of designing a software system to provide services to either end-user applications or to other services distributed in a network, via published and discoverable interfaces" (Michael P. Papazoglou, 2007). This software architecture is characterized by standardized service contracts, service loose coupling, service abstraction, service reusability, service autonomy, service discoverability, service composability, service-orientation and interoperability (Arcitura Education Inc., 2013).

With the aim of building a SOA, a highly distributable communication and integration backbone is required (M. P Papazoglou & van den Heuvel, 2007). This functionality is provided by an ESB, middleware application that provides interoperability between different communication protocols (Davis, 2009) and can be used as an integration platform that enables existing applications to be exposed as services (Rademakers & Dirksen, 2009).

According to Rademakers & Dirksen (2009), the main benefits of an ESB are: necessity to integrate applications, heterogonous environment and reduction of total cost of ownership. Besides, its core functionalities are: location transparency, transport protocol conversion, message transformation, message routing, message enhancement, security, and monitoring and management.

Event-Driven Architecture

EDA is an architectural style in which one or more of the components in a software system are decoupled and event-driven, i.e., these components act when they recognize an event (Chandy & Schulte,

2010). This architecture is characterized by using asynchronous messaging –normally publication/subscription– and ESBs or intermediaries in order to transport messages. Moreover, it does not depend on a central controller (Taylor et al., 2009).

An application which implements EDA must report current events without specifying actions to be performed by event consumers. On the one hand, event producers must push notifications and "forget" them without waiting for a reply from the event consumer. On the other hand, event consumers must immediately respond after recognizing an event (Chandy & Schulte, 2010).

Event-Driven Service-Oriented Architecture

As previously mentioned, ED-SOA is also known as SOA 2.0. Basically, SOA 2.0 is an evolution of traditional SOA in which the communication between users and services is done by events, instead of remote procedure calls (Luckham, 2012). Therefore, services are triggered by events and react to events, reacting to input events and generating output events.

It is important to highlight that SOA and EDA are complementary, and not alternatives to be chosen. According to Etzion and Niblett (2010) an event-driven approach can be joined to request-response components in a SOA in two ways: (1) a component can provide or consume a request-response interface and also be an event producer or event consumer, (2) the SOA infrastructure hosting the SOA components can provide instrumentation that produces events on behalf of request-response style services. In this chapter, we have implemented SOA 2.0 following the first approach.

Complex Event Processing

CEP (Luckham, 2002) is a technology that provides a set of techniques for helping to discover complex events by analyzing and correlating other basic and complex events. A basic event occurs at a point in time and it is indivisible and atomic, while a complex event can happen over a period of time, it is aggregated from basic or other complex events and contains more semantic content. Some of these techniques are: detecting causality, membership or timing relationships between events, abstracting event-driven processes and detecting event patterns. Therefore, CEP allows detecting complex and meaningful events, known as situations, and inferring valuable knowledge for end users.

The main advantage of using CEP to process complex events is that the latter can be identified and reported in real time, unlike in traditional software for event analysis, therefore reducing the latency in decision making. Thus, CEP is a fundamental technology for applications that (1) must respond quickly to situations that change rapidly and asynchronously and where interactions do not have to be transactional, (2) must support management by exception, (3) must rapidly react to unusual situation and (4) require loose coupling and adaptability (Chandy & Schulte, 2010).

CEP has some similarities and differences with SOA. The main similarity is that both approaches provide modularity, loose coupling and flexibility. Some of the main differences are shown in the following lines:

- SOA interactions are based on services (a user must know the service producer and interface in advance in order to send requests to it). However, event-driven CEP is reactive and more decoupled since events are generated by event producers, and event consumers are responsible for intercepting and processing them.
- While SOA processes use events to drive control flow (Havey, 2009) (these processes can both send and receive events), CEP engines continuously analyze and correlate these events to assess if they meet the conditions defined in any of the event patterns stored in them.

OUR ARCHITECTURE INTEGRATING IOT, SOA 2.0 AND CEP

Overview

As previously mentioned, CEP is an emerging technology that allows us to analyze and correlate data in form of events in order to detect relevant or critical situations in real time. In order to detect these situations in heterogeneous systems, the integration of CEP and SOA 2.0 is required. Furthermore, there is a need to process this real data provided by different and heterogeneous sensors distributed around the world. Therefore, this integration should be joined to IoT.

In efforts to address this necessity, we propose a solution based on the integration of IoT, SOA 2.0 and CEP (see Figure 1). An ESB is the key element of the integration, which allows us to combine these approaches. As shown in Figure 1, event producers are sensors, i.e., devices that monitor the environment to capture information (temperature, light, rain, etc.), which is then transmitted to IoT platforms using the controller integrated into them. This way, this information will be available for different applications and users authorized to access these platforms.

The data obtained from IoT platforms (event producers in our architecture) is published into the ESB. For this purpose, the ESB will use an HTTP endpoint in order to receive this data. An HTTP endpoint allows to send requests and to receive requests over HTTP transport protocol, and uses one of two message exchange patterns: *request-response* or *one-way*. The one-way message exchange pattern is used in this architecture.

Then, the ESB will normalize and transform the received data into the correct format in form of events. Afterwards, these events will be sent to a CEP engine. This engine will contain event patterns specifying the conditions to identify relevant situations and the actions to be carried out. Every time that an event pattern is detected, a complex event will be created and immediately published into the ESB.

Finally, such complex events (alerts) generated by the CEP engine will be notified to the event consumers that have subscribed to them. Concretely, these consumers can be an email server and a NoSQL (*Not only SQL*) database («NOSQL Databases», 2013), an emerging database management system for dealing with huge amounts of data. Therefore, users will receive the alerts which they are interested in by email. Moreover, these alerts will be stored as a historical event repository.

Figure 1. An approach for the integration of IoT, SOA 2.0 and CEP

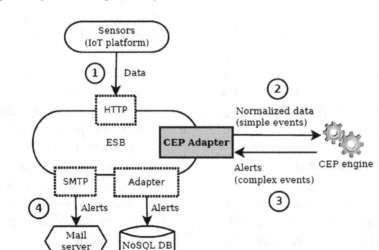

Implementation Issues

In this subsection, we will explain the implementation details of our architecture proposal for integrating IoT, SOA 2.0 and CEP.

This architecture is implemented making use of Xively IoT platform (event producer), Esper CEP engine (EsperTech Inc., 2013), Mule ESB (MuleSoft, 2013a), and Gmail and MongoDB database (MongoDB, 2013a) (event consumers). The steps followed to implement this architecture are enumerated and described below.

IoT Platform and ESB Integration

We have selected Xively as IoT platform because it provides about 250 million devices, it has 17 million users and integration capabilities with open source libraries.

Moreover, we have used Mule as the ESB for implementing our architecture. This ESB was evaluated by Rademakers and Dirksen (2009) as the best-of-breed products currently available according to the following criteria: ESB core functionality, quality of documentation, market visibility, active development and support community, custom logic, transport protocols and connectivity options, integration capabilities with open source frameworks, and tool support.

In addition, some companies have reported Mule as an excellent product (MuleSoft, 2013c). For example, TiVo reported 75% gains in development productivity with Mule ESB enterprise, while Ebay adopted standard service framework with Mule ESB at core, among others.

As a first step, we have integrated Xively IoT platform with Mule ESB. In order to facilitate this task, we have used Mule Studio (MuleSoft, 2013b), an integrated, two-way environment for developing, debugging, and deploying Mule ESB applications that provides developers with a choice of free software tools (a visual, drag-and-drop editor and an XML code editor). Besides, both editors work in tandem, thus making "round-trip" editing true.

CEP Engine and ESB Integration

Once Xively has been integrated with Mule, the next step has been the connection of Mule and the Esper CEP engine. According to EsperTech (2013), the company developing Esper, this engine can process around 500,000 events/s on a workstation, and between 70,000 and 200,000 events/s on a laptop.

The use of a CEP engine instead of a rule engine provides substantial benefits. According to Chandy and Schulte (2010) there are some differences between CEP and rule engines: normally, rule engines are request driven, i.e., when an application needs to make a decision it will invoke this engine to derive a conclusion from a set of premises. The general model for a rule engine is *If some-condition then do-action-X*. In most applications, a large number of rules will have to be analyzed before making a decision, thus becoming a problem for real-time decision making. However, CEP engines are event-driven and run continuously, and according to EDA principles, they can process notification messages as soon as they arrive. In this case, the general model for a CEP engine is a *when-then rule* (known as a complex event pattern). When *something-happens-or-some-condition-is-detected* then *do-action-X*, instead of an *if-then-else* rule. Thus, event patterns use time as another dimension. Moreover, CEP engines are faster and more efficient in handling and receiving notifications.

Sending events from the Mule ESB to the Esper engine, and vice versa, is possible thanks to a module which we have implemented in this architecture.

In order to detect relevant or critical situations in real time (in our architecture), it is necessary to implement specific event patterns. These patterns have been implemented in Esper EPL (*Event Processing Language*). Several reasons have motivated EPL choice: firstly, the learning curve is not steep since its syntax is very close to SQL, widely known worldwide. Besides, EPL natively supports multiple event format types:

Java/.NET objects, maps and XML documents, what facilitates its use in multiple platforms. Even more, it is also possible to customize not only the language but also the Esper engine, which is written in Java and is open source. Moreover, this engine allows us to add new event patterns in runtime, should it be necessary.

At this point, Xively, Mule and Esper are fully integrated.

Mail Server, NoSQL Database and ESB Integration

With the aim of notifying relevant or critical situations (complex events) detected by the Esper engine, it is necessary to integrate Mule ESB with different event consumers. In order to achieve this, we have integrated this ESB with Gmail and MongoDB. In this manner, notifications will be received by different users in their Google accounts and read from, for example, their smart phones. Furthermore, these notifications will be stored in a NoSQL database.

We have chosen this type of database because it provides the following advantages (Meijer & Bierman, 2011): NoSQL has asynchronous BASE (Basically Available, Soft state, Eventual Consistency) updates rather than synchronous ACID (Atomicity, Consistency, Isolation, Durability), it is optimized to react to changes (not to manage transactions), it does not require neither schemes nor data types definitions, it is also distributed, easily horizontally scalable and very efficient for managing huge amounts of data.

Moreover, we have used MongoDB because it is the leading NoSQL database (MongoDB, 2013b). Some of its main features are: simple and powerful JSON-style documents with dynamic schemas, indexing on any attribute, replication and high availability, document-based queries, horizontal scaling without compromising functionality, and flexible aggregation and data processing.

CASE STUDY

In recent years, the number of smart homes including sensors for monitoring environmental conditions has increased. These sensors can measure temperature, energy or gas consumption, among others. Furthermore, there is a tendency to share the information collected by these sensors into IoT platforms.

This scenario becomes interesting when it is necessary to process this data in real time to detect relevant or critical situations in a house. For example, it may be desirable to be notified when there is irresponsible electricity consumption. This way, we could be more careful about how we use our electrical appliances.

Therefore, we have applied our architecture to the field of home automation.

Data Source Description

As previously mentioned, we have used data provided by the Xively platform. Concretely, Table 1 summarizes the names and URLs of the data feeds which we have chosen, the country where

Table 1. Xively feeds with home automation data used in this case study

N°	Feed Name	Country	URL	Update Freq.
F1	Residential information	The Netherlands	https://xively.com/feeds/62988	1 min
F2	HAC Center	Poland	https://xively.com/feeds/103216	1 min
F3	Current Cost Bridge	Spain	https://xively.com/feeds/89125	5 min
F4	Hirsch House Data	United States	https://xively.com/feeds/24319	5 min

the sensors associated with each feed are located, and their update frequency.

Notice that the name and number of data types provided by each feed is variable and some of them are presented in different units. For instance, temperature in *Hirsch House Data* feed is in Fahrenheit, while the rest is in Celsius degrees. For this reason, it was necessary to normalize the data from these four feeds (F1 - F4), as shown in Table 2. This table specifies the name we assigned to each data, its type and description, and if it is available in the specific feed (marked with an "X" if so). This data will be stored in an object class called *HomeEvent*.

Event Patterns for Home Automation

In the following paragraphs, we define some complex event patterns to detect relevant or critical situations in smart homes.

Irresponsible Energy Consumption Pattern

This complex event pattern can detect situations in which high energy consumption (greater than 1500 watts) arises in a time interval of 10 minutes. The implementation of this pattern in EPL is:

```
@Name("Irresponsible Energy Consump-
tion")
insert into IrresponsibleEnergyCon-
sumption
select e.timestamp as timestamp,
e.home as home,
e.location as location,
e.energyConsumption as energyConsump-
tion
from pattern [every e =
HomeEvent(energyConsumption > 1500)
].win:time_batch(10 min)
```

First of all, we define the event pattern making use of the *from pattern* clause. Next, the *HomeEvent* events whose energy consumption is greater than 1500 W are selected by using the *every* pattern operator. In order to refer these events later, it is necessary to assign them an alias (in this case, *e*).

As shown in this event pattern, it also has a time window, *win: time_batch (10 min)*, which means

Table 2. Format used to normalize data from Xively feeds

Data	Type	Description	F1	F2	F3	F4
Home	String	Feed name	X	X	X	X
Sensor	String	Feed URL	X	X	X	X
Location	String	City, country	X	X	X	X
Latitude	Float	Sensor latitude	X	X	X	X
Longitude	Float	Sensor longitude	X	X	X	X
Timestamp	String	Timestamp	X	X	X	X
EnergyConsumption	Float	Energy consumption (W)	X	X	X	X
RoomTemperature	Float	Home room temperature (°C)	X	X	X	X
OutdoorTemperature	Float	Home outdoor temperature (°C)		X		X
RoomHumidity	Float	Home room humidity (%)	X	X		
OutdoorHumidity	Float	Home outdoor humidity (%)		X		X
TVConnection	Float	TV Connection (on /off)			X	X

that this window batches events and releases them every 10 minutes.

Finally, properties to be selected from the events matching the pattern conditions are specified. These properties are: timestamp, the house where the situation has been detected, its location, and the energy consumption value. The *insert into* clause specifies that this pattern will create a new complex event pattern with such properties: *IrresponsibleEnergyConsumption (timestamp, home, location, energyConsumption)*. Figure 2 illustrates this implementation.

Irresponsible Stove Use Pattern

This complex event pattern detects situations where a stove is being used when it is not necessary but causing high energy consumption. In this pattern, we consider that it is an irresponsible stove use when the outdoor temperature is under 19° C and the room temperature is higher than 21° C. The implementation of this pattern in EPL is:

```
@Name("Irresponsible Stove Use")
insert into IrresponsibleStoveUse
select e.timestamp as timestamp,
```

Figure 2. Illustration of Irresponsible Energy Consumption pattern

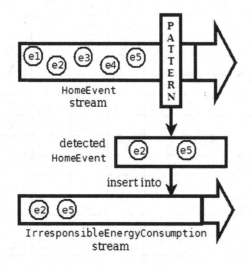

```
e.home as home,
e.location as location,
e.outdoorTemperature as outdoorTem-
perature,
e.roomTemperature as roomTemperature
from pattern [every e = HomeEvent
(outdoorTemperature < 19
and roomTemperature > 21)].win:time_
batch(10 min)
```

Fire Pattern

This pattern would detect if a house is burning. In this case, after analyzing home temperature, if it increases more than 20° C in the following minute, then we can deduce that there is a fire in the house. Logically, it is unlikely that the temperature can vary more than 20° C in only one minute, even though a stove is heating the room, unless there is a fire. The implementation of this pattern in EPL is:

```
@Name("Fire")
insert into Fire
select e2.timestamp as timestamp,
e2.home as home, e2.location as loca-
tion,
e1.roomTemperature as initialRoomTem-
perature,
e2.roomTemperature as finalRoomTem-
perature
from pattern [every (e1 = HomeEvent
-> (timer:interval(1 min)
and e2 = HomeEvent(home = e1.home and
(roomTemperature -
e1.roomTemperature) > 20)))]
```

Power Failure Pattern

This pattern detects when there is a power outage. It can be detected when the power consumption is greater than 0 watts at a specific moment and after that, the power consumed in the house is equal to 0 watts. Notice that we assume that the regular energy consumption at home will never be 0 watts, since there will always be an appliance plugged into the outlet, for instance, a fridge. The implementation of this pattern in EPL is:

```
@Name("Power Failure")
insert into PowerFailure
select e2.timestamp as timestamp,
e2.home as home,
e2.location as location,
e1.energyConsumption as initialEner-
gyConsumption,
e2.energyConsumption as finalEnergy-
Consumption
from pattern [every (e1 =
HomeEvent(energyConsumption > 0)
-> e2 = HomeEvent(home = e1.home and
energyConsumption = 0))]
```

Irresponsible Television Use Pattern

This pattern attempts to detect situations in which we forget to turn off the television before leaving our houses. It can be detected if a television is turned on during 6 hours. Notice that we assume that people do not spend more than 6 hours in front of a television. Otherwise, we should increase the number of hours imposed on this pattern. The implementation of this pattern in EPL is:

```
@Name("Irresponsible Television Use")
insert into IrresponsibleTelevision-
Use
select e1.timestamp as initialTime-
stamp,
e2.timestamp as finalTimestamp,
e2.home as home, e2.location as loca-
tion,
e1.TVconnection as initialTVconnec-
tion,
e2.TVconnection as finalTVconnection
from pattern [every (e1 =
HomeEvent(TVconnection = true)
```

```
-> (timer:interval(6 hours) and not
e2 = HomeEvent(
home = e1.home and TVconnection =
false)))]
```

Applying our Architecture to Home Automation

As explained before, we have implemented our architecture for integrating IoT, SOA 2.0 and CEP making use of Xively IoT platform, Esper CEP engine, Mule ESB, Gmail and MongoDB database. In order to check the usefulness of this architecture, we have applied it to such a case study of home automation.

In this case study we have created two Mule flows (See Figure 3). A Mule flow is a combination of message sources and message processors that does not have a fixed format. It can be as simple or as complex as required, and can include, for instance, processing by multiple components before any output is performed. A message source receives or generates new messages to be processed by Mule while a message processor processes such messages through a flow (MuleSoft, 2013a).

The first Mule flow is responsible for processing the information between Xively and Esper engine. The second one will receive complex events (alarms) detected by event patterns previously defined in the CEP engine, and this flow will also send these alarms to interested event consumers. Notice that the figure does not show this second flow in full for space limitation reasons.

Therefore, the first Mule flow has been called as *Home automation*. Firstly, we have used the *composite source*, a Mule scope where two or more message sources can be placed in order to accept incoming messages from multiple input channels. Thus, this scope allows the Mule flow to obtain data from various external sources. In this case, we have connected four Xively data feeds to the ESB, making use of HTTP endpoints. These endpoints must specify a Xively username

Figure 3. Integration of IoT, SOA 2.0 and CEP applied to home automation

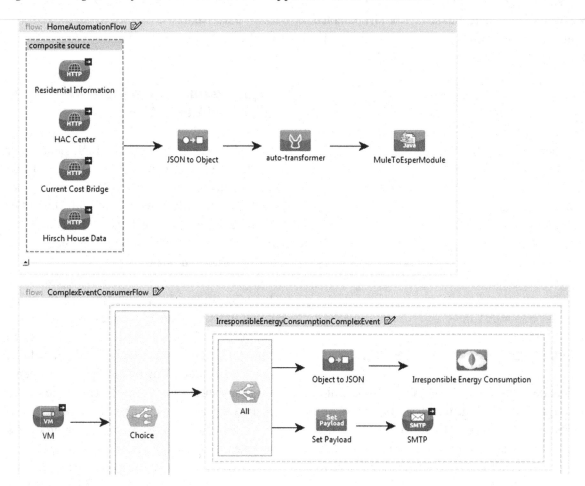

and password account so that the ESB can access the information from this platform, as well as the URLs of such data feeds and the format (CSV, JSON or XML) in which the data will be retrieved –JSON in this case.

Then, the information obtained in JSON format is converted to Java objects. These objects will be received by the transformer we have implemented to normalize data and to convert them into the appropriate event format (see Table 2). Finally, these events will be sent to the Esper engine, using the *MuleToEsperModule* that we have implemented to integrate Mule with Esper, allowing the data transmission in both directions. Additionally, the event patterns to be inserted into the CEP engine can be implemented into this module.

When detecting complex events into the Esper engine, they will be sent to the *VM (Virtual Machine) component*, which is located in the second Mule flow called as *ComplexEventConsumerFlow*. This "in memory transport" can be used for intra-JVM communication between Mule Flows that uses in-memory queues by default.

Afterwards, the *Choice* flow control is connected to the VM component. This flow control dynamically routes messages based on message payload or properties. Thus, it will detect which type of complex event has been received and will route the event to the first routing option in the scope that matches the routing configurations. Routing options are: *IrresponsibleEnergyConsumptionComplexEvent, IrresponsibleStoveUseComplexEvent,*

FireComplexEvent, PowerFailureComplexEvent and *IrresponsibleTelevisionUseComplexEvent.*

Every routing option has an *All* flow control which sends the same message (complex event) to multiple message processors. Particularly, every event will be transformed into JSON and stored in a specific MongoDB database collection for this type of complex event. Moreover, the *Set Payload* transformer will set the payload of such an event to the string describing the alert; the latest will be sent by email to the users interested in it. To this end, the SMTP connector has been used for sending messages over SMTP through the use of the *javax.mail* API. We have configured some attributes of this connector with server (*host*, *port*, *user* and *password*) and email information (*to*, *from* and *subject*—the name of the detected alarm).

Results and Evaluation

Our architecture used for detecting relevant or critical situations in smart homes has been tested during 12 hours, from 8:19 h. to 20:19 h. (UTC) on 17th July 2013.

Figure 4 shows values of energy consumption, room temperature and television connection data in *Current Cost Bridge* home during such 8 hours. It is important to highlight that the *Irresponsible Energy Consumption* pattern has been fired 5

times, every 10 minutes when the energy consumption has been greater than 1500 watts. Therefore, 5 *Irresponsible Energy Consumption* complex events have been created by the Esper engine. Afterwards, these events have been sent to Mule ESB which has sent them by email to this house's owners in order to warn them about these relevant situations. In addition, these complex events have been stored in a historical event database.

Figure 5 sketches values of energy consumption, room temperature, outdoor temperature, outdoor humidity and television connection data in *Hirsch House Data* home during such 8 hours. In this occasion, the *Irresponsible Energy Consumption* pattern has been detected 38 times. Moreover, the *Irresponsible Stove Use* pattern has been fired 24 times, when the outdoor temperature has been under 19° C and the room temperature has been higher than 21° C. It means that, in general, this house has high energy consumption and its owners should consider how to reduce this consumption in order to reduce the electricity bill every month.

Figure 6 and Figure 7 show values of such data in *HAC Center* and *Residential Information* houses. As can be seen, none of the event patterns for home automation proposed in this chapter has been detected in these houses. Thus, house's owners have not been warned about any relevant or

Figure 4. Monitoring data from Current Cost Bridge's sensors

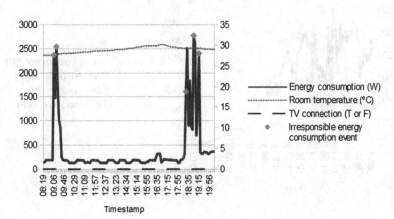

Figure 5. Monitoring data from Hirsch House Data's sensors

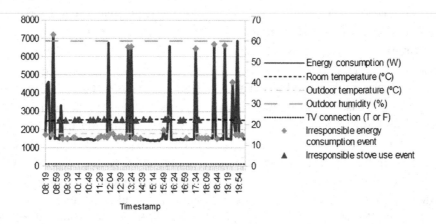

Figure 6. Monitoring data from HAC Center's sensors

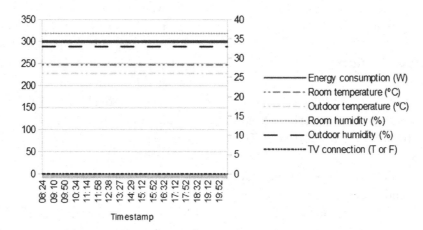

Figure 7. Monitoring data from Residential Information's sensors

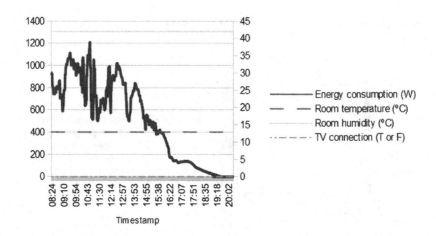

critical situations. Notice that *HAC Center*'s values have not changed during all the execution. It could be caused because the sensors are not working properly.

In conclusion, these results confirm that our architecture can be applied to home automation in order to automatically detect relevant and critical situations in real time in houses located around the world. It is easily scalable since we can connect more data feeds belonging to other home sensors and can add new complex event pattern for home automation in order to detect other situations. For this purpose, we should add an HTTP endpoint per each new data feed and specify the new event patterns in the *Choice* flow control.

RELATED WORK

In recent years, CEP has become one of key technologies for detecting relevant and critical situations in real time. CEP can be applied to different areas: fraud detection and security (Michael Edward Edge & Falcone Sampaio, 2009), transportation and traffic management (Dunkel, Fernández, Ortiz, & Ossowski, 2011), health care (Yuan & Lu, 2009), energy and manufacturing (Vikhorev, Greenough, & Brown, 2013), location-based services (Uhm, Lee, Hwang, Kim, & Park, 2011), financial systems and operations (Michael E. Edge & Falcone Sampaio, 2012), and operational intelligence in business (Chaudhuri, Dayal, & Narasayya, 2011), among others.

There are some works that propose the integration of CEP with IoT and SOA 2.0. Da et al. (2010) propose a SOA that provides user-centric services in a cost-effective and highly scalable way, making use of an ESB and the Drools rule engine (JBoss Community, 2013). To this end, they have proposed a RFID CEP framework for business process with two phases: to process data stream gathered by RFID readers and generate

events, and to integrate these events into complex events. As previously mentioned, we use Esper CEP engine in our architecture, rather than a rule engine, since CEP engines are faster than rule engines (Chandy & Schulte, 2010).

Furthermore, Walczak et al. (2012) describe an approach for machine-to-machine communication and processing data in Future Internet applications. Concretely, applications in domains of video and sensor surveillance (MobiWatch) and energy consumption monitoring and management (HomeNetEnergy) are developed in this work. The XMPP protocol is used as a base of machine-to-machine communication between sensors and services and it is also used to send notifications about the detected events. Thus, an ESB is not used to integrate IoT and CEP. In addition, events are described in form of rules, instead of event patterns, and a Drools engine is also used. CEP engines make easier the addition of new types of event patterns to be detected, should it be necessary.

On the other hand, there are other works that integrate SOA and IoT, applying it to the field of home automation, but these works do not use CEP technology to process information. For instance, Miori and Russo (2012) implement specific ontologies that automatically take information from the context and use knowledge-based environment representation. In order to detect relevant situations without direct human intervention they have developed an intelligent ecosystem applying machine learning and artificial intelligence techniques. Concretely, they have proposed a semantic DomoNet platform architecture based on DomoML, an XML-compliant language to be applied in any home automation context. Therefore, while our architecture using CEP can be easily applied to different domains, DomoNet can only be used in home automation domain.

Ye and Huang (2011) propose a cloud-based architecture for smart homes which provides different Web services to identify relevant situations in houses. This architecture has three layers: infrastructure layer which consists of physical resources designed for the delivery of Cloud services, platform layer that is the core of this architecture for managing resources and security, and the service layer which is responsible for the interaction between service providers and smart home users. This architecture is also limited to the home automation domain.

Sleman and Moeller (2011) describe a distributed operating system based on SOA which manages data and events by using SOA-messages in XML or JSON formats. These events can be exchanged between the embedded devices in a home network. This architecture has four layers: hardware layer which represents all devices in the home network, bridging layer which enables access to embedded devices, SOA distributed operating system layer that manages events and tasks for the communication between the different embedded devices and also dispatches the information to one of device's services, and the application layer. In this architecture, a queue is used for managing user requests and different modules are implemented to manage information routing, services, events, devices and databases. Our architecture uses an ESB which provides more efficient and heterogeneous functionalities than such modules in Sleman's architecture.

FUTURE RESEARCH DIRECTIONS

In our near future work we will complete our architecture with the integration of other event producers and event consumers. These producers and consumers will be easily integrated into our architecture thanks to the ESB, which helps to increase the flexibility of heterogeneous environments.

On the one hand, we will use other existing IoT platforms as event producers, such as Thing-Speak (2013). ThingSpeak is an open application platform designed to enable connections between things and people; thereby it is similar to Xively –the IoT platform used in this work. Other event producers to be integrated into our architecture are existing Web services, applications and sensors. Indeed, we will make and configure our own sensors to obtain specific real data which is not provided by existing IoT platforms.

On the other hand, Web services, applications and actuators will be integrated into our architecture as event consumers. Particularly, the use of actuators will be a benefit because some mechanical actions would be taken at home when detecting specific complex event pattern. For instance, if the *IrresponsibleStoveUse* event pattern is detected, then the stove would be automatically turned off.

We are also planning to apply our architecture in different domains to prove its versatility and to evaluate the results in such varied domains. Moreover, we would like to improve our proposal in order to anticipate critical situations before occurrence, i.e., it will be reactive and pro-active.

Last but not least, we are going to provide a user-friendly interface for the definition of the home automation event patterns defined in this work and new ones. We have already proposed a metamodel and implemented an editor for facilitating user-friendly design of complex event patterns in (Boubeta-Puig, Ortiz, & Medina-Bulo, 2014). It is important to highlight that this editor is independent of both the domain where CEP technology is needed to be applied to, and the concrete EPL required by a particular CEP engine. In concrete, non-experts on CEP will use our editor for graphically defining home automation patterns; afterwards, the editor will automatically transform these event patterns into the EPL code understandable by Esper engine. Finally, this code will be automatically inserted into the CEP engine. In this manner, our architecture will be able to detect new critical or relevant situations described by these event patterns added to the engine at runtime.

CONCLUSION

In this chapter we have proposed and implemented an architecture for integrating IoT, CEP and SOA 2.0 to facilitate an efficient detection of relevant and critical situations in SOA scenarios. Thanks to this architecture, when relevant situations arise from the detection of certain predefined event patterns, real time alerts are sent to the interested parties.

Furthermore, this architecture has been applied to a home automation case study with the aim of evaluating its usefulness. In particular, we have used data from sensors available in Xively IoT platform. This data has been published into the Mule ESB which transforms it into normalized events and sends them to the Esper CEP engine. This engine has been used to detect complex events which specify relevant or critical situations happening in smart houses at a point in time. Then, the ESB has notified these situations to houses' owners by email. In addition, these situations have been stored in a historical event database.

Although we have taken the example of home automation, once new complex event patterns are defined, our system could be used for detecting relevant situations in other fields, should it be necessary.

Therefore, we conclude that our architecture integrating Mule ESB with Esper CEP engine and Xively IoT platform can analyze and process real events from heterogeneous environments shared every day by thousands of individuals, organizations and companies. Moreover, this architecture makes possible the automatic and real-time detection of relevant and critical situations defined by event patterns for different domains which can be added to the CEP engine at runtime.

ACKNOWLEDGMENT

This work was funded by the Spanish Ministry of Science and Innovation under the National Program for Research, Development and Innovation, project MoD-SOA (TIN2011-27242). We would like to specially thank Víctor Ayllón and Juan Manuel Reina, Novayre managers, for their fruitful comments and discussions on the topic dealt with in this chapter.

REFERENCES

Arcitura Education Inc. (2013). *ServiceOrientation.com*. Retrieved August 6, 2013, from http://serviceorientation.com/serviceorientation/service_loose_coupling

Atzori, L., Iera, A., & Morabito, G. (2010). The internet of things: A survey. *Computer Networks*, *54*(15), 2787–2805. doi:10.1016/j.comnet.2010.05.010

Boubeta-Puig, J., Ortiz, G., & Medina-Bulo, I. (2014). A model-driven approach for facilitating user-friendly design of complex event patterns. *Expert Systems with Applications*, *41*(2), 445–456. doi:10.1016/j.eswa.2013.07.070

Chandy, K. M., & Schulte, W. R. (2010). *Event processing: Designing IT systems for agile companies*. New York: McGraw-Hill.

Chaudhuri, S., Dayal, U., & Narasayya, V. (2011). An overview of business intelligence technology. *Communications of the ACM*, *54*(8), 88–98. doi:10.1145/1978542.1978562

Da, Z., Bo, C., Yang, Z., & Junliang, C. (2010). Future service provision: Towards a flexible hybrid service supporting platform. In *Proceedings of Services Computing Conference (APSCC)*, (pp. 226 -233). IEEE.

Davis, J. (2009). *Open source SOA*. Manning Publications.

Dunkel, J., Fernández, A., Ortiz, R., & Ossowski, S. (2011). Event-driven architecture for decision support in traffic management systems. *Expert Systems with Applications*, *38*(6), 6530–6539. doi:10.1016/j.eswa.2010.11.087

Edge, M. E., & Falcone Sampaio, P. R. (2009). A survey of signature based methods for financial fraud detection. *Computers & Security*, *28*(6), 381–394. doi:10.1016/j.cose.2009.02.001

Edge, M. E., & Falcone Sampaio, P. R. (2012). The design of FFML: A rule-based policy modelling language for proactive fraud management in financial data streams. *Expert Systems with Applications*, *39*(11), 9966–9985. doi:10.1016/j.eswa.2012.01.143

EsperTech Inc. (2013). *Esper - Complex event processing*. Retrieved September 19, 2013, from http://esper.codehaus.org/

Etzion, O., & Niblett, P. (2010). *Event processing in action*. Stamford, CT: Manning.

Gubbi, J., Buyya, R., Marusic, S., & Palaniswami, M. (2013). Internet of things (IoT), a vision, architectural elements, and future directions. *Future Generation Computer Systems*, *29*(7), 1645–1660. doi:10.1016/j.future.2013.01.010

Haller, S., Karnouskos, S., & Schroth, C. (2009). The internet of things in an enterprise context. In J. Domingue, D. Fensel, & P. Traverso (Eds.), *Future internet – FIS 2008* (Vol. 5468, pp. 14–28). Berlin: Springer-Verlag. doi:10.1007/978-3-642-00985-3_2

Havey, M. (2009). *CEP and SOA: Six letters are better than three*. Retrieved July 15, 2013, from http://www.packtpub.com/article/cep-complex-event-processing-soa-service-oriented-architecture

JBoss Community. (2013). *Drools fusion*. Retrieved November 13, 2010, from http://www.jboss.org/drools/drools-fusion.html

LogMeIn. (2013). *Xively - Public cloud for the internet of things*. Retrieved July 19, 2013, from https://xively.com/

Luckham, D. (2002). *The power of events: An introduction to complex event processing in distributed enterprise systems*. Reading, MA: Addison-Wesley.

Luckham, D. (2012). *Event processing for business: Organizing the real-time enterprise*. Hoboken, NJ: Wiley.

Meijer, E., & Bierman, G. (2011). A co-relational model of data for large shared data banks. *Queue*, *9*, 30–48. doi:10.1145/1952746.1961297

Miori, V., & Russo, D. (2012). Anticipating health hazards through an ontology-based, IoT domotic environment. In *Proceedings of 2012 Sixth International Conference on Innovative Mobile and Internet Services in Ubiquitous Computing (IMIS)* (pp. 745-750). IMIS.

Mongo, D. B. (2013a). *MongoDB*. Retrieved July 19, 2013, from http://www.mongodb.org/

Mongo, D. B. (2013b). *The leading NoSQL database*. Retrieved November 15, 2013, from http://www.mongodb.com/leading-nosql-database

MuleSoft. (2013a). *Mule ESB*. Retrieved November 13, 2013, from http://www.mulesoft.org/

MuleSoft. (2013b). *Mule studio documentation*. Retrieved November 13, 2013, from http://www.mulesoft.com/mule-studio

MuleSoft. (2013c). *Integration case studies.* Retrieved November 13, 2013, from http://www.mulesoft.com/case-studies

NOSQL Databases. (2013). Retrieved July 19, 2013, from http://nosql-database.org/

Papazoglou, M. P. (2007). *Web services: Principles and technology.* Upper Saddle River, NJ: Prentice Hall.

Papazoglou, M. P., & van den Heuvel, W. J. (2007). Service oriented architectures: Approaches, technologies and research issues. *The VLDB Journal, 16*(3), 389–415. doi:10.1007/s00778-007-0044-3

Rademakers, T., & Dirksen, J. (2009). *Opensource ESBs in action.* Greenwich, CT: Manning.

Sleman, A., & Moeller, R. (2011). SOA distributed operating system for managing embedded devices in home and building automation. *IEEE Transactions on Consumer Electronics, 57*(2), 945–952. doi:10.1109/TCE.2011.5955244

Sosinsky, B. (2011). *Cloud computing bible.* Hoboken, NJ: Wiley.

Taylor, H., Yochem, A., Phillips, L., & Martinez, F. (2009). *Event-driven architecture: How SOA enables the real-time enterprise.* Reading, MA: Addison-Wesley.

ThingSpeak. (2013). *Internet of things - ThingSpeak.* Retrieved July 19, 2013, from https://www.thingspeak.com/

Uhm, Y., Lee, M., Hwang, Z., Kim, Y., & Park, S. (2011). A multi-resolution agent for service-oriented situations in ubiquitous domains. *Expert Systems with Applications, 38*(10), 13291–13300. doi:10.1016/j.eswa.2011.04.150

Vikhorev, K., Greenough, R., & Brown, N. (2013). An advanced energy management framework to promote energy awareness. *Journal of Cleaner Production, 43*, 103–112. doi:10.1016/j.jclepro.2012.12.012

Walczak, D., Wrzos, M., Radziuk, A., Lewandowski, B., & Mazurek, C. (2012). Machine-to-machine communication and data processing approach in future internet applications. In *Proceedings of 8th International Symposium on Communication Systems, Networks Digital Signal Processing (CSNDSP)* (pp. 1 -5). CSNDSP.

Ye, X., & Huang, J. (2011). A framework for cloud-based smart home. In *Proceedings of 2011 International Conference on Computer Science and Network Technology (ICCSNT)* (Vol. 2, pp. 894-897). ICCSNT.

Yuan, S.-T., & Lu, M.-R. (2009). An value-centric event driven model and architecture: A case study of adaptive complement of SOA for distributed care service delivery. *Expert Systems with Applications, 36*(2), 3671–3694. doi:10.1016/j.eswa.2008.02.024

ADDITIONAL READING

Bo, D., Kun, D., & Xiaoyi, Z. (2008). A High Performance Enterprise Service Bus Platform for Complex Event Processing. *Seventh International Conference on Grid and Cooperative Computing (GCC)* (pp. 577-582).

Boubeta-Puig, J., Ortiz, G., & Medina-Bulo, I. (2011). An Approach of Early Disease Detection using CEP and SOA. *The Third International Conferences on Advanced Service Computing* (pp. 143-148), Rome, Italy.

Chappell, D. A. (2004). *Enterprise Service Bus.* USA: O'Reilly Media.

Cugola, G., & Margara, A. (2012). Processing flows of information: From data stream to complex event processing. *ACM Comput. Surv., 44*(3), 15:1–15:62.

Domingo, M. C. (2012). An overview of the Internet of Things for people with disabilities. *Journal of Network and Computer Applications*, *35*(2), 584–596. doi:10.1016/j.jnca.2011.10.015

Erl, T. (2005). *Service-oriented architecture: concepts, technology, and design*. Upper Saddle River, NJ: Prentice Hall Professional Technical Reference.

Event Processing Technical. (2013). Event Processing Glossary - Version 2.0. Retrieved July 15, 2013, from http://www.complexevents.com/wpcontent/uploads/2011/08/EPTS_Event_Processing_Glossary_ v2.pdf

Gad, R., Boubeta-Puig, J., Kappes, M., & Medina-Bulo, I. (2012). *Leveraging EDA and CEP for Integrating Low-level Network Analysis Methods into Modern, Distributed IT Architectures* (pp. 13–26). Universidad de Almería, Spain: VIII Jornadas de Ciencia e Ingeniería de Servicios.

Haller, S., Karnouskos, S., & Schroth, C. (2009). The Internet of Things in an Enterprise Context. En J. Domingue, D. Fensel, & P. Traverso (Eds.), Future Internet – FIS 2008 (Vol. 5468, pp. 14-28). Berlin, Heidelberg: Springer-Verlag.

He, M., Zheng, Z., Xue, G., & Du, X. (2008). Event Driven RFID Based Exhaust Gas Detection Services Oriented System Research. *4th International Conference on Wireless Communications, Networking and Mobile Computing, 2008. WiCOM '08.* (pp. 1-4). Dalian, China.

Kopetz, H. (2011). *Internet of Things. Real-Time Systems* (pp. 307–323). Springer, US: Real-Time Systems Series. doi:10.1007/978-1-4419-8237-7_13

Kortuem, G., Kawsar, F., Fitton, D., & Sundramoorthy, V. (2010). Smart objects as building blocks for the Internet of things. *IEEE Internet Computing*, *14*(1), 44–51. doi:10.1109/MIC.2009.143

Leavitt, N. (2009). Complex-Event Processing Poised for Growth. *Computer*, *42*(4), 17–20. doi:10.1109/MC.2009.109

Levina, O., & Stantchev, V. (2009). Realizing Event-Driven SOA. *Fourth International Conference on Internet and Web Applications and Services, 2009. ICIW '09* (pp. 37-42).

Li, G., Muthusamy, V., & Jacobsen, H.-A. (2010). A distributed service-oriented architecture for business process execution. *ACM Trans. Web*, *4*(1), 2:1–2:33.

Metzger, A., Pohl, K., Papazoglou, M., Di Nitto, E., Marconi, A., & Karastoyanova, D. (2012). Research challenges on adaptive software and services in the future Internet: towards an S-Cube research roadmap. *Workshop on European Software Services and Systems Research - Results and Challenges (S-Cube)*, 2012 (pp. 1-7).

Michelson, B. M. (2006). *Event-driven architecture overview: Event-Driven SOA Is Just Part of the EDA Story*. Patricia Seybold Group. doi:10.1571/bda2-2-06cc

Newcomer, E., & Lomow, G. (2004). *Understanding SOA with Web Services (Independent Technology Guides)*. Addison-Wesley Professional.

Papazoglou, M. (2012). *Web services and SOA: principles and technology*. Essex, England, New York: Pearson Education.

Sosinsky, B. (2011). *Cloud Computing Bible*. Indiana, USA: Wiley.

Sottara, D., Manservisi, A., Mello, P., Colombini, G., & Luccarini, L. (2009). A CEP-based SOA for the management of Waste Water Treatment Plants. *IEEE Workshop on Environmental, Energy, and Structural Monitoring Systems (EESMS)* (pp. 58-65). Crema, Italy.

Spiess, P., Karnouskos, S., Guinard, D., Savio, D., Baecker, O., Souza, L., & Trifa, V. (2009). SOA-Based Integration of the Internet of Things in Enterprise Services. *IEEE International Conference on Web Services, 2009. ICWS 2009* (pp. 968-975).

Wang, W., Lee, K., & Murray, D. (2013). Building a generic architecture for the Internet of Things. *2013 IEEE Eighth International Conference on Intelligent Sensors, Sensor Networks and Information Processing* (pp. 333-338).

Wieland, M., Martin, D., Kopp, O., & Leymann, F. (2009). SOEDA: A Method for Specification and Implementation of Applications on a Service-Oriented Event-Driven Architecture. In W. Abramowicz (Ed.), *Business Information Systems* (Vol. 21, pp. 193–204). Berlin, Heidelberg: Springer Berlin Heidelberg. doi:10.1007/978-3-642-01190-0_17

Wu, E., Diao, Y., & Rizvi, S. (2006). High-performance complex event processing over streams. *Proceedings of the 2006 ACM SIGMOD international conference on Management of data* (pp. 407-418). Chicago, IL, USA: ACM.

Xia, F., Yang, L. T., Wang, L., & Vinel, A. (2012). Internet of Things. *International Journal of Communication Systems*, 25(9), 1101–1102. doi:10.1002/dac.2417

KEY TERMS AND DEFINITIONS

Complex Event: It is an event which contains more semantic meaning, summarizing a set of other events.

Complex Event Processing: It consists of processing and identifying the most meaningful events within an information system, analyzing their impact, and taking subsequent actions in real time.

Enterprise Service Bus: It is a software architecture model used to facilitate interaction and communication between service-oriented applications.

Event: It can be defined as anything that happens or could happen.

Event-Driven Architecture: It is an architecture which reacts to multiple events under several conditions.

Event Pattern: It is a template where the conditions describing the situations to be detected in real time are specified.

Event Processing Language: It is a type of language for defining event patterns.

Service-Oriented Architecture: It is an architectural style, based on services.

Web Service: It is a modular application that can be invoked through the Internet following some established standards.

Chapter 15
A Demand–Driven Cloud–Based Business Intelligence for Healthcare Decision Making

Shah Jahan Miah
Victoria University, Australia

ABSTRACT

Technology development for process enhancement has been a topic to many health organizations and researchers over the past decades. In particular, on decision support aids of healthcare professional, studies suggest paramount interests for developing technological intervention to provide better decision-support options. This chapter introduces a combined requirement of developing intelligent decision-support approach through the application of business intelligence and cloud-based functionalities. Both technological approaches demonstrate their usage to meet growing end users' demands through their innovative features in healthcare. As such, the main emphasis in the chapter goes after outlining a conceptual approach of demand-driven cloud-based business intelligence for meeting the decision-support needs in a hypothetical problem domain in the healthcare industry, focusing on the decision-support system development within a non-clinical context for individual end-users or patients who need decision support for their well-being and independent everyday living.

INTRODUCTION

Health organizations have randomly been made substantial investments in improving their processes through assistance of new technology over the past decades. As their technological intervention, most of the cases they aim at developing ways to delivering timely and accurate health or medical information to the right people, at a right time, to enable and enhance various operational and strategic decision-making (Carte et al. 2005). In particular on decision support aids previous studies suggest two main emphasizes on developing technological intervention to provide better deci-

DOI: 10.4018/978-1-4666-5884-4.ch015

sion support mechanisms. First emphasis goes on such decision support system that helps various practitioners in a clinical environment in relation to information management perspective. On the other hand, second emphasis goes on decision support system development within a non-clinical context for individual end-users or patients who need decision support for their well-being and independent every-day living.

Developing intelligent decision support systems within the medical domain for improving clinical activities is not a novel research area. Over the past decades many studies have identified different problems of intelligent solution developments for different purposes. Examples includes Zhuang, Wilkin & Ceglowski (2013) for pathology test ordering; Corchado, Bajo, Paz & Tapia (2008) for monitoring Alzheimer patients; Lin, Hu & Sheng (2006) for lower back pain diagnosis and Haghighi et al. (2013) for the improvement of emergency management systems. These studies employ various intelligent techniques to improve clinical practices for medical professionals. However, the intelligent systems design should not only focus on the problem analysis and relevant technology design for process improvement, but also focus to meet the client's domain-specific on-site information demands within the new technological provisioning platform that would provide better user-access and flexibility (Miah, 2012a). Other line of relevant studies highlight their interventions on non-clinical care domain, for example the study on home based care delivery (Barjis, Kolfschoten & Maritz, 2013), web-based patients intervention (Liang et al. 2006) and wireless patient monitoring (Varshney, 2008). These studies compliment the research done in the direction of telemedicine or telehealthcare domain for decision support (Karim & Bajwa, 2011). Drawing from this the key focus of this chapter goes on how an approach of demand-driven cloud-based Business Intelligence (BI) can be conceptualized to benefit of end users for their well-being and independent

every-day living through the application of new technological provisioning platform such as cloud computing.

The importance of decision support systems (DSS) have increasingly identified as an enabler to the achievement of medical industry's strategic and operational objectives over the many decades. DSS promises to provide timely and relevant information in addition to analytical capabilities to assist effective decision-making (Turban & Aronson, 2001). Keen & Scott Morton (1978, p 1-2) identified four major characteristics of DSS:

- Impact on decision in which there is sufficient structure for computer and analytic aids to be of interest,
- Payoff is in extending the range and capability of decision process to help improve effectiveness,
- The relevance for users is in the creation of a supportive tool, under their own control, and
- Applications are no routine as needed.

As the demand of DSS to support effective decision making have increased, so have the terms used to describe them: data warehousing, knowledge management, data mining, collaborative systems, online analytical processing, with Business Intelligence tending to encompass all (Gibson et al, 2004). Business Intelligence (BI) can be considered as the combination of processes and technologies to assist in decision making for managers and end users. The BI systems have been well-recognized for enhancing the effectiveness of information management and decision making. It is suggested that BI provides comprehensive decision support mechanism to meet all levels of demands for decision makers through applications such as decision support systems, query and reporting, online analytical processing (OLAP), statistical analysis, forecasting, and data mining (Stasieńko, 2010).

The advantage of cloud computing is that it is capable to offer a cloud-based (e.g. Internet or web-based provisioning) decision support service to meet the health professionals and end users decision needs. Other known benefit is that it can bring access and service flexibility both for service users and service providers (Miah, 2012b). With the benefit, it is important to understand and develop conceptual approach for designing the service delivery technology. In this chapter, our study is relevant to such a service design, namely an intelligent DSS application for the provision of cloud computing. As such, this book chapter will analyze current decision support issues of health organizations and professionals in order to develop a demand-driven cloud-based BI solution approach. The chapter will also identify fundamental issues in developing such a combined decision support mechanism by employing ontology and rules-based techniques. The mechanism could ensure decision support processes for management of information from three particular views such as professionals-oriented, patient-care oriented and organization and government settings oriented to their decision making aid.

BACKGROUND

Healthcare data provides wide variety of purposeful meanings to influence on decisions making. In health informatics, the need of decision making has generally been addressed for various practitioners as professional users (such as patients, hospital carers and healthcare professionals) as well as end users (such as patients and private and government health organizations). Health organizations and professionals nowadays are suffering from difficulties to effectively manage, process, and use the bombarded health information which has influence on their decisions making. They use various piecemeal e-health approaches for retrieving, displaying, analyzing, transferring

and sharing such a huge amount of information offline and online to meet their regular demands of decision support.

Jackson (2009) mentioned that the current economic crisis is having a severe impact on many healthcare providers as "the financial market's decline has reduced available investment income funds that offset declining reimbursements and falling philanthropic donations" and "the rising unemployment associated with the downturn has lowered admissions and elective procedures and increased uncompensated care" (pp.3). Jackson (2009) also described that continuing rising costs for qualified personnel in almost every roles within a healthcare provider's organization and the cost of supplies essential to the delivery of care have been of significant strategic issue in terms of implementing and monitoring continuous improvements in patient safety and quality of care delivery. This problem became a common headache all over the world. Patient groups also deliberately suffer from the dilemma as it is more than a simple matter of having more information systems available to resolve the delivery issue of appropriate care and decision support process to targeted stakeholders.

Web services are Internet-based application components provide universally available standard interface for various users. With enormous development of the Internet and the web service technologies over the past decade, web services have been very successful in e-commerce, e-business, artificial intelligence (AI), and service computing. They have also offered a number of strategic advantages such as mobility, flexibility, interactivity and interchangeability in comparison with traditional services (Hoffman, 2003). Web services are Internet-based application components that have been offered provisions to deliver healthcare information in a better accessible way and much more affordable way. The newly rising Cloud computing have also been used as a modern architecture of shared computing service in many areas for minimizing labor and implementation expenses (Santos, Gummadi & Rodrigues, 2009). However, the use of cloud based services for the effective decision making of multiple parties is still largely overlooked given its potential benefits. The service is mainly supported through computing utility rental by service providers. After the introduction of web-based utility services by Amazon. com, many web service providers became increasingly interested in the cloud-computing platform for launching new services to meet clients' demands as the cloud-based provision involves minimal labor and implementation expense (Santos et al. 2009). Nurmi, Wolski, & Grzegorczyk (2010) described an open-source software framework for cloud computing in which computing resources are considered as an Infrastructure as a Service. Santos et al. (2009) addressed requirements of confidentiality and integrity in data access and process in order to deliberately propose a trusted cloud computing platform for facilitating a closed box execution and storage in a virtual environment (p.2). This implies that the cloud-based provision must provide secure functionalities with a concurrent trusted storage facility. However, it is important to bring new insights that could improve the decision-making process within the provider communities as well as end users. As mentioned earlier BI techniques help create timely, accurate, and integrated knowledge that transforms healthcare with important outcomes including higher quality services, patient satisfaction, operational efficiency and financial and operational performance (Jackson, 2009; Stasieńko, 2010). In the same way, it is important to formalize the growing requirements of new problem-specific intelligent application design with better service benefits in terms of providing domain-specific decision support to the decision makers through cloud-based functionalities. This is the central motivation of the chapter.

MAIN FOCUS OF THE CHAPTER

The section introduces cloud computing as a central topic and how it can be used in healthcare decision making. This section also describes the targeted decision support in the three particular perspectives such as professionals-oriented, patient-care oriented and organization and government settings oriented to their decision making aid. The main aim is to identify relevant need of decision support technologies in order to reinforce cloud computing-based decision support mechanisms to professionals and end users in delivering the health or medical decision services.

As outlined in many latest journal articles cloud computing is still a developing paradigm. The definition attributes, and characteristics of the cloud computing provisions will be evolving over time. In a literature review, Vaquero, Rodero-Merino, Caceres & Lindner (2008) found more than 20 definitions of cloud computing as of significance definitions containing the essential characteristics. Based on the study Vaquero et al. (2008, p. 51) provided a definition as follows:

Clouds are a large pool of easily usable and accessible virtualized resources (such as hardware, development platforms and/or services). These resources can be dynamically re-configured to adjust to a variable load (scale), allowing also for an optimum resource utilization. This pool of resources is typically exploited by a pay-per-use model in which guarantees are offered by the Infrastructure Provider by means of customized Service-Level Agreements.

This implies that clouding computing is about the way of use to meet demands of users and organizations. The basis of the demand is service oriented rather than process or product oriented requirements. Kuo (2011) suggested three typical models of cloud computing from a service point of view such as: software, platform, and infrastructure.

They are namely: Software as a service (SaaS), Platform as a service (PaaS) and Infrastructure as a service (IaaS). In SaaS, software applications are accommodated by a cloud service provider and made available to users and organizations over the Internet. Platform as a service refers to operation platforms or system environments that are hosted on cloud and accessed through users' browser. With PaaS, organizations can employ and develop various web based applications without installing any tools on their local computer, and then deploy those software applications without any specialized maintenance and administrative requirements. Finally, with IaaS, the computing equipment such as hardware, servers, and networking components are hosted for cloud users to use for business support operations, such as for storage, manipulation and processing. The provider of cloud service owns the equipment and is responsible for accommodating, operating, and maintaining the technology. Cloud user typically pays on a per-use basis such as per transactions (Kuo, 2011).

According to IBM & Juniper Networks Solutions (2009) and Kuo (2011) there are models of cloud computing from a deployment point of views (Kuo, 2011). These are as follows:

- **Public Cloud:** A cloud service provider makes resources such as applications and storage environment available over the Internet on a per-use basis. For instance, the Amazon Elastic Compute Cloud (EC2) (as cloud service) allows users to rent virtual computing resources on which to operate their own applications. The cloud service runs within Amazon's network infrastructure and data centers and allows users and public organizations to pay only for what they use.
- **Private Cloud:** A cloud infrastructure is operated solely for sole organization. In this case the proprietary networks such

as data center provide hosted services to a certain group of users. For instance, Microsoft Azure enables customers to develop the foundation for a private cloud using windows server with the dynamic data center toolkit (Kuo, 2011).

- **Community Cloud:** A cloud infrastructure is shared by several organizations with common concerns such as security requirements, policy and compliance considerations. For instance, the Google GovCloud provides the Los Angeles City Council with a segregated data environment to store applications and data that are deliberately accessible only to the city's agencies (Kuo, 2011).
- **Hybrid Cloud:** This type of cloud infrastructures contains more than one cloud (e.g. private, public, community). In this cloud service, an organization provides and manages some resources within its own data center and has others provided externally. For example, IBM collaborates with Juniper Networks to deliver a hybrid cloud infrastructure to users and their organizations to extend their private clouds to remote servers (IBM & Juniper Networks Solutions, 2009).

Cloud Computing in Healthcare Decision Support

Many health professionals and experts believe that the cloud computing technologies can improve healthcare services by changing the face of current static health information technology, although it is still emergent to its widespread adoption in many aspects. The potential benefits of cloud computing have been reported in many studies to improve healthcare services. Studies proposed different frameworks to improve health care service (for example the study by Wang & Tan, 2010). Rolim et al. (2010) described a cloud computing solution to automate the process of collecting patients' vital data via a network of sensors connected to legacy medical devices. This system is used to deliver the data to a medical center's cloud for storage, processing, and distribution. Rolim et al. (2010) suggested that the system provides users at anytime from anywhere, real-time data collecting, eliminates manual collection work and the possibility of typing errors, and eases the deployment process. This system mainly makes healthcare data available for the medical professionals. Rao et al. (2010) reported a pervasive cloud initiative called "Dhatri", which integrates the cloud computing functionalities with wireless technologies to enable physicians to access patient health record at anytime from anywhere. Koufi et al. (2010) proposed a cloud-based solution for emergency medical system for the Greek National Health Service that integrates the emergency system with personal health record systems to provide physicians with easy access to patient records. It implies that cloud computing has been considered as effective solution platform to create automated information support in healthcare sector.

The key functionalities of cloud computing is that it is demand-oriented, self-managed and based on self-service Internet infrastructure that enables the user organizations to access computing resources. It can be seen as an out-sourced infrastructure for computing services as a new model of employing information technologies resources. As mentioned earlier, it is yet to have useful functionalities in this service so relevant decision makers in this sector can have better option to use this as decision support technology. For example, functionalities of DSS can be on cloud for the decision support aid of government and healthcare professionals in healthcare organisations. In designing DSS Haghighi et al. (2013) proposed ontology based knowledge repository for putting appropriate knowledge reasoning with better interpretations for individual's decision support in medical emergency management. For well-defined domains, it is claimed that ontology,

as a conceptual modeling technique, has the potential to improve the structuring of knowledge in decision making aid. Apart from this, healthcare sector requires continuous and systematic innovation in order to remain cost effective, efficient, and timely, and to provide high-quality services (Kuo, 2011; Koufi et al., 2010). As indicated in many studies promising innovations through the use of cloud computing have been demonstrated to improve the decision support provisions to targeted user groups. In the scope of this chapter, three particular perspectives are only focused such as professionals-oriented, patient-care oriented and organization and government settings oriented that could help create a platform to support automated data gathering in decision making aid.

Professionals-Oriented Decision Support

Clinical decision support systems (CDSS) are one of the appropriate examples of professionals oriented decision support. CDSS analyses medical data to help professionals make clinical decisions. The system commonly used for the support of medical business management. Rouse (2010) suggested that CDSS provide supports for physicians, nurses and other health care professionals to prepare a diagnosis and to review the diagnosis as a means of improving the final medical result and its interpretations. Within the approach most of the cases data mining techniques are used to examine the patient's medical history in conjunction with relevant clinical research, in order to predict potential events, which can range from drug interactions to disease symptoms. Under this specific class of DSS, many example studies exist that are used to provide help decision support to medical professionals. Zhuang, Wilkin & Ceglowski (2013) for pathology test ordering; Corchado, Bajo, Paz and Tapia (2008) for monitoring Alzheimer patients; Lin, Hu & Sheng (2006) for lower back pain diagnosis; and Haghighi et al. (2013) for emergency management.

Zhuang, Wilkin & Ceglowski (2013) described a decision support framework that assists general practitioners (GPs) in ordering pathology tests effectively. The study developed a concept of an integrated intelligent approach that combines knowledge discovery and case-based reasoning technique to capture the contextual requirements for an evidence-based and situation-relevant solution. The key innovation of Zhuang's et al. (2013) approach is that the approach helps GPs to have new understanding about the use of pathology tests by discovering and extracting practical and relevant knowledge from past pathology request data, from both patient-centric and clinical situation-centric perspectives. The approach provides guidance for practitioners through fulfilling ordering needs as it is situation oriented. As diagnostic support tool, Lin, Hu & Sheng (2006) described an intelligent DSS approach to support clinicians' diagnosis of lower back pain (LBP), a usual medical problem that requires appropriate responses to several challenging characteristics. It is because the diagnosis process of LBP required highly specialized knowledge that involves a complex anatomical and physiological structure (Lin et al. 2006). Lin's et al. diagnosis support approach is used multiple complementary methods to acquire the targeted knowledge from two highly experienced domain experts who practice in different clinics and used verbal probability estimation to capture uncertainty. Based on that, they developed a voting scheme for knowledge inference on the basis of consensus. However, Lin's et al. (2006) web-based approach is designed for the clinicians only that consist of a knowledge base, an inference engine, a case repository, and two interfaces for convenient system access and update.

Patient Care Oriented Decision Support

Liang, Xue & Berger (2006) suggested that web-based decision support mechanism has received considerable attention in the healthcare arena for patients specially for transforming healthcare, since Web technologies have been introduced. This decision support approach shares knowledge about providing tailored interventions to individual patients. As part of providing healthcare support the approach helps patients with chronic diseases make decisions about their medication persistency through motivating patients to continue taking their medications. The approach is developed as an initiative in fulfilling consumers' increasing requests of health-related information specific diseases and treatments, especially to support delivery of health services such as behavioral interventions (Liang et al. 2006). Corchado, Bajo, Paz & Tapia (2008) introduced intelligent decision support for monitoring Alzheimer patients' health care in execution time in elderly residences. The AGALZ (Autonomous aGent for monitoring ALZheimer patients) is an autonomous deliberative case-based planner tool designed to plan the nurses' working time dynamically, to maintain the standard working reports about the nurses' activities, and to guarantee that the patients assigned to the nurses are given the right care.

Barjis, Kolfschoten & Maritz (2013) introduced a healthcare decision support recently for providing home-based healthcare services to patients. The approach can be seen as a patient monitoring systems for fulfilling the requirements of medical staff (nurses, doctors) to decide on the course of intervention or further treatment based on the vital signs of the rural patients on a regular basis. The decision support approach provides patient information flow from home-based care workers to a local clinic or hospital, where the information is presented on a desktop computer used by clinic nurses and doctors for monitoring the patients' health and speeding up decision making (Barjis et al. 2013). The proposed system by Barjis et al. has been tested through a proof of concept prototype, which is applied in practice and generating data for evaluation.

Organization and Government Settings Oriented Decision Support

Organizations and governments also seek for decision support aids in improving healthcare service delivery. E-health systems can be seen as appropriate examples of organization and government oriented decision support approach. For example, Shavit (2009) identified the need of government decision making in the allocation of public resources for improving health focusing on needs of the population. The study identifies the importance of analyzing range of technological interventions available for characterizing the need in order to meet the demand of national health goals. Similarly, Moisil & Jitaru (2006) reported on government initiatives of e-health situation in Romania. Barjis, Kolfschoten & Maritz (2013) introduced a healthcare decision support recently for administering home-based healthcare services. From an organizational point of view the approach can be viewed as a patient monitoring systems for fulfilling the requirements of medical staff (nurses, doctors) to decide on the course of intervention in service delivery to mass people. The intervention can be described as further treatment of the rural patients that are tele-monitored by the healthcare organization. Eichler et al. (2004) identified issues of healthcare resource allocation decision making. The study provides an overview of the development of debate on thresholds, reviews threshold figures in relation to cost per unit of health gain, currently proposed for resource-allocation decisions in addition to explore how thresholds may emerge. Eichler's research contributes to the need of transparent and consistent decision-making for government organizations. De Meo et al. (2008) described a decision support approach aiming to support government agency decision makers to design new services tailored to citizen profiles in a complex and distributed e-government scenario. The approach is used to meet design need of citizen's expected access highly personalized services which has been at the basis of many public services such as health education and public housing.

PROPOSED CONCEPTUAL APPROACH

To meet the demand from the perspectives of patient-care, practitioners and organization or government oriented decision support, our study outlines a combined intelligent system approach. Our approach is influenced by a "one-size-fits-all" approach of De Meo et al. (2008), which has been of interest at the basis of many public healthcare services. The proposed conceptual approach of intelligent system focuses on extending a DSS approach introduced by Miah, Kerr & von-Hellens (2013) for the decision support aid of government professionals, domain experts and end users in the rural business context. An Ontology based knowledge repository has been employed for putting appropriate knowledge reasoning with better interpretations for individual's decision support. For well-defined domains, it is claimed that ontology, as a conceptual modeling technique, has the potential to improve the structuring of knowledge. Ontology refers to a particular view of the properties that comprise the problem domain, and how those properties relate to each other (Gennari et al. 2003). The use of ontology to model knowledge can lead towards the development of a solid, contextually relevant cognitive base that enables effective knowledge representation for a specific problem domain (Evermann, 2005). This can result in a useful knowledge-based platform for the development of a contextually relevant knowledge-base. The ontology has been extensively used for DSS developments, such as in the domain of medical emergency management for mass gatherings (Haghighi et al. 2013). The study by Haghighi et al. (2013) used ontology to resolve inconsistencies of terminology to enhance communication support among medical emergency personnel. Our study uses such domain ontology for better knowledge management in decision support across users and organisations, in terms of providing common vocabulary for effective knowledge sharing to different group of users.

The approach works in three layers of functional processes in that it allows three groups of users' decision support as it is important to recognize different classes of user as defined by specific industry requirements and the relevant managerial responsibility. Whilst scientifically informed domain models will be built by healthcare professionals, the choice and focus of these is a policy matter, and their use and customization is an end-user or patients matter. The first (layer at left-hand side in Figure 1) is an authorization layer for organizational users such as healthcare/government managers who allocate resources to assign one or more healthcare professionals to specific domain (e.g. diseases knowledge and relevant expertise). The second layer (middle) allows access to the knowledge acquisition component of the system where the healthcare professionals/experts on particular diseases (targeted domain) will develop decision-making rules and identify cases through the inference engine calibrations using real data on specific diseases. Findings suggested that most intelligent systems simply use rules-based methodology although they may employ various AI techniques varying from agent-based to case-based decision support approaches (Miah, Kerr & Gammack, 2009). However, a set of expert rules for decision making can be determined from domain experts, which are then used to generate the target-relevant rules (such as business logics) of decision support to the end users decision making requirements. This layer employs rules and case based reasoning for providing advisory and monitoring services. The final layer (right-hand side) allows patients access to the system, thus enabling them to achieve their advisory support specific to their own disease management through the support of healthcare information that will be delivered. The authorization layer is required to control resources allocations and to provide accountability in healthcare. The last two layers, namely knowledge acquisition from the specific health service domain (e.g. diseases domain) and specific options to diseases management for

targeted patient groups are essential to identify decision support functionality. Figure 1 shows the overall conceptual model in which the three functional processes are given for the three user layers.

For the patient's layer of advisory functionalities, we employ the MYCIN (an earlier expert systems (1970) developed at Stanford for medical professionals to diagnose and recommend treatment for certain blood infections) concept to functionalize the patient's need. The four metaphorical stage tasks are: 1) decide which organisms, if any, cause significant disease; 2) determine the likely identify of the significant organisms; 3) decide which drugs can be potentially used and finally; 4) select the best drug or set of plan for drugs. We utilized this metaphor in providing advisory support to specific patients groups. Figure 2 illustrates the possible architectural consideration of the proposed DSS on cloud.

In the cloud based architectural design, the proposed DSS on cloud is based on private and public cloud using hybrid cloud deployment in that the strategy is to share technologies for application servers, however the storage server can still seat at their own premises. Hybrid cloud deployment can offer an unprecedented opportunity to reduce the cost of IT, while improving functionalities of cloud services by employing DSS provisions to meet decision support requirements. In the aspect of the proposed DSS on hybrid cloud, ontology based knowledge will be hosted on public cloud to provide voculabury consistency specially to enhance communication support among medical emergency personnel and meeting their domain need. Database will be still located at private cloud, considering its sensitivity of privacy and security concerns. The ontology layer will integrate the business logics and inference rules of the targeted specific domain in order to display data according to user requests. Our study uses the ontology for better knowledge management in decision support across users and organisations, in terms of providing common

Figure 1. The overall architecture of the combined decision support approach

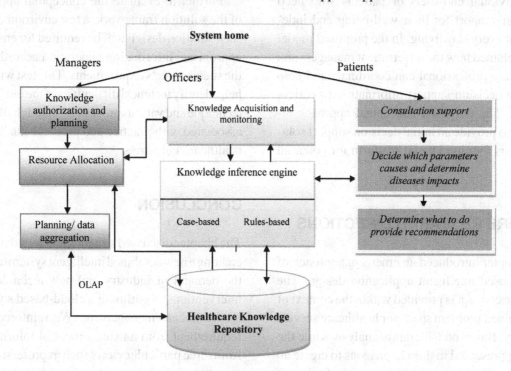

Figure 2. Proposed DSS design clusters on cloud computing

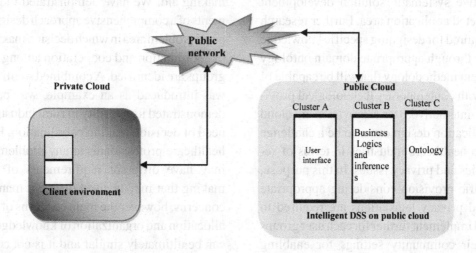

vocabulary for effective knowledge sharing to different group of patients/users. However, health organization should outline their strategic planning to examine user and service delivery factors such as information demands, targeted users, information service delivery procedure, technologies,

standard rules and policy in healthcare information delivery, and relevant government regulations that may have impact to achieve the goal of implementing such cloud based services. It is important to consider these factors prior to moving the service into the cloud within a non-clinical context for individual end-users or patients who need decision support for their well-being and independent every-day living. In the proposed model it is explained how the government managers and healthcare professional can coordinate and help provide decision support information to patient groups. The proposed conceptual approach attempts to provide an initial decision support solution basis for cloud based platform for potential users.

FUTURE RESEARCH DIRECTIONS

The chapter introduced an emergent approach of cloud based intelligent application design. The solution concept is provided within the context of a combined problem space for healthcare service delivery. Based on a literature analysis while the finding presented in this chapter was to create an initial basis of a concept on a review of relevant research, it only represents an early stage research of innovative systematic solution development in the targeted application area. Further research will be required for designing specific knowledge repository through appropriate domain ontology development methodology that will be capable of working with contemporary technological provision. The interactive user's provision in cloud based application design can also be a challenge relevant to healthcare industries in terms of security, ethics and privacy issues. In this purpose, user specific provision considering appropriate ethical and privacy legislations are required to define and implement further for each user groups within their community settings for enabling better decision making or action taking through effective collaboration. An in-depth evaluation study will also be required for system integration and acceptability considering a wide range of healthcare or medical support situations and to ensure compatibility of different technological components within an operating environment.

Further to evaluate the conceptual approach of the solution framework, a test environment for such solution design will be required for ensuring appropriate information generation according to the stakeholder's requirements. This test will also help identify technical difficulties of the intelligent technique and various process-oriented challenges associated with practice and protocol standard in healthcare industries.

CONCLUSION

The chapter discussed a theoretical foundation of creating a new combined intelligent system to meet the demand of industry and new technological interventions of outlining a cloud-based solution for healthcare management. We reinforced the requirement from a management of information from three particular views such as professionals-oriented, patient-care oriented and organization and government settings oriented to their decision making aid. We have demonstrated the requirements of a comprehensive approach design in a targeted problem area in which decision making needs of coordination and cooperation among different groups are identified. A combined solution model was introduced as an example, was previously demonstrated its usability in rural industry for the need of decision making coordination. However, healthcare professionals at any problem domain may have different requirements of decision making that may be used different management concerns, however the main concerns of resource allocation and organization of knowledge domain can be ultimately similar and it is not covered in this chapter. Many organizations may not have appropriate resources and infrastructure associated with healthcare management. Although the cloud-based solution can support flexibility and easier access to real-time data, it involves security and privacy of information and data resources including access control policy concerns.

The collaboration of cloud computing in healthcare industry can be seen as a big step for the healthcare delivery since computing era began. The cloud computing can be a potential answer to enable many services in healthcare organizations that may improve clinical and non-clinical services, especially through the use of intelligent applications. Although intelligent techniques have grown to a sophisticated level, the combination of these services with cloud-based computing is still in an emergent stage. Many relevant tools and technologies are still being developed. The topic area introduced in the chapter for the aid of decision support of targeted professionals' decision making is still just a concept. There is a need for considerable research on initial design and testing prior to implementation of the relevant technology in practice and need to suit the standard protocol of industry. The author attempts to bring a multidisciplinary application area of intelligent cloud techniques to enhance readers' knowledge and understanding in the field.

REFERENCES

Barjis, J., Kolfschoten, G., & Maritz, J. (2013). A sustainable and affordable support system for rural healthcare delivery. *Decision Support Systems*. doi:10.1016/j.dss.2013.06.005 PMID:23729945

Carte, T. A., Schwarzkopf, A. B., Shaft, T. M., & Zmud, R. W. (2005). Advanced business intelligence at cardinal health. *MIS Quarterly Executive*, *4*(4), 413–424.

Corchado, J. M., Bajo, J., de Paz, Y., & Tapia, D. I. (2008). Intelligent environment for monitoring Alzheimer patients, agent technology for health care. *Decision Support Systems*, *44*, 382–396. doi:10.1016/j.dss.2007.04.008

De Meo, P., Quattrone, G., & Ursino, D. (2008). A decision support system for designing new services tailored to citizen profiles in a complex and distributed e-government scenario. *Data & Knowledge Engineering*, *67*, 161–184. doi:10.1016/j.datak.2008.06.005

Eichler, H. G., Kong, S. X., Gerth, W. C., Mavros, P., & Jönsson, B. (2010). Determinants of continuous usage intention in web analytics services. *Electronic Commerce Research and Applications*, *9*, 61–72. doi:10.1016/j.elerap.2009.08.007

Evermann, J. (2005). Towards a cognitive foundation for knowledge representation. *Information Systems Journal*, *15*, 147–178. doi:10.1111/j.1365-2575.2005.00193.x

Gennari, J. H., Musen, M. M., Fergerson, R. W., Grosso, W. E., Crubezy, M., & Eriksson, H. et al. (2003). The evaluation of Protégé: An environment for knowledge based systems development. *International Journal of Human-Computer Studies*, *58*, 89–123. doi:10.1016/S1071-5819(02)00127-1

Gibson, M., Arnott, D., & Carlsson, S. (2004). Evaluating the intangible benefits of business intelligence: Review & research agenda. In *Proceeding of the Decision Support in an Uncertain and Complex World: The IFIP TC8/WG8.3 International Conference*, (pp. 295-305). Preto, Italy: IFIP.

Haghighi, P. D., Burstein, F., Zaslavsky, A., & Arbon, P. (2013). Development and evaluation of ontology for intelligent decision support in medical emergency management for mass gatherings. *Decision Support Systems*, *54*, 1192–1204. doi:10.1016/j.dss.2012.11.013

Hoffman, K. D. (2003). Marketing + MIS = e-service, e-services: A cornucopia of digital offerings ushers in the next net-based evolution. *Communications of the ACM*, *46*(6), 53–55. doi:10.1145/777313.777340

IBM and Juniper Networks Solutions. (2009). *Website IBM and Juniper networks: Delivering solutions that transform your networking infrastructure*. Retrieved from ftp://public.dhe.ibm.com/common/ssi/ecm/en/jns03002usen/JNS03002USEN.PDF

Jackson, L. (2009). *Leveraging business intelligence for healthcare providers* (Oracle White Paper). Redwood Shores, CA: Oracle Corporation.

Jiang, S., Fang, L., & Huang, X. (2009). An idea of special cloud computing in forest pests control. *Lecture Notes in Computer Science, 5931,* 615–620. doi:10.1007/978-3-642-10665-1_61

Karim, S., & Bajwa, I. S. (2001). Clinical decision support system based virtual telemedicine. In *Proceedings of 2011 Third International Conference on Intelligent Human-Machine Systems and Cybernetics*. Academic Press.

Keen, P. G. W., & Morton, M. S. (1978). *Decision support system*. Reading, MA: Addison Wesley.

Koufi, V., Malamateniou, F., & Vassilacopoulos, G. (2010). Ubiquitous access to cloud emergency medical services. In *Proceedings of the 2010 10th IEEE International Conference on Information Technology and Applications in Biomedicine (ITAB)*. Corfu, Greece: IEEE.

Kuo, A. M. H. (2011). Opportunities and challenges of cloud computing to improve health care services. *Journal of Medical Internet Research, 13*(3), e67. doi:10.2196/jmir.1867 PMID:21937354

Liang, H., Xue, T. Y., & Berger, B. A. (2006). Web-based intervention support system for health promotion. *Decision Support Systems, 42,* 435–449. doi:10.1016/j.dss.2005.02.001

Lin, L., Hu, P. J. H., & Sheng, O. R. L. (2006). A decision support system for lower back pain diagnosis: Uncertainty management and clinical evaluations. *Decision Support Systems, 42,* 1152–1169. doi:10.1016/j.dss.2005.10.007

Miah, S. J. (2012a). The role of end user in e-government application development: A conceptual model in the agricultural context. *Journal of Organizational and End User Computing, 24*(3), 69–85. doi:10.4018/joeuc.2012070104

Miah, S. J. (2012b). Cloud based DSS development for emergency medical professionals. In *Multidisciplinary computational intelligence techniques: Applications in business, engineering and medicine* (pp. 47–60). Hershey, PA: IGI Global. doi:10.4018/978-1-4666-1830-5.ch004

Miah, S. J., Kerr, D., & Gammack, J. (2009). A methodology to allow rural extension professionals to build target-specific expert systems for Australian rural business operators. *Journal of Expert Systems with Applications, 36,* 735–744. doi:10.1016/j.eswa.2007.10.022

Miah, S. J., Kerr, D., & von-Hellens, L. (2013). A collective artefact design of decision support systems: Design science research perspective. *Information Technology & People, 27*(3).

Moisil, I., & Jitaru, E. (2006). E-health progresses in Romania. *International Journal of Medical Informatics, 75,* 315–321. doi:10.1016/j.ijmedinf.2005.08.013 PMID:16275159

Nurmi, D., Wolski, R., Grzegorczyk, C., Obertelli, G., Soman, S., Youseff, L., & Zagorodnow, D. (2010). The eucalyptus open-source cloud-computing system. In *Proceedings of 9th IEEE/ACM International Symposium on Cluster Computing and the Grid*. IEEE. Retrieved on 22 April, 2011, from http://www.cca08.org/papers/Paper32-Daniel-Nurmi.pdf

Park, J., Kim, J., & Koh, J. (2010). An e-health platform for the elderly population: The butler system. *Electronic Commerce Research and Applications, 9*, 61–72. doi:10.1016/j.elerap.2009.08.007

Rao, G. S. V. R. K., Sundararaman, K., & Parthasarathi, J. (2010). Dhatri: A pervasive cloud initiative for primary healthcare services. In *Proceedings of the 2010 14th International Conference on Intelligence in Next Generation Networks (ICIN)*. Berlin, Germany: IEEE.

Rolim, C. O., Koch, F. L., Westphall, C. B., Werner, J., Fracalossi, A., & Salvador, G. S. (2010). A cloud computing solution for patient's data collection in health care institutions. In *Proceedings of the 2nd International Conference on eHealth, Telemedicine, and Social Medicine*. New York, NY: IEEE.

Rouse, M. (2010). *Definition of clinical decision support system (CDSS)*. Retrieved from http://searchhealthit.techtarget.com/definition/clinical-decision-support-system-CDSS

Santos, N., Gummadi, K. P., & Rodrigues, R. (2009). *Towards trusted cloud computing*. Retrieved on 22 April, 2011, from http://www.mpi-sws.org/~gummadi/papers/trusted_cloud.pdf

Stasieńko, J. (2010). Business intelligence as a decision support system. In G. Setlak, & K. Markov (Eds.), *Methods and instruments of artificial intelligence* (pp. 141–148). Rzeszow, Poland: Academic Press.

Turban, E., & Aronson. (2001). *Decision support systems and intelligent systems* (6th Ed.). Hoboken, NJ: Prentice Hall, Inc.

Vaquero, L. M., Rodero-Merino, L., Caceres, J., & Lindner, M. (2008). A break in the clouds: towards a cloud definition. *ACM SIGCOMM Computer Communication Review, 39*(1), 50–55. doi:10.1145/1496091.1496100

Varshney, U. (2008). A framework for supporting emergency messages in wireless patient monitoring. *Decision Support Systems, 45*, 981–996. doi:10.1016/j.dss.2008.03.006

Wang, X., & Tan, Y. (2010). Application of cloud computing in the health information system. In *Proceedings of the 2010 International Conference on Computer Application and System Modeling (ICCASM)*. New York, NY: IEEE.

Zhuang, Z. Y., Wilkin, C. L., & Ceglowski, A. (2013). A framework for an intelligent decision support system: A case in pathology test ordering. *Decision Support Systems, 55*, 476–487. doi:10.1016/j.dss.2012.10.006

ADDITIONAL READING

Buzolic, J., Mladineo, N., & Knezic, S. (2009). Decision support system for disaster communications in Dalmatia. *International Journal of Emergency Management, 1*(2), 191–201. doi:10.1504/IJEM.2002.000520

Cox, P. G. (1996). Some Issues in the Design of an Agricultural Decision Support Systems. *Agricultural Systems, 52*, 355–381. doi:10.1016/0308-521X(96)00063-7

Evermann, J. (2005). Towards a cognitive foundation for knowledge representation. *Information Systems Journal, 15*, 147–178. doi:10.1111/j.1365-2575.2005.00193.x

Fischer, G. (1999). Domain-Oriented Design Environments: Supporting Individual and Social Creativity. In J. Gero, & M. L. Maher (Eds.), *Computational Models of Creative Design IV* (pp. 83–111). Sydney, Australia: Key Centre of Design Computing and Cognition.

Haghighi, P. D., Burstein, F., Zaslavsky, A., & Arbon, P. (2013). Development and evaluation of ontology for intelligent decision support in medical emergency management for mass gatherings. *Decision Support Systems*, *54*, 1192–1204. doi:10.1016/j.dss.2012.11.013

Hayman, P. T., & Easdown, W. J. (2002). An ecology of a DSS: reflections on managing wheat crops in the North-eastern Australian grains region with WHEATMAN. *Agricultural Systems*, *74*, 57–77. doi:10.1016/S0308-521X(02)00018-5

Mackrell, D., Kerr, D. V., & von Hellens, L. (2009). A qualitative case study of the adoption and use of an agricultural decision support system in the Australian cotton industry: the socio-technical view. *Decision Support Systems*, *47*, 143–153. doi:10.1016/j.dss.2009.02.004

Maio, C. D., Fenza, G., Gaeta, M., Loia, V., & Orciuoli, F. (2011). (in press). A knowledge-based framework for emergency DSS. *Knowledge-Based Systems*.

Marston, S., Li, Z., Bandyopadhyay, S., Zhang, J., & Ghalsasi, A. (2011). Cloud computing — The business perspective. *Decision Support Systems*, *51*, 176–189. doi:10.1016/j.dss.2010.12.006

McCown, R. L. (2002). Changing systems for supporting farmer's decisions: problems, paradigms, and prospects. *Agricultural Systems*, *74*, 179–220. doi:10.1016/S0308-521X(02)00026-4

Miah, S. J. (2008), An ontology based design environment for rural decision support, Unpublished PhD Thesis, Griffith University, Brisbane, Australia.

Miah, S. J. (2009). A new semantic knowledge sharing approach for e-government systems, 4th IEEE International Conference on Digital Ecosystems, Dubai, UAE, pp. 457-462, 2010.

Miah, S. J. (2012). An Emerging Decision Support Systems Technology for Disastrous Actions Management. In S. J. Miah (Ed.), *Emerging Informatics - Innovative Concepts and Applications* (pp. 101–110). Rijeka, Croatia: InTech Open Access. doi:10.5772/2393

Miah, S.J., Kerr, D., & Gammack, J. (2009). A methodology to allow rural extension professionals to build target-specific expert systems for Australian rural business operators, Journal of Expert Systems with Applications, (36), pp. 735-744.

Michalowski, W., Rubin, S., Slowinski, R., & Wilk, S. (2003). Mobile clinical support system for pediatric emergencies, Decision Support Systems, 36 (2), 161-176 Microsoft Azure Services, Retrieved on 12, January, 2012 from URL: http://www.microsoft.com/azure/default.mspx

Mirfenderesk, H. (2009). Flood emergency management decision support system on the Gold Coast, Australia. *Australian Journal of Emergency Management*, *24*, 2.

Mirfenderesk, H. (2009). Flood emergency management decision support system on the Gold Coast, Australia, The Australian Journal of Emergency Management, Vol. 24 No. 2, May 2009

Muntermann, J. (2009). Towards ubiquitous information supply for individual investors: a decision support system design. *Decision Support Systems*, *47*, 82–92. doi:10.1016/j.dss.2009.01.003

Nurmi, D., Wolski, R., Grzegorczyk, C., Obertelli, G., Soman, S., Youseff, L., & Zagorodnow, D. (2010). The Eucalyptus Open-source Cloud-computing System, the 9th IEEE/ACM International Symposium on Cluster Computing and the Grid, retrieved on 22 April, 2011, from http://www.cca08.org/papers/Paper32-Daniel-Nurmi.pdf

Otten, J., Heijningen, B., & Lafortune, J. F. (2004) The virtual crisis management centre. An ICT implementation to canalise information, International Community on Information Systems for Crisis Response (ISCRAM2004) Conference, 3–4 May 2004, Brussels, Belgium.

Qin, J., & Paling, S. (2001). Converting a controlled vocabulary into an ontology: the case of GEM. *Information Research*, 6(2), 1–11.

Vouk, M.A. (2008). Cloud Computing – Issues, Research and Implementations, Journal of Computing and Information Technology – CIT, 16 (4), 235–246

KEY TERMS AND DEFINITIONS

Case Based Method: Case-based method uses case based reasoning (CBR) that is the process of solving new problems based on the solutions of similar past problems.

Clinical DSS: CDSS provide supports for physicians, nurses and other health care professionals to prepare diagnosis and to review the diagnosis as a means of improving the final medical result and its interpretations.

Cloud Computing: Cloud computing can be seen as a large pool of easily usable and accessible virtualized resources. The key functionalities of cloud computing are demand-oriented, self-managed and based on self-service Internet infrastructure that enables users to access computing resources.

Business Intelligence: Business Intelligence (BI) can be considered as a combination of processes and technologies to assist in decision making for managers and end users.

Decision Support Systems: Decision Support Systems (DSS) is a computer-based application that provides information support to various organizational decision-making activities. This application enables the management, operations, and planning levels of an organization and help to make decisions for effective businesses.

Rules Based Method: Rule-based methods use rule discovery or rule extraction from data. This method is one of the data mining techniques aimed at understanding data structures to provide comprehensible description.

Chapter 16
Web and Cloud Management for Building Energy Reduction:
Toward a Smart District Information Modelling

Patrizia Lombardi
Politecnico di Torino, Italy & Università di Torino, Italy

Andrea Acquaviva
Politecnico di Torino, Italy

Enrico Macii
Politecnico di Torino, Italy

Anna Osello
Politecnico di Torino, Italy

Edoardo Patti
Politecnico di Torino, Italy

Giulia Sonetti
Politecnico di Torino, Italy & Università di Torino, Italy

ABSTRACT

ICT is recognized as being a key player against climate change: pervasive sensors and actuators can efficiently control the whole energy chain. On the other side, advances on 3D modelling, visualization, and interaction technologies enable user profiling and real-time feedback to promote energy-efficient behaviours. The study presented in this chapter illustrates the development of a Web service-oriented, open platform with capabilities of real-time district level data processing and visualization. The platform will allow open access with personal devices and A/R visualization of energy-related information to client applications for energy and cost-analysis, tariff planning and evaluation, failure identification and maintenance, energy information sharing. The expected results are a consistent reduction in both energy consume and CO2 emissions by enabling more efficient energy distribution policies, according to the actual characteristics of district buildings and inhabitants as well as a more efficient utilization and maintenance of the energy distribution network, based on social behaviour, users lifestyles, and singular demands.

DOI: 10.4018/978-1-4666-5884-4.ch016

INTRODUCTION

According to the EU directive on the energy performance of buildings (EPBD-recast 2010), more than 40% of energy consumption in Europe is due to the operations of heating, cooling and lighting in buildings. Although an innovative technological approach in recent years has allowed the construction of more efficient buildings, we must point out that an increase in demand and energy (EC, 2010) consumption by end-users shows a total energy consumption on the rise since 1990.

Despite the significant progresses achieved in newly constructed buildings, existing buildings, and the historical ones in particular, still need special-purpose attention, as well as methods and tools for increasing their energy efficiency and for their proper automation. Moreover, the district/quarter level is still not sufficiently addressed and integrated with the other levels.

Energy efficiency is at the heart of the EU's Europe 2020 Strategy for smart, sustainable and inclusive growth and of the transition to a resource efficient economy. More specifically, the Union has set itself a target for 2020 of saving 20% of its primary energy consumption compared to projections and this objective was identified in the Commission's Communication on Energy 2020 as a key step towards achieving our long-term energy and climate goals (Lombardi and Trossero, 2013).

Although substantial steps have been taken towards this objective, recent Commission estimates suggest that the EU is on course to achieve only half of the 20% objective. Responding to the call of the European Council of 4 February 2011 to take 'determined action to tap the considerable potential for higher energy savings of buildings, transport and products and processes', the Commission has therefore developed this comprehensive Energy Efficiency Plan (COM/2011/0109 final).

This will be pursued consistently with other policy actions under the Europe 2020 Strategy's Flagship Initiative for a Resource Efficient Europe, including the 2050 roadmap for a low-carbon economy, to ensure policy coherence, assess trade-offs between policy areas and benefit from potential synergies. The strategy focuses on instruments to trigger the renovation process in public and private buildings and to improve the energy performance of the components and appliances used in them. It proposes to accelerate the refurbishment rate of public buildings through a binding target and to introduce energy efficiency criteria in public spending. It also foresees obligations for utilities to enable their customers to cut their energy consumption.

European Commission is stressing the importance of ICT for energy reduction and sustainability (Lombardi, 2011). ICT is a key player against climate change offering the possibility of 7,8 Gt reduction of CO_2 emission in 2020. ICT systems can efficiently control the whole energy chain, from production, to consumption, transportation and storage (Kelly, 2010). For the above mentioned reasons, ICT has been identified as one possible means to design, optimize, regulate and control energy use within existing and future (smart) buildings.

Existing activities and softwares are mentioned to understand gaps and opportunities to be implemented, such as 3D modeling, visualization and interaction technologies that enable user profiling and real-time feedback to promote energy efficient behaviours.

To unlock the potentiality of these technologies, the study focuses on the development of a "smart" integrated unique digital network and cloud archive for the city, using existing Smart Grid that comprises the networking and control of intelligent generation, storage, consumers and interconnected elements of energy distribution and transmission systems by the means of ICT. A specific objective of the study is to experiment a co-designing approach to adapt the existing information platform to householders needs in order to facilitate their habit changing. The co-design approach oriented to consumer practices asks for innovative solutions to stimulate behavioural changes among specific groups. A further contribution is to mobilise and revitalise these groups to reach more efficient models of energy consumption and to indicate further research on this field (Deakin et al., 2011).

The chapter is organized as follows. The following section - Background - provides some context modelling and social behaviour analysis. Then, an illustration of the middleware and Web services for data integration is provided. This will lead to a District Information Modelling and Management for Energy Reduction. Finally, future research directions will be presented as well as some conclusions.

BACKGROUND

The European Commission (EC) has currently a set of policies for developing EU strategies to promote ICTs for Energy Efficiency in Buildings. For instance, the EC requires Member States to ensure that minimum energy performance requirements of buildings are set with a view to achieving cost optimal levels using a comparative methodology framework established by the Commission. Cost optimal performance level means the energy performance in terms of primary energy leading to minimum life cycle cost. Member States have to provide cost optimal calculations to evaluate the cost optimality of current minimum requirements. The following documents are relevant for development:

- Ad-Hoc Advisory Group Report - ICT for Energy Efficiency aware of the issues and opportunities faced by the European Union in transforming to a low carbon economy society;
- Public consultation on "Information and Communication Technologies for a Low Carbon Society," ICT for Sustainable Growth, Sept 2009;

- Energy performance of buildings, included in the Directive 2010/31/EU of the European Parliament and of the Council, May 2010.

Through these and others, the European Commission is encouraging efforts in research, development and validation of results, aimed at a more efficient and optimal management of energy systems, on the way in which energy consumption may be reduced whilst maintaining indoor comfort, safety and security conditions and technological solutions always maintained closed to the state-of-the-art.

ICT can help changing behaviour at the level of final users. Aware that information and real-time information is able to influence and change around the 20% of energy consumption behaviour at household level, ICTs are positively involved in transforming everyday practices of energy consumption. The objective of the project is to experiment a co-designing approach to adapt the existing information platform to householders needs in order to facilitate their habit changing. The co-design approach oriented to consumer practices asks for innovative solutions to stimulate behavioural changes among specific groups. The project's contribution is to mobilise and revitalise these groups to reach more efficient models of energy consumption. People living in the districts used as demonstrator have the competence and consumer culture to make the best use of technical innovation and participate in co-design activities to develop new user-friendly technologies.

Many context-modelling approaches are known in scientific literature. Strang (Strang, 2012) provides a list of different context modelling approaches: 1) Key-value models, 2) Mark-up scheme models, 3) Graphical models, 4) Object-oriented models, 5) Logic based models and 6) Ontology based models.

Despite of advantages and disadvantages introduced by each approach, the goal of using common typical models and languages is to handle the acquisition, transmission and sharing of context. Furthermore, different approach affect to different context complexity: there is no 'one solution' particular language, but modelling approaches can differ in terms of expressiveness, interoperability, performance efficiency, programming effort required, reasoning support provided, ambiguity and incompleteness information management. Behavioural modelling is necessary in many different vertical scenarios from various application domains. This necessity is driven by the need to understand human behaviour of a single individual or of a group of individuals as a whole. Hereafter will be provided overviews of techniques used for this type of modelling, focusing on how activities are identified and classified.

The recent development of micro-electronics and computer systems has driven the creation of various smart environments, which has introduced many novel applications leveraging on intelligent behaviour detection, but significant development challenges are still open because of the complexity and unpredictability of human behaviour. One of these challenges is to understand and early detect typical human behaviour in different contexts, e.g. providing profiles (which are models) of individual or group. In this case the challenge is

create a profile enough accurate. But the profile, even if accurate, is not useful without a correlation with the environment, because rule-based systems need to leverage on both which user(s) behaviours and boundary conditions. The challenges are so further increasing, because both behaviours and external conditions could evolve over time and randomly (Knutsson, 2006).

Figure 1 explains the steps to recognize human activities and behaviours. The environment provides external data to infer any individual-related condition (location, tasks, activities), which are analyzed and sensed consistently with individual and boundary conditions. This has the scope of both learn common behaviour patterns and detect the context, in order to provide real time context-aware support (in the case of the project, the energy optimization). Standing to the proliferation of portable, fully computational, geo-located, wireless devices and sensors (Park, S-J., 2004), retrieving and sensing environmental context is feasible but is not yet deployed at user level in order to change and optimize energy consumption at room/building/district level. Instead, a lot of researches and EU funded project in the field of e-health, where the human observation is primary, focuses on different aspect of context aware detection, for example it

Figure 1. Behavioural context awareness detection

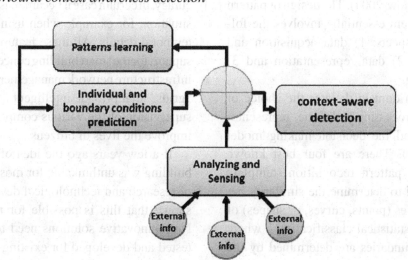

is possible to monitor people with severe problem or disease in order to prevent dangerous mistakes (e.g.: patients with Parkinson's disease who leave home alone), or to support the user's cognitive state and prevent cognitive decline, to detect abnormal events (such as falls) or unexpected behaviours that may be related to a health problem or to early detect future problems (e.g.: diet observation to prevent cardiovascular disease). In these cases the keyword "Ambient Assisted Living (AAL)" is used, which represent those system addressing complex activity recognition, usually based on raw sensor readings and some higher intelligent level able to semantically represent data, filter them and look for relevant features and patterns in order to satisfy some requirement (Fernandez-Luque, F. J., 2013).

Standing to the already available researches in the field of human observation and monitoring, the aim of the study presented in this chapter is to inquire into how to observe and classify the user from the energy-consumption point of view, making a long term trend analysis of daily behavioural information, focusing and exploiting the potential of all possible ICT technologies currently available on the market. Machine learning is the science concerning with enabling machines to learn patterns from historical data and allows for the creation of algorithms through the analysis them (T.T. Chow, 2004). The design of pattern recognition system essentially involves the following three aspects: 1) data acquisition and pre-processing, 2) data representation and 3) decision making.

The problem domain dictates the choice of sensor(s), pre-processing technique, representation scheme, and the decision making model (Sohraby, 2007). There are four best known approaches for pattern recognition: template matching - used to determine the similarity between two entities (points, curves, or shapes) of the same type; statistical classification – where the decision boundaries are determined by the probability patterns distributions; syntactic or

structural matching - where a pattern is viewed as being composed of simple sub-patterns which are themselves built from yet simpler subpatterns; artificial neural networks (ANNs) – information processing computational models based on complex parallel interconnections of simple neurons. These models are not necessarily independent and sometimes the same pattern recognition method exists with different interpretations. Various types of mainly deterministic task and activity models exist. The motivation of these more formal models is to leverage domain information that is already available. The following list considers models that focus on activity feature selection and classification: 1) Semantic formal modelling of tasks and activities with ontology; 2) Process-oriented and workflow-based activity models; 3) Concurrent task trees; 4) Petri nets; 5) Constructing and learning task models.

This list does not consider activity models where the original input of the data to construct these models comes from sensors or applications. Although activity recognition systems where high level, symbolic activities are inferred directly from low-level, continuous sensors are most common in the literature, but these sensor based classification, techniques have sometimes shown to be ineffective. Moreover, they require large amounts of annotated data for better classification and accuracy. In certain case it became easy to distinguish situation, for example when using location and temporal details. All these features are valuable support for the smart building concept. It integrates infrastructure network management, the so-called "grids," that provide intelligent and harmonized supervision of the various components to really improve the lives of citizens.

If a few years ago the idea of a zero energy building was unthinkable for most people, years of research and technological development have shown that this is possible for new buildings. Now innovative solutions need to be explored, tested and developed for existing buildings, and even for the historical ones, where the constraints are more and not always easy to resolve. There are still three essential elements to be developed which require specific technical-scientific or technological solutions:

1. Development of innovative technologies that can be used in valuable buildings historical and/or artistic work;
2. Reduction of installation and maintenance costs of the technologies to be used;
3. Empowerment of users.

Indeed, a proper design of Smart Building starts with the knowledge and then the analysis of the plants and consumption streams in different areas as well as quality requirement within different rooms. After the identification of intervention areas and plant efficiency and innovative services in smart optics, allocation of consumption to the respective spending centres, implementation of security controls and definition of energy saving measures, the management will set signalling alarms, control and command of technological systems, utilities (water, gas, light) and security services communications and broadcasting.

MIDDLEWARE AND WEB SERVICES FOR DATA INTEGRATION

This study proposes a strategy for smart building management and control leverages upon an ICT infrastructure made of heterogeneous monitoring and actuation devices. Moreover, in order to improve backwards compatibility, the infrastructure supports wired devices work with different protocols, such as BACnet, LogWork, etc. An innovative Web service oriented software infrastructure has already overcome those problems by an intelligent ICT-based service monitoring and managing the energy consumption. According to a shared definition (Borges et al, 2004), a SOA (Service Oriented Architecture) "is an architectural style that encourages the creation of loosely coupled business services that are interoperable

and technology-agnostic" enabling business flexibility. A SOA solution consists of a composite set of business services that realize an end-to-end business process. Each service provides an interface-based service description to support flexible and dynamically re-configurable processes. It is not properly new, but there are now some standard technologies (such as Web Services) that make it much easier to implement, in particular for business services inked together to implement business processes (Heinzelman,.2004). For instance, the recent SEEMPubS project (http://seempubs. polito.it/) used the LinkSmart middleware to provide interoperability between heterogeneous devices and networks, both existing and to be deployed (Osello et al. 2013). The infrastructure allows easy extension to other networks, thus representing a contribution to the opening of a market for ICT-based customized solutions integrating numerous products from different vendors (Eisenhauer, 2009). The system manages energy efficiently and WSNs are preferred to simplify the integration of new sensors into and also to avoid overloading of cables in historical buildings. As many SOA, this solution prefers flexibility over efficiency, since machine cycles and network traffic are less important then being able to quickly implement and change business processes The software infrastructure provides the following main functionalities:

*   It enables the interfacing to the application layer by means of Web services, through which the sensor data is read and can be used for visualization or to feed energy management policies;
*   It collects environmental data coming from the sensor nodes into the local database and this data can be accessed in an asynchronous way and preserved from network failures;
*   It allows the remote reconfiguration of sensor node parameters such as the sampling rates of physical quantities which are to be monitored;

- It allows the remote control of actuator devices;
- It enables interoperability among heterogeneous networks, characterized by different communication protocols, microcontrollers and sensors.

As shown in Figure 2, the software runs in a PC-Gateway (GW) and communicates directly with the heterogeneous networks. The dedicated Interface represents the lowest layer of our proposed stack, and receives information coming from various devices, regardless of the adopted communication protocols, hardware or the network topology. Hence, each network needs a specific software interface, which interprets the environmental information (e.g. temperature, humidity, etc.) and stores them in an integrated database (DB), in order to make the whole infrastructure flexible and reliable with respect to backbone network problems, since data are locally stored. The Web-service layer, implemented using

LinkSmart, interfaces the device networks to the Web, making the remote management and control easier. Moreover it exports to the application client layer, the last in our stack, all the environmental data that was stored in the DB. At this layer, the information is available to the end-user and ready to be post-processed or to be shown via computers, tablets or smart phones. Particular emphasis was given to the possibility to reconfigure each node, changing, for instance, some parameters about power management. In this scenario, the end-user sends the new configuration via Web-services to the GW and stores it in the DB. Then, the new settings will be automatically sent to the receiver mote, when it wakes up from the sleeping period, through the specific network software Interface.

The configurable parameters change depending on the hardware and the Operating System running on the end node. However, using this software infrastructure, the user can choose only the right settings ignoring the real physical hardware related to the virtual device. About power

Figure 2. The structure of the SEEMPubS middleware

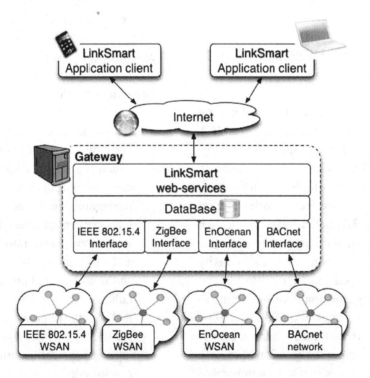

management, it is worth noting that there is no standard that indicates how controls and configuration settings are to be sent to the mote via the protocol packet payload. Hence, the proposed network software Interface is hardware dependent only for the way in which these parameters are formatted. However, from the communication point of view, it is protocol standards compliance. The goal of this study, from ICT side, is to bring information models from building level to district level enable the communication between heterogeneous and commercial devices for the real time interaction/visualization of virtual district distribution network models.

TOWARD A DISTRICT INFORMATION MODELING FOR ENERGY REDUCTION

As shown in Fig.3, this study intend to put together progresses in real-time monitoring and BIM to create a district information modelling and

simulation framework able to collect, process and remotely visualize district level energy usage. The overall objective is to create a District Information Model and Management system to represent in real-time and using 3D models of the buildings and the heating/cooling/electricity networks of the district. The system will collect information provided by users using their personal devices and represent in real-time information collected by sensors installed in the buildings and along the distribution networks. A processing engine will compute user-feedback actions in terms of suggestions where possible in real-time, about energy-positive and economically convenient actions. A number of client applications will be developed that are able to interact with the core system to collect and visualize district information remotely to end-users. One of the key challenges addressed by this study is to exploit information about buildings, energy distribution grid (both thermal and electric) and user behaviour to optimize energy efficiency. For instance, to create smarter energy distribution policies based on

Figure 3. The concept of the DIMMER project

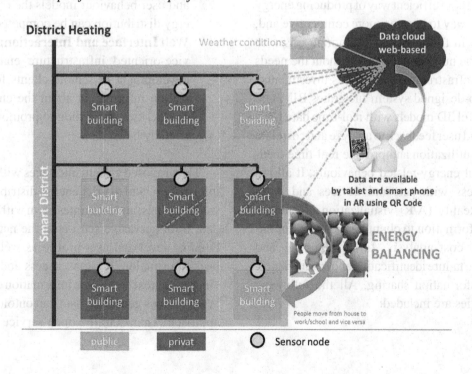

building intrinsic thermal characteristics and user behaviour in public buildings, enabling a flatter energy demand during the day by convincing users to make a smarter usage of variable tariffs in private ones are examples of possible optimizations. To achieve this target, a software system where information about buildings, their usage as well as user requirements is collected and feedbacks are provided to the stakeholders must be realized. A final product will be a Web-service oriented, open platform with capabilities of real-time district level data processing and visualization. Thanks to the Web-service interface, applications can be developed exploiting such an interface to monitor and control energy consumption and production from renewable sources. For public buildings like schools or university campuses, applications can visualize in real-time energy utilization leading to a considerable educative impact. Energy suppliers can provide their own set of client applications displaying clients energy consumptions, providing comparisons between client or groups of them as to change "not-smart" behaviours and, at the end, aiming at developing a smarter way of producing and distributing energy. For an energy producer, defining a more efficient way of producing energy is the only way to become more competitive and, especially in this period of economic crisis, to increase the number of clients without the needs of costly infrastructures and plants investments.

The so-designed system integrates BIM and district level 3D models with real-time data from sensors and user feedback to analyze and correlate buildings utilization and provide real-time feedback about energy-related behaviours. It allows open access with personal devices and Augmented Reality (A/R) visualization of energy-related information to client applications for energy and cost-analysis, tariff planning and evaluation, failure identification and maintenance, energy information sharing. All the following technologies are included:

- **Real-Time Data Collection:** Exploitation of real time data from pervasive sensors in buildings to provide actual information about buildings usage and their thermal characteristics.
- **Advanced Middleware Technology For Data Integration:** Integration of heterogeneous monitoring systems exploiting state-of-art middleware technologies.
- **Simulation and Virtual Visualization:** Virtual model of district based on BIM models of energy distribution plants to enable simulation and interactive visualization of energy flows, building real-time parameters and people behaviour and profiling.
- **User/Social Profiling, Visualization and Feedback:** Integration of a social behaviour model used to enable the virtual observation of user behaviours in the virtual visualization framework.
- **Energy Efficiency and Cost Analysis Engine:** Exploiting real-time information from buildings and from smart district heating/cooling and grid, building models and user behaviour models the optimal energy distribution can be computed.
- **Web Interface and Interaction:** Web service-oriented infrastructure enabling the development of remote clients for visualization information about the energy efficiency, user interaction to promote energy-friendly behaviour.

The proposed system interfaces with building information, and district energy distribution networks models, and integrates them with real-time data from pervasive sensors at the network and building level and user-profile as well as feedback information. It allows access and visualize "in-the-context" real-time information exploiting Web services generated using an ontology-based approach. Thanks to the open service based interface, client applications can be developed to: i) Visualize in real-time energy related information in the building and district environment; ii) Correlate user profiling and feedback information with building and district utilization to opportunities for energy distribution optimization; iii) Optimize policies based on more fine information real-time energy production/consumption and environmental conditions; iv) Perform cost and energy analysis that would enable the offer of personalized tariff plans and their evaluation on the basis of profiled use of energy. Various traders can propose their applications and promote alternative and competitive tariff plans. This will represent a new instrument that will also make the user more conscious about economic implications of their actions and of possible trader migration. In the study, each components of the system will enable the integration of Building Information Models (BIM), distribution network models, sensor data (both from environmental and energy production/consumption monitoring systems) and user feedback through QR Codes and Web portals. Moreover, the project will evaluate the ICT tools integration into social practices and their implications for the energy intensity of these practices. A qualitative research on ICT use in household and public buildings – indoor and outdoor – and the implications of ICT use for energy consumption will be carried out, by means e.g. of questionnaires and in-depth interviews addressed to samples of the district energy users.

A set of client applications for three types of users has been thought: energy suppliers, facility managers and district habitants. Energy suppliers will use/develop applications implementing energy optimization policies and visualization of distribution network for monitoring/ maintenance purposes. Facility managers will develop applications for monitor user behaviour, collect their feedback and promote a better utilization of building infrastructures thanks to real-time visualization and A/R capabilities. Building habitants will receive real-time feedback about their behaviours

during normal building utilization and will provide feedback about comfort level to facility managers. In particular, specific applications for students can be designed for educational purposes. Households (we specifically target condos in this project) will exploit applications allowing the energy and cost impact of home appliance utilization as well as the evaluation of economic impact of alternative tariff plans.

Collected data will be classified according to different grades of privacy, and made available just second that classification. In line with national and EU principles, data will be processed only when certain conditions are met: transparency, legitimate purpose and proportionality. If the proposed classification provides higher grade of privacy and security, a certain class of data will be totally closed to the public, and may be used only for statistical purposes in anonymous form. However, since the overall aim of the project concerns energy optimization features, interoperability of district energy production/consumption, environmental conditions real time visualization and user feedback data, the project aims to preserve also the Open Data principle. Several mechanisms may restrict access to or reuse certain sub-set of data, but the strategy includes commitments to publish with no inequalities that beneficial information for user awareness and decision tool enhancing. The right to access data is strengthened in legislation, vehicles for redress will also be enhanced and standards for higher data usability introduced.

Concerning energy optimization, the study envisions two levels of policies: i) Energy optimization policies based on sensors on the district heating/cooling network (e.g. water temperature and pressure, building temperature, environmental temperature) and building characteristics from BIM models (materials, location, orientation). These policies are based on objective data from sensors and building models leading to immediate control actions; ii) Speculative and statistically based policies based on user profiling and feedback actions, analysis of building utilization

Figure 4. The scheme of the DIMMER system

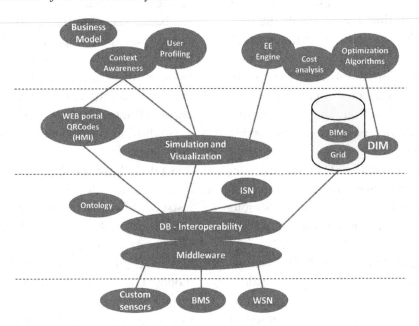

and predicted user behaviours. The scheme is described in Figure 4.

The whole system will by composed by a middleware, a database system, a BIM/DIM interface, and a set of client applications. Expected key client applications are: cost and energy analysis engine, A/R engine to visualize energy-related info over building and network models, user profiling and feedback collection engine, QR codes and energy Web portals.

The middleware interfaces sensor nodes and provides a set of Web services to allow client application to access sensor data in a hardware independent way. Sensors and actuators can be either present as separate networks (e.g. Enocean, Zigbee) or part of a BMS - Building Management System (e.g. Siemens Desigo). Custom sensor nodes can are also foreseen. A DBMS will collect energy related information provided by sensors and user profiling. The designed system interfaces BIM/DIM databases like ArchiBUS to retrieve building/district related information about 3D models and building characteristics (materials, location, orientation, underground

infrastructures). All the data related to building and district infrastructures and sensors will be available through Web-services by means of the developed middleware. These information will be exploited by the cost and energy analysis engine, the A/R engine and the user profiling and feedback engine.

The visualization engine is aimed at integrating sensor data with 3D virtual models providing the interface to personal devices for remote real-time visualization purposes of sensor information. On the other side, the energy analysis and cost engine exploits the Web-service based interface of the middleware to collect energy-related information.

Once real-time data are processed by software for controlling, managing, optimizing energy use at apartment/building/district level, a reverse data flow use the same network connection to come back to users and sensor. This contribution will be a friendly-user feedback with facts and figures about energy waste or bad habits, offering advice to improve energy efficiency and save money; but it can also act as switch for electrically controlled devices (for instance, stand-by appliance, louvers, gas and water circuit breakers) or as a remote tuning/adjusting of benchmarks, or as a company check-point for bills. The underlying vision is that by making available district energy production and consumption information using a natural, visual, and Web-service oriented interface to client applications would increase the energy efficiency by promoting local balancing and exploitation of renewable energy, increasing also market flexibility.

Part of these feedback flows can be stored on the cloud, published on the Web, remain within company data memories or sent directly to the user, depending on the transversal utility they can have for other building managers and the confidentiality of the information.

Indeed, different levels of communication relying on the same database with different processors allow a one to one building data access, optimization, transferability and interconnectivity, enhancing the optimization of the information exchange based on ICT, the creation of a "smart" digital archive unique for the city and giving support for the strategic plan of the city.

Regarding results exploitation, academic activities will follow two main directions: external exploitation, to increase its international visibility and thus its chances of establishing cooperation with private companies and universities, as well as to enable the participation to publicly funded projects, at the national and international levels. Internal exploitation, to increase the know-how of researchers and students on topics. The impact of research activities will allow a progress on knowledge in different topics, like data interoperability, energy optimization at district level, visualization of real-time energy information. The increased knowhow will have a direct commercial implication; in fact, the research partners will consider exploiting it indirectly by making agreements for its exploitation through third parties.

All R&D and academic partners will contribute to the dissemination of the project's results through technical presentations at international conferences and workshops, technical articles in journals and magazines addressing energy efficiency in buildings, participation to fairs and exhibits, lectures and seminars in the context of international schools and training initiatives.

FUTURE RESEARCH DIRECTIONS

The development of a District Information Model and Management system as described in this chapter requires collaboration between private and public enterprises as well as university. These activities are planned in a three-years time scale. The expected impacts are as follows:

- Improvement of the design of user profiles. Make households be able to monitor their energy consumption, receive real-time guidelines about green behaviours through innovative visualization and interaction instruments (e.g. A/R, ambient visualization, QR Codes), adapt to tariff changes, control loads by scheduling ON and OFF switching of their plug loads.
- Optimize information exchanged on ICT new platform and database, converging IT data flow and classification, building occupational profile and data-focused services.
- Enhance environmental education methods. Inform users and make them aware of the importance of their energy-related actions. This approach also aims at controlling the dynamics of energy demand in buildings and enable optimal management by energy supply companies, giving them the possibility to use their producers in a smarter way and connect more final user with limited impact.
- Study model for decentralization of EU energy market and therefore improve coordination between smart grid managers, energy providers, big and small final users and local energy producer.

- Create a "smart" integrated unique digital network and cloud archive for the city, using existing Smart Grid that comprises the networking and control of intelligent generation, storage, consumers and interconnected elements of energy distribution and transmission systems by the means of ICT.
- Maximize the benefits of the smart distribution network, ensuring proper levels of interoperability among sensors, devices and feedback information, data availability and security, and finally decision support system for both citizens and city managers.

CONCLUSION

This study has shown how ICT pervasive use can enable the integration of different processes, applications, systems and technologies in order to visualize and manage district energy consumption. To handle the acquisition, transmission and sharing of data, many context-modelling approaches have been analysed. An innovative Web service oriented software infrastructure plus a number of client applications is going to be developed to interact with the core system and collect and visualize district information remotely to end-users. The proposed solution relies on the assumption that ICT can be a valid help in changing the user behaviour, since to be aware of real-time and ex-post data information and analysis has been proved to influence and change around the 20% of energy consumption at household level. This software, Web-service oriented, building integrated and application based on data mining & energy use analysis implies a definition of a BIM model and a digital simulation for the comparison of data between different solutions regarding energy efficiency. The so-designed system integrates BIM and district level 3D models with real-time data from sensors and user feedback to analyse and correlate buildings utilization and

provide real-time feedback about energy-related behaviours. Further outcomes will be the definition and implementation of an infrastructure that combines decision support systems on all levels (energy, economic, political) via social and market simulations, capable of modelling behaviour and energy consumption trends of citizens.

If the smartest way to achieve efficiency in our energy consumption relies in the user involvement and awareness, this study could represent a significant step towards the definition of a new conceptual model of low energy society, aiming at assessing an economic value for each stakeholder and identifying innovative business, products, and services models that may emerge in the Smart City of the future. The implementation of such energy monitoring/evaluating systems can become a proper decision support able to define guidelines in the political, economic and environmental framework, compliant with the criteria given by the regional, national, and European legislation, therefore providing effective mechanisms that encourage consumers to an efficient energy usage and a better production/distribution energy network.

REFERENCES

Arsanjani, A., Borges, B., & Holley, K. (2004). Service-oriented architecture: Components and modeling can make the difference. *Web Services Journal*, *9*(1), 34–38.

Chow, T. T. (2004). Energy modelling of district cooling system for new urban development. *Energy and Building*, *36*(11), 1153–1162. doi:10.1016/j.enbuild.2004.04.002

Deakin, M., Lombardi, P., & Cooper, I. (2011). The IntelCities community of practice: The capacity-building, co-design, evaluation and monitoring of eGov services. *Journal of Urban Technology*, *18*(2), 13–38. doi:10.1080/10630732.2011.601107

Eisenhauer, M. R. (2009). A development platform for integrating wireless devices and sensors into ambient intelligence systems. In *Proceedings of Sensor, Mesh and Ad Hoc Communications and Networks Workshops*. IEEE. doi:10.1109/SAHCNW.2009.5172913

European Commission (EC). (2010a). *Energy efficiency in Europe: EU adopted the energy performance of buildings directive 2010/31/EU (EPBD)*. Brussels: EC.

European Commission (EC). (2010b, May 19). The directive 2010/31/EU on the energy performance of buildings. *Official Journal of the European Union*.

Fernandez-Luque, F. J., Pérez, D., Martínez, F., Domènech, G., Navarrete, I., Zapata, J., & Ruiz, R. (2013). An energy efficient middleware for an ad-hoc AAL wireless sensor network. *Ad Hoc Networks*, *11*(3), 907–925. doi:10.1016/j.adhoc.2012.10.003

Heinzelman, W., Murphy, A., Carvalho, H., & Perillo, M. (2004). Middleware to support sensor network applications. *IEEE Network*, *18*(1), 6–14. doi:10.1109/MNET.2004.1265828

Kelly, S. P. (2010). An assessment of the present and future opportunities for combined heat and power with district heating (CHP-DH) in the United Kingdom. *Energy Policy*, *38*(11), 6936–6945. doi:10.1016/j.enpol.2010.07.010

Knutsson, D. (2006). HEATSPOT—A simulation tool for national district heating analyses. *Energy*, *31*, 278–293. doi:10.1016/j.energy.2005.02.005

Lombardi, P. (2011). Managing the green IT agenda. *Intelligent Buildings International*, *13*(3), 8–10.

Lombardi, P., & Trossero, E. (2013). Beyond energy efficiency in evaluating sustainable development in planning and the built environment. *International Journal of Sustainable Building Technology and Urban Development*.

Osello, A., Acquaviva, A., Aghemo, C., Blaso, L., Dalmasso, D., & Erba, D. et al. (in press). Energy saving in existing buildings by an intelligent use of interoperable ICTs. *Energy Efficiency*. doi:10.1007/s12053-013-9211-0

Park, S.-J., Vedantham, R., Sivakumar, R., & Akyildiz, I. F. (2004). A scalable approach for reliable downstream data delivery in wireless sensor networks. In *Proceedings of MobiHoc* (pp. 78–89). ACM. doi:10.1145/989459.989470

SEEMPubS. (2010). Retrieved from http://seempubs.polito.it/

Sohraby, K., Minoli, D., & Znati, T. (2007). *Wireless sensor networks: Technology, protocols, and applications*. Hoboken, NJ: John Wiley and Sons. doi:10.1002/047011276X

Strang, K. D. (2012). Importance of verifying queue model assumptions before planning with simulation software. *European Journal of Operational Research*, *218*(2), 493–504. doi:10.1016/j.ejor.2011.10.054

ADDITIONAL READING

Barry, K. D. (2003). *Web Services and Service-Oriented Architectures: The Savvy Manager's Guide*. Morgan Kaufmann.

Candido, G., Colombo, A., Barata, J., & Jammes, F. (2009), Service-oriented infrastructure to support the deployment of evolvable production systems. In IEEE Transaction on Industrial Informatics, vol. 7, no. 4

Chase, C. W. (2013). *Demand-Driven Forecasting: A Structured Approach to Forecasting*. John Wiley & Sons Inc.

Eastman C., Teicholz P., Sacks R., Liston K. (2008). *BIM Handbook: A Guide to Building Information Modeling for Owners, Managers, Designers, Engineers and Contractors*. London: John Wiley & Sons Inc.

Erl, T. (2005). *Service-Oriented Architecture: Concepts, Technology and Design*. Prentice Hall.

Falud, R. (2011). *Building Wireless Sensor Networks: with ZigBee, XBee, Arduino, and Processing*. O'Reilly.

Finith E.,(2007), *BIG BIM little bim: The Practical Approach to Building Information Modeling-integrated Practice Done the Right Way!*, United States: 4Site Press

Gezer, C., & Buratti, C. (2011), A zigbee smart energy implementation for energy efficient buildings. In *Vehicular Technology Conference, ser. VTC Spring*, Denver, Colorado, USA, pp. 1–5.

Guinard, D., Trifa, V., Karnouskos, S., Spiess, P., & Savio, D. (2010). Interacting with the soa-based Internet of things: Discovery, query, selection, and on-demand provisioning of Web services, *Services Computing. IEEE Transactions*, 3(3), 223–235.

Ibrahiem, M. M. El Emary, S. Ramakrishnan, (2014), Wireless Sensor Networks: From Theory to Applications, Taylor and Francis gruop, US

Josuttis, M. N. (2007). *SOA in Practice: The Art of Distributed System Design*. US: O'Reilly media.

Karnouskos, S. (2009), The cooperative Internet of things enabled smart grid. In *Proceedings of the 14th IEEE International Symposium on Consumer Electronics, ser. ISCE2010*, Braunschweig, Germany.

Kiviniemi, A. (2011), The Effects of Integrated BIM in Processes and Business Models. In Kocaturk T., Medjdoub B., Distributed Intelligence in Design, Chichester UK, Wiley Blackwell

Milgram, P., Takemura, H., Utsumi, A., & Kishino, F. (1995), Augmented Reality: A Class of Displays on the Reality-virtuality Continuum. In Telemanipulator and Telepresence Technologies, SPIE 2351.

Munasinghe, M., & Meier, P. (2008). *Energy Policy Analysis and Modelling, Cambridge Energy and Environment Series*. Cambridge University Press.

Murphy, M., McGovern, E., & Pavia, S. (2013). *Historic Building Information Modelling – Adding intelligence to laser scanner and image based surveys of European classical architecture, ISPR Journals of Photogrammetry and Remote sensing* (pp. 89–102). Elsevier.

Osello, A. (2012). *Il futuro del disegno con il BIM per ingegneri e architetti*. Palermo: Dario Flaccovio.

Polimeni, J. M., Mayumi, K., Giampietro, M., & Alcott, B. (2009). *The Myth of Resource Efficiency: The Jevons Paradox*. Oxford: Earthscan.

Portland Sustainability Institute (PoSI). (2010). *The EcoDistricts Initiative: Accelerating sustainability at a district scale – framework*. Portland, OR: Portland Sustainability Institute.

Robinson, D. (2011). *Computer Modelling for Sustainable Urban Design: Physical Principles, Methods and Applications*. Earthscan.

Rogers, R. (1997). *Small Cities for a Small Planet*. London: Faber and Faber.

Stavropoulos, T. G., Gottis, K., Vrakas, D., & Vlahavas, I. (2013). Awe- some: A Web service middleware for ambient inteigence. *Expert Systems with Applications*, 40(11), 4380–4392. doi:10.1016/j.eswa.2013.01.061

Stone, D., Jarrett, C., Woodroffe, M., & Minocha, S. (2005). *User Interface Design and Evaluation Interactive Technologies*. Morgan Kaufmann as an imprint of Elsevier.

Suzuki, et al. (2010). *Eco2 Cities: Ecological Cities as Economic Cities*. The World Bank. doi:10.1596/978-0-8213-8046-8

Underwood, C., & Yik, F. (2004). *Modelling Methods for Energy in Buildings*, Blackwell, UK W. Rees and M. Wackernagel,(1996), *Urban ecological footprints: Why cities cannot be sustainable and why they are a key to sustainability*. *Environmental Impact Assessment Review, 16*, 223–248.

Warmer, C., Kok, K., Karnouskos, S., Weidlich, A., Nestle, D., Selzman, P., et al. (2009), Web services for integration of smart houses in the smart grid. In Grid-Interop - The road to an interoperable grid, Denver, Colorado, USA

Yang W.-B., Chen M.-B., Yen Y.-N. 2011. An application of digital point cloud to historic architecture in digital archives. Advances in Engineering Software 42, Elsevier, 2011, pp. 690-699.

KEY TERMS AND DEFINITIONS

Advanced Data Visualization: Advanced visualization of district infrastructures with real-time visualization of district cooling sensor data, inefficient domestic energy sources, 3D visualization of distribution network infrastructures and real-time collected values in A/R using QR codes to localize the user and visualize sensor values.

Ambient Assisted Living (AAL): Those system addressing complex activity recognition, usually based on raw sensor readings and some higher intelligent level able to semantically represent data, filter them and look for relevant features and patterns in order to satisfy some requirement.

District Modelling: 3D parametric models both at building and district level by proposed standard for interoperability between BIM softwares.

Energy Efficiency Algorithms: Improved policies for district heating distribution exploiting building characteristics, 3D models, inner comfort levels and weather sensors to improve user energy demand behaviour, flatten demand peaks and take into account renewable energy sources.

Middleware Framework: A framework that defines an abstraction layer on top of heterogeneous communication protocols. It provides services to application developers, hiding the complexity of underlying device specifics. It solves the compatibility issues among heterogeneous devices by abstracting them with Web Services in a Service Oriented Architecture (SOA) environment, under which the details of the communication between the devices is hidden.

Real-Time Data Collection: Network of sensors for ubiquitous, self-powered pervasive data acquisition and gathering, allowing monitoring of building and distribution network monitoring to assess energy utilization, waste, comfort parameters, water temperature, ambient temperature, humidity, CO_2, etc.

User Profiling: Interaction with the public energy awareness community Web portal by developing open, portable, real-time and user-attractive services. This is in order to understand and early detect typical human behavior in different contexts, e.g. providing profiles (which are models) of individual or group matched with related boundary conditions.

Chapter 17
E-Business in Education:
The Case of Delta State University

Edwin Iroroeavwo Achugbue
Delta State University, Nigeria

ABSTRACT

This chapter is anchored on previous research to examine e-business in education, with emphasis on the Delta State University Abraka, Delta State, Nigeria. The study focused on the concept of e-business, e-business in education, and explored the various educational routines, such as e-learning, tele-learning, research, and administration. The study examined classification of e-business, e-business tools, such as e-mail, Websites, message boards, online catalogs, and telephone and e-business activities in education. It also focused on e-payment of fees, students' registration, checking of results, and online application as part of e-business routines in administration. Finally, the study looked at the barriers to e-business adoption in education using diffusion theory of innovation. A conclusion and recommendations are then made.

INTRODUCTION

Universities and other tertiary institutions all over the world are already developing new technologies for educational and administrative support, with the emergence of virtual learning environments (Ford, 2008). Thus according to Buller (2008) there is no doubt that advances in information and communication technologies have been huge over the last few years and that they continue to accelerate. Information and communication technologies (ICTs) have become an essential part of our lives. In the past decade, the use of ICT throughout society really took off with the emergence of the Internet. The Internet started mainly as a network for researchers that gave the opportunity to share information and ideas. An important step in the commercialization of the Internet was the an-

DOI: 10.4018/978-1-4666-5884-4.ch017

nouncement of the World Wide Web (WWW) in 1991 by Tim Berners-Lee of CERN (Kalakota & Whinston, 1996; & Amamuah-Mensah, 2009).

In today's contemporary society, there is hardly any form of transaction either in business (i.e. buying, selling, financial transaction) or education (i.e. administration, registration, purchase of form, checking of result, examination, teaching and learning) that is done without ICT. This use of ICT in almost all aspects of human transaction occasioned by the World Wide Web (www) has introduced the concept of e-business, e-commerce, e-learning, e-registration, e-transaction, e-banking, which of course are covered by e-business. One of the factors that have promoted e-business is the Internet. According to Azumah, Koh and Maguire (2006). The Internet has gone from being a communication tool, used by a small sector of professional society (academics and military) to something that has permeated much of the business, corporate, and consumer world. Some of the largest and most technological and information consuming organizations have seen this as an opportunity to create a totally new market for their product and services. Furthermore, in the 21st century and beyond the Internet is one area of technological development that has and will continue to revolutionize modern organizations and the communication world like nothing before. It is also a medium of collaboration and interaction between individuals, their computers and many business and non-business organizations without regard for geographical location.

From the above, it is clear that the emergence of Internet is a catalyst to the development of e-business (Azumah, Koh and Maguire, 2006). In Nigeria and particularly higher Institutions, e-business is now the alternative and convenient way of conducting all types of business. Akintola, Akinyede and Agbonifo (2011) note that Nigeria being the giant of Africa is not only in numerical strength but also an economic power and intellectualism. According to *business times* cited in Akintola, Akinyede and Agbonifo (2011),

there were just a small number of dial-up e-mail providers in Nigeria before the year 1998, today, well over 400 ISPs have been licensed. The present ISPs and often users with online advertising chances as well as Internet banking security and very small aperture terminal (VSAT) services which help to promote e-learning, e-registration and distance learning programs. The use of mobile phones is also another means of promoting e-business education within and out of the Universities and other tertiary institutions. Many youths and adults who are versatile with the mobile phones are getting Internet connections from their WAP-enabled mobile phones, PDA's, smart phones and from their personal computers (PCs). All these education activities carried out online make education e-service oriented, the objective of this study therefore is to examine e-business in education, with focused on Delta State University, Abraka Nigeria.

CONCEPT OF E-BUSINESS

The concept of e-business followed the emergence of the Internet by the U.S. Government, which was initially used by technical audience of government agencies, academic researchers and scientists. By the 1970s, innovations like electronic fund transfer (ETF) fund routed electronically from one organization to another began to emerge, though it was limited to large corporations then. Although in the 60s electronic data interchange (EDI)which is the act of transferring documents electronically was introduced. this also followed the introduction of inter-organizational system (IOS) which includes travel reservation systems and stock trading was introduced. By the 1990s the Internet was commercialized and users flocked to participate in the form of dot-coms, or Internet start-ups. Innovative applications ranging from online direct sales to e-learning experiences also evolved. This led most organizations to have a Web site, while others that are large have comprehensive portals. Since the evolution of the Internet many concepts began to emerge, prominent among them being the concept of e-business which is sometimes referred to as e-commerce, though broader than e-commerce. According to Georgia (2009) and Shih (2005), e-business was largely based in the United State of America (USA) in the earlier years, but today the concept is widely used in business and education globally.

Zwass and Melao cited in Amamuah-Mensah (2009) also noted that e-business probably began with electronic data interchange (EDI) in the 60s. However, it was only in the 90s, primarily via the Internet that e-business emerge as a core features of organizations. Further believed that e-business would revolutionize the ways in which organizations interact with customers, employees, suppliers and partners. The above situation suggests that most human transactions either in commerce or education are done electronically, this process being what is referred to as e-business. The term e-business is very broad and has different applications in different fields but has the same meaning. E-business (electronic business) can be defined as concepts, methodologies and processes for the support and automation of business transactions through information and communication technologies (ICTs). The above definition covers all ICT, supports for all processes related to the development, production, distribution of information, goods and services and education. Sometimes, e-commerce (electronic commerce) is often used synonymously with e-business. This refers to concepts, methodologies and processes for the support and automation of commercial transactions through the use of information and communication technologies (Pawlowski and Adelsberger (2002). From the above definitions, it clear that e-business is broader and encompasses e-commerce.

Clark cited in Pawlowski and Adelsberger (2002) asserts that transactions such as licensing processes (e-registration), research and development process, court administration and education are only directly related to trade of goods and services. It means therefore, that e-business covers a wider range of transactions. Building on the above frame-work, Swatman and Chan (2001) note that e-business is developing at a tremendous pace over the past few years, since the creation of the NASDAQ index. As a result, e-business has become one of the most widely discussed and rapidly growing parts of the business world. However, due to this development in e-business, different types of businesses are evolving. Education is also undergoing significant changes due to the development of ICT.

Emphasizing the concept of change, occasioned by the world wide Web (www) Achugbue and Ochonogor (2011) affirm that ICTs have made remarkable progress in education and business transactions, which impact has resulted in e-business concept. Furthermore, e-business according to the European Commission(2007), are business processes that run through the entire value chain, such as electronic purchasing and supply, chain management, processing, orders electronically, handling customer service, operating with business partners, it also include educational transactions of the Internet and seeing as integrations of the Internet and related ICTs into the business organization. From the foregoing, Elcoteq cited in Maijata (2004) assert that e-business is a higher level term which could be divided into four lower level terms that include e-collaboration, e-commerce, e-learning and e-marketing. The concept of e-collaboration means the process of working together dynamically and electronically, either through the Internet, a company local area network (LAN), or through wireless devices. Distance education was the first form of electronic learning. E-learning is a way of providing training, educational or learning material by some electronic means, like computer or a mobile phone. Electronic learning can be online (over the Internet and intranet) or offline (CD-ROM and DVD). E-marketing, e-marketing is the act of providing marketing services or goods from seller to buyer that involves one or more electronic methods or media (Ghosh, 1998, Heeter, 1999 and Maijata, 2007).

From all the various definitions given, it is obvious that e-business encompasses all human transaction either in goods and services or teaching and learning which are e-commerce and e-learning respectively. To that extent, the definition given by the European Commission, Ghosh, Heeter and Maijata look appropriate in the context of the above discussion, because they have posited that e-business is any transaction which involves education and commerce which is the focus of this discussion. It is the integration of the Internet and other ICTs into business transaction which may take the form of goods and services (commerce) and education which is teaching and learning. It could take the form of tele-learning, tele-collaboration, tele-conferencing, e-learning, distance learning, messaging in form of e-mail and even research which include e-documents (soft copies) of research either sent or distributed online. However, between 1999-2001 emphases of e-business shifted from B2C to B2B and from B2B to B2E, e-commerce, e-government, e-learning and m-commerce. E-business will continue to shift as a result of emerging technologies.

CLASSIFICATION OF E-BUSINESS

Academic and business organization all over the world have already drawn up a number of framework for classifying e-business but each one tends to approach it from a particular perspective. Although some author and literature tend to describe e-business as e-commerce which is not very correct. In this research, e-commerce is treated as part of e-business. E-commerce (EC) describes the buying and selling of products, services, and information via computer networks including the Internet. E-business is the conduct of business on the Internet, not only buying and selling but also servicing customers and collaborating with

business partners. These descriptions suggest that e-commerce is embedded in e-business, because e-business is the transformation of key business processes through the use of Internet technologies.

Accordingly, Parreuras(nd), Risdah(2007), Zutshi, Zutshi and Sohal (2006) classified e-business as follows:

- **Business to Consumer (B2C):** This involves online transactions that are made between businesses and individual consumer. It could be buying of goods and services, in form of commodities books or payment of fees and other financial transactions Online. It could be sending of journal articles, manuscripts for Business to review and publications via the Internet.

- **Business-to-Business (B2B):** B2B is online transactions with other businesses, such as the likes of service rendering organizations including Universities, and other tertiary institutions, banks of different types and agencies.

- **E-Commerce (EC):** Electronic training of physical goods and of intangibles such as information. A common thing associated with e-business is e-commerce which can be described as technology to conduct business transactions, such as buying and selling goods and services. However e-commerce involves using the Internet for commerce and conducting electronic transactions (Hardcastle, 2011).

- **E-Learning (EL):** An online delivery of information for purposes of training or education. E-Learning has become the most significant recent development in the field of education. It can be considered as the highest achievement of using ICT in education. E-Learning is viewed as the delivery of course content via electronic media (Millawithanachchi and Jayasundara, nd) this is the core activity of e-business in education. As noted by Volery and Lord

(2000), literature with respect to online delivering in the field of education has change since the 1990s especially with the advent of the Internet.

- **E-Government (EG):** Is an e-commerce model in which a government entity buys or provides goods, services, or information to businesses or individual citizens.

- **Business-to-Employees (B2E):** Is an e-commerce model in which an organization delivers services, information, or products to its individual employees.

- **Intra-Business:** Is a category that includes all Internet organizational activities that involve the exchange of goods, services, or information among various units and individuals in an organization.

- **Electronic Banking:** Refers to the use of technology which allows customers to perform banking transactions electronically.

- **Internet Banking (IB):** Internet banking is the ability to use one's personal computer to communicate with one's bank. Internet banking and online banking is an outgrowth of PC banking. PC banking enables customers to execute bank transactions from their personal computer via a modem through financial software of the bank (Sethi and Bhatia, 2007).

- **Peer-to-Peer (P2P):** These are technology that enables networked peer computers to share data and processing with each other directly, they can be used in C2C, B2B, and B2C e-commerce.

- **Business-to-Business-to-Consumer (B2B2C):** E-commerce model in which a business provides some product or services to a client business that maintain its own customers.

- **Electronic Data Interchange (EDI):** This involves business-to-business exchange of data via e-mail and fax and their use as media for reaching prospects and established customers, such as newsletters.

Other classifications of e-business according to Ketel (2003) include:

- E-tailing
- The security of business transactions
- E-enterprise
- E-registration etc.

These classifications suggest that e-business is a catalyst to nearly all human activities.

E-BUSINESS IN EDUCATION

E-business in education is about the application of information and communication technologies in dealing with education routines, in all education institutions. It may be primary, secondary or tertiary institutions. For Universities and other institutions, e-business is first and foremost about improving services to their diverse clientele. E-business will radically change the service culture of the University and greatly improve the efficiency and effectiveness of service delivery (Kvavik, 2002). This means that educational institutions that are not utilizing ICT in education service delivering cannot be effective in this technology driven age. However, the above situation pertains to mostly developing countries educational system.

Shrivestava cited in Kvavik (2002) while explaining e-business in education, noted that learning occurs from interaction in the network and from learning materials and data bases. Furthermore, e-business is about changing how we teach and learn computer-mediated and interactive instruction to Web-linked learning communities together with new public or private teaching form a good platform for this teaching process. From the onset, information and communication technology is a catalyst in this teaching process.

E-business encompasses a vest array of activities such as:

- Distribution of information which include content distribution and communication, such as Web searching news, reference tools and digitized library materials, data bases and conversion of hard copies to electronic or soft copies, e-mail, and chat groups.
- Education and training, such as technology enhance learning (TEL) Web-based courses, online examination and evaluation, video steaming, course delivery to distributed locations, multi-instructional and consortia-based education programs, tele-learning, e-learning, teleconferencing and e-health or health care delivery.
- Provision of staff and students services via the Web and a common portal, providing referrals and dynamic links to other ISPs-creating in effect a one stop service.
- Optimization of human process through link transaction, automation and self-help which include online applications and payment of admission fees, online purchasing of forms and filling e-registration and loan programs.
- Online collaboration research.
- Selling and buying of goods and services.
- Management and support of relationships with and among Universities.

Accordingly, Swatman and Chan (2001) assert that over the past two years, the rate at which e-business University programs have been introduced around the world has escalated dramatically. The success of electronic education market (EEM) highly depends on the interoperability of the systems involved. In e-business education there must be compatibility of ICT facilities. E-business and education sometimes referred to as electronic education market (EEM) change the characteristics of business and education process at different levels. At the micro level, developer's teachers and learners are confronted with the use of new technologies and applications. What it

means is that developers, teachers and students need some basic ICT skill to enable them utilize these e-business ICT facilities. This is because at other levels the role of the user and the environment changes significantly using (EEM) for design and development processes or learning in the environment of an (EEM). This leads to changes on the part of the individual as well as organizational changes. In an e-business education, there are certain activities which are different from e-commerce. There are key players or actors and there is also a process that is supposed to follow, a model of e-business education highlighting the e-business in education is below:

A Model of E-Business Education Activities

- **Business model**
  - Actors/process
  - Developer
  - Acquiring information
  - Designing and learning environments
  - Implementing learning environments
- **Learner**
  - Selecting learning activities
  - Learning
  - Collaborating
  - Receiving accreditation/certification
- **Teacher**
  - Developing learning environments
  - Teaching/facilitation courses
  - Monitoring and performance/ Evaluation
- **Content provider**
  - Researching specific content
  - Developing content
  - Distributing content
- **Manager**
  - Supporting collaborations/team management
  - Administrating actors and
  - Trading functions

It is important to note that the activities may not be limited to the ones highlighted above, because of innovation and development of new learning ideas and skills in the teaching and learning process. For example, developer, leaner, teacher, content provider and manager are all players in e-business education with their distinguishing roles such that the application of the facilities enables the process to be successful. However, Powell (2008) argued that the accelerating growth of e-business has raised interest in transforming traditional business models or developing new ones that better exploit the opportunities enabled by technology innovations. One of the consequences of the above situation on education is the significance of e-business opportunities in education. Though the impact of e-business in education or application differs from that of customers centered business transaction, for example e-business from customer's point of view according to Mitchell (2004) symbolizes ATMs the World Wide Web and online banking, meaning that e-business is about user choice and instantaneous, just-for-me, personalized service.

However, in this information age, customers in any capacity, students, teachers, marketers or consumable demand driven customers may want learning materials and education routine activities to be available in digital format to have electronic access. Customers may want to have access at any time and any place by being able to personalize the digital information.

E-Business Tools in Education

The Internet offers a variety of communication options, many of which can help to conduct business more effectively and efficiently (Risdahl, 2007). Accordingly, each of these tools can be used to perform business task more quickly than the traditional means, some basic e-business tools include the following:

- **Electronic Mail:** Electronic mail or (e-mail) is an Internet service through wich individuals who have created an e-mail address (accounts) use to send and receive electronic messages or letters. E-mails are much like postal letters, except that they are delivered much faster than s nail mail when sending over long distances and are usually free (Achugbue, 2011).
- **E-Book:** Is an online version of printed books, accessed via the Internet: there are two types of e-book, the electronic version of a whole text e.g. books that already exist in a print or a data base of linked materials (Leaff, 2003). Although most authors and librarians include data base version as part of e-book. The term is not limited to electronic version of discrete books only as many lecturers, academics and students would probably believe. It encompasses all online versions of printed resources.

In the current educational systems, the use of e-book in education business is very essential. This is because libraries, which are the hub of institutional resources in developed, developing and even most underdeveloped countries are engaging in the business of retrospective conversion of print resources to electronic resources. This is to enable them take part in the 21st century education practice which is mainly driven by the application of information and communication technology in the teaching and learning process. E-books are basic technological information which can be read through an e-book reader. This are software that is necessary and may be downloaded from the intent, this include, Microsoft reader and Adobe, Acrobat e-book reader. E-books differ from e-journals, because academics don't expect to buy e-journals themselves. They are bought either by the main library or departmental library. A book according to Leaf (2003) is conceived as an entity, whereas a journal consists of services of small discrete entities which do not benefit from being read in conjunction with each other. The World Wide Web provides a standard method for exchanging and publishing information on the Internet. The medium is based on standard document formats such as HTML (hypertext markup language) which has been widely adopted because it offers a wide range of formatting facilities that makes documents easier to read on different access device. This entire platform enhances the utilization of e-books (Hardcastle, 2011)

- **Web Sites:** These may come in a variety of forms, including Corporate Web sites, online catalogs, marketing sites, and blogs.
- **Message Boards:** Are an online user forum where information is posted online, sometimes referred to as posting boards.
- **Online Catalogs:** This type of Web site where e-business is propagated uses a shopping cart to facilitate secure online purchases (Risdahl, 2007).
- **Telephone:** Mobile telephone is one of the many ICT tools or facilities that have enhanced e-business services, either in real business practice or education.

Social media is another platform that is use to render educational services, as part of e- business in education. Social media according to Wikinvest cited in Taprial and Kanwar (2010), is a websites that allow users to share content, media, etc. examples are the popular social networking sites like Friendster, Facebook, MySpace, etc. Social media also includes You Tube, Photobucket, Flickr, and other sites aimed at photo and video sharing,. News aggregation and online reference sources, examples of which are Digg and Wikipedia, are also counted in the social media bucket, Micro blogging sites such as twitter are all part of social network. Today's students are visually sophisticated and accustomed to digital media. Most student prefer to work digitally, due to wide access to personal learning devices that gives teachers and students greater control over access to content and collaborations (Cisco, 2011). Accordingly, Educator and students use these devices daily to record videos, access to digital media, and content to friends, colleagues,

and families in real time. As part of the spread of social media in education, our expectation is that facilities like videoconferencing adoption inn teaching and learning is expected to consist of increased student collaborative projects and student's creation and delivery of content, which will include a shift to desktop videoconferencing and other collaborative technologies over time. This will help drive Wave III as a result of their rapid adoption of Internet-based tools like You Tube.

One of the major projects in Africa that really position education on e- service platform is the Pyramid Research project. According to Pyramid Research (2010), mobile technology and connectivity (Internet) are bringing significant benefit to education globally. Most significantly, mobile services are helping to improve communication between teachers, classmates and colleagues. Across all levels and age groups, mobile phones are allowing instant access and sharing of time-critical information, this also applies to communication between teachers and parents, ultimately benefiting students. Mobile connectivity is also helping to change the way education is being conducted. Students in distance learning programs and online Universities access educational information and programs at their comfort. Table 1 is an e-business education sample programs leveraging mobile technology and connectivity in emerging market.

The impact of the project was to bring the benefit of mobile technology and connectivity to education globally. This service has helped to improve communication between teachers, classmates and colleagues. The project enable students in distance learning programs and online and online universities access educational information and programs from the comfort of their home. Another major breakthrough on e-business in education, is the input collected from student by learning2Go the largest collaborative mobile learning project, which is an aspect of the social media services it provide a wide range of perceived benefits and usage for mobile education application. In the emerging e business environment,

Table 1. E-business education sample programs leveraging mobile technology and connectivity in emerging market

Project	Country	Details
Dr. Math	South Africa	Dr. Math leverages Mxit, a mobile social networking tool, to provide math tutoring and education.
Elimu Kwa Teknolojia	Tanzania	The program allow teachers to download video to support their courses.
Longman Ladybird Mobile Reading	Nigeria	Reading, spelling and grammar activities downloaded to mobile phones.
SNDT WOMEN'S UNIVERSITY	India	A mobile education program for remote teaching and learning in rural communities.
K-Neet	North Carolina, US	Help improve student's math's skills through mobile access to a social networking tool.

Adopted from: Pyramid Research, 2010.

with respect to mobile learning 2.5G+ networks including EDGE, GPRS, HSPA, UMTS are becoming essential for connectivity in general given the lack of fixed infrastructure. These networks are allowing governments, NGOs, and school bodies to introduce Internet connectivity to students. Additionally, a multitude of education-focused applications are also making their way into students' and teachers' handsets. The availability of this application provided a better platform for the practice of e-services in Higher Institutions in Nigeria.

Examples of Countries within West Africa sub region where mobile technology in education sector is fully utilized include South Africa, Tanzania and Nigeria, India in Asian and North Carolina in the United States. In South Africa, Dr. Math, a math tutoring and teaching program, leverages a social networking program was launched in January 2007. 2.5G+ networks are also being used to introduce media content to the classroom. Media content is a very appealing tool for students, Dr. Maths provides mathematics solutions to pupils from Grade 3 to Grade 12 with an instant online tutor. The application uses MXit, the hugely popular mobile social network, as a platform, MXit is a mobile instant messaging platform used by an estimated 8-10m children in South Africa. The idea behind Dr. Maths model is that there

is a buddy on your contact list, and students can ask questions online. Tutors and teachers make themselves available at certain times of the day (between 2pm and 8pm) to answer questions, the program utilizes the services of students from the Universities of Pretoria's Engineering, Built Environment and Information Technology Department, who are required as part of their study to complete 40 hours of community service, such students are called Dr. Maths. The program induces prompt online when tutors are available, and students then send questions, today the user base has grown geometrically. However, in Tanzania, an extensive partnership of organization is helping to introduced locally tailored media content to classrooms with impressive results. The program titled (education through technology) was launched in Tanzania in 2007, it was a partnership between the International Youth Foundation (IYF), the ministry of Education and Vocational Training (MoEVT), the Forum for Africa Woman Educationist (FAWE), Nokia Corporation and the Pearson Foundation. The Program leverages mobile technology in other to bring interactive multimedia education programs to teachers and students between the ages of 10 and 12. In Nigeria there is still a significant educational gap, According to UNESCO Institute for Statistics Data Base cite in Pyramid (2010), Nigeria's adult literacy rate of 72% exceeds Sub-Saharan Africa's average of 62%, and better than some Northern African countries such as Morocco and Egypt. In view of the above, Longman Nigeria introduces Mobile reading to Nigeria. Longman Nigeria PLC is a subsidiary of Pearson Education Limited, introduced Ladybird Mobile Reading program in July 2009. The program was lunched as a pilot in seven schools in Lagos State. The content is based on the Ladybird Keywords Reading books, the program is focused on students between 5-9 years old. The program allow students to download, spelling and grammar activities to their parents' mobile phones, students complete the activities at home and discuss them with teachers in class. Each activity has time duration and the application is a WAP-based and requires a GPRS or 3G handset and an Internet connection to run.

Technology is changing constantly, even though when some authorities categorize Internet as one of e-business tool. In the real sense e-business cannot be possible without the presence of Internet. It means that Internet governs all the activities of e-business. However, according to Parreuras (nd), Internet, intranet and extranet can also be classified as tools that facilitate the process of e-business.

E–Business involves several key activities including improving business processes which enhance communication and providing means to carry out business transactions. E-business is a part of Internet economy which encompasses all of the activities that involves using the Internet for commerce. As a result, the advantage of e-business will include reduced costs, improved efficiency and access to larger markets by automating many of the administrative tasks associated with ordering (Hardcastle, 2011). This could be ordering of books or acquisition of library materials both print and non-print, and even the process of acquiring stationaries for administrative work within in educational institution. This process is known as e-procurement, it is used to reduce administrative cost and purchase of goods at lower prices. Adopt-

ing e-business approach, can help to enhance the three main areas of business production processes, customer focused processes and internal management processes. With respect to customer focused e-business, this will lead to efficiency of customer services through the introduction of help desk on the Web site or institution porters. Such facility will also help to reduce cost and pressure on other support services, such as telephone helplines. Additionally, the adoption of e-business approach in education can help institutions to reach a larger global academic audience.

E-Business Activities in Education

The benefit of using the Internet these days is that you can scale your activities to the size of your business, the size of your customer base and possibly your budget. Some common e-business activities are:

- Building and maintaining a basic Web site presence.
- Conducting business with clients and vendors via e-mail and the Web.
- Building and leveraging online communities.
- Provide online customer service.
- Selling product and services online.
- Engaging in e-mail marketing campaigns.

In education specifically, Achugbue (2013) posited that there are core e-business activities in education. Particularly, in the teaching and learning process, accordingly, these activities are ICT based. This involves the use of ICT in the teaching and learning process, it also includes Administration and management of education particularly in education routine services. Some of these e-business activities in core education routine services are:

- **E-Libraries:** Also known as virtual library, digital library or library without wall. Electronic library therefore, is a library in which collections are stored in digital formats (as opposed to print, microform or other media) and accessible by computers. The content is digital and may be stored locally or accessed remotely via computer networks.

- **E-Learning:** Comprises of all forms of electronically supported learning and teaching. However, the information and communication systems, whether networked learning or not, serve as specific media to implement the learning process. E-learning is essentially the computer and network enabled transfer of skills and knowledge. E-learning applications and processes include Web-based learning, computer based learning and digital collaboration. In this learning process, content is delivered via Internet, intranet and extranet, audio tape, satellite TV and CD-ROM.

- **E-Registration:** Is Web based registration or online registration where students do registration of courses in order to secure their eligibility for a new session. This form of registration can be done from anywhere with an Internet connection.

- **E-Application:** Is the purchase and filling of forms online other form of e-business activities are related to financial transactions and mainly associated with the payment of fees and management of money. Such as:

- **E-Transact**
- **E-Payment**
- **E-Banking**
- **Credit Cards**
- **Debit Cards**
- **Electronic Fund Transfer**
- **Recharge Cards**

Internet banking (Seth, 2007, Akintola, Akinyede and Agbonifo, 2011 and Gbola, 2013)

Suffice to say that all the above e-business activities take place in all tertiary institutions. However, in Nigeria according to Gbola (2013), it has become expedient for academic institutions and universities to have their cooperate presence in the Web, within the last five years. The National Universities Commission (NUC) which is the regulatory body of Universities in Nigeria and other international bodies in tertiary education have come up with a Web-metrics of Universities and to highlight the growing importance of the Web to the running and administration of Universities (www.nuc.edu.ng)

E-Business Model in Education

Basically, there are three domains where e-business occurs in educational originations or institution. Figure 1 captures the three domains where doing education business electronically occurs (Commonwealth of Australia, 2002).

- In the front office, interacting with customers and community
- In the back office, performing functions such as the provision of internal financial services and
- With the supply chain, interacting with suppliers and partners

The diagram in Figure 1 also shows organizational groups in each domain. The three domains where e-business occurs in educational institutions:

On the basis of Figure 1, an e-business model for education is considered necessary for understanding of the changes in educational institutions occasioned by the emergence of information and communication technology. Such model is strongly tied to the strategies and goals of education.

Business model in education will be modelled along educational goals and strategies. According to Drozdova (2008), the class model as shown in Figure 2 is mostly frequently used in education

Figure 1. Three domains where doing education business electronically occurs
Adapted from: Commonwealth of Australia (2002).

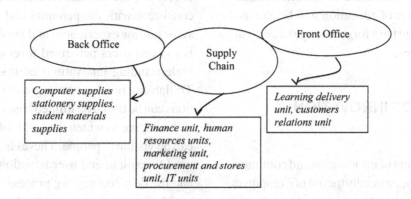

need to be changed into different one with using information and communication technologies and further stated that the vision of a complete online education is too brave, the electronic support of education called e-learning or e-education occurs in the strategies of all educational institutions. From the foregoing, it is clear that there is a shift from the traditional educational platform to modern educational learning environment which many authors qualify as e-learning, e-education, or e-institution. This is because the educational system is driven by information and communication technologies (ICTs) as illustrated in the model in Figure 2. This innovation occasioned by the use of ICTs is necessary for all educational institutions to strive in the current dispensation. However,

creating the e-business model of educational institutions according to Drozdova (2008), we can use the general business model for GII services (Global Information Infrastructure services). This is because the new business model of educational institutions providing e-education will contain at the meta- level basic elements of the educational system and element of the information communication system. Figure shows clearly the metal level business model of educational institution and was created according to the general business model for Global Information Services. The model expresses the connections between structural task of education system and elements of information communication systems which created the infrastructure. The model present a new type

Figure 2. Business model of educational Institutions providing e-education tasks of education system
Adopted from: Drozdova (2008)

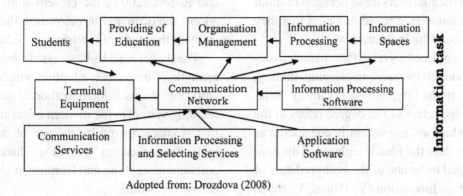

Adopted from: Drozdova (2008)

of educational institutions which means that by implementation of information-communications system a new form of education will be changed first of all, but must not forget change of contents or further changes.

DIFFUSION OF INNOVATION THEORY

Rapid development of information and communication technology, especially the use of Computers, Internet, social network, social media and other forms of ICT facilities which are new innovations in the teaching and learning process, are the main drivers of education in the 21st century. This innovation and diffusion of ICT in educational institutions, is what is referred to as e-business in education. However, to understand the penetration of e-business in education the Diffusion of Innovation Theory seems to be more appropriate.

Research on Diffusion of Innovation has been widely applied in disciplines such as education, sociology, communication, agriculture marketing and information technology (Rogers, 1995, Agarwal, Sambamarthy & stair, 2000, Yi-Hsuan, Yi-chuan & Chi-Ning, 2011). According to Rogers (1995), an innovation is an idea, practice or object that is perceived as new by an individual or another unit of adoption. It is a process by which diffusion is communicated through certain channels over time among members of a social system. The Theory of Diffusion of Innovation argues that potential users make decision to adopt or reject an innovation based on belief that they conceived about the innovation.

Diffusion of innovation has five characteristics which include relative advantage, compatibility, complexity, trialability, and observability. Relative advantage refers to the degree refers to the degree to which an innovation is considered as being better than the idea it replaced. This construct is found to be one of the best predators of adoption of an innovation (Yi-Hsuan, Yi-chuan & Chi-Ning, 2011). Compatibility is define as the degree to which an innovation is regarded as being consistent with the potential end users, existing values, prior experiences and needs. Complexity is the end users perceived level of difficulty in understanding innovations ad their ease of use. Trialability refers to the degree to which innovations can be tested on limited bases. Observability is the degree to which the result of an innovation can be visible to people. These characteristics are used to explain end user adoption of innovation and the decision making process.

The theory represents a number of sub-theories that collectively studies the process of adoption and use of a new technology. While much of this theory emanates from rural sociology, its established framework has been used in diverse areas such as business, education and information and communication. Since Rogers uses the terms innovation and technology interchangeably, the diffusion of innovation theory seems particularly suitable for the study of e-business in education. Rogers provides a useful summary in his early research on diffusion of innovation theory, and notes that potential relevance of such factors as relative advantage, compatibility, complexity, trialability and observability towards change will affect either positively or negatively the adoption of a new technology. Rogers's model could help a researcher to consider the basic forces which affect both adoption rates, and the factors which may lead to the rejection of innovation. Since these variables are elastic according to Cauros (2003), and Rogers (2003), the present study therefore adopts the diffusion of innovation theory in the study in the study of e-business in education.

The study viewed e-business in education as an example of innovation adoption which reflects a shift from the traditional method of teaching and learning system to the modern e-learning system that is characterized by the use of information and communication technology hardware and software in teaching and learning in Universities across the World.

Figure 3, provides the research model. The objective is to examine key factors that influence e-business in education. Therefore, the factors theorized as having strong influences in diffusion of e-business in education are adopted from Rogers Diffusion of Innovation theory. These factors were then associated to e-business tools, ICT facilities (hardware and software), users of e-business tools for teaching and learning, learners, content providers, managers/administrators of university institutions and output which include teaching, learning, research and administration to form the research model.

Diffusion of Innovation Theory has elicited studies in various disciplines. Malcolm and Godwyl (2008) used the theory in their study of diffusion of Information and Communication Technology in selected Ghanaian Schools. Robertson and Gatignon (1989) Kwon and Zmud (1987) developed a framework for studying organizational adoption and diffusion, using diffusion of innovation theory and concluded that five contextual factors such as, user community characteristics, organizational characteristics, technology characteristics, task characteristics and environmental factors, each of which may impact

on acceptance of information and communication technology.

Attewell (1992) studied Technology Diffusion and organizational learning, in a business computing, using Diffusion of Innovation Theory and posited that knowledge is a barrier to adoption of a new technology. However, for some technology tends to get lower over time. Generally, diffusion of innovation theory was strongly supported in the context of individual adoption of technologies and usage. According to Davis, Bogazzi and Warsaw (1989), Huff and Munro (1989), favourable perceptions of innovation characteristics are positively related to adoption and possible use of technology. Adopters are differently influenced by different information channel types and sources at different adoption decision stages.

Accordingly, Raho, Belohlar and Fevder (1987), used Diffusion of Innovation Theory to study assimilation of new technology into an organization and found a relationship in the level of education as an influencing factor in the use of computers. Due to the novelty of e-business in education, most studies concerning e-business are mainly in the areas of e-business transactions (goods and services)

Figure 3. Research model
Adopted from Rogers Diffusion of Innovation Theory (1995)

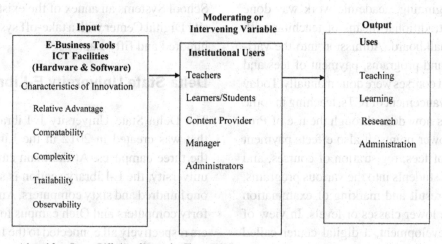

Adopted from Rogers Diffusion of Innovation Theory (1995)

CASE STUDY: DELTA STATE UNIVERSITY

Delta State University has been historically recorded as a Center of Education. It started as a Government Teachers' Training College during the colonial era and some years into the post-colonial era. It became a College of Education that awarded Nigeria Certificate of Education (N.C.E) from 1971-1985. In 1981 it was affiliated to the then University of Benin, Benin city, in the South South of Nigeria and consequently offered degree programs from 1981 till 1985, when it became the faculty of Education of the then Bendel State University with its main campus at Ekpoma. The creation of Edo and Delta States in August 1991 and the conversion of the main campus of the then Bendel State University Ekpoma to become Edo State University in December 1991 necessitated the establishment of an autonomous Delta State University, Abraka on 30th April 1992 by the then Executive Governor of the State, Olorogun Felix Ibru. Delta State University, Abraka started with five faculties. In 1995, the state Governor introduced a policy of having three campuses that should be spread within the three senatorial districts in the State. In view of this policy, three campuses were established to include the main campus in Abraka, Anwai-Asaba and Oleh campuses.

In the beginning, academic work was done through the traditional means of teaching with the use of chalkboard. Admission into the various courses and programs, payment of fees and registration of courses were done manually. Today due to the advancement of ICTs, teaching in some department is now done through the use of Projector and power points. It also effects payment of all types of fees, registration of courses, and admission of students into the various programs, checking of result and marking of examination scripts at the lower classes or levels. In view of the above development, a digital center called Delta State University Digital Center was opened in 2007 and the Delta State University E-Library in 2012 respectively.

Delta University Digital Center

The center has about one thousand desktop computers (1000), with the Delta University porter created which allow students to log in and also create their individual porter to enable them have access to their individual records. At the Digital Center, the following e-services are carried out.

- E-Payment of fees
- E-Registration of course
- E-Checking of results and uploading of results
- E-Compilation and computation of results
- E-Generation of reference pin
- E-Management of Student's academic records
- Student's research and projects
- Electronic information for teaching and learning and
- Training of staff and students on the use of e-business facilities

In view of this growing awareness on e-business in education and to cope with the challenges of e-services in education in the 21st century, the University established a new Digital section call School Systems an annex of the existing University Digital Center with a take-off system of three hundred and fifty Laptops.

Delta State University E-Library

The Delta State University E-Library is a unit that was created in 2012 in the Library across the three campuses. At the main campus of the university, the E-Library section is stocked with one hundred and sixty computers, Anwai campus forty computers and Oleh campus forty computers respectively all connected to the Internet. The purpose of the E-Library was to meet up with the University mission and policy of providing quality education to the student's. The E-Library provided electronic resources to both staff and student's, as the Library subscribed to databases that enable staff and student's to have access to electronic journals. However, the establishment of the University Digital Center and the University E-Library has contributed to teaching and learning in the institution. It has exposed both staff and student's to E-Education (Electronic Education) which has also enhance student's skill on the use E-Business facilities in carrying out academic activates. Students at the Delta State University can now post assignment online, do registration and payment of fees, checking of results and downloading of course materials online. However, the system is faced with the following challenges.

BARRIERS TO E-BUSINESS ADOPTION

Despite the impact of e-business in education, there are considerable barriers to e-business adoption in education. According to Parreuras (2009) the barriers are both technological and non-technological.

- Technological Barriers to E-Business:
  - There is a lack of universally accepted standards for quality, security and reliability.
  - The tele-communication bandwidth is insufficient especially for m-commerce.
  - Software development is still evolving.
  - Internet accessibility is still very expensive and inconvenient.
  - There is need for automated warehouses to facilitate B2C services.
- Non-technological Barriers to E-Business.
  - Security and privacy issues still remain largely unresolved.

- Doubt arising from lack of trust in EC is a matter of concern.
- Some E-Business players are still not satisfied with paperless, faceless transactions.
- There is an increasing amount of fraud on the Internet.

Other substantial barriers to the application of e-Business to education (teaching and learning) according to Mitchell cited in Mitchell (2003) including the following:

- Educator resistance to integration of technological platforms for online learning.
- Security of digital data is still a matter of concern.
- Lack of standard in E-Business.
- Lack of collaborating parties in supply chain affects B2B E-Business.
- Customer's resistance to change lack of interest or skills or inability to pay often stalls business to customer's initiatives.
- A number of these barriers above are not easily overcome without huge finance investment and development of skills in educational institutions.

CONCLUSION AND RECOMMENDATIONS

E-business provides physical and non-physical environment for transaction of business and education routine service. With advances in information and communication technology the introduction of the Internet. E-business will continue to flourish. This will include new business design and new approach to teaching and learning. While this research focuses on the concept of e-business, which followed the introduction of the Internet by the U.S, It also attempt to examine e-business in education, which include all education activities that are supported by ICT or that are carried out electronically. Classification of e-business forms was also examined. This focuses on B2C, B2B e-commerce, e-learning, e-government EDI, Internet banking (IB) and electronic banking among others. E-business tools and activities in education and barriers to e-business adoption was also part of this study.

REFERENCES

Achugbue, I. E. (2011). Electronic mail security. In *Handbook of research on information communication technology policy: Trends issues and advancements*. Hershey, PA: IGI Global.

Achugbue, I. E. (2013). E-libraries & e-learning. In *Reading in general studies*. Abraka, Nigeria: University Press Delta State University.

Achugbue, I. E., & Ochonogor, W. C. (2011). The role and challenges of ICT in educational development in Nigeria higher institutions. In *Proceedings of the 2011 Annual International Conference*. Faculty of Education, Delta State University Abraka.

Agarwal, R., Sambamurthy, V., & Stair, R. M. (2000). The evolving relationship between general and specific efficacy: An empirical assessment. *Information Systems Research*, *11*(4), 418–430. doi:10.1287/isre.11.4.418.11876

Akintola, K.G., Akinyede, R.O., & Agbonifo, C.O. (2011). Appraising Nigeria readiness for e-commerce towards achieving vision 2020. *IJRRAS, 9*(2).

Amamuah-Mensah, E. (2009). *E-business adoption in the banking industry in Ghana*. (Unpublished Masters thesis). Lulea University of Technology.

Attewell, P. (1992). Technology diffusion and organizational Learning: The case of business computing. *Organization Science, 3*, 21–27. doi:10.1287/orsc.3.1.1

Beez, A., Kechiche, B., & Sylwia, B. (2010). The impact of mobile services in Nigeria: How mobile technologies are transforming economic and social activities. *Pyramid Research.* Retrieved June 16, 2013 from www.pyramidresearch.com

Buller, W. (2008). Learning from e-business. In *The e-revolution and post compulsory education: Using e-business models to deliver quality education*. New York: Routledge.

Cauros, A. (2003). *Innovation change theory and the acceptance of new technologies: A literature review*. Retrieved on the 18 of June 2013, from www.http://paperecor.mpg.de/evo/discussion paper

Darozdova, M. (2008). *New business model of educational institutions*. Retrieved March 3, 2013 from www.custom.kbbark.c2/e%2Bm/0Ldrozdova.pdf

Davis, F., Bagazzi, R., & Warsaw, R. (1989). User acceptance of computer technology: A comparison of two theoretical models. *Management Science, 35*, 982–1003. doi:10.1287/mnsc.35.8.982

Gbola, O. (2013). *Students perceptions of e-registration at Ladoke Akintola University of Technology*. Nigeria: Ogbomoso.

Georgia, B. R. (2009). E-business education worldwide on the right track? *International Journal of Management, 8*(2).

Hardcastle, E. (2011). *Business information systems*. Elizabeth Hardcastle and Ventus publishing ApS.

Huff, S. L., & Munro, M. C. (1989). Managing micro proliferation. *Journal of Information Systems Management*, 72-75.

Kalakota, R., & Whinston. (1998). *Frontiers of electronic commerce*. Reading, MA: Addison-Wesley Publications Company Inc.

Kvawik, R. B. (2002). E-business in higher education. In *Web portals and higher education, technologies to make IT personal*. Jossey-Bass Inc.

Kwon, T. H., & Zmud, R. W. (1987). Unifying the fragmented model of information systems implementation. In J. R. Boland, & R. Hirsheim (Eds.), *Critical issues in information systems research*. New York: John Wiley.

Leaf, G. (2003). *Promoting the uptake of e-books in higher and further education: The joint information systems committee report*.

Maijals, V. (2004). *Outlook of information security in e-business*. (Unpublished master thesis). Helsinki University of Technology, Helsinki, Finland.

Malcolm, E., & Godwyl. (2008). *Diffusion of information communication technology in selected Ghanaian schools*. Retrieved, August 20, 2011 from mak.ac.ugldocuments/markfiles/thesis/Tminomujuni_justus.pdf

Parreiras, F. S. (2009). *E-business: Challenges and trends*. Retrieved July 16, 2013 from www.oghavidell.ir/pdf/ebus.pdf

Pawlowski, J. M., & Adelsbery, H. H. (2002). *E-business and education*. University of Esen, Germany. Retrieved July 16, 2013 from citeseerx.ist.psu.edu/view/doc/download?

Powell, J. (2008). What sort of e-business is post primary education. In *The e-revolution and post-compulsory education: Using e-business model to deliver quality education*. New York: Routledge.

Pyramid Research. (2010). *The impact of mobile services in Nigeria: How Mobil technologies are transforming economic and social activities*. Retrieved July 16, 2013 from www.pyramidresearch.com

Risdahl, A. (2007). *E-commerce*. Adams Media.

Robertson, T. S., & Gatignon, H. (1989). Technology diffusion: An empirical test of competitive effects. *Journal of Marketing, 53*, 35–49. doi:10.2307/1251523

Rogers, E. M. (1995). *Diffusion of innovations* (4th ed.). New York: Free Press.

Rogers, E. M. (2003). *Diffusion of innovation* (5th ed.). New York: Free Press.

Sethi, J., & Bhatia, N. (2007). *Element of banking and insurance*. New Delhi, India: Prentice Hall of India.

Shih, C. F., Dedrick, D., & Kreamer, K. L. (2005). Rule of law and the international diffusion of e-commerce. *Communications of the ACM, 48*(1).

Swatman, P. M. C., & Chan, E. S. K. (2001). E-commerce/e-business education: Pedagogy or new product development. In *Reading in e-commerce*. Berlin: Springer-Verlag. doi:10.1007/978-3-7091-6213-2_9

Volery, T., & Lord, D. (2000). Critical success factor in online education. *International Journal of Educational Management, 14*(14), 216–223. doi:10.1108/09513540010344731

Yi-Hsuan, L., Yi-Chuan, H., & Chia-Ning, H. (2011). Adding innovation diffusion theory to technology acceptance model: Supporting employees' intentions to use e-learning systems. *Journal of Educational Technology & Society, 14*(4), 124–137.

Zhao, F. (2006). *Entrepreneurship and innovations in e-business: An integrative perspective*. London: Idea Group Publishing. doi:10.4018/978-1-59140-920-5

Zutshi, A., Zutshi, S., & Sohal, A. (2006). How e-entrepreneurs operate in the context of open source software. In *Entrepreneurship and innovations in e-business: An integrative perspective.* London: Idea Group Publishing. doi:10.4018/978-1-59140-920-5.ch004

ADDITIONAL READING

Alara, N. (2013). Including social media marketing with GOMC in an e-business course: A preliminary examination. *The Online Journal of New Horizons in Education, 3*(3), 2–11.

Balasubramanian, K. Clarke-Okan, W. Daniel, J., Ferreira, F., Kanwar, A., Kwan, A., Lesperance, J., Mallet, J., Abdurrahman, U., & West, P. (2009). ICT for higher education: Background paper from Commonwealth of learning. UNESCO World Conference on Higher education. Paris: UNESCO.

Chen, L. (2007). *Library 2.0 initiatives in academic libraries.* Chicago: Association of Research Libraries.

Collins, B., & Van der Wende, M. (2002). Model of technology and change in higher education: An international Comperative survey on the current and future use of ICT in higher education. Center for higher education and policy studies.

Davis, D., & Ellisson, L. (2003). *The new strategic direction and the school.* London: Routledge Falmer. doi:10.4324/9780203428184

Deng, L., & Yuen, A. (2009). Blogs in higher education: implementation and issues. *TechTrends, 53*(3), 95–98.

Eberhardt, D. M. (2007). Facing up facebook. *About Campus, 12*(4), 18–26. doi:10.1002/abc.219

Fry, H., Ketteridge, S., & Marshell, S. (2007). *Hand book for teaching and learning in higher Education: Enhance academic practice. New academic practice.* New York: Routledge.

Ganster, L., & Schumacher, B. (2007). Expanding beyond our library wells: Building an active online community through facebook. *Journal of Web Librarianship, 3*(2), 111–123. doi:10.1080/19322900902820929

Harris, K. (2008). Using social networking sites as student's engagement tools. *Diverse Issues in Higher Education, 25*(18), 40.

Hazari, S., North, A., & Moreland, D. (2009). Investigating pedagical value of wiki technology. *Journal of Information Systems Education, 20*(2), 187–199.

Junco, R., & Cole-Avent, G. A (2008). An introduction to technologies commonly used by college students. *New Directions for Students Services* (124) 3-17.

Kettunen, J. (2002). Competative strategies in higher education. *Journal of Institutional Research, 11*(2), 38–47.

Miller, S. E., & Jensen, L. A. (2007). Connecting and Communicating with students on face book. *Computers in Libraries, 27*(8), 18–22.

Nelson, M. R., & Hains, E. (2010). E-books in higher education: Are we there E-books in higher education: Are we there yet? EDUCAUSE: Center for applied research.

Risdahl, A. (2007). *E-Commerce.* Massachusetts: Adams Media.

Robbins-Bell, S. (2008). Higher education as virtual conversation. *EDCAUSE Revew, 43*(5), 24.

Rowley, J. (2004). Just another channel? Marketing communication in e-business. *Marketing Intelligence & Planning, 22*(1), 24–41. doi:10.1108/02634500410516896

Senwyh, N. (2009). Face working: Exploring Students education related use of facebook. *Learning, Media and Technology, 34*(2), 157–174. doi:10.1080/17439880902923622

Venkatranman, N. (1994). IT enable business transformation: From automation to business scope redefinition. *Sloan Management Review, 35*(2), 73–87.

Violino, B. (2009). The buzz on campus: Social networking takes hold. *Community College Journal, 79*(6), 28–30.

Wandel, T. (2008). Colleges and Universities want to be your friend: Community via online social networking. *Planning for Higher Education, 37*(1), 35–48.

Wanke, I. C. (2009). Management education using social media. *Organisation Managemnt Journal, 6*(4), 251–262.

Weller, D. (2013). Current advantages and disadvantages of using e-textbooks. *Focus on Colleges, Universities, and Schools., 7*(1), 1–6.

Woodard, A. (2007). From zero to Web part 2. *Computers in Libraries, 29*(9), 41–43.

KEY TERMS AND DEFINITIONS

E-Collaboration: Process of monitoring citing, and cooperating in a project or program by using Internet, e-mails or groupware.

E-Commerce: The buying and selling of products and services by business and consumers through an electronic medium without using any paper documents.

E-Journals: A digital version of a print journal made available through the Web.

E-Learning: Is a learning that takes place in the context of using information and communication facilities.

E-Resources: Materials consisting of data and are manipulated by computers.

E-Tailing: The sales of goods and through the Internet it includes business to business and to consumer sales.

Extranet: A computer network which allows controlled access from the outside for a specific business or educational purposes.

Intranet: A computer network that uses Internet protocol technology to share information, operational systems or computing services within an organization.

Chapter 18
Elastic Application Container System:
Elastic Web Applications Provisioning

Sijin He
Imperial College London, UK

Li Guo
University of Central Lancashire, UK

Yike Guo
Imperial College London, UK

ABSTRACT

Cloud applications have been gaining popularity in recent years for their flexibility in resource provisioning according to Web application demands. The Elastic Application Container (EAC) system is a technology that delivers a lightweight virtual resource unit for better resource efficiency and more scalable Web applications in the Cloud. It allows multiple application providers to concurrently run their Web applications on this technology without worrying the demand change of their Web applications. This is because the EAC system constantly monitors the resource usage of all hosting Web applications and automatically reacts to the resource usage change of Web applications (i.e. it automatically handles resource provisioning of the Web applications, such as scaling of the Web applications according to the demand). In the chapter, the authors firstly describe the architecture, its components of the EAC system, in order to give a brief overview of technologies involved in the system. They then present and explain resource-provisioning algorithms and techniques used in the EAC system for demand-driven Web applications. The resource-provisioning algorithms are presented, discussed, and evaluated so as to give readers a clear picture of resource-provisioning algorithms in the EAC system. Finally, the authors compare this EAC system technology with other Cloud technologies in terms of flexibility and resource efficiency.

DOI: 10.4018/978-1-4666-5884-4.ch018

INTRODUCTION

Driven by the rapid growth of the demand for efficient and economical computational power, cloud computing (Zhang, Cheng, & Boutaba, 2010), has led the world into a new era. By enabling virtualisation technology on physical machines (PMs), it not only gives immense benefits in terms of reliability, efficiency, and scalability, but also provides virtual computational services, such as computing power, storage and network, in such a way cloud users are able to consume them over the Internet as utilities.

Most notable cloud providers, such as, Amazon EC2 (Amazon, 2010), RightScale (Adler, 2011), offer Virtual Machines (VMs) as a service to cloud users and allow the users to host their web applications on the VMs. We refer this type of approach as VM + web applications approach as shown in Figure 1(a). It allows cloud users to directly control its underlying computing resources, such as VM operations, scaling, networking, etc. In addition, this approach allows the resources of a single PM

to be shared across multiple VMs for maximum efficiency. However, setting up and maintaining a working environment for web applications are complex and time consuming for cloud users, and VM resource management is a heavy-weight task for the cloud providers in this approach. In practice, we have identified two scenarios showing VM + web applications approach less feasible and less resource-efficient.

Heavyweight VM Migration: VM migration over LAN (Local Area Network) is one of the most common VM resource management operations for cloud providers. However, the VM migration over LAN is a heavyweight task. In a shared-storage environment, a VM live migration requires transferring the working state and memory from one PM to another over LAN. It consumes a large amount of I/O and network traffics in the LAN environment (He, Guo, & Guo, 2011). In a WAN (Wide Area Network) environment, mechanisms for migrating VMs remain elusive. The VM-based migration across IDCs over the Internet (Wood, Ramakrishnan,

Figure 1. (a) Architecture of VM + web application approach (b) Architecture of server + web application approach

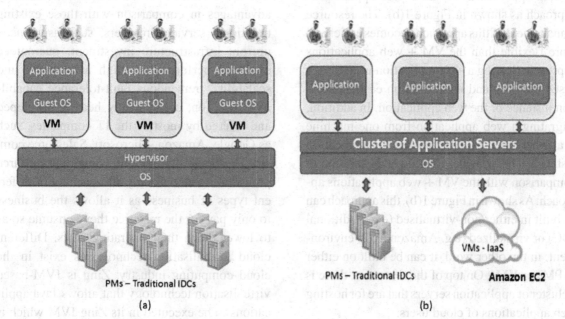

377

van der Merwe, & Shenoy, 2010) also requires a huge amount of I/O for both IDCs and costs a great amount of time for replicating a VM from one IDC to another. This is because a VM generally consists of a guest OS and applications in which the size of the VM can vary from hundred megabytes to 50 gigabytes or more depending on the sizes of the OS and web applications as shown in Figure 1(a). This makes the VM resource management in WAN infeasible.

Overhead in the VM + Web application Approach: A VM generally consists of a guest operating system (OS) for running applications. The guest OS in the VM always occupies a considerable amount of VM resources, this causes the overhead in a VM. As number of VMs increases, the total amount of overhead in VMs increases in the cloud system. Therefore, the overhead in VMs consumes a great amount of cloud resources. This leads to resource-inefficiency in this approach.

In contrast, cloud providers, such as Google App Engine (Zahariev, 2009), OpenShift (Schabell), offer application servers to cloud users and allow cloud users to directly manage their web applications without considering the underlying computer resource consumption. We refer this type of approach as server + web applications approach as shown in Figure 1(b). The resource management of this approach becomes easier and more flexible than the VM + web applications approach. Scaling a web application is no longer based on VMs and it is based on each application instance of the web application. In addition, migrating a web application from one machine to another machine only transfers the application instance. This provides a lightweight solution in comparison with the VM + web applications approach. As shown in Figure 1(b), this approach can be built in either non-virtualised (e.g. traditional IDC) or virtualized (e.g. Amazon EC2) environment, in the other word, it can be built on either in PMs or VMs. On top of the resources, there is a cluster of application servers that are for hosting web applications of cloud users.

In this chapter, we propose an elastic web application provisioning system based on the server + web application approach. This system is called Elastic Application Container system (EAC system). It automatically controls its underlying computer resources so that cloud users can concentrate on their core web applications. In general, EAC system enables the cloud users to efficiently develop and deliver lightweight, elastic, multi-tenant, and portable web applications. The EAC system provides a lightweight resource management solution in comparison with the cloud providers offering VMs. Each EAC in the EAC system is a virtual resource unit hiding all its abstractions of the underlying VMs for delivering better resource efficiency and more scalable cloud web applications. Furthermore, it natively supports automatic scaling of web applications that allows resources used by each web service is tracked and adjusted as needed.

BACKGROUND

Cloud computing (Zhang et al., 2010) has been extremely popular for hosting and delivering web applications over the Internet. It has many advantages in comparison with those existing traditional service providers, such as reduced upfront infrastructure investment, guaranteed expected performance, high availability and scalability, tremendous fault-tolerance capability and so on, consequently heavily developed and offered by most of the IT companies, such as Google, Amazon, Microsoft, Salesforce.com, etc. The flexibility of cloud computing resource provisioning increasingly attracts a lot of different types of business as it allows the business to only pay for the resource they consume so as to lower down their operating costs. Different cloud virtualisation technologies exist in the cloud computing industry. Zing is JVM-based virtualisation technology that allows Java applications to be executed in its Zing JVM which is

ing an entire VM for one single application may introduce unnecessary overhead and cost due to under-utilisation. Allocating one or more full VMs per application incurs unnecessary costs, due to a large number of under-utilised VMs. Therefore, sharing a VM with multiple cloud users is a feasible solution to solve this VM under-utilisation problem.

The Architecture of the EAC System

The server + web applications approach is a cost-effectiveness approach that is based on the idea of sharing VM resources by deploying multiple applications per VM and thereby reducing the number of required VMs. Hosting multiple applications per VM enables multi-tenancy for this approach. Therefore, we propose architecture for this approach called Elastic Application Container system (EAC system). Similar to the concept of a VM, an EAC in an EAC system is a much less weight abstract representation of an application. It offers lightweight resource provision mechanisms for the application providers and cloud users.

Instead of adding or removing one full VM for a particular application in the cloud, the EAC system allows multiple applications from different

cloud users to be run across different VMs. In this way, fewer VMs can be used to run applications and avoid unnecessary costs with an efficient application-scaling algorithm to compromise the desired Quality of Service (QoS). In addition, the EAC system can be hosted in the virtualised environment, this gives more flexible resource provisioning and cheaper operating costs.

The model of the EAC System is shown in Figure 2. The EAC system supports deployment and scaling of multiple simultaneous applications per VM. This allows us to share VM resources among deployed applications, reducing the number of required VMs. As we can see from the model, on top of the PMs, there are VMs hosted in the PMs, i.e. the EAC system is hosted on the virtualised environment. In this way, the number of VMs in the EAC system can be scaled up and down according to the system performance.

On top of each VM, there is a conventional OS where an Elastic Application Server (EAS) is installed. The EAS is a shared application container that offers a higher degree of elasticity and agility that is similar to the VM hypervisor software that can host multiple application instances from different applications simultaneously. Most of the functionality expected of a traditional ap-

Figure 2. The model of the Elastic Application Container system

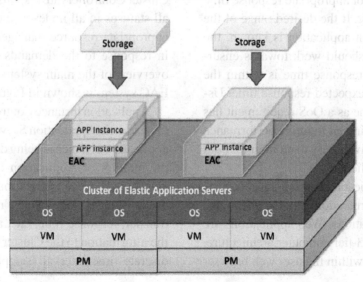

plication server is still expected from the EAS, for example, a runtime container to host the application logic and provide some degree of access and Quality of Service (QoS) of the application execution, plus the technology must be extended to accommodate the use scenario of a cloud service deployment, including most notably potential massive computing processing, tenant isolation, multi-tenancy, and fine-grained use metering etc. The EASs are connected together to form a cluster of EASs. The cluster of EASs not only provides an environment for running applications, but is also responsible for application instance resource management, such as application instance scaling.

An Elastic Application Container (EAC) are created across the cluster of EASs. Each EAC can host only one application. Each application may have one or more application instances hosted across the cluster of the EASs. The numbers of application instances of an application in an EAC depend on QoS of the applications, i.e. varies according to the application demand. In general, an EAC running across a cluster of EASs is an isolated abstract representation for hosting one application at a time across different EASs. The data storage is also provided data for the hosting application.

A common Quality of Service (QoS) requirement for web applications is to ensure the response time within a range of appropriate response time for each user request. If the desired range of the response time for an application is known, the scaling algorithms should work towards ensuring that the actual response time is within the desire range of the expected response time. Using the response time as a QoS requirement has the advantage of being an intuitive performance measure that is relatively easy to monitor for both the server and the client.

The type of application running in an EAC is specifically for a certain domain of applications, such as web applications. Web applications are often deployed in a 3-tier computer architecture. The client tier runs within the user web browser while the application and database tiers run in the remote server infrastructure. Both the application and the database tiers often use a computer cluster in the same data centre to be able to process many cloud user requests simultaneously.

The architecture of the EAC system is flexible and modular with a hierarchical design which is common in many cloud architecture, such as Eucalyptus (Nurmi et al., 2009), IC Cloud (Guo et al., 2010), as shown in Figure 3(a). Using this design is beneficial for scaling the EAC system as clusters can be added or removed dynamically in response to real-time demands of the system. In this way, different clusters in different data centres can easily join or leave the EAC system. This makes cross-data centre resource management feasible.

Components of the EAC System

There are four high-level components in this hierarchical system, each with its own web service interface. Application Instance Controller controls the life cycle of an application instance, the fundamental computing resource unit of the EAC system. On top of the Application Instance Controllers, there are Node Controllers that are designed for managing the node and monitor application instances running in the EAC system. Cluster Controllers are responsible for monitoring all statuses in all nodes in the cluster and make appropriate resource management on the nodes in response to the demands of the nodes. The overview of the main system components in the EAC system is shown in Figure 3(b).

Application Instance Controller is a component of an Elastic Application Server (EAS). While an application instance is being deployed to an EAS, the monitor of Application Instance Controller keeps track of the application instance resource usage, such as CPU cycles, memory used, data transfer, response time, etc., and then propagate the information to the Cluster Controller in every discrete time interval (sampling interval). The

Figure 3. (a) The hierarchical design of the EAC system (b) An overview of the logical relation among EAC system

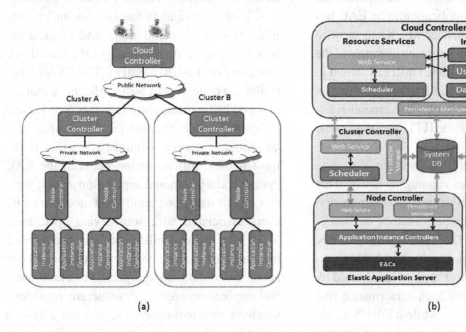

(a)　　　　　(b)

Cluster Controller makes scaling decisions on application according to its application instances resource usage reported by the Application Instance Controller.

Node Controller controls the execution and termination, and monitor resource usage of a node. The node can be either a PM or a VM, i.e. non-virtualised logical machine and virtualised logical machine. For monitoring in a non-virtualised environment, the monitor keeps track of the resource usage of the PM including CPU time, memory, I/O operations and network traffics, etc., in a fixed sampling interval. For monitoring a virtualised environment, the monitor calls external monitoring APIs of the cloud provider in a fixed sampling interval in order to obtain information about the resource usage of the VM. The resource usages for both cases are then propagated to the Cluster Controller that makes scaling decisions.

Cluster Controller generally executes on a machine that has network connectivity to the machine running the Cloud Controller and to the nodes running the Node Controllers. It has a scheduler

module that is responsible for resource management of its nodes and applications. For example, it gathers information of nodes and applications from the Node Controllers and Application Instance Controllers respectively in a cluster. It is responsible for adding or removing nodes from the cluster that can be manually scaled by the EAC system providers or auto-scaled in response to the resource utilisation of nodes in the cluster. The Cluster Controller is also responsible for controlling the lifecycle of applications running in EACs. In addition to that, it is also responsible for application instance placement to one of the EASs in a cluster and removal from EASs in a cluster. For example, the Cluster Controller can scale up an application by replicating an application instance from an EAS to another EAS, and scale down an application by removing a replicated application instance from an EAS. The EAC system comes with the auto-scaling functionality that is to assure efficient use of shared resources. With automatic scale enabled in an application, the Cluster Controller closely monitors each application instance in an EAS and properly scales in response to the change of the application instance usage. Each application in an EAC has an application load-balancer which can forward application requests to application instances of the same application in the same cluster as shown in Figure 4(a). Different load-balancing strategies can be applied. For simplicity, we use round-robin (Hahne, 1991) to distribute HTTP requests to the application instances.

The Storage Controller provides a storage service for applications running in EACs. This storage service must co-locate with an application in EAC for maintaining performance and integrity of applications. The EAC system usually cannot operate without a co-located DBMS or a file system, because most applications hosted by the EAC system require high-performance real time access to their data. While a DBMS is not part of the EAC infrastructure, it is an integral part of its context. The scheduler of the Storage Controller is responsible for scaling up or down the storage cluster in response to resource usage of the storage. In addition to that, it is also responsible for provisioning storage resource for an

application, such as total data storage, number of concurrent database requests for each application.

Cloud Controller is the entry-point into the EAC system for cloud users and application-based providers. It also manages the underlying resources of the EAC system. The Cloud Controller is a collection of web applications that are grouped by their roles into Interface Service and Resource Service. The Interface Service provides one-to-many service administration that is the most notable differentiation between the EAC system and a traditional application server. It offers one-to-many and retail-style model to cloud users associated with self-service operations. To deliver this capability, the Interface Service presents user-visible interfaces (EAC portal, User account and data storage portal) to cloud users and application-based infrastructure providers, handling user authentication, providing system statistics and management tools. It allows new EACs to be added automatically in real time, with all business and technical arrangements also handled automatically as shown in Figure 5.

In Figure 4(b), it shows the life cycle of an application in an EAC by the Cluster Controller. Upon verifying the authorisation, only the cloud

Figure 4. (a) Load balancer of the EAC system (b) The life cycle of an application in an EAC

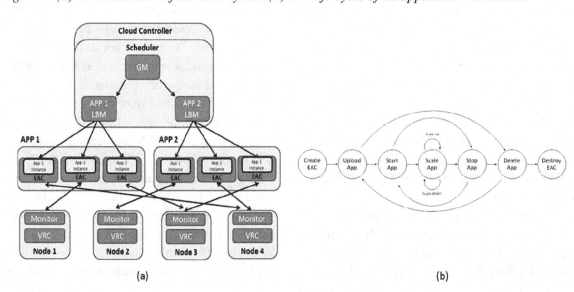

(a)

(b)

Figure 5. (a) Application management portal for Cloud users (b) Statistics of application memory (c) Statistics of response time of an application (d) Management tools

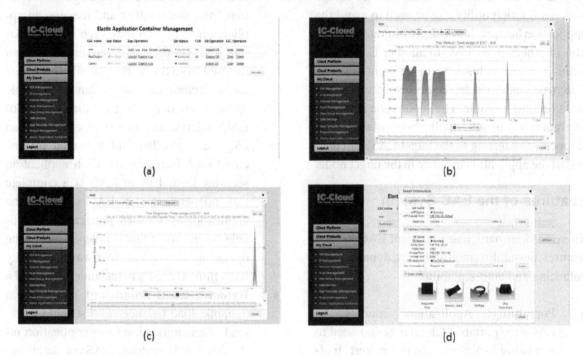

(a)

(b)

(c)

(d)

user of an EAC or the application administrator is allowed to control the life cycle. To start deploying an application in an EAC, a cloud user must firstly create an EAC, and then upload an application to the EAC. On receiving a request of creating an EAC, the Cluster Controller decides the best EAS for an application instances to be placed in the cluster, and then it instantiates a new Application Instance Controller for monitoring its resource usage. While an application instance is being deployed to an EAS, the monitor keeps track of the application instance resource usage, such as CPU cycles; memory used, data transfer, etc., and then reports to the Cluster Controller. The Cluster Controller will make decisions on scaling the application according to its application resource usage. To destroy an EAC, the EAC Controller firstly stops the application running in the EAC, including its application instances, and then deletes the files and its data associated with the application.

Cloud users must have a certain degree of explicit control over the amount or resources dynamically allocated to de-allocated from them. For example, the number of application instances hosted for an EAC can be defined and controlled by cloud users. This can effectively control excessive consumption of resources stemming from a software bug in an application. Unlimited scaling-up without any restriction could cause unreasonably high costs to cloud users.

The Resource Service has a scheduler that is responsible for managing the following main functionalities in the EAC system. Upon receiving an EAC creation request from a cloud user, the Cloud Controller requires deciding a suitable cluster for hosting an application which is based on the following factors: resource usage of the cluster, geographical locations of the cluster and incoming requests, etc. We apply reactive placement algorithms (Malet & Pietzuch, 2010) to find the most suitable cluster for an EAC to be hosted, i.e. finding a cluster according to the real-time demand. The Resource Service equips with a migration utility can be used to avoid the application hotspot. It can easily migrate application instances in an EAC to another EAS either within the same cluster or to different clusters. This makes the cross-data centre resource management become possible. The application instances migration requires the application instance to be stopped, transferring to the target EAS, and then restart the application instance in the target node.

Features of the EAC System

There are four particular important EAC system features, portability, multi-tenancy, dynamic load balancing and auto-scalability.

- **Portability:** Applications running on EACs are portable. Cloud users no need to fear being locked into the technology. It allows the cloud users to reuse existing code instead of creating new code when moving an application from an environment to another. In order to make EAC portable, we use some popular existing computing paradigms, such as popular programming languages (e.g. Java, PHP, .Net etc.), traditional relational databases (e.g. MySQL, PostgreSQL, etc.), instead of inventing a new computing paradigm. Further, the EAC system does not provide programming interfaces and abstractions that cloud users need to know. In this way, the cloud users can use their favourite programming tools to develop their applications and upload them via a web-based portal that give an easier and more flexible way for application development.
- **Multi-Tenancy:** Multi-tenancy implies that the same application server is used to support execution of multiple instances of one or more applications, each as a separate logical tenant. The EAC system sup-

ports multi-tenancy which allows cloud users using EACs operate in virtual isolation from one another and manage an application as though they each have a separate VM, yet their data remain secure and insulted from the activity of all other cloud users. A cloud user allows having multiple applications depending on the number of EACs the one has. However, one EAC can only be controlled and managed by one cloud user. Furthermore, each application securely hosted in an EAC is a complete and independent unit. EAC separates the application in its own protected and reliable environment that is independent of the operating system and hardware, and only has a limited access to the underlying VMs.

- **Dynamic Load Balancing:** We deploy a dynamic load balancer to distribute workload of an application to its application instances across multiple EASs or databases to achieve optimal resource utilisation of VMs, maximise throughput, minimise response time, and avoid overload of the application. The architecture of EAC system load balancing is shown in Figure 4(a). Multiple Applications co-exist in the EAC system. The EAC system consists of a cluster of nodes. Each node has at most one application instance of each application. There are two levels of load balancing managers in the EAC system: Global Manager (GM) and Application Load Balancing Manager (Application LBM). Every application has its Application LBM, while there is only one GM in the Cloud Controller of the EAC system. Whenever an HTTP request for a new user session arrives at the GM, the GM dispatches requests it receives to the Application LBMs of the corresponding applications. If the Application LBM of an application finds that the application instances of the application are deployed on more than one EASs, it distributes the new session requests based on the current session-to-server allocation policy. The typical policies are: round-robin, lowest number of sessions, and lowest load average.

- **Auto-Scalability:** Elasticity of an EAC enables its computing processing power and data storage to be increased or decreased instantly in response to demand of an application running on the EAC. Auto-scalability of the EAC system allows the computing resources of the system increase seamlessly during demand spikes to maintain the overall system performance, and decrease automatically during demand lulls to minimise costs. Increasing computing resources allows the system to create more EACs for computation, and decreasing computing resources allows the application-based provider to save operating costs of VMs. As we mentioned earlier, both EASs and databases in the EAC system provide auto-scalability for maintaining a healthy EAC system performance.

RESOURCE PROVISIONING IN THE EAC SYSTEM

In this section, we present a reactive web application auto-scaling algorithms for the EAC system which provide automatic scaling of web applications in the EAC system so as to maintain a desired Quality of Service (QoS). The web application auto-scaling algorithm applies an automatic reactive scaling mechanism similar to mechanisms applied by Amazon EC2 (Amazon, 2010) and RightScale (Adler, 2011) which only scale when a predefined threshold is met. In this way, web applications in the EAC system can be created and destroyed instantaneously according to the current workload.Before making scaling decisions, the EAC system firstly profiles the newly deployed application over a period of time

. The algorithm detects if there is an outlier in the profiled response time distribution by taking the past and current response time of an application as input. Once an outlier is detected, an application is either scaled up or down. For scaling-up, a new application instance is created in one of the application server, the incoming requests are then automatically re-distributed to the application instances and the monitor instantaneously monitor the response time of the application instance. For scaling-down, an application instance is removed and all application requests to those instances are re-distributed to other application instances.

Profiling Web Applications

As we mentioned earlier, a common Quality of Service (QoS) requirement for web applications is to ensure the response time within a range of appropriate response time for each user request. If the desired range of the response time for an application is known, the scaling algorithms should work towards ensuring that the actual response time is within the desire range of the expected response time. Using the response time as a QoS requirement has the advantage of being an intuitive performance measure that is relatively easy to monitor for both the server and the client. The response time is required to be defined for each web applications in the EAC system so as to guarantee QoS. However, the expected response time of applications are difficult to define, this is because an application may have different expected response times for different request types.

In the EAC system, cloud users do not normally know the response time of their web applications, thus they are not required to specify the expected range of the response time of their web applications. When an application is uploaded and deployed to the EAC system, there is no historical response time data of the application, the EAC system is required to decide the response time of web applications by continuously monitoring the web applications before determining and performing any web application resource provisioning.

Given that a web application has been monitored for a period of time t in the EAC system, we can partition the time t into n fixed length time intervals t_i where $t_i \in T$ and $1 < i < n$. For each time interval t_i of a running web application, there is a set of response time generated from different types of requests *req* sent by end users of the web application. However, the response time of the different types of the application requests varies depending on the resource consumption (e.g. CPU and memory usage, etc.) of the application requests. Therefore, we classify the response time of the application in the time interval t_i into m categories according to the m type of application requests req_j where $1 < j < m$. For each request type req_j, we have a set of o number of response time $req_j = \left\{ rt_1^{req_j}, rt_2^{req_j}, \ldots, rt_o^{req_j} \right\}$ for a certain type of application requests req_j in the time interval t_i. The average response time, rt^{req_j}, of application requests of a certain type req_j over a period of time t_i is $rt^{req_j} = \dfrac{\sum_{i=1}^{o} rt_i}{o}$.

As we mention earlier, there are m types of application requests in an application in the EAC system, the expected response time for all types of web application requests in the time interval t_i is defined as shown follows. Suppose a response time variable RT^{t_i} can take the response time of req_1, denoted as rt^{req_1} with probability p_1, the response time of req_2, denoted as rt^{req_2}, with probability p_2,, and so on, up to the response time of req_m, denoted as rt^{req_m}, with probability p_m, i.e. m number of types of application requests. Then the expected response time of the response time variable RT^{t_i} for m number of types of application requests in a fixed time interval t_i is defined as:

$$E\left[RT^{t_i}\right] = rt^{req_1} p_1 + rt^{req_2} p_2 + \ldots + rt^{req_m} p_m$$

where rt^{req_j} represents the response time of a type of the application request req_j and the probability p_j is the likelihood of the type of the application request occurring in the application in a fixed time interval t_i, i.e. the ratio of the number of application requests for a certain type to all types of application requests for the application in a fixed time interval t_i is defined as:

$$p_j = \frac{\left| req_j \right|}{\sum_{k=1}^{m} \left| req_k \right|}.$$

Given that the response times of all application requests in an application have been monitored for a period of time T, we partitioned T into m fixed length time intervals. For each time interval, we obtained the corresponding m expected response time of the application. Thus, we have a set of the expected response times for m fixed length time intervals in T, $T = \left\{ E\left[RT^{t_1}\right], E\left[RT^{t_2}\right], \ldots, E\left[RT^{t_m}\right] \right\}$.

Web Application Auto-Scaling Algorithm

Given that there are m applications running in the EAC system $A = \{a_1, a_2, \ldots, a_m\}$ where $a_i \in A$ and $1 < i < m$. Assume that each application a_i has been profiled for a period of time T and takes n number of discrete readings of the response time of the application during the time interval T. Each reading is taken in a fixed-length time interval and $E\left[RT_{a_i}^{T}\right]$ represents the response time for the application a_i over a period of time T. In addition, $E\left[RT_{a_i}^{t_o}\right]$ represents the current observed response time for the application a_i. The application auto-scaling algorithm is shown in Algorithm 1. The algorithm constantly monitors applications' response time at a constant time interval and obtain their current observed response time $E\left[RT_{a_i}^{t_o}\right]$ (line 3). The algorithm then determines whether the current observed response time is an outlier (line 4). Note that different outlier detection can be applied, in the current EAC system, Dixon's Q test (Dixon & Mood, 1946) and Grubbs' test (Grubbs, 1969) are used. If an outlier is detected and the current observed response time $E\left[RT_{a_i}^{t_o}\right]$ is greater than $E\left[RT_{a_i}^{T}\right]$, it indicates that the observed application is over-utilised. This is because the application takes a longer time to complete a request than usual. Hence, scaling up the application, i.e. adding one application instance to the application is required. Otherwise, the observed application is under-utilised, scaling down the application, i.e. removing one application instance from the application is required (line 5 to line 9).

Algorithm 1. Web application auto-scaling algorithm

```
1. while at least one application is
running do
2. for each a_i in A do
3. Monitor and obtain E[RT_{a_i}^{t_o}] at a
constant time interval
4. if IsOutlier(E[RT_{a_i}^{t_o}]) then
5. if E[RT_{a_i}^{t_o}] > E[RT_{a_i}^{T}] then
6. Scale up a_i by adding one of its
application instances
7. else
8. Scale down a_i by removing one of
its application instances
9. end if
10. end if
11. end for
12. end while
```

Application providers in the EAC system must have a certain degree of explicit control over the amount of resources dynamically allocated to or de-allocated from. For example, the EAC system allows application providers to specify the maximum number of application instances to be scaled. Without specifying the maximum number of the application instances, excessive consumption of resources stemming from a software by in an application will easily happen as unlimited scaling-up without any restriction could cause unreasonably high costs to tenants. By scaling up an application, theoretically, it can be expected that the completion time of a web application request would decrease as the computing resource being consumed increases. Application scaling-down is in a similar fashion to the application scaling-up. Scaling down an application requires removing an application instance from the application. Therefore, we choose an application instance that is the least active among all application instances of the same application, i.e. removing the application instance results in the minimum impact on the performance of the application. The number of sessions of an application instance can be used to determine the numbers of users are currently using the application instance. In this way, a long-term inactive application should ideally have no sessions. Therefore, we choose an application instance that has the least number of sessions. In order to ensure an uninterrupted service to any such sessions, all sessions belonging to the application instance will be moved to an application server where another application instance of the same application is deployed.

Implementation of the EAC System

The prototype of the EAC system is implemented in Java and has been deployed on the IC cloud. All system components in the EAC system are implemented as web applications in Java, which makes the system platform independent. The prototype is not dependent on any web development framework, but has initially been tested for web applications developed and hosted in Apache Tomcat application servers. The Apache Tomcat application server is an open source framework for developing Java Servlet-based applications, i.e. the Apache Tomcat application server has been modified to be a cloud-enable application server. When running multiple web applications on a Java application server, all web applications are usually placed in the same Java Virtual Machine (JVM). For the storage cluster, we use MySQL cluster which is stable and well-supported. The HTTP requests are routed through a high performance HTTP load balancer. Therefore, we use Apache HTTP Server, which balances the load of requests for new user sessions among EASs. The user interface is implemented using HTML and JavaScript. Figure 5 show the application management portal that provides cloud users with all necessary information about their applications. The cloud users not only can directly control their applications, such as creation and deletion of EACs, deployment of applications, etc., but also can monitor their application resource usages that give a brief overview of the amount of resources have been used.

EXPERIMENTS AND EVALUATION

In this section, we firstly evaluate the resource-efficiency of the EAC system and compare it with the VM + web application approach. We then evaluate the outliner detection methods that is the most suitable for the EAC system.

Resource-Efficiency

In this section, we compare the EAC system and IC Cloud (Guo et al., 2010) in terms of resource efficiency. To measure the resource efficiency for both systems, we examine the change of HTTP response time as the number of VMs or EACs increases in a PM. We setup the experiment by using two PMs with exactly the same hardware configuration, i.e. 2 cores of CPUs and 4GB RAM. The IC Cloud platform was installed in PM 1 and the EAC system was installed in PM 2. For each VM we create in the IC Cloud platform, we also use CentOS to run an unmodified Tomcat server where a computing-intensive application is deployed. The computing-intensive application is used for calculating by using Gregory's series (Gupta, 1973) which slowly converges to .

We decide to calculate 100,000 terms for the series, where $n = 100,000$. For each EAC we create, we also deploy the same application for calculating π. In order to conduct the experiment for VMs, at the first iteration, step 1 is to start with creating one VM, denoted as VM_{11} where the first 1 represents the first iteration and the second 1 represents the index of the VM. The capacity of VM_{11} is equivalent to the current remaining capacity of the PM, i.e. after taking away the overhead of the hypervisor and the hosted OS, and other applications, and then start the VM_{11} to run the target application. Step 2 is to invoke an HTTP request dispatcher to send 1000 HTTP requests to the target application in order to obtain the HTTP response time per 1000 requests for the target application in VM_{11}, denoted as $Rt_{VM_{11}}$.

Step 3 is to repeat the step 2 for 10 times and calculate the average HTTP response time per 1000 requests for the target application in VM_{11}, denoted as $\overline{Rt}_{VM_{11}}$. We then set it as the average response time at iteration 1, denoted as P_1. At the second iteration, we delete VM_{11} and then we create and start two new VM, VM_{21} and VM_{22}. Each VM has the resource capacity equivalent to $\frac{1}{n}$ of the current remain capacity of the PM, where n represents the number of the VMs in this iteration. We invoke the HTTP request dispatcher to send 1000 HTTP requests to the target applications in those two VMs respectively. We then repeat the HTTP dispatching process for 10 times in order to calculate $\overline{Rt}_{VM_{21}}$ and $\overline{Rt}_{VM_{22}}$. We then calculate p_2 which is the mean of $\overline{Rt}_{VM_{21}}$ and $\overline{Rt}_{VM_{22}}$. At the third iteration, we delete VM_{21} and VM_{22} and create three VMs, and so on. We finally obtain a list of average response time $\{p_1, p_2, ..., p_n\}$ from iteration 1 to n. The experiment for EACs was also conducted in a similar fashion.

We have performed 13 iterations for VMs and EACs, the results are shown in Figure 6. In Figure 6(a) shows the HTTP response remains relatively steady as the number of VMs increases from 1 to 10, but there is a sudden increase in the HTTP response time as the number of VMs increases from 10 to 13. This is due to the fact that there is insufficient resource in a VM to process the incoming HTTP requests. As we mention earlier, each VM consists of a guest OS and applications. In this experiment, a VM consumes 294 MB RAM overhead in average for running CentOS and Tomcat Server. As the number of VMs increases, the resource capacity of a VM decreases provided the PM resources remain constant. Hence, the remaining resource capacity in a VM for processing HTTP requests decreases given that the overhead is constant. This causes insufficient resources for processing the HTTP requests and leads to slower HTTP response time. Figure 6(b) shows the HTTP response time stays steady as the number of EACs increases. This is because an EAC doesn't need an OS to run an application. It only consumes a small amount of overhead for each application running in an EAC. In the experiment, an EAC consumes only 10 MB RAM in average which is 29.4 times smaller than the VM. Each EAC has sufficient resource to run its application. Therefore, the EAC system is more resource-efficient than the VM + web application approach for running the same number of applications.

Even though VM + application approach offers VMs which allows a variety of applications to be executed, we stress that the EAC system is not a replacement solution for VM + web application approach. The EAC system is an efficient approach specifically for a certain domain of applications, such as web applications. The VM + web applications approach is not suitable for web applications this is because web applications require a more scalable and flexible environment, but the resource management of the VM + web applications approach is heavyweight as demonstrated in the previous section. Currently, the EAC system only supports one type of programming language, Java. By Using the EAC system, application servers for different programming languages can be modified for supporting multi-tenant cloud use.

Figure 6. (a) Relationship between number of VMs and response time (b) Relationship between number of EACs and response time

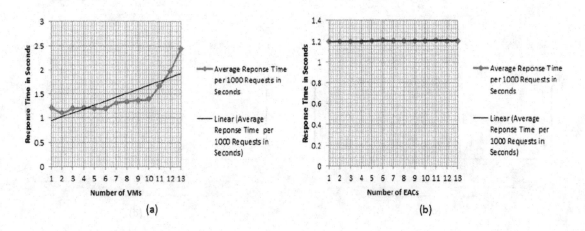

(a)

(b)

Comparisons between Outlier Tests in the Web Application Auto-Scaling Algorithm

The web application auto-scaling algorithm has been implemented and integrated into the EAC system which has been deployed in IC Cloud. In this experiment, we mainly compare the characteristics of the two outlier tests, i.e. Dixon's Q test and Grubbs' test. Before conducting the experiment, we provisioned a total of 6 VMs, each of them allows hosting one application instance. Note that the configuration of each VM is 1 virtual CPU and 1GB memory and the sampling interval of the auto-scaling algorithm is 20 seconds. The web application we deployed on the EAC system in this experiment is an online bookstore. We deploy

Siege (Manolios & Srinivasan, 2005) to simulate the activities of concurrent users using the online bookstore. There are two types of workloads that have been deployed in this experiment. In general, we aim to design Workload 2 to exhibit more volatile than Workload 1. Workload 1 generates a workload by a total of 1500 simulated concurrent users. The sessions start with 100 concurrent users and are increased by 100 new users every 2 minutes. When the total number of concurrent users reaches 1500, it is then reduced by 100 users every 2 minutes until it reaches 100 concurrent users. The number of requests generated by the simulated concurrent users of Workload 1 is shown in Figure 7(a) and 7(b) respectively. Workload 2 generates a more random load than Workload 1. The number of concurrent users fluctuates between

Figure 7. (a) Number of application instances in response to workload 1 using Dixon's Q test (b) Response time and number of application instances in response to workload 1 using Dixon's Q test (c) Number of application instances in response to workload 1 using Grubbs' test (d) Response time and number of application instances in response to workload 1 using Grubbs' test

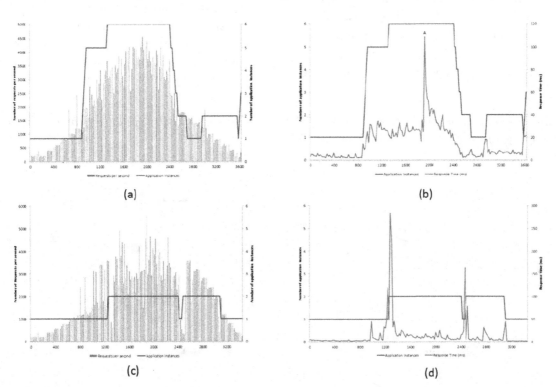

100 and 1500, i.e. the number of concurrent users is increased or decreased randomly by a number of users. Thus, the number of requests generated by the simulated concurrent users of Workload 2 is shown in Figure 7(c) and 7(d) respectively.

At the beginning of the experiment, we upload an online bookstore application to the EAC system. It is then deployed to one of the EAS among 6 VMs. Note that we only allow maximum one application instance to be run on each EAS. We use Siege to simulate concurrent users sending requests to the web application for an hour. The EAC system determines whether the application instances of the online bookstore is required to be scaled according to the application auto-scaling algorithm every 20 seconds. The maximum number of application instances can be scaled is 6. In this way, we conducted experiments using two types of workloads with Dixon's Q test and Grubbs' test. As we discussed earlier, the workload in Workload 1 is not volatile in comparison with Workload 2 as it increases and then decreases gradually. In terms of number of application scaling for Workload 1, the number of application scaling using Dixon's Q test is 10 as shown in Figure 7(a) and using Grubbs' test is 4 as shown in Figure 7(b). For Workload 2, the number of application scaling using Dixon's Q test is 7 as shown in Figure 7(c) and using Grubbs' test is 6 as shown in Figure 7(d). This shows that the experiments with Dixon's Q test is more sensitive to the change of workload, this is because it compares the latest few number of the response time of the application and scales more promptly according to the change of work load. This could lead to unnecessary use of scaling cloud resources. However, application scaling is inexpensive. Rapid scaling in such a short period of time is acceptable and does not consume a great amount of resources.

In Figure 8, there is a significant peak (Point A) of the response time for Workload 1, but there is no increase in the number of the application

instances, this is due to the maximum number of application instances allowed to be scaled is 6. Once the number of application instances reaches the pre-defined maximum, no scaling would be performed. Similar situation can also be found (Point B) Workload 2 in Figure 8(b), as the minimum number of application instance is 1 which could not be scaled down.

For non-volatile workload, such as Workload 1, a sudden change in response time can instantly invoke application scaling for both outlier tests. However, for volatile work load, such as Workload 2, the experiments with Dixon's Q test always scales when there is sudden change (Point C) as shown in Figure 8(b). However, the experiments with Grubbs' test for Workload 2 slowly reacts to the change of response time (Point D and E) as shown in Figure 8(d), this is because the Grubbs' test takes a relatively larger historical data set than the Dixon's test. In terms of resource efficiency, using Grubbs' test is more efficient than using Dixon's Q test as the Grubb's test is less sensitive to the change of response time which often leads to unnecessary application scaling. Due to the inexpensive application scaling, resource efficiency is no longer an important factor to be taken into account for application scaling. However, for some volatile workload, using Grubbs' test is not beneficial for instantly scaling an application due to it is less sensitive to the change of the response time. In overall, Dixon's Q test is more preferable; this is due to its sensitivity to the change of workload and inexpensive of application scaling.

FUTURE RESEARCH DIRECTIONS

Future research will expand on several dimensions of our work here. On the theoretical side, we intend to more deeply explore efficiency and pricing mechanisms for EACs. We are also studying some alternatives algorithms which perform

Figure 8. (a) Number of application instances in response to workload 2 using Dixon's Q test (b) Response time and number of application instances in response to workload 2 using Dixon's Q test (c) Number of application instances in response to workload 2 using Grubbs' Q test (d) Response time and number of application instances in response to workload 2 using Grubbs' test

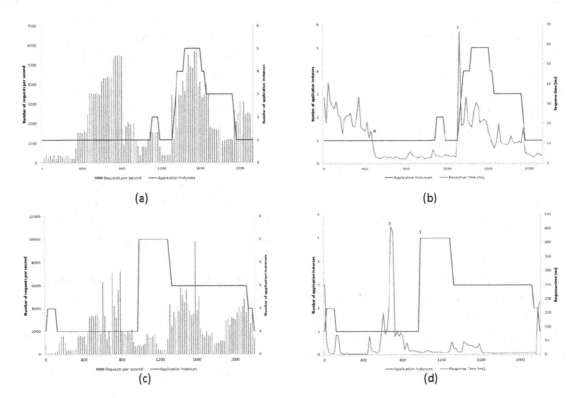

(a)

(b)

(c)

(d)

best for resource management operations. On the implementation side, we will carry on supporting more programming languages using different application servers for multi-tenant cloud use and allow the EAC system to be portable in other cloud infrastructure.

CONCLUSION

In this paper, we proposed a lightweight resource management model that is called Elastic Application Container (EAC) for delivering scalable cloud applications. We presented the architecture of the EAC system and an algorithm for EAC resource provisioning. We then described an implementa-

tion of the EAC system based on modifying a Tomcat Server to support multi-tenant cloud use. Our evaluation included experiments to compare the VM + web applications and EAC approaches in terms of resource-efficiency of resource management. The experiments show that EAC system offers lightweight resource management operations and more resource-efficiency than the VM-based approach. Furthermore, we have made an EAC system available for trials to all who wish to try the system in our computing department. The feedbacks so far have been very positive. Furthermore, in order to achieve high agility and respond to rapid demand fluctuations, the web application auto-scaling algorithm uses reactive model that automatically allocates and de-allocates application resources according to response time based on finding an outlier in the near real-time data. We then integrated the algorithms into the EAC system. In this experiment section, we conducted an experiment to compare the two outlier detection methods (Dixon's Q test and Grubbs' test) in the application auto-scaling algorithm.

REFERENCES

Adler, B. (2011). *Building scalable applications in the cloud: Reference architecture & best practices*. RightScale Inc.

Amazon, E. (2010). *Amazon elastic compute cloud (Amazon EC2)*.

Ashraf, A., Byholm, B., Lehtinen, J., & Porres, I. (2012). *Feedback control algorithms to deploy and scale multiple web applications per virtual machine*. Paper presented at the Software Engineering and Advanced Applications (SEAA). New York, NY.

Aversa, L., & Bestavros, A. (2000). *Load balancing a cluster of web servers: Using distributed packet rewriting*. Paper presented at the Performance, Computing, and Communications Conference, 2000. New York, NY.

Bacigalupo, D. A., Van Hemert, J., Chen, X., Usmani, A., Chester, A. P., He, L., & Jarvis, S. A. (2011). Managing dynamic enterprise and urgent workloads on clouds using layered queuing and historical performance models. *Simulation Modelling Practice and Theory, 19*(6), 1479–1495. doi:10.1016/j.simpat.2011.01.007

Barham, P., Dragovic, B., Fraser, K., Hand, S., Harris, T., Ho, A., & Warfield, A. (2003). Xen and the art of virtualization. *ACM SIGOPS Operating Systems Review, 37*(5), 164–177. doi:10.1145/1165389.945462

Bi, J., Zhu, Z., Tian, R., & Wang, Q. (2010). *Dynamic provisioning modeling for virtualized multi-tier applications in cloud data center*. Paper presented at the Cloud Computing (CLOUD). New York, NY.

Cardellini, V., Colajanni, M., & Yu, P. S. (1999). Dynamic load balancing on web-server systems. *IEEE Internet Computing, 3*(3), 28–39. doi:10.1109/4236.769420

Chieu, T. C., Mohindra, A., Karve, A. A., & Segal, A. (2009). *Dynamic scaling of web applications in a virtualized cloud computing environment*. Paper presented at the e-Business Engineering, 2009. New York, NY.

Dixon, W. J., & Mood, A. M. (1946). The statistical sign test. *Journal of the American Statistical Association, 41*(236), 557–566. doi:10.1080/016 21459.1946.10501898 PMID:20279351

Goldsack, P., Guijarro, J., Lain, A., Mecheneau, G., Murray, P., & Toft, P. (2003). *SmartFrog: Configuration and automatic ignition of distributed applications*. HP OVUA.

Grubbs, F. E. (1969). Procedures for detecting outlying observations in samples. *Technometrics, 11*(1), 1–21. doi:10.1080/00401706.1969.1049 0657

Guo, L., Guo, Y., & Tian, X. (2010). *IC cloud: A design space for composable cloud computing*. Paper presented at the Cloud Computing (CLOUD). New York, NY.

Gupta, R. C. (1973). The Madhava-Gregory series. Math. Ed, 7.

Habib, I. (2008). Virtualization with KVM. *Linux Journal*, (166), 8.

Hahne, E. L. (1991). Round-robin scheduling for max-min fairness in data networks. *IEEE Journal on Selected Areas in Communications, 9*(7), 1024–1039. doi:10.1109/49.103550

He, S., Guo, L., & Guo, Y. (2011). *Real time elastic cloud management for limited resources.*

Infrastructure, G. (2009). *GoGrid cloud hosting.*

Jennings, R. (2010). *Cloud computing with the Windows Azure platform.* Wrox.

Malet, B., & Pietzuch, P. (2010). *Resource allocation across multiple cloud data centres.* Paper presented at the 8th International Workshop on Middleware for Grids, Clouds and e-Science. New York, NY.

Manolios, P., & Srinivasan, S. K. (2005). A parameterized benchmark suite of hard pipelined-machine-verification problems. In *Correct hardware design and verification methods* (pp. 363–366). Berlin: Springer. doi:10.1007/11560548_32

Natis, Y. (2008). *Key issues for cloud-enabled application infrastructure, 2008.* Gartner Research (G00155751).

Nurmi, D., Wolski, R., Grzegorczyk, C., Obertelli, G., Soman, S., Youseff, L., & Zagorodnov, D. (2009). *The eucalyptus open-source cloud-computing system.* Paper presented at the Cluster Computing and the Grid, 2009. New York, NY.

Pepple, K. (2011). *Deploying OpenStack.* Sebastopol, CA: O'Reilly.

Platform, G. (2002). *White paper.* New York, NY: GigaSpaces Technologies Ltd.

Rosenblum, M. (1999). *VMware's virtual platform™.* Paper presented at the Hot Chips. New York, NY.

Schabell, E. D. (n.d.). OpenShift primer. *Developer Press.*

Ungureanu, V., Melamed, B., & Katehakis, M. (2008). Effective load balancing for cluster-based servers employing job preemption. *Performance Evaluation, 65*(8), 606–622. doi:10.1016/j.peva.2008.01.001

Urgaonkar, B., Shenoy, P., Chandra, A., & Goyal, P. (2005). *Dynamic provisioning of multi-tier internet applications.* Paper presented at the Autonomic Computing, 2005. New York, NY.

Urgaonkar, B., Shenoy, P., Chandra, A., Goyal, P., & Wood, T. (2008). Agile dynamic provisioning of multi-tier internet applications. *ACM Transactions on Autonomous and Adaptive Systems, 3*(1), 1. doi:10.1145/1342171.1342172

Van Vliet, J., Paganelli, F., van Wel, S., & Dowd, D. (2011). *Elastic beanstalk.* Sebastopol, CA: O'Reilly Media, Inc.

Velte, A., & Velte, T. (2009). *Microsoft virtualization with hyper-V.* New York: McGraw-Hill, Inc.

Weissman, C. D., & Bobrowski, S. (2009). *The design of the force.com multitenant internet application development platform.* Paper presented at the SIGMOD Conference. New York, NY.

Wood, T., Ramakrishnan, K., van der Merwe, J., & Shenoy, P. (2010). *Cloudnet: A platform for optimized wan migration of virtual machines* (Technical Report TR-2010-002). Boston: University of Massachusetts.

Xian-Qong, Z. J.-H. D. (2000). Approaching technique in longjump. *Journal of Chehgdu Physical Education Institute, 5*, 021.

Zahariev, A. (2009). *Google app. engine.* Helsinki, Finland: Helsinki University of Technology.

Zhang, Q., Cheng, L., & Boutaba, R. (2010). Cloud computing: State-of-the-art and research challenges. *Journal of Internet Services and Applications, 1*(1), 7–18. doi:10.1007/s13174-010-0007-6

ADDITIONAL READING

Alamri, A., Ansari, W. S., Hassan, M. M., Hossain, M. S., Alelaiwi, A., & Hossain, M. A. (2013). A Survey on Sensor-Cloud: Architecture, Applications, and Approaches. *International Journal of Distributed Sensor Networks*. doi. *Artn, 917923*. doi: doi:10.1155/2013/917923

Alhamad, M., Dillon, T., & Chang, E. (2011). A Survey on SLA and Performance Measurement in Cloud Computing. On the Move to Meaningful Internet Systems: Otm 2011. *Pt Ii, 7045*, 469–477.

Andrikopoulos, V., Binz, T., Leymann, F., & Strauch, S. (2013). How to adapt applications for the Cloud environment. *Computing, 95*(6), 493–535. doi:10.1007/s00607-012-0248-2

Beloglazov, A., Buyya, R., Lee, Y. C., & Zomaya, A. (2011). A Taxonomy and Survey of Energy-Efficient Data Centers and Cloud Computing Systems. *Advances in Computers, 82*(82), 47–111. doi:10.1016/B978-0-12-385512-1.00003-7

Ghanem, M., Chortaras, A., & Guo, Y. (2004). Web service programming for biological text mining. Paper presented at the Proceedings of SIGIR Workshop on Search and Discovery in Bioinformatics held in conjunction with the 27th Annual International ACM SIGIR Conference, Sheffield, UK, July 2004.

Guo, L., Guo, Y., & Tian, X. (2010). IC Cloud: A Design Space for Composable Cloud Computing. Paper presented at the Cloud Computing (CLOUD), 2010 IEEE 3rd International Conference on.

Han, R., Ghanem, M. M., Guo, L., Guo, Y., & Osmond, M. (2012). Enabling cost-aware and adaptive elasticity of multi-tier cloud applications. *Future Generation Computer Systems*.

Han, R., Guo, L., Ghanem, M. M., & Guo, Y. (2012). Lightweight Resource Scaling for Cloud Applications. Paper presented at the Cluster, Cloud and Grid Computing (CCGrid), 2012 12th IEEE/ACM International Symposium on.

He, S., Ghanem, M., Guo, L., & Guo, Y. (2013). Cloud Resource Monitoring for Intrusion Detection. Paper presented at the 5th IEEE International Conference on Cloud Computing Technology and Science.

He, S., Guo, L., Ghanem, M., & Guo, Y. (2012). Improving Resource Utilisation in the Cloud Environment using Multivariate Probabilistic Models. Paper presented at the Cloud Computing (CLOUD), 2012 IEEE 5th International Conference on.

He, S., Guo, L., & Guo, Y. (2011a). Elastic Application Container. Paper presented at the Grid Computing (GRID), 2011 12th IEEE/ACM International Conference on.

He, S., Guo, L., & Guo, Y. (2011b). Real time elastic cloud management for limited resources. Paper presented at the Cloud Computing (CLOUD), 2011 IEEE International Conference on.

He, S., Guo, L., Guo, Y., Wu, C., Ghanem, M., & Han, R. (2012). Elastic Application Container: A Lightweight Approach for Cloud Resource Provisioning. Paper presented at the Advanced Information Networking and Applications (AINA), 2012 IEEE 26th International Conference on.

Li, Y., Guo, L., & Guo, Y. (2012). CACSS: TOWARDS A GENERIC CLOUD STORAGE SERVICE. Paper presented at the 2nd International Conference on Cloud Computing and Services Science.

KEY TERMS AND DEFINITIONS

Application Instance Controller: This controller keeps track of the application instance resource usage, such as CPU cycles, memory used, data transfer, response time, etc., and then propagate the information to the Cluster Controller in every discrete time interval.

Cloud Controller: This controller is the entry-point into the EAC system for cloud users and application-based providers, and manages the underlying resources of the EAC system.

Cluster Controller: This controller generally executes on a machine that has network connectivity to the machine running the Cloud Controller and to the nodes running the Node Controllers. It has a scheduler module that is responsible for Resource management of its nodes and applications.

Elastic Application Container (EAC): An EAC running across a cluster of EASs is an isolated abstract representation for hosting one application at a time across different EASs. Each application may have one or more application instances hosted across the cluster of the EASs.

Elastic Application Container System (EAC System): A technology delivers a lightweight virtual resource unit for better resource efficiency and more scalable web applications in the cloud.

Elastic Application Server (EAS): A shared application container offers a higher degree of elasticity and agility that is similar to the VM hypervisor software that can host multiple application instances from different applications simultaneously.

Node Controller: This controller controls the execution and termination, and monitor resource usage of a node.

Server + Web Application Approach: An approach offering application servers to cloud users and allow cloud users to directly manage their web applications without considering the underlying computer resource consumption.

Storage Controller: This controller provides a storage service for applications running in the EAC system.

VM + Web Application Approach: An approach offering Virtual Machines (VMs) as a service to cloud users and allow the users to host their web applications.

Web Application Auto-Scaling Algorithm: The algorithm provides automatic reactive scaling of web applications in the EAC system so as to maintain a desired Quality of Service.

Chapter 19
Artificial Neural Network for Industrial and Environmental Research via Air Quality Monitoring Network

Tianxing Cai
Lamar University, USA

ABSTRACT

Industrial and environmental research will always involve the study of the cause-effect relationship between emissions and the surrounding environment. The techniques of artificial intelligence such as artificial neural network can be applied in the industrial and environmental research. Chemical facilities have high risks to originate air emission events (e.g. intensive flaring and toxic gas release). They are caused by various uncertainties like equipment failure, false operation, nature disaster, or terrorist attack. Through an air-quality monitoring network, data integration is applied to identify the possible emission source and dynamic emission profiles. In this chapter, the above-mentioned application has been illustrated. It has the capability to identify the potential emission profile and characterize spatial-temporal pollutant dispersion. It provides valuable information for accidental investigations and root cause analysis for an emission event; meanwhile, it helps evaluate the regional air quality impact caused by such an emission event.

INTRODUCTION

Chemical facilities, where large amounts of chemicals and fuels are processed, manufactured, and housed, present high risks to seed potential air emission events. The normal emissions are those routine emissions that are expected during plant normal operations, which will have a large impact on the pollution concentration profile in the surrounding region. The air emission events may also be caused by severe process upsets due to planned operations such as plant scheduled turnarounds

DOI: 10.4018/978-1-4666-5884-4.ch019

(start-up or shut down). Therefore, industrial and environmental research will always involve the study of the cause-effect relationship between the emission and the surrounding environment. For example, an olefin plant with ethylene productivity of 544,000 ton/yr can easily flare about 2,268 tons of ethylene during a single start-up(Xu, Yang, Liu, Li, Lou, Gossage, 2009), resulting in at least 18 tons of CO, 3.4 tons of NOx, and 45.4 tons of HRVOCs (defined in Texas air quality regulation as ethylene, propylene, isomers of butene, and 1,3-butadiene). If all the other flaring species (ethane, propylene, propane, and etc.) are also accounted, tremendous air emissions will be produced within a short-time period. Chemical plant emission events can also be caused by uncontrollable and unpredictable uncertainties such as emergency shutdown, nature disaster, or terrorist attack. For example, an oil refinery at eastern Japan exploded with huge amounts of toxic emissions due to Japan's tsunami and earthquake occurred on March 11th of 2011(NDTV, 2011). In another emission event on March 22nd of 2011, the blast of a carbide plant in Louisville, Kentucky, fired calcium carbide and produced a large amounts of inhalation hazardous gases (United States Chemical Safety Board, 2013). The air-quality impacts from chemical plant emission events can be serious to both local communities and their surrounding environments. One of the major concerns is the exposure of acute or short-term toxicity. Release of acutely toxic contaminants, such as SO2 and chlorine, would likely be transported to a populated area and pose an immediate threat to the public health and environment quality. Generally, the plant personnel should document and report emission details in response to an emission event, so that valuable information of hazardous releasing rate, possible transportation speed and directions, and potential harmful impacts on exposed populations and ecosystems can be estimated to support responsible decision makings. Since such responsible decisions are very critical, independent supporting information such

as real-time measurements from a local air-quality monitoring network is vitally needed, especially in industrial zones populated heavily by various chemical facilities.

A local air-quality monitoring network can measure and record multiple pollutant concentrations simultaneously and alarm dangerous events in a real-time fashion. Meanwhile, based on measurement data from each monitoring station, plus regional meteorological conditions during the event time period, a monitoring network could help estimate possible emission source locations or even their emission rates. This inverse characterization of abnormal emission sources is very valuable to all stake holders, including government environmental agencies, chemical plants, and residential communities.

In the bulk of previous research, inverse modeling ideas were originated by the adoption of atmospheric dispersion models, which was normally used in the forward modeling problem to determine downwind contamination concentrations with given meteorological conditions and emission rates. "Gaussian Plume Model" is an approximate analytical method for point-source emissions for calculation of air pollutant concentration in the downwind area (Pasquill, 1961 and 1974; Turner, 1979 and 1994; Hanna et al., 1982; Seinfeld, 1986; Slade, 1986; Halitsky, 1989; Griffiths, 1994; Turner et al., 1989; Bowman, 1996). Even though inverse modeling methods based on Gaussian plume models have been reported(Hogan, Cooper, Wagner, and Wallstrom, 2005; Jeong, Kim, Suh, Hwang, Han, and Lee, 2005; MacKay, McKee, and Mulholland, 2006), they are generally used to estimate emission rates of point sources in an average long-time period based on measurements from multiple monitoring stations. It means their emissions are assumed under steady-state conditions and their values are treated as constants. Therefore, there is still a lack of studies on the reverse modeling for abnormal emission identifications with the consideration of dynamic emission rates of point emission sources.

Based on an available air-quality monitoring network, the data integration technologies will be applied to identify the scenarios of the possible emission source and the dynamic pollutant monitor result, so as to timely and effectively support diagnostic and prognostic decisions. Qualitative and mixed methods researchers have employed information and communication technology (ICT) tools, simulated or virtual environments, information systems, information devices and data analysis tools in this field. With the collection and information representation in a range of ways, software tools have been created to manage and store these data. This data management enables more efficient searching ability for digitized information in various types. Various technologies have made the work of research more efficient. The results of the qualitative or mixed methods research may be integrated to reach the research target. Right now, a lot of software tools are available for the analysis to identify knowledge patterns and represent new meanings. The programs extend the capabilities of the researcher in terms of information coding and meaning-making. Machine-enhanced analytics has enabled the identification of aspects of interest such as correlations and anomalies from large datasets.

Among all the above mentioned techniques, one of the commonly used methodologies is artificial neural network. In computer science and related fields, artificial neural networks are models inspired by animal central nervous systems that are capable of machine learning and pattern recognition. They are usually presented as systems of interconnected "neurons" that can compute values from inputs by feeding information through the network. Like other machine learning methods, neural networks have been used to solve a wide variety of tasks that are hard to solve using ordinary rule-based programming, including computer vision and speech recognition.

Generally, it involves a network of simple processing elements exhibiting complex global behavior determined by the connections between the processing elements and element parameters. Commonly, though, a class of statistical models will be called "neural" if they

1. They consist of sets of adaptive weights, i.e. numerical parameters that are tuned by a learning algorithm, and
2. They are capable of approximating non-linear functions of their inputs.

The adaptive weights are conceptually connection strengths between neurons, which are activated during training and prediction.

Neural network models in artificial intelligence are usually referred to as artificial neural networks (ANNs); these are essentially simple mathematical models defining a function of $f : X \rightarrow Y$ or a distribution over X or both X and Y, but sometimes models are also intimately associated with a particular learning algorithm or learning rule. A common use of the phrase ANN model really means the definition of a class of such functions where members of the class are obtained by varying parameters, connection weights, or specifics of the architecture such as the number of neurons or their connectivity.

The word network in the term 'artificial neural network' refers to the inter–connections between the neurons in the different layers of each system. An example system has three layers. The first layer has input neurons, which send data via synapses to the second layer of neurons, and then via more synapses to the third layer of output neurons. More complex systems will have more layers of neurons with some having increased layers of input neurons and output neurons. The synapses store parameters called "weights" that manipulate the data in the calculations.

An ANN is typically defined by three types of parameters:

- The interconnection pattern between different layers of neurons.

- The learning process for updating the weights of the interconnections.
- The activation function that converts a neuron's weighted input to its output activation.

In this chapter, the application of artificial neural networks for such applications have been developed according to the real application purpose. It includes two stages of modeling and optimization work: i) the determination of background normal emission rates from multiple emission sources and ii) single-objective or multi-objective optimization for impact scenario identification and quantification. They will have the capability to identify the potential emission profile and spatial-temporal characterization of pollutant dispersion for a specific region, including reversely estimation of the air quality issues. It provides valuable information for accidental investigations and root cause analysis for an emission event; meanwhile, it helps evaluate the regional air quality impact caused by such an emission event as well. Case studies are employed to demonstrate the efficacy of the developed methodology.

MOTIVATION

The basic mission of the industrial and environment research with Web service is to preserve and improve the air quality of our living environment. To accomplish this, we must be able to evaluate the status of the atmosphere as compared to clean air standards and historical information. The following are some of the topics associated with monitoring air pollution.

In USA, the Clean Air Act requires every state to establish a network of air monitoring stations for criteria pollutants, using criteria set by OAQPS for their location and operation. The monitoring stations in this network are called the State and Local Air Monitoring Stations (SLAMS). The states must provide OAQPS with an annual summary of monitoring results at each SLAMS monitor, and detailed results must be available to OAQPS upon request. To obtain more timely and detailed information about air quality in strategic locations across the nation, OAQPS established an additional network of monitors: the National Air Monitoring Stations (NAMS). NAMS sites, which are part of the SLAMS network, must meet more stringent monitor siting, equipment type, and quality assurance criteria. NAMS monitors also must submit detailed quarterly and annual monitoring results to OAQPS.

Between the years 1900 and 1970, the emission of six principal pollutants increased significantly. These six pollutants, also called criteria pollutants, are: particulate matter, sulfur dioxide, carbon monoxide, nitrogen dioxide, ozone, and lead. In 1970, the Clean Air Act (CAA) was signed into law. The CAA and its amendments provides the framework for all pertinent organizations to protect air quality. EPA's principal responsibilities under the CAA, as amended in 1990 include:

- Setting National Air Quality Standards (NAAQS) for pollutants considered harmful to the public health and environment.
- Ensuring the air quality standards are met or attained (in cooperation with the States) through national standards and strategies to control air emission standards from sources.
- Ensuring the sources of toxic air pollutants are well controlled.
- Monitoring the effectiveness of the program.

One way to protect and assess air quality was through the development of an Ambient Air Monitoring Program. Air quality samples are generally collected for one or more of the following purposes:

- To judge compliance with and/or progress made towards meeting ambient air quality standards.

- To activate emergency control procedures that prevent or alleviate air pollution episodes.
- To observe pollution trends throughout the region, including non-urban areas.
- To provide a data base for research evaluation of effects: urban, land-use, and transportation planning; development and evaluation of abatement strategies; and development and validation of diffusion models.

With the end use of the air quality samples as a prime consideration, the network should be designed to meet one of four basic monitoring objectives listed below:

- To determine highest concentrations expected to occur in the area covered by the network;
- To determine representative concentrations in areas of high population density;
- To determine the impact on ambient pollution levels of significant sources or source categories;

- To determine general background concentration levels.

These four objectives indicate the nature of the samples that the monitoring network will collect which must be representative of the spatial area being studied.

The EPA's ambient air quality monitoring program is carried out by State and local agencies and consists of three major categories of monitoring stations, State and Local Air Monitoring Stations (SLAMS), National Air Monitoring Stations (NAMS), and Special Purpose Monitoring Stations (SPMS), that measure the criteria pollutants. Additionally, a fourth category of a monitoring station, the Photochemical Assessment Monitoring Stations (PAMS), which measures ozone precursors (approximately 60 volatile hydrocarbons and carbonyl) has been required by the 1990 Amendments to the Clean Air Act.

Figure 1. State and local monitoring(SLAMS) network

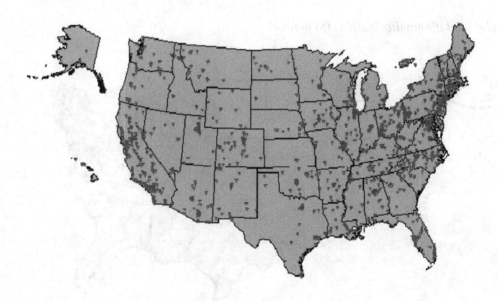

STATE AND LOCAL AIR MONITORING STATIONS (SLAMS)

The SLAMS (Figure 1) consist of a network of ~ 4,000 monitoring stations whose size and distribution is largely determined by the needs of State and local air pollution control agencies to meet their respective State implementation plan (SIP) requirements.

NATIONAL AIR MONITORING STATIONS (NAMS)

The NAMS (1,080 stations, shown in Figure 2) are a subset of the SLAMS network with emphasis being given to urban and multi-source areas. In effect, they are key sites under SLAMS, with emphasis on areas of maximum concentrations and high population density.

SPECIAL PURPOSE MONITORING STATIONS (SPMS)

Special Purpose Monitoring Stations provide for special studies needed by the State and local

agencies to support State implementation plans and other air program activities. The SPMS are not permanently established and, can be adjusted easily to accommodate changing needs and priorities. The SPMS are used to supplement the fixed monitoring network as circumstances require and resources permit. If the data from SPMS are used for SIP purposes, they must meet all QA and methodology requirements for SLAMS monitoring.

PHOTOCHEMICAL ASSESSMENT MONITORING STATIONS (PAMS)

A PAMS network (Figure 3) is required in each ozone nonattainment area that is designated serious, severe, or extreme. The required networks will have from two to five sites, depending on the population of the area. There will be a phase-in period of one site per year starting in 1994. The ultimate PAMS network could exceed 90 sites at the end of the 5-year phase-in period.

The AirData website gives you access to air quality data collected at outdoor monitors across the United States, Puerto Rico, and the U. S. Virgin Islands. The data comes primarily from

Figure 2. National air monitoring(NAMS) network

Figure 3. Photochemical assessment monitoring network

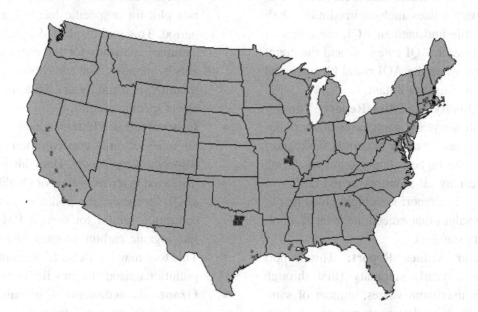

the AQS (Air Quality System) database. You can choose from several ways of looking at the data:

- Download data into a file (or view it on the screen)
- Output the data into one of AirData's standard reports
- Create graphical displays using one of the visualization tools
- Investigate monitor locations using an interactive map

AirData assists a wide range of people, from the concerned citizen who wants to know how many unhealthy air quality days there were in his county last year to air quality analysts in the regulatory, academic, and health research communities who need raw data.

AirData lets you display and download monitored hourly, daily, and annual concentration data, AQI data, and speciated particle pollution data. If you need data that AirData does not have (such as emissions data) please see Other Sources of Data.

There are four main parts of the AirData website: Download Data, Reports, Visualize Data, and the Interactive Map.

Download Data

This part of the website has two query tools. The first tool provides daily summary concentrations and Air Quality Index values for the criteria pollutants for each monitoring site in the location you select. The second tool provides raw data for a specific location and time for any pollutant.

Reports

This part of the website provides a way to generate customized reports based on criteria you select (pollutant, location, etc.). The About Reports page explains exactly what is in each report, including individual column descriptions.

- **Air Quality Index (AQI) Report:** This report displays a yearly summary of AQI values in a county or city (specifically a

CBSA - Core Based Statistical Area) . The summary values include maximum, 90th percentile and median AQI, the count of days in each AQI category, and the count of days when the AQI could be attributed to each criteria pollutant.

- **Air Quality Statistics Report:** This report shows yearly summaries of air pollution values for a city or county. The report shows the highest values reported during the year by all monitors in the CBSA or county. The report uses highlighted text to show values that exceed the level of an air quality standard.
- **Monitor Values Report:** This report shows a yearly summary (first through fourth maximum values, number of samples, etc.) of the measurements at individual monitors and provides descriptive information about the sites.
- **Air Quality Index Daily Values Report:** This report provides daily Air Quality Index values for the specified year and location.

Visualize Data

Sometimes "seeing" the data is the best way to understand it. AirData's visualization tools display data in unique and helpful ways.

- **AQI Plot:** Compare AQI values for multiple pollutants for a specific location and time period. This tool displays an entire year of AQI values – two pollutants at a time - and is useful for seeing how the number of unhealthy days can vary throughout the year for each pollutant.
- **Tile Plot:** Plot daily AQI values for a specific location and time period. Each square or "tile" represents one day of the year and is color-coded based on the AQI level for that day. The legend tallies the number of days in each AQI category.

- **Concentration Plot:** Generate a time series plot for a specific location and time period. This tool displays daily air quality summary statistics for the criteria pollutants by monitor. You can choose to plot all monitors in a county or CBSA, or you can select specific monitors.
- **Concentration Map:** Generate an animated series of daily concentration maps for a specific time period. Daily air quality is displayed in terms of the Air Quality Index (AQI) for the criteria pollutants, or in concentration ranges for certain PM species like organic carbon, nitrates, and sulfates. This tool may be useful for tracking an air pollution episode like a wildfire event.
- **Ozone Exceedances:** Compare 8-hour ozone "exceedances" from this year with previous years. Comparisons are presented in three ways. The first plot shows the comparisons by MONTH. The second plot shows the comparisons by DAY (for cumulative counts). The third plot shows the comparisons by YEAR.

The Interactive Map

Use the interactive map to see where air quality monitors are located, get information about the monitor, and download data from the monitor. You can select which monitoring networks to display on the map.

There are also other sources of air data about the monitoring network files and air quality data (Table 1). From the Web service, below information is available.

Types of Data

Monitoring Data

Ambient (outdoor) concentrations of pollutants are measured at more than 4000 monitoring stations owned and operated mainly by state envi-

Table 1. Sources of air data

Name	Type of Data
AirNow	Air quality forecasts and real-time data in a visual format for public health protection
AirCompare	AQI summaries for comparison of counties
AirTrends	Trends of air quality and emissions
Air Emission Sources	Emissions - national, state, and county-level summaries for criteria pollutant emissions
The National Emissions Inventory	Emissions - a comprehensive and detailed estimate of air emissions of both Criteria and Hazardous air pollutants from all air emissions sources
AQS Data Mart	Monitored ambient air quality data from AQS; for those who need large volumes of data
AQS Data Page	The most requested data from the Air Quality System (AQS) are posted on this Web page
CASTNET	The Clean Air Status and Trends Network (CASTNET) is the nation's primary source for data on dry acidic deposition and rural, ground-level ozone
Remote Sensing Information Gateway (RSIG)	Air quality monitoring, modeling, and satellite data
Radiation Monitoring Data	Air quality and emissions; Links to databases and maps
EPA Data Finder	Air, Water, other EPA data
Visibility Information Exchange Web System (VIEWS)	Air quality monitoring, modeling, emissions, and satellite data
DataFed	Air quality monitoring, modeling, emissions, and satellite data
Data.Gov	Air, Water, other U.S. Federal Executive Branch datasets

ronmental agencies. The agencies send hourly or daily measurements of pollutant concentrations to EPA's database called AQS (Air Quality System). AirData retrieves data from AQS.

Emissions Data

EPA keeps track of the amount of pollution that comes from a variety of sources such as vehicles, power plants, and industries. The emissions data reported to EPA by state environmental agencies can be an actual reading taken at a source or an estimate made using a mathematical calculation. AirData does not contain emissions data at this time. Emissions data can be obtained from the Air Emissions Sources website (for general summaries) and the NEI browser (for detailed reports).

Types of Air Pollutants

Criteria Air Pollutants

EPA sets national air quality standards for six common pollutants, also called criteria pollutants, to protect public health. Monitoring sites report data to EPA for these six criteria air pollutants:

- Ozone (O_3)
- Particulate matter (PM10 and PM2.5)
- Carbon monoxide (CO)
- Nitrogen dioxide (NO2)
- Sulfur dioxide (SO2)
- Lead (Pb)

   (PM10 includes particles less than or equal to 10 micrometers in diameter. PM2.5 includes particles less than or equal to 2.5 micrometers and is also called fine particle pollution.)

Hazardous Air Pollutants (HAPs)/Toxic Air Pollutants

Hazardous air pollutants (HAPs) (also called toxic air pollutants or air toxics) are pollutants that are known or suspected to cause serious health problems such as cancer. There are 188 hazardous air pollutants. Examples of toxic air pollutants include benzene, which is found in gasoline; perchlorethlyene, which is emitted from some dry cleaning facilities; and methylene chloride, which is used as a solvent and paint stripper. Examples of other listed air toxics include dioxin, asbestos, toluene, and metals such as cadmium, mercury, chromium, and lead compounds. The National-Scale Air Toxics Assessment (NATA) is EPA's ongoing comprehensive evaluation of air toxics in the U.S.

The AQI (Air Quality Index)

AirData uses the Air Quality Index (AQI) in some of its reports and tables and to display data using the visualization tools. The AQI is an index for reporting daily air quality. It tells how clean or polluted the air is, and what associated health effects might be a concern, especially for ground-level ozone and particle pollution.

Think of the AQI as a yardstick that runs from 0 to 500. The higher the AQI value, the greater the level of air pollution and the greater the health concern. For example, an AQI value of 50 represents good air quality with little potential to affect public health, while an AQI value over 300 represents hazardous air quality.

An AQI value of 100 generally corresponds to the national air quality standard for the pollutant, which is the level EPA has set to protect public health. AQI values below 100 are generally thought of as satisfactory. When AQI values are above 100, air quality is considered to be unhealthy-at first for certain sensitive groups of people, then for everyone as AQI values get higher. The AQI is divided into six categories as shown in Table 2.

Table 2. Six categories of AQI

Air Quality Index (AQI) Values	Levels of Health Concern	Colors
When the AQI is in this range:	*..air quality conditions are:*	*...as symbolized by this color:*
0-50	Good	Green
51-100	Moderate	Yellow
101-150	Unhealthy for Sensitive Groups	Orange
151 to 200	Unhealthy	Red
201 to 300	Very Unhealthy	Purple
301 to 500	Hazardous	Maroon

Each category corresponds to a different level of health concern. The six levels of health concern and what they mean are:

- **Good:** AQI is 0 - 50. Air quality is considered satisfactory, and air pollution poses little or no risk.
- **Moderate:** AQI is 51 - 100. Air quality is acceptable; however, for some pollutants there may be a moderate health concern for a very small number of people. For example, people who are unusually sensitive to ozone may experience respiratory symptoms.
- **Unhealthy for Sensitive Groups:** AQI is 101 - 150. Although general public is not likely to be affected at this AQI range, people with lung disease, older adults and children are at a greater risk from exposure to ozone, whereas persons with heart and lung disease, older adults and children are at greater risk from the presence of particles in the air.
- **Unhealthy:** AQI is 151 - 200. Everyone may begin to experience some adverse health effects, and members of the sensitive groups may experience more serious effects.
- **Very Unhealthy:** AQI is 201 - 300. This would trigger a health alert signifying that

everyone may experience more serious health effects.

- **Hazardous:** AQI greater than 300. This would trigger health warnings of emergency conditions. The entire population is more likely to be affected.

METHODOLOGY

1. Modeling of Emission Patterns

Chemical plant emissions include normal routine emissions and abnormal emissions. Abnormal emissions are caused by planned, unpredictable, or uncontrollable events that will significantly upset or damage equipment, process facility, ventilation system, or flare control system, which in turn generate large amounts of emissions. Emissions due to process turnaround operations (e.g., start-up and shutdown) as well as equipment leakage, rupture, or explosions are typical examples. Conceivably, abnormal emissions emitted from chemical plants bear several typical dynamic emission profiles

To quantitatively characterize each abnormal emission patterns in Table 3, a general mathematical model shown in Equation (1) has been developed.

$$
m_i^D(t) = \sum_{k \in K_i} \left[\frac{a_{i,k}\left(b_{i,k}\,t + c_{i,k}\right)}{1 + \exp\left(d_{i,k}\left|t - e_{i,k}\right| + d_{i,k}\left|t - f_{i,k}\right|\right)} \right] \tag{1}
$$

where $m_i^D(t)$ means the dynamic emission rate from emission source i at time t; k represents the emission peak index of $m_i^D(t)$; K_i represents the set of emission peak index of $m_i^D(t)$; $a_{i,k}$, $b_{i,k}$, $c_{i,k}$, $d_{i,k}$, $e_{i,k}$, and $f_{i,k}$ are corresponding parameters. Coupling these parameters together can help characterize three major elements of a dynamic emission pattern: emission peak number, peak duration, and peak decreasing trend. As examples, Table 3 provides the value range for the key parameters, which could be used to generate corresponding dynamic emission patterns.

Table 3. Parameter characterization of various emission patterns

Dynamic Emission Patterns	$b_{i,k}$	$e_{i,k}$ and $f_{i,k}$	Dimension of set K_i
Single Acute Peak	0	$e_{i,k} = f_{i,k}$	1
Single Plain Peak	0	$e_{i,k} \neq f_{i,k}$	1
Single Inclining Peak	1	$e_{i,k} \neq f_{i,k}$	1
Multiple Acute Peak	0	$e_{i,k} = f_{i,k}$	Number of Peaks
Multiple Plain Peak	0	$e_{i,k} \neq f_{i,k}$	Number of Peaks
Multiple Inclining Peak	1	$e_{i,k} \neq f_{i,k}$	Number of Peaks

2. Problem Statement

Based on the aforementioned, the studied problem is to develop a systematic methodology to reversely detect the emission source from a list of candidates (local chemical plants) according to the abnormal air-quality measurements from an available monitoring network, so as to support diagnostic and prognostic decisions timely and effectively. The outcome of the developed methodology should provide information of emission source location, starting time, time duration, total emission amount, and dynamic emission rate and pattern from the abnormal emission sources. The methodology will firstly determine the background normal emission rates for a given list of candidate emission sources in the region. Next, an optimization model will be employed for reverse emission source detection based on abnormal air-quality measurements. For clarity, the problem statements are summarized below.

- **Assumptions:**
  - An air-quality event in a region is caused by abnormal emissions from one and only one emission source based on a given list of candidate emission sources, whose abnormal emission pattern belongs to one of those shown in Table 1;
  - Each candidate emission source has a constant emission rate during its normal operational conditions;
  - Emission transportation follows Gaussian dispersion model and there is no secondary consumption or generation of the pollutant during its air transportation;
  - When the emitted pollutant reached ground through dispersion, it will be absorbed, i.e., there is no pollutant reflection from the ground during its air transportation;

  - Meteorological conditions (e.g., local wind direction and wind speed) during the considered scheduling time horizon are constant (or near constant) in the region.
- **Given Information:**
  - Spatial locations of each emission sources and monitoring stations;
  - Emission source stack parameters, such as stack height and outlet temperature;
  - Dynamic monitoring results at each monitoring station;
  - Meteorological conditions in the studied region during the event time period.
- **Information to be Determined:**
  - Which emission source caused the investigated pollutant concentration pattern;
  - What are the emission pattern and dynamic emission rate for the identified emission source.

3. General Methodology

The input parameters at the modeling stage include geographical information (locations of every possible emission source and monitoring station), meteorological condition (e.g., wind direction, speed, and atmospheric stability), measurements at each monitoring station, and emission source data (e.g., stack height, exit diameter and outlet temperature). The next step is to map locations of candidate emission sources and monitoring stations into a rectangular coordinator system (see Appendix). Then, the firs- stage modeling aims at the determination of normal emission rates from every emission source. The task is accomplished through a regression model based on Gaussian-dispersion model to minimize the sum of squared error (SSE) between the model calculated results and monitoring results from multiple monitoring stations. Since the normal emission rate of each emission source is the background emission during plant steady-state operational conditions, it is also called steady-state emission rate.

This regression model is to identify the normal emission rate for each candidate emission source by minimizing SSE between the model predicting results and the monitoring results from multiple monitoring stations at normal emission status (without emission events).

3.1 Objective Function

$$\varphi_1 = \min_{m_i^S} \sum_{t \in T^D} \sum_{j \in J} \left(\bar{C}_j - C_{j,t}^S \right)^2 \qquad (2)$$

where j represents the index of monitoring stations grouped by set J; T^S represents a selected steady-state time set when each emission source has a normal emission rate. T^S contains multiple time instants indexed by t. $\bar{C}_j$ and $C_{j,t}^S$ respectively represents model calculated and measured pollutant concentrations at the j-th monitoring station at time t. Equation (2) suggests the objective function is to minimize SSE between $\bar{C}_j$ and $C_{j,t}^S$.

The model calculated pollutant concentration at the j-th monitoring station ($\bar{C}_j$) should be the cumulative of $\bar{C}_{i,j}$ from all the emission sources, which can be formulated by Equation (3).

$$\bar{C}_j = \sum_{i \in I} \bar{C}_{i,j}, \ \forall \ j \in J \qquad (3)$$

3.2 Dispersion Transportation Principle

Note that $\bar{C}_{i,j}$ should be calculated by the following Equation (4). It represents pollutant dispersion from emission sources to monitoring stations under the impact of meteorological conditions. The associated details of Equation (4) can be referenced in the Appendix.

$$\bar{C}_{i,j} = \frac{m_i^s \, f\left(Z_{i,j}, H_i\right)}{2U_i \, \pi \, \sigma_{Y_{i,j}} \, \sigma_{Z_{i,j}}} \exp\left[-\frac{1}{2}\left(\frac{Y_{i,j}}{\sigma_{Y_{i,j}}} \right)^2 \right]$$
$$\forall \ i \in I, \ j \in J \qquad (4)$$

where $\bar{C}_{i,j}$ is the pollutant concentration at the j-th monitoring station caused by the emission from the i-th emission source; $Y_{i,j}$ is the projection of $d_{i,j}$ along Y direction (Here, X direction is the same as the wind direction; Y direction is horizontally perpendicular to X direction); $Z_{i,j}$ is the ground height difference between the i-th emission source to the j-th monitoring station; H_i is the plume height above the ground for source i; $\sigma_{Y_{i,j}}$ and $\sigma_{Z_{i,j}}$ are the standard deviations of the emission plume's probability distribution function along Y and Z directions, respectively; $f(Z_{i,j}, H_i)$ is a function with respect to $Z_{i,j}$ and H_i; m_i^s represents the constant emission rate at the i-th emission source in the normal condition.

The related equations and procedures to calculate the parameters shown in Equation (4) has been included in the Gaussian dispersion model area (Pasquill, 1961, 1974; Turner, 1979, 1994; Hanna et al., 1982; Seinfeld, 1986; Slade, 1986; Halitsky, 1989; Griffiths, 1994; Turner et al., 1989; Bowman, 1996).

3.3 Artificial Neural Network Model

To train the artificial neural network we obtain a generalized transfer function of the values of emission rate and the pollutant concentrations which are normalized in the procedure of model preparation (Figure 6). The normalized features were used to give the training on the neural network with the Lavenberg - Marquardt back propagation algorithm. Different numbers of hidden neurons were used and we found a good approximation and generalization with 1000 neurons (Figure 5). Riva-Rocci based measurement is used as the target values. The measurement of the dynamic emission rate changes is not easy because the systolic and diastolic values are measured at different time instances. There are total 7000 samples have participated the modeling of the artificial neural network. 70% of the samples are training samples, which are presented to the network during training, and the network is adjusted according to its error.15% of the samples are validation samples, which are used to measure network generalization, and to halt training when generalization stops improving. The rest 15% of the samples are testing samples. These have no effect on training and so provide an independent measure of network performance during and after training.

15% of the samples are validation samples, which are used to measure network generalization, and to halt training when generalization stops improving. The rest 15% of the samples are test-

ing samples. These have no effect on training and so provide an independent measure of network performance during and after training.

CASE STUDY

To demonstrate the efficacy of the developed systematic methodology, two case studies including the detection of a real SO_2 emission event are conducted.

As shown in Figure 4, the studied involves five chemical emission sources (E1, E2, E3, E4, and E5 represented by red dots) and four monitoring stations (S1, S2, S3, and S4 represented by green dots) distributed in a squared region (30 km×30 km). The entire region is gridded and the edge length of each gridded cell is 1 km. The surface wind blows from the southwest to northeast as

Figure 4.Percentage selection of the samples for validation and test Data

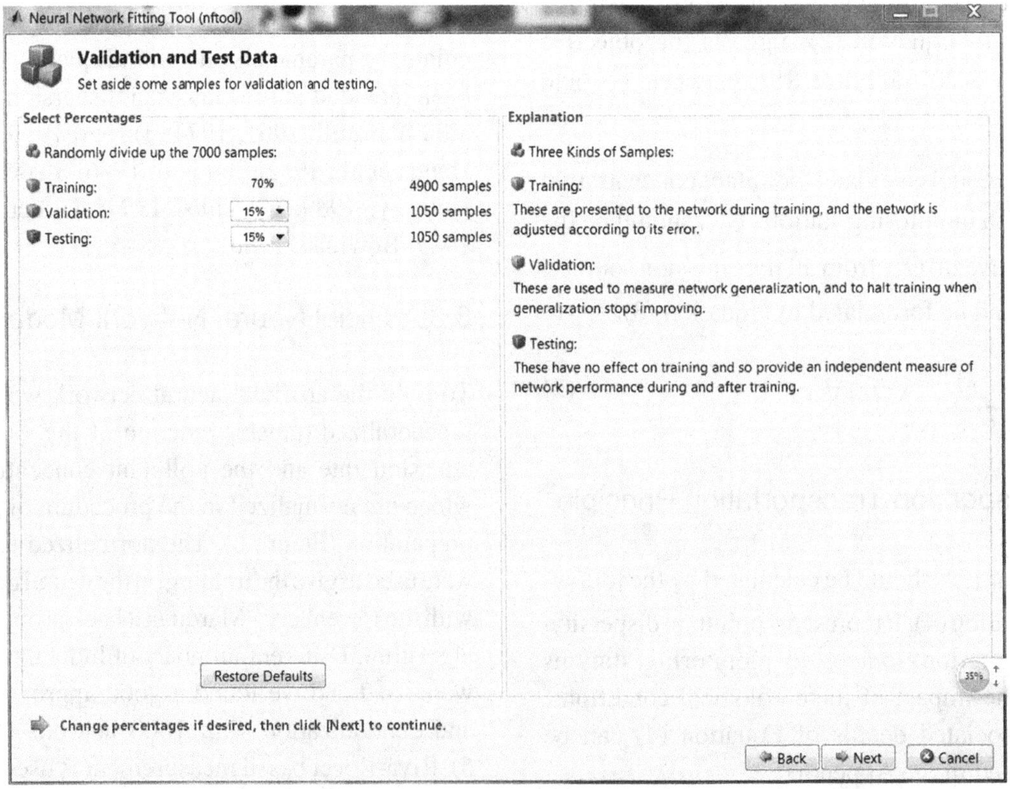

Figure 5.Setting for the hidden neurons

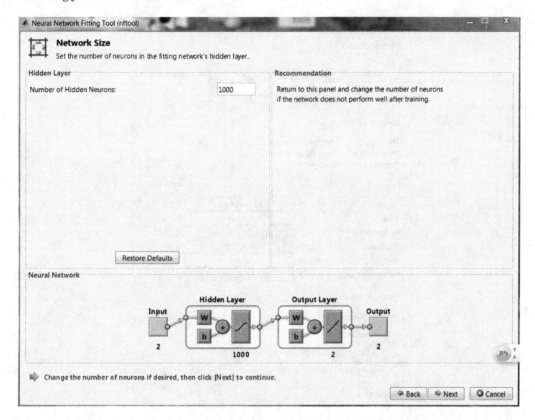

shown in Figure 7. A common pollutant emitted from these five emission sources is monitored by the monitoring stations through hourly measurements.

The plume and stack parameters of the five emission sources are given in Table 4. During the event time period, the lapse rate was 4 K/km, the wind speed was 1.6m/s at 10-meter height, and the ambient temperature was 20 °C. For the investigation, the entire time period has been separated into two parts: steady-state time period and dynamic time period. The data in the steady-state has been applied to determine the normal emission rates for each emission source.

The modeling result for the developed artificial neural network has been plot in the Figure 8.It can be seen that the training has the R square value of 0.41802 while the validation and test has the R-square of 0.15516 and 0.13702 respec-

tively. It can be seen that the R square value among the periods of training, validation and test are quite similar and the overall R square value has been 0.16433.This has shown that the artificial neural network model can give the quantitative identification of the normal emission rate. The results of m_1^s through m_5^s are identified as 10.8, 10.5, 10.1, 9.2, and 9.8 kg/h, respectively.

CONCLUSION

A local air-quality monitoring network has potentials to proactively identify abnormal emission events. In this chapter, a systematic methodology for simultaneous identification of a emission source and its emission rate has been developed to conduct regression for background emission rate determination and emission source identification

Figure 6.Training neural network

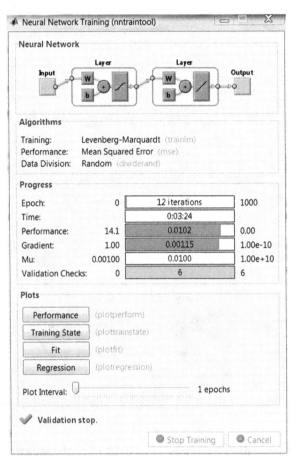

Figure 7. Spatial scope of case study

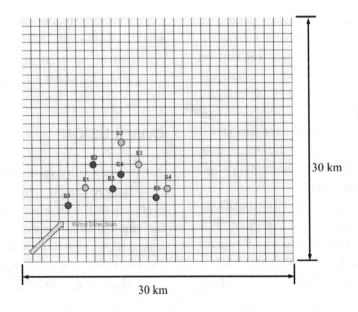

and quantification. The case study is employed to demonstrate the efficacy of the developed methodology. This study lays out a solid foundation for multiple stake holders on diagnostic and prognostic decisions in face of an industrial air-pollution event, including government environmental agencies, regional chemical plants, and local communities. Based on an available air-quality monitoring network, the data integration technologies will be applied to identify the scenarios of the possible emission source and the dynamic pollutant monitor result, so as to timely and effectively support diagnostic and prognostic decisions. The application of artificial neural networks for such applications have been developed according to the real application purpose.

Table 4. Plume and stack parameters for each emission source

Chemical Emission Sources	E1	E2	E3	E4	E5
Stack Height H_i *(m)*	80	110	95	100	105
Stack Exit Temperature $T_{s,i}$ *(K)*	480	400	460	440	430
Stack Exit Velocity $V_{s,i}$ *(m/s)*	17.5	13.0	15.6	14.2	16.1
Stack Exit Diameter $D_{s,i}$ *(m)*	1.6	1.9	1.5	1.7	1.8

Figure 8. Regression result for training, validation and test

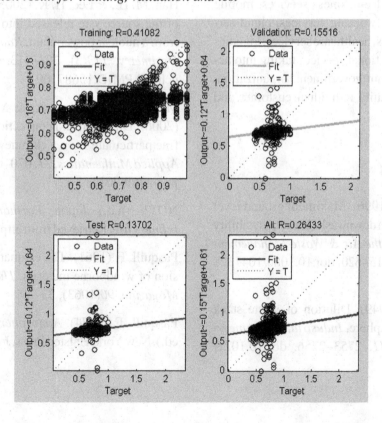

FUTURE RESEARCH DIRECTIONS

This study can not only determine emission source location, starting time, and time duration responsible for an observed emission event, but also reversely estimate the dynamic emission rate and the total emission amount from the accidental emission source. It provides valuable information for accidental investigations and root cause analysis for an emission event; meanwhile, it helps evaluate the regional air-quality impact caused by such an emission event as well. It lays out a solid foundation for multiple stake holders on diagnostic and prognostic decisions in face of an industrial air-pollution event, including government environmental agencies, regional chemical plants, and local communities.

It is necessary to further extend the current research to be integrated into the website service of environmental protection agency. Similar case studies and applications in using technologies and fundamental theory can be applied and demonstrated in the representative service domains with the combination of e-business services, mobile services, social networking services, cloud services, legal services, healthcare services, logistics services and educational services taking into account demands from government, organization, enterprise, community, individual, customer, and citizen.

REFERENCES

Bowman, W. A. (1996). Maximum ground level concentrations with downwash: The urban stability mode. *Journal of the Air & Waste Management Association*, *46*, 615–620. doi:10.1080/10473289.1996.10467495

Church, P. E. (1949). Dilution of waste stack gases in the atmosphere. *Industrial & Engineering Chemistry*, *41*, 2753–2756. doi:10.1021/ie50480a022

Goldsmith, J. R., & Friberg, L. T. (1976). Effects of air pollution on human health, air pollution. In *The effects of air pollution* (3rd ed.). New York: Academic Press.

Griffiths, R. F. (1994). Errors in the use of the Briggs parameterization for atmospheric dispersion coefficients. *Atmospheric Environment*, *28*(17), 2861–2865. doi:10.1016/1352-2310(94)90086-8

Halitsky, J. (1989). A jet plume model for short stacks. *Journal of the Air Pollution Control Association*, *39*(6), 856–858.

Hogan, W. R., Cooper, G. F., Wagner, M. M., & Wallstrom, G. L. (2005). *An inverted Gaussian Plume model for estimating the location and amount of release of airborne agents from downwind atmospheric concentrations (RODS Technical Report)*. Pittsburgh, PA: Real Time Outbreak and Disease Surveillance Laboratory, University of Pittsburgh.

Jeong, H. J., Kim, E. H., Suh, K. S., Hwang, W. T., Han, M. H., & Lee, H. K. (2005). Determination of the source rate released into the environment from a nuclear power plant. *Radiation Protection Dosimetry*, *113*(3), 308–313. doi:10.1093/rpd/nch460 PMID:15687109

MacKay, C., McKee, S., & Mulholland, A. J. (2006). Diffusion and convection of gaseous and fine particulate from a chimney. *IMA Journal of Applied Mathematics*, *71*, 670–691. doi:10.1093/imamat/hxl016

NDTV. (n.d.). *Japan: Earthquake triggers oil refinery fire*. Retrieved from http://www.ndtv.com

Pasquill, F. (1961). The estimation of the dispersion of windborne material. *The Meteorological Magazine*, *90*(1063), 33–49.

Pasquill, F. (1974). *Atmospheric diffusion* (2nd ed.). New York: Halsted Press, John Wiley & Sons.

Seinfeld, J.H. (1986). *Atmospheric chemistry and physics of air pollution*. New York: J. Wiley. Hanna, S.R., Briggs, G.A., & Kosker, R.P. (1982). *Hand book on atmospheric diffusion*. Springfield, VA: NTIS, DE81009809(DOE/TIC-22800).

Slade, D. H. (Ed.). (1986). *Meteorology and atomic energy*. Washington, DC: U.S. Atomic Energy Commission, Air Resources Laboratories, Research Laboratories, Environmental Science Services Administration, U.S Department of Commerce.

Turner, D. B. (1979). Atmospheric dispersion modeling. *Journal of the Air Pollution Control Association, 29*(5), 502–519. doi:10.1080/0002 2470.1979.10470821

Turner, D. B. (1994). *Workbook of atmospheric dispersion estimates: An introduction to dispersion modeling* (2nd ed.). Boca Raton, FL: Lewis Publishers.

Turner, D. B., Bender, L. W., Pierce, T. E., & Petersen, W. B. (1989). Air quality simulation models from EPA. *Environmental Software, 4*(2), 52–61. doi:10.1016/0266-9838(89)90031-2

United States Chemical Safety Board. (n.d.). Retrieved from http://www.csb.gov

Xu, Q., Yang, X., Liu, C., Li, K., Lou, H. H., & Gossage, J. L. (2009). Chemical plant flare minimization via plant-wide dynamic simulation. *Industrial & Engineering Chemistry Research, 48*(7), 3505–3512. doi:10.1021/ie8016219

ADDITIONAL READING

Benjamin, R. I. (1983). Information technology: a strategic opportunity.

Bouwman, H., & van der Duin, P. (2003). Technological forecasting and scenarios matter: research into the use of information and communication technology in the home environment in 2010. foresight, 5(4), 8-19.

Carbonara, N. (2005). Information and communication technology and geographical clusters: opportunities and spread. *Technovation, 25*(3), 213–222. doi:10.1016/S0166-4972(03)00095-6

Castells, M., & United Nations Research Institute for Social Development. (1999). Information technology, globalization and social development.

Cohen, W. W., & Richman, J. (2002, July). Learning to match and cluster large high-dimensional data sets for data integration. In Proceedings of the eighth ACM SIGKDD international conference on Knowledge discovery and data mining (pp. 475-480). ACM.

Dayhoff, J. E., & DeLeo, J. M. (2001). Artificial neural networks. *Cancer, 91*(S8), 1615–1635. doi:10.1002/1097-0142(20010415)91:8+<1615::AID-CNCR1175>3.0.CO;2-L PMID:11309760

Goodhue, D. L., Wybo, M. D., & Kirsch, L. J. (1992). The impact of data integration on the costs and benefits of information systems. *Management Information Systems Quarterly*, 293–311.

Halevy, A., Rajaraman, A., & Ordille, J. (2006, September). Data integration: the teenage years. In Proceedings of the 32nd international conference on Very large data bases (pp. 9-16). VLDB Endowment.

Hevner, A. R., March, S. T., Park, J., & Ram, S. (2004). Design science in information systems research. *Management Information Systems Quarterly, 28*(1), 75–105.

Hopfield, J. J. (1988). Artificial neural networks. *Circuits and Devices Magazine, IEEE, 4*(5), 3–10. doi:10.1109/101.8118

Ives, Z. G., Florescu, D., Friedman, M., Levy, A., & Weld, D. S. (1999, June). An adaptive query execution system for data integration. []. ACM.]. *SIGMOD Record, 28*(2), 299–310.

Jain, A. K., Mao, J., & Mohiuddin, K. M. (1996). Artificial neural networks: A tutorial. *Computer, 29*(3), 31–44. doi:10.1109/2.485891

Lal, K. (2001). Institutional environment and the development of information and communication technology in India. *The Information Society, 17*(2), 105–117. doi:10.1080/019722401750175649

Lenzerini, M. (2002, June). Data integration: A theoretical perspective. InProceedings of the twenty-first ACM SIGMOD-SIGACT-SIGART symposium on Principles of database systems (pp. 233-246). ACM.

McQuail, D. (1987). *Mass communication theory: An introduction.* Sage Publications, Inc.

Odendaal, N. (2003). Information and communication technology and local governance: understanding the difference between cities in developed and emerging economies. *Computers, Environment and Urban Systems, 27*(6), 585–607. doi:10.1016/S0198-9715(03)00016-4

Patterson, D. W. (1998). *Artificial neural networks: theory and applications.* Prentice Hall PTR.

Peterson, C., & Soderberg, B. (1993). Artificial neural networks. Modern heuristic techniques for combinatorial problems, 197-242.

Schreyer, P. (2000). *The contribution of information and communication technology to output growth: a study of the G7 countries (No. 2000/2).* OECD Publishing. doi:10.1787/151634666253

Townsend, A. M., DeMarie, S. M., & Hendrickson, A. R. (1998). Virtual teams: Technology and the workplace of the future. *The Academy of Management Executive, 12*(3), 17–29.

Unwin, T., & Unwin, P. T. H. (Eds.). (2009). *ICT4D: Information and communication technology for development. Cambridge University Press. Dutton, W. H. (1996). Information and communication technologies: Visions and realities.* Oxford University Press, Inc.

Vaishnavi, V. K., & Kuechler, W. Jr. (2007). *Design science research methods and patterns: innovating information and communication technology.* CRC Press. doi:10.1201/9781420059335

van den Hooff, B., & van de Wijngaert, L. (2005). Information and communication technology in organizations: adoption, implementation, use and effects. *Sage (Atlanta, Ga.).*

Yegnanarayana, B. (2004). *Artificial neural networks.* PHI Learning Pvt. Ltd.

KEY TERMS AND DEFINITIONS

Air Pollution: Air pollution is the introduction into the atmosphere of chemicals, particulates, or biological materials that cause discomfort, disease, or death to humans, damage other living organisms such as food crops, or damage the natural environment or built environment.

Air Quality Index: An air quality index (AQI) is a number used by government agencies to communicate to the public how polluted the air is currently or how polluted it is forecast to become. As the AQI increases, an increasingly large percentage of the population is likely to experience increasingly severe adverse health effects. Different countries have their own air quality indices which are not all consistent. Different countries also use different names for their indices such as Air Quality Health Index, Air Pollution Index and Pollutant Standards Index.

Air Quality Monitoring Network: The monitoring network provides data concerning regional air quality so that the assess of compliance with the National Ambient Air Quality Standards (NAAQS) is available as required by the Federal Clean Air Act.

Artificial Neural Network: In computer science and related fields, artificial neural networks are computational models inspired by animal central nervous systems (in particular the brain) that are capable of machine learning and pattern recognition. They are usually presented as systems of interconnected "neurons" that can compute values from inputs by feeding information through the network.

Data Integration: Data integration involves combining data residing in different sources and providing users with a unified view of these data.

Information and Communication Technology: Information and communications technology (ICT) is often used as an extended synonym for information technology (IT), but is a more specific term that stresses the role of unified communications and the integration of telecommunications, computers as well as necessary enterprise software, storage, and audio-visual systems, which enable users to access, store, transmit, and manipulate information.

NAAQS: The National Ambient Air Quality Standards (NAAQS) are standards established by the United States Environmental Protection Agency under authority of the Clean Air Act (42 U.S.C. 7401 et seq.) that apply for outdoor air throughout the country.

Compilation of References

Abbott, P., Zheng, Y., Du, R., & Willcocks, L. (2013). From boudary spanning to creolization: A study of Chinese software and services outsourcing vendors. *The Journal of Strategic Information Systems*, *22*, 121–136. doi:10.1016/j.jsis.2013.02.002

Accenture. (2009). *Research & insights: Web 2.0 and the next generation of public service.* Retrieved from http://www.epractice.eu/en/library/309027

ACELG. (2011). *Local government and community engagement.* Sydney: Australian Centre of Excellence for Local Government, University of Technology, Sydney.

Achugbue, I. E., & Ochonogor, W. C. (2011). The role and challenges of ICT in educational development in Nigeria higher institutions. In *Proceedings of the 2011 Annual International Conference.* Faculty of Education, Delta State University Abraka.

Achugbue, I. E. (2011). Electronic mail security. In *Handbook of research on information communication technology policy: Trends issues and advancements.* Hershey, PA: IGI Global.

Achugbue, I. E. (2013). E-libraries & e-learning. In *Reading in general studies.* Abraka, Nigeria: University Press Delta State University.

Adamic, L., & Adar, E. (2005). How to search a social network. *Social Networks*, *27*(3), 187–203. doi:10.1016/j.socnet.2005.01.007

Adler, B. (2011). *Building scalable applications in the cloud: Reference architecture & best practices.* RightScale Inc.

Agarwal, S., Kenkre, S., Pandit, V., & Sengupta, B. (2011). Studying the evolution of skill profiles in distributed, specialization driven service delivery systems through work orchestration. In *Proceedings of the 2011 Annual SRII Global Conference* (pp. 201-213). Washington, DC: IEEE Computer Society.

Agarwal, R., Sambamurthy, V., & Stair, R. M. (2000). The evolving relationship between general and specific efficacy: An empirical assessment. *Information Systems Research*, *11*(4), 418–430. doi:10.1287/isre.11.4.418.11876

Agarwal, S. (2010). Remote health monitoring using mobile, phones and web services. *Telemedicine Journal and e-Health*, *16*(5), 603–607. doi:10.1089/tmj.2009.0165 PMID:20575728

Ahmad, A. A., & Zink, S. D. (1998). Information technology adoption in Jordanian public sector organizations. *Journal of Government Information*, *25*(2), 117–134. doi:10.1016/S1352-0237(97)00094-4

Ahmadi, H., & Kong, J. (2012). User-centric adaptation of web information for small screens. *Journal of Visual Languages and Computing*, *23*(1), 13–28. doi:10.1016/j.jvlc.2011.09.002

Ai, F., & Wang, M. (2007). On China mobile's service model evolution. *Market Modernization*, (4), 346.

Ajzen, I. (1974). Effects of information on interpersonal attraction: Similarity versus affective value. *Journal of Personality and Social Psychology*, *29*(3), 374–380. doi:10.1037/h0036002 PMID:4814127

Ajzen, I. (1976). Uniqueness of behavioral effects in causal attribution. *Journal of Personality, 44*(1), 98. doi:10.1111/j.1467-6494.1976.tb00586.x

Ajzen, I. (1977). Intuitive theories of events and the effects of base-rate information on prediction. *Journal of Personality and Social Psychology, 35*(5), 303–314. doi:10.1037/0022-3514.35.5.303

Ajzen, I. (1978). Use and misuse of Bayes' theorem in causal attribution: Don't attribute it to Ajzen and Fishbein either. *Psychological Bulletin, 85*(2), 244. doi:10.1037/0033-2909.85.2.244

Ajzen, I. (2012). Martin Fishbein legacy: The reasoned action approach. *The Annals of the American Academy of Political and Social Science, 640*(1), 11–27. doi:10.1177/0002716211423363

Ajzen, I., & Fishbein, M. (1969). The prediction o f behavioral intentions in a choice situation. *Journal of Experimental Social Psychology, 5*(1), 400–416. doi:10.1016/0022-1031(69)90033-X

Ajzen, I., & Fishbein, M. (1973). Attitudinal and normative variables as predictors of specific behaviors. *Journal of Personality and Social Psychology, 27*(1), 41. doi:10.1037/h0034440

Ajzen, I., & Fishbein, M. (2004). Questions raised by a reasoned action approach: Comment on Ogden (2003). *Health Psychology, 23*(4), 431–434. doi:10.1037/0278-6133.23.4.431 PMID:15264981

Ajzen, I., & Fishbein, M. (2008). Scaling and testing multiplicative combinations in the expectancy value model of attitudes. *Journal of Applied Social Psychology, 38*(9), 2222–2247. doi:10.1111/j.1559-1816.2008.00389.x

Akintola, K.G., Akinyede, R.O., & Agbonifo, C.O. (2011). Appraising Nigeria readiness for e-commerce towards achieving vision 2020. *IJRRAS, 9*(2).

Al-Ali, A., Zualkernan, I., & Aloul, F. (2010). A mobile GPRS-sensors array for air pollution monitoring. *IEEE Sensors Journal, 10*(10), 1666–1671. doi:10.1109/JSEN.2010.2045890

Alam, S., & Walker, D. (2011). The public Facebook: A case of Australian government Facebook pages and participation. In *Proceedings of ACIS 2011*. Sydney, Australia: ACIS.

Aldrich, M. (2011). *Inventor's story*. Retrieved from http://www.aldricharchive.com/inventors_story.html

Alibaba Group. (2013). *Company overview*. Retrieved June 29, 2013, from http://news.alibaba.com/specials/aboutalibaba/aligroup/index.html

Allaire, J. (2009). *Building new business models on the web*. SYS-CON Media Inc.

Al-Masah, A. S., & Al-Sharafi, A. M. (2013). Benefits of cloud computing for network infrastructure monitoring service. *International Journal of Advances in Engineering and Technology*, 46-51.

Almeida, F., Terra, B. M., Dias, P. A., & Gonçalves, G. (2010). Adoption issues of multi-agent systems in manufacturing industry. In *Proceedings of Fifth International Multi-Conference on Computing in the Global Information Technology* (pp. 238–244). Valencia, CA: Conference Publishing Services - IEEE. doi:10.1109/ICCGI.2010.48

Alonso, G., Casati, F., Kuno, H., & Machiraju, V. (2004). *Web Services: Concepts, Architectures and Applications*. Berlin: Springer-Verlag.

Amamuah-Mensah, E. (2009). *E-business adoption in the banking industry in Ghana*. (Unpublished Masters thesis). Lulea University of Technology.

Amazon, E. (2010). *Amazon elastic compute cloud (Amazon EC2)*.

Amazon. (2013). *Amazon Web Services*. Retrieved 9 8, 2013, from http://aws.amazon.com/

Ambler, S. (2012). *Encapsulating database access: An agile best practice*. Retrieved from http://www.agiledata.org/essays/implementationStrategies.html

American Global Standards. (2013). *Virtual Cert™ program - American global standards*. Retrieved April 25, 2013, from http://www.americanglobal.org/process/virtual-cert/

Anastasio, T. J., Ehrenberger, K. A., Watson, P., & Zhang, W. (2012). *Individual and collective memory consolidation - Analogous processes on different levels.* Cambridge, MA: MIT Press.

Anderson, P. (2007, February). What is web 2.0? Ideas, technology and implications for education. *JISC Technology and Standards Watch.*

Anderson, G. W. (2011). *Sams teach yourself SAP in 24 hours.* Indianapolis, IN: Pearson Education, Inc.

Anderson, L., & Krathwohl, D. (2001). *A taxonomy for learning, teaching and assessing: A revision of Bloom's taxonomy of educational objectives.* New York, NY: Longman.

Andrews, A. (2009). *Social networks face challenging 2009, must monetise or die.* Retrieved July 1, 2012, from http://paidcontent.co.uk/article/419-social-networks-face-challenging-2009-must-monetise-or-die/

Andrews, A. (2009). *Facebook shows off polls in davos, new business model or just cool toy?* Retrieved July 1, 2012, from http://www.washingtonpost.com/wp-dyn/content/article/2009/02/02/AR2009020200876.html

Ante, S. (2012, January 7). Avoiding innovation's terrible toll. *Wall Street Journal,* 3-4.

Anthony, R. N. (1965). *Planning and control systems: A framework for analysis.* Boston: Division of Research, Graduate School of Business Administration, Harvard University.

Anttiroiko, A. V. (2010). Innovation in democratic e-governance: Benefitting from web 2.0 applications in the public sector. *International Journal of Electronic Government Research, 6*(2), 18–36. doi:10.4018/jegr.2010040102

Appadurai, A. (1998). *The social life of things: Commodities in cultural perspective.* Cambridge, UK: Cambridge Uniersity Press.

Arcitura Education Inc. (2013). *ServiceOrientation.com.* Retrieved August 6, 2013, from http://serviceorientation.com/serviceorientation/service_loose_coupling

Arlbjern, J. S., & Haug, A. (2010). *Business process optimization.* Aarhus, Denmark: Academica.

Arsanjani, A., Zhang, L.-J., Ellis, M., Allam, A., & Channabasavaiah, K. (2007, March 28). *Design an SOA solution using a reference architecture.* Retrieved april 18, 2013, from http://www.ibm.com/developerworks/library/ar-archtemp/

Arsanjani, A., Borges, B., & Holley, K. (2004). Service-oriented architecture: Components and modeling can make the difference. *Web Services Journal, 9*(1), 34–38.

Ashraf, A., Byholm, B., Lehtinen, J., & Porres, I. (2012). *Feedback control algorithms to deploy and scale multiple web applications per virtual machine.* Paper presented at the Software Engineering and Advanced Applications (SEAA). New York, NY.

Attewell, P. (1992). Technology diffusion and organizational Learning: The case of business computing. *Organization Science, 3,* 21–27. doi:10.1287/orsc.3.1.1

Atzori, L., Iera, A., & Morabito, G. (2010). The internet of things: A survey. *Computer Networks, 54*(15), 2787–2805. doi:10.1016/j.comnet.2010.05.010

Australian Government. (2009). *Engage: Getting on with government 2.0, report of the government 2.0 taskforce.* ACT: Australian Government Information Management Office.

Avast. (2013). *Virtualization parameters.* Retrieved April 22, 2013, from http://avast.helpmax.net/en/additional-protection/sandbox/expert-settings/virtualization-parameters/

Aversa, L., & Bestavros, A. (2000). *Load balancing a cluster of web servers: Using distributed packet rewriting.* Paper presented at the Performance, Computing, and Communications Conference, 2000. New York, NY.

Aye, N., Khin, H. S., & Win, T. T. KoKo, T., Than, M. Z., Hattori, F., & Kuwabara, K. (2013). Multi-domain public key infrastructure for information security with use of a multi-agent system. In *Proceedings of the 5th Asian Conference on Intelligent Information and Database Systems* - (pp. 365-374). Heidelberg, Germany: Springer-Verlag.

Bacigalupo, D. A., Van Hemert, J., Chen, X., Usmani, A., Chester, A. P., He, L., & Jarvis, S. A. (2011). Managing dynamic enterprise and urgent workloads on clouds using layered queuing and historical performance models. *Simulation Modelling Practice and Theory, 19*(6), 1479–1495. doi:10.1016/j.simpat.2011.01.007

Badger, L., Grance, T., Patt-Corner, R., & Voas, J. (2012). *Draft cloud computing synopsis and recommendations.* Gaithersburg, MD: NIST.

Baker, J. (2012). The technology–organization–environment framework. In *Information systems theory: Explaining and predicting our digital society* (Vol. 1, pp. 231–245). Springer Link. doi:10.1007/978-1-4419-6108-2_12

Baltzan, P. K, L., & P, B. (2013). Business Driven Information Systems. Sydney: McGraw Hill Australia.

Banerjee, S., & Pedersen, T. (2002). An adapted Lesk algorithm for word sense disambiguation using WordNet. In *Computational linguistics and intelligent text processing* (pp. 136–145). Berlin: Springer. doi:10.1007/3-540-45715-1_11

Bantoft, K., & Wouters, P. (2006). *Openswan building and integrating virtual private networks.* Birmingham, UK: Packt Publishing.

Barabási, A. L., & Albert, R. (1999). Emergence of scaling in random networks. *Science, 286*(5439), 509–512. doi:10.1126/science.286.5439.509 PMID:10521342

Barbot, C. (2013). A model of consumer choice with vertically differentiated goods: Reassessing the traditional demand theory and an application to tourism. *Journal of Transport Literature, 7*(1), 52–64. doi:10.1590/S2238-10312013000100003

Barham, P., Dragovic, B., Fraser, K., Hand, S., Harris, T., Ho, A., & Warfield, A. (2003). Xen and the art of virtualization. *ACM SIGOPS Operating Systems Review, 37*(5), 164–177. doi:10.1145/1165389.945462

Barjis, J., Kolfschoten, G., & Maritz, J. (2013). A sustainable and affordable support system for rural healthcare delivery. *Decision Support Systems.* doi:10.1016/j.dss.2013.06.005 PMID:23729945

Barr, J., Varia, J., & Wood, M. (2006). *Amazon EC2 Beta.* Retrieved Nov 27, 2012, from Amazon Web Services Blog: http://aws.typepad.com/aws/2006/08/amazon_ec2_beta.html

Barreiros, M., & Lundqvist, P. (2011). *QOS-enabled networks.* West Sussex, UK: John Wiley & Sons, Ltd. doi:10.1002/9780470976814

Basak, D., Toshniwal, R., Maskalik, S., & Sequeira, A. (2010). Virtualizing networking and security in the cloud. *SIGOPS Operating Systems Review,* 86-94.

Bauer, B., & Odell, J. (2005). UML 2.0 and agents: How to build agent-based systems with the new UML standard. *Engineering Applications of Artificial Intelligence, 18*(2), 141–157. doi:10.1016/j.engappai.2004.11.016

Bauer, E., & Adams, R. (2012). *Reliability and availability of cloud computing.* New York: John Wiley & Sons. doi:10.1002/9781118393994

BCS The Chartered Institute for IT. (2012). *Cloud computing: Moving IT out of the office.* Swindon, UK: British Informatics Society Limited.

Beez, A., Kechiche, B., & Sylwia, B. (2010). The impact of mobile services in Nigeria: How mobile technologies are transforming economic and social activities. *Pyramid Research.* Retrieved June 16, 2013 from www.pyramidresearch.com

Behavioural Precursors and HIV Testing Behaviour among African American Women. (2012). *Health Education Journal, 71*(1), 102-114.

Bell, G. (2006). The age of thumb: A culture reading of mobile technologies from Asia. *Knowledge, Technology & Policy, 19*(2), 41–57. doi:10.1007/s12130-006-1023-5

Bellifemine, F., Caire, G., Poggi, A., & Rimassa, G. (2008). JADE: A software framework for developing multi-agent applications: Lessons learned. *Information and Software Technology Journal, 50,* 10–21. doi:10.1016/j.infsof.2007.10.008

Belzarena, P., Bermolen, P., & Casas, P. (2010). End-to-end quality of service-based admission control using the fictitious network analysis. *Computer Communications, 33,* S157–S166. doi:10.1016/j.comcom.2010.04.024

Bergenti, F., Rossi, L., & Tomaiuolo, M. (2009). Towards automated trust negotiation in MAS. In *Proceedings of WOA 2009.* Parma, Italy: WOA.

Berry, M. J. A., & Linoff, G. S. (2004). *Data mining techniques: For marketing, sales, and customer relationship management* (2nd ed.). Indianapolis, IN: Wiley Publishing.

Betz, C. T. (2007). *Architecture and patterns for IT service management, resource planning, and governance: Making shoes for the cobbler's children: Making shoes for the cobbler's children.* San Francisco: Morgan Kaufmann Publishers Inc.

Bi, J., Zhu, Z., Tian, R., & Wang, Q. (2010). *Dynamic provisioning modeling for virtualized multi-tier applications in cloud data center.* Paper presented at the Cloud Computing (CLOUD). New York, NY.

Bistarelli, S., Montanari, U., & Rossi, F. (1997). Semiring-based constraint satisfaction and optimization. *Journal of the ACM, 44*(2), 201–236. doi:10.1145/256303.256306

Bitner, M. J., Brown, S. W., & Meuter, M. L. (2000). Technology infusion in service encounters. *Journal of the Academy of Marketing Services, 28*(1), 138–149. doi:10.1177/0092070300281013

Blake, M. B., Cummings, D. J., Bansal, A., & Bansal, S. K. (2012). Workflow composition of service level agreements for web services. Elsevier Science Publishers B. V., 234-244.

Bleistein, S. J., Cox, K., & Verner, J. (2006). Validating strategic alignment of organizational IT requirements using goal modeling and problem diagrams. *Journal of Systems and Software, 79*(3), 362–378. doi:10.1016/j.jss.2005.04.033

Bordini, R. H. (2009). *Multi-agent programming: Languages, tools and applications.* Berlin, Germany: Springer.

Borec, T. (2012, October 2). *EU: What are eservices?* Retrieved November 4, 2013, from http://ebiz.pwc.com/2012/10/eu-what-are-eservices/

Bose, R. J. C., & van der Aalst, W. (2010). Trace alignment in process mining: Opportunities for process diagnostics. In *Business process management* (pp. 227–242). Berlin: Springer. doi:10.1007/978-3-642-15618-2_17

Botti, V., & Boggino, A. C. (2008). *ANEMONA - A multi-agent methodology for holonic manufacturing systems.* London: Springer-Verlag.

Boubeta-Puig, J., Ortiz, G., & Medina-Bulo, I. (2014). A model-driven approach for facilitating user-friendly design of complex event patterns. *Expert Systems with Applications, 41*(2), 445–456. doi:10.1016/j.eswa.2013.07.070

Bowman, W. A. (1996). Maximum ground level concentrations with downwash: The urban stability mode. *Journal of the Air & Waste Management Association, 46,* 615–620. doi:10.1080/10473289.1996.10467495

Boyd, D. M., & Ellison, N. B. (2007). Social network sites: Definition, history, and scholarship. *Journal of Computer-Mediated Communication, 13*(1), 210–230. doi:10.1111/j.1083-6101.2007.00393.x

Boyne, G. A. (2002). Public and private management: What's the difference? *Journal of Management Studies, 39*(1), 97–122. doi:10.1111/1467-6486.00284

Brandt, E. (2007). How tangible mock-ups support design collaboration. *Knowledge, Technology & Policy, 20*(3), 179–192. doi:10.1007/s12130-007-9021-9

Bredies, K., Chow, R., & Joost, G. (2010). Addressing use as design: A comparison of constructivist design approaches. *The Design Journal, 13*(2), 156–179. doi:10.2752/175470710X12735884220853

Breidbach, C. F., Kolb, D. G., & Srinivasan, A. (2013). Connectivity in service systems: Does technology-enablement impact the ability of a service system to co-create value? *Journal of Service Research.* doi:10.1177/1094670512470869

Brogan, C. (2011). *An insider's guide to social media etiquette.* Retrieved July 1, 2012, from http://www.chrisbrogan.com/socialmediaetiquette/, ChrisBrogan.com. 24 February.

Brooks, J. F. (1995). *The mythical man-month: Essays on software engineering* (2nd ed.). Chicago: Addison Wesley Longman, Inc.

Buera, F. J., & Kaboski, J. P. (2012). The rise of the service economy. *The American Economic Review, 102*(6), 2540. doi:10.1257/aer.102.6.2540

Buller, W. (2008). Learning from e-business. In *The e-revolution and post compulsory education: Using e-business models to deliver quality education.* New York: Routledge.

Burgess, C. (2012). *The rise of the employee brand.* Retrieved July 1, 2012, from http://www.business-2community.com/branding/the-rise-of-the-employee-brand-0140637

Burstien, M. et al. (2005). A semantic Web services architecture. *IEEE Internet Computing*, 9(5), 72–81. doi:10.1109/MIC.2005.96

Buskens, V. (1995). *Social networks and the effect of reputation on cooperation*. The ISCORE discussion papers. Retrieved April 1, 2013, from http://www.uu.nl/SiteCollectionImages/Fac_SW/SOC/Iscore%20Papers/IscorePaper42_Buskens1995.pdf

Buti, A. L., Eakins, D., Fussell, H., Kunkel, L. E., Kudura, A., & Mccarty, D. (2013). Clinician attitudes, social norms and intentions to use a computer-assisted intervention. *Journal of Substance Abuse Treatment*, 44(4), 433. doi:10.1016/j.jsat.2012.08.220 PMID:23021495

Büttcher, S., Clarke, C. L., & Cormack, G. V. (2010). *Information retrieval: Implementing and evaluating search engines*. Cambridge, MA: MIT Press.

Buyya, R., Broberg, J., & Goscinski, A. M. (2011). *Cloud computing: Principles and paradigms*. New York: Wiley. doi:10.1002/9780470940105

Canadi, I., Barford, P., & Sommers, J. (2012). Revisiting broadband performance. In *Proceedings of the 2012 ACM Conference on Internet Measurement Conference* (pp. 273-286). New York: ACM.

Capozzi, C. (2013). *Business model vs. revenue model*. Retrieved July 1, 2012, from http://www.ehow.com/info_7760925_business-model-vs-revenue-model.html

Cardellini, V., Colajanni, M., & Yu, P. S. (1999). Dynamic load balancing on web-server systems. *IEEE Internet Computing*, 3(3), 28–39. doi:10.1109/4236.769420

Carlson, N. (2010, March 5). At last – The full story of how Facebook was founded. *Business Insider*.

Carr, P., May, T., & Stewart, S. (2012). *Australia's trusted infrastructure-as-a-service cloud provider market 2012*. Retrieved November 28, 2012, from http://www.longhausshop.com/reports/single-user-online-version-1.html

Carrera, P., & Caballero, A., & Muã'Oz, D. (2012). Futureâ€ oriented emotions in the prediction of bingeâ€ drinking intention and expectation: the role of anticipated and anticipatory emotions. *Scandinavian Journal of Psychology*, 53(3), 273–279. doi:10.1111/j.1467-9450.2012.00948.x PMID:22448916

Carstensen, J., Morgentha, J., & Golden, B. (2012). *Cloud computing assessing the risks*. Ely: IT Governance Publishing.

Carte, T. A., Schwarzkopf, A. B., Shaft, T. M., & Zmud, R. W. (2005). Advanced business intelligence at cardinal health. *MIS Quarterly Executive*, 4(4), 413–424.

Casillas, J., & Martínez-López, F. J. (2009). Mining uncertain data with multiobjective genetic fuzzy systems to be applied in consumer behaviour modelling. *Journal of Expert Systems with Applications*, 36(2), 1645–1659. doi:10.1016/j.eswa.2007.11.035

Castellani, A. P., Gheda, M., Bui, N., & Rossi, M. (2011). Web services for the internet of things through CoAP and EXI. In *Proceedings of IEEE International Conference on Communications Workshops*. IEEE.

Caudle, S. L., Gorr, W. L., & Newcomer, K. E. (1991). Key information systems management issues. *Management Information Systems Quarterly*, 15(2), 171–188. doi:10.2307/249378

Cauros, A. (2003). *Innovation change theory and the acceptance of new technologies: A literature review*. Retrieved on the 18 of June 2013, from www.http://paperecor.mpg.de/evo/discussion paper

Chaffey, D. (2009). *E-Business and E-Commerce Management: Strategy, Implementation and Practice* (4th ed.). Harlow, England: Prentice Hall.

Chaffey, D. (2011). *Business Information Management* (2nd ed.). Harlow, England: Prentice Hall.

Chandy, K. M., & Schulte, W. R. (2010). *Event processing: Designing IT systems for agile companies*. New York: McGraw-Hill.

Chang, A. M., & Kannan, P. (2008). *Leveraging web 2.0 in government*. IBM Centre for the Business of Government.

Chappell, C., & Feindt, S. (2000). Analysis of e-commerce practice in SMEs. *Communications and Strategies*, 37(1), 49–70.

Chard, K., Caton, S., Rana, O., & Bubendorfer, K. (2010). Social cloud: Cloud computing in social networks. In *Proceedings of 2010 IEEE 3rd International Conference on Cloud Computing* (pp. 99-106). Miami, FL: IEEE.

Charmaz, K. (2006). *Constructing grounded theory: A practical guide* (2nd ed.). London, UK: Sage.

Chaudhuri, S., Dayal, U., & Narasayya, V. (2011). An overview of business intelligence technology. *Communications of the ACM, 54*(8), 88–98. doi:10.1145/1978542.1978562

Chen, D. (2012). Modern service industry calls for discipline construction services. *China University Teaching,* (6), 29-31.

Chen, L., Yang, G., Wang, D., & Zhang, Y. (2010). WordNet-powered web services discovery using kernel-based similarity matching mechanism. In *Proceedings of Service Oriented System Engineering (SOSE), 2010 Fifth IEEE International Symposium on* (pp. 64-68). IEEE.

Chen, S., Nepal, S., & Liu, R. (2011). Secure connectivity for intra-cloud and inter-cloud communication. In *Proceedings of International Conference on Parallel Processing Workshops* (pp. 154 - 159). Taipei, Taiwan: Elsevier.

Chen, Z., Deng, C., & Lu, Y. (2007). Classification and analysis of mobile services and adoption models. *Statistics and Decision,* (21), 57-60.

Cheng, H.-H., & Huang, S.-W. (2013). Exploring antecedents and consequence of online group-buying intention: An extended perspective on theory of planned behavior. *International Journal of Information Management, 33*(1), 185–198. doi:10.1016/j.ijinfomgt.2012.09.003

Cheng, P.-Y., Hsu, P.-K., & Chiou, W.-B. (2012). Undergraduates' intentions to take examinations for professional certification: Examinations of four competing models. *Asia Pacific Education Review, 13*(4), 691–700. doi:10.1007/s12564-012-9229-6

Chieu, T. C., Mohindra, A., Karve, A. A., & Segal, A. (2009). *Dynamic scaling of web applications in a virtualized cloud computing environment.* Paper presented at the e-Business Engineering, 2009. New York, NY.

China Academy of Telecommunicatoin Research of MIIT. (2012). *Cloud computing white paper.* Beijing: China Academy of Telecommunicatoin Research of MIIT.

China Internet Network Information Center. (2013). *The 32nd China internet development statistics report.* Retrieved July 19, 2013, from www.cnnic.cn

China Internet Watch. (2013). *The story of China's biggest social network: Qzone.* Retrieved September 15, 2013, from http://www.chinainternetwatch.com/category/social-media/

China Mobile. (2012). *Annual report 2012.* Retrieved July 12, 2013, from http://www.chinamobileltd.com/en/global/home.php

China Mobile. (2013). *Business review.* Retrieved July 10, 2013, from http://www.chinamobileltd.com/en/business/business.php

Chorlton, K., Conner, M., & Jamson, S. (2012). Identifying the psychological determinants of risky riding: An application of an extended theory of planned behaviour. *Accident; Analysis and Prevention, 49,* 142. doi:10.1016/j.aap.2011.07.003 PMID:23036391

Chou, W. (2002). Inside SSL: The secure sockets layer protocol. *IT Professional, 4*(4), 47–52. doi:10.1109/MITP.2002.1046644

Chow, T. T. (2004). Energy modelling of district cooling system for new urban development. *Energy and Building, 36*(11), 1153–1162. doi:10.1016/j.enbuild.2004.04.002

Chukmol, U., Benharkat, A. N., & Amghar, Y. (2008). Enhancing web service discovery by using collaborative tagging system. In *Proceedings of Next Generation Web Services Practices* (pp. 54–59). IEEE. doi:10.1109/NWeSP.2008.29

Chung, J.-Y., Lin, K., & Mathieu, R. G. (2003). Guest editors' introduction: Web services computing—Advancing software interoperability. *Computer, 36*(10), 35–37. doi:10.1109/MC.2003.1236469

Church, P. E. (1949). Dilution of waste stack gases in the atmosphere. *Industrial & Engineering Chemistry, 41,* 2753–2756. doi:10.1021/ie50480a022

Chwelos, P., Benbasat, I., & Dexter, A. S. (2001). Empirical test of an EDI adoption model. *Information Systems Research, 12*(3), 304–321. doi:10.1287/isre.12.3.304.9708

Ciancetta, F., D'Apice, B., Landi, C., & Pelvio, A. (2007). *Mobile sensor network architecture for environmental monitoring.* Retrieved from http://www.imeko.org/publications/tc19-2007/IMEKO-TC19-2007-064.pdf

Cisco. (2003). *Designing VPN security.* Cisco Press.

Cisco. (2007). *Cisco router and security device manager.* Retrieved July 30, 2013, from http://www.cisco.com/en/US/prod/collateral/routers/ps5318/product_data_sheet0900aecd800fd118.html

Cisco. (2012). *SSL VPN configuration guide* (Cisco IOS release 15M&T). Cisco Press.

Cohen, R., & Kaempfer, G. (2000). On the cost of virtual private networks. *IEEE/ACM Transactions on Networking, 8*(6), 775–784. doi:10.1109/90.893873

Comodo Group. (2013). *The virtual kiosk.* Retrieved April 26, 2013, from http://help.comodo.com/topic-72-1-451-4738-The--Virtual-Kiosk.html

Computenext. (2013). *What is Cloud Service Brokerage?* Retrieved 9 8, 2013, from https://www.computenext.com/cloud-service-brokerage/

Connell, B. (2008). What is service-oriented architecture (SOA)? *SearchSOA.* Retrieved April 30, 2013, from http://searchsoa.techtarget.com/definition/service-oriented-architecture

Contos, B. T., Hunt, S., & Derodeff, C. (2007). *Physical and logical security convergence: Powered by enterprise security management.* Burlington, MA: Syngress Publishing.

Cooper, A. (1999). *The inmates are running the asylum: Why high tech products drive us crazy and how to restore the sanity.* Indianapolis, IN: SAMS. doi:10.1007/978-3-322-99786-9_1

Corchado, J. M., Bajo, J., de Paz, Y., & Tapia, D. I. (2008). Intelligent environment for monitoring Alzheimer patients, agent technology for health care. *Decision Support Systems, 44,* 382–396. doi:10.1016/j.dss.2007.04.008

Cormode, G., & Krishnamurthy, B. (2008). Key differences between web 1.0 and web 2.0. *First Monday, 13*(6), 2. doi:10.5210/fm.v13i6.2125

Coronado-Garcia, L. C., & Perez-Leguizamo, C. (2011). A mission-critical certification authority architecture for high reliability and response time. *International Journal of Critical Computer-Based Systems,* 6-24.

Coronel, C., Morris, S., & Rob, P. (2013). *Database Systems: Design, Implementation, and Management* (10th ed.). Boston: Course Technology, Cengage Learning.

Costa, P., Migliavacca, M., Pietzuch, P., & Wolf, A. L. (2012). NaaS: Network-as-a-service in the cloud. In *Proceedings of the 2nd USENIX Conference on Hot Topics in Management of Internet, Cloud, and Enterprise Networks and Services, Hot-ICE.* Berkeley, CA: USENIX Association.

Creotivo. (2013). *100 Social Networking Statistics & Facts for 2012.* Retrieved 9 24, 2013, from http://visual.ly/100-social-networking-statistics-facts-2012

Creswell, J. W. (2009). *Research design: Qualitative, quantitative, and mixed methods approaches* (3rd ed.). Thousand Oaks, CA: Sage. doi:10.1037/e599802009-001

Cummins, F. A. (2009). *Building the agile enterprise: With SOA, BPM and MBM.* San Francisco: Morgan Kaufmann Publishers Inc.

Currie, W. L., & Parikh, M. A. (2006). Value creation in web services: An integrative model. *The Journal of Strategic Information Systems, 15*(2), 153–174. doi:10.1016/j.jsis.2005.10.001

Czepiel, J. A. (1990). Service encounters and service relationships: Implications for research. *Journal of Business Research, 20*(1), 13–21. doi:10.1016/0148-2963(90)90038-F

Da, Z., Bo, C., Yang, Z., & Junliang, C. (2010). Future service provision: Towards a flexible hybrid service supporting platform. In *Proceedings of Services Computing Conference (APSCC),* (pp. 226 -233). IEEE.

Dadashzadeh, M. (2010). Social media in government: From eGovernment to eGovernance. *Journal of Business & Economics Research, 8*(11), 81–86.

Daft, R. L., Lengel, R. H., & Trevino, L. K. (1987). Message equivocality, media selection, and manager performance: Implications for information systems. *Management Information Systems Quarterly, 11*(3), 355. doi:10.2307/248682

Daigneau, R. (2011). *Service design patterns - Fundamental design solutions for SOAP/WSDL and RESTful web services.* Reading, MA: Addison-Wesley Professional.

Damanpour, F. (1987). The adoption of technological, administrative, and ancillary innovations: Impact of organizational factors. *Journal of Management, 13*(4), 675–688. doi:10.1177/014920638701300408

Dan, A., Davis, D., Kearney, R., Keller, A., King, R., Kuebler, D., & Youssef, A. (2004). Web services on demand: WSLA-driven automated management. *IBM Systems Journal, 43*(1), 136–158. doi:10.1147/sj.431.0136

Darozdova, M. (2008). *New business model of educational institutions*. Retrieved March 3, 2013 from www.custom. kbbark.c2/e%2Bm/0Ldrozdova.pdf

Dasgupta, D., & Dasgupta, R. (2010). *Social networks using web 2.0, part 2: Social network as a service (SNaaS)*. Retrieved from http://www.ibm.com/developerworks/webservices/library/ws-socialpart2/index.html?ca=drs

David, C. L. (2012). *Event processing for business: Organizing the real-time enterprise*. Hoboken, NJ: Wiley.

Davies, J. (2011). *Implementing SSL / TLS using cryptography and PKI*. Hoboken, NJ: John Wiley & Sons.

Davis, F. D. (1989). Perceived usefulness, perceived ease of use, and user acceptance of information technology. *Management Information Systems Quarterly, 13*(1), 319–340. doi:10.2307/249008

Davis, F., Bagazzi, R., & Warsaw, R. (1989). User acceptance of computer technology: A comparison of two theoretical models. *Management Science, 35*, 982–1003. doi:10.1287/mnsc.35.8.982

Davis, J. (2009). *Open source SOA*. Manning Publications.

Dayananda, S. M., & Kumar, A. (2012). Architecture for inter-cloud services using IPSec VPN. In *Proceedings of Advanced Computing & Communication Technologies (ACCT), 2012 Second International Conference* (pp. 463-467). Rohtak: IEEE Computer Society.

De Capua, C., Meduri, A., & Morello, R. (2010). Smart ECG measurement system based on web-service-oriented architecture for telemedicine applications. *IEEE Transactions on Instrumentation and Measurement, 59*(10), 2530–2538. doi:10.1109/TIM.2010.2057652

de Kool, D., & van Wamelen, J. (2008). Web 2.0: A new basis for e-government? In *Proceedings of the 3rd International Conference on Information & Communication Technologies: From Theory to Applications (ICTTA 2008)*. ICTTA.

De Meo, P., Quattrone, G., & Ursino, D. (2008). A decision support system for designing new services tailored to citizen profiles in a complex and distributed e-government scenario. *Data & Knowledge Engineering, 67*, 161–184. doi:10.1016/j.datak.2008.06.005

De Reuver, M. (2009). *Governing mobile service innovation in co-evolving value-network*. Infrastructure Systems & Services. Next Generation Infrastructures Foundation.

De, P., Chodhury, P., & Choudhury, S. (2010). A framework for performance analysis of client/server based SOA and P2P SOA. In *Proceeedings of International Conference on Computer and Network Technology ICCNT'10*, (pp. 79-83). ICCNT.

Deakin, M., Lombardi, P., & Cooper, I. (2011). The IntelCities community of practice: The capacity-building, co-design, evaluation and monitoring of eGov services. *Journal of Urban Technology, 18*(2), 13–38. doi:10.1080/10630732.2011.601107

Deitel, H. M., Deitel, P. J., DuWadt, B., & Trees, L. (2004). *Web Services: A technical Introduction*. Upper Saddle River, NJ: Prentice Hall.

Delen, D., & Demirkan, H. (2012). Data, information and Anlytics as services, available online. *Decision Support Systems*. doi: doi:10.1016/j.dss.2012.05.044 PMID:23552280

Demirkan, H., & Delen, D. (2013). Leveraging the capabilities of service-oriented decision support systems: Putting analytics and big data in cloud. *Decision Support Systems, 55*(1), 412–421. doi:10.1016/j.dss.2012.05.048

Denaro, G., Pezze, M., Tosi, D., & Schilling, D. (2006). Towards self-adaptive service-oriented architectures. In *Proceedings of 2006 workshop on Testing, Analysis, and Verification of Web Services and Applications* (pp. 10 – 16). New York: ACM.

DePietro, R., Wiarda, E., & Fleischer, M. (1990). *The context for change: Organization, technology and environment*. Lexington, MA: Lexington Books.

Dewar, R. D., & Dutton, J. E. (1986). The adoption of radical and incremental innovations: An empirical analysis. *Management Science, 32*(11), 1422–1433. doi:10.1287/mnsc.32.11.1422

Di Martino, B. (2009). Semantic web services discovery based on structural ontology matching. *International Journal of Web and Grid Services*, 5(1), 46–65. doi:10.1504/IJWGS.2009.023868

Didarloo, A. R., Shojaeizadeh, D., Gharaaghaji, R., Habibzadeh, H., Niknami, S., & Pourali, R. (2012). Prediction of self-management behavior among Iranian women with type 2 diabetes: Application of the theory of reasoned action along with self-efficacy (ETRA). *Iranian Red Crescent Medical Journal*, 14(2), 86–95. PMID:22737561

Diedrich, A., Terrados, J., Arroyo, N. L., & Balaguer, P. (2013). Modeling the influence of attitudes and beliefs on recreational boaters' use of buoys in the Balearic Islands. *Ocean and Coastal Management*, 78, 112. doi:10.1016/j.ocecoaman.2013.02.027

Dierks, T., & Rescorla, E. (2008). *The transport layer security (TLS) protocol version 1.2.* Retrieved June 18, 2013, from http://datatracker.ietf.org/doc/rfc5246/?include_text=1

Diewert, W. E. (2012). Afriat's theorem and some extensions to choice under uncertainty. *The Economic Journal*, 122(560), 305–331. doi:10.1111/j.1468-0297.2012.02504.x

Dijkman, R., & Van Gorp, P. (2011). BPMN 2.0 execution semantics formalized as graph rewrite rules. In *Business process modeling notation* (pp. 16–30). Berlin: Springer. doi:10.1007/978-3-642-25160-3

DIR. Texas. (2012). *Datacenter service: Capgemini contract.* Retrieved 25 June, 2013, from http://www.dir.texas.gov/SiteCollectionDocuments/DCS/_CAP/Exhibit%202/CAP_Exhibit%202.1_Multisourcing%20Service%20Integrator%20SOW_20111228.pdf

Dixon, W. J., & Mood, A. M. (1946). The statistical sign test. *Journal of the American Statistical Association*, 41(236), 557–566. doi:10.1080/01621459.1946.10501898 PMID:20279351

Djajadiningrat, J. P., Gaver, W. W., & Fres, J. W. (2000). Interaction relabeling and extreme characters. In *Proceedings of the Conference on Designing Interactive Systems Processes, Practices, Methods, and Techniques - DIS '00* (pp. 66–71). New York: ACM Press.

Dong, D., Sun, L., & Sun, Z. (2014). Web Services in China. In Z. Sun, & J. Yearwood, Demand-Driven Web Services: Theory, Technologies and Applications. IGI-Global.

Dong, T.-P., Cheng, N.-C., & Wu, Y.-C. J. (2013). A study of the social networking website service in digital content: industries: The Facebook case in Taiwan. *Computers in Human Behavior.* doi:http://dx.doi.org/10.1016/j.chb.2013.07.037

Dong, L., & Tomlin, B. (2012). Managing disruption risk: The interplay between operations and insurance. *Management Science*, 58(10), 1898–1915. doi:10.1287/mnsc.1120.1524

Drejer, I. (2004). Indentifying innovation in surveys of services: A Schumpeterian perspective. *Research Policy*, 33, 551–652. doi:10.1016/j.respol.2003.07.004

Dreyfus, H. L. (1991). *Being-in-the-world : A commentary on Heidegger's Being and Time, division I.* Cambridge, MA: MIT Press.

Duncan, G. (1996). Waiting with Beta'd breath. *TidBITS*, 328.

Dunkel, J., Fernández, A., Ortiz, R., & Ossowski, S. (2011). Event-driven architecture for decision support in traffic management systems. *Expert Systems with Applications*, 38(6), 6530–6539. doi:10.1016/j.eswa.2010.11.087

Durfee, E. H. (1999). Distributed problem solving and planning. In G. Weiss (Ed.), *Multiagent systems: A modern approach to distributed artificial intelligence* (pp. 121–164). Cambridge, MA: MIT Press.

Dustdar, S., & Schreiner, W. (2005). A survey on web services composition. *International Journal Web and Grid Services*, 1(1), 1–30. doi:10.1504/IJWGS.2005.007545

Dutta, S., & Pinder, A. J. (2011). *Service intelligence and performance management - Moving beyond the rearview mirror.* Retrieved Mars 19, 2013, from http://www.mercedsystems.com/m2/resource_library/Aberdeen%20Group%20Whitepaper%20-%20Service%20Intelligence%20and%20Performance%20Management.pdf

Edge, M. E., & Falcone Sampaio, P. R. (2009). A survey of signature based methods for financial fraud detection. *Computers & Security*, 28(6), 381–394. doi:10.1016/j.cose.2009.02.001

Edge, M. E., & Falcone Sampaio, P. R. (2012). The design of FFML: A rule-based policy modelling language for proactive fraud management in financial data streams. *Expert Systems with Applications*, *39*(11), 9966–9985. doi:10.1016/j.eswa.2012.01.143

Edirisuriya, A., & Johannesson, P. (2009). On the alignment of business models and process models. In *Business process management workshops* (Vol. 17, pp. 68–79). Berlin: Springer. doi:10.1007/978-3-642-00328-8_7

Eggers, W. D. (2007). *Government 2.0: Using technology to improve education, cut red tape, reduce gridlock, and enhance democracy*. Rowan & Littlefield Publishers, Manhattan Institute.

Ehn, P. (1988). *Work-oriented design of computer artifacts*. Stockholm: Arbejdslivscentrum.

Ehn, P., & Kyng, M. (1991). Cardboard computers: Mocking-it-up or hands-on the future. In J. M. Greenbaum, & M. Kyng (Eds.), *Design at work: Cooperative design of computer systems* (pp. 169–195). Hoboken, NJ: Lawrence Erlbaum Associates.

Eisenhauer, M. R. (2009). A development platform for integrating wireless devices and sensors into ambient intelligence systems. In *Proceedings of Sensor, Mesh and Ad Hoc Communications and Networks Workshops*. IEEE. doi:10.1109/SAHCNW.2009.5172913

Eldon, E. (2008). *2008 growth puts Facebook in better position to make money*. San Francisco: VentureBeat.

Elgazzar, K., Aboelfotoh, M., Martin, P., & Hassanein, H. (2012). Ubiquitous health monitoring using mobile web services. *Procedia Computer Science*, *10*, 332–339. doi:10.1016/j.procs.2012.06.044

Erden, Z., & Von Krogh, G. (2012). Knowledge sharing in an online community of volunteers: The role of community munificence. *European Management Review*, *9*(4), 213–227. doi:10.1111/j.1740-4762.2012.01039.x

EsperTech Inc. (2013). *Esper - Complex event processing*. Retrieved September 19, 2013, from http://esper.codehaus.org/

Estrin, J. (2009). *Closing the innovation gap: Reigniting the spark of creativity in a global economy*. New York: McGraw-Hill.

Etzion, O., & Niblett, P. (2010). *Event processing in action*. Stamford, CT: Manning.

European Commission (EC). (2010). *Energy efficiency in Europe: EU adopted the energy performance of buildings directive 2010/31/EU (EPBD)*. Brussels: EC.

European Commission (EC). (2010b, May 19). The directive 2010/31/EU on the energy performance of buildings. *Official Journal of the European Union*.

Evermann, J. (2005). Towards a cognitive foundation for knowledge representation. *Information Systems Journal*, *15*, 147–178. doi:10.1111/j.1365-2575.2005.00193.x

Fabian, B., Kunz, S., & Konnegen, M., MüLler, S., & GüNther, O. (2012). Access control for semantic data federations in industrial product-lifecycle management. *Computers in Industry*, *63*(9), 930–940. doi:10.1016/j.compind.2012.08.015

Ferber, J., Gutknecht, O., & Michel, F. (2004). From agents to organizations: An organizational view of multi-agent systems. In *Agent-oriented software engineering IV* (pp. 214–230). Berlin, Germany: Springer. doi:10.1007/978-3-540-24620-6_15

Ferguson, B. (2012). *CompTIA network+ review guide exam: N10-005*. Hoboken, NJ: John Wiley & Sons.

Fernandez-Luque, F. J., Pérez, D., Martínez, F., Domènech, G., Navarrete, I., Zapata, J., & Ruiz, R. (2013). An energy efficient middleware for an ad-hoc AAL wireless sensor network. *Ad Hoc Networks*, *11*(3), 907–925. doi:10.1016/j.adhoc.2012.10.003

Fichman, R. G. (2000). The diffusion and assimilation of information technology innovations. In R. Zmud (Ed.), *Framing the domains of IT management: Projecting the future through the past*. Pinnaflex Publishing.

Finn, A., Vredevoort, H., Lownds, P., & Flynn, D. (2012). *Microsoft private cloud computing*. Hoboken, NJ: John Wiley & Sons.

FIPA. (2000, August 28). *FIPA agent management specification*. Retrieved May 15, 2013, from http://www.fipa.org: http://www.fipa.org/specs/fipa00023/XC00023H.html

FIPA. (2013). *FIPA specifications*. Retrieved November 18, 2013 from http:www.fipa.org

Firat, A. F., & Venkatesh, A. (1995). Liberatory post-modernism and the reenchantment of consumption. *The Journal of Consumer Research*, (3): 239–267. doi:10.1086/209448

Fisher, C. S. (1977). *Networks and places: Social relations in the urban setting*. New York: Free Press.

Focus Group. (2012). *Focus group on cloud computing technical report part 1*. Geneva: International Telecommunication Union.

Foner, L. (1997). Yenta: A multi-agent, referral-based matchmaking system. In *Proceedings of First International Conference on Autonomous Agents* (pp. 301-307). Marina del Rey, CA: ACM.

Fornara, N., & Colombetti, M. (2002). Operational specification of a commitment- based agent communication language. In *Proceedings of the 1ˢᵗ International Joint Conference on Autonomous Agents & MultiAgent Systems (AAMAS'2002)*, (pp. 536-542). Bologna, Italy: AAMAS.

Fortinet. (2013). *FortiOS™ handbook SSL VPN for FortiOS 5.0*. Fortinet.

Fountain, J. (2001). Paradoxes of public sector customer service. *Governance: An International Journal of Policy, Administration and Institutions*, *14*(1), 55–73. doi:10.1111/0952-1895.00151

Fox, G. C., Kamburugamuve, S., & Hartman, R. (2012). Architecture and measured characteristics of a cloud based internet of things API. In *Proceedings of International Conference on Collaboration Technologies and Systems CTS' 2012*, (pp. 6-12). CTS.

Foxall, G. R., Yan, J., Oliveira-Castro, J. M., & Wells, V. K. (2011). Brand-related and situational influences on demand elasticity. *Journal of Business Research*, *66*(1), 73. doi:10.1016/j.jbusres.2011.07.025

Franchi, E., & Poggi, A. (2011). Multi-agent systems and social networks. In M. Cruz-Cunha, G. D. Putnik, N. Lopes, P. Gonçalves, & E. Miranda (Eds.), *Business social networking: Organizational, managerial, and technological dimensions* (pp. 84–97). Hershey, PA: IGI Global. doi:10.4018/978-1-61350-168-9.ch005

Fremantle, P., Weerawarana, S., & Khalaf, R. (2002). Enterprise services. *Communications of the ACM*, *45*(10), 77–82. doi:10.1145/570907.570935

Fu, L., Yu, L., Chen, Y., & Qin, W. (2013). Overview on development trends of mobile internet 2012-2013. *China Internet*, (2), 1-7.

Fu, N., & Shi, Y. (2007). The comparative research on electronic services in China and the U.S. *Sci-Tech Information Development & Economy*, *17* (36), 133-134.

Fuglsang, L. (2010). Bricolage and invisible innovation in public service innovation. *Journal of Innovation Economics*, *5*(1), 67. doi:10.3917/jie.005.0067

Fujii, K., & Suda, T. (2005). Semantics-based dynamic service composition. *IEEE Journal on Selected Areas in Communications*, *23*(12), 2361–2372. doi:10.1109/JSAC.2005.857202

Fulk, J., & Steinfield, C. W. (1990). *Organizations and communication technology*. Newbury Park, CA: Sage Publications.

Füller, J., Mühlbacher, H., Matzler, K., & Jawecki, G. (2009). Consumer empowerment through internet-based co-creation. *Journal of Management Information Systems*, *26*(3), 71–102. doi:10.2753/MIS0742-1222260303

Future Summit Blog. (2008). *New business models: Get the world innovating for you for free*. Retrieved July 1, 2012, from http://www.futuresummit.org/blog/new-business-models-get-the-world-innovating-for-you-for-free/

Gallouj, F. (2002). *Innovation in the service economy*. Cheltenham, UK: Edward Elgar. doi:10.4337/9781843765370

Galloway, B., & Hancke, G. P. (2012). Introduction to industrial control networks. *Introduction to Industrial Control Networks*, *15*(2), 860–880.

Galluccio, L., Morabito, G., & Palazzo, S. (2011). On the potentials of object group localization in the internet of things. In *Proceedings of IEEE International Symposium on World of Wireless, Mobile and Multimedia Networks WoWMoM'2011*, (pp. 1-9). IEEE.

Gambetta, D. (2000). Can we trust trust? In D. Gambetta (Ed.), *Trust: Making and breaking cooperative relations* (pp. 213–237). Oxford, UK: Department of Sociology, University of Oxford.

Gartner. (2013). *Gartner IT glossary*. Retrieved September 14, 2013, from http://www.gartner.com/it-glossary/Web-services/

Gbola, O. (2013). *Students perceptions of e-registration at Ladoke Akintola University of Technology*. Nigeria: Ogbomoso.

Genesereth, M. R. (1997). An agent-based framework for interoperability. In J. M. Bradshaw (Ed.), *Software agents* (pp. 317–345). Cambridge, MA: MIT Press.

Genesereth, M. R., & Ketchpel, S. P. (1994). Software agents. *Communications of the ACM, 37*(7), 48–53. doi:10.1145/176789.176794

Gennari, J. H., Musen, M. M., Fergerson, R. W., Grosso, W. E., Crubezy, M., & Eriksson, H. et al. (2003). The evaluation of Protégé: An environment for knowledge based systems development. *International Journal of Human-Computer Studies, 58*, 89–123. doi:10.1016/S1071-5819(02)00127-1

Gentry, P. B. (2001). What is a VPN? *Information Security Technical Report, 6*(1), 15–22. doi:10.1016/S1363-4127(01)00103-0

George, G., & Bock, A. J. (2011). The business model in practice and its implications for entrepreneurship research. *Entrepreneurship Theory and Practice, 35*(1), 83–111. doi:10.1111/j.1540-6520.2010.00424.x

George, G., & Bock, A. J. (2012). *Models of opportunity: How entrepreneurs design firms to achieve the unexpected*. Cambridge, UK: Cambridge University Press. doi:10.1017/CBO9780511984815

Georgia, B. R. (2009). E-business education worldwide on the right track? *International Journal of Management, 8*(2).

Ghose, A. K., & Lê, L. K, H.-K., & Morrison, E. D. (2010). The business service representation language: A preliminary report. In Service modelling and representation techniques. Academic Press.

Gibson, M., Arnott, D., & Carlsson, S. (2004). Evaluating the intangible benefits of business intelligence: Review & research agenda. In *Proceeding of the Decision Support in an Uncertain and Complex World: The IFIP TC8/WG8.3 International Conference*, (pp. 295-305). Preto, Italy: IFIP.

Giddens, A. (1984). *The constitution of society: Outline of the theory of structuration*. Berkeley, CA: University of California Press.

Gisolfi, D. (2001). *Web services architect: Part 1*. Retrieved 7 14, 2013, from http://www.ibm.com/developerworks/library/ws-arc1/

Glaser, B. G., & Holton, J. (2005). Basic social processes, the grounded theory review. *International Journal of Grounded Theory Review, 4*(3), 1–27.

Gleeson, B., Lin, A., Heinanen, J., Armitage, G., & Malis, A. (2000). *A framework for IP based virtual private networks*. Retrieved March 26, 2013, from http://www.rfc-editor.org/rfc/rfc2764.txt

GNS3. (2013). *What is GNS3?* Retrieved June 5, 2013, from http://www.gns3.net/

Gold-Bernstein, B., & Ruh, W. (2004). *Enterprise integration: The essential guide to integration solutions*. Reading, MA: Addison-Wesley Professional.

Goldreich, O. (2004). Foundations of cryptography: Volume 2, basic applications. Cambridge, UK: Cambridge University Press.

Goldsack, P., Guijarro, J., Lain, A., Mecheneau, G., Murray, P., & Toft, P. (2003). *SmartFrog: Configuration and automatic ignition of distributed applications*. HP OVUA.

Goldsmith, J. R., & Friberg, L. T. (1976). Effects of air pollution on human health, air pollution. In *The effects of air pollution* (3rd ed.). New York: Academic Press.

Golicic, S. L., & Smith, C. D. (2013). A meta-analysis of environmentally sustainable supply chain management practices and firm performance. *Journal of Supply Chain Management, 49*(2), 78–95. doi:10.1111/jscm.12006

Google. (2013). *Traveling made simplier in 3D Google earth and maps*. Paper presented at the Google IO Developers Conference. San Francisco, CA.

Gopinath, G., & Chellammal, S. (2010). An approach to identify candidate services for semantic web service discovery. In Proceedings of Service-Oriented Computing and Applications (SOCA), (pp. 321-324). IEEE.

Gordijn, J., Soetendal, J., & Paalvast, E. (2005). VA3: Governance selection in value webs. In *Challenges of expanding internet: E-commerce, e-business, and e-government* (Vol. 189, pp. 17–31). Academic Press. doi:10.1007/0-387-29773-1_2

Gottschalk, K. e. (2001). *Web Services architecture overview. retrieved.* Retrieved July 15, 2009, from http://www.ibm.com/developerworks/webservices/library/w-ovr/

Gou, Q.-D., & Liu, Y.-H. (2012). Dynamic IPsec VPN architecture for private cloud services. In *Proceedings of 2012 International Conference on Wavelet Active Media Technology and Information Processing* (pp. 250-253). Sichuan, Canada: IEEE Xplore.

Gould, R., & Lee, K.-I. (2012). Predicting congregate meal program participation: Applying the extended theory of planned behavior. *International Journal of Hospitality Management, 31*(3), 828–836. doi:10.1016/j.ijhm.2011.09.019

Gov, U. S. A. (2002, December 17). *LAW 107–347.* Retrieved from http://frwebgate.access.gpo.gov/cgi-bin/getdoc.cgi?dbname=107_cong_public_laws&docid=f:publ347.107.pdf

Government, A. (2012). *Interacting with Government: Australians' use and satisfaction with e-government services—2011.* Retrieved 11 11, 2013, from http://www.finance.gov.au/publications/interacting-with-government-2011/index.html

Greenwood, D., & Calisti, M. (2004). Engineering web service-agent integration. In *Proceedings of 2004 IEEE International Conference on Systems, Man and Cybernetics* (Vol. 2, pp. 1918-1925). The Hague, The Netherlands: IEEE.

Gregory, J. (2003). Scandinavian approaches to participatory design. *International Journal of Engineering Education, 19*(1), 62–74.

Gregory, R., Prifling, M., & Beck, R. (2009). The role of cultural intelligence for the emergence of negotialted culture in IT offshore outsourcing projects. *Information Technology & People, 22,* 223–241. doi:10.1108/09593840910981428

Griepentrog, B. K., Harold, C. M., Holtz, B. C., Klimoski, R. J., & Marsh, S. M. (2012). Integrating social identity and the theory of planned behavior: Predicting withdrawal from an organizational recruitment process. *Personnel Psychology, 65*(4), 723–753. doi:10.1111/peps.12000

Griffiths, R. F. (1994). Errors in the use of the Briggs parameterization for atmospheric dispersion coefficients. *Atmospheric Environment, 28*(17), 2861–2865. doi:10.1016/1352-2310(94)90086-8

Groen, B. A. C., & Wouters, M. J. F. (2012). Why do employees take more initiatives to improve their performance after co-developing performance measures? A field study. *Management Accounting Research, 23*(2), 120–141. doi:10.1016/j.mar.2012.01.001

Grönroos, C. (1990). *Service management and marketing: Managing the moments of truth in service competition.* Lexington, MA: Lexington Books.

Grubbs, F. E. (1969). Procedures for detecting outlying observations in samples. *Technometrics, 11*(1), 1–21. doi:10.1080/00401706.1969.10490657

Gubbi, J., Buyya, R., Marusic, S., & Palaniswami, M. (2013). Internet of things (IoT), a vision, architectural elements, and future directions. *Future Generation Computer Systems, 29*(7), 1645–1660. doi:10.1016/j.future.2013.01.010

Guo, L., Guo, Y., & Tian, X. (2010). *IC cloud: A design space for composable cloud computing.* Paper presented at the Cloud Computing (CLOUD). New York, NY.

Guo, R., Le, J., & Xia, X. (2005). Capability matching of web services based on OWL-S. In *Proceedings of Database and Expert Systems Applications* (pp. 653–657). IEEE.

Gupta, P., & Verma, A. (2012). Concept of VPN on cloud computing for elasticity by simple load balancing technique. *International Journal of Engineering and Innovative Technology,* 274-278.

Gupta, R. C. (1973). The Madhava-Gregory series. *Math. Ed, 7.*

Habib, I. (2008). Virtualization with KVM. *Linux Journal,* (166), 8.

Haerder, T., & Reuter, A. (1983). Principles of transaction-oriented database recovery. *ACM Computing Surveys,* (15): 287–317. doi:10.1145/289.291

Hagger, M. S., Lonsdale, A. J., Hein, V., Koka, A., Lintunen, T., & Pasi, H. et al. (2012). Predicting alcohol consumption and binge drinking in company employees: An application of planned behaviour and self-determination theories. *British Journal of Health Psychology, 17*(2), 379. doi:10.1111/j.2044-8287.2011.02043.x PMID:22106875

Haghighi, P. D., Burstein, F., Zaslavsky, A., & Arbon, P. (2013). Development and evaluation of ontology for intelligent decision support in medical emergency management for mass gatherings. *Decision Support Systems, 54*, 1192–1204. doi:10.1016/j.dss.2012.11.013

Hahne, E. L. (1991). Round-robin scheduling for max-min fairness in data networks. *IEEE Journal on Selected Areas in Communications, 9*(7), 1024–1039. doi:10.1109/49.103550

Hakes, W. (2012). *Big Data Analytics: The Revolution Has Just Begun*. Retrieved 10 20, 2013, from Analytics 2012 Conference: http://www.youtube.com/watch?v=ceeiUAmbfZk

Halitsky, J. (1989). A jet plume model for short stacks. *Journal of the Air Pollution Control Association, 39*(6), 856–858.

Haller, S., Karnouskos, S., & Schroth, C. (2009). The internet of things in an enterprise context. In J. Domingue, D. Fensel, & P. Traverso (Eds.), *Future internet – FIS 2008* (Vol. 5468, pp. 14–28). Berlin: Springer-Verlag. doi:10.1007/978-3-642-00985-3_2

Halpert, B. (2011). *Auditing Cloud Computing A Security and Privacy Guide*. Canada: John Wiley & Sons, Inc. doi:10.1002/9781118269091

Hamburg, I., & Zaharia, M. H. (2000). Tools for a participative computer aided modeling of flows in production. [Goshen, KY: Integrated Technology Systems.]. *Proceedings of, EDA2000*, 627–632.

Hamzeh, K., Pall, G. S., Verthein, W., Taarud, J., Little, W. A., & Zorn, G. (1999). *Point-to-point tunneling protocol (PPTP)*. The Internet Society.

Hansen, D., Shneiderman, B., & Smith, M. A. (2010). *Analyzing social media networks with NodeXL*. Morgan Kaufmann.

Hansen, T., & Risborg, M. S. N. (2012). Understanding consumer purchase of free-of cosmetics: A value-driven TRA approach. *Journal of Consumer Behaviour, 11*(6), 477–486. doi:10.1002/cb.1397

Hao, F., Lakshman, T. V., Mukherjee, S., & Song, H. (2010). Secure cloud computing with a virtualized network infrastructure. In *Proceedings of 2nd USENIX Conference on Hot Topics in Cloud Computing* (pp. 16-16). Boston, MA: USENIX.

Hardcastle, E. (2011). *Business information systems*. Elizabeth Hardcastle and Ventus publishing ApS.

Harding, C. (2011). *Cloud computing for business -The open group guide. Zaltbommel*. Van Haren Publishing.

Harris, J., & Henderson, A. (1999). A better mythology for system design. In *Proceedings of the SIGCHI Conference on Human Factors in Computing Systems the CHI is the Limit - CHI '99* (pp. 88–95). New York: ACM Press.

Haselmann, T., Thies, G., & Vossen, G. (2010). Looking into a REST-based universal API for database-as-a-service systems. In *Proceedings of IEEE Conf. on Commerce and Enterprise Computing CEC'10*, (pp. 17-20). IEEE.

Hata, H., Kamizuru, Y., Honda, A., Hashimoto, T., Shimizu, K., & Yao, H. (2010). Dynamic IP-VPN architecture for cloud computing. In *Proceedings of 8th Asia-Pacific Symposium on Information and Telecommunication Technologies* (pp. 1-5). Kuching: NTT Communications.

Havey, M. (2009). *CEP and SOA: Six letters are better than three*. Retrieved July 15, 2013, from http://www.packtpub.com/article/cep-complex-event-processing-soa-service-oriented-architecture

He, S., Guo, L., & Guo, Y. (2011). *Real time elastic cloud management for limited resources*.

Heidegger, M. (1967). *Sein und zeit*. Tübingen, Germany: M. Niemeyer.

Heinzelman, W., Murphy, A., Carvalho, H., & Perillo, M. (2004). Middleware to support sensor network applications. *IEEE Network, 18*(1), 6–14. doi:10.1109/MNET.2004.1265828

Henriksen, H. Z., & Mahnke, V. (2005). E-procurement adoption in the Danish public sector. *Scandinavian Journal of Information Systems, 17*(2), 85–106.

Henten, A. (2012). Innovations from the ICT-based service encounter. *Info, 14*(2), 42–56. doi:10.1108/14636691211204851

Hildebrandt, T., Mukkamala, R. R., & Slaats, T. (2011). Declarative modelling and safe distribution of health-care workflows. In *Proceedings of First International Symposium*. FHIES.

Hildebrandt, T., Mukkamala, R. R., & Slaats, T. (2011). Designing a cross-organizational case management system using dynamic condition response graphs. In *Proceedings of 15th International Enterprise Distributed Object Computing Conference*. Academic Press.

Hinge, K., Ghose, A. K., & Koliadis, G. (2009). Process seer: A tool for semantic effect annotation of business process models. In *Proceedings of 13th IEEE International eDoc Conference*. IEEE.

Hoesch-Klohe, K., Ghose, A. K., & Le, L.-S. (2010). Towards green business process management. In *Proceedings of the IEEE International Services Computing Conference*. IEEE.

Hofacker, C. F., Goldsmith, R. E., Bridges, E., & Swilley, E. (2007). E-services: A synthesis and research agenda. In H. Evanschitzky, & R. I. Gopalkrishnan (Eds.), *E-services: Opportunities and threats* (pp. 13–44). DUV. doi:10.1007/978-3-8350-9614-1_3

Höfer, C. N., & Karagiannis, G. (2011). Cloud computing services: Taxonomy and comparison. *Journal of Internet Services and Applications*, 81-94.

Hoffman, K. D. (2003). Marketing + MIS = E-Services. *Communications of the ACM, 46*(6), 53–55. doi:10.1145/777313.777340

Hogan, W. R., Cooper, G. F., Wagner, M. M., & Wallstrom, G. L. (2005). *An inverted Gaussian Plume model for estimating the location and amount of release of airborne agents from downwind atmospheric concentrations (RODS Technical Report)*. Pittsburgh, PA: Real Time Outbreak and Disease Surveillance Laboratory, University of Pittsburgh.

Holtzblatt, K. (2005). Customer-centered design for mobile applications. *Personal and Ubiquitous Computing, 9*(4), 227–237. doi:10.1007/s00779-004-0324-5

Hong, S., Nag, B. N., & Yao, D. Q. (2009). Improving e-trade auction volume by consortium. In V. Sugumaran (Ed.), *Distributed artificial intelligence, agent technology, and collaborative applications* (pp. 91–115). Hershey, PA: IGI Global.

Horling, B., & Lesser, V. (2005). A survey of multi-agent organizational paradigms. *The Knowledge Engineering Review, 19*(4), 281–316. doi:10.1017/S0269888905000317

Hornsby, A., & Leppanen, T. (2011). event.Hub: An event-driven information hub for mobile devices. In *Proceedings of the 8th International Conference on Ubiquitous Intelligence and Computing* (pp. 209-223). Banff, Canada: Springer-Verlag.

Howard, A. E. (2012). *Connecting with communities: How local government is using social media to engage with citizens*. ANZSOG Institute for Governance at the University of Canberra and Australian Centre of Excellence for Local Government.

Howden, N., Rönnquist, R., Hodgson, A., & Lucas, A. (2001). JACK intelligent agents – Summary of an agent infrastructure. In *Proceedings of 5th International Conference on Autonomous Agents*. Montreal, Canada: ACM.

Hsiao, D. K. (1992). Federated databases and systems: Part II --- A tutorial on their resource consolidation. *The VLDB Journal*, 285–310. doi:10.1007/BF01231702

Hsu, C. H. C., & Huang, S. (2012). An extension of the theory of planned behavior model for tourists. *Journal of Hospitality & Tourism Research (Washington, D.C.), 36*(3), 390–417. doi:10.1177/1096348010390817

Huang, C., Smith, P., & Sun, Z. (2014). Securing network for cloud services. In Z. Sun, & J. Yearwood, Demand Driven Wen Services. IGI-Global.

Huang, H., & Trauth, E. M. (2007). Cultural influences and globally distributed information systems development: Experience from Chinese IT professionals. In *Proceeding of the 2007 ACM SIGMIS CPR Conference on Computer Personnel Reaearch* (pp. 36-45). ACM.

Huang, S.-Y., Chang, C.-M., & Kuo, S.-R. (2013). User acceptance of mobile e-government services: An empirical study Government Information Quarterly,. *Vol.30(1), pp.33-44, pp.77-82.*

Huang, H. (2012). Push a variety of new ICT production for cloud computing. *Communications World Weekly, 9*(10), 33–34.

Huang, H.-C. (2012). Factors influencing intention to move into senior housing. *Journal of Applied Gerontology, 31*(4), 488–509. doi:10.1177/0733464810392225

Huberman, A. M., & Miles, M. B. (1994). Data management and analysis methods. In N. K. Denzin, & Y. S. Lincoln (Eds.), *Handbook of qualitative research* (pp. 428–444). Thousand Oaks, CA: Sage.

Huff, S. L., & Munro, M. C. (1989). Managing micro proliferation. *Journal of Information Systems Management*, 72-75.

Huhns, M. N., Singh, M. P., Burstein, M., Decker, K., & Durfee, K. E., Finin, … Zavafa, L. (2005). Research directions for service-oriented multiagent systems. *IEEE Internet Computing, 9*(6), 65–70. doi:10.1109/MIC.2005.132

Hurwitz, J., Kaufman, M., Halper, F., & Kirsch, D. (2012). *Hybrid cloud for dummies*. Hoboken, NJ: John Wiley & Sons.

Hu, W., Almansoori, A., Kannan, P. K., Azarm, S., & Wang, Z. (2012). Corporate dashboards for integrated business and engineering decisions in oil refineries: An agent-based approach. *Decision Support Systems, 52*(3), 729–741. doi:10.1016/j.dss.2011.11.019

Hyland, P. E., Mclaughlin, C. G., Boduszek, D., & Prentice, G. R. (2012). Intentions to participate in counselling among front-line, at-risk irish government employees: An application of the theory of planned behaviour. *British Journal of Guidance & Counselling, 40*(3), 279–299. doi:10.1080/03069885.2012.681769

IBM and Juniper Networks Solutions. (2009). *Website IBM and Juniper networks: Delivering solutions that transform your networking infrastructure.* Retrieved from ftp://public.dhe.ibm.com/common/ssi/ecm/en/jns03002usen/JNS03002USEN.PDF

ICWS. (2009). *ICWS2009.* Retrieved from http://conferences.computer.org/icws/2009/

Infrastructure, G. (2009). *GoGrid cloud hosting.*

INFSO D.4 Networked Enterprise & RFID INFSO G.2 Micro & Nanosystems. (2008). Internet of things in 2020. *Roadmap for the Future, 1*, 1-27.

Ioannidis, J. (2011). IPsec. In H. C. Tilborg, & S. Jajodia (Eds.), *Encyclopedia of cryptography and security* (pp. 635–638). New York: Springer US.

Irani, D. et al. (2011). Modeling unintended personal-information leakage from multiple online social networks. *Internet Computing, 15*, 13–19. doi:10.1109/MIC.2011.25

ITU-T. (2005). *ITU internet reports 2005: The internet of things.* Retrieved from http://www.itu.int/osg/spu/publications/internetofthings/

Jackson, L. (2009). *Leveraging business intelligence for healthcare providers* (Oracle White Paper). Redwood Shores, CA: Oracle Corporation.

JADE. (2013). *Jade software web site.* Retrieved November 18, 2013, from http://jade.tilab.com/

Jaffe, M., & Shine, T. (2011, April 19). *S&P's credibility under fire as agency issues US debt warning.* Retrieved Mars 25, 2013, from http://abcnews.go.com/Politics/standard-poors-credibility-fire-us-debt-warning/story?id=13407823

Jaha, A. A., Shatwan, F. B., & Ashibani, M. (2008). Proper virtual private network (VPN) solution. In *Proceedings of the Second International Conference on Next Generation Mobile Applications, Services and Technologies* (pp. 309-314). IEEE Computer Society.

Jain, R., Chiu, D.-M., & Hawe, W. (1998). A quantitative measure of fairness and discrimination for resource allocation in shared computer systems. In *Proceedings of CoRR.* CoRR.

James, J., & Clarke, R. (2010). Transforming the relationship between citizens and local councils using web 2.0 technologies. In H. Yeatman (Ed.), *The SInet 2010 eBook: Proceedings of the SInet 2009 conference.* University of Wollongong.

Jamil, D., & Zaki, H. (2011). Cloud computing security. *International Journal of Engineering Science and Technology, 3*, 4.

JBoss Community. (2013). *Drools fusion.* Retrieved November 13, 2010, from http://www.jboss.org/drools/drools-fusion.html

Jennings, N. R., Faratin, P., Lomuscio, A. R., Parsons, S., Sierra, C., & Wooldridge, M. (2001). Automated negotiation: Prospects, methods and challenges. *Group Decision and Negotiation, 10*(2), 199–215. doi:10.1023/A:1008746126376

Jennings, R. (2010). *Cloud computing with the Windows Azure platform.* Wrox.

Jeong, H. J., Kim, E. H., Suh, K. S., Hwang, W. T., Han, M. H., & Lee, H. K. (2005). Determination of the source rate released into the environment from a nuclear power plant. *Radiation Protection Dosimetry, 113*(3), 308–313. doi:10.1093/rpd/nch460 PMID:15687109

Jeyaraj, A., Rottman, J. W., & Lacity, M. C. (2006). A review of the predictors, linkages, and biases in IT innovation adoption research. *Journal of Information Technology, 21*(1), 1–23. doi:10.1057/palgrave.jit.2000056

Jiang, J. J., & Conrath, D. W. (1997). Semantic similarity based on corpus statistics and lexical taxonomy. In *Proceedings of International Conference on Research in Computational Linguistics* (pp. 19-33). Academic Press.

Jiang, S., Fang, L., & Huang, X. (2009). An idea of special cloud computing in forest pests control. *Lecture Notes in Computer Science, 5931*, 615–620. doi:10.1007/978-3-642-10665-1_61

Jin, D., Chai, K.-H., & Tan, K.-C. (2012). Organizational adoption of new service development tools. *Managing Service Quality, 22*(3), 233–259. doi:10.1108/09604521211230978

Josephson, S. G. (1994). *Abductive inference: Computation, philosophy, technology.* Cambridge, UK: Cambridge University Press. doi:10.1017/CBO9780511530128

Joshi, J. (2008). *Network security.* Burlington, MA: Elsevier.

Jun, L. (2009). *Five business models for social media start-ups.* Retrieved July 1, 2012, from http://mashable.com/2009/07/14/social-media-business-models/

Kalakota, R., & Whinston. (1998). *Frontiers of electronic commerce.* Reading, MA: Addison-Wesley Publications Company Inc.

Kamal, M. M. (2006). IT innovation adoption in the government sector: Identifying the critical success factors. *Journal of Enterprise Information Management, 19*(2), 192–222. doi:10.1108/17410390610645085

Kang, W., Son, S. H., & Stankovic, J. (2009). PRIDE: A data abstraction layer for large-scale 2-tier sensor networks. In *Proceedings of IEEE Communications Society Conf. on Sensor, Mesh and Ad Hoc Communications and Networks, SECON'09.* IEEE.

Kaplan, A. M., & Haenlein, M. (2010). Users of the world, unite! The challenges and opportunities of Social Media. *Business Horizons, 53*, 59–68. doi:10.1016/j.bushor.2009.09.003

Kapustka, P. (2013). *Where cloud is going: Service as a service.* Retrieved 9 27, 2013, from IT World: http://www.itworld.com/cloud-computing/348931/where-cloud-going-service-service

Karakostas, B., & Kardaras, D. (2012). *Services customization using web technologies.* Hershey, PA: IGI Global.

Karim, S., & Bajwa, I. S. (2001). Clinical decision support system based virtual telemedicine. In *Proceedings of 2011 Third International Conference on Intelligent Human-Machine Systems and Cybernetics.* Academic Press.

Karimpour, R., & Taghiyareh, F. (2009). Conceptual discovery of web services using WordNet. In *Proceedings of Services Computing Conference,* (pp. 440-444). IEEE.

Kauffman, R. J., Srivastava, J., & Vayghan, J. (2012). Business and data analytics: New innovations for the management of e-commerce. *Electronic Commerce Research and Applications, 11*, 85–88. doi:10.1016/j.elerap.2012.01.001

Kautz, H., Selman, B., & Shah, M. (1997). Combining social networks and collaborative filtering. *Communications of the ACM, 40*(3), 63–65. doi:10.1145/245108.245123

Keen, M., Acharya, A., Bishop, S., Hopkins, A., Milinski, S., Nott, C., & Verschueren, P. (2004). *Patterns: Implementing an SOA using an enterprise service bus the business process/services layer*. Boulder, CO: IBM.

Keen, P. G. W., & Morton, M. S. (1978). *Decision support system*. Reading, MA: Addison Wesley.

Kelly, S. P. (2010). An assessment of the present and future opportunities for combined heat and power with district heating (CHP-DH) in the United Kingdom. *Energy Policy, 38*(11), 6936–6945. doi:10.1016/j.enpol.2010.07.010

Khmelevsky, Y., & Voytenko, V. (2010). Cloud computing infrastructure prototype for university education and research. In *Proceedings of the 15th Western Canadian Conference on Computing Education*. Kelowna: WCCCE.

Khomyakov, M., & Bider, I. (2000). Achieving workflow flexibility through taming the chaos. In *Proceedings of 6th International Conference on Object Oriented Information Systems*. Academic Press.

Kim, D., Squyres, J., & Lumsdaine, A. (2006). The introduction of the OSCAR database API (ODA). In *Proceedings of International Conference on High-Performance Computing in an Advanced Collaborative Environment*. Academic Press.

Kim, Y., Ryu, Y., & Yoo, J. (2012). Cloud services based mobile monitoring for photovoltaic systems. In *Proceedings of IEEE International Conference on Cloud Computing Technology and Science CloudCom'2012*, (pp. 578 – 580). IEEE.

Klusch, M., & Kaufer, F. (2009). WSMO-MX: A hybrid semantic web service matchmaker. *Web Intelligence and Agent Systems, 7*(1), 23–42.

Knutsson, D. (2006). HEATSPOT—A simulation tool for national district heating analyses. *Energy, 31*, 278–293. doi:10.1016/j.energy.2005.02.005

Kodali, R. R. (2005). What is service-oriented architecture? *JavaWorld*. Retrieved April 30, 2013, from http://www.javaworld.com/javaworld/jw-06-2005/jw-0613-soa.html

Kokash, N. (2006). A comparison of web service interface similarity measures. *Frontiers in Artificial Intelligence and Applications, 142*, 220–231.

Koliadis, G., Ghose, A., & Padmanabhuni, S. (2008). Towards an enterprise business process architecture standard. In *Proceedings of IEEE Congress on Services* (pp. 239-246). IEEE.

Koliadis, G., & Ghose, A. (2006). Relating business process models to goal-oriented requirements models in kaos. In *Advances in knowledge acquisition and management* (Vol. 4303, pp. 25–39). Berlin: Springer. doi:10.1007/11961239_3

Kommalapati, H. (2010). *Windows Azure for enterprises*. Retrieved November 28, 2012, from http://msdn.microsoft.com/en-us/magazine/ee309870.aspx

Kopecky, J., Vitvar, T., Bournez, C., & Farrell, J. (2007). Sawsdl: Semantic annotations for WSDL and XML schema. *IEEE Internet Computing, 11*(6), 60–67. doi:10.1109/MIC.2007.134

Kotabe, M., & Helsen, K. (2010). *Global marketing management* (5th ed.). Newark, NJ: John Wiley & Sons.

Kotler, P., & Keller, K. (2009). *A framework for marketing management* (4th ed.). Upper Saddle River, NJ: Prentice-Hall.

Kotuliak, I., Rybár, P., & Trúchly, P. (2011). Performance comparison of IPsec and TLS based VPN technologies. In *Proceedings of 9th International Conference on Emerging eLearning Technologies and Applications* (pp. 217-221). IEEE.

Koufi, V., Malamateniou, F., & Vassilacopoulos, G. (2010). Ubiquitous access to cloud emergency medical services. In *Proceedings of the 2010 10th IEEE International Conference on Information Technology and Applications in Biomedicine (ITAB)*. Corfu, Greece: IEEE.

Kreger, H. (2001). *Web Services Conceptual Architecture (WSCA 1.0)*. Retrieved 8 27, 2013, from http://www.cs.uoi.gr/~zarras/mdw-ws/WebServicesConceptualArchitectu2.pdf

Kuan, K. K. Y., & Chau, P. Y. K. (2001). A perception-based model for EDI adoption in small businesses using a technology-organization-environment framework. *Information & Management, 38*(8), 507–512. doi:10.1016/S0378-7206(01)00073-8

Kulkarni, G., Gambhir, J., & Palwe, R. (2011). Cloud computing-Software as service. *International Journal of Computer Trends and Technology*, 178-182.

Kulkarni, P., Nazeeruddin, M., & McClean, S. (2006). Building a controlled delay assured forwarding class in differentiated services network. In *Proceedings of the 2006 SIGCOMM Workshop on Internet Network Management* (pp. 11-16). New York: ACM.

Kumar, N., Stern, L. W., & Anderson, J. C. (1993). Conducting interorganizational research using key informants. *Academy of Management Journal*, *36*(6), 1633–1651. doi:10.2307/256824

Kuo, A. M. H. (2011). Opportunities and challenges of cloud computing to improve health care services. *Journal of Medical Internet Research*, *13*(3), e67. doi:10.2196/jmir.1867 PMID:21937354

Kvawik, R. B. (2002). E-business in higher education. In *Web portals and higher education, technologies to make IT personal*. Jossey-Bass Inc.

Kwon, T. H., & Zmud, R. W. (1987). Unifying the fragmented model of information systems implementation. In J. R. Boland, & R. Hirsheim (Eds.), *Critical issues in information systems research*. New York: John Wiley.

Kyusakov, R., Eliasson, J., Delsing, J., van Deventer, J., & Gustafsson, J. (2011). Integration of wireless sensor and actuator nodes with IT infrastructure using service-oriented architecture. *IEEE Transactions on Industrial Informatics*, *6*(1), 1–9.

Laudon, K., & Traver, C. (2013). *E-Commerce 2013: Business, Technology, Society* (9th ed.). Harlow, England: Pearson.

Laurel, P. (2008). *Social media monetization and revenue, under Australia, featured, featured articles, monetization, money, online communities, ROI, consumer economy, digital economy, peer2peer, revenue, web 2.0 presentation at PANPA (part) and web directions 2008 (full)*. Retrieved July 1, 2012, from http://laurelpapworth.com/social-media-monetization-and-revenue/

Laurel, P. (2009). *Monetization: Facebook revenue and business model, under featured, metrics, monetization, money, business, revenue*. Retrieved July 1, 2012, from http://laurelpapworth.com/monetization-facebook-revenue-and-business-model/

Le Pape, C. (1990). A combination of centralized and distributed methods for multi-agent planning and scheduling. In *Proceedings of 1990 IEEE International Conference on Robotics and Automation* (pp. 488-493). Cincinnati, OH: IEEE.

Leacock, C., & Chodorow, M. (1998). Combining local context and WordNet similarity for word sense identification. *WordNet: An Electronic Lexical Database*, *49*(2), 265–283.

Leaf, G. (2003). *Promoting the uptake of e-books in higher and further education: The joint information systems committee report*.

Ledoux, T., & Kouki, Y. (2012). SLA-driven capacity planning for Cloud applications. In *Proceedings of the 2012 IEEE 4th International Conference on Cloud Computing Technology and Science (CloudCom)* (pp. 135-140). Washington, DC: IEEE Computer Society.

Lee, A. S., & Baskerville, R. L. (2003). Generalizing generalizability in information systems research. *Information Systems Research*, *14*(3), 221–243. doi:10.1287/isre.14.3.221.16560

Letier, E., & van Lamsweerde, A. (2002). Deriving operational software specifications from system goals. *SIGSOFT Softw. Eng. Notes*, *27*(6), 119–128. doi:10.1145/605466.605485

Lewin, K. (1936). *Principles of topological psychology*. New York: McGraw Hill. doi:10.1037/10019-000

Lewin, K. (1952). Field theory in social science. In D. Cartwright (Ed.), *Selected theoretical papers*. London, UK: Tavistock.

Lewis, M. (2006). *Comparing, designing, and deploying VPNs*. Cisco Press.

Li, L., & Gao, H. (2013). WeChat: 300 million users behind. *News and Writing*, 34-36.

Li, X., Zhang, B., Lu, T., Niu, H., Hou, Y., & Zhu, L. (2012). *E-commerce in China: Taobao*. Retrieved August 2, 2013, from http://www.dwastell.org/MSc/Group6.pdf

Liang, H., Xue, T. Y., & Berger, B. A. (2006). Web-based intervention support system for health promotion. *Decision Support Systems*, *42*, 435–449. doi:10.1016/j.dss.2005.02.001

Liang, X., & Song, F. (2008). *E-businessman wins the most*. Beijing, China: CITIC Press.

Liao, W., & Su, S. (2011). A dynamic VPN architecture for private cloud computing. In *Proceedings of 4th IEEE/ACM International Conference on Cloud and Utility Computing* (pp. 409-414). Melbourne, Australia: IEEE.

Li, C., & Bernoff, J. (2008). *Groundswell: Winning in a world transformed by social technologies*. Cambridge, MA: Harvard Business Press.

Li, D., Lai, F., & Wang, J. (2010). E-business assimilation in China's international trade firms: The technology-organization-environment framework. *Journal of Global Information Management*, *18*(1), 39–65. doi:10.4018/jgim.2010091103

Lilien, G. L., Morrison, P. D., Searls, K., Sonnack, M., & von Hippel, E. (2002). Performance assessment of the lead user idea-generation process for new product development. *Management Science*, *48*(8), 1042–1059. doi:10.1287/mnsc.48.8.1042.171

Liljander, V., Gillberg, F., Gummerus, J., & van Riel, A. (2006). Technology readiness and the evaluation and adoption of self-service technologies. *Journal of Retailing and Consumer Services*, *13*(3), 177–191. doi:10.1016/j.jretconser.2005.08.004

Lim, S. B., & Palacios-Marques, D. (2011). Culture and purpose of web 2.0 service adoption: A study in the USA, Korea and Spain. *The Service Industries Journal*, *31*(1), 123–131. doi:10.1080/02642069.2010.485634

Lin, D. (1998). An information-theoretic definition of similarity. In *Proceedings of ICML* (Vol. 98, pp. 296-304). ICML.

Lin, L., Hu, P. J. H., & Sheng, O. R. L. (2006). A decision support system for lower back pain diagnosis: Uncertainty management and clinical evaluations. *Decision Support Systems*, *42*, 1152–1169. doi:10.1016/j.dss.2005.10.007

Liu, D. (2008). Models on Web-based information gap between e-goverment and citizens. *2008 ISECS International Colloquium on Computing, Communication, Control, and Management* (pp. 156-160). It is a very low quality CP paper. Read 02 10 13: IEEE Computer Society. doi:DOI 10.1109/CCCM.2008.61

Liu, J., Kit, H. C., Hambi, M., & Tsui, C. Y. (2002). Stable round-robin scheduling algorithms for high-performance input queued switches. In *Proceedings of Symposium on High Performance Interconnects*, (pp. 43-51). Academic Press.

Liu, Q. (2012). Huawei's cloud plan. *CEOCIO*, *1*(5), 47–48.

LogMeIn. (2013). *Xively - Public cloud for the internet of things*. Retrieved July 19, 2013, from https://xively.com/

Lombardi, P., & Trossero, E. (2013). Beyond energy efficiency in evaluating sustainable development in planning and the built environment. *International Journal of Sustainable Building Technology and Urban Development*.

Lombardi, P. (2011). Managing the green IT agenda. *Intelligent Buildings International*, *13*(3), 8–10.

Losee, R., & Church, L. J. (2004). Information retrieval with distributed databases: Analytic models of performance. *IEEE Transactions on Parallel and Distributed Systems*, 18–27. doi:10.1109/TPDS.2004.1264782

Loukis, E., Pazalos, K., & Salagara, A. (2012). Transforming e-services evaluation data into business analytics using value models. *Electronic Commerce Research and Applications*, *11*(2), 129–141. doi:10.1016/j.elerap.2011.12.004

Low, C., Chen, Y., & Wu, M. (2011). Understanding the determinants of cloud computing adoption. *Industrial Management & Data Systems*, *111*(7), 1006–1023. doi:10.1108/02635571111161262

Lowson, B., King, R., & Hunter, A. (1999). *Quick response managing the supply chain to meet consumer demand.* West Sussex, UK: John Wiley & Sons Ltd.

Lu, Y., Zhao, L., & Wang, B. (2010). From virtual communities members to C2C e-commerce buyers: Trust in virtual communities and its effect on consumers' purchase attention. *Electornic Commerce Research and Applications*, 346-360.

Luckham, D. (2002). *The power of events: An introduction to complex event processing in distributed enterprise systems.* Reading, MA: Addison-Wesley.

Lu, J., Wang, Z. L., & Hayes, A. L. (2012). How do technology readiness platform functionality and trust influence C2C user satisfaction? *Journal of Electronic Commerce Research*, *13*(1), 50–69.

Luo, J., Li, W., Liu, B., Zheng, X., & Dong, F. (2010). Multi-agent coordination for service composition. In *Agent-based service-oriented computing. series: Advanced information and knowledge processing, XIII* (pp. 47–79). London: Springer-Verlag Limited. doi:10.1007/978-1-84996-041-0_3

Lusch, R. F., & Vargo, S. (2006). *The service-dominant logic of marketing: Dialog, debate, and directions.* Armonk, NY: M.E. Sharpe.

Lv, Q., Zhou, J., & Cao, Q. (2009). Service matching mechanisms in pervasive computing environments. In *Proceedings of Intelligent Systems and Applications* (pp. 1–4). IEEE. doi:10.1109/IWISA.2009.5073110

Ly, L., Rinderle-Ma, S., Göser, K., & Dadam, P. (2012). On enabling integrated process compliance with semantic constraints in process management systems. *Information Systems Frontiers*, *14*(2), 195–219. doi:10.1007/s10796-009-9185-9

Lyytikainen, H. (2012). *Designing web services for location-aware mobile devices, case: Traffic monitoring service.* Retrieved from http://lib.tkk.fi/Dipl/2012/urn100645.pdf

Maamar, Z., Faci, N., Badr, Y., Krug Wives, L., Bispo dos Santos, P., Benslimane, D., & Palazzo Moreira de Oliveira, J. (2011). Towards a framework for weaving social networks principles into web services discovery. In *Proceedings of the International Conference on Web Intelligence, Mining, and Semantics (WIMS'2011)*. Sogndal, Norway: WIMS.

Maamar, Z., Faci, N., Krug Wives, L., Yahyaoui, H., & Hacid, H. (2011). Towards a method for engineering social web services. In *Proceedings of the IFIP WG8.1 Working Conference on Method Engineering (ME'2011)*. Paris, France: IFIP.

Maamar, Z., Bentahar, D., Faci, N., & Thiran, P. (2013). Social web services research roadmap: Present & future. In *Distributed computing innovations for business, engineering, and science*. Hershey, PA: IGI Global Publishing.

Maamar, Z., Faci, N., Boukadi, K., Sheng, Q. Z., & Yao, L. (2013). *Commitments to regulate social web services operation.* IEEE Transactions on Services Computing.

Maamar, Z., Faci, N., Krug Wives, L., Badr, Y., Bispo dos Santos, P., & Palazzo Moreira de Oliveira, J. (2011). Using social networks to web services discovery. *IEEE Internet Computing*, *15*(4), 48–54. doi:10.1109/MIC.2011.27

Maamar, Z., Hacid, H., & Hunhs, M. N. (2011). Why web services need social networks. *IEEE Internet Computing*, *15*(2), 90–94. doi:10.1109/MIC.2011.49

Maamar, Z., Krug Wives, L., Badr, Y., Elnaffar, S., Boukadi, K., & Faci, N. (2011). LinkedWS: A novel web services discovery model based on the metaphor of social networks. *Simulation Modelling Practice and Theory*, *19*(10), 121–132. doi:10.1016/j.simpat.2010.06.018

Maaradji, A., Hacid, H., Daigremont, J., & Crespi, N. (2010). Towards a social network based approach for services composition. In *Proceedings of the 2010 IEEE International Conference on Communications (ICC'2010)*. Cape Town, South Africa: IEEE.

Maciá-Pérez, F., Marcos-Jorquera, D., & Gilart-Iglesias, V. (2007). Embedded web services for industrial TCP/IP services monitoring. In *Proceedings of IEEE Conference on Emerging Technologies and Factory Automation,* (pp. 1115-1122). IEEE.

MacKay, C., McKee, S., & Mulholland, A. J. (2006). Diffusion and convection of gaseous and fine particulate from a chimney. *IMA Journal of Applied Mathematics, 71,* 670–691. doi:10.1093/imamat/hxl016

Macmillan. (2007). *Macmillan English Dictionary for Advanced Learners.* London: Macmillan.

Ma, H. (2011). On China mobile 3G business development strategy and its future trends. *Information & Communications, 113,* 113–114.

Maijals, V. (2004). *Outlook of information security in e-business.* (Unpublished master thesis). Helsinki University of Technology, Helsinki, Finland.

Malcolm, E., & Godwyl. (2008). *Diffusion of information communication technology in selected Ghanaian schools.* Retrieved, August 20, 2011 from mak.ac.ugldocuments/markfiles/thesis/Tminomujuni_justus.pdf

Malet, B., & Pietzuch, P. (2010). *Resource allocation across multiple cloud data centres.* Paper presented at the 8th International Workshop on Middleware for Grids, Clouds and e-Science. New York, NY.

Malik, S. (2002). *Network security principles and practices.* Cisco Press.

Manolios, P., & Srinivasan, S. K. (2005). A parameterized benchmark suite of hard pipelined-machine-verification problems. In *Correct hardware design and verification methods* (pp. 363–366). Berlin: Springer. doi:10.1007/11560548_32

Mao, Z. (1966). *A single spark can start a prairie fire.* Beijing: Foreign Languages Press.

Markova, I. (2009). *Web 2.0 technology adoption by government departments.* Carleton University.

Marks, E. A. (2008). *Service-oriented architecture governance for the services driven enterprise.* Hoboken, NJ: John Wiley & Sons, Inc.

Marsh, S. P. (1994). *Formalising trust as a computational concept.* (Unpublished doctoral dissertation). Stirling, UK.

Marshall, M. N. (1996). Sampling for qualitative research. *Family Practice, 13*(6), 522–526. doi:10.1093/fampra/13.6.522 PMID:9023528

Martínez-López, F. J., & Casillas, J. (2009). Marketing intelligent systems for consumer behaviour modelling by a descriptive induction approach based on genetic fuzzy systems. *Industrial Marketing Management, 38*(7), 714–731. doi:10.1016/j.indmarman.2008.02.003

Massad, N., Heckman, R., & Crowston, K. (2006). Customer satisfaction with electronic service encounters. *International Journal of Electronic Commerce, 10*(4), 73–104. doi:10.2753/JEC1086-4415100403

Mathis, R. L., & Jackson, J. H. (2009). *Human resource management.* Mason, GA: Cengage Learning.

Matur, V., Dhopesshwarkar, S., & Apte, V. (2009). MASTH proxy: An extensible platform for web overload control. In *Proceedings of the International Conference on World Wide Web,* (pp. 1113-1114). WWW.

Mausbach, B. T., Moore, R. C., Davine, T., Cardenas, V., Bowie, C. R., & Ho, J. et al. (2013). The use of the theory of planned behavior to predict engagement in functional behaviors in schizophrenia. *Psychiatry Research, 205*(1-2), 36. doi:10.1016/j.psychres.2012.09.016 PMID:23031803

McGovern, J., Tyagi, S., Stevens, M., & Mathew, S. (2003). *Java web services architecture.* San Francisco: Morgan Kaufmann.

McGrath, C., & Zell, D. (2001). The future of innovation diffusion research and its implications for management: A conversation with Everett Rogers. *Journal of Management Inquiry, 10*(4), 386–391. doi:10.1177/1056492601104012

McLaughlin, H. (2009). What's in a name: Client, patient, customer, consumer, expert by experience, service user--What's next? *British Journal of Social Work, 39*(6), 1101–1117. doi:10.1093/bjsw/bcm155

Medjahed, B., & Bouguettaya, A. (2011). *Service composition for the semantic web.* New York: Springer Science Business Media. doi:10.1007/978-1-4419-8465-4

Medjahed, B., Rezgui, A., & Bouguettaya, A. (2003). Infrastructure for E-Government Web Services. *IEEE Internet Computing, 7*(1), 58–65. doi:10.1109/MIC.2003.1167340

Meijer, A., & Thaens, M. (2010). Alignment 2.0: Strategic use of new internet technologies in government. *Government Information Quarterly, 27*(2), 113–121. doi:10.1016/j.giq.2009.12.001

Meijer, E., & Bierman, G. (2011). A co-relational model of data for large shared data banks. *Queue, 9*, 30–48. doi:10.1145/1952746.1961297

Mell, P., & Grance, T. (2011). *The NIST definition of cloud computing.* Washington, DC: National Institute of Standards and Technology.

Merritt, A. (2000). Culture in the cockpit: Do Hofstede's dimensions replicate? *Journal of Cross-Cultural Psychology, 3*, 283–301. doi:10.1177/0022022100031003001 PMID:11543415

Meuter, M. L., Ostrom, A. L., Roundtree, R. I., & Bitner, M. J. (2000). Self-service technologies: Understanding customer satisfaction with technology-based service encounters. *Journal of Marketing, 64*, 50–64. doi:10.1509/jmkg.64.3.50.18024

Miah, S. J. (2012). The role of end user in e-government application development: A conceptual model in the agricultural context. *Journal of Organizational and End User Computing, 24*(3), 69–85. doi:10.4018/joeuc.2012070104

Miah, S. J. (2012). Cloud based DSS development for emergency medical professionals. In *Multidisciplinary computational intelligence techniques: Applications in business, engineering and medicine* (pp. 47–60). Hershey, PA: IGI Global. doi:10.4018/978-1-4666-1830-5.ch004

Miah, S. J., Kerr, D., & Gammack, J. (2009). A methodology to allow rural extension professionals to build target-specific expert systems for Australian rural business operators. *Journal of Expert Systems with Applications, 36*, 735–744. doi:10.1016/j.eswa.2007.10.022

Miah, S. J., Kerr, D., & von-Hellens, L. (2013). A collective artefact design of decision support systems: Design science research perspective. *Information Technology & People, 27*(3).

Middlestadt, S. E. (2012). Beliefs underlying eating better and moving more: Lessons learned from comparative salient belief elicitations with adults and youths. *The Annals of the American Academy of Political and Social Science, 640*(1), 81–100. doi:10.1177/0002716211425015

Milgram, S. (1967). The small world problem. *Psychology Today, 1*(1), 61–67.

Millard, J. (2010). Government 1.5: Is the bottle half full or half empty. *European Journal of ePractice, 9*(1), 35-50.

Miller, G. A., Beckwith, R., Fellbaum, C., Gross, D., & Miller, K. J. (1990). Introduction to wordnet: An on-line lexical database. *International Journal of Lexicography, 3*(4), 235–244. doi:10.1093/ijl/3.4.235

Miori, V., & Russo, D. (2012). Anticipating health hazards through an ontology-based, IoT domotic environment. In *Proceedings of 2012 Sixth International Conference on Innovative Mobile and Internet Services in Ubiquitous Computing (IMIS)* (pp. 745-750). IMIS.

Modgil, S., Faci, N., Rech Meneguzzi, F., Oren, N., Miles, S., & Luck, M. (2009). A framework for monitoring agent-based normative systems. In *Proceedings of the 8ᵗʰ International Conference on Autonomous Agents and MultiAgent Systems (AAMAS'2009).* Budapest, Hungary: AAMAS.

Moisil, I., & Jitaru, E. (2006). E-health progresses in Romania. *International Journal of Medical Informatics, 75*, 315–321. doi:10.1016/j.ijmedinf.2005.08.013 PMID:16275159

Mokhtar, S. B., Kaul, A., Georgantas, N., & Issarny, V. (2006). Towards efficient matching of semantic web service capabilities. In *Proceedings of International Workshop on Web Services–Modeling and Testing (WS-MaTe 2006)* (pp. 137-152). WS-MaTe.

Mongo, D. B. (2013). *MongoDB.* Retrieved July 19, 2013, from http://www.mongodb.org/

Mongo, D. B. (2013). *The leading NoSQL database.* Retrieved November 15, 2013, from http://www.mongodb.com/leading-nosql-database

Monk, A., Wright, P., Haber, J., & Davenport, L. (1993). *Improving your human - computer interface: A practical technique.* Upper Saddle River, NJ: Prentice Hall International.

Moran, M. J. (2011). *Semantic service oriented architecture - Component model, reference architecture and evaluated prototype.* (Unpublished doctoral dissertation). Galway, Ireland.

Moreno, J. L. (1934). *Who shall survive?* New York: Beacon Press.

Morrison, E. D., Ghose, A. K., Dam, H. K., Hinge, K. G., & Hoesch-Klohe, K. (2012). Strategic alignment of business processes. In Proceedings of Service-Oriented Computing, ICSOC 2011 Workshops (pp. 9-21). ICSOC.

Mosher, L., Helmbock, J., Hogan, J., McCarthy, C., & O'Mara, M. (2006, April 7). *Demand-driven IT service management through enterprise resource planning for IT: IBM IT service management strategy and vision.* Retrieved April 6, 2013, from http://www-935.ibm.com/services/fr/cio/ optimise/optit_wp_gts_demanddriven.pdf

Moutinho, L., Rita, P., & Li, S. (2006). Strategic diagnostics and management decision making: A hybrid knowledge-based approach. *Intell. Sys. Acc. Fin. Mgmt, 14,* 129–155. doi:10.1002/isaf.281

MuleSoft. (2013). *Mule ESB.* Retrieved November 13, 2013, from http://www.mulesoft.org/

MuleSoft. (2013). *Mule studio documentation.* Retrieved November 13, 2013, from http://www.mulesoft.com/mule-studio

MuleSoft. (2013). *Integration case studies.* Retrieved November 13, 2013, from http://www.mulesoft.com/case-studies

Mundbrod, N., Kolb, J., & Reichert, M. (2012). Towards a system support of collaborative knowledge work. In *Proceedings of 1st International Workshop on Adaptive Case Management.* Academic Press.

Muscariello, M., Mellia, M., Meo, M., Marsan, A., & Cigno, R. (2005). Markov models of internet traffic and a new hierarchical MMPP model. *Computer Communications, 28*(16), 1835–1851. doi:10.1016/j.comcom.2005.02.012

Musion. (2013, February 19). *Musion to present its futuristic holographic technology at international confex & live experience.* Retrieved April 14, 2013, from http://www.it-analysis.com/business/innovation/news_release.php?rel=36660

Nam Ko, M., Cheek, G. P., Shehab, M., & Sandhu, R. (2010). Social-networks connect services. *IEEE Computer, 43*(8), 37–43. doi:10.1109/MC.2010.239

Nam, T. (2011). Towards the new phase of e-government: An empirical study on citizens' attitude about open government and government 2.0. In *Proceedings of the 11th Public Management Research Conference.* Maxwell School of Syracuse University.

Narayan, S., Brooking, K., & Vere, S. D. (2009). Network performance analysis of VPN protocols: An empirical comparison on different operating systems. In *Proceedings of 2009 International Conference on Networks Security, Wireless Communications and Trusted Computing.* IEEE Computer Society.

Natis, Y. (2008). *Key issues for cloud-enabled application infrastructure, 2008.* Gartner Research (G00155751).

Nayak, R., & Lee, B. (2007). Web service discovery with additional semantics and clustering. In *Proceedings of Web Intelligence* (pp. 555–558). IEEE. doi:10.1109/WI.2007.82

NCOIC. (2013). *Design phase service integration capability pattern.* Retrieved June 28, 2013, from https://www.ncoic.org/apps/group_public/document.php?document_id=15964

NDTV. (n.d.). *Japan: Earthquake triggers oil refinery fire.* Retrieved from http://www.ndtv.com

Negnevitsky, M. (2005). *Artificial Intelligence: A Guide to Intelligent Systems* (2nd ed.). Harlow: Addison-Wesley.

Newswire, P. R. (2013, March 20). *Tencent announces 2012 fourth quarter and annual results.* Retrieved September 14, 2013, from http://www.prnewswire.com/news-releases/tencent-announces-2012-fourth-quarter-and-annual-results-199130711.html

Newton, J. D., Ewing, M. T., Burney, S., & Hay, M. (2011). Resolving the theory of planned behaviour's â€˜expectancy-value muddleâ€™ using dimensional salience. *Psychology & Health,* 1–15.

Ng, T., Fung, J., Chan, L., & Mak, V. (2010). *Understanding IBM SOA foundation suite - Learning visually with examples.* Crawfordsville: IBM Press, Pearson plc.

Nguyen, C. D., Perini, A., Tonella, P., Miles, S., Harman, M., & Luck, M. (2009). Evolutionary testing of autonomous software agents. In *Proceedings of the 8th International Conference on Autonomous Agents and Multiagent Systems* (vol. 1, pp. 521-528). Richland: International Foundation for Autonomous Agents and Multiagent Systems.

Nguyen, X. T. (2005). Demonstration of WS2JADE. In *Proceedings of Fourth International Joint Conference on Autonomous Agents and Multi-Agent Systems* (pp. 135–136). Utrecht, The Netherlands: ACM.

Nimetz, J. (2007). *Emerging Trends in B2B Social Networking.* Retrieved 9 24, 2013, from Marketing-jive: http://www.marketing-jive.com/2007/11/jody-nimetz-on-emerging-trends-in-b2b.html

Normann, R., & Ramírez, R. (1993, July-August). From value chain to value constellation: Designing interactive strategy. *Harvard Business Review*, 65–77. PMID:10127040

NOSQL Databases . (2013). Retrieved July 19, 2013, from http://nosql-database.org/

Nurmi, D., Wolski, R., Grzegorczyk, C., Obertelli, G., Soman, S., Youseff, L., & Zagorodnov, D. (2009). *The eucalyptus open-source cloud-computing system.* Paper presented at the Cluster Computing and the Grid, 2009. New York, NY.

O'Shaughnessy, J., & O'Shaughnessy, N. J. (2011). Service-dominant logic: a rejoinder to Lusch and Vargo's reply. *European Journal of Marketing*, *45*(7/8), 1310–1318. doi:10.1108/03090561111137732

Oberle, D., Barros, A., Kylau, U., & Heinzl, S. (2013). A unified description language for human to automated services. *Information Systems*, *38*(1), 155–181. doi:10.1016/j.is.2012.06.004

OECD. (1999). *Economic and social impact of e-commerce: Preliminary findings and research agenda (OECD Digital Economy Papers, No. 40).* Paris: OECD Publishing.

OECD. (2012, April 30). *Procedural fairness and transparency 2012 - Key points.* Retrieved April 20, 2013, from www.oecd.org: http://www.oecd.org/daf/competition/mergers/50235955.pdf

Oliveira, T., & Martins, M. F. (2010). Understanding e-business adoption across industries in European countries. *Industrial Management & Data Systems*, *110*(9), 1337–1354. doi:10.1108/02635571011087428

O'Neill, N. (2010). *Facebook squeezes digg into a new business model.* Retrieved July 1, 2012, from http://www.allfacebook.com/2010/03/facebook-digg-business/

Oppliger, R. (2009). *SSL and TLS: Theory and practice.* Norwood, NJ: Artech House.

Oracle Corporation. (2009). *Documentation.* Retrieved June 5, 2013, from https://www.virtualbox.org/wiki/Documentation

O'Reilly, T. (2007). What is web 2.0: Design patterns and business models for the next generation of software. *Communications & Strategies*, *65*(1), 17–37.

Orriols-Puig, A., Martínez-López, F. J., & Casillas, J. (2012). (in press). A Soft-Computing-based Method for the Automatic Discovery of Fuzzy Rules in Databases: Uses for Academic Research and Management Support in Marketing. *Journal of Business Research*.

Osello, A., Acquaviva, A., Aghemo, C., Blaso, L., Dalmasso, D., & Erba, D. et al. (n.d.). Energy saving in existing buildings by an intelligent use of interoperable ICTs. *Energy Efficiency.* doi: doi:10.1007/s12053-013-9211-0

Osimo, D. (2008). *Web 2.0 in government: Why and how?.* Institute for Prospective Technological Studies (IPTS), Joint Research Centre, European Commission, EUR No. *23358* EN.

Osterwalder, A. (2005). *What is a business model?* Retrieved July 1, 2012, from http://business-model-design.blogspot.com/2005/11/what-is-business-model.html

Osterwalder, A., Pigneur, Y., & Smith, A. (2010). *Business model generation.* Hoboken, NJ: John Wiley & Sons Inc.

Ou, C. X., & Davison, M. R. (2009). Why ebay lost to TaoBao in China: The global advantage. *Communications of the ACM, 52*, 145–148. doi:10.1145/1435417.1435450

Paczkowski, J. (2008). *Facebook and the Duke Nukem Forever of business models.* Retrieved July 1, 2012, from http://digitaldaily.allthingsd.com/20081010/facebook-and-the-duke-nukem-forever-of-business-models/

Pan, S., & Mao, Q. (2013). Case study on web service composition based on multi-agent system. *Journal of Software, 8*(4), 900–907. doi:10.4304/jsw.8.4.900-907

Paolucci, M., Shehory, O., Sycara, K., Kalp, D., & A., P. (2000). A planning component for RETSINA agents. In N. Jennings & Y. Lesperance (Eds.), *Lecture Notes in Computer Science* (LNCS), (vol. 1757, pp. 147-161). Heidelberg, Germany: Springer-Verlag.

Paolucci, M., Kawamura, T., Payne, T. R., & Sycara, K. (2002). Semantic matching of web services capabilities. In I. Horrocks, & J. Hendler (Eds.), *The semantic web - ISWC 2002, (LNCS)* (pp. 333–347). Berlin, Germany: Springer.

Papazoglou, M. P. (2003). Service -Oriented Computing: Concepts, Characteristics and Directions. In Proceedings of 4th Intl Conf on Web Information Systems Engineering (WISE2003). pp. 3-12.

Papazoglou, M. P. (2007). *Web services: Principles and technology.* Upper Saddle River, NJ: Prentice Hall.

Papazoglou, M. P. (2008). *Web services: Principles and Technology.* Harlow, England: Pearson Prentice Hall.

Papazoglou, M. P., & Georgakopoulos, D. (2003). Service-oriented computing. *Communications of the ACM, 46*(10), 25–28.

Papazoglou, M. P., & van den Heuvel, W. J. (2007). Service oriented architectures: Approaches, technologies and research issues. *The VLDB Journal, 16*(3), 389–415. doi:10.1007/s00778-007-0044-3

Pappu, M., & Mundy, R. A. (2002). Understanding strategic transportation buyer-seller relationships from an organizational learning perspective: A grounded theory approach. *Transportation Journal, 4*(41).

Park, E. C., & Choi, C. H. (2003). Adaptive token bucket algorithm for fair bandwidth allocation in DiffServ networks. In *Proceedings of IEEE Global Telecommunications Conference GLOBECOM'03*, (pp. 3176-3180). IEEE.

Park, J., Kim, J., & Koh, J. (2010). Determinants of continuous usage intention in web analytics services. *Electronic Commerce Research and Applications, 9*(1), 61–72. doi:10.1016/j.elerap.2009.08.007

Park, K.-W., & Park, K. H. (2011). ACCENT: Cognitive cryptography plugged compression for SSL/TLS-based cloud computing services. *ACM Transactions on Internet Technology, 11*(2), 1–30. doi:10.1145/2049656.2049659

Park, S.-J., Vedantham, R., Sivakumar, R., & Akyildiz, I. F. (2004). A scalable approach for reliable downstream data delivery in wireless sensor networks. In *Proceedings of MobiHoc* (pp. 78–89). ACM. doi:10.1145/989459.989470

Parreiras, F. S. (2009). *E-business: Challenges and trends.* Retrieved July 16, 2013 from www.oghavidell.ir/pdf/ebus.pdf

Parveen, F. (2012). Impact of social media usage on organizations. In *Proceedings of the 16th Pacific Asia Conference on Information Systems (PACIS 2012).* Ho Chi Minh City, Vietnam: PACIS.

Pasquill, F. (1961). The estimation of the dispersion of windborne material. *The Meteorological Magazine, 90*(1063), 33–49.

Pasquill, F. (1974). *Atmospheric diffusion* (2nd ed.). New York: Halsted Press, John Wiley & Sons.

Paulini, M., Murty, P., & Maher, M. L. (2012). Design processes in collective innovation communities: A study of communication. *CoDesign*, 1–24.

Pautasso, C., & Alonso, G. (2005). From web service composition to megaprogramming. In M. Shan, U. Dayal, & M. Hsu (Eds.), *Technologies for e-services (LNCS)* (pp. 39–53). Heidelberg, Germany: Springer. doi:10.1007/978-3-540-31811-8_4

Pawlowski, J. M., & Adelsbery, H. H. (2002). *E-business and education.* University of Esen, Germany. Retrieved July 16, 2013 from citeseerx.ist.psu.edu/view/doc/download?

Payer, M., & Gross, T. R. (2011). Fine-grained user-space security through virtualization. *ACM SIGPLAN Notices, 46*(7), 157–168. doi:10.1145/2007477.1952703

Pěchouček, M., & Mařík, V. (2008). Industrial deployment of multi-agent technologies: Review and selected case studies. *Autonomous Agents and Multi-Agent Systems*, *17*(3), 397–431. doi:10.1007/s10458-008-9050-0

Pedersen, T., Patwardhan, S., & Michelizzi, J. (2004). WordNet: Similarity: Measuring the relatedness of concepts. In Demonstration papers at HLT-NAACL 2004 (pp. 38-41). Association for Computational Linguistics.

Peppard, J., & Rylander, A. (2005). Products and services in cyberspace. *International Journal of Information Management*, *25*, 335–345. doi:10.1016/j.ijinfomgt.2005.04.005

Pepple, K. (2011). *Deploying OpenStack*. Sebastopol, CA: O'Reilly.

Perego, A., Carminati, B., & Ferrari, E. (2009). The quality of social network: A collaborative environment for personalizing web access. In *Proceedings of the International Conference on Collaborative Computing: Networking, Applications, and Worksharing (CollaborateCom'2009)*. Washington, DC: CollaborateCom.

Petrie, C., & Genesereth, M. e. (2003). Adding AI to Web services. In D. V. van Elst L, AMKM 2003, LNAI 2926 (pp. 322-338).

Pinzón, C., Francisco de Paz, J., Tapia, D. I., Bajo, J., & Corchado, J. M. (2012). Improving the security level of the FUSION@ multi-agent architecture. *Expert System Application*, *39*(8), 7536–7545. doi:10.1016/j.eswa.2012.01.127

Platform, G. (2002). *White paper*. New York, NY: GigaSpaces Technologies Ltd.

Polanyi, M. (1983). *The tacit dimension*. Gloucester, MA: Peter Smith.

Ponsard, C., Massonet, P., Molderez, J., Rifaut, A., Lamsweerde, A., & Van, H. (2007). Early verification and validation of mission critical systems. *Formal Methods in System Design*, *30*, 233–247. doi:10.1007/s10703-006-0028-8

Popi, C., & Festor, O. (2009). Flow monitoring in wireless MESH networks. In *Proceedings of the 3rd International Conference on Autonomous Infrastructure, Management and Security: Scalability of Networks and Services* (pp. 134-146). Enschede, The Netherlands: Springer-Verlag.

Powell, J. (2008). What sort of e-business is post primary education. In *The e-revolution and post- compulsory education: Using e-business model to deliver quality education*. New York: Routledge.

Premkumar, G., Ramamurthy, K., & Nilakanta, S. (1994). Implementation of electronic data interchange: An innovation diffusion perspective. *Journal of Management Information Systems*, *11*(2), 157–186.

Pruitt, J., & Grudin, J. (2003). Personas. In *Proceedings of the 2003 Conference on Designing for User Experiences - DUX '03* (pp. 1–15). New York: ACM Press.

Pryyantha, B., Kansal, A., Goraczko, M., & Zhao, F. (2008). Tiny web services: Design and implementation of interoperable and evolvable sensor networks. In *Proceedings of 6th ACM Conference on Embedded Network Sensor Systems*, (pp. 253-266). ACM.

Pudjianto, B., Zo, H., Ciganek, A. P., & Rho, J. J. (2011). Determinants of e-government assimilation in Indonesia: An empirical investigation using a TOE framework. *Asia Pacific Journal of Information Systems*, *21*(1), 49–80.

Purser, K. (2012). Using social media in local government: 2011 survey report. Australian Centre of Excellence for Local Government, University of Technology.

Pyramid Research. (2010). *The impact of mobile services in Nigeria: How Mobil technologies are transforming economic and social activities*. Retrieved July 16, 2013 from www.pyramidresearch.com

Qu, X., Feng, J., & Sun, W. (2008). United access of distributed biological information database based on web service and multi-agent. In *Proceedings of Conf. Control and Decision*, (pp. 4257 – 4260). Academic Press.

Qu, X., Sun, H., Li, X., Liu, X., & Lin, W. (2009). WSSM: A WordNet-based web services similarity mining mechanism. In Proceedings of Future Computing, Service Computation, Cognitive, Adaptive, Content, Patterns, (pp. 339-345). IEEE.

Quin, L. (2012, January 24). *Extensible markup language (XML)*. Retrieved April 5, 2013, from www.w3.org: http://www.w3.org/XML/

Rademakers, T., & Dirksen, J. (2009). *Open-source ESBs in action*. Greenwich, CT: Manning.

Radware. (2012). *LDAP network challenges: Radware carrier solutions*. Retrieved April 5, 2013, from http://www.radware.com/: http://www.radware.com/

Rainbird, M. (2004). Demand and supply chains: The value catalyst. *International Journal of Physical Distribution & Logistics Management, 34*(3/4), 230–250. doi:10.1108/09600030410533565

Rainey, D. L. (2012). A model for improving the adoption of sustainability in the context of globalization and innovation. In F. Nobre, D. Walker, & R. Harris (Eds.), *Technological, managerial and organizational core competencies: Dynamic innovation and sustainable development* (pp. 18–39). Hershey, PA: IGI Global. doi:10.4018/978-1-4666-0882-5.ch306

Ramayah, T., Yeap, J. A. L., & Ignatius, J. (2013). An empirical inquiry on knowledge sharing among academicians in higher learning institutions. *Minerva: A Review of Science. Learning and Policy, 51*(2), 131–154.

Ramos, V., Delamer, I., & Lastra, J. (2011). Embedded service oriented monitoring, diagnostics and control: Towards the asset-aware and self-recovery factor. In *Proceedings of IEEE International Conference on Industrial Informatics*, (pp. 497 – 502). IEEE.

Rao, G. S. V. R. K., Sundararaman, K., & Parthasarathi, J. (2010). Dhatri: A pervasive cloud initiative for primary healthcare services. In *Proceedings of the 2010 14th International Conference on Intelligence in Next Generation Networks (ICIN)*. Berlin, Germany: IEEE.

Rao, J., & Su, X. (2005). A survey of automated web service composition methods. In *Proceedings of the First International Conference on Semantic Web Services and Web Process Composition* (pp. 43-54). Heidelberg, Germany: Springer-Verlag.

Redl, C., Breskovic, I., Brandic, I., & Dustdar, S. (2012). Automatic SLA matching and provider selection in grid and cloud computing markets. In *Proceedings of the 2012 ACM/IEEE 13th International Conference on Grid Computing* (pp. 85-94). Washington, DC: IEEE Computer Society.

Reichheld, F. (2013). *Net promoter score™ (NPS) measuring overall satisfaction with the customer experience, and predicting customer loyalty*. Satmatrix Corporation, Bain & Company.

Ren, K., Chen, J., Xiao, N., Song, J., & Li, J. (2008). Building quick service query list using wordnet for automated service composition. In *Proceedings of Asia-Pacific Services Computing Conference,* (pp. 297-302). IEEE.

Ren, Z. (2001). *The winter of Huawei*. Retrieved 4 24, 2013, from http://blog.roodo.com/shanks02/archives/11641667.html

Ren, Z. (2003). What to learn from the American. *Chinese Entrepreneur,* (11), 34-35.

Ren, Z. (2010). The right direction comes from compromise. *China Businessman*, 26-28.

Ren, Z. (2013). *Ren Zhengfei (任正非)*. Retrieved from http://baike.baidu.com/view/23495.htm

Ren, Z. (2008). Learn to think in grey. *Business Review (Federal Reserve Bank of Philadelphia)*, 1–1.

Resnik, P. (1999). Semantic similarity in a taxonomy: An information-based measure and its application to problems of ambiguity in natural language. *Journal of Artificial Intelligence Research, 11*, 95–130.

Review, H. B. (2009). *Harvard business review on business model innovation*. Cambridge, MA: Harvard Business School Press.

RFC. (2012). *RFC editor*. Retrieved Nov 15, 2013, from http://www.rfc-editor.org/

Richetin, J., Perugini, M., Conner, M., Adjali, I., Hurling, R., Sengupta, A., & Greetham, D. (2012). To reduce and not to reduce resource consumption? That is two questions. *Journal of Environmental Psychology, 32*(2), 112–122. doi:10.1016/j.jenvp.2012.01.003

Richter, A., & Koch, M. (2008). Functions of social networking services. In *Proc. Intl. Conf. on the Design of Cooperative Systems* (pp. 87-98). Berlin: Springer.

Ried, S. (2011). *Sizing the cloud*. Washington, DC: Forrester.

Rimal, B., Choi, E., & Lumb, I. (2010). A taxonomy, survey, and issues of cloud computing ecosystems. In *Cloud computing: Principles, systems and applications* (pp. 21–46). London: Springer. doi:10.1007/978-1-84996-241-4_2

Rinderle-Ma, S., Reichert, M., & Weber, B. (2008). Relaxed compliance notions in adaptive process management systems. In *Proceedings of Conceptual Modeling - ER Conference* (Vol. 5231, pp. 232-247). Berlin: Springer.

Risdahl, A. (2007). *E-commerce*. Adams Media.

Robbins, S. P., & Judge, T. A. (2012). *Organizational behavior*. Upper Saddle River, NJ: Pearson Education.

Robertson, T. S., & Gatignon, H. (1989). Technology diffusion: An empirical test of competitive effects. *Journal of Marketing, 53*, 35–49. doi:10.2307/1251523

Rocheleau, B., & Wu, L. (2002). Public versus private information systems. *American Review of Public Administration, 32*(4), 379. doi:10.1177/027507402237866

Rogers, E. M. (1995). *Diffusion of innovations*. New York: Free Press.

Rogers, E. M. (2003). *Diffusion of innovation* (5th ed.). New York: Free Press.

Rolim, C. O., Koch, F. L., Westphall, C. B., Werner, J., Fracalossi, A., & Salvador, G. S. (2010). A cloud computing solution for patient's data collection in health care institutions. In *Proceedings of the 2nd International Conference on eHealth, Telemedicine, and Social Medicine*. New York, NY: IEEE.

Rosenblum, M. (1999). *VMware's virtual platform™*. Paper presented at the Hot Chips. New York, NY.

Rosenschein, J. S. (1982). Synchronization of multi-agent plans. In *Proceedings of Second National Conference on Artificial Intelligence* (pp. 115–119). Pittsburgh, PA: AAAI Press.

Ross, D. F. (2011). *Introduction to supply chain management technologies* (2nd ed.). Boca Raton, FL: CRC Press.

Rouse, M. (2009). *Storage as a service (SaaS)*. Retrieved July 11, 2013, from http://searchstorage.techtarget.com/definition/Storage-as-a-Service-SaaS

Rouse, M. (2010). *Definition of clinical decision support system (CDSS)*. Retrieved from http://searchhealthit.techtarget.com/definition/clinical-decision-support-system-CDSS

Rouse, M. (2011). *Cloud services*. Retrieved July 03, 2013, from http://searchcloudprovider.techtarget.com/definition/cloud-services

Ruscitti, F. (2012). On the boundary behavior of the excess demand function. *Research in Economics, 66*(4), 371. doi:10.1016/j.rie.2012.05.001

Rusli, E. (2010). *How Facebook and Twitter are changing business models, shaping brand identity*. Retrieved July 1, 2012, from http://techcrunch.com/2010/05/13/how-facebook-and-twitter-are-changing-business-models-shaping-brand-identity-video/?utm_source=feedburner&utm_medium=feed&utm_campaign=Feed:+Techcrunch+(TechCrunch)

Russell, S. J., & Norvig, P. (2010). *Artificial intelligence: A modern approach*. Englewood Cliffs, NJ: Prentice Hall.

Rust, R. T., & Kannan, P. K. (2003). E-service: A new paradigm for business in the electronic environment. *Communications of the ACM, 46*(6), 37–42. doi:10.1145/777313.777336

Şah, M., & Wade, V. (2012). Automatic metadata mining from multilingual enterprise content. *Web Semantics: Science. Services and Agents on the World Wide Web, 11*, 41–62. doi:10.1016/j.websem.2011.11.001

Saldanha, T. J. V., & Krishnan, M. S. (2012). Organizational adoption of web 2.0 technologies: An empirical analysis. *Journal of Organizational Computing and Electronic Commerce, 22*(4), 301–333. doi:10.1080/10919392.2012.723585

Salton, G., & McGill, M. (1983). *Introduction to modern information retrieval*. New York: McGraw Hill.

Salzer, J. M. (1960). Data processing. In *Papers presented at the May 3-5, 1960, western joint IRE-AIEE-ACM computer conference on - IRE-AIEE-ACM '60 (western)*. New York: ACM Press.

Samuel, A. (2009). Waiting for government 2.0: Why do public agencies take so long to embrace social media? In J. Gotze, & J. Bering Pedersen (Eds.), *State of the eUnion: Government 2.0 and onwards* (pp. 109–122). Academic Press.

Santos, N., Gummadi, K. P., & Rodrigues, R. (2009). *Towards trusted cloud computing*. Retrieved on 22 April, 2011, from http://www.mpi-sws.org/~gummadi/papers/trusted_cloud.pdf

SAP. (2005, December 18). *Microsoft, IBM, SAP to discontinue UDDI web services registry effort*. Retrieved from http://soa.sys-con.com/node/164624

Sarwar, B. M., Karypis, G., Konstan, J. A., & Riedl, J. T. (2000). Application of dimensionality reduction in recommender system -- A case study. In *Proceedings of ACM WEBKDD Workshop*. ACM.

Sauter, V. L. (2011). *Decision support systems for business intelligence*. Hoboken, NJ: John Wiley & Sons. doi:10.1002/9780470634431

Schabell, E. D. (n.d.). OpenShift primer. *Developer Press.*

Schalkoff, R. J. (2011). *Intelligent Systems: Principles, Paradigms, and Pragmatics*. Boston: Jones and Bartlett Publishers.

Schellong, A. R. M. (2008). Government 2.0: An exploratory study of social networking services in Japanese local government. *Transforming Government: People. Process and Policy, 2*(4), 225–242.

Schmutzler, J., Wolff, A., & Wietfeld, C. (2008). Comparative performance evaluation of web services and JXTA for embedded environmental monitoring systems. In *Proceedings of Conference on Enterprise Distributed Object Computing*, (pp. 369-376). Academic Press.

Schneider, G. (2011). *Electronic Commerce* (9th ed.). Australia: Course Technology.

Schneider, G. P. (2013). *Electornic commerce* (10th ed.). Australia: Coourse Technology CENGAGE Learning.

Scott, W. R. (1987). The adolescence of institutional theory. *Administrative Science Quarterly, 32*(4), 493–511. doi:10.2307/2392880

Scupola, A., Henten, A., & Westh Nicolajsen, H. (2009). E-services: Characteristics, scope and conceptual strengths. *International Journal of E-Services and Mobile Applications, 1*(3), 1–16. doi:10.4018/jesma.2009070101

SEEMPubS. (2010). Retrieved from http://seempubs.polito.it/

Seinfeld, J.H. (1986). *Atmospheric chemistry and physics of air pollution*. New York: J. Wiley. Hanna, S.R., Briggs, G.A., & Kosker, R.P. (1982). *Hand book on atmospheric diffusion*. Springfield, VA: NTIS, DE81009809(DOE/TIC-22800).

Sekaran, U. (2003). *Research methods for business* (4th ed.). New York: John Wiley & Sons.

Sellis, T., Skoutas, D., & Staikos, K. (2008). Database interoperability through web services and ontologies. In *Proceedings of International Conference on BioInformatics and BioEngineering*. BIBE.

Sensis. (2012). *Yellow social media report*. Sensis Pty Ltd.

Sermersheim, J. (2006, June 1). *Lightweight directory access protocol (LDAP), the protocol*. Retrieved April 9, 2013, from http://tools.ietf.org/html/rfc4511

Sethi, J., & Bhatia, N. (2007). *Element of banking and insurance*. New Delhi, India: Prentice Hall of India.

Shafiq, M. O., Ali, A., Ahmad, H. F., & Suguri, H. (2005). AgentWeb gateway - A middleware for dynamic integration of multi agent system and web services framework. In *Proceedings of 14th IEEE International Workshops on Enabling Technologies: Infrastructure for Collaborative Enterprise* (pp. 267–270). Washington, DC: IEEE.

ShaikhAli. A., Rana, O., Al-Ali, R., & Walker, D. (2003). UDDIe: An extended registry for web services. In *Proceedings of the 2003 Symposium on Applications and the Internet Workshops* (pp. 85-89). San Leandro, CA: IEEE Computer Society.

Shan, T. (2009). *Cloud taxonomy and ontology*. Retrieved August 1, 2013, from http://tonyshan.ulitzer.com/node/1469454

Sharif, M., Troshani, I., & Davidson, R. (2014). Adoption of Social Media Services: The Case of Local Government Organizations in Australia. In Z. Sun, & J. Yearwood (Eds.), *Demand-Driven Web Services: Theory, Technologies, and Applications*. IGI-Global.

Shelby, Z. (2010). Embedded web services. *IEEE Wireless Communications, 17*(6), 52–57. doi:10.1109/MWC.2010.5675778

Shenker, S., & Wroclawski, J. (1997, September 1). *General characterization parameters for integrated service network elements*. Retrieved April 6, 2013, from https://tools.ietf.org/rfc/rfc2215.txt

Shih, C. F., Dedrick, D., & Kreamer, K. L. (2005). Rule of law and the international diffusion of e-commerce. *Communications of the ACM, 48*(1).

Shin, D.-H., & Choo, H. (2012). Exploring cross-cultural value structures with smartphones. *Journal of Global Information Management, 20*(2), 67–93. doi:10.4018/jgim.2012040104

Silverstein, M. J., Singhi, A., Liao, C., & Michael, D. (2012). *The $10 trillion prize captivating the newly affluent in China and India*. Boston: Harvard Business Review Press.

Singh, M. P., Chopra, A. K., & Desai, N. (2009). Commitment-based service-oriented architecture. *Computer, 42*(11), 72–79. doi:10.1109/MC.2009.347

Singh, P. M., & Huhns, N. M. (2005). *Service-oriented computing: Semantics, processes, and agents*. Chichester, UK: John Wiley & Sons, Ltd.

Sitaram, D., & Manjunath, G. (2011). *Moving to the cloud developing apps in the new world of cloud computing*. Burlington, MA: Elsevier Science.

Sivashanmugam, K., Miller, J. A., Sheth, A. P., & Verma, K. (2005). Framework for semantic web process composition. *International Journal of Electronic Commerce, 9*(2), 71–106.

Skroch, O. (2010). Multi-criteria service selection with optimal stopping in dynamic service-oriented systems. In *Proceedings of the 6th International Conference on Distributed Computing and Internet Technology* (pp. 110-121). Berlin: Springer-Verlag.

Slade, D. H. (Ed.). (1986). *Meteorology and atomic energy*. Washington, DC: U.S. Atomic Energy Commission, Air Resources Laboratories, Research Laboratories, Environmental Science Services Administration, U.S Department of Commerce.

Sleman, A., & Moeller, R. (2011). SOA distributed operating system for managing embedded devices in home and building automation. *IEEE Transactions on Consumer Electronics, 57*(2), 945–952. doi:10.1109/TCE.2011.5955244

Smith, R., & Davis, R. (1980). The contract net protocol: High level communication and control in a distributed problem solver. *IEEE Transactions on Computers, 29*(12), 1104–1113. doi:10.1109/TC.1980.1675516

Smyth, B., Briggs, P., & Coyle, M. (2009). A Case-Based Perspective on Social Web Search, LNCS. In *Case-Based Reasoning*[]. Berlin: Springer.]. *Research for Development, 5650*, 494–508.

Social.advantages. (2009). *The new effective social business model – Facebook wins*. Retrieved July 1, 2012, from http://social.advantages.us/2009/11/15/the-new-effective-social-business-model-facebook-wins/

Sohali, A., & Zamanifar, K. (2009). Matching model for semantic web services discovery. *Journal of Theoretical and Applied Information Technology, 7*(2), 139–144.

Sohraby, K., Minoli, D., & Znati, T. (2007). *Wireless sensor networks: Technology, protocols, and applications*. Hoboken, NJ: John Wiley and Sons. doi:10.1002/047011276X

Song, H. (2003). E-services at FedEx. *Communications of the ACM, 46*(6), 45–46. doi:10.1145/777313.777338

Sørensen, J. K. (2011). *The paradox of personalisation: Public service broadcasters' approaches to media personalisation technologies*. University of Southern Denmark. SDU.

Sosinsky, B. (2010). *Cloud computing bible*. Hoboken, NJ: John Wiley & Sons.

Soto, E. L. (2006). FIPA agent messaging grounded on web services. In *Proceedings of 3rd International Conference on Grid Service Engineering and Management* (pp. 247-248). Erfurt, Germany: Academic Press.

Spink, K. S., Wilson, K. S., & Bostick, J. M. (2012). Theory of planned behavior and intention to exercise: Effects of setting. *American Journal of Health Behavior, 36*(2), 254. doi:10.5993/AJHB.36.2.10 PMID:22370262

Stasieńko, J. (2010). Business intelligence as a decision support system. In G. Setlak, & K. Markov (Eds.), *Methods and instruments of artificial intelligence* (pp. 141–148). Rzeszow, Poland: Academic Press.

State Services Commission. (2008). *New Zealand e-government 2007: Progress towards transformation.* Wellington, New Zealand: New Zealand Government.

Steinberg, J., & Speed, T. (2005). *SSL VPN understanding, evaluating and planning secure, web-based remote access.* Birmingham, AL: Packt Publishing.

Stephens, T. R. (2007). *Business model 2.0.* Retrieved July 1, 2012, from http://www.rtodd.com/collaborage/2007/10/business_model_20.html

Steward, A. (2012). *Progress on government 2.0.* Retrieved from http://agimo.govspace.gov.au/2012/07/06/progress-on-government-2-0/#more-3982

Stewart, J. M., & Chapple, M. (2011). *CISSP certified information systems security professional study guide.* Hoboken, NJ: John Wiley & Sons.

Stoicu-Tivadar, V., Stoicu-Tivadar, L., Puscoci, S., Berian, D., & Topac, V. (2012). WebService-based solution for an intelligent telecare system. In *Recent advances in intelligent engineering systems.* Berlin: Springer. doi:10.1007/978-3-642-23229-9_18

Stoneseed. (2013). *You can download our multisourcing whitepaper here.* Retrieved June 24, 2013, from http://stoneseed.co.uk: http://stoneseed.co.uk/blog/wp-content/themes/vulcan/download.php

Strachey, C. (1959). Time sharing in large fast computers. In *Proceedings of International Conference on Information Processing Congress* (pp. 336–341). Paris: UNESCO.

Strang, K. D. (2012a, January 26). *Evaluating marketing investment projects in the uranium mining industry.* Paper presented at the System of Systems Conference. El Paso, TX.

Strang, K. D. (2009). Assessing team member interpersonal competencies in new product development e-projects. *International Journal of Project Organisation and Management, 1*(4), 335–357. doi:10.1504/IJPOM.2009.029105

Strang, K. D. (2010). Comparing learning and knowledge management theories in an Australian telecommunications practice. *Asian Journal of Management Cases, 7*(1), 33–54. doi:10.1177/097282011000700104

Strang, K. D. (2010). *Effectively teach professionals online: Explaining and testing educational psychology theories* (2nd ed.). Saarbruecken, Germany: VDM Publishing.

Strang, K. D. (2011). A grounded theory study of cellular phone new product development. *International Journal of Internet and Enterprise Management, 7*(4), 366–387. doi:10.1504/IJIEM.2011.045112

Strang, K. D. (2011). Leadership substitutes and personality impact on time and quality in virtual new product development. *Project Management Journal, 42*(1), 73–90. doi:10.1002/pmj.20208

Strang, K. D. (2012). Importance of verifying queue model assumptions before planning with simulation software. *European Journal of Operational Research, 218*(2), 493–504. doi:10.1016/j.ejor.2011.10.054

Strang, K. D. (2012). Group cohesion, personality and leadership effect on networked marketing staff performance. *International Journal of Networking and Virtual Organisations, 10*(2), 187–209. doi:10.1504/IJNVO.2012.045734

Strang, K. D. (2012). Investment selection in complex multinational projects. *International Journal of Information Technology Project Management, 3*(2), 1–13.

Strang, K. D. (2012). Nonparametric correspondence analysis of global risk management techniques. *International Journal of Risk and Contingency Management, 1*(3), 1–24. doi:10.4018/ijrcm.2012070101

Strang, K. D. (2012). Prioritization and supply chain logistics as a marketing function in a mining company. *Journal of Marketing Channels, 19*(2), 1–15. doi:10.1080/1046669X.2012.667763

Strang, K. D. (2013). Homeowner behavioral intent to evacuate after flood warnings. *International Journal of Risk and Contingency Management, 2*(3), 1–28. doi:10.4018/ijrcm.2013070101

Strang, K. D. (2013). Risk management research design ideologies, strategies, methods and techniques. *International Journal of Risk and Contingency Management, 2*(2), 1–26. doi:10.4018/ijrcm.2013040101

Strang, K. D. (Ed.). (2008). *Collaborative synergy and leadership in e-business*. Hershey, PA: IGI Global.

Strang, K. D., & Chan, C. E. L. (2010). Simulating e-business innovation process improvement with virtual teams across Europe and Asia. *International Journal of E-Entrepreneurship and Innovation*, *1*(1), 22–41. doi:10.4018/jeei.2010010102

Strebe, M. (2006). *Network security foundations: Technology fundamentals for IT success*. Hoboken, NJ: John Wiley & Sons, Inc.

Strijbosch, K. (2011). *Adaptive case management: A new way of supporting knowledge work*. (Unpublished Doctoral Dissertation). Radboud Universiteit Nijmegen.

Stroulia, E., & Wang, Y. (2005). Structural and semantic matching for assessing web-service similarity. *International Journal of Cooperative Information Systems*, *14*(4), 407–437. doi:10.1142/S0218843005001213

Sun, Z., & Finnie, G. (2004; 2010). Intelligent Techniques in E-Commerce: A Case-based Reasoning Perspective. Heidelberg Berlin: Springer-Verlag.

Sun, Z., & Firmin, S. (2012). A strategic perspective on management intelligent systems. In J. Casillas et al, Management Intelligent Systems, AISC 171 (pp. 3-14). Springer.

Sun, Z., Yearwood, J., & Firmin, S. (2013). A technique for ranking friendship closeness in social networking services. Submitted to ACIS2013 Melbourne.

Sundbo, J., Sundbo, D., & Henten, A. (2013). Service co-innovation service encounters as basis for innovation. In *Proceedings of RESER 2013*. RESER.

Sun, Z., Dong, D., & Yearwood, J. (2011). Demand driven web service. In H.-F. Leung, D. K. Chiu, & P. C. Hung (Eds.), *Service intelligence and service science: Evolutionary technologies and challenges* (pp. 35–54). Hershey, PA: IGI Global.

Sun, Z., & Finnie, G. (2004). *Intelligent Techniques in E-Commerce: A Case-based Reasoning Perspective*. Heidelberg, Berlin: Springer-Verlag. doi:10.1007/978-3-540-40003-5

Sun, Z., Finnie, G., & Yearwood, J. (2010). Case based web services. In I. Lee (Ed.), *Encyclopedia of e-business development and management in the global economy* (pp. 871–882). Hershey, PA: Business Science Reference. doi:10.4018/978-1-61520-611-7.ch087

Sun, Z., & Lau, S. K. (2007). Customer experience management in e-services. In J. Lu, D. Ruan, & G. Zhang (Eds.), *E-Service Intelligence: Methodologies, Technologies and Applications* (pp. 365–388). Berlin, Heidelberg: Springer Verlag. doi:10.1007/978-3-540-37017-8_17

Sun, Z., Wang, M., & Dong, D. (2010). Decision making in multiagent web services based on soft computing. In J. Casillas, & F. J. Martínez-López (Eds.), *Marketing intelligent systems using soft computing* (pp. 389–415). Berlin: Springer. doi:10.1007/978-3-642-15606-9_22

Sun, Z., Zhang, P., Dong, D., Kajan, E., Dorloff, F.-D., & Bedini, I. (2012). Customer decision making in web services. In *Handbook of research on e-business standards and protocols: Documents, data, and advanced web technologies*. Hershey, PA: IGI Global. doi:10.4018/978-1-4666-0146-8.ch010

Swatman, P. M. C., & Chan, E. S. K. (2001). E-commerce/e-business education: Pedagogy or new product development. In *Reading in e-commerce*. Berlin: Springer-Verlag. doi:10.1007/978-3-7091-6213-2_9

Sycara, K., Paolucci, M., Ankolekar, A., & Srinivasan, N. (2003). Automated discovery, interaction and composition of semantic web services. *Web Semantics: Science. Services and Agents on the World Wide Web*, *1*(1), 27–46. doi:10.1016/j.websem.2003.07.002

Syeda-Mahmood, T., Shah, G., Akkiraju, R., Ivan, A. A., & Goodwin, R. (2005). Searching service repositories by combining semantic and ontological matching. In *Proceedings of Web Services* (pp. 13–20). IEEE. doi:10.1109/ICWS.2005.102

Tabein, R., Moghadasi, M., & Khoshkbarforoushha, A. (2008). Broker-based Web service selection using learning automata. *2008 International Conference on Service Systems and Service Management, June July 2008, pp.1-6.*

Tang, J. C. (2007). Approaching and leave-taking.[–es.]. *ACM Transactions on Computer-Human Interaction*, *14*(1), 5. doi:10.1145/1229855.1229860

Tang, Z. (1995). Confucianism, Chinese culture, and reproductive behavior. *Population and Environment*, *16*(3), 269–284. doi:10.1007/BF02331921

Taobao. (2013). *Taobao English guide*. Retrieved August 1, 2013, from http://taobaofocus.com/faq

Tapia, D. I., Rodríguez, S., Bajo, J., & Corchado, J. (2009). FUSION@, a SOA-based multi-agent. In J. M. Corchado, S. Rodríguez, J. Llinas, & J. Molina (Eds.), *International symposium on distributed computing and artificial intelligence 2008, advances in soft computing architecture,* (vol. 50, pp. 99-107). Heidelberg, Germany: Springer.

Tapsns.com. (2009). *Facebook and business model 2.0*. Retrieved July 1, 2012, from http://www.tapsns.com/blog/index.php/2009/01/facebook-and-business-model-20/

Tawileh, A., Rana, O., & Mcintosh, S. (2008). A social networking approach to F/OSS quality assessment. In *Proceedings of the International Conference on Computer Mediated Social Networking (ICCMSN' 2008)*. Dunedin, New Zealand: ICCMSN.

Taylor, S. (2012). *Service intelligence, improving your bottom line with the power of IT service management*. Crawfordsville: Pearson Education.

Taylor, H., Yochem, A., Phillips, L., & Martinez, F. (2009). *Event-driven architecture: How SOA enables the real-time enterprise*. Reading, MA: Addison-Wesley.

Tencent. (2013). *E-commerce*. Retrieved Aug. 29, 2013, from http://www.tencent.com/en-us/ps/ecommerce.shtml

Themistocleous, M., Irani, Z., Kuljis, J., & Love, P. E. D. (2004). Extending the information systems lifecycle through enterprise application intergration. In *Proceedings of the 37th Hawaii International Conference on System Sciences*. IEEE.

ThingSpeak. (2013). *Internet of things - ThingSpeak*. Retrieved July 19, 2013, from https://www.thingspeak.com/

Thirumaran, M., Naga Venkata Kiran, G., & Dhavachel-van, P. A. (2012). Collaborative Framework for Managing Run-Time Changes in Enterprise Web Services. *International Journal of Web & Semantic Technology*, *3*(3), 85. doi:10.5121/ijwest.2012.3306

Thomas, M., Yoon, V., & Redmond, R. (2009). Extending loosely coupled federated information systems using agent technology. In V. Sugumaran (Ed.), *Distributed artificial intelligence, agent technology, and collaborative applications* (pp. 116–131). Hershey, PA: IGI Global.

Thomas, P. Y. (2012). Harnessing the Potential of Cloud Computing to Transform Higher Education. In L. Chao (Ed.), *Cloud Computing for Teaching and Learning Strategies for Design and Implementation* (pp. 147–158). USA: IGI Global. doi:10.4018/978-1-4666-0957-0.ch010

Tonchev, A., & Tonchev, C. (2010). *Social networks: A quality perspective*. The Big Q Blog. Retrieved from http://www.juran.com/blog/?p=127

Tong, H., Cao, J., Zhang, S., & Li, M. (2009). A distributed agent coalition algorithm for web service composition. In *Proceedings of 2009 World Conference on* Services (pp. 62-69). Los Angeles, CA: IEEE.

Tonino, H., Bos, A., de Weerdt, M., & Witteveen, C. (2002). Plan coordination by revision in collective agent based systems. *Artificial Intelligence*, *142*(2), 121–145. doi:10.1016/S0004-3702(02)00273-4

Towns, S. (2010). *Will Facebook replace traditional government websites*. Retrieved from http://www.govtech.com/e-government/Will-Facebook-Replace-Traditional-Government-Web.html

Trevino, L. K., Daft, R. L., & Lengel, R. H. (1990). Understanding managers' media choices: A symbolic interactionist perspective. In C. W. Steinfield, & J. Fulk (Eds.), *Organizations and communcation technology* (pp. 71–94). Newbury Park, CA: Sage Publications.

Treviño, L. K., Webster, J., & Stein, E. W. (2000). Making connections: Complementary influences on communication media choices, attitudes, and use. *Organization Science*, *11*(2), 163–182. doi:10.1287/orsc.11.2.163.12510

Trongmateerut, P., & Sweeney, J. T. (2013). The influence of subjective norms on whistle-blowing: A cross-cultural investigation. *Journal of Business Ethics*, *112*(3), 437–451. doi:10.1007/s10551-012-1270-1

Troshani, I., Jerram, C., & Rao Hill, S. (2011). Exploring the public sector adoption of HRIS. *Industrial Management & Data Systems*, *111*(3), 470–488. doi:10.1108/02635571111118314

Turban, E., & Aronson. (2001). *Decision support systems and intelligent systems* (6th Ed.). Hoboken, NJ: Prentice Hall, Inc.

Turban, E., & Volonino, L. (2011). *Information technology for management: Improving strategic and operational performance*. Hoboken, NJ: John Wiley & Sons, Inc.

Turchik, J. A., & Gidycz, C. A. (2012). Prediction of sexual risk behaviors in college students using the theory of planned behavior: A prospective analysis. *Journal of Social and Clinical Psychology, 31*(1), 1. doi:10.1521/jscp.2012.31.1.1

Turner, D. B. (1979). Atmospheric dispersion modeling. *Journal of the Air Pollution Control Association, 29*(5), 502–519. doi:10.1080/00022470.1979.10470821

Turner, D. B. (1994). *Workbook of atmospheric dispersion estimates: An introduction to dispersion modeling* (2nd ed.). Boca Raton, FL: Lewis Publishers.

Turner, D. B., Bender, L. W., Pierce, T. E., & Petersen, W. B. (1989). Air quality simulation models from EPA. *Environmental Software, 4*(2), 52–61. doi:10.1016/0266-9838(89)90031-2

Turner, M., Budgen, D., & Brereton, P. (2003). Turning software into a service. *Computer, 36*(10), 38–44. doi:10.1109/MC.2003.1236470

Tzeng, G. H., & Huang, J. J. (2011). *Multiple attribute decision making: Methods and applications*. Boca Raton, FL: CRC Press, Taylor & Francis Group.

Ugurlu, S., & Erdogan, N. (2005). A secure communication framework for mobile agents. In *Proceedings of the 20th International Conference on Computer and Information Sciences* (pp. 412-421). Heidelberg, Germany: Springer-Verlag.

Uhm, Y., Lee, M., Hwang, Z., Kim, Y., & Park, S. (2011). A multi-resolution agent for service-oriented situations in ubiquitous domains. *Expert Systems with Applications, 38*(10), 13291–13300. doi:10.1016/j.eswa.2011.04.150

Ungureanu, V., Melamed, B., & Katehakis, M. (2008). Effective load balancing for cluster-based servers employing job preemption. *Performance Evaluation, 65*(8), 606–622. doi:10.1016/j.peva.2008.01.001

United States Chemical Safety Board. (n.d.). Retrieved from http://www.csb.gov

Urgaonkar, B., Shenoy, P., Chandra, A., & Goyal, P. (2005). *Dynamic provisioning of multi-tier internet applications*. Paper presented at the Autonomic Computing, 2005. New York, NY.

Urgaonkar, B., Shenoy, P., Chandra, A., Goyal, P., & Wood, T. (2008). Agile dynamic provisioning of multi-tier internet applications. *ACM Transactions on Autonomous and Adaptive Systems, 3*(1), 1. doi:10.1145/1342171.1342172

Usdod. (2013). *History of the ARPAnet*. Washington, DC: United States Department of Defense (USDOD).

Van Der Aalst, W. M. P. (1998). The application of petrinets to workflow management. *Journal of Circuits. Systems and Computers, 8*(1), 21–66.

Van Lamsweerde, A. (2001). Goal-oriented requirements engineering: A guided tour. In *Proceedings of Requirements Engineering Conference* (pp. 249-262). Academic Press.

Van Vliet, J., Paganelli, F., van Wel, S., & Dowd, D. (2011). *Elastic beanstalk*. Sebastopol, CA: O'Reilly Media, Inc.

Vandermerwe, S., & Rada, J. (1988). Servitization of business: Adding value by adding services. *European Management Journal, 6*(4), 314–324. doi:10.1016/0263-2373(88)90033-3

Vaquero, L. M., Rodero-Merino, L., Caceres, J., & Lindner, M. (2008). A break in the clouds: towards a cloud definition. *ACM SIGCOMM Computer Communication Review, 39*(1), 50–55. doi:10.1145/1496091.1496100

Varshney, U. (2008). A framework for supporting emergency messages in wireless patient monitoring. *Decision Support Systems, 45*, 981–996. doi:10.1016/j.dss.2008.03.006

Vedder, A. (1999). KDD: The challenge to individualism. *Ethics and Information Technology, 1*(4), 275–281. doi:10.1023/A:1010016102284

Velte, A., & Velte, T. (2009). *Microsoft virtualization with hyper-V*. New York: McGraw-Hill, Inc.

Venkatesh, V., Morris, M. G., Davis, G. B., & Davis, F. D. (2003). User acceptance of information technology: Toward a unified view. *Management Information Systems Quarterly, 27*(3), 425–478.

Venkateswaran, R. (2001). Virtual private networks. *IEEE Potentials,* (1), 11-15.

VentureDig. (2010). *Monetizing social networks: The four dominant business models and how you should implement them in 2010.* Retrieved July 1, 2012, from http://venturedig.com/tech/monetizing-social-networks-the-four-dominant-business-models-and-how-you-should-implement-them-in-2010/

Vercellis, C. (2009). *Business intelligence, data mining and optimization for decision making.* Cornwall, UK: John Wiley & Sons.

Vidyarthi, N. (2010). *Opinion: Will Google's smart TV finally bring apps and web browsing to the living room?* Retrieved August 09, 2013, from http://socialtimes.com/opinion-will-googles-smart-tv-finally-bring-apps-and-Web-browsing-to-the-living-room_b13046

Vikhorev, K., Greenough, R., & Brown, N. (2013). An advanced energy management framework to promote energy awareness. *Journal of Cleaner Production, 43*, 103–112. doi:10.1016/j.jclepro.2012.12.012

VirtualBox. (2009). *Welcome to VirtualBox.org.* Retrieved June 5, 2013, from https://www.virtualbox.org/

Vitvar, T. (2007). SESA: Emerging technology for service-centric environments. *IEEE Software, 24*(6), 56–67. doi:10.1109/MS.2007.178

Vitvar, T., Mocan, A., Kerrigan, M., Zaremba, M., Zaremba, M., & Moran, M. et al. (2007). Semantically-enabled service oriented architecture: Concepts, technology and application. *Service Oriented Computing and Applications, 1*(2), 129–154. doi:10.1007/s11761-007-0009-9

Vitvar, T., Zaremba, M., Moran, M., & Mocan, A. (2008). Mediation using WSMO, WSML and WSMX. In C. Petrie, H. Lausen, M. Zaremba, & T. Margaria-Steen (Eds.), *Semantic web services challenge: Results from the first year (semantic web and beyond)* (pp. 72–83). Heidelberg, Germany: Springer.

Volery, T., & Lord, D. (2000). Critical success factor in online education. *International Journal of Educational Management, 14*(14), 216–223. doi:10.1108/09513540010344731

Vu, H. T., & Leez, T.-T. (2013). Soap operas as a matchmaker: A cultivation analysis of the effects of South Korean TV dramas on Vietnamese women's marital intentions. *Journalism & Mass Communication Quarterly, 90*(2), 308–330. doi:10.1177/1077699013482912

Walczak, D., Wrzos, M., Radziuk, A., Lewandowski, B., & Mazurek, C. (2012). Machine-to-machine communication and data processing approach in future internet applications. In *Proceedings of 2012 8th International Symposium on Communication Systems, Networks Digital Signal Processing (CSNDSP)* (pp. 1 -5). CSNDSP.

Walker, R. M. (2006). Innovation type and diffusion: An empirical analysis of local government. *Public Administration, 84*(2), 311–335. doi:10.1111/j.1467-9299.2006.00004.x

Wang, L. (2009). State of the art and trends of social networking sites. *Modern Science & Technology of Telecommunications,* (6), 9-13.

Wang, X., & Tan, Y. (2010). Application of cloud computing in the health information system. In *Proceedings of the 2010 International Conference on Computer Application and System Modeling (ICCASM).* New York, NY: IEEE.

Wang, H., & Ghose, A. K. (2010). Green strategic alignment: Aligning business strategies with sustainability objectives. In B. Unhelkar (Ed.), *Handbook of research in green ICT* (pp. 29–41). Academic Press. doi:10.4018/978-1-61692-834-6.ch002

Wang, Z. (2001). *Internet QoS - Architectures and mechanisms for quality of service.* San Francisco: Morgan Kaufmann.

Wasserman, S., & Faust, K. (1994). *Social network analysis: Methods and applications.* Cambridge, UK: Cambridge University Press. doi:10.1017/CBO9780511815478

Waters, D. (2006). Demand chain effectiveness-supply chain efficiencies: A role for enterprise information management. *Journal of Enterprise Information Management, 19*(3), 246–261. doi:10.1108/17410390610658441

Weaver, A. C. (2006). Secure sockets layer. *Computer*, 88–90. doi:10.1109/MC.2006.138

Weber, A., Dwyer, T., & Mummery, K. (2012). Morphine administration by paramedics: An application of the theory of planned behaviour. *Injury*, *43*(9), 1393. doi:10.1016/j.injury.2010.12.006 PMID:21215396

Webster, J., & Treviño, L. K. (1995). Rational and social theories as complementary explanations of communication media choices: Two policy-capturing studies. *Academy of Management Journal*, *38*(6), 1544–1572. doi:10.2307/256843

Weischedel, B., & Huizingh, E. K. R. E. (2006). Website optimization with web metrics. In *Proceedings of the 8th International Conference on Electronic Commerce the New E-Commerce: Innovations for Conquering Current Barriers, Obstacles and Limitations to Conducting Successful Business on the Internet - ICEC '06* (pp. 463–470). New York: ACM Press.

Weissenberger-Eibl, M. A., & Spieth, P. (2006). Knowledge transfer: Affected by organisational culture? In K. Tochtermann & H. Maurer (Eds.), *Proceedings of I-KNOW '06, 6th International Conference on Knowledge-Management* (pp. 68-75). Hedelberg, Germany: Springer.

Weiss, G. (2000). *Multiagent systems: A modern approach to distributed artificial intelligence*. Cambridge, MA: MIT Press.

Weiss, G. (2013). *Multiagent systems* (2nd ed.). Cambridge, MA: MIT Press.

Weissman, C. D., & Bobrowski, S. (2009). *The design of the force.com multitenant internet application development platform*. Paper presented at the SIGMOD Conference. New York, NY.

Wellman, B. (1979). The community question: The intimate networks of East Yorkers. *American Journal of Sociology*, *84*, 1201–1231. doi:10.1086/226906

Wellman, B., & Berkowitz, S. D. (1988). *Social structures: A network approach*. Cambridge, UK: Cambridge University Press.

Wernerfelt, B. (1984). A resource-based view of the firm. *Strategic Management Journal*, *5*(2), 171–180. doi:10.1002/smj.4250050207

Wigand, F. D. L. (2010). Adoption of web 2.0 by Canadian and US governments. In *Comparative e-government*. New York: Springer. doi:10.1007/978-1-4419-6536-3_8

Wikipedia. (2013, May 6). *Comparison of agent-based modeling software*. Retrieved May 13, 2013, from http://en.wikipedia.org/wiki/Comparison_of_agent-based_modeling_software

wikipedia-CP. (2013). *Cloud Computing*. Retrieved 8 28, 2013, from wikipedia: http://en.wikipedia.org/wiki/Cloud_computing

Wikipedia-SNS. (2013, 9 20). *Social Networking Service*. Retrieved 9 24, 2013, from Wikipedia: http://en.wikipedia.org/wiki/Social_networking_service

Wikipeidia-SN-List. (2013, 7 26). *List of social networking websites*. Retrieved 9 24, 2013, from Wikipeidia: http://en.wikipedia.org/wiki/List_of_social_networking_websites

Wilkinson, N. (2005). *Managerial Economics: A Problem-Solving Approach*. Cambridge: Cambridge University Press. doi:10.1017/CBO9780511810534

Williams, A. (2009). *The feds, not forrester, are developing better definitions for cloud computing*. Retrieved July 03, 2013, from http://readwrite.com/2009/10/13/forrester-says-we-need-better#awesm=~oav2lHYSPRCOcG

Williams, M. (2000). Interpretivism and generalization. *Sociology*, *34*(2), 209–224. doi:10.1177/S0038038500000146

Wittgenstein, L. (1953). *Philosophical investigations*. Oxford, UK: B. Blackwell.

Wolf, G. (2004, September). Steve Jobs: The next insanely great thing. *Wired Magazine*, 1-5.

Wolfe, R. A. (1994). Organizational innovation: Review, critique and suggested research directions. *Journal of Management Studies*, *31*(3), 405–431. doi:10.1111/j.1467-6486.1994.tb00624.x

Wood, T., Ramakrishnan, K., van der Merwe, J., & Shenoy, P. (2010). *Cloudnet: A platform for optimized wan migration of virtual machines* (Technical Report TR-2010-002). Boston: University of Massachusetts.

Wood, T., Ramakrishnan, K. K., Shenoy, P., & Merwe, J. V. (2012). Enterprise-ready virtual cloud pools: Vision, opportunities and challenges. In *Special focus on security and performance of networks and clouds* (pp. 995–1004). Academic Press. doi:10.1093/comjnl/bxs060

Wooldridge, M. (2002). *An Introduction to Multiagent Systems*. Chichester, England: John Wiley & Sons Ltd.

Wooldridge, M. J., & Jennings, N. R. (1995). Intelligent agents: Theory and practice. *The Knowledge Engineering Review*, *10*(2), 115–152. doi:10.1017/S0269888900008122

Wright, P. C., & Monk, A. F. (1991). A cost-effective evaluation method for use by designers. *International Journal of Man-Machine Studies*, *35*(6), 891–912. doi:10.1016/S0020-7373(05)80167-1

Wu, Q., Iyengar, A., Subramanian, R., Rouvellou, I., Silva-Lepe, I., & Mikalsen, T. (2009). Combining quality of service and social information for ranking services. In *Proceedings of ServiceWave 2009 Workshops held in Conjunction with the 7th International Conference on Service Service-Oriented Computing (ICSOC'2009)*. Stockholm, Sweden: ICSOC.

Wu, Z., & Palmer, M. (1994). Verbs semantics and lexical selection. In *Proceedings of the 32nd Annual Meeting on Association for Computational Linguistics* (pp. 133-138). Association for Computational Linguistics.

Wu, D., Parsia, B., Sirin, E., Hendler, J., & Nau, D. (2003). Automating DAML-S web services composition using SHOP2. In D. Fensel, K. Sycara, & J. Mylopoulos (Eds.), *The semantic web - ISWC 2003, (LNCS)* (Vol. 2870, pp. 195–210). Berlin, Germany: Springer. doi:10.1007/978-3-540-39718-2_13

Wu, J., & Wu, Z. (2005). Similarity-based web service matchmaking.[). IEEE.]. *Proceedings of Services Computing*, *1*, 287–294.

Xian-Qong, Z. J.-H. D. (2000). Approaching technique in longjump. *Journal of Chehgdu Physical Education Institute, 5*, 021.

Xiao, Z. (2012). Correlates of condom use among Chinese college students in Hunan province. *AIDS Education and Prevention*, *24*(5), 469–482. doi:10.1521/aeap.2012.24.5.469 PMID:23016507

Xie, X., Du, B., & Zhang, Z. (2008). Semantic service composition based on social network. In *Proceedings of the 17th International World Wide Web Conference (WWW'2008)*. Beijing, China: WWW.

Xinhua. (2013). *Tencent president: Wechat will remain free*. Retrieved September 15, 2013, from http://news.xinhuanet.com/english/china/2013-04/07/c_132290364.htm

Xu, Q., Yang, X., Liu, C., Li, K., Lou, H. H., & Gossage, J. L. (2009). Chemical plant flare minimization via plant-wide dynamic simulation. *Industrial & Engineering Chemistry Research*, *48*(7), 3505–3512. doi:10.1021/ie8016219

Xu, S., Zhu, K., & Gibbs, J. (2004). Global technology, local adoption: A cross country investigation of internet adoption by companies in the United States and China. *Electronic Markets*, *14*(1), 13–24. doi:10.1080/1019678042000175261

Yahyaoui, H., Maamar, Z., Lim, E., & Thiran, P. (2013). Towards a community-based, social network-driven framework for web services management. *Future Generation Computer Systems*, *29*(6), 1363–1377. doi:10.1016/j.future.2013.02.003

Yan, Q. (2011). Huawei's cloud computing. *China Internet Week*, 22-24.

Yang, J., & Park, H. (2008). A design of open service access gateway for converged web service. In *Proceedings of International Conference on Advanced Communication Technology*, (pp. 1807-1810). Academic Press.

Yang, J., Zhang, Z., & Zhao, Y. (2010). Analysis on database connection mechanism of web application system in dreamweaver. In *Proceedings of International Conference on Internet Technology and Applications*, (pp. 1- 4). Academic Press.

Yang, L., & Liu, X. (2009). Analysis on the successful strategies of Taobao's e-commerce. In *Proceedings of the 2009 International*, (pp. 202-205). Academic Press.

Yang, Y. (2011). *How could computing leads us towards ICT*. Retrieved July 8, 2013, from http://www.ciotimes.com/cloud/cyy/43789.html

Yang, B., Tan, F., Dai, Y.-S., & Guo, S. (2009). Performance evaluation of cloud service considering fault recovery. In M. G. Jaatun, G. Zhao, & C. Rong (Eds.), *Cloud computing* (pp. 571–576). Berlin: Springer. doi:10.1007/978-3-642-10665-1_54

Yang, J. (2008). The concept and connotation of e-service. *Information Studies: Theory & Application, 31*(5), 670–674.

Yang, J. (2012). Predicting cheating behavior: A longitudinal study with Chinese business students. *Social Behavior and Personality, 40*(6), 933. doi:10.2224/sbp.2012.40.6.933

Yan, L. (2008). *The internet of things: From RFID to the next-generation pervasive networked systems.* New York: Auerbach. doi:10.1201/9781420052824

Yau, O. H. M., & Wu, W.-Y. (2012). Feng Shui principles in residential housing selection. *Psychology and Marketing, 29*(7), 502–518. doi:10.1002/mar.20538

Ye, X., & Huang, J. (2011). A framework for cloud-based smart home. In *Proceedings of 2011 International Conference on Computer Science and Network Technology (ICCSNT)* (Vol. 2, pp. 894-897). ICCSNT.

Yeo, C. S. (2008). *Market-oriented cloud computing: Vision, hype, and reality for delivering IT services as computing utilities.* Paper presented at the High Performance Computing and Communications. Melbourne, Australia.

Yeo, C. S., Venugopal, S., Chu, X., & Buyya, R. (2010). Autonomic metered pricing for a utility computing service. *Future Generation Computer Systems, 26*(8), 1368–1380. doi:10.1016/j.future.2009.05.024

Yi-Hsuan, L., Yi-Chuan, H., & Chia-Ning, H. (2011). Adding innovation diffusion theory to technology acceptance model: Supporting employees' intentions to use e-learning systems. *Journal of Educational Technology & Society, 14*(4), 124–137.

Yin, R. K. (2009). *Case study research: Design and methods.* Thousand Oaks, CA: Sage Publications.

Ylirisku, S., & Buur, J. (2007). *Designing with video.* London: Springer London.

Younglove, R. W. (2000). Virtual private networks - How they work. *Computing & Control Engineering Journal, 11*(6), 260–262. doi:10.1049/cce:20000602

Yu, B., & Singh, M. (2003). Searching social networks. In Proceedings of Second International Joint Conference on Autonomous Agents and Multiagent Systems (pp. 65-72). New York: ACM.

Yuan, S.-T., & Lu, M.-R. (2009). An value-centric event driven model and architecture: A case study of adaptive complement of SOA for distributed care service delivery. *Expert Systems with Applications, 36*(2), 3671–3694. doi:10.1016/j.eswa.2008.02.024

Zahariev, A. (2009). *Google app. engine.* Helsinki, Finland: Helsinki University of Technology.

Zhang, B., Yang, S., & Bi, J. (2013). Enterprises' willingness to adopt/develop cleaner production technologies: An empirical study in Changshu, China. *Journal of Cleaner Production, 40*, 62. doi:10.1016/j.jclepro.2010.12.009

Zhang, M. (2011). Mobile VAS value analysis from user demands perspective. *Information Research, 166*(8), 7–9.

Zhang, Q., Cheng, L., & Boutaba, R. (2010). Cloud computing: State-of-the-art and research challenges. *Journal of Internet Services and Applications, 1*(1), 7–18. doi:10.1007/s13174-010-0007-6

Zhao, F. (2006). *Entrepreneurship and innovations in e-business: An integrative perspective.* London: Idea Group Publishing. doi:10.4018/978-1-59140-920-5

Zhuang, Z. Y., Wilkin, C. L., & Ceglowski, A. (2013). A framework for an intelligent decision support system: A case in pathology test ordering. *Decision Support Systems, 55*, 476–487. doi:10.1016/j.dss.2012.10.006

Zhu, K., & Kraemer, K. L. (2005). Post-adoption variations in usage and value of e-business by organizations: Cross-country evidence from the retail industry. *Information Systems Research, 16*(1), 61–84. doi:10.1287/isre.1050.0045

Zhu, K., Kraemer, K., & Xu, S. (2003). Electronic business adoption by European firms: A cross-country assessment of the facilitators and inhibitors. *European Journal of Information Systems, 12*(4), 251–268. doi:10.1057/palgrave.ejis.3000475

Zhu, W.-D., Kirchner, M., Ko, T., Oland, M., Prasad, B., Prentice, M., & Ruggiero, M. A. (2013). *Advanced case management with ibm case manager*. IBM Redbooks.

Zimmermann, O., Doubrovski, V., Grundler, J., & Hogg, K. (2005). Service-oriented architecture and business process choreography in an order management scenario: Rationale, concepts, lessons learned. In *Companion to the 20th annual ACM SIGPLAN conference on object-oriented programming, systems, languages, and applications* (pp. 301-312). New York: ACM.

Zoellner, J., Krzeski, E., Harden, S., Cook, E., Allen, K., & Estabrooks, P. A. (2012). Qualitative application of the theory of planned behavior to understand beverage consumption behaviors among adults. *Journal of the Academy of Nutrition and Dietetics, 112*(11), 1774. doi:10.1016/j.jand.2012.06.368 PMID:23102176

Zutshi, A., Zutshi, S., & Sohal, A. (2006). How e-entrepreneurs operate in the context of open source software. In *Entrepreneurship and innovations in e-business: An integrative perspective*. London: Idea Group Publishing. doi:10.4018/978-1-59140-920-5.ch004

About the Contributors

Zhaohao Sun is currently a senior lecturer in Information Systems at the School of Science, Information technology and Engineering, University of Ballarat, Australia, and adjunct professor of Hebei Normal University, China. He worked as a full professor of computer science and technology and the head of the School of Computer Science and Technology at Hebei Normal University, China, for two years. Dr. Sun previously held academic positions also at Hebei University, RWTH Aachen, TU Cottbus, Bond University, University of Wollongong, and other universities. He has 4 books and over 110 refereed publications of journals, book chapters, and conference proceedings. His current research interests include intelligent information systems, e-commerce, Web services, case-based/experience-based reasoning, multiagent systems, Web intelligence, service computing. He is a PC member for dozens of international conferences, and a reviewer for many international journals. He is an associate editor of *Journal of Intelligent and Fuzzy Systems*. He is a senior member of ACS, a member of the AIS and the IEEE.

John Yearwood is Professor and Dean of School of Science, Information Technology, and Engineering, University of Ballarat, Australia. His research spans areas of pattern recognition, argumentation, reasoning, decision support, Web services, and their applications. He has been chief investigator on a number of ARC projects in these areas. His work has involved the development of new algorithms and approaches to classification based on modern non-smooth optimization techniques, new frameworks for structured reasoning, and their application in decision support and knowledge modelling. Some important outcomes relate to the use of text categorization techniques for detecting drugs responsible for adverse reactions. He is currently an ARC research fellow working in the area of argumentation and narrative structures. He is an associate editor for the *Journal of Research and Practice in Information Technology*. He has over 210 refereed journal and conference publications.

* * *

Iroroeavwo Edwin Achugbue is lecturer in the department of Library and Information Science, Faculty of Education, Delta State University Abraka, Nigeria. He holds a Diploma in Library science, B.Sc. (Ed) in Library Science, M.Sc in Library and Information Science. He is currently a PhD student at the time of this research in the Department of Library and Information Science, Delta State University. He has published in local, national and international journals. His areas of publication include ICT in Nigeria Universities, ICT policy in developing countries, Librarian attitude towards digital libraries, ICT and information needs of rural farmers, ICT and education, email security, and social networking.

Andrea Acquaviva is Assistant Professor at the Department of Control and Computer Engineering of Politecnico di Torino (DAUIN - EDA Group). He received his M. Sc. degree (summa cum laude) at University of Ferrara, Italy and Ph.D. degree in electrical engineering from Bologna University, Italy. He was research intern at Hewlett Packard Labs in Palo Alto, CA, USA from 2001 to 2003 and Visiting Researcher in the Ecole Politechnique Federale de Lausanne from 2005 to 2007. He has been research consultant for Freescale Semiconductor from 2004 to 2006. His research interests focus on (1) Multicore and multiprocessor architectures, including low-power, thermal aware system level design, variability and aging-aware design of next generation nanoscale electronics; (2) Computer modellsing and simulatio of biological systems, with special emphasis on the optimization on parallel architectures; (3) Wireless sensor networks. In these fields, he is co-author of more than 70 publications in international journals and peer-reviewed international conference proceedings as well as 8 book chapters.

Juan Boubeta-Puig received his first-class Honours Degree in Computer Systems Management in 2007 and his BSc in Computer Science in 2010 at the University of Cádiz (Spain). He has been working at the Department of Computer Science and Engineering as an Assistant Professor since 2009. He is currently doing his PhD research focused on the integration of complex event processing into event-driven service-oriented architectures, and the model-driven development of advanced user interfaces. Moreover, he has served as a program and organizing committee member in conferences and workshops and has published several peer-reviewed papers in conferences and journals over the last years.

Tianxing Cai is a researcher in the Dan. F Smith Department of Chemical Engineering, Lamar University. Tianxing specialized in the research fields of modeling, simulation, and optimization for the industrial operation, process safety, and environment protection. His major research is the development of optimization models (Linear Programming, Quadratic Constraint Programming, Nonlinear Programming, Mixed Integer Programming, Relaxed Mixed Integer Programming, Mixed Integer Quadratic Constraint Programming, Mixed Integer Nonlinear Programming, Relaxed Mixed Integer Quadratic Constraint Programming) to realize the synthesis of energy and water systems, manufacturing planning and scheduling and plant wide optimization. Besides that, he also involves the software application of Aspen, HYSYS, ProII, MATLAB, and gPROMS to conduct simulation and optimization for the process design, environment impact reduction, and safety assessment.

Te Fu Chen is an Assistant Professor at Department of Business Administration, Lunghwa University of Science and Technology, MBA, St. John's University, Taiwan. Dr Chen received his MBA degree in business and information management from MBA, Provindence University Taiwan in 1999; and Ph.D. degree in management from the University of Western Sydney, Australia, in 2007. His research interests include business model innovation, knowledge-based innovation, knowledge management, e-commerce/e-business, CRM, SCM, international marketing, service innovation management, tourism and leisure marketing, and cultural innovation and creative industry. Dr Chen has published over hundred papers and books in international journals global publishers. He has been the editor-in-chief and the editor and reviewer of many referred journals. Currently, he is the editor-in-chief of *International Journal of Digital Humanities and Creative Innovation Management*.

Hoa Khanh Dam is currently a lecturer at the University of Wollongong, located in one of the most beautiful settings in Australia, just an hour's drive south of Australia's largest city, Sydney. He has been lecturing/coordinating both undergraduate and postgraduate subjects in Software Engineering at the School of Computer Science and Software Engineering (SCSSE) since 2009. He's also the degree coordinator for the Bachelor of Computer Science and the research coordinator at SCSSE. Hoa holds PhD and Master degrees in Computer Science from RMIT University and a Bachelor of Computer Science degree from the University of Melbourne in Australia. His PhD thesis on proposing a novel agent-oriented approach to support change propagation in the evolution of software systems was highly commended as "strongly competitive at international levels" by external examiners. He has taught Software Engineering courses at RMIT International University Vietnam. He also has extensive work experience in the industry at various positions, including a technical architect, project manager and software engineer. Hoa's research has been published in the top venues in AI and intelligent agents (AAMAS, JAAMAS), software maintenance and evolution (ICSM), service-oriented computing (ICSOC), and enterprise computing (EDOC). He is a research participant of the 120 million CRC Smart Services project, which involves seven major industry players and six universities in Australia. Hoa has also been involved in the organisation of some recent editions of the International Conference on Principles and Practice of Multi-Agent Systems (PRIMA) where he was the workshop co-chair (PRIMA 2010), deputy program co-chair and local organization co-chair (PRIMA 2011), and senior program committee member (PRIMA 2013).

Robyn Davidson is a Senior Lecturer in Financial Accounting at the University of Adelaide Business School. She holds a PhD (Information Systems) and a BCom (Accounting and Computer Science) from Flinders University (South Australia). Robyn teaches in financial accounting and information systems and has an interest in innovative teaching methods. Robyn's research interests are in technology use in teaching, information systems, electronic service quality, Web 2.0, and business models. She has published in education and business journals.

Dong Dong is an associate professor of computer science and software engineering at Hebei Normal University, China. He received his B.S. degree in mathematics from Hebei Normal University, a M.S. in software engineering from Beijing University of Technology, China, and another M.S. degree in computer science from Asian Institute of Technology (Thailand). He is a member of CCF and ACM. His research has appeared in many journals including *Computer Engineering and Design, Computer Education, Journal of Hebei Normal University, Computer Application and Software.* His two books: *Computer Algorithms and Programming Practice* and *Foundation of Java Programming* have been published by Tsinghua Press. He has published a couple of book chapters in *Advanced Intelligent Computing Theories and Applications with Aspects of Artificial Intelligence* (Springer), *Handbook of Research on Complex Dynamic Process Management, Service Intelligence, and Service Science* (IGI Global), and LNAI. His research interests include Web information systems, recommender systems, data mining applications, and intelligent systems.

Noura Faci is an Associate Professor at the University Lyon 1, France, since October 2008. Her research interests include dependable e-business systems, service computing, and social computing. Noura also held a research associate position at King's College London in Agents and Intelligent Systems Group, where she led a work package as part of an European IT Research Project entitled "CONTRACT." She graduated for her PhD in Computer Sciences from Reims University in France in 2007.

Enrico Franchi received from the University of Parma a B.Sc. in Mathematics and Computer Science, a M.Sc. in Computer Science, and a Ph.D. in Information Technologies under the supervision of Prof. Agostino Poggi. His main interests are related to multi-agent and distributed systems, social networks, artificial intelligence, and software engineering. He is currently investigating the mutual relationships between social networks and multi-agent systems, with a special regard to simulations.

Gopinath Ganapathy is a Professor in Computer Science at Bharathidasan University, India. He published around 30 research papers in International Journals and Conferences. He has 23 years of experience in academia, industry, research and consultancy services. He has around 8.5 years of International experience in US and UK. His research interests include semantic web, auto programming, natural language processing, and text mining.

Aditya Ghose holds PhD and MSc degrees in Computing Science from the University of Alberta, Canada (he also spent parts of his PhD candidature at the Beckman Institute, University of Illinois at Urbana Champaign and the University of Tokyo), and a Bachelor of Engineering degree in Computer Science and Engineering from Jadavpur University, Kolkata, India. While at the University of Alberta, he received the Jeffrey Sampson Memorial Award. His research has been funded by the Australian Research Council (Chief Investigator on 8 ARC Discovery and Linkage Projects), the Canadian Natural Sciences and Engineering Research Council, the Japanese Institute for Advanced Information Technology (AITEC), and various Australian government agencies as well as companies such as Bluescope Steel, CSC, and Pillar Administration. His research has been published in the top venues in service-oriented computing (SCC and ICSOC), software modelling (ER), software evolution (IWSSD, IWPSE), and AI (Artificial Intelligence Journal, AAAI, AAMAS, and ECAI). He has been an invited speaker at the Schloss Dagstuhl Seminar Series in Germany and the Banff International Research Station in Canada. He has also been a keynote speaker at several conferences, and program/general chair of several others. He is a senior technical advisor to several companies in the areas of constraint programming and business process management, both in Australia and Canada. He serves as assessor (Ozreader) for the Australian Research Council and as an external reviewer for the research funding agencies of Canada, Austria, The Netherlands, Ireland, and South Africa. Professor Ghose is a Research Leader in the Australian Cooperative Research Centre for Smart Services, Co-Director of the Centre for Oncology Informatics at the Illawarra Health and Medical Research Institute, Co-Leader of the University of Wollongong Carbon-Centric Computing Initiative and Co-Convenor of the Australian Computer Society NSW SIG on Green ICT. He is Vice-President of CORE, Australia's apex body for computing academics. He is also President of the Service Science Society of Australia.

Li Guo is Lecturer at the School of Computing, Engineering and Computer Science at the University of Central Lancashire. He has PhD from the University of Edinburgh (2007) and has worked as research associate at Imperial College London. His research interests are in cloud computing, distributed sensor informatics, big data analysis and intelligent multi-agent systems, and has more than 40 peer-reviewed publications in these areas. He has contributed to many EPSRC and EU research projects and was the chief architect of the Imperial College Cloud (IC Cloud) system currently in use in a wide variety of Digital Economy projects, and was also chief architect for EU FP6 project-GridEcon providing computational facilities for data analysis services from a variety of sources and devices.

Yike Guo has been working in the area of data intensive analytical computing since 1995. During last 15 years, he has been leading the data mining group to carry out many research projects, including UK e-science projects such as: Discovery Net on Grid based data analysis for scientific discovery; MESSAGE on wireless mobile sensor network for environment monitoring; BAIR on system biology for diabetes study; iHealth on modern informatics infrastructure for healthcare decision making; UBIO-PRED on large informatics platform for translational medicine research; Digital City Exchange on sensor information-based urban dynamics modelling. He was the Principal Investigator of the Discovery Science Platform grant from UK EPSRC where he is leading the team to build the IC Cloud system for large scale collaborative scientific research. He is now the Principal Investigator of the eTRIKS project, a 23M Euro project in building a cloud-based translational informatics platform for global medical research.

Sijin He received a BSc in Mathematics (1st Class Honour) from University College London in 2007 and a MSc in Computing Science from Imperial College London in 2008. In August 2013, he received PhD in Computer Science at Imperial College London on cloud computing. His main research interests are cloud resource management and cloud security. He is now working on cloud computing and big data at Discovery Science Group (DSG). He was also chief architect for a UK Ministry of Defence project, Rogue Virtual Machine Identification in DaISy Clouds, providing a cloud-monitoring framework for intrusion detection in the cloud environment.

Anders Henten is Professor with special responsibilities at center for Communication, Media, and Information Technologies (CMI) at the Department of Electronic Systems at Aalborg University in Copenhagen. He is a graduate in communications and international development studies from Roskilde University in Denmark (1989) and holds a Ph.D. from the Technical University of Denmark (1995). He has worked professionally in the area of communications economy and policy for more than 25 years. He has participated in numerous research projects financed e.g. by the European Community, the Nordic Council of Ministers, Danish Research Councils and Ministries, and in consultancies, financed by World Bank, UNCTAD, ITU, Danish Ministries, etc. He has published nationally and internationally – more than 250 academic publications in international journals, books, conference proceedings, etc.

Chengcheng Huang is a HDR student studying Masters by research in Computing Science at the University of Ballarat at Australia. His supervisors are Dr. Zhaohao Sun and Dr. Phil Smith. Chengcheng earned his Bachelor degree in Information Technology in 2010 and Honours degree in Computing Science in 2011 from University of Ballarat, Australia sequentially. He is finalizing his thesis and applying for a PhD research position. Chengcheng earned CCNA certificate since 2007. He has also been a valuable member of Golden Key International Honours Society since 2012. His current research interests include networking technology, cloud computing and cloud services.

Ejub Kajan teaches at the State University of Novi Pazar, Serbia. He holds a PhD and MSc in Computer Science from University of Niš, Serbia, and diploma degree in Electronic Engineering from University of Split, Croatia. His current research focuses on e-commerce in general, e-commerce architectures, social networks, semantic interoperability, computer networks, and decision support systems. He published in various outlets, including ACM, IEEE, IGI, and Ivy League Publishing journals and in IGI Global and Springer books. He is a Senior Member of the ACM, and a member of IEEE, IADIS, and ISOC. He also serves editorial boards of *International Journal of Distributed Systems and Technologies* (IJDST) and *Journal of Information, Information Technology, and Organization* (JIITO). In the past, he worked as software engineer and general manager in the computer industry.

Katayoun Khodaei holds a postgraduate diploma in Computer Science from the University of Canterbury and is due to complete a Masters of Computer Science degree from the University of Wollongong studying the area of eHealth Business Process Management. She has a strong background and industry experience as an International trade specialist and business process analyst at the Parsian Bank.

Patrizia Lombardi (PhD, MSc, BA/MA) is Full Professor of Urban Planning Evaluation and Project Appraisal and Head of the Interuniversity Department of Regional and Urban Studies and Planning of Politecnico and Università di Torino. She is an established figure in the field of evaluating smart and sustainable urban development for over 20 years, publishing widely in the subject area and coordinating, or serving as lead partner, in several Pan-European Projects related to Sustainable built environment, Smart Cities, Post carbon society and Cultural heritage. She is Scientific Coordinator of the UNESCO Master "World Heritage and Cultural Projects for Development" managed by the Turin School of development of the International Labour Organization and member of a number of Scientific Committees, including the Consortium for Information Systems of the Piemonte Region and the EIT-ICT Lab of Trento Rise.

Zakaria Maamar is a full professor in the College of Technological Innovation at Zayed University, Dubai, U.A.E. His research interests include Web services, social networks, and context-aware computing. He has a PhD in computer science from Laval University, Canada.

Enrico Macii was born in Torino, Italy, on February 7, 1966. He is a Full Professor of Computer Engineering at Politecnico di Torino. Prior to that, he was an Associate Professor (from 1998 to 2001) and an Assistant Professor (from 1993 to 1998) at the same institution. From 1991 to 1997 he was also an Adjunct Faculty at the University of Colorado at Boulder. He holds a Laurea Degree in Electrical Engineering from Politecnico di Torino (1990), a Laurea Degree in Computer Science from Università di Torino (1991) and a PhD degree in Computer Engineering from Politecnico di Torino (1995). Since 2007, he is the Vice Rector for Research and Technology Transfer at Politecnico di Torino, and since 2012 also the Rector's Delegate for International Affairs. His research interests are in the design of electronic digital circuits and systems, with particular emphasis on low-power consumption aspects. In the field above he has authored around 450 scientific publications (H-index = 36, G-index = 67, Total citations: 5721, Most cited paper: 693 citations – Source: Google Scholar, November 20, 2013).

Inmaculada Medina-Bulo received her PhD in Computer Science at the University of Seville (Spain). She has been a Professor in the Department of Computer Science and Engineering of the University of Cádiz (Spain) since 1995. She held the post of Department Secretary in 1997 and has been a member of the Council of the School of Engineering (ESI) as well as a Socrates/Erasmus Program Coordinator for several years. From July 2010 to July 2011 she was appointed Degree Coordinator for the Computer Science Studies and a member of the Board of the ESI. Her research was supported by research stays at the USA, the UK and Germany. She has served in program and organizing committees at different conferences. She has published numerous papers in international journals and conferences. She is the main researcher of the UCASE Software Engineering Research Group.

Alex Menzies holds a bachelors degree in ICT, Software Engineering, Business Information Systems. Alex is currently a senior consultant providing deep insights and practical advice to clients in the utilities, finance and mining industries. He has strong core BA skills and experience in dynamic environments that enable him to work efficiently and accurately, to deliver successful business transformation. Alex is a member of the Decision Systems Laboratory and a founding member of the Expert & Decision Support Systems Institute. Alex has worked throughout the entire project life cycle as a catalyst for change in both business and IT focused projects. His previous experience includes native mobile application and service project, a program of work for financial advisers and mortgage brokers which delivered a new online platform, and numerous transformations of the internal applications and business processes.

Shah J. Miah is a Lecturer in Information Systems (IS) at Victoria University, Melbourne, Australia. Prior to this position, he had academic positions at the University of the Sunshine Coast, Griffith University, and James Cook University, Australia. He has received his PhD (in the area of Decision Support Systems), jointly from the Institute for Integrated and Intelligent Systems and Griffith Business School, Griffith University, Australia. Shah is an early career researcher who has lead authored over 50 peer reviewed publications include research book chapters, journal and conference papers in different IS areas and taught over 20 different IS/IT subjects for both postgraduate and undergraduate levels. His current research interests are decision support systems for industries, design science research methodologies, e-Service design for businesses and healthcare information systems development.

Evan Morrison holds a Bachelors Degree in Computer Science from the University of Wollongong with majors in Secure Distributed Systems and Software Development. Evan is due to complete a PhD in Computer Science in mid-2014, where his research and applied interests are in the area of Business Service Management and Requirements Engineering. His research is funded by partners in the Australian Smart Services CRC including the Queensland Government, Suncorp, and Infosys. He is a director for eHealth startup Progression Logic, which specialises in ehealth business intelligence systems. Evan has also played crucial roles in the support and development team of the Centre for Oncology Informatics, the Wollongong Carbon-Centric Computing Initiative, the Australian Service Science Society, and the Decision Systems Laboratory. He has given presentations around the country and internationally in New Zealand, South East Asia, and Europe. Evan even has prepared a handful of patent applications based on search technologies.

Guadalupe Ortiz completed her PhD in Computer Science at the University of Extremadura (Spain) in 2007, where she worked, since graduating in 2001, as Assistant Professor and research engineer. In 2009, she joined the University of Cádiz as Professor in the Department of Computer Science and Engineering. She has published numerous peer-reviewed papers in international journals, workshops and conferences. She has participated in various programme and organization committees of scientific workshops and conferences and acts as a reviewer for several journals. Her research interests embrace aspect-oriented and model-driven techniques as a way to improve service context-awareness and their adaptation to mobile devices. Additionally, her research focuses on trending topics such as the integration of complex-event processing in service-oriented architectures.

Anna Osello was born in Locana (Turin, Italy) on 30.09.1967. She obtained her degree in Building Engineering from Politecnico di Torino in 1992 and her Doctorate degree in Drawing and Survey of Buildings in 1996 from l'Università degli Studi la Sapienza in Rome. Since 1999, she is Associate Professor of Drawing at Politecnico di Torino where she coordinates a working group denominated POLItoBIM with the goal of carrying out theoretical and applied research on the issues of BIM and software interoperability. The innovative character of her research on Drawing as a communication language derives from the interdisciplinary exchange and collaboration with colleagues expert in ICT, Energy and Structure Mechanics. She is presently engaged in several research projects, among which Smart Energy Efficient Middleware for Public Spaces – SEEMPubS and Distric Information Modelling and Management for Energy Reduction – DIMMER (FP7 programme). She is the author of about 100 publications including the book Osello A., The future of Drawing with BIM for Engineers and Architects, Flaccovio, Palermo, 2012.

Edoardo Patti received the B.Sc. and M.Sc. degree in Computer Engineering at University of Palermo in 2007 and Politecnico di Torino in 2010 respectively. He joined the Department of Control and Computer Engineering, Politecnico di Torino, as Ph.D. student from January 2011. From October 2013 he is Visiting Researcher at the University of Manchester. He is also involved in various FP7 European funded projects focused on Smart Building and Smart City. His research interests concern: 1) Ubiquitous Computing; 2) Internet of Things; 3) Smart Systems and Cities, with particular emphasis on Service-Oriented Architectures for enabling interoperability between heterogeneous devices; 4) Augmented and Virtual Reality for Building/District Information Modeling (BIM/DIM).

Evelina Pencheva received her Master degree in mathematics from University of Sofia, Bulgaria, and PhD degree in telecommunication networks from Technical University of Sofia. Her current position is full Professor at Faculty of Telecommunications, Technical University of Sofia. Her interests include multimedia communications, service delivery platforms and network protocols. She has experiences in development of next generation mobile applications and middleware platforms. She is author/co-author of over 200 scientific publications, textbooks, and books.

Agostino Poggi is full professor of Computer Engineering at the Faculty of Engineering of the University of Parma. He coordinates the Agent and Object Technology Lab, and his research focuses on agent and object-oriented technologies and their use to develop distributed and complex systems. He is author of more than a hundred technical papers in refereed journals and conferences and his scientific contribution has been recognized through the "System Research Foundation Outstanding Scholarly Contribution Award" and the "System Innovation Award." Moreover, he is in the editorial board of the following scientific journals: *Software Practice & Experience, International Journal of Hybrid Intelligent Systems, International Journal of Agent-Oriented Software Engineering, International Journal of Multiagent and Grid Systems*, and *International Journal of Software Architecture*.

Manikandan Sethunarayanan Ramasamy is an Assistant Professor in Mathematics at Bharathidasan University Constituent College, Lalgudi, TamilNadu, India. He received his Ph.D. in graph theory. He has 12 years of research and 7 years of academic experience. He published 10 research papers in international high impact journals and conferences. His research interests include graph theory and optimization research.

Mohd Hisham Mohd Sharif is currently a PhD student in Information Systems at the University of Adelaide Business School. He holds an MSc (Computer Science) from Malaysian University of Technology and a degree (Information Systems) from Malaysian Northern University. His research interests include design and development of software application and adoption of technological applications including social media and accounting application in government organisations. Currently, he is working on a research project to explore the adoption of social media application in Australian local government organisations.

Phil Smith is a senior lecturer in Information Technology in the School of Science, Information Technology and Engineering, University of Ballarat. Phil received his Ph.D. from Deakin University in the area of Novice Programming Environments, which studies ways to instil appropriate conceptual models of programming in students. He has worked for several years with Dr. David Stratton in the Distributed Simulation Laboratory in collaboration with the DSTO (Defense Simulation and Technology Office) before becoming interested in the development and teaching of mobile applications. His current research interests are mobile computing and cloud computing.

Giulia Sonetti graduated from University of Naples "Federico II" in 2009 with a BArch+MArch in Architecture. She worked as environmental consultant in architectural offices both in Italy and in Spain, focusing on sustainability evaluations and Life Cycle Assessment. She then completed a MSc in Renewable Energy and Architecture in the University of Nottingham (2011), and the first course "New strategies for energy generation, conversion and storage" in the Energy School by the European Physics Society joint Italian Physics Society in 2012. She is currently attending a PhD school in Estimate and Evaluation at the Interuniversity Department of Regional & Urban Studies and Planning in Politecnico di Torino and Università di Torino. Her research focuses on the themes of sustainability evaluation tools in the changing scenario toward a low energy society, particularly exploring the relationship among energy and economy efficiency, user involvement and policy effectiveness at district level.

Jannick Kirk Sørensen is Assistant Professor at Center for Communication, Media, and Information Technology (CMI) at Aalborg University Copenhagen. His research fields are interaction design, service innovation, personalisation, and user involvement, particularly in the field of media technology. He holds a PhD degree from University of Southern Denmark (2011) on the topic of personalised Webpages for public service broadcasters. Prior to his academic career, he worked in the media industry as a journalist, interaction designer, and sound engineer.

Kenneth David Strang has a Doctorate in Project Management (business research, high distinction), an MBA (honors), a BS (honors), as well as a Business Technology diploma (honors). He is a certified Project Management Professional® from Project Management Institute, and is a Fellow of the Life Management Institute (distinction, specialized in actuary statistics and pension systems), from Life Office Management Association. His research interests include leadership, multicultural e-learning, marketing new product development, knowledge management, and e-business project management. He designs and teaches multidisciplinary subjects in business, informatics and educational psychology, in class and online distance education. He supervises PhD and doctorate students. He is chief editor and associate/area editor on several journals. Finally, Ken is Professor and Coordinator of the Business Administration degree program in the State University of New York, Plattsburgh at Queensbury campus (USA).

Lizhe (Lee) Sun is currently an associate with the Boston Consulting Group (BCG), Sydney, Australia. Lee holds First Class Honours degree in Engineering and combined Bachelors degree in Engineering and Commerce from the University of New South Wales. He was also a visiting undergraduate scholar at Harvard University. Lee has experiences working in Asia with research interest for the Asian IT landscape. He worked as a tutor at the Australian School of Business and the School of Civil Engineering, University of New South Wales for more than two years. Prior to joining BCG, Lee also worked as an engineering consultant with Evans and Peck (WorleyParsons) specializing in cost engineering and construction management. Lee interned at Morgan Stanley as an Investment Banking Analyst focusing on Mergers and Acquisition execution, with experiences in industrials and emerging small caps. Lee previously worked as a summer analyst at Goldman Sachs in the securities division, focusing on fixed income, currencies and credit strategies. He also worked as an analyst on the buy side with Challenger Life specializing in credit markets and annuity pricing.

Chellammal Surianarayanan is an Assistant Professor in Computer Science at Bharathidasan University Constituent College for Women, Orathanadu, TamilNadu, India. She has 12 years of experience in research and academic services. She is a research scholar in the School of Computer Science and Engineering, Bharathidasan University, India. Her research interests include semantic web services, semantic web and data mining.

Michele Tomaiuolo is a researcher at the University of Parma, Department of Information Engineering. He obtained a master degree in Information Engineering at the University of Parma, defending a thesis on the "Definition and Realization of Tools to Manage the Security in Multi-Agent Systems," about the introduction of multiuser capabilities, authentication, and encryption in JADE, an agent framework developed in Java by the University of Parma in conjunction with Telecom Italia Lab. He obtained a PhD in "Information technologies," at the University of Parma, Department of Information Engineering, in 2006, defending a thesis on "Models and Tools to Manage Security in Multiagent Systems." His current research activity is focused in particular on security and trust management, but it also deals with multi-agent systems, semantic web, rule-based systems, peer-to-peer networks.

Indrit Troshani is a Senior Lecturer in Information Systems at the University of Adelaide Business School. He holds a PhD (Computer Science) from Edith Cowan University (Western Australia) and an MSc (Computer-based Information Systems) from the University of Sunderland (UK). His research interests include adoption and diffusion of network innovations including digital reporting and accounting innovations (e.g. XBRL), Green IS/IT, e-health, and mobile services. His work has been published in several journals including *Information Technology & People, Electronic Markets, Journal of Computer Information Systems, Journal of Engineering and Technology Management, European Journal of Innovation Management,* and *Industrial Management & Data Systems.*

Emir Ugljanin is teaching assistant at the State University of Novi Pazar, Serbia. He is a PhD student of Computer Sciences at University of Niš, Serbia, and has diploma on master studies from Technical faculty of University of Novi Sad, Serbia. His current research focuses on e-commerce, social networking, geoweb, semantic web, and decision support systems.

Mihai Horia Zaharia is currently an associate professor at the Computer Engineering Department from "Gheorghe Asachi" Technical University. He received a Ph.D. in Computer Science from the same university in 2002. The research interest areas are related to distributed systems, parallel computer architecture, computer networks security, design patterns, microprocessor applications, decision support systems, distributed artificial intelligence, social networks, social modeling, psychology, and mobile computing/Internet of things. He received several research grants from The National University Research Council of Romania as director. In addition, it was involved in some European projects from Leonardo or FP7 frameworks as technical director. He published over 70 papers as author or co-author in national or international publications. In addition, he published as author or as co-author eight books at national level.

Index